UNLOCKING AFRICA'S SUSTAINABLE DEVELOPMENT

*What Africans have forgotten in order
to promote continuous flow of
sustainable positive change in their
communities whilst
protecting future generations' ability
to meet their needs ...*

PATRICK SSEMPEERA

UNLOCKING AFRICA'S SUSTAINABLE DEVELOPMENT
WHAT AFRICANS HAVE FORGOTTEN IN ORDER TO PROMOTE CONTINUOUS FLOW OF SUSTAINABLE POSITIVE CHANGE IN THEIR COMMUNITIES WHILST PROTECTING FUTURE GENERATIONS' ABILITY TO MEET THEIR NEEDS …

Copyright © 2022 Patrick Ssempeera.

All rights reserved. No part of this book may be used or reproduced by any means, graphic, electronic, or mechanical, including photocopying, recording, taping or by any information storage retrieval system without the written permission of the author except in the case of brief quotations embodied in critical articles and reviews.

iUniverse books may be ordered through booksellers or by contacting:

iUniverse
1663 Liberty Drive
Bloomington, IN 47403
www.iuniverse.com
844-349-9409

Because of the dynamic nature of the Internet, any web addresses or links contained in this book may have changed since publication and may no longer be valid. The views expressed in this work are solely those of the author and do not necessarily reflect the views of the publisher, and the publisher hereby disclaims any responsibility for them.

ISBN: 978-1-5320-9705-8 (sc)
ISBN: 978-1-5320-9706-5 (hc)
ISBN: 978-1-5320-9707-2 (e)

Library of Congress Control Number: 2021923756

Print information available on the last page.

iUniverse rev. date: 01/13/2022

Dedication

To my late Dad, Fred Ssempeera & my mother, Serina Betty Nakimera.

To Peace, Joan, Alex, Mark, Patricia, Charlotte, Oprah, and Martin.

Unlocking Africa's Sustainable Development

Reclaiming Our Position

Disclaimer Statement

This book expresses my views and opinions on how I wish Africa's sustainable development should aim. They do not intend to harm anyone in any way, provoke, insult, or disrespect. I do share my experiences, insights, and observations with the world.

Patrick Ssempeera

2021

Foreword

Superpowers have fought wars and won many. However, the complex war to fight in the 21st century is between humanity and climate change. The World Bank reports that by 2030, climate change will push more than 100 million people globally back into poverty.[1] The report concludes that Sub-Saharan Africa and South Asia will be hit the hardest. Therefore, we must struggle to sustain the planet earth by stopping the extinction of creatures, stopping the exhaustion of natural resources, and promoting renewability. Giants play decisive roles in the campaign to save the planet earth, but the fighting arena is entirely a responsibility for all. The battlefield management does no discrimination. It includes big economies and emerging economies. Superpowers are doing well to lead the sustainability campaign. However, saving the planet in a world of political insurgencies is more about creating peace between humans and other living beings.

To solve the collision between human civilization and the ecological system is undoubtedly a responsibility for all. Innovation can do great wonders to reduce climate change, but the best solution lies in fostering a tremendous shift in consumer behaviours, especially the regulation of the massive luxury economies. The masses should understand why they need to contribute to the campaign to save the planet. Peace between the planet and humankind will be created majorly by understanding but not only enacting policies. Developing countries need to understand the sustainability mission to contribute to saving the planet from a well-informed point of view.

Chapter 8, "Integrations", leads continuous improvement in the sustainable development pillars in the African context, whilst the other Chapters unlock sustainability hence the book title, *"Unlocking Africa's sustainable development."* When you unlock development pathways, then you have to lead and manage sustainable development. Therefore, Chapter 8, "Integrations", provides integrated solutions to lead and manage sustainability in several African countries. Other Chapters are about "unlocking", but Chapter 8 is strictly about leading and managing sustainable development.

I clustered the chapters as follows: Cluster A has two chapters, 1 and 2, i.e. "Culture and Religion" and "Our Politics", respectively. Cluster B has chapters 3 and 4, i.e. "Education system" and "Optimism and Positivity", respectively. Cluster C has chapters 5 and 6, i.e. "Phenomenology and Probability" and "Women and Youth Empowerment", respectively. Cluster D has chapters 7 and 8, i.e. "Industrialization and Globalization" and "Integrations", respectively.

I define sustainability, and many others have defined it: as minding about future generations being able to meet their needs as we live now. In the African context, I triangulate my definition to capture the preservation of the planet earth and promote the dignity of African humankind. The high-income countries were able to develop many years ago, and they have been able to sustain their development.

---

[1] Stephane Hallegatte, Mook Bangalore, Laura Bonzanigo, Marianne Fay, Tomaro Kane, Ulf Narloch, Julie Rozenberg, David Treguer, and Adrien Vogt-Schilb, *Shock Waves: Managing the Impacts of Climate Change on Poverty* (Washington, D.C: The World Bank, 2016), 02.

However, they cannot claim that their development is sustainable because of the world's threats, such as climate change, mineral exhaustion, terrorist attacks, and many other kinds of extremisms.

The 21st century requires emerging countries to aim for sustainable development because the sustainability topic has come when many African countries have failed to undergo full structural transformation. Hence the book title is aimed at unlocking sustainable development but not sustained development. Many African countries have little economic progress to sustain.

Unlocking Africa's sustainable development is a book written for Africans to awaken them on what they have forgotten to promote the continuous flow of sustainable positive change in their communities. The book aims to prevent foreigners from taking advantage of a continued mess in Africa. Others have exploited Africa for its high levels of ignorance, wrong attitude, and a lack of knowledge on achieving real growth and development. In simple terms, on average, Africa can be described as a mendicant compared to other continents. Remember, no one can make you feel inferior without your consent. We have consented beyond doubt to the inferiority complex through our attitudes.

At some point, we have been described as imitations of a human being either explicitly or implied, and we do not bother to ask ourselves why. This book has found the reasons. I have found out that the major hindrance to genuine development in Africa is not about the lack of money as many people think or limited to poor leadership and bad governance; it rather heavily lies in the relatively minor issues overlooked. It is more than that usually thought. As an African, in an attempt to read the details of this book, free your mind to avoid getting neurotic, and do not stage an immature defence mechanism. There is room to contribute to this script. Feel free; your ideas are welcome. It is still a work-in-progress—continual and collective struggle to achieve our dream of standing on our own as Africans is required.

If you find many problems with this book, it is because of the education system I went through, as I explained in Chapter Three. Otherwise, I have tried my best to create an African Self-Help Project on Self-driven Sustainable Development. However, I apologise for the errors found. Genuine self-driven sustainable development calls on us to be objective. To understand Africa's oddness, avoid going defensive. Not to be on the defensive, avoid subjectivity. Otherwise, there is no need to progress to the eight Chapters of this book.

I have organized the book into eight (8) Chapters. In my opinion, genuine self-driven sustainable development for Africa lies in correcting the issues described in the Chapters; Africa shall never have genuine self-driven sustainable development without being corrected. I have expressly provided the interdependence that all issues have with one another across all Chapters, showing what we ought to do and why. I have provided the likely impacts Africa will face if some of these bottlenecks are not addressed. I have, therefore, provided a roadmap, and in my opinion, it serves as a development action plan for Africa.

Although I made several constructs for some statements to look subjective, many of these behavioural, attitude and planning issues are overt. Vesting all hindrances and bottlenecks to sustainable development in poor leadership, bad governance, imperialism, colonialism, and neocolonialism is like focusing on trees rather than the forest. I have focused on the forest rather than the trees. I have taken typical population samples, case studies, making empirical observations, and bringing parent issues that hinder sustainable, steady, and accelerated growth and development to book in ways that matter to all Africans—a holistic view. I believe in empiricism.

We are a reflection of the quality of leaders we have. The leaders are a part of "us". We should start by blaming ourselves before pointing to our leaders. I have sampled some African countries and used them as examples and case studies. What we share in common is that we are all Africans and once colonized. The problems we face cut across many African countries, hence the book title, "Unlocking Africa's sustainable development." These sampled states are a subsystem within the complex system called "Africa". I counted on inductive arguments by reasoning that a number of similarities make further similarities likely. Therefore, case studies in the mentioned developing countries were more likely to identify with other developing countries in Africa. The claims I made support some degree of probability for the conclusions' truth, but not their certainty. In none of the arguments, I made in this book do the facts guarantee the truth of the conclusions I drew, but I made it more likely that the conclusions are true.

Most summits on Africa's sustainable development are biased to debate unemployment, socioeconomic relations, welfare, foreign policies, diplomatic relations, security, climate change, economic integrations, information technology and globalization. That is expressly the obvious, but genuine development is not very much about diplomacy. We need more summits on motivation, awakening, cognition, attitude, and perception as far as African masses are concerned.

The 1987 Brundtland Report defined sustainability as "meeting the needs of the present without compromising the ability of the future generations to meet their own needs."[2] Africa's sustainable development is impossible when the express focus is limited to the three main pillars of sustainable development as proposed by the United Nations Paris Summit of 2015, which many African states ratified. The balance of the three pillars, social, economic, and environment, depends on each nation's moral framework. I am not disputing the pillars, but I am exploring what seems to be extraneous variables that I believe inform the three pillars. Sustainability as the dependent variable is informed by the three independent pillars/variables.

This book philosophizes what I believe should be the moral framework to guide Africans while on the road to achieve self-driven sustainable development. It is still a challenge to meet mutual consent about sustainability in Africa because people believe morality is rooted in faith or religion more than the Rule of Law. Many countries have developed by adopting an integrated approach hence beating moral dilemmas, but sustained development differs from sustainable development. Sustainable development forecasts what is likely to happen in 100+ years—by not necessarily sticking only to objectivism but also employing some form of relativism to be culturally bound. Some successful self-sustaining and promising sustainable societies understand that morality and Rule of Law are rooted in each other and faith and religion are concerned with salvation.

Sustainable development looks at the conservation of the natural system whilst meeting human needs. The biggest issue in this is the non-renewable resources which will eventually get exhausted to meet the demands of the population explosion. Africa's development is not self-sustained. Self-sustained is when

---

[2] *Report of the World Commission on Environment and Development: Our Common Future (Brundtland Report)* (Oslo: World Commission on Environment, 20 March 1987), Article 3(27).

you create and recreate by yourself whilst sustainable development is keeping a target goal of human-ecosystem equilibrium for now and for the generations to come. Self-sustenance and sustainability cannot be achieved when risk factors and causal factors appearing extraneous from the entire spectrum are not addressed.

The industrial revolution, which promotes linear economic models, entirely looks unsustainable. The world leaders in industrial processes are now focusing on more sustainable economic models, e.g. the circular model. Except for a few sectors, today's industrial development in Africa broadly encourages a "take-make-dispose" economic model. This model will eventually lead to exhaustion of the non-renewable resources. The developmental strategy is: balancing the social, economic, and environmental aspects for any activity to be deemed sustainable. If we care for future generations, the best approach that would explicitly appear as number one in the sustainable development objectives would be promoting circular economies.

The linear economic model of industrial development and associated sustainability models is understandable, but mathematics invalidates the entire process. Why? The projected world population of over 9.7 billion people by 2050 renders the entire proposed human-ecosystem equilibrium strategy invalid. The competitive capitalistic models the modern world nurtures through democratic ideals trigger people to yearn for more than enough materialistic needs to satisfy their egos. You cannot talk of satisfying wants and needs without talking about the products of the industrial revolution. Because of the repercussions of the 4th industrial revolution, integrated probabilistic models show that many African people will swing into poverty because of natural catastrophes resulting from climate change like floods, extreme heat, droughts, wildfires, hurricanes, and tornadoes. These shall predispose humanity to various sorts of diseases, chronic hunger and famine, and shall destroy the registered economic growth.

Africa's sustainability agenda should nurture thinking out of the box and around the box. The best solution to protect the ability of future generations to meet their needs is to think around the box and outside the box, but not limited to the box. As time goes on, the need to protect future generations will see many nations shifting from being wholly capitalistic to one-tenth—governments wholly taking on the housing sector and controlling luxury. It is not uncommon to find a family or one person owning two to three or even more saloon cars in a developing country. There are homes with many refrigerators, TV sets, gas cookers, and other gadgets, feeding on non-renewable energy. Today, in developing countries, on-average one-in-three mobile phone user holds more than one mobile phone. The number of people who recycle smartphones and computer batteries remains unclear in many parts of Africa. Each day I drive on the road alone in the car, I ask myself whether the activity I am driving for is worth the emission I emit in the environment. I realize luxury drives take on a slightly more considerable proportion of the drives I make.

The effective way to protect future generations is to stay put on highly environmental degrading luxuries and promote: circular economies, sharing economies, putting purpose before profit, human rights before money, and 'Just-Enough-To-Live' models and moving away from just minimizing environmental degradation and negative social impacts to stopping. Therefore, thinking "future generations" might require governments to take on the manufacturing and production of goods and services to a large extent to meet the demands of the population. Tapping into green infrastructure, green vehicles, green technologies for the housing sector, and recyclable production—leaning more on socialist policies in some African countries where democratic ideals seem premature to meet social conditions. Otherwise, if capitalism continues uncontrolled with linear models, very little might be achieved as far as protecting the future generations is concerned, and it renders the whole efforts of developmental agencies insignificant.

Why this book? I was insinuated by talks from non-Africans on social media platforms and particularly by the controversial tweet remarks made by the 45th President of the United States of America on African countries in early 2018 that resonated, blowing much attention globally. I did not go defensive, and because of having some ideas I felt worth sharing on how development could be achieved, I got motivated to give an expert opinion as a practising professional civil engineer by *drafting a process*. I brainstormed on several ideas that I have compiled to author this book. In my view, once implemented, I have a strong belief that Africa's sustainability agenda will be unlocked. The gist of the matter primarily lies on when I can fetch Gold underneath the strata with my technology, human resources, and cash, keeping the economist's comparative advantage constant.

Throughout this book, I have used sustainability in two contextual versions, but both culminate into the need to protect the future African generations. I find the need to address the concept of sustainable development in the African context different from other territories, clearly addressing the roots to promote sustainability. Sustainability in the African context is simply about minding about the future generation's ability to live and be treated with dignity by others and be able to stand on their own as we live now. Dismissing all claims made by non-Africans on Africans as sour grapes and getting prone to self-deceptive rationalization will only keep Africans odd. Some of my opinions and thoughts are hypotheses, not facts. Anyone can scrutinize and further examine them.

As a practising civil engineer, I have given my opinions that anyone can replicate to nullify or deduce their validity. This authorship can be agreed or nullified by research into the hypotheses and claims forethought. It is a *collection of ideas* that I have generated over the years about transforming and sustaining Africa and its future generations. These ideas are for Africans to question and think about them. It is not a unique kind of overgeneralization, but I document my observation which anyone can critique. I have used mixed approaches and integrated reasoning, either deductively or inductively, to conclude as appropriate, not forgetting that observation is good enough to premise arguments. I have authoritatively backed some claims, though.

No man is an island, and nobody is a custodian of knowledge. Therefore, I am very open to criticism and ideas from well-wishers to improve the fate and image of Africans. I bring forward my ideas and encourage others to front theirs to collectively harmonize our ideas to improve the best ideals to propel Africa to the destination we wish it to be in the digital era, making information flow easy. Freeing our minds, conquering fear, and innovating our styles to define what sustainable development means for Africa is essential because nobody will help us treat the root cause of our predicaments. Many are treating symptoms.

One primary question should haunt every African, considering the African economy of about US$ 2.43 Trillion (IMF GDP estimates, 2019).[3] As Africans, if we get rid of all long-serving heads of states since the revolution is already taking shape as I author this book, are we guaranteed to achieve self-driven

---

[3] "GDP, Current Prices," International Monetary Fund, 2021, https://www.imf.org/external/datamapper/NGDPD@WEO/OEMDC/ADVEC/WEOWORLD/AFQ

sustainable development? The Sub-Saharan economy only, which has some of the poorest countries in the world, is about US$ 1.77 Trillion making about 2.02% of the World Economy (The World Bank GDP estimates, 2019).[4] By "African", I mean aboriginal native African, by colour and blood but not naturalization, i.e. the indigenous peoples. If all long-serving heads of states individualizing states resigned today, are we composed well-enough to have no more excuses hindering self-sustenance without depending on foreign hands?

Colonial war veterans, long-serving heads of state are significantly believed to cause suppression and oppression of the masses. That they hold the keys to sustainable development and that they perpetuate being a slave variable. Masses view them as the number one bottleneck to the bright future of Africa. I find this hypothetical, and I nullify it by empiricism. They are just a drop in the ocean or just a sample representative of the population of causes. I can never call them the root cause. They are a mere cause and perpetuating conduits but not a root. Good governance includes leaders stepping down, but we are shielded from thinking of a solution to the real problem but rather cling to only long-serving regimes as the bottleneck.

It is worth noting that even some developed nations have manipulative tendencies in their politics; leadership transitions appear democratically inclined. However, things are different when you get to the bottom. Some developed countries, including a G20 member, have had their leaders assume leadership transitions democratically but with actual leaders clinging in the same circles for nearly three decades, creating an environment close to a tyrannical oligarchy. These people are the first to congratulate long-serving African leaders whenever they rig elections, forgetting that their countries work to earn, but Africa begs to earn. Some leaders in the developed countries interfere and influence the outcomes of elections in other sovereign countries. I believe genuine self-driven development for African countries is not only bottlenecked by power struggles, but other factors which need to be addressed honestly might take precedence. This means that it is not more on who leads but more on us.

In the many collectivistic African cultures where situational attributions are considered first and individual messes considered last, genuine self-driven development becomes complex. It is becoming a song to attribute all challenges to the long-serving regimes. The biggest problem long-serving war veterans create is to appear as if they were sent to stage guerrilla wars fighting for freedom in a bid to meet the demands of a social contract. As I wrote this book, nobody sent me to do so. I cannot impose my ideas on others. Fighting for humanity does not mean owning humanity.

The great Nelson Mandela was jailed for twenty-seven (27) years but stepped down after serving for five (5) years; who are you not step down? In history, many people served humanity; they made sacrifices the world lives to remember; you are not the first. If we concur to this debate, you and I can avoid oppressive and unaccountable leadership in just a couple of hours. That justifies that our leaders represent who we are, and the solution lies in holistically identifying the problem and change. More lies in doing than talking and improving one–on–one relationships that will break the underlying deep-seated selfishness. These egocentric tendencies arise especially out of distorting collectivism. Therefore, we need to do much on nurturing emotional capital for the young generations by exploring alternatives and restoring a

---

[4] "World Development Indicators," The World Bank, September 15th 2021, https://databank.worldbank.org/reports.aspx?source=2&country=SSF#

sense of shame in political leaders. Doing much to make people understand that development is "doing it or leading it by yourself".

The book presents an analysis of the African behaviour, socio-environment, socioeconomic and sociopolitical perception, understanding, and attitude towards; time, work, space and land, politics, governance, resources and a comparison with the rest of the world. Within this context, change is inevitable for steady and accelerated genuine self-driven sustainable growth and development. Once we recognize our role as Africans in creating our predicaments, we shall also realize that and only that, we have the power to change the prevailing situation. We struggle to nullify fate as a predicament and the claim that we are falling towards the nature-end of the spectrum of the larger nature and nurture debate.

Unemployment, stunted growth and development, corruption and embezzlement of resources, loss of power, facing the effect of neocolonialism and imperialism from others, state of meaninglessness, increased criminalities, poverty, poor standard of living, and poor nutrition are all our predicaments. The whys and wherefores are explicitly outlined in the Chapters. Chapter 8, "Integration", leads continuous improvement in the sustainable development pillars whilst the other Chapters are about unlocking sustainability hence the book title, *"Unlocking Africa's sustainable development."* When you unlock development pathways, then you have to lead and manage sustainable development. Therefore, Chapter Eight, "Integrations", provides integrated solutions required to solve crises whilst leading and managing sustainability in several African countries. Other Chapters are about "unlocking", but Chapter 8 is strictly about leading and managing sustainable development.

To accelerate and cope with the rest of the world, Africa needs integrated approaches or a holistic view in all matters but not to blame long-serving leaders or oppressive governance alone. Lastly, those Africans who feel fine or graduates must know that they occupy the top few, maybe 2-5%, and I am focusing on the forest. Sometimes it is easier for others to say that he is Spanish than European but not easier to say he is Ugandan than African. If you happen to have graduated from the forest, help those still in the forest also to graduate so that we can collectively celebrate and enjoy our beautiful Africa endowed with natural resources. Otherwise, if you do not, your grandchildren and many other generations to come shall dive back into colonialism and imperialism. It is, therefore, more of nurturing the African masses on how things work and how to achieve genuine self-driven sustainable development. After reading this book, you will note that it summarizes the "Upholding the Rule of Law" as the tool to unlock and lead continuous improvement in sustainability.

The Question

The planet earth has seven continents, of which people inhabit only six. These are North America, South America, Europe, Asia, Africa, Australia, and Antarctica. Of all the six inhabited continents, Africa has the greatest socioeconomic crisis. Other continents like Asia and South America, too, have a low human development index in a good number of states. The rate at which states in dire need to improve living standards is more promising at the level of do-it-yourself, or lead-it-yourself, in other states than on the African land.

Africa is the second-largest continent with an area of 29,648,481Km^2 after Asia, which has an area of about 31,033,131Km^2. Africa is still the second most populated continent with about 1.307bn people, second to Asia with a population of 4.55bn (2019 estimates). Africa has some of the world's wealthiest mineral deposited countries like the Democratic Republic of Congo (DRC). Unfortunately, Africa has the least Gross Domestic Product (GDP) and houses some of the world's poorest countries. Several agencies have made predictions and noted that Africa's economy would supersede many developed nations in not far time. Development agencies still report that Africa has 6/10 of the world's fastest-growing economies (2018 data). In this way, agencies look at GDP and not at the "who" leads in the GDP growth, which risks a wrong prediction on the sustainability of Africa's economy.

In history, many territories have once been colonized by others. African countries gained independence at about the same time as many other developed countries, but they have since been crippled. While some other African states recently gained independence in early 2011 and 1990s, many have had independence for more than 50 years. Several African countries faced an abysmal start post-colonial era characterized by wars, genocides, antidemocratic governments, and power seizures, which greatly affected their accelerated growth and development.

I had the following hypotheses to draw on what still seals Africa's fate:

- *Africa has; bad leaders, autocratic or antidemocratic governments, balkanization and poor political ideologies.*
- *Africa is not asking the right questions.*
- *Africa was ruined by colonialism and then gained independence immaturely and risked an invisible hand crippling success.*

This authorship intended to explore and make conclusions on the correct hypothesis, possibly rank the order, to guide Africa in the right direction by answering Africa's modern oddness amongst the other continents.

Analytical findings

Africa is not asking the right questions and puts much trust in whoever promises free things. I instead vanish than prolonging myself to live in free things forever. We are called human beings because of the intelligence we hold to lead other living beings. As Africans, depending on others to survive forever makes us a little sub-human. All living beings put themselves first, and it is a modern-day deception to believe that they can wish the other to live better than them. Africa ought to learn to live by its own making by asking the right questions and treating others equally. In geopolitics, none is better or fairer than the other on African matters. Bad leadership comes second, whilst the invisible hand that cripples Africa's success comes last.

UNLOCKING AFRICA'S SUSTAINABLE DEVELOPMENT

Factors That Describe Africa's Situation

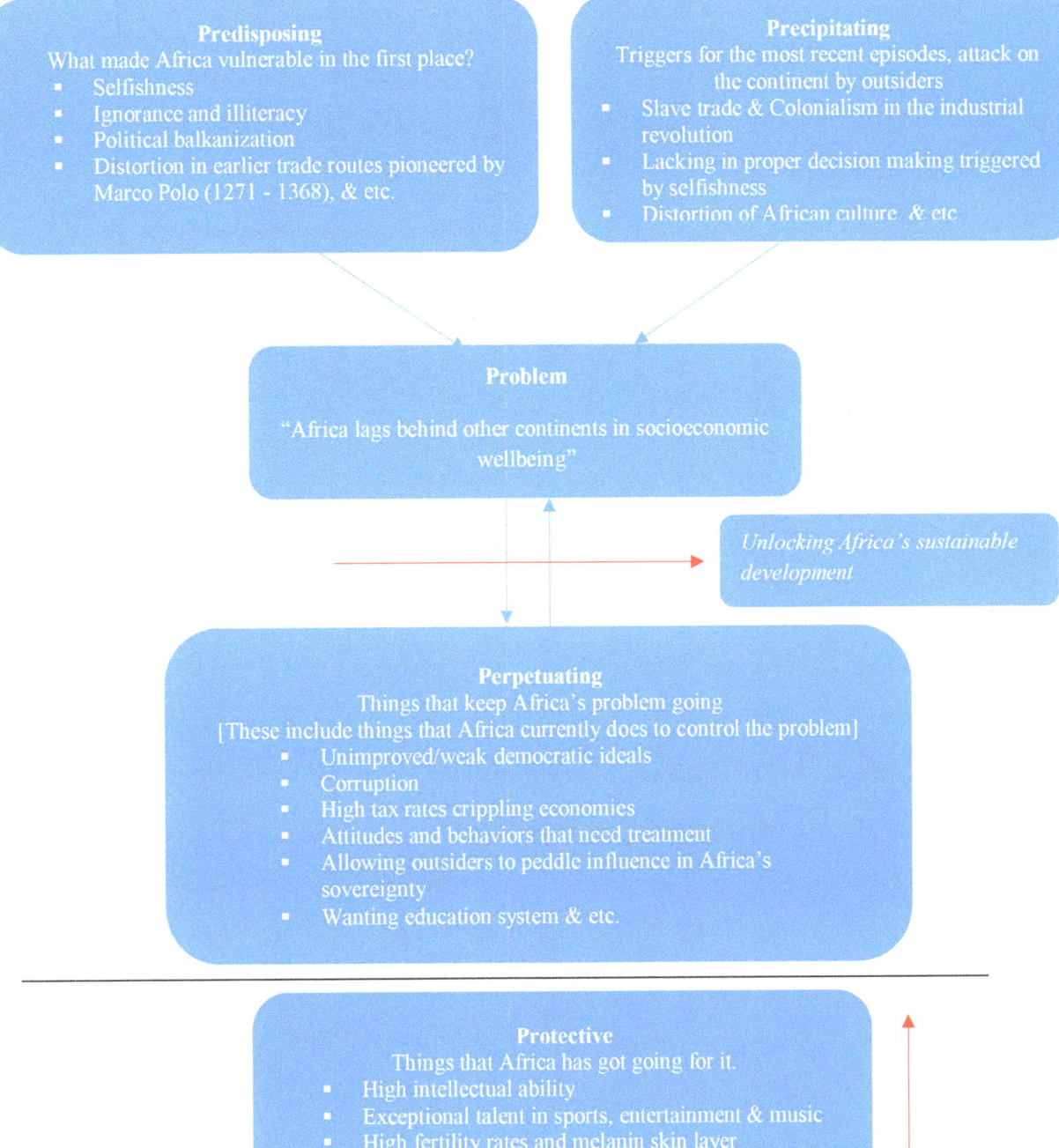

Note: **Unlocking Africa's sustainable development** seeks to break the perpetuating factors and motivate protective factors.

Patrick Ssempeera
January, 2022.
Kampala, UG

Capter One: Culture and Religion

"Spirituality and psychology are rooted in the same source."

Religion • Culture • Psychology
=== Patrick Ssempeera ===

Chapter Organization

Quick Insights

Culture

Africa's Ethnicities

Religion

Conventional Religions

Africa's Position in the World of Conventional Religions

- Christianity
- Islam

Africa's Traditional Religions: What would be a sustainable religion for Sub-Saharan Africa?

Other World's Famous Religions

- Buddhism and Hinduism
- Judaism

Required Spiritual Leader's Competence in Sustainable Development

Effect of Conventional Religions to Africans

Cognitive Restructuring of African Masses—dealing with African thoughts and core beliefs

Socratic Questioning on the influence of the Western World in Africa following timelines

Spirituality, Psychology, and 21st Century Sustainable Development

Conclusion

Quick Insights

I'm an African "Muganda" of Bantu ethnic descent in Uganda's central before I become anything else. Living as a "Muganda" calls for cherishing values, norms, beliefs, morals, and the tradition of the Baganda culture. I descend from Ssekabaka Kintu of the "Ngo" clan in Buganda in Uganda's central. I strongly detest homogenization embraced and spearheaded by a particular faction of people. Many problems we have had in Africa are a result of displacing African values. The latest inculcation by some religious leaders to instil confidence in Africans to appreciate their cultural values is such an excellent opportunity to spearhead socio-economic transformation for the African child. Labelling several African values satanic by some others was such a big mistake that is owed an apology. Therefore, something worth noting is that self-awareness initiatives are a solid foundation to enable the sustainable social transformation of any society. Failure to recognize one's roots and what they are is not only dangerous but threatens self-driven sustainable development, more especially where an illusion of knowledge dominates. It must dominate where the ancestral knowledge is not grown and extended further. To grow somebody's intellect, one ought to understand where they are coming from to appreciate why they live. Leading continuous improvement in societal systems must benchmark on the understanding of how particular societies have evolved.

"A people without the knowledge of their past history, origin, and culture is like a tree without roots." Marcus Garvey (1887 – 1940)

Africa is owed an apology for the way others introduced foreign religions and theologies in the land. The process was not the most suitable. It led to a rapid disintegration of traditional values. The process was associated with opportunism, something they should have realized and stopped. However, most religions' great moral teachers look foreign, but strong history shows the presence of Africans succouring in some of the world's great religions across ages. The architects of great religions could not explicitly bring out Africa's connection with these religions. It takes great courage and vivid logic to comprehend Africa's position in many domineering religions. The opportunism I have described made all domineering religions look non-African. A close look at the books of salvation demonstrates that Africans and the domineering religions of Islam and Christianity have been close allies across ages.

One of the most potent weapons to use to soften the masses is to create a religion. It works better than any scientific innovation can do. The growth of psychology in the 20th century has brought out new evidence depicting that it could be sharing a source with spirituality. For example, accepting people for who they are; guides several doctrines in the world's famous religions, and it is also a psychological principle commonly known as *"unconditional positive regard."* Optimistic thinking, identifying negative thoughts, and having empathy for others are ideals in psychological interventions. These ideals equate to the spiritual conviction of effective faith. Psychological techniques of relaxation, active listening, principles of reciprocity, and being nonjudgmental have meeting points in religion and cultural domains.

Many similarities show that psychology and spirituality might have the same source. However, by the end of the 21st century, psychology is destined to lead several domains of understanding humanity. Another arguer may look at holy texts as a tool guiding spirituality, religions, and psychology at some point. However, modern psychology studying; the mind, the neurons, brain activities, and cognition are at crossroads with some doctrines of the world's major religions. Some cognitive behavioural psychologists and neuroscientists believe that it is much more on how we think to solve our problems that matter but not the core beliefs we hold in our respective religions and associated doctrines. In the bid to solve the world's humane problems, psychological interventions are proving the best techniques than core religious beliefs and doctrines, which place more focus on prayer and meditation.

In some African cultures, which were attacked and replaced with other cultures in the form of religions, we credit our ancestors for psychological interventions of creating peace among humans and other living beings, especially in marriage and family systems. Although ancestors lacked formal expression of ideas in writing to have a unique language, which loosened their philosophy to be coined ethno-philosophies in some parts of Africa, we cannot take their wisdom for granted. We need not forget that labelling them ethno-philosophy is already a philosophy of its kind! That greatest weakness in searching for knowledge by some African ancestors, especially in the Sub-Sahara, created many problems we live to make clear.

Although organized philosophy is just starting to grow in some parts of Africa, there was philosophy but not as pronounced as in Europe, the Americas, and Asian territories. It is entirely untrue to say Africa lacked philosophy completely. The world has always had people in leading positions, and at some point, Africans will reclaim their position to steer the wheel for many generations ahead of us. Despite the partitioning of Africa by colonialists, Africa was a single block that would highly progress if it remained as a single block or if Africans made the partitioning. Saying that Africa lacked philosophers is outright deception that we ought to recognize because Egypt and associated lands have had great philosophers right from the ancient past. Many of these philosophers have shaped the world into what we are today. Unless claims emerge backed with evidence that Egypt and associated lands are not a part of Africa. Creating peace is the ultimate goal of anyone claiming to bring good to the world. It is upon this clause that I cannot fail to mention that:

> *"If somebody's religion brings you hatred, you must be sick, especially when you are of the same colour, blood, ethnicity, and culture. You have been indoctrinated and cannot think outside the doctrines of the religion." Patrick Ssempeera*

Anyone who believes their religion is superior to others and prejudices others' religions needs to be crushed totally in the modern world. We are born defaulted already in different religions introduced to Africa. Many of us claim/believe our religion commands others—that it has been proven beyond doubt through spiritual conviction by modern and ancient men of the Supreme Being and scholars of different times. By default, here means being preselected for an option and adopt a religion of no choice but one gained in a similar way that we obtain a domicile of origin. You get the energy and core belief of the truthfulness of the religion of domicile in infancy. We grow in a culture that brainwashes our ancestral instincts and grows us in fear of living in the natural environment selectively but wholly in the artificial world.

Culture. Many scholars spanning from ancient times to the present day modern world have laboured to study people's culture across the globe. Various scholars have provided explanations on what culture is and at some point fail to reach a consensus, but in my view:

> *"Culture would be best described as a set of organized instinct overt behaviours which influence a person's attitude towards life and the cognition that one develops over time and portrays inherently passed on from his ancestors or learned from their natural and built environments. It is characterized by: a unique way of life, the unique norms, the unique way of thinking, the unique type of food, the unique type of music, the unique type of clothing, the unique type of dance, the unique symbolic meanings attributed to different objects or events, the unique language and dialect, the unique method of worship, the unique beliefs, the unique medicines and herbs, the unique disorders, the unique folk illnesses, the unique attitudes, stereotypes, characters, and temperaments."*

Several modern scholars describe culture as a way of life. Contemporary scholars such as Stuart McPhail Hall (1932-2014)[5] and Raymond Henry Williams (1921-1988)[6] from the United Kingdom identified culture with consumption of goods and leisure activities such as art, music, film, food, sports, and clothing. However, the description of culture by the two scholars did not explicitly provide for norms and the language or dialect as associative attributes for a culture. The English Oxford dictionary defines "norms" as standards of behaviour that are typical of or accepted within a particular group or society. The Merriam-Webster dictionary defines the word "norms" as a principle of right action binding upon the group members and serving to guide, control, or regulate proper and acceptable behaviour.

In Africa, we have specific cultural norms attributed to each independent ethnic group and tribe. Our ancestors laid a strong foundation within these cultural norms to give us unique identities and specific manners. As rational creatures, we ought to carry on norms that protect our motherland. And suppose you provide high-quality education to a culturally sound person. In that case, it produces overarching results that are sustainable and much felt by the visitors to their homeland on the spot.

Culture, Heritage, and Sustainability

The effort to enact laws and regulations to preserve cultural heritage and nature conservation in Africa might not yield proper, reliable, and sustainable results when African culture is deteriorating day and night at the expense of the western culture. This is equivalent to a wastage of time because you cannot preserve and conserve what you do not love and believe in well enough. For example, people sometimes abuse and drop traditional African recipes to adopt foreign recipes in many African societies, spoiling identity.

---

[5] Stuart McPhail Hall was a Jamaican-born British Marxist sociologist, cultural theorist, and political activist.

[6] Raymond Henry Williams was a Welsh socialist writer, academic, novelist and critic influential within the New Left and in wider culture.

The most significant feature of the 1972 UNESCO World Heritage Convention was linking together the concepts of nature conservation and the preservation of cultural properties in a single document.[7] The Convention recognized how people interact with nature and the fundamental need to balance the two, and mathematics shows us that it is imperative and true. A sustainable and optimal solution is obtained when a plot of cultural heritage preservation is directly proportional to nature conservation. There is no better solution than prevention—it is better to preserve, conserve, prolong, and defend our cultures as we interact with nature.

We need to preserve our customs, objects, places, values, artistic expressions, and other symbols. These symbols protect and defend our identity. We need to preserve our artefacts such as objects, pictures, and books and documents. Each culture has its own built environment that signifies the identity, such as archaeological remains, buildings, and townscapes. Also, cultures identify with the natural environment, such as agricultural heritage, coasts and shorelines, and rural landscapes. In the interest of sustainable development, all these should be protected and preserved to be enjoyed by future generations.

In February 2017, China issued ambitious plans to build vertical forests as towers that would produce 60-kgs of oxygen per day. The towers would be home to more than 1,100 trees and 2,500 cascading plants, and they were estimated to absorb about 25-tons of carbon dioxide every year.[8] To put things in perspective, saving 25 tons of CO_2 would be equivalent to taking five cars off the road for a year. Chinese cities have some of the most polluted air in the world.

Carbon dioxide is one of the naturally occurring greenhouse gases responsible for global warming. Greenhouse gases help in the absorption and emission of infrared radiation in the atmosphere. Global warming results from the continual increase of greenhouse gases, superseding the naturally occurring amounts in the atmosphere. The increased industrialization pumps vast amounts of carbon dioxide into the atmosphere. Therefore, Chinese cities have some of the most polluted air globally because of the high industrialisation, yet China is rich in cultural heritage. How will it be in Africa 100-years from today, where masses seem not to understand the role of preserving cultural heritage as we get on to the road to industrialize fully?

China's ambitious plans cannot compete with nature conservation because it is treatment, not prevention. Understanding the ecological system through the conception, design, implementation, commissioning, maintenance, decommissioning, removal, management, and procurement of projects is paramount to conserve nature. In this regard, therefore, the UN-HABITAT would highly recommend and prioritize more culturally triggered shelters and industries for ecological sustainability.

The tendency to view your culture as unimportant or backward has a lasting effect on your motherland, offspring, and many generations to come. That is outright ignorance not to master the growth of your own culture because even those cultures you admire have grown through centuries. Therefore, a wise person

---

[7] "Convention Concerning the Protection of the World Cultural and Natural Heritage: The General Conference of the United Nations Educational, Scientific and Cultural Organization meeting in Paris from 17 October to 21 November 1972, at its seventeenth session." United Nations Educational, Scientific and Cultural Organization (UNESCO), accessed October 6th 2021. https://whc.unesco.org/en/conventiontext/.

[8] Rosamond Hutt, "China is about to get its first vertical forest," World Economic Forum, May 4th 2017, https://www.weforum.org/agenda/2017/05/china-is-about-to-get-its-first-vertical-forest/.

maintains and grows their culture and does not adopt a foreign one; culture grows just like language. It is our responsibility to preserve our culture and document the facts through generations.

In the interest of self-driven sustainable development, one would first need to be culturally sound to embrace any form of religion. One would need to be grown very strong in the cultural tradition. In several parts of the world, including Africa, religion has consistently intermarried with culture until conventional religions separated the two.

In some areas, people have entirely dropped ancestral culture to adopt foreign religions. According to the 2015 UN Paris Agreement, self-driven sustainable development depends on the three pillars, i.e., social, economic, and environment; both culture and religion are essential. In the context of culture, UNESCO put it right: "Heritage is our legacy from the past, what we live with today, and what we pass on to future generations. Our cultural and natural heritage are both irreplaceable sources of life and inspiration." We should preserve our cultural heritage because when our cultures deteriorate, we risk creating unsustainable communities.

Culture, Mindfulness Exercises, and Sustainability

There has been the comprehensive promotion of conventional religions by providing educative material to the masses, but we do a minimal campaign to promote cultures in Africa. The effect of this to the African child is total belief in their culture as backward and unworthy. The Chinese have recently started promoting their culture worldwide, promoting the Chinese mandarin language taught in several African universities. The language is taught together with kung-fu and taichi, a Chinese cultural style of aerobics. They know well that it is the language on which culture revolves or hinges. The same applies to yoga—a Hindu philosophy, a spiritual and ascetic discipline that teaches you how to control your body and mind in the belief that you can become united with the spirit of the universe in this way.

Both kung-fu and yoga were derived from cultural practices of China and India, respectively. They are now spreading worldwide. They seem easy to understand in the abstract, though not when you get to the details. Also, they seem easy to understand because they are associated with physical exercises; but do you think African cultures lacked such exercises or related activities? According to psychologists, the scientific explanation proves body fitness (work-out) exercises and relaxation techniques valuable, and that is all. They are termed mindfulness exercises grouped under third-wave cognitive behavioural therapies.

Leonardo Da Vinci (1642-1726) had one of the greatest minds in history and believed that we should accept personal responsibility for our health and well-being. He further made remarks that a healthy body leads to a healthy mind. His contribution to physiology and neuroscience has brought about profound success in the areas of modern physiology. Physical exercises are purely a scientific phenomenon, although cultural or religious beliefs have been associative facts way back. At least the advancement in science has clearly shown us the relevancy of physical exercises, especially when sustainability has become the essential topic of the 21st century.

There is no need for specialized activities appearing new for a person who takes full responsibility for their health and wellbeing. Keeping fit is an activity that many people have not invested in, especially on the African continent. Therefore, any confusion brought in this area can easily win their conscience. Here,

I am not contesting yoga, but I am reminding you that it is not an innovation to attract much attention and excitement. It is a Hindu philosophy that promotes oneness, a social construct that juggles religion and the Hindu people's cultural tradition. Because of the spread of Hinduism across the globe, the Yoga community has so far celebrated more than five international Yoga days, starting on June 21st 2015.

Yoga works on both the mental and physical preparedness of the body, which is an ideal therapy. The breathing and meditation done in yoga relaxes the body and eradicates stress. Yoga is more just–specific and focuses on physical fitness, which is not a new order of physical exercise. This Hindu philosophy is starting to be embraced by Africa's Christians, and sometimes, I wonder whether Africans appreciate the cause of events in their lives. The fact is, Yoga is more than just physical exercise for the Hindu people. However, the continued embracing of meditational exercises at the expense of African facts and labelling African philosophies as backward, satanic, and mere ethno-philosophies spoils Africa's identity significantly.

Europeans and Arabs introduced conventional religions to Africa through missionary work and colonialism. We labelled almost everything African as backward and awkward because of being less travelled, unexposed, illiterate, and highly ignorant in that perspective hence justifying the meaning of the word "black" and the associated words which stem from the word "black." If you are not among that group that justifies the word black, you are probably in the top 2%. They could not think of yellow, red, or something else as explicitly shown in the English Oxford dictionaries for reasons we continuously justify up-to-date. It is high time we proved this wrong. We intake everything that comes into our motherland, and we *blacklist* our own, hence justify the meaning of the word *blacklist*.

The white man travelled a lot and learnt a lot from wherever he went whilst some of our ancestors were busy hunting. Because of his curiosity and confidence, he managed to rule. If you are less travelled, less exposed, and ignorant in some spheres, you should not *blacklist* your deeds without justification or evidence. The inferiority complex exhibited by the Africans to date has left many cultures in tatters. A group of Pentecostals are labelling many African cultural norms and traditions as satanic—which is just a man's social construct.

In some cases, what they labelled satanic supported the constant renewal of humankind in those days—those were the ancestors that produced the adherents of modern religions who are failing on the topic of sustainability. Now, satan's adherents renewed humanity, and the adherents of good-doing threaten the 6th earth's mass extinction. Because of the short-sightedness of most of our people, they cannot see the long term impact of adherence to such modern oppression.

Africa's Ethnicities

Africa's population is divided into seven linguistic groups. These are Khoisan (Southern Africa's Bushmen); the Nilo-Saharan (Hamitic, Nilotic and Nilo-Hamitic); the Niger-Congo (Kwa), The Bantu; the Afro-Asiatic (Arabic, Tigrinya and Amharic); Indo-European and Austronesian. There are about one hundred languages widely used for inter-ethnic communication in Africa. The map below shows the major divisions of African languages.

The traditional language families spoken in Africa:

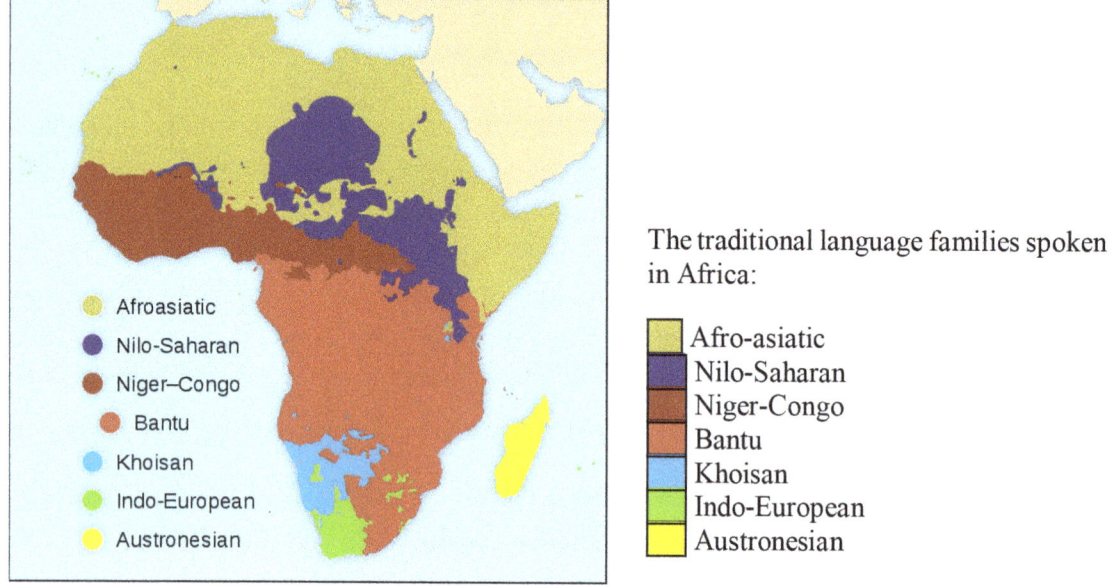

Africa's Linguistic Groups[9]

Religion

Religion. There has been no precise definition of what counts as a religion. However, several scholars have laboured to explain religion, but American anthropologist Clifford James Geertz (1926-2006) has one of the best descriptions of religion. He argues that religion relates humanity to a cosmic 'order of existence'.[10] Therefore, different religions may or may not contain various elements ranging from the divine, sacred things, faith, a Supernatural Being or Supernatural Beings and transcendence that provides norms and power for the rest of life. In my view:

"Religion consists of a set of strongly shared beliefs, values and attitudes, an object, practice, cause, or activity that somebody is completely devoted to, designated behaviours and practices, texts, morals, sanctified places, prophesies, ethics and organizations, particular institutionalized or personal system of beliefs and practices that relates humanity to a Supreme Being, transcendental, or spiritual elements. Religion is, therefore, an architectural process of learning about the Supreme Being, a way of life—a cultural system."

Africa's indigenous religions are referred to as traditional religions, and those religions introduced to Africa by the Arabs, Europeans, and others, are referred to as conventional religions. *In Africa's context,* conventional religions include Christianity, Islam, and Judaism. In some cases, some Africans are adherents to Hinduism and Buddhism, which are Asian traditional religions. Conventional religions

---

[9] User:SUM1, *Languages of Africa*, image, https://commons.wikimedia.org/wiki/File:Map_of_African_language_families.svg. Creative Commons License (CC BY-SA 4.0), https://creativecommons.org/licenses/by-sa/4.0/.

[10] Clifford Geertz, *The Interpretation of Cultures* (New York: Basic Books, 1973). See chapter 4, "Religion as a Cultural System."

are organized religions with official doctrines and practices. However, traditional religions are ethnic or regional customs under the umbrella of religion; they take on the fork-cultural dimension.

The majority of Africans are adherents of Christianity or Islam. According to Stastista survey conducted in 2010, about 60% of Africans are Christians, 30% are Islamic, 3% are folk religions, and 3% are unaffiliated.[11] Therefore, Christians and Muslims make up about 89% of Africa's population. **Note:** The population of Africa was estimated at 1.307 billion in 2019, with Nigeria as the most populated country taking up about 15.38%. I attempt to discuss the leading conventional religions henceforth in comparison to Africa's traditional religions.

Conventional Religions

The leading conventional religions in Africa are Christianity and Islam. Christianity is an Abrahamic monotheistic religion based on the life and teachings of Jesus Christ, who serves as the focal point for the religion. Christian theology is summarized in creeds such as the Apostles' Creed and Nicene Creed. Throughout its history, Christianity has weathered schisms and theological disputes that have resulted in many distinct churches and denominations. Worldwide, the three largest branches of Christianity are the Roman Catholic Church, the Eastern Orthodox Church, and the various denominations of Protestantism. Islam is a religion that was founded by Prophet Mohammad, who reigned between 570CE – 632CE. The Islamic religion believes that Mohammad was God's messenger who was sent to extend monotheism previously preached by Adam, Abraham, Moses, Jesus, and other prophets.

Africa's Position in the World of Conventional Religions

The three great religions of the world, i.e. Christianity, Judaism, and Islam, were somewhat aided by Africa at some point. In other words, they have roots in Africa, but Africans never defined their architecture. For example, Jesus Christ is believed to have spoken Aramaic for preaching. Interestingly, Aramaic and associated Ethiopic languages have been written in their scripts for over 3000 years. These languages serve as liturgical languages in Christianity and Judaism. Both languages belong to the Semitic subgroup of the Afro-Asiatic family.

On the other hand, the New International Version (NIV) in the Christian Bible reports that Joseph, a son of Jacob, saved Jews from starvation in 1567BC when he took them to Egypt, where he had been sold as a slave. In the same line of reasoning, King Herod ordered the killing of infants when Jesus was a baby. According to 13 When they had gone, an angel of the Lord appeared to Joseph in a dream. "Get up," he said, "take the child and his mother and escape to Egypt. Stay there until I tell you, for Herod is going to search for the child to kill him."

[14] So he got up, took the child and his mother during the night and left for Egypt, in the Christian Bible, Jesus Christ as a baby then, escaped death when he was hidden in Egypt. All these facts demonstrate a strong connection of Christianity with Africa in the beginning, particularly North Africa.

---

[11] Statista Research Department, "Percentage of population in Sub-Saharan Africa that belonged to major religious groups in 2010, by religion," Statista, April 4th 2014, accessed September 3rd 2021, https://www.statista.com/statistics/374727/population-in-sub-saharan-africa-by-religion/.

Christians

The Christian faith hinges on the resurrection of Jesus Christ. The holy text for Christians is the Bible (Old and New). The Christian denominations include but are not limited to Catholics, Protestants, Pentecostals and et cetera. The oldest denomination is the Catholics. The legislation of Christianity by Emperor Constantine I of the Roman Empire in 313AD helped the Christian church gain traction. The enemies of Christ coined the word Christians to denote/label the followers of Jesus Christ.

Catholics. The Roman Catholic Church is the largest Christian Church, with more than 1.29 billion members worldwide. The Bishop of Rome, known as the Pope, heading the Church, summarised the church's doctrines in the Nicene Creed. Its central administration, "the Holy See", is in the Vatican City, enclaved within Rome, Italy. The Catholic Church teaches that it is the *one true church founded by Jesus Christ,* that its bishops are the successors of Christ's apostles, and that the Pope is the successor to Saint Peter. The Catholic Church maintains that the doctrine on faith and morals that it declares as definitive is infallible. The first use of the term "Catholic" to describe the Christian Church was in the early 2nd century to emphasize its universal scope. In the context of Christian ecclesiology, it has a rich history and several usages. Catholic means universal.

The Catholic and Eastern Orthodox churches broke communion with each other in the East-West Schism of 1054. Since the East-West Schism of 1054, the Eastern Church has taken the adjective "Orthodox" as its distinctive epithet. The contemporary Orthodox Church had shared communion with the contemporary Roman Catholic Church until the East-West Schism of AD 1054, which had been triggered by disputes over doctrine, especially the authority of the Pope. The Eastern Orthodox Church teaches that it is the One, Holy, Catholic and Apostolic Church established by Jesus Christ in his Great Commission to the apostles. It practices what it understands to be the original Christian faith and maintains the sacred tradition passed down from the apostles. Eastern Orthodoxy is Christianity that developed in the Greek-speaking Eastern part of the Roman Empire and continued later in the Byzantine Empire and beyond.

Protestantism. Protestantism came into existence in the Reformation of the 16th century, splitting from the Roman Catholic Church. The word "Protestant" stems and derives its meaning from the word "protest", which means to—disagree with or disapprove of something. Therefore, Protestant literally means to protest a Catholic.

Protestantism is a form of Christianity that originated with the Reformation, a movement against what its followers considered errors in the Roman Catholic Church. It is one of the three major divisions of Christendom, together with Roman Catholicism and Orthodoxy. The term (Protestantism) derives from the letter of protestation from German Lutheran princes in 1529 against an edict of the Diet of Speyer condemning the teachings of Martin Luther as heretical. Martin Luther (1483–1546) was a German professor of theology, composer, priest, monk and a seminal figure in the Protestant Reformation. Martin Luther initiated the 1517 schism from the Roman Catholic Church to Reform Protestantism and continued by John Calvin, Huldrych Zwingli, and other early Protestant Reformers in 16th Century Europe.

Most experts on the subject consider the publication of the Ninety-Five Theses by Martin Luther in 1517 as its starting point. His refusal to renounce all of his writings at the demand of Pope Leo X in 1520 and the Holy Roman Emperor Charles V at the Diet of Worms in 1521 resulted in his excommunication by the Pope and condemnation as an outlaw by the Emperor. Martin Luther's marriage to Katharina von Bora, a former nun, set a model for clerical marriage, allowing Protestant clergy to marry. With its origins in Germany, Protestants reject the notion of papal supremacy and deny the Roman Catholic doctrine of transubstantiation but disagree among themselves regarding the real presence of Christ in the Eucharist. They emphasize the priesthood of all believers, the doctrine of justification by faith alone rather than by or with good works, and a belief in the *Bible alone as the highest authority in matters of faith and morals*.

Pentecostalism. Pentecostalism is a renewal movement within Protestant Christianity that emphasises a direct personal experience of God through baptism with the Holy Spirit. They can be described as second degree Protestants. In the early 20th century, Pentecostalism emerged among radical adherents of the Holiness movement, energized by revivalism and expectation for the imminent Second Coming of Christ. Believing that they were living in the end times, they expected God to spiritually renew the Christian Church, thereby bringing to pass the restoration of spiritual gifts and the evangelization of the world.

In 1900, Charles Parham, an American evangelist and faith healer, began teaching that speaking in tongues was the Bible evidence of Spirit baptism. The three-year-long Azusa Street Revival, founded and led by William J. Seymour (1870–1922) in Los Angeles, California, resulted in the spread of Pentecostalism throughout the United States of America. As visitors to the USA, the rest of the world carried the Pentecostal experience back to their home churches or felt called to the mission field. While virtually all Pentecostal denominations trace their origins to Azusa Street in Los Angeles, California, the movement has experienced a variety of divisions and controversies.

The Azusa Street Revival was a historic Pentecostal revival meeting in Los Angeles, California and is the origin of the Pentecostal movement. William J. Seymour, an African American preacher, led the movement. It began with a meeting on April 9th 1906, and its legacy extends to the present day. Ecstatic spiritual experiences accompanied by claims of physical healing miracles were part of the revival, dramatic worship services, speaking in tongues, and inter-racial mingling. The secular media and Christian theologians criticised the participants for behaviours considered outrageous and unorthodox, especially at the time. Today, historians consider the revival as the primary catalyst for the spread of Pentecostalism in the 20th century. Pentecostalism comprises over 700 denominations and many independent churches, and there is no central authority/structure governing it; however, many denominations are affiliated with the Pentecostal World Fellowship.

Other Christians include Orthodoxies, Seventh Day Adventists, Jehovah's Witnesses and etcetera. Ideally, since all Christians believe in Jesus Christ as the ultimate saviour, there would be no factions. However, because of human imperfections, factions are inevitable.

Islam

Islam is a religion founded by Prophet Mohammad, who reigned between 570CE – 632CE. It is one of the Abrahamic religions. The Islamic religion believes that Mohammad was Allah's messenger sent to extend monotheism previously preached by Adam, Abraham, Moses, Jesus and other prophets. The holy book of Islam is the Quran. Upon his death, the Prophet left about one hundred thousand Muslims on the Arabian Peninsula. The early years of Islam were characterized by two divisions that originated from the death of Prophet Mohammad in the 7th century. These groups opposed each other on who was the lawful successor of Prophet Mohammad.

Unlike the Christians, where Jesus Christ assigned Simon Peter as his successor, Prophet Mohammad did not leave a clear message on who should succeed him. This caused two divisions, the Shi'as and Sunnis within the Islamic faith. The arguments raised by the two groups revolved around the sociopolitical and spiritual responsibility on who was the rightful custodian to further the Prophet's work in both dimensions. Shi'as argue that the Prophet chose Ali (son-in-law) as the next leader, whilst the Sunnis argue that the Prophet named Abu Bakr (close companion) as the next leader (caliph). Like the Christian faith, Islam has experienced a widening schism between immediate leaders and upcoming leaders over the years. This psychological fact has created divisions within divisions—the question of *core beliefs* development. Most of the Islamic beliefs and practices derive from the teachings and practices of Prophet Mohammad. The "Sunnis" is the most populous Islamic group to date, making up over 85% of Muslims worldwide. Muslims also believe in the existence of the Supreme Being and Eternal Self.

Africa's Traditional Religions: What would be a sustainable religion for Sub-Saharan Africa?

Africa's traditional/indigenous religions are those religious beliefs held by African peoples before Europeans and Arabs introduced conventional religions and are still held to date by some Africans who cherish traditionalism. They are oral traditions, not scriptural, and hence they associate with no holy texts. Some Africans are traditionalists, meaning they still follow their natural cause, whilst most converted to conventional religions. At some point, African people often combine the practice of traditional belief with the practice of Abrahamic religions. Of recent, they have also started embracing Hinduism and Buddhism, sometimes not knowing. Hinduism and Buddhism are Asian traditional religions of Indian origin. It is worth noting that some of the conventional religions such as Islam, Judaism, and Christianity approximate to traditional religions of some Asians and Europeans. And it is, therefore, a difficult task to appreciate to which point along a continuum the conventional religions, rather traditional religions for some others, become religions and not cultures.

African traditional religions would be developed and homogenized into one great African indigenous religion founded and rooted in "Ubuntu philosophy" for the Niger-Congo and Bantu peoples. We would need a *fusion* of various African cultures and traditions to corroborate the Ubuntu philosophy. Similarly, philosophies from other Africa's ethnicities in the same scheme of things would be borrowed. If this happened, it was the kind of religion that would propel Africa to self-driven sustainable development. The correct African religion for the Niger-Congo and Bantu peoples would be rooted in the African Ubuntu Philosophy. Ubuntu is an African philosophy that emphasizes "Being self through others". The Sub-Saharan peoples ought to have their religion.

> *"A person is a person through other persons. None of us comes into the world fully formed. We would not know how to think, or walk, or speak, or behave as human beings unless we learned it from other human beings. We need other human beings in order to be human. I am because other people are. A person is entitled to a stable community life, and the first of these communities is the family."* **Archbishop Desmond Tutu**

The most pronounced attribute of the African traditional religions is belief in veneration of the dead, how the dead influence the living ones and pilgrimage to sacred sites. Other attributes include the *belief in spirits* and the use of African traditional medicine to heal the sick. They try to harmonize nature with the supernatural. However, one wonders whether the word *spirit* is African—and how it was constructed to gain meaning and enter the English dictionaries, i.e. the *holy* and *evil* spirits. These spirits are everywhere across the globe for those who believe regardless of conventional religions. For that matter, the dead are not dead everywhere, not only in Africa! Now that the world has graduated to several platforms, we need to *go evidence-based approach* in the interest of self-driven sustainable development, i.e. the self-awareness perspective. We need a phenomenological stance! This is because Africa is begging for its people to survive merely. Yet, conventional religions are doing well in Africa better than any other institution, and poverty-ridden Sub-Saharan Africa is among the most religious places in the world. This is where the *problem statement roots.*

The correct unified African traditional religion, mainly for the Sub-Saharan peoples, would be rooted in the Ubuntu philosophy and the companioning philosophies of other ethnicities. This would be *similar* to Asian fork religions, e.g. the Chinese folk religion. The Shenism Chinese fork religion, for example, believes in the exorcism of harmful drives, the veneration of forces of nature and ancestors, and a belief in the rational order of nature, which can be influenced by people and their leaders as well as spirits and gods. It is the most widely practised religion by the Chinese people. To the conventionalists, these people are perceived to miss eternal life. My greatest worry is their potential to lead Africans and support Africa's cause massively, especially in funding infrastructure and associated technologies when the conventionalist is looking on. And instead, the conventionalists extort money directly from the surviving African either by reciprocal cognitive restructuring means or through unlawful means in the eyes of a sustainable development activist.

Africa's sustainable religion would be a solid and organized fusion of the word of the great moral teachers of the leading holy texts and Ubuntu philosophy or similar African philosophies of other ethnicities. None of the great moral teachers founded a unique faction. Claiming their word into our religious architecture was the right and sustainable move. Some great religions seem to compartmentalize the African way of life, making it unsustainable in the long run. This is the root cause of many problems facing Africa. Africa's way of life, i.e. collectivism, moves as a whole. Therefore, the sustainable African way of life for a wholesome enterprising, healthy, and believer of African descent is shown as a jigsaw that constantly moves as a whole and is never departmentalized. It consists of four dimensions, i.e. spiritual, psychological, biological, and social dimensions. They are interconnected and interdependent, and all these dimensions move as a whole. Once one dimension is neglected and postponed for a future date, trouble ensues. There can be many problems, and our lives become difficult to manage—hence, resorting to many unnecessary activities, practices, and prophecies. Without Africans grasping this concept, they will *never* stand on their own. The continent's prospects will continue to be defined by others. This is not the sustainable development Africans are eyeing. We need a self-driven future!

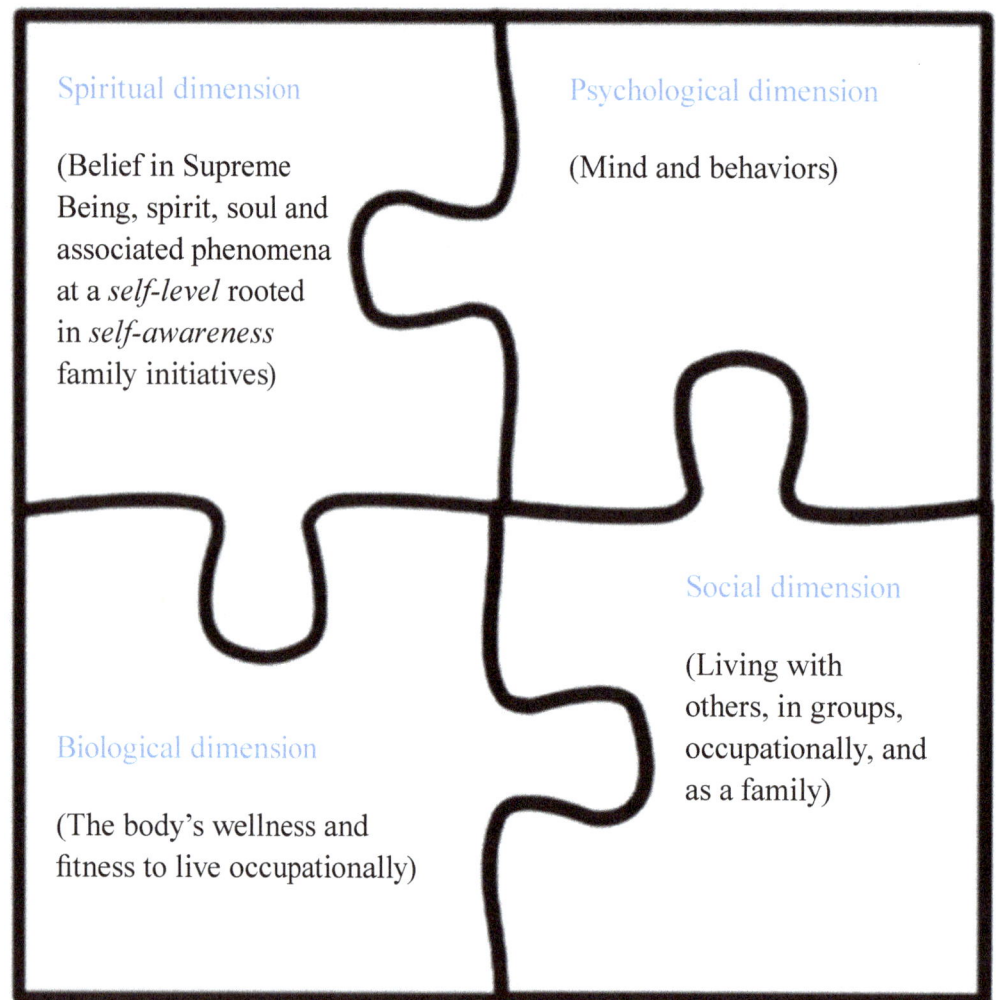

The Four Interconnected Dimensions that make an Enterprising African

Explanation

To graduate as an accountant, you must have read an accounting degree. You must not be socially impaired to live with others while studying and after. Your body must be healthy and physically fit without experiencing a severe medical or clinical problem to be able to achieve the degree. You must be spiritually sound and competent at a phenomenological level. A level that tracks phenomena at the family level through self-awareness family initiatives. These initiatives ought to be multigenerational, especially in collectivistic cultures. Tracking this multigenerational cultural influence on our lives is critical in making a successful and enterprising human being. If all this effort meets a creative mind, there is no doubt that one will succeed. All these four dimensions work together every day throughout our lives, and there is no magic.

Interestingly, the architecture of traditional religions believes in the Supreme Being or the Supernatural and the corresponding devil, which is synonymous with what conventional religions, e.g. Christians call "God" and corresponding "Satan", respectively. The traditionalists understand what doing good to humanity entails. The Supernatural is regarded as one that bestows life and wellbeing, and the Devil is explained in the belief in evil spirits and the use of magic or *evil spirits* to influence one's events and the events of another person without their consent—usually labelled as having no faith in the living word. The traditionalists acknowledge *the world of spirits;* Conventionalists also acknowledge *the world of spirits.* This world has both evil and good spirits. The same architecture, for example, in Buganda where I originate, and which I know most, the traditional religion has rituals very similar to what some conventional religions perform. They also have prophets and philosophers whom scholars have failed to recognize. For example, the belief in good spirits influencing people's lives is seen from a good point of view, and the use of evil spirits and magic to shape events is viewed from a negative perspective (the evil).

A culturally sound Muganda only needs to pay tribute to African ancestors following norms, values, and beliefs. This is what society constructed as good which believers of the living word find noncompliant with the process to get to the heavens. Interestingly, the spirits of African ancestors who are claimed to have done the good while in conventionalism are worshipped. I find this a psychological technique. At some point not so different from the cultural tradition of paying tribute to the spirits of African ancestors. If any spirit prayed through provides what *society calls the good for society but not what the individual labels as good for themselves*, I find it naïve to label this spirit an evil spirit simply because it has not been canonized in conventionalism. A positive result cannot be argued from a negative premise.

The psychological assumption the architects make in drafting religions and which is good, but Africans failed to recognize is the claim that praying through a good/holy spirit enables one to reach the High of Creation. Africans also had/have good spirits regardless of conventional religions. Not all spirits of Africa's dead are evil. Many people elsewhere claim to know Africans more than Africans themselves, but there is still a lot that remains uninvestigated and unexamined, which requires more effort to draw patterns and interrelationships. The most outstanding feature of many African collectivistic cultures in understanding the world of spirits is their capability to settle evil spirits from negatively influencing people's lives—they know how to maintain and update firewalls to safeguard you from viruses. This norm which a certain fraction of Christians find non-compliant with what they believe when adequately evaluated, would be an excellent treatment of the complex spectrum of the African dissociative identity disorders. In my opinion, faith is simply doing good to humanity, other living beings, and the environment.

The one who uses magic and evil spirits to influence events can be understood in the psychological dimension by answering why he believes in magic and evil spirits. The cognitive distortions of the sort! These distortions are far-stretching and would necessitate defining spectrums. This would enable us to define several unique maladaptive behaviours. If cultural norms, values, and beliefs are reexamined in laboratories, we can document purposeful results that could help draw a line between the common good and the evil. These laboratories would benchmark on spiritual and psychological dimensions which share the same source. The psychological dimension does not discriminate or segregate. It knows no boundary; whether conventionalist or traditionalist, you can be profiled along the same continuum. Why you believe and not believe are psychological facts. The circumstances leading to why you believe or not are unique from one person to another, justifying that the psychological dimension must share a source with spirituality. These are phenomenological stances.

One finds great joy in a conventional religion only when they have nothing to do with earning their livelihood. However, do you know why we have mushrooming religions, which is a psychological fact? Deriving the most incredible enthusiasm to fish people has come with many rewards to complement the exercise in the 21st century. Because Europeans authored much of what Africans follow today, they think they know much about Africans, which is false. I have meditated on several occasions and found that self-awareness, i.e. *evidence-based initiatives*, ought to revive the glory of African humankind. We shall regain our lost glory when we refresh our minds to believe in our cause. Understanding Africans is purely an African issue for Africans, and it is solvable by Africans. One ought to experience an African phenomenon that makes them weigh the odds in matters related to spiritual conviction and the sustainability of this beautiful continent.

The process of praying, for example, by kneeling and standing, is shared in both the traditional and conventional religions. Secondly, appreciating phenomena, visiting sacred sites, special hills, and the love for humanity are all embraced in both the traditional and conventional religions. Correct enlightenment of African masses would be to embrace the great moral philosophers as outlined in the holy texts and scriptures, in an architectural process that would be rooted in the great African Ubuntu Philosophy and associated philosophies. In this way, the Ubuntu African conventional religion would borrow more wisdom and understanding of the Supreme Being from the holy texts. The traditional religions that interweaved with cultures would remain intact as cultural facts. The God of conventional religions never founded a unique faction. His word needed to be embraced and integrated into the admirable "Ubuntu Philosophy" for the Bantu, creating an African religion that would conserve Africa's identity and the environment. Conventional religions were formulated to streamline people to grow spiritually, and we could not afford to miss our African religion. The Ubuntu African religion would not have to report anywhere, just like many other religious formations and reformations throughout history. This is the best way that self-driven sustainable development would be possible.

Following many phenomenological pieces of evidence gathered to date, especially in many cultures across Africa, it is clear that the Africans knew and understood the Supreme Being before conventional religions were introduced in Africa. In Uganda, the Baganda peoples call the Supreme Being, "Katonda" which means the one who created the universe—and was considered the High Spirit. Katonda comes from the Luganda verb, "Tonda", which means create. The word, "Katonda" on which the Baganda proverb, *"Katonda agoba ensoonga: nga tasse wuwo"*, is premised, has existed way back before conventional religions. The English version of this proverb is, "God will have had his special purpose (in letting a certain person die) : (so you say) if he has not killed your own (e.g. father or child)." The hidden meaning is, "when someone wins a case against another, that person can always say God makes his decision following the highest moral standards of reason." The argument in this proverb demonstrated how people expressed dismay, similar to how someone would feel when they lose a court case. It is believed that "Katonda" was considered the Supreme command that would follow the highest moral values of humanity, the "virtues".

Today, in Buganda culture, the Supreme Being is referred to as Katonda throughout all conventional religions. Why not coin another terminology for the Supreme Being following the introduction of conventional religions? That is where the second problem statement roots; using psychological techniques to expand conventional religions. This demonstrates that the Baganda people, of Bantu ethnicity, understood that a Supreme Being exists above all. However, because of being illiterate, they failed to document the facts throughout history. Otherwise, they would coin a great African religion rooted in the "Ubuntu philosophy" in collaboration with other Bantu. This religion would heavily protect, defend, and conserve Africa's identity and the environment.

How would Africans be enlightened? The great African conventional religion would accompany the study into traditional healers, spiritual leaders, and their cultures. It would seek to enlighten more on what they called holy by fusing the word of the great moral teachers into their mainstream work and practices. This is because the limits of the spiritual dimension in collectivism are not known. Trying to do away with what we owe to traditionalists goes with some assets we cannot afford to lose in the sustainability agenda, the reason why Africa lags.

Traditional spiritual leaders experience unique phenomena not anyone else experiences. Even if one studies and graduates with a PhD, if they do not receive a phenomenological favour, they can never become traditional spiritual leaders, except those who fake in the interest of extorting money from the public. The psychosocial and psycho-spiritual work of traditional spiritual leaders produces positive results when socially objectivized. In the same domain, the positives, those who enlighten the traditionalists ought to experience a similar phenomenon. And that phenomenon should be for the good of African peoples, not against sustainability. That God's calling would not be tagged on what man socially constructs like wealth, marriage, education, and ability. This should not be a *core requirement or essential* but rather *desirable*. God's calling cannot be tagged on whether your parents are/were married or not or whether you have a degree or not. It is a phenomenon for those that God's favour has landed on. This equation of traditionalists versus conventionalists must be answered for Africa's sustainability.

Africans going overboard in conventionalism is because of this equation that was not solved. I believe the Supreme Being who created the universe wishes to have the planet earth conserved. Not answering Africa's spiritual equation within the sustainability framework leaves very little hope. Honestly, a competent African spiritual leader should be able to heal some illnesses beyond psychosocial stressors. Some conventionalists who have tried to blend Africanisms with conventional ideals are doing well to rehabilitate, treat, and heal many spiritual and psychosocial illnesses. Masses turn to spiritual leaders whenever things become very tight in their way, and they should be able to obtain holistic spiritual services that produce results. In this way, they should be guided and empowered to adopt tools and techniques within holistic therapeutic interventions that move within God's word and sustainability of the beautiful African continent.

A human's sufferance in the belief of following the living word requires more studies on the African masses. Many psychosocial stressors and illnesses can be treated in the cultural tradition, which some conventionalists debar. Through an integrated approach of praying and conforming to the good Africanisms will see Africans become livelier and successful. Africa's ancient secretive illiterate philosophers left us a big job to draw a line between good and evil in our cultures. Therefore, the aggregate of the good, fused with the word of the great moral philosophers in the leading holy texts and scriptures, would emerge the great African conventional religion to protect Africa's nature and identity. There was a difference between human beings and other living beings before conventionalism depicting God's presence in humanity. Man has led in all corners of the globe regardless of what. This management and leadership bestowed on man in the social constructionism cannot be claimed all hopeless before conventionalism.

Other World's Famous Religions

Buddhism and Hinduism

Gautama Buddha [480BC – 400 BC] was a Hindu. The Hindu people are found in India. Therefore, Buddhism forms part of the ethos, which is essentially Hindu. Hinduism is the world's third-largest religion and the oldest in the world. It is a fusion of various Indian cultures and traditions. Hinduism is believed to have no founder. Just as Christianity and Islam have faced several schisms that created a number of waves and divisions within divisions, Hinduism and Buddhism are not any different. They, too, have been inseparable twins at some point in history, with Buddhism being one of the stains of Hinduism. Buddhism, with roots in India, declined after the Gupta era and at some point disappeared from India around the 11th Century CE. It is, therefore, a religion more populous in other Asian countries outside India, especially China and Japan. The most important attribute about Buddhism as preached by Buddha is that nobody or no moral teacher can claim that their teachings help humanity reach the highest good in the universe.

Although Buddhism does not expressly dispute the existence of the Supreme Being, the teachings are more focused on oneness. Therefore, nobody should claim that they can reach the highest good in the universe through their teachings. In this line of faith, the Buddhists dispute the priests of Hinduism, the formal rituals of Hinduism, and the caste system, thereby focusing on Buddha's great message of seeking enlightenment through *meditation*. Buddhism is, therefore, considered as one of the strains of Hinduism in India.

South Africa holds the largest Buddhist population in Africa, estimated to be between 100 and 150 thousand people, whilst Mauritius holds the largest population of Hinduism in Africa, estimated to be over 55% of the population. Themes in Hindu beliefs include the four proper goals or aims of human life, i.e. ethics, prosperity, passions, and liberation. Various kinds of Yogas in Hindu beliefs are aimed at getting liberated from the cycle of death and salvation. The practice of Yoga is connected to the religious beliefs and practices of both Hinduism and Buddhism, although there are distinct variations in Yoga usage. Some of the major scriptures of Hinduism include the Vedas and the Upanishads, among others.

Case Study on a Chinese Buddhist—a Personal Experience

A Chinese colleague who is a Buddhist once asked me, "Do you know how Catholics offended other people?" He had bought a book that put him more defensive as a Buddhist—a book written to defame Catholics highly. He told me, "Your God is within you and me, right here, but he is never up in the skies as you think."

In my internship training while still in school, I was posted to a Chinese construction site. Since I am a Christian, I used to pray in Jesus' name before taking a meal until a Chinese manager confronted me, asking me whether it was Jesus who had served me the food. At first, I thought the gentleman was joking, but surprisingly, the incident went on for many days until when he was greatly offended at some point trying to push me off the dining. I learnt two lessons here; nobody knows the truth thoroughly, and one needs to adhere to the morals and values in a foreign jurisdiction. This is because each jurisdiction invents its morality to live with others—the moral and public philosophy. It is only in Africa where you can introduce things anyhow and at any time you wish. This Chinese construction contractor believed I did not have to bring my religion to his camp whenever he served me food and that I had to bow before him but not saying a prayer through Jesus, who has not been there when preparing the meal. I had to respect the manager so that I would complete the training.

Judaism

According to the Christians' New Testament and the Muslims' Quran, Mary, the mother of Jesus Christ, was a Galilean Jewish woman of Nazareth. Judaism is the *ethnic religion* of the Jewish people and is considered the expression of the covenant that God established with the Israelites. Judaism emphasizes the *Oneness* of God and rejects the Christian concept of God in human form. The holy text of Judaism is the Hebrew Bible, and Judaism evolved from ancient Israelite religions around 500BCE. It comprises the collective religious, cultural and legal tradition and civilization of the Jewish people.

What did the great moral philosophers' coming, i.e. Prophet Mohammad, Jesus Christ, Siddhartha Gautama (the Buddha), and others, mean to the World? Did they come to blur cultures? A personal view

The moral philosophers came to the world to communicate the greatness of the Supreme Being. They emphasised that the Supreme Being is a spirit; there is a Supreme spirit above all spirits. They came to communicate how to do the good. And the good is done by being non-judgmental and through forgiveness.

In brief, all the great moral teachers communicated almost the same message that enlightened the world about the greatness of the Supreme Being who is the one to judge for us those who cause us pain. That when someone causes you pain, pray for them to change for good and move on. Do not attempt revenging or reciprocating.

Never reciprocate when you feel anger; when you start using the devil's tools, at some point, you graduate as a devil itself. The level of evildoing goes maturing, and you can never return to doing the good. That guilty conscience you develop trying to get back to good-doing makes your life uncertain. When you reciprocate, that means you judge the person who wronged you, but you can never know 100% why that person wronged you; they might be suffering from a disorder, perhaps.

A broad spectrum of spiritual and psychological disorders exists. When you reciprocate or revenge, you apologise that you both have the same disorders as the person who wronged you; sometimes, the believers label it "being taken over by satan". Therefore, vengefulness shows that you also have that problem that the person who harmed you has. Even if you know 100% why they harmed you, forgive; when you forgive, you release those negative emotions from you and pass on an example to the person who harmed you; that could make that person slowly adapt to good doing. That is what brought moral philosophers to enlighten the world.

When you understand that that person has a problem, it ceases to be a problem to you; you seek the solution to that problem. The problem is not always the problem but the way you perceive the problem is the problem. Ultimately, this differentiates a healthy conscience from a sick conscience; predetermines the one with a healthy personal relationship with the Supreme Being.

The great moral teachers preached about love, hope, and forgiveness. They preached how to live a way of life that does good things to humans, other living beings, and the environment. Also, they preached about how to have a healthy personal relationship with the Supreme Being.

The karma principle and associated twelve (12) laws are some of the fundamentals coined by those who understood the coming of the great moral philosophers. They teach us how to live a healthy personal relationship with the Supreme Being. The 12 laws are well-understood and practised by a good fraction of Buddhists and Hindus. In my opinion, the twelve (12) karma laws approximately equate to the ten (10) commandments in Abrahamic religions.

One's relationship with the Supreme Being is a phenomenon that differs from one person to another. Through praying and meditation, one improves their relationship with the Supreme Being. Therefore, the great moral teachers' coming meant to shape a healthy relationship with the Supreme Being, to learn how to do good whilst living in your culture. People did a lot of evil things in several cultures across the globe. Our ancestors lived in the darkness, failing to know whom the good resides in, and the great moral teachers brought light to the world.

The opportunists, because they failed to forgive one another, created shockwaves and schisms throughout history!

I have found out that several other moral teachers in Sub-Saharan Africa and other parts of the world did not emerge out as great, and their work significantly contributed to the well-being of humanity. *Sometimes, the world misinterpreted them and labelled them evildoers.*

A Personal Insight into some Religious Schisms Faced in History

A close look at many religious schisms faced throughout history, the people's refusals to adhere to many social constructs in spiritualism and the disagreements in worshipping and the form of Supreme Being or what one calls Supreme depicts that most of the causal factors were/are psychological facts. Jesus Christ, for example, being born from a Jewish mother and the subsequent upholding of Judaism tradition and laws by Jews whilst many parts of the world embraced Christianity leaves a big question that is well answerable in the psychological dimension. Jesus was a Jew, but his claims to be a son of God threw mixed reactions in the community where he originated. Even though much evidence occurred during Jesus' lifetime and after Jesus' resurrection, as reported by holy texts, Jews firmly hold their beliefs to date. Therefore, at some point, several interpretations of monotheism that existed in Judaism gave rise to Christianity. These variations in interpretations are psychological facts of human nature. The same people from whom Jesus was born disagree within themselves that Jesus Christ was a son of God, then what about other peoples who derive faith in this fact?

The Shi'as and Sunnis disagreement and many thousands of disagreements faced by Muslims throughout history are all psychological facts that emanate from the need to hold power. Martin Luther was a scholar whose theses landed into the hands of people that had yearned for liberation for many years. They felt having got a golden opportunity which was a way out of conservatism. All these facts can be profiled in a psychological dimension, what ordinary man calls human imperfections. What disturbs some hypnotic faiths' leaders to think they know most that their religion or movement is better than others is explainable in the psychological dimension—the personality development, the compliance and conforming techniques concerning power, and man's survival state most of the time.

One man's temple meeting his demands following what Abraham Maslow (1908 – 1970) postulated as the hierarchy of needs makes him derive much pleasure in extending and preaching what he calls right.[12] The fact that these men and women of the Supreme Being advertise on TVs, the internet, Radios, and other Media in the modern world is enough evidence of a psychological fact being a causal factor in a number of schisms throughout history—the subject of power, what Maslow postulated in his hierarchy of needs. All kinds of behaviours that spiritual leaders portray at some point can be profiled in the psychological dimension.

I am convinced that if one wakes up one day and proposes using digital technologies in worshipping centres, churches and mosques, they might face stiff resistance. They rally Africans to make offertory through digital platforms, and this collection goes to the needy children fund, and none of it goes to the magistrates; there can be protests. Why?

Buddha is central in Buddhism, Jesus Christ is central in Christianity, and Mohammad is central in Islam. These can be collectively referred to as moral philosophers. They help humanity appreciate the highest good. At some point, Christianity, Judaism and Islam are referred to as Abrahamic religions, of which Africa has aided somewhere in history. The surrounding architecture of these religions was drawn following cultural psychologies and traditions of who led the schism in that particular time in history. All moral philosophers on which religions are hinged taught about "doing the good to humanity" and never preached the kind of architecture required in doing the good. This architecture of doing the good to humanity, in behaviours, thoughts, and actions, cannot run away from the psychological facts of humanity, i.e. the human imperfections—implying psychology and spirituality have the same source. They are inseparable twins whose study could help humans to achieve sustainable life on earth.

More on Conventional Religions and Sustainable Development

Anyone who wishes their country sustainable socioeconomic success cannot wish for a state religion. Similarly, democratic ideals are abused the moment freedom of expression and human rights are oppressed. The advantage of having an opposition is that it helps expose the wrongdoings of the current regime. The opposition is best termed as the advisory arm of the current system. Jesus Christ was not a Christian, neither was Mohammed a Shi'a or a Sunni. When one listens to all religious factions within the Islamic faith and Christianity, they all have sound reasons for their identity. The amusing bit of it is

---

[12] In a 1943 paper titled "A Theory of Human Motivation," American psychologist Abraham Maslow theorized that human decision-making is undergirded by a hierarchy of psychological needs. Maslow proposed that five core needs form the basis for human behavioral motivation. Those needs are physiological needs, safety needs, love and belonging needs, esteem needs, and self-actualization needs. See more from: http://www.maslow.com

that they all believe in Jesus Christ and Mohammed as the ultimate saviour for Christians and Muslims, respectively. Another amusing scenario is that the Quran prohibits division in Islam. Holy Quran: 006.159 "Indeed, those who divide their religion and break up into sects, you have no part with them in the least: their affair is with God: He will, in the end, tell them the truth of all that they used to do."

The world changes every second, and one cannot rule out the loathsome capital gains as one crucial factor that triggers religious factions to explode day by day. The struggle for power in the modern world has now changed goalposts from one we knew at our thumbprints to one which cons, indoctrinates, wins and traumatizes the people's minds to live in fear in broad daylight. We have theology, philosophy, psychology, and history scholars to help improve and sustain the future. People who have not mastered or have not been exposed chronologically to theology, philosophy, psychology, and history preaching for any change, say spiritual change and salvation relying on God's grace alone as the catalyst is a challenge. In the interest of self-driven national development, this is invalid over 2000-years into time following the birth of Jesus Christ. I am convinced that in the 21st century, one may get closer to God without reading his word well-enough, perhaps. However, one may never sustainably get others closer to God without reading and being studied enough. The more you read and know, the more you appreciate God's love for the universe. You need to know a spectrum of things to fish people get closer to God

To transform from the African traditional religion to Christianity or Islam or another appropriate African conventional religion or faith harmoniously needed training and exposure. A typical example is a Ugandan-based Christian preacher who burnt the Christian bible in Kampala in April 2017. This is because the bible read "holy ghost". On July 6th, 2017, The Daily Monitor wrote, "In April this year, the celebrated preacher stunned the public when he allegedly burned Bibles of King James Version (KJV) and Good News version which he collected from his 6,000-strong flock on Easter Sunday. The core reason for burning the version of the Bibles was that they bore the words "Holy Ghost" as opposed to "Holy Spirit.""[13]

We are left stranded in the desert with such modern oppression, and genuine self-driven development is impossible because development starts within the mind. When you sit back and reflect pretty well, you realize that psychology works hand in hand with spirituality; and are likely to have the same source. Some training in psychopathology to track mental disorders would present a good opportunity for spiritual leaders vying for counselling, guidance and pastoring to heal as many Pentecostals claim—only emphasizing the point from a sustainable development agenda, not opportunistic pastoring.

The Islamic and Christian doctrines are constitutional, and anyone who thinks about national development, peace and stability can quickly understand them. Fitting in societies of different cultural settings would ideally require doctrines to safeguard culture for national development, peace and stability. Suppose all faith that is not purely streamlined to follow doctrines and to have a structure is not put to an end, with the short-sightedness of many African people, partially sighted people, false attitude and laziness. In that case, there is no bright future for Africa, only to remain mendicants.

For example, all conventional religions at some point agree that cohabitation and fornication are not good deeds. Initially, marriage was neither formal nor legalized. Neither Jesus was a Christian nor was Mohamed a Shia or Sunni. Buddha was also not a Buddhist! Man has created many ideals by himself

---

[13] "Court summons Pastor Bugingo over burning Bibles," The Daily Monitor, July 6th, 2017.

through social construction. Many but not all of these ideals aim to create peace, stability, and equity. If society does not provide such ideals, living in peace would not be easy because of the desire for power that humans yearn for every day in spirit, politics, leadership, and governance.

To everyone with a free mind and not corrupt, the need for doctrines can easily be understood although human-made. Formalizing and legalizing marriage must have been decided following several religious teachings and the holy texts. On the other hand, safeguarding family institutionalism and the people's lineage would require a more organized approach hence building up laws. Otherwise, people would produce like animals. The question remains why is it so difficult to believe in other doctrines because it is not God who openly said that formal marriage is when a church magistrate weds the couple? [4] "Haven't you read," he replied, "that at the beginning the Creator 'made them male and female,'[and said, 'For this reason a man will leave his father and mother and be united to his wife, and the two will become one flesh'? So they are no longer two, but one flesh. Therefore what God has joined together, let no one separate. It is a doctrine to safeguard marriage made by man. Doctrines are formulated to make humans more organized in faith, more united, create peace and stability whilst improvising a roadmap to sustainable development. You cannot leave people to do whatever they want under the sun because you believe in God's Grace and whatever a man does democratically to shape and sustain the faith is against God's word. If you are an open-minded person, scientist or psychologist, this can easily be understood. With the population explosion, you can easily understand why there is a need to regulate all sorts of religions and faiths.

The need for doctrines can be justified. They serve as guidelines to create social order among believers. As a believer, you need to follow protocol in the church. Doctrines are the organized principles that govern a community of believers—and well-educated believers who carry out relevant research formulate them. We need well-educated spiritual leaders to lead sustainability.

The need for education can be justified. For example, Jesus Christ, like most Jewish children, is believed to have been educated. Several scholars believe that Jesus could have been able to speak at least three languages; Hebrews, Greek, and Aramaic. Scholars have a wide consensus that Aramaic was the primary language Jews of the first century spoke, and Jesus is believed to have spoken Aramaic for preaching. The most exciting fact is that the Ethiopic languages of Ethiopia and Aramaic languages belong to the Semitic subgroup of the Afro-Asiatic family. Jesus is believed to have learned from His parents at home about the Scriptures (the Old Testament) and Jewish history and culture.

All Jewish males were also offered free public education, instituted for all male students in the first century BC. As part of their education, all of the boys were taught Scripture and law but also included reading, writing, history, elementary sciences and mathematics.

According to Luke (Luke 4:16), we know that Jesus knew how to read since He read the Scriptures in the temple and knew how to write (John 6:6, 8). It was written of Jesus that "the child grew and became strong, filled with wisdom. And the favour of God was upon him" (Luke 2:40). Once, when Jesus' parents attended the Feast of Passover, they left to return to Nazareth only to find that Jesus was not with them.

When they searched for Him, it was "After three days they found him in the temple, sitting among the teachers, listening to them and asking them questions. And all who heard him were amazed at his understanding and his answers" (Luke 2:46-47).

Jesus astounded many because "Jesus increased in wisdom and in stature and in favour with God and man" (Jesus increased in wisdom and in stature and in favour with God and man). Luke is the second-longest of the four gospels of the Christian bible, and together with Acts of the Apostles, the pair make up a two-volume work from the same pen, called Luke-Acts. A gospel is a written account of the career and/or teachings of Jesus of Nazareth.

The four gospels of the New Testament—Matthew, Mark, Luke and John – are almost the only source of information on Jesus and thus occupy a uniquely important place in Christianity. They were all written in the period between c.70 AD and the end of the 1st century by anonymous authors and stand at the end of a process of oral and written tradition that began on, or even before, the death of Jesus. For various reasons, modern scholars are cautious of relying on them uncritically; nevertheless, they do provide a good idea of the public career of Jesus, but nothing on private life and critical study can attempt to distinguish the original ideas of Jesus from those of the later authors.

The early church fathers ascribed to Luke authorship of both the Gospel according to Luke and the book of Acts of the Apostles, which would mean Luke contributed over a quarter of the text of the New Testament, more than any other author. Many scholars believe that *Luke was a Greek physician* who lived in the Greek city of Antioch in Ancient Syria, though some other scholars and theologians think Luke was a Hellenic Jew. Luke, the evangelist, was born in Antioch and believed by profession to be a physician. He had become a disciple of the apostle Paul and later followed Paul until his martyrdom. It is believed that having served the Lord continuously, unmarried and without children, filled with the Holy Spirit, he died at the age of 84 years. This is where some churches and religions partly derive a section of their doctrines—to serve God wholeheartedly; you ought not to be diverted by marriage.

St. Paul writes, "So the man who marries does well, but the one who doesn't, does even better." (So the man who marries does well, but the one who doesn't, does even better.). The superiority of celibacy is contested by several factions that went off the Catholic doctrine to formulate other religious factions. In my opinion, going unmarried lowers the risk of *multigenerational baggage* resulting from the sexual fusion of man and woman hence allowing the spiritual leader to serve God wholeheartedly. Several African cultures prescribe going six months or more without indulging in sexual intercourse to win battles, sociocultural stress, and related problems. Therefore, it is a therapeutic intervention. Adherents to conventional ideals call it fasting but it is part of cultural norms.

The Hindu people of India also found it quite essential to serve God wholeheartedly, minus being married when they said, "If prayer overtakes a man, he does not need human love of marriage." The Hindus believe that the love of God supplants that love. They, too, go to the forest, unmarried, and spend most of their time in prayer and meditation. In my opinion, when one is married, they would have to do away with many things because marriage calls for a high level of discipline and self-examination. Therefore, to wholeheartedly serve God would necessitate doing away with the marriage captivity. Otherwise, you would spend a fraction of your time pursuing to learn the personality or uniqueness of your partner. However, because of this conservatism, some people fell off the doctrine. And I do not see any harm in this fallout – they developed their beliefs.

The fact that Luke, a physician, contributed more than a quarter of the Gospel explicitly shows the power of education. Reading the Gospel, you can even see that Luke's Gospel is outstanding. Theologian scholars have proved that Jesus Christ was educated and attained an equivalence of tertiary education in the modern-day. If you understand what education means, you will not believe that Africa lacked education before colonialists. You will undoubtedly ask yourself what Jesus Christ did between 12-years to 30-years before embarking on his public career.

It is over 2000 years AD, and we still have people who doubt the relevance of education. They can hardly attend school while certain groups believe that to be a man of God and preach the word of God, you do not need any schooling or theological classes but just God's favour. Today's an educated person is more dangerous than one who lived in ancient times simply because the ancient people were also comparatively educated in their way, at home and in their societies. Today, education is done holistically in schools and not in homes. Today, if one fails to attend school, he is more badly a fit in society than the ancient societies. If people learn what they call "equivalence", they would understand that the ancient also had professors.

The births of some of the African chiefdoms and kingdoms are believed to occur after the birth of Jesus Christ, the ultimate saviour for Christians and others slightly after the birth of Prophet Mohammed, the ultimate saviour for Muslims. One of the oldest notable empires to ever live in Africa was the Axum or Aksum Empire in Eritrea and Northern Ethiopia, existing from approximately 100AD to 940AD. The Kingdom of Ghana, centred in what is today Senegal and Mauritania, dominated West Africa between about 750 and 1078 A.D. The great Musa Keita I of the wealthy West African Mali Empire, a Muslim by religion, reigned from (1312 – 1337). Clearly, if we are to follow Christianity, +2000 years AD, some people have adamantly decided not to believe in Jesus Christ as a saviour or Prophet Mohammed as their saviour.

Even at the time Jesus Christ lived, some people witnessed the miracles he performed, but they refused to believe in his prophecy and being a son of God, i.e. when he walked on water; when he healed the sick; when he resurrected the dead; when he converted water into wine; when he served two loaves of bread to over 5000 people; when he ascended to heaven, and still, people in his time refused to believe; what about now? And more importantly, Jesus Christ had been prophesied in the Old Testament. And today, with the IT facilities, education and modernity, it is indicative that it is their will to do so – not to believe. So, let us not antagonize them.

According to (Matthew 13:5-6), an evangelist of the Christian bible, i.e. New Testament, "Some fell on rocky places, where it did not have much soil. It sprang up quickly because the soil was shallow. But when the sun came up, the plants were scorched, and they withered because they had no root." These could be the ones talked about. It is their will to make such a decision because education and modernity have made each of us choose his or her belief. You decide on what to believe, unlike in the ancient time when people were less exposed and coerced. We are now living in an era of *evidence.* Maybe, God's will has not been to their opportunity. If you claim to help them endure everlasting life, it is more amplified when not opportunistically done.

Let us focus on a common goal which is sustainable development. Let us pave a way to create peace and stability—desist state religions, desist uncontrolled or ungoverned faith, and learn to respect others' faith. This means all sorts of faith must be clearly and explicitly regulated to avoid opportunism resulting from uncontrolled religious factions which sprout out almost every day. India and China are some of the fastest-growing economies in the world. They are believed to have started with cottage industries. However, in Africa, such industries are replaced with opportunistic worshipping centres in homes or a community of a few households. When you ask people why they do so, they tell you that powerful charismas started small. Here, I am using China and India as typical examples because they lived below the poverty line in the 1950s. Today, they emerge as the world's role models in creating good roadmaps to sustained growth and development.

The need for education for spiritual leaders should be non-negotiable. A faction of the highly charismatic faiths, especially some factions of Pentecostals, argue that Pentecostalism is not a religion but rather a movement within Christianity. They call themselves "believers". The Oxford English Dictionary (8th Ed.) defines the word "believer" as "a person who believes in the existence or truth of something especially somebody who believes in a god or religious faith." Who is then not a believer? Almost all human beings are believers. It does not matter what you believe. You are automatically a believer if you believe in the order of human existence, i.e. supremacy above all. In 1924 philosopher Hans Vaihinger (1852-1933) philosophized that none of us can know the truth completely.

Therefore, we ought to respect each other's beliefs—species of truth should be allowed to co-occur. This faction only forgets that the so-called movement has become a cultural tradition in many societies today, and religion is part of the culture. They have their style of music, unique mode of praying, their dances, their unique worshipping times such as overnights, unique testimony deliverance, et cetera. Hence, Pentecostalism is a religion. An excellent conventional religion must have a structure and doctrines to safeguard, promote and conserve sovereignty, nurture prudence, promote morality, promote safety and orderliness, and conserve the environment.

Some conventional religions, wherever they extended, ensured that conserving the environment was the number one priority. Quite a large number of their worshipping centres are raised on hills. The recently sprouted false prophets are mindless about the environment. They build wherever they wish, whether wetlands or designated landfills;—they do not care, especially in Africa. Cases of land grabbing as a result of the unregulated prophecy are on the rise. This is highly motivated by opportunistically designed charismatic movements, which are heavily personalized to rotate around the founder of the worshipping community. I have seen halls used as bars at night and turn into worshipping centres during the day. Health, safety, and environmental aspects are essential issues in socio-economic transformation and religions must be designed to calm people therapeutically. A hall juggling as a bar during the night and a worshipping centre during the day violate the human sense of right and wrong. The opportunistically designed personality cults seem to care less about the health and safety of the neighbourhood.

In 1992, The International Labor Organization (ILO) issued the Code of Practice for Safety and Health in workplaces, especially construction activities. Little did it note that the noise from the worshipping centres is of more decibels than that of construction activities. This noise is a public nuisance, and no immediate laws are put in place to safeguard the rights of others in many African countries. Noise from these worshipping centres can psychologically harm others. For example, noise interferes with sleep, and many worshipping centres are built in public places or dwelling places. A person who sleeps amidst too much noise finds difficulty concentrating the following morning as the brain has difficulty accessing the temporary memory.

In the interest of sustainability, carbon emissions and noise reduction are current global issues. This is because high decibel noise from worshipping centres might cause secondary effects such as stress, loss of concentration, and headaches to those who are not a party to the worshipping centres, especially the neighbouring communities. Such excessive noise may cause acute tinnitus. The level or frequency of the noise may or may not be overwhelming in some cases. However, the prolonged duration of exposure taking on the overnights in most cases exceeds the morally acceptable exposure limit values for many recently mushroomed worshipping centres.

We need to control noise from the recently sprouted spiritual beliefs. Health is always first, speaking from a sustainable development agenda, not from the spiritual context. Good health and safety practice recommend noise control measures. Since we desisted state religions or faiths, we should not inconvenience others. Eat whatever you want but do not lure others into your dishes unwillingly. Think the way you want but behave like others if you want to live with them. If you wish not to, then isolate yourself, and as far as I know, Mars is not wholly occupied. If life cannot be fairly supported on Mars, as far as I know from the spiritual beliefs of some charismatic faiths, prayers can change everything. Stephen Hawking (1924-2018) once said, "I have noticed even people who claim everything is predestined, and that we can do nothing to change it, look before they cross the road." The ILO and sister organizations ought to do something on this issue, especially on halls juggling as worshipping centres during the day and as bars at night. Such worshipping centres contribute a considerable proportion to the tax pool to many African developing countries, but we need to weigh the odds—putting human rights first.

"I have noticed even people who claim everything is predestined, and that we can do nothing to change it, look before they cross the road." Stephen Hawking (1924-2018)

Required Spiritual Leader's Competence (Skill, Knowledge, and Ability) to Lead Sustainable Development in the 21st Century

The Venn diagram below hypothesizes the required competence from the spiritual leaders that wish to lead sustainable development in Africa.

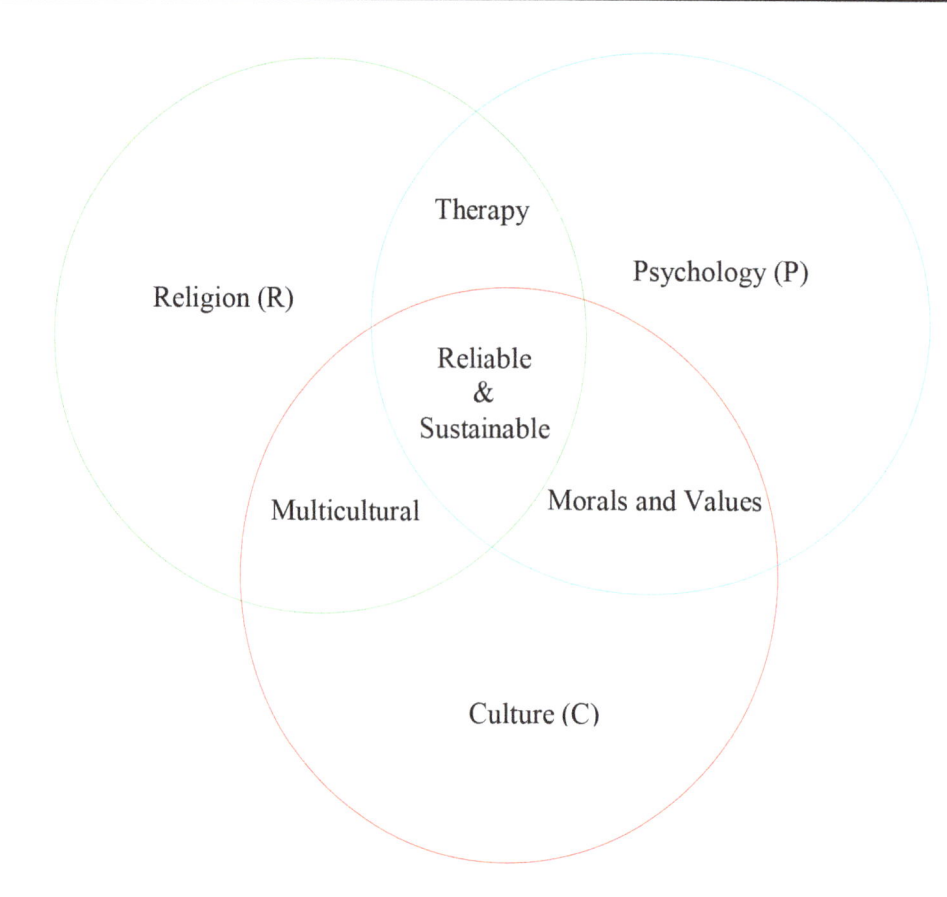

```
                    Therapy
                                    Psychology (P)
  Religion (R)
                    Reliable
                       &
                   Sustainable
          Multicultural    Morals and Values


                    Culture (C)
```

Required Competence from the Spiritual Leaders

Guiding Sustainable Development Assumption

Faith means having a strong belief in the doctrines of a religion based on spiritual conviction rather than proof. Faith is doing the good to humanity and nature. Faith starts where reasoning stops. Meditation is the gateway to learning about the Supreme Being but not through reason. Religions house faith and facilitate the learning about the Supreme Being, and religion contains symbolisms. Because religions associate with symbolisms, they deduce evidence on specific facts symbolized. Therefore, religion can be traditional or conventional. Traditional religion is for indigenous peoples, and conventional religion brings several indigenous peoples into the same umbrella. However, conventional religion is also traditional to some peoples, i.e. the pioneers.

The Venn diagram above existed intact before Europeans invaded Africa. Psychology was in the form of ethno-philosophies (proverbs, sayings, and poems) that guided morals and values. Culture, as rich as it was, intertwined with traditional religions. These traditional religions appreciated the Supernatural Being in their way before conventionalists told them that that supernatural was not supreme than theirs. For example, the remarkable psychological interventions adopted by Africans in preparing girls for marriage cannot be underestimated. Today's psychology is scientifically driven.

Conventional religions largely drove out traditional religions without knowing the extent required because the drivers did not understand what ought to go and remain in the *context of sustainability*. Our cultures were intertwined/embedded with traditional religions to a high significance level that we ought to recognize and conserve, and they influenced each other *reciprocally*. It was not easy to recognize the point along a continuum at which our traditional religions and associated symbolisms crossed cultures. That would be the ideal point to learn about what ought to be conserved in the bid to embrace conventional religions.

Because this ideal point was never appreciated, it caused compartmentalizing the African lifestyle. Yet, African peoples moved holistically in all matters—traditional religions intertwined with cultural lifestyles. We never had dualistic lifestyles, unlike the westerners. Departmentalization is thus costing us a lot! It is one of the reasons why African peoples are disunited. Cultural norms and virtues are getting worn out, leading to intense individualism, which has never been an African lifestyle—and now we wish to reclaim sharing values as if it is a new norm in Africa!

Therefore, as shown in the Venn diagram, an African spiritual leader must be competent to spearhead sustainable development. In other words, they should learn theology, psychology, and cultures before getting licenses or permits to do their work. The spiritual leader must be able to lead counselling and psychotherapy interventions in humanity. This way, Africa's self-driven sustainable development can be achieved. True African spiritual leaders ought to bring Africans back to where they belong by ensuring that Africans move holistically but not departmentalized lifestyles to develop sustainably. This can be done by blending Africanisms with conventional ideals. It is upon this insight experienced as a phenomenon that I believe Africa's glory is destined for people who move the social, biological, spiritual, and psychological dimensions as a unified whole through self-awareness models. True African spiritual leaders leading sustainable development must understand these concepts.

Religion is the belief in God or gods' existence and the activities connected with worshipping. Such activities associated with religions intertwine with cultures, hence religion being part of the culture. This demonstrates that there was religion in Africa before introducing Christianity, Hinduism, Buddhism, Islam, etcetera. A sustainable society calls for *multicultural competent spiritual leaders.* A spiritual leader who is trained in culture, religion, and psychology would enormously contribute to sustainable development.

A spiritual leader must have the ability to lead masses sustainably. Therapies exist between religions and psychology, which can be tapped into by the spiritual leader. On the other hand, cultures shape morals and values due to multigenerational social constructs, and these find a meeting point in the psychological domain. To be multicultural, the spiritual leader should understand how a particular society has evolved. To sustainably lead a religion, the spiritual leader must have sound knowledge of the culture of a particular society—and their emphasis while pastoring should be aimed at doing the good. In doing the good, they should research all tools and techniques that unite people. They should protect and conserve the environment.

Note: In ancient Africa, the spiritual leaders and secretive philosophers labelled some tree species, water bodies, hills, mountains, rocks, and caves as spiritual icons—that they belonged to territorial spirits to protect and conserve the environment. People would not dare to cut down the trees, or dump garbage in water bodies, or destroy caves and mountains because of the perceived danger that would result, which was a psychological mechanism of defending the environment. However, in modern Africa, these social constructs or beliefs are abused as traditionally satanic, and we are now tensed up due to the temperature rise, extreme heat, and floods. Development agencies now spend billions of dollars in combating temperature rise globally—at least not to rise above 2°C. *In this case, who is fooling whom?*

Charismatic movements. The greatest danger of some charismatic movements is the lack of structure and *incompetence in multicultural dynamics,* which are a necessity in self-driven sustainable development. The effect of such movements on followers is that they nurture less cogitative people, viewing it from a sustainable development agenda, not the spiritual context. People, growing too conservative in their thinking towards work and time. They cannot cogitate well enough listening to the basic human sense of right and wrong for sustainable development. These movements are producing extremists—people who are far outside the mainstream attitudes of society. For example, multicultural competent spiritual leaders can understand the limits of holy books in the interest of sustainability. For example, in Proverbs 13:24 in the Christian Bible, "He who spares the rod, spoils the child" contradicts Child Physical Abuse Statutes.

The western world, the architect of some domineering conventional religions, tends to view human beings as having compartmentalized dimensions. In contrast, the Middle East and Asia view things as a unified whole. North Africa, which shares attributes with the Middle East at some point, also holistically views a human being. Sub-Saharan Africa also viewed things as a whole until when conventional religions restructured their beliefs. It just does not flow logically for an individualist to change things of a collectivistic.

Many highly charismatic spiritual leaders, especially from the prophecy faiths, use hypnotics to treat their followers. You cannot rule out the possibility of using Africanisms to treat followers while distancing their congregation from using Africanisms. This is where hypnotherapy appears rooted between Faith and Psychology. However, many followers of the charismatic movements that claim to heal are not in the know or pretend not to be. A few of God's chosen messiahs that heal live in a fantasy world; it is difficult to recognize them.

On the other hand, according to clinicians, some mental disorders, especially the bipolar disorders that charismatic spiritual leaders claim to treat primarily, can heal with or without therapy. And these are the majority of disorders many spiritual leaders claim to treat. Similarly, some maladaptive behaviours and maladjustments in people can heal with or without treatment. Chronic poverty is one detrimental factor in others that causes too many psychological problems and consequently perpetuates or leads to many mental/behavioural disorders that leave people with many unanswered questions. They ultimately end up in charismatic movements led by personality cults that appear to treat wounded areas and disorders from the people. Such spiritual leaders take advantage of the high ignorance levels and diversity of today's problems. Therefore, a good movement faith or religion that is not opportunistically designed must understand the diversity of today's problems and their sources. And should make necessary referrals but not bury their congregation in the spiritual conviction for every psychosocial stressor.

A firm believer argues that the God Almighty or Supreme Being can handle all problems because he is above all, but kindly note what I meant with *opportunistically* centred religions. Any Christian or Muslim, for example, believes in God or Allah being above all. No matter one's religious inclination or faction, believers would ideally believe in supremacy above all.

Much as majority faiths promote the Kingdom of God, sustaining the earth planet is equally vital. They both belong to the Supreme Being, and none of them should be wished extinction. Sustainability of the earth calls for core competencies in the clergy and pastoral ministries. The spiritual dimension is streamlined to function better when the spiritual leader well comprehends the social crises. *Accepting development in many other spheres and succumbing to complacency in spiritualism, yet we wish to keep the planet earth green is outright innocence that makes daydreamers.*

As far as belief in the existence of the Supreme Being is concerned, Pentecostals logically present the best *theory* of ordaining spiritual leaders. Their argument of God's messiah logically manifests itself to anyone who labours to listen to the voice of reason. How many religions existed after God created the universe? Faith should not be limited by any boundaries such as traditions, education level, income level, or any other sorts of demographics. Once you are God's chosen messiah, you do not have to have a rich autobiography that society constructs to sheep.

According to Pentecostals, being a messiah is a calling from the creator of the universe. The biggest challenge is that if all of us claimed to be messiahs, what would be the likely outcome? I believe in *order*. Yes, believers usually answer this question, saying God's grace works upon the fantasists and masqueraders and that the Holy Spirit speaks to the messiahs. As a sustainable development forward-looker, I find this not happening in real-time to catch space. If you leave messianic claimants to explode day and night, the effects can be irreversible.

Well, movement faiths claim that policy limitations imposed on their faith would violate the entire concept or philosophy, but they should get reminded of Africa's situation. Catholicism's sustainability agenda is seen to be unshakable then, in this context. If Catholicism were not founded nearly about 2000 years ago, Pentecostals would not exist the way they are today. They would probably appear differently. Catholicism is the founding platform for many other Christian denominations. It is now over 500 years since theologian Martin Luther published the 95 Theses of criticism of Catholicism, creating shockwaves that eventually changed the face of Christianity. The role of Catholicism in global transformation, sustainability, and development is heroic and cannot be underestimated—in law, education, science, and political governance. We need streamlined religions that answer people's questions.

I borrow a leaf from the program management profession, which plans, organizes, staffs, controls and executes. A program is continuous. I do not think it does any harm to be programmatic. However, the population explosion, science, and technological advancement keep Catholicism's conservatism in a tricky situation. Psychological distresses among Christians caused by socio-economic crises, political crises, natural disasters, climate change, and all other sorts of catastrophes in Africa will push people towards faiths that house a high degree of; hypnotherapies, motivational speakers, dancing, and dancing singing most of the time. When people with psychosocial problems go to these places, they feel psychologically treated, appear livelier, more social, more concerned with, more anxiety and depression free, happier, more motivated, and meaningful. This, coupled with a belief in messiahs being God's chosen people and therefore need no prior laws or social order constructs to oversee their deliverances, leaves a big question.

See The Big Bang and the Supreme Being.[14] One explains the reason for the other because the *"why"* questions are not exhausted fully, especially in the Big Bang. Theological schools endeavour to ague the *"whys"* far better than the Big Bang. The Big Bang is very good at the *"how"*, whilst some religions are very good at the *"why"*, which explains the likelihood of spirituality connecting with science.

Science has had far-reaching success in many spheres. Do not be surprised to learn about today's and future scholars and scientists discovering a slight lack of parallelism within holy texts. For example, higher-order cognition and hypotheses on the Markan Priority, Lukan Priority, and Matthean Priority clearly provide a platform for different theories arguing who used the others' synopses to compile the gospel for Christians. There has been a recent proposal to review the Christians' prayer, "Our Father in Heaven," not because it is invalid, but perhaps its construction needs review. This depicts advancement in thought which is more psychological than meditational.

Not being exposed to the knowledge sources before preaching the word of God poses a great danger to our societies and must stop. At some point, the great moral teachers' message to the world, i.e. Jesus Christ, Mohammad, and Buddha, communicate the same information. Thinking outside the box shows that if Asian travellers, specifically Indians, had moved a bit faster than the: Europeans, Arabs, and Christian missionaries, most Africans would be Buddhists and/or would convert to Hinduism. Although Africa is a focal point for human evolution and religion, according to a particular faction of historians and theologians, the widespread of Islam and Christianity was introduced in the land by foreigners. Thus, the modern conflicts over religion are meaningless, purposeless, and a wastage of time.

The believers ought to know that the Supreme Being, or whatever they denote Supreme, is bigger than any religion, bigger than any faith, bigger than any church or temple. Therefore, they should not confuse religious magistrates or church magistrates and Supreme Being's presence in humanity. Understanding the presence of Supreme Being in humanity makes the mode or medium of communicating with him not to be a problem. There was no religion in the beginning. Some Buddhists and Hinduists, who are not Christians, understand the management of humanitarian crises more than many Christian factions worldwide. In Africa, they have been at the forefront of extending humanitarian aid and soft loans in some cases in the recent past whilst fighting for global peace and reconciliation. This is where nature and nurture forces interplay to make human personality a complex model and partly nullify religion as a better ideal to train/shape moral behaviour. The unconscious and subconscious forces, biological and natural, develop internally, being made at inaccessible levels of the mind, and religion seems to do very little to streamline morality—a good reason why false prophets find it difficult to live to the standard pastoring calls for. With the so many factions sprouting out of Christianity and Islam every day over one leader Jesus Christ and Mohammad, respectively, Buddhism is left to rule the world and contribute immensely to sustainable development. At least, its rate of division is not rampant.

---

[14] See p. 116, §3.

Culture, Religion, and Disorders

As Africans, we have many problems, crises, diseases, and disorders that cannot be answered well enough by conventional religions, embracing the western lifestyle, or the treatment plans available on the market. These problems need careful examination by Africans through African methods. For example, the prevalence of *complex dissociation* or *dissociative identity disorders* and other symptoms of the kind is more pronounced in Africa than anywhere else by empirical observation. Dissociation is when a human being appears detached from self, mind, and body and at times appears to have altered identities or simply appears possessed.

Many people have, at some point, ever appeared dissociated for some reason. Sustainable development is impossible if we continue observing at the surface and fail to dig to the bottom of the sea. A study into Africa's witchcraft beliefs versus clinical disorders is a must if we dream of achieving Africa's sustainable development. If you asked fellow Africans: whether they believed in the existence of witchcraft, a majority would say to some extent "yes", and some others would say "no". We wish to know this extent and the cause. Over-reliance on western and American information to pave sustainability is an utter wrong. We need our evaluation of our people in the African context to agree or nullify the speculations.

Modern forensic psychologists use *signatures* to track criminals, but signatures have several interpretations in several African cultures. I am convinced that besides the scientific method of treatment and the spiritual context, a third unknown African therapy juggles between the two, and it is not yet brought to book. As Africans, we have not made a thorough philosophical inquiry into our being.

China has been criticized for using unscientifically proven medical herbs, but the life expectancy of Chinese people ranks high globally. Incuriousness makes people fail to document empirical and historical events. Not every phenomenon that causes positive change can be explained scientifically or spiritually; some cannot. We would thus ask ourselves why some people healed in the ancient world using unscientifically proven herbs? How did the ancestors learn about these herbs? Both these questions must be answered without bias with things like the Creator of the universe decided so. We would explore these facts and bring all of them to book.

All forms of dissociative identity disorders in Africa, where a person suddenly alters personality states, especially in the rural areas, are attributable to some form of spirits or being possessed by ghosts. However, possession-form identities in dissociation make an individual appear supernatural or as if an external person has taken control. The individual, thus, speaks and acts in a manner that is a little deviant from the normal. In such circumstances, most African cultures believe that a ghost replaces the person's identity. This is where personality cult's faiths take advantage to confuse the people—some of these disorders are caused by past traumatic events that cause a wash away of the brain memory of the individual, causing depersonalization and derealization, which creates two or more personality identities.

In most rural African beliefs, unless otherwise corrected through vivid research, all personality states that alter to create two or more identities in humans are attributable to being possessed by demons and spirits. Therefore, immediate intervention is in the form of praying. The possibility of traumatic events in a believed possessed person's childhood may necessity a *multicultural competent spiritual leader,* as illustrated in the figure above, to make an archaeological dig to output a well-informed evaluation report for the individual.[15]

---

[15] See p. 27-29, §1.

A more ambitious and strategic plan is to create laboratories for traditional healers to work with modern scientists to process this scattered information into knowledge and wisdom. And we try to answer lots of unanswered questions in the African setting. A significant study on possession-dissociative Identity disorders is essential to avoid overgeneralizing ghosts to have disordered the individual. We need to integrate knowledge from traditional healers with that of modern scientists to correctly classify the dissociation disorders and bring them to book in an African style.

I am firmly convinced by empirical deduction that many mental disorders affecting African people are not classified anywhere, for example, in the American Diagnostic Statistical Manual (DSM-5) or the International Classification of Mental Disorders (ICD). We need our Manuals and Standards. For example, the importation of unnecessary wigs to make artificial hairstyles that mimic whites, high level breaching with cancerous stimulus chemicals, excessive embezzlement of the donor or government funds and unreasonable luxury lifestyles amidst high poverty levels might call for an investigation into the cause.

Many government officials who excessively embezzle government funds need psychological/personality profiling. Lots of them are more than just being psychopaths. For example, I cannot imagine a normal person living above middle-income status to consistently and repetitively steal money meant for HIV/AIDS patients, the poor and refugees.

Many standardized tests constructed by Westerners and Americans for diagnosing mental disorders, personality disorders, and other kinds of maladaptive behaviours are culturally biased and cannot conform to the African context, e.g. the Wechsler Intelligence Test for Children (WISC), cannot provide a reliable Intelligence test for an African child. It is, therefore, high time we made African standards for the African person in the African context. Africa has for long been with traditional healers who have treated people with herbs that are unscientifically proven. Ignoring traditional healers from the equation is ignorance, and I wonder how the continent's sustainability and ecological conservation will be achieved when little attention is provided to traditionalists. *There are lots of knowledge gaps that need to be filled.*

In ancient Africa, most of the diseases, if not all, were attributed to spirits and many people died because there were no hospitals and other people were cured with the available herbs. Surprisingly, all diseases today are, to a considerable extent, believed to have a *scientific cause.* You cannot scientifically treat a disease whose prognosis is unscientific, for example, culture-bound syndromes. In other words, if you cannot thoroughly diagnose the problem, that means you do not fully understand it. Unfortunately, a few medical practitioners who understand this problem lack the zeal to make correct referrals. Some of the problems facing Africa cannot be solved by Western models but rather the African style.

Conventional religions worsen the situation since they only focus on great moral teachers and ignore the African moral teachers who did not get out as great but contributed to what we are today. At some point, the disorders and the problems we face emanate from distorting our instinctual moral fibres. Still, at some point, conventional religions blackmailed all African innovations and made them look satanic. In brief, relevant cultural studies, as pointed out above, should be done first for all cultures. Otherwise, even if developmental agencies keep pouring money, money, money and money into Africa without these studies being carried out and results documented for treatment and referral, it is a wastage of time. A line has to be drawn to delineate what causes what and why. Africa has too many unanswered questions and unprocessed data. Real development is at a personal level, i.e. the mind—self-awareness.

Not long ago, Uganda issued a Witchcraft Act CAP 124 of 1957.[16] You cannot enact such Acts of a sort when prior studies have not been made to have a reference. Without a reference, such an Act is baseless and fakery founded. And by the way, the truth of the matter reveals its importance, but Law operates more on logic and evidence but not so much on truth. That explains that too many personality cults and false prophets emerge because of a lack of reference material to track these criminalities. Most prophets who claim to treat may probably be dealing with patients who, in most cases, malinger. A team of researchers from 70 years ago until now have consistently found out that more than 20% of criminals worldwide fake symptoms of amnesia.[17] Do not be surprised when studies reveal that more than 20% of the patients who claim to be treated by personality cults are probably malingerers.

In developing countries, Penal Code Act is still young, defences are only based on empirical evidence, but research and scientific diagnosis of evidence is still limited. Many defences in the interest of insanity, diminished responsibility, and accidents still challenge the "proof beyond reasonable doubt" principle used when convicting the accused person. Here, personality cults and false prophets are taking advantage of a lack of documentation to confuse the masses. Yet, they are criminals themselves or aid criminals like the malingerers to keep perpetuating the problem. Nigerian filmmakers are fond of acting movies that greatly emphasize witchcraft and bizarre delusions, throwing more confidence in the public that a person's body or mental functioning and health can be controlled remotely by another. To draw a clear distinction between a delusion and a firmly held idea or belief presents enormous challenges. Sometimes, it partially depends on the degree of conviction with which the belief is held despite contradictory evidence in relation to its accuracy. We need vivid researches to draw a line for the possible coexistence of bizarre and non-bizarre delusions, if at all possible.

Culture and What Goes Unexpected or as Expected

"My mother produced at 18 years. Here I am, I'm producing at 20 years also." Janet narrated. "My mother never wedded and died at the young age of 28 years. I have heard that even our ancestors have a similar story somewhere at some point. It is as if there is some kind of a curse moving with us onwards." She added. This should not scare anyone the moment you sense it; you have the conscious advantage to attack it from anywhere. The moment you recognize the likelihood of unexpected or expected cultural events happening in your life, attack them—capable of turning into culture-bound syndromes. Do not run away from these events by embracing a new cultural lifestyle that you fail to understand very well. Running away (avoidance) has never been a better remedy—you should investigate the root cause and work on it appropriately. When you run away from the events, you repress them, and they reoccur to you or another person in your lineage at a future date. It is better to find out why using methods that communicate in the same language and style—the evidence-based approach.

---

[16] The Principle law governing Witchcraft in Uganda is the Witchcraft Act Cap 124. Section 2(1) of that law provides that any person who directly or indirectly threatens another with death by witchcraft or by any other supernatural means commits an offence and is liable on conviction to imprisonment for life.

[17] Marko Jelicic, "Testing Claims of Crime-Related Amnesia," Journal of Frontiers in Psychiatry, November 21st 2018, https://www.frontiersin.org/articles/10.3389/fpsyt.2018.00617/full. or https://doi.org/10.3389/fpsyt.2018.00617.

"Many of the superstitions, myths, values, predispositions, cultural traits, beliefs, and norms are keeping us in poverty," Rogers said. Rogers and I belong to the same social group. "How?" I asked. "For example, to say that money collected from a funeral service when your beloved passes away can only be used to buy edibles and not belongings is outdated. I find it improper and keeps us in poverty." He tried to give an example. "Not really," I replied. "Some of these norms and beliefs were constructed as safeguards to morality. Don't you think African morality is on a decline in society today, which could otherwise reflect growth in the schooled ones and elites?"

The Baganda ancestors from where I originate understood very well the role played by symbolisms in sustaining culture. They debarred to use money collected at the funeral to buy belongings because it would symbolize a person who has passed away and look as if the death amused the survivors and descendants of that person. And this has never been good news to someone who is morally shaped in the African context. They, therefore, avoided appearing luxurious after the death of a beloved one. Their failure to expound on the assumptions they held and kept secretive in nature makes them look dysfunctional, and some of our core beliefs are seen as a myth. Yet, the overarching goal was to keep society in order and have a purposeful social transformation that promotes sustainability.

Africa has had one of the best moral philosophies, and at times I wonder why people do away with African norms to adopt foreign ones. In Africa, a foreigner can find a genuine welcome smile that is distributed equally in the face. Somewhere else, in some territories, they just open their mouths for a couple of seconds but never smile genuinely. Our hospitality in many African places is beyond what we can describe.

My friend, who has lived in the developed world for more than four decades, lamented how his immediate neighbour passed away and rotted in his house but only to be discovered after a week. And this is the sustainable development that the developed world *sometimes* talks about because they have all gone clean energy—to loosen in values because technology has driven the world to greater heights. Regardless of whether Christianity or Islam, Buddhism or Hinduism, was introduced or not in the African land, African values could not promote such kind of individualism—the advantage that collectivism which is very rich in the sustainability of the planet, could bring to the table.

Technology has created a revolution of intense individualism and loosened values, with Japan releasing robots to meet care home shortfalls and Americans releasing AI Sophia 2019. It is not very good news to learn that when people grow older are taken to retirement homes. Development, which loses a sense of humanity and replaces with technology and AI, is not sustainable because the cost of AI and technological gadgets is higher than preserving humanistic values. Africans ought to recognize that they hold the flag to lead the planet and get relieved from the bug caught by some people, expanding and growing day in and day out. It is so unfortunate that Africans have not had the way to create their social platforms yet, but they needed independent technologies to keep their values intact. The topic of sustainable development cannot leave humanistic values out of the equation.

Our ancestors' lack of structured documentation in many parts of Sub-Saharan Africa costs us a lot today. That is something wrong the ancestors did not foresee not inventing and keeping structured historical information for future generations. It is, therefore, the lack of structured documentation for the meaning of norms that keep us in poverty but not the norms themselves. Philosophers argue that the whole concept of a particular way of thinking, reflecting, and reasoning is new to most parts of Africa. That African philosophy is starting to grow, which is not valid.

African philosophy is treated as not explicit; it is implicit in the languages and beliefs of African cultures. It is the lack of a structured information flow that makes African philosophy a new thing. Philosophy itself is the way of thinking about thinking. The way Africans viewed the universe, the mind and the body is unique to Africa. It is modern-day deception to think that our ancestors did not have a purposeful way to think about the universe, the mind, and the body. Many African norms are philosophical in nature and hold water. Some have been in existence for many hundreds of years ago but remain valid to date.

The tenets of psychoanalysis, a psychological theory developed by psychologists, and which is a field that originated from philosophy, shares some knowledge and understanding on raising children in the African setting. For example, in the Baganda culture, in central Uganda, I have grown up with a proverb below:

Luganda: Akaakyama amamera: tekagololekeka; bw'ogolola omenya bumenyi. (akati)

English translation: What grew crooked when young: cannot be straightened (later). Just as the twig is bent, the tree is inclined—a child must be taught (corrected) when young.

The hidden meaning is that trying to correct a person nurtured wrongly is almost impossible. Our personality, characters, attitudes, and temperaments are *shaped* in infancy, adolescence and early adulthood while still living with parents or family of origin. They emphasized that all people, whatever characters and attitudes and beliefs they hold about the self, the environment and others, are due to which family they grew up from. This is the reason why our ancestors came up with psychological interventions to keep order in society. The only challenge they had was being secretive and never revealing the overarching goal by storing information in a permanent medium, transferrable from one generation to another. And to have it processed for everlasting meaning to support today's sustainability challenge. The task we have today as Africans, since we are educated, and have the tools such as computers, is to reexamine the work of the secretive African philosophers but not to rubbish their work as unimportant and hopeless. Without doing this, we shall fail to solve the problems that make us appear odd in the world.

Back in the days, a well-differentiated person, who is also well-groomed, with acceptable societal characters and attitudes had to be very strong in the vernacular literacies as foreigners have labelled them so. Yet, these were the tenets on which the foundation of education would be built. Rubbishing ancestors' collectivistic ideologies stretching over 10,000 years ago in some African territories and calling them mere ethno-philosophy that do not have an overarching effect is cheating ourselves in broad daylight. A close look at western philosophy, the writings of the prominent people in the western world, I strongly believe many articles, wisdom and knowledge were obtained from Africa on the assumption that African integrity was posed on mere ethno-philosophy and, therefore, had little value to lay a foundation for modern life.

I have seen several psychoanalysts struggling with making archaeological digs and applying many therapeutic techniques to treat African problems. Psychoanalysts go back to the past, shaping the present, which is not a new concept in Africa. African problems that western therapies and techniques can solve are limited. It is modern-day deception to use western therapies to treat African problems in several spheres. People are dying day in and day out due to the hopelessness of insisting on applying western ideologies and philosophies on African humankind. The 21st debate of nurture versus nature is not a new topic on the African land. Sigmund Freud, one of the pioneers of the psychoanalysis theory, emphasized that the first five years of a human being are the formative years which aligns well with the proverb I have just described above (see page 37). A full narrative on the said proverb can be authored, explaining how and from where the proverb originated and its relevance in the African land. Our ancestors are the most extraordinary moral teachers that we owe a lot to recognize and salute, in both the religions and cultures, instead of rubbishing their work as unphilosophical and unimportant. They knew well that cure has never defeated prevention.

A close look at the so-called ethno-philosophy of African humankind, I realize that everything African is undervalued. These indigenous philosophical systems are unique to ourselves, and there is no single day we wish to become exotic in our native African land. Then, why not use these philosophical systems as a foundation for freedom. The kinds of freedoms we envision include financial and economic freedoms, justice for all, and prosperity. Our ancestors appreciated family power structure, family systems dynamics and multigenerational issues quite well. Today, well organized scholars package many humanistic studies to look utterly new to the African land. I have tried to draw patterns, making inquiries into African ethno-philosophy claims and using logic to conclude. I found ethno-philosophy claims carrying a vast meaning that masses have not laboured to use but rather to entertain foreign packaged kinds of literature that we call new and modern.

The argument about African philosophy consisting of shared beliefs, values, and assumptions implicit in languages spoken on the African land is quite valid. That was its uniqueness, and it ought to be recognized for that. However, Africa's languages, which many have not been uniquely symbolized to remain dialects, are rich in vocabulary. The philosophy of African languages, the collection of proverbs, adages, and idioms house much meaning. Our ancestors' failure to create a structured program or way to pass on information from one generation to another and kept it by word of mouth has affected the continent very much. It is one of the reasons that explain the penetration of colonialism into Africa. You can look at Ethiopia and think about the many reasons why it did not fully catch the bug. The failure to uniquely symbolize our languages is partly the reason they are called dialects. Ancient African philosophers (Sub-Saharan) can best be described as secretive philosophers because they failed to expressly reveal the meaning of reality for how they viewed the universe as they made studies.

Some of the proverbs and norms held by ancestors carry much meaning. Researchers have reached beautiful discoveries, but they still find these African proverbs rich and valid. The African thinking philosophies embedded in language dialects as ethno-philosophy claims are examined for truth and validity. Failure to make clear documentation puts this truth and validity in a doubtful position. Only those who live to examine their lives can really learn to appreciate the meanings of our ancestral knowledge. Joseph Lule, in his book, "The hidden wisdom of the Baganda: Amagezi g'Omuganda Amakusike", elaborates on the meanings and philosophies of the secretive African philosophers I have described.[18] A book that every curious African humanistic scholar should endeavour to purchase and read. Such similar

---

[18] Joseph Lule, *The hidden wisdom of the Baganda: Amagezi g'Omuganda Amakusike* (Arlington, VA: Humbolt & Hartmann, Inc.), 2006.

books are available in different cultures across the African continent. The book is written in Luganda and English. It is a collection of the proverbial expressions, aphorisms, and wise sayings of the Baganda.

Now that we have appreciated the shortfalls in our background, what's the way forward? The way forward is to piece together what is remaining and call on Africans to understanding how our race can be sustained in the global sustainable development campaign. It is not too late to unite, understand ourselves, create self-awareness initiatives, develop our languages, maintain values, and think of solutions for Africa in an African fashion and style.

The Other Side of Foreign Religions

Christians as a Case Study

The Christian denomination is premised on the argument that Jesus is the son of God who resurrected from the dead and ascended to heaven. *Is Christianity a religion?* Let us begin by understanding what religion is all about. I understand scholars have laboured to agree on a unified religious definition that is universally accepted, but they are still failing to reach a consensus. However, when I try to piece together the existing knowledge and understating of what religion is all about, the following stands valid in the interim:

> *Religion consists of: a set of strongly shared beliefs, values and attitudes, an object, practice, cause, or activity that somebody is completely devoted to, designated behaviours and practices, texts, morals, sanctified places, prophesies, ethics and organizations, particular institutionalized or personal system of beliefs and practices that relates humanity to a Supreme Being, transcendental, or spiritual elements. Religion is, therefore, a way of life—a cultural system.*

Christianity, therefore, conforms to the definition above to a good significance level. The common mantra that Christianity is not a religion seems to be false looking at the keywords in the definition. The vital question to ask is; why then do we have many Christian denominations? The opportunists would reason as below:

Religion is man's attempt to reach God

Christianity is God's attempt to reach man

Therefore, Christianity is not a religion.

Not many people can believe *without evidence*. Jesus's crucifixion is a good example—despite the fact that many prophets had prophesized his coming as a son of God, it justifies the claim. Out of anger, jealousy, and the struggle for power, the rulers and chiefs of that time could not spare Jesus Christ. However, upon Christ's resurrection from the dead, as documented, it proved enough evidence that he was different from other people, perhaps a son of God. This would subsequently weaken the powers of those that took his moral teachings as mere claims to be a living word. However, this documentation is disputed by some others who believe in God not taking on a human form.

Based on logic, those early years after Jesus Christ ascended into heaven according to the Christian Bible, there must have been politics on the rightful custodian of Christ's message to the world. Despite Jesus Christ leaving disciples and many other followers, the winds of the world could not spare them to spread his word peacefully. In my opinion, on recognising that the evidence-based approach is a powerful stimulus that can elicit many followers and weaken the existing social, financial, and economic systems, several opportunists could not wait to follow Christ. Therefore, they got his word into their mainstream work and politics to capture others but not to further his good word.

Therefore, the claim that Christianity is not a religion is motivated, triggered and perpetuated by modern-day opportunists. Thousands of different kinds of Christian churches and religions are mushrooming globally. Over 10,000 of such kinds of distinct religions mushroom every day worldwide; a significant fraction claims to follow Jesus Christ but disagreeing with each other at some point is a result of opportunistic traits and power greed. On the contrary, they teach their followers that the love for power and earthly things is the root cause of all trouble we see in the world today. Interestingly, their temples are labelled, and they advertise on TVs and other Media to get an extensive outreach. Thus, extending and applying psychology in religious practices.

There is no genuine reason why a universally accepted church of Christ—the church for all, all-embraced, can have different labels, like eastern and western denominations. How possible can this be defended in the faith of the living word of Christ? If it does not pose anxiety in your heart, why not ignore it but remain faithful to the church and its congregation? Why split? In the interest of sustainable development and sustaining African humankind, we ought to redefine the means and processes to reach our God, the "Universal God".

Some people have become atheists because of the many religious leaders who have failed to keep Jesus Christ's image and his word, i.e. *the do as I do but not only the do as I say.* Of the two aforementioned, which one runs faster, is much powerful, and is sustainable? When we talk of sustaining the planet earth, we cannot stop thinking and reflecting on the diversity issues threatening the planet. Borrowing a leaf from symbolic interactionism and psychology, how can you defend the fact that many churches are not selling Christ's word, if not Christ himself? Where is sustainability in the global equation? I believe many are doing business.

An African, whose philosophers have been abused as carrying little impact in influencing knowledge and wisdom in the modern world, is under significant threat, especially in this era when sustainable development is the anxious-inducing topic. I wish to call upon all Africans and ask them a simple question: what is your position and interest in this world? Are you following Jesus Christ as a Christian or Mohammed as a Muslim, or an organized, institutionalized set of cultural beliefs from and for others? Look at yourself and the future of Africa, the future of the children of our grand grandchildren; what is their position in the sustainable development equation?

You need to reflect and imagine whether we can take a man out of the foreign religion or the foreign religion out of a man and sustain the African race and this planet at large? Which one does excellent magic in the African interest and African mindset? Wherever you are, reflect on how much is drained either directly or indirectly from the African people who have been made poor by the same people associating themselves with categorical religious denominations. In return, Africans bend to beg for assistance, yet the texts they are taught to comprehend, in the same religious factions, are unambiguous on what ought to be done by a righteous-making person.

Religion and Africa's Post-Independence Political Systems

The Buganda Kingdom in Uganda as a Case Study

https://www.buganda.or.ug/

In the 1840s, Buganda Kingdom found in Uganda effectively controlled Lake Nalubaale using fleets of war canoes. It was considered the most powerful kingdom in East and Central Africa before European invaders. It was difficult for others to fight the battle with Buganda and win it because of the solid political system and the army Buganda had at that time. Barter trade was the system of exchange where goods or services were directly exchanged for others without involving a medium of exchange such as money or bitcoins. On November 30, 1953, the protectorate government deported the Buganda King under clause 6 of the 1900 Agreement, where the governor signed a declaration withdrawing British recognition from Ssekabaka Muteesa as the Native Ruler of Buganda.[19] The mind and heart weakening programs managed to soften Buganda, which had a strong army back then, and this made it possible for others to penetrate it and pick the Ssekabaka (King) as they wished.

Uganda got independence from the British in 1962. The weakening of the Buganda people through colonialism and religion made it possible for others to successfully attack the Kingdom in 1966. On May 24th 1966, the Ugandan federal army attacked the Kingdom, and the King was thrown into exile in a battle that lasted less than a day. The King (Ssekabaka) had been trapped in a building that was set on fire. However, with the help of priests from Lubaga, a place near the kingdom, he managed to escape.

The coalition of the Kabaka Yekka and Uganda People's Congress (KY-UPC) movement led October 9th 1962. with the Ssekabaka (King) as head of state and Milton Obote as prime minister.[20] The politics behind the grievous mistake of creating less intimate coalitions was fueled by the divisions that conventional

---

[19] 1900 Buganda Agreement Clause 6: So long as the Kabaka, chiefs, and people of Uganda shall conform to the laws and regulations instituted for their governance by Her Majesty's Government, and shall cooperate loyally with Her Majesty's Government in the organisation and administration of the said Kingdom of Uganda. Her Majesty's Government agrees to recognise the Kabaka of Uganda as the native ruler of the province of Uganda under Her Majesty's protection and over-rule. The King of Uganda shall henceforth be styled His Highness the Kabaka of Uganda. On the death of a Kabaka, his successor shall be elected by a majority of votes in the Lukiko, or native council. The range of selection, however, must be limited to the Royal Family of Uganda, that is to say, to the descendants of King Mutesa.

[20] KY party and UPC Party leaders were Muteesa II and Obote respectively. The former came from Buganda region and the latter came from Nothern Uganda.

religions had created.[21] They brought less intimate people together because they had converted to the same conventional religious faction (Protestant). In this way, they strongly opposed Benedict Kiwanuka of the Democratic Party (DP), who belonged to another conventional religion (Catholic) but was a servant of King Muteesa.

On the other hand, conventional ideals rapidly disintegrated traditional values, and Benedicto Kiwanuka perceived his education as more relevant than Baganda's core beliefs. He faulted when he wanted the King to have the same lenses viewing the world as himself, which contradicted the traditional values. This created a collision in Buganda power structure, and some Baganda perceived him as a threat. That was primarily triggered and perpetuated by conventional ideals and the illusion of knowledge. If conventional religions did not rapidly disintegrate the cultural tradition of paying allegiance to the King, Buganda and Uganda would not face the 1966 crisis whose effects we face today. We evidence Benedicto's illusion of knowledge in his acceptance of working as Chief Justice in Idi Amin's autocratic government. What kind of justice was he going to deliver? One of the main theories suggests that Benedicto Kiwanuka was killed on September 21st 1972, at Makindye military prison on the orders of Amin when he tried to show him how knowledgeable he was administering the rule of law. Benedicto persisted and demonstrated his skills while many people distanced themselves from Amin's autocratic government, indicating that he lacked sound political and professional judgement as a lawyer based on knowledge and understanding of Amin's administration. The current Buganda leaders might have to draw lessons from Chief Justice Benedicto Kiwanuka of the 1960s and Sir Apollo Kaggwa of the 1900s because the country has again graduated into autocracy. In the interest of sustainability, I would want to remind all the current leaders that a personal value does not weigh heavier than a scientific fact—the definition of Buganda is "our native land" —and we fight to keep it green. Therefore, leaders need to self-critique and self-examine their ideas working for a state where democracy is nonfunctioning.

The KY-UPC opposing DP was characterized by many contradictions and heavily adversarial on the grounds of belonging to different religious factions. This kind of deception, to look at your fellow brother and sister as an enemy because they belong to different religions, cannot in any way contribute to sustainable development. I am awfully sorry, but I cannot find it anywhere crucial in Africa's sustainability. It has caused more loss than benefit for Africa's humankind. Many people who learned about Uganda and Buganda's story believe that Baganda's political intrigue failed Ben Kiwanuka to make a coalition with King Edward Muteesa. Yet, in my opinion, it was the *invisible hand of conventional religions*. This invisible hand continues to shape Uganda's politics and Africa in general to a large extent. Today, Baganda people continue to suffer in Uganda's central due to the deception spearheaded by conventional ideals.

Conventional ideals sub-divided Buganda's fifty-six (56) clans. Some are adherents of Christianity and others are adherents of Islam. It would be better, if the Buganda region subscribed to one conventional religion. In that case, it would promote sustainability much better.

---

[21] See p. 360, §8.

Psychology in Religion and Culture

Many religions use psychological interventions to win followers. Hypnotherapies and cognitive restructuring are some of the techniques employed to win masses. It is important to note that it is all about the way we think but not so much about the doctrines of religion. Many religious leaders are using psychological interventions to win followers, creating many kinds of personality cults. Psychological interventions are more effective at winning African masses, and that is why most campaigns done by others in Africa use psychological interventions to succeed. Our cultures are pivoted on a unique psychological foundation on which morals had been premised. Unfortunately, these ethno-philosophies were abused that they carry little developmental ideologies to aid social transformation because they lacked proper documentation and sound historical foundations. I have investigated some knowledge and wisdom held by ancestors and realized that behavioural science is not entirely new in Africa.

As mentioned earlier, most African adages, proverbs, and morals were meant to keep order in society. The ultimate need for studying religion is to praise the Supreme Being and bring love and joy in this world—to keep order in societies. For example, forgiveness is not a new thing in Africa. We cannot claim that it was introduced through foreign religions. It has existed in African traditional religions—culturally. In psychological explanations, the person's emotions, behaviour, and cognition are interworked. They are interrelated and interdependent. Our ancestors had not studied much of cognition but had made great efforts to read behaviours and emotions on which they premised many adages, sayings, and proverbs on forgiveness and other topics that are still valid. In modern psychology, we learn that you can never know what your neighbour thinks 100%, but you can only conclude their thought pattern by reading their emotions, body physiology, and behaviours. Why do you then rubbish African ancestors' efforts to communicate wisdom through proverbs, sayings, adages, and maxims?

The good question to ask ourselves is: How and why did they (ancestors) coin these proverbs that rotated around behaviours and are still valid in the modern-day?

In trying to explain forgiving, how and why it occurs—is to let go of negative emotions such as vengefulness. A person forgives when they release the offender from the indebtedness, however legally or morally justified it might be. I am interested in forgiveness because it cuts across conventional religions, psychology, and traditional African cultures. One of the essential attributes of religious teachings is forgiveness, and it is central to many religious ethics. Forgiveness is a frequent topic in theological works and sermons, considered in the form of redemption. Forgiveness is a moral value that I believe is not rooted in any religion but rather the Supreme Being's presence in humanity.

It is more about how we think about the self, the environment around us, and others. Our core beliefs are predetermined by the environment in which we are born and grow. Have you ever wondered why women are generally more religious than men, particularly among Christians, globally? According to the Pew Research Centre, an estimated 83.4% of women worldwide identify with a faith group, compared with 79.9% of men.[22] In my opinion, it is a psychological explanation that can answer this question. Our

---

[22] "The Gender Gap in Religion around the World: Women are generally more religious than men, particularly among Christians." Pew Research Centre: Demographic studies, March 22nd 2016, https://www.pewforum.org/2016/03/22/the-gender-gap-in-religion-around-the-world/.

defence mechanisms vary across men and women. We tend to get sad, angry, depressed, or anxious when threatening or provoking stimulus elicits a response from us. Some stimuli are multigenerational effects that we have found in place at birth, like texts. Once we read these texts, the interpretation can vary across people and with age.

Other stimuli which are dominated by the effects of the industrial and technological revolutions have put our survival and sustainability at a worrying state because of the competition it creates. These elicit a considerable kind of anxiousness and sadness in the hearts and minds of the weakest Africans. Consequently, our defence mechanisms are activated, confusing humility with immature defence mechanisms. Many religious teachings are so good at this, nurturing, watering, and perpetuating immature defensive mechanisms as humility for an African person suppressing constructive aggression and assertiveness.

In the introduction of conventional religions, many of Africa's cultural instincts were repressed, forgetting that repressed material can never disappear. Many masses are good at repressing and denying cultural values, norms and meanings around African symbolisms because of the anxiousness the introducers of conventional religion instilled in the beginning by labelling African symbolisms evil. The most important thing to note is that the sustainability of the African race is not well-considered in the global sustainability equation. By mere living anyhow does not count, but the quality in which we live relative to others matters, especially in the world they have created and dominated.

Because neurotic defences naturally dominate women, they are good at repressing material, displacing anger and fear elsewhere, and reaction formation. This is the reason why cognitive restructuring and paradoxical interventions work best on women because they highly employ neurotic defences, especially reaction formation, as their defence mechanism. The justification of reaction formation is rooted in the way African women, especially mothers grown strong in vernacular literacies, manage to greet with a smile most of the time and a sweet and sound voice tone across the continent regardless of the crises in which we live. With this explanation, one cannot fail to understand why history's most influential religious leaders tend to be predominantly, if not exclusively, male. Yet, it often appears that women dominate the ranks of the faithful.

Cognitive Restructuring of African Masses—Dealing With African Thoughts and Core Beliefs

The Western travellers labelled everything found in Africa negative about the Supreme Being and that whatever was thought and ran in the minds of Africans at that time was negative and naïve, which were maladaptive thoughts and beliefs *without providing evidence or proof*. They instilled a culture of dogmatism and fanaticism, making *Africans go overboard* in conventional religions. Some Africans feel somewhat guilty when they name their children ancestral names, and they have resorted to dropping them. That is something that spoils identity to a big extent.

Conventionalists associated themselves with the products of the industrial revolution like guns, watches, boats/ships, shoes, clothes, and et cetera, which made it easy to induce the typical African native of that time to learn by association and as well get conditioned to follow whatever was taught because they received gifts they had never seen in the locale before. The introduction of conventional religions in many African parts after the industrial revolution had begun/expanded posed unique challenges to Africans.

Several foreign religions were introduced in Africa, especially Sub-Saharan Africa, after the slave trade, which leaves many questions unanswered.

I cannot fail to deduce by logic that some Africans learnt and thought that good things like the guns, the clothes and shoes associated with white travellers were obtainable due to accepting the faith they associated with. There is no way a typical native of that time would not admire the industrial revolution's products that travellers associated themselves with. With little knowledge and exposure, one would attribute gaining such nice things to acceptance of the religion of the Western travellers.

Labelling negativity for African symbolisms and interactionism whilst labelling positivity for western travellers' items, symbolisms and their Supreme Being was a taboo to Africa. It predisposed Africa to several unique disorders. The core beliefs were offset rapidly without solidified preparations. The minds of Africans were not well prepared to constructively receive the white travellers' message amidst the industrial revolution.

As an ideal, the shaping of Africans into what was required by the white missionaries and those who accompanied them thereafter forgot the sustainability equation. It was done opportunistically. There was some bit of a bias in the introduction. The overarching goal was lost somehow. They were fascinated by the mineral wealth they found in Africa, and constructive introduction of religion could not be done without bias—we have to lead, and they follow, dilemmas. Thus, the negative thoughts held by many African masses about African things and symbolisms are motivated as a result of the indoctrination done on their minds—which is becoming a multigenerational problem. The foreigners instilled anxiety into the hearts of many masses across the continent without proper justification. That African things are taboo, so they needed to follow western culture but not to grow theirs—for example, growing our cultures by doing away with what was bad and develop with the good ones.

Existing African beliefs were labelled as maladaptive thoughts/beliefs. That we are children of a lesser God and that African beliefs were false and rationally unsupported. Therefore, all existing traditional religious beliefs were maladaptive beliefs without limits. The lack of a structured system of information flow, storage, and documentation predisposed Africans to the bug and, at the same time, accelerated it. African beliefs and thought processes were hence labelled faulty cognitive processes. Because western travellers had associated themselves with lovely things like clothes and shoes, guns and other items, they looked pretty prudent and promising. Without boundaries and limits, all African traditional beliefs and symbolism were generalized as evil. They made global descriptions of African cultural beliefs hence instilling anxiety and fear in the hearts and minds of Africans. It was a psychological attempt to restructure the way Africans thought about their native beliefs and objects.

Religion itself is a cultural system of beliefs. Unless you dispute the Supreme Being's presence in humanity, that is when you can disagree that religion is culture. It required a clear boundary on what ought to be followed and what to leave out to embrace a new cultural system of beliefs for the betterment and socioeconomic transformation of the continent. Religions within religions demonstrate opportunism and partially explain why the sustainability of the African continent is becoming a big challenge.

Your works should seek to know the goodness of the Supreme Being but not to find economic gain from him. Ultimately, morals are now predetermined by the foreign travellers' newly modified cultural and social values but not God's message that the foreign travellers carried to Africans. The point to note in this is that the process of introduction of religions within religions was opportunistically and selfishly done without minding the sustainability of Africans. God's presence in humanity needs no texts; God's presence in the wildlife, the environment, and the universe needs no human imposing himself over another. It is purely *meditational and phenomenological.* Africans have lost it. Very few can think, reflect, and comprehend that religion is culture and that our native cultures risk dying. The Supreme Being's presence in humanity has always existed regardless of what and who.

The foreigners induced a particular cognitive distortion in African masses, "black-and-white thinking" about African culture. This can be defined as "the failure in a person's (African's) thinking to bring together the dichotomy of both positive and negative qualities of their (culture), cultural values, predispositions, symbolism, norms, and others into a cohesive, realistic whole." They were elicited to fail to spot a grey area between their cultures and religions introduced. Ultimately, everything found in African beliefs was labelled evil and satanic.

I strongly detest the fact that morality is rooted in any kind of religion. Therefore, it is rooted in the Supreme Being's presence in humanity, which is why every culture invents its morality. Ultimately, without having met to unify moralities, you find that several morals from different cultures communicate the same message. And it is because of God's presence in humanity that we have universal morals but not religion. Two morals to look at:

a. The love your neighbour as you love yourself, which is the foundation of societal order.

b. Incest.

Regardless of what kind of religion you adhere to, almost all cultures cannot allow crossing the prohibited degrees in marriage. **Why?**

The topic of sustainable development is hot, especially for Africa. Many things, events, creatures, flora and fauna, and humans are disordered in Africa due to opportunism spearheaded by some other peoples. Africans are dependent on free meals because they have been conditioned to live as so. Many native species in Africa are getting extinct due to others' intervention in Africa's matters. People are very sensitive about what they believe. And the approach to change someone in belief, if you ought to do it sustainably, must be formally organized and *evidenced* because conflicting results are pretty many.

A majority of the Chinese, Koreans, Japanese, and Indians supporting Africa are not Christians. However, when you argue with a very religious person, they say you contradict faith with earthly things. But what good do you benefit to live as an odd man out? Understanding the extent of this concern is through the support Africans provide to the businesses established by Chinese and Indian Buddhists compared to Christian counterparts in telecommunications, banking, education, manufacturing, construction, insurance, et cetera, especially in Sub-Saharan Africa. Why don't you support fellow Christians business largely?

I constantly refer to Sub-Saharan Africa because they cannot do away with the Sub-Saharan region if one mentions socioeconomic sufferance. That shows that the need to fulfil economic status weighs more than religious status at a national level. We need to work on closing the gaps in religious inclinations for accelerated self-driven sustainability. Religious differences should not deter our socioeconomic progress. If you need oxygen in the hospital, you do not mind whether a Christian, Muslim, or Traditionalist supplies it. At that time, a witch can give you oxygen, and you accept it.

What is The Solution for Africa?

It is never too late for an optimist. Self-awareness initiatives at a family level are critical to self-driven sustainable socioeconomic transformation. Understanding and praising the Supreme Being is rooted in self-awareness. What is limiting you? Evaluate it from all sides without fear or bias. We are in the struggle to sustain the African continent in the global sustainability equation. All claims that African youths do not want to work are mere allegations and sour grapes. Our failures to succeed occupationally, professionally, and innovatively are explainable in our failure to know ourselves—self-awareness—thorough self-examination.

We have lost considerable values and swapped them with those of others. That our cultures are wanting, religious beliefs are everything. How can we utilize the new religious beliefs for our good? Let us piece together what is remaining and claim ownership of the new product. I mention the African school, the African church, the African mosque, the African religion, the African museum, the African education system, the African English, the African French, the African mandarin, the African movement, the African bishops, clerics leading the African church, and et cetera. Let us forge ultimate ownership of the new product.

There are very few African people with a lazy, not-to-work attitude. The African struggler culture was destroyed after anxiety was fueled in the hearts and minds of Africans through several religions introduced to swap for African cultures. The Supreme Being should be one and is not affiliated with any religion. His word can be heard and understood by those who seek to find it in any way they wish—a philosophical inquiry into our universal existence in the universe.

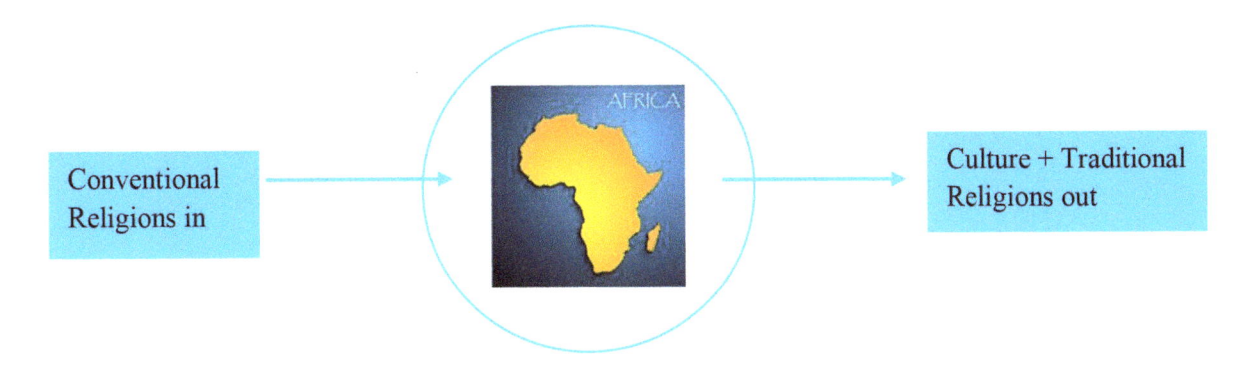

Conventional Religions displaced African Values

If culture was not swapped for various forms of religion in Africa and quality education was given a strong foundation, Africa's sustainability, growth, and development would not pose many challenges. Unnecessary anxiety is driving Africans in a very hopeless direction. And the education system is also less promising because of the opportunism embedded in the introduction of religion.

The *Shaka Zulu African struggle culture* was swapped in religions. *Our own religious beliefs on which effective and efficient work ethics revolved were killed.* Our hospitable culture, collectivistic-centred, struggle-oriented, long-term, arduous struggle culture was abused. This was the religious belief that earned us independent survival. Today, with all the religions we have, we, instead, cannot survive on our own. The tithes, offerings and other collections are channelled without question right from the smallest unit into individualized worshipping centres and out of Africa.

The struggler culture can be reintroduced by owning the new product, a religious belief conditionally developed in us, not reporting to others unnecessarily—putting ourselves first before anything else, loving ourselves and appreciating our identity—the cultural identity. To create lasting change, we recognize the past to improve the future. However, we cannot dwell on it because we cannot fight the old and people over 150 years into our time, but rather build the new systems by claiming the new religious product as ours and benchmarking on it to forge new improvement plans.

Earlier, I demonstrated how Africa has a strong connection with the world's great religions, although the architecture is not ours. It is high time we redefine our architecture. This is evident, in a way, Africans demonstrate a new moral think tank when it comes to contemporary issues that are shaking religious denominations, e.g. the LGBT community. Another issue is about the treatment that African religious leaders experience before the architects of some famous religions. Even though there has been remarkable progress in this area (how African religious leaders are treated), the underlying questions remain unanswered satisfactorily. When we claim what we have become by highly benchmarking on a moral school of thought that is driven by African cultures that promote politeness, we shall recognize that we need a unification of traditional cultural holidays with religious holidays so that we can scale down on the number of national holidays that consume a considerable fraction of our time.

Socratic Questioning on the Influence of the Western World and Associated Religions in Africa Following Timelines

The table below provides dates for monumental events that once influenced the life of Africans. It is provided for reflection.

Event	Year
Christianity in North Africa	1AD and 2AD
Islam in Africa	7th Century
Roman Empire	27 BC – 286 AD
Marco Polo, Italian merchant's silk route	13th Century, (1217 – 1295)
Vasco Da Gama, Portuguese explorer in Africa	14th & 15th Century (1497 – 1502)
Christopher Columbus, an Italian explorer in the Americas	1492
Christianity in Sub-Saharan Africa	15th – 19th Century
Beginning of Slavery in Central and West Africa	16th Century
Landing of the first slave in the USA	August 1619
Martin Luther King Theses publication	1517
First attempt to abolish the slave trade in UK and the USA	1807
Berlin Conference	1884
Buddhism in Africa (South Africa)	Traces began in the 1680s, official introduction in 19th Century
Hinduism in Africa (South Africa)	19th Century
Industrial Revolution	1765, 18th Century

Mind Mapping Questions

After reflecting on monumental events in the table above, the questions below can be answered by linking the events. Thoughts should radiate out from the table above to find answers to the questions below.

- Why did the Berlin Conference happen after introducing Christianity in Africa and after the beginning of the industrial revolution?

- Meditate about the feasible locations of the headquarters of conventional religions

- The distance between Medina and Mecca is 210 miles (338 km), and the distance between Rome and Jerusalem is 1434 miles (2307.8 km)

- Why was the most feasible and viable location of St. Peter's Basilica in 4AD found to be Rome and not any other place?

- Why the most feasible and viable location for protestants' religious headquarters was found to be England and not any other place?

Why did the new Basilica, which replaced the old St. Peters Basilica, begin in 1506 and Martin Theses published in 1515? These two dates associate quite well with historical timelines. What can we learn from this?

Why was the beginning of Pentecostalism in the USA and spearheaded explicitly by African—Americans?

Jesus Christ was mothered by a Jewish woman whose traditional religion is Judaism. Why do the same peoples find it difficult to accept God in human form whilst other peoples of the world believe so?

Why did the Chinese and some other Asians manage to fight invaders? Would the Chinese achieve sustained progress if they had not fought invaders and left them to introduce Christianity and Islam along with colonialism? Compare and contrast.

Why did Eritreans and Ethiopians fight colonialism? Why couldn't other African territories defend themselves against the invaders? Could it be political balkanization or a more significant psychological fact?

Imagine, if Buddhists had moved earlier than Christian missionaries, what would happen to Africa, especially Sub-Saharan Africa?

For Christians, how did "The Church of Christ Lord" miss the 1st – 4th centuries as the universally accepted name? It sounds to be the best ideal name for those in charge of Jesus Christ's furtherance of God's message to the world.

What could have been the influence of the Roman Empire on Africa?

Why is North Africa dominated by Afro-Asiatic (Arabic, Tigrinya and Amharic) and other African parts occupied by other linguistic groups, Niger-Congo (Bantu and Kwa); the Nilo-Saharan (Hamitic, Nilotic and Nilo-Hamitic) and South African Khoisan?

Why did Christianity take over 14 centuries to get to some parts of Sub-Saharan Africa?

Of what significance is religion in fostering colonialism in Africa? How did religion shape our political beliefs and independence?

Why is North Africa always paired with the Middle East while reporting economic data by development agencies? What does this association depict? *Why does sub-Saharan Africa remain the poorest, yet it performs very well in conventional religions?*

Arabs introduced Islam in Africa, and the slave trade was pioneered by Arabs and later followed by Portuguese and Spaniards. There is an association between the two. Of what significance can this be?

What is the likely estimate of slaves that were taken out of Africa between the 16th Century and 1807? Of what significance can this be?

The major *Atlantic slave trading (1619–1804) nations,* ordered by trade volume, were: the Portuguese, the British, the French, the Spanish, and the Dutch Empires. Arabs pioneered the Arab slave trade between the medieval era and the early 20th Century. We significantly see African-Americans in the Americas and a few blacks in Europe; where are they in the Arab peninsula? What can we learn from this?

Why Africa? Regarding geographical convention and following linguistic groups, couldn't we have two continents out of Africa we know today? Why do we have Asia and Europe, yet there exists the most significant overland boundary out of the three that exist on earth, i.e. along the Turkish Straits, the Caucasus and the Urals?

Personal Insight on Mind Mapping Questions

We need to forgive our ancestors. They could not desist invaders. The invaders were educated and had great philosophers who laboured to put ink on paper. It is important to note that great philosophy is the foundation of whatever we see, learn and appreciate. Because invaders associated themselves with religion and development, education, hospitals and welfare, it was very hard for an African who was ignorant in that dimension not to admire them. The intertwined fingers below are meant to show you that everything done in our motherland by invaders was interconnected. The power of invaders to influence the world wherever they went was primarily a result of having great philosophers. These philosophers made it easy to streamline religions and core beliefs and forge cases to influence many other territories.

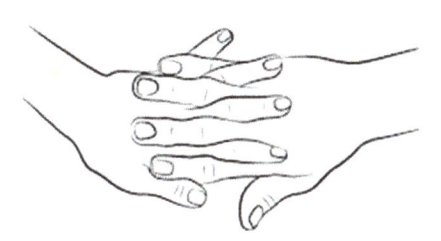

Fingers intertwined

Because of Africa's ignorance, as defined earlier, the invaders could take advantage to influence Africans in all possible ways. The Chinese could resist colonialism because they had great leaders and philosophers who were educated and had a strong language. They could convey messages from one generation to another. China has a well-documented history that goes beyond 5000 years, actually far more than the pioneers of the industrial revolution. In my analysis, I believe reading/writing has an emotional attachment and wisdom it nurtures. That is perhaps why Ethiopia and Eritrea could fight the Italian invaders in the 1896 Adua battle. It is implicit.

Although the invaders in Egypt successfully conquered, they still ruled in parallel to the Egyptian government. It is, of course, not a clear point that everyone can appreciate, but organized information flow is magical. Expressing ideas by writing and recording history in writing has a solid philosophical bone that can trigger the mind to resonate the yesterday, the now and the future in a better way than a person who gets just mere skeletons of their history typical of many African societies. How can one process wisdom from skeletons of history? As Africans, let us appreciate the weakness deep into our hearts and minds! The reliability of our cultural beliefs is very low in some dimensions. Therefore, we need to do more work by drawing patterns and lines on what should be the pillars of our identity. For that matter, Eritreans and Ethiopians are very confident living in their cultures wherever they go!

It is good to appreciate that leadership is not only about the influence but also the impact created matters. The impact that colonialists caused to Africans is a permanent wound. Unless that wound is treated, we will continue to live while pestering others to survive. There will always be leaders at any point in time who will influence others for as many generations to come. The Roman Empire played its role in history, and the contemporary/modern Roman Empire still influences the world to date. The industrial revolutionists played their part in history and are still shaping the world, especially in matters related to environmental conservation and sustainability. The Greeks, Egyptians, Phoenicians, Holland, Spain, Portugal, and the Soviet Union did their part. The Americans and Chinese are doing their part. And many others are doing their part. By the time we realize to wake up, the Chinese influence in Africa will be insurmountable. Africa's failure to resist invaders was inevitable in the past. It was a structural problem, and we live to forgive our ancestors.

However, the current educated generations are to blame for doing worse than our ancestors because we still follow the Western way of life. Yet, we have gained from the education they introduced, and we should be able to free our minds and start seeing things differently. We are making a great mistake which future generations will live to regret on us. And they will not forgive us. I find not many mistakes in the African chiefs who failed to fight colonialism, but I find grievous mistakes in the living African generation. At that time, they used holy texts to penetrate Africa; now, they use free meals. What is the difference?

In my analysis, I find some of the colonialists' approaches somehow lawful to a small extent because they had advanced in technology following the industrial revolution. In many areas they went, they made agreements before forming protectorate governments. And there was no way, viewing things from a psychological perspective, Africans could not admire to live better in education and welfare. However, establishing whether there was free will and undue influence in making contract agreements is quite problematic. They had to mistakenly give in and welcome the Europeans due to the lack of foresight precipitated and perpetuated by ignorance and illiteracy. Therefore, at some point, the Europeans never used violent means to enter and settle in many African territories but rather psychological influence. It is because they led the industrial revolution that presented them with the opportunity to reach and conquer places.

The only overt unlawful aspect, probably, is making contract agreements with illiterate and ignorant persons. Today, Africans have the education but are insisting on the westernized cultural values to live their lives—as if the instinctual assets of African humankind can be repressed in virtue of living a western life. Africans appear odd in some circumstances because they try to suppress instinctual fabrics so that they remain unconscious in virtue of living the western life—and it is difficult to hide the unconscious. You cannot solve your problems when you dislike your unconscious. One who dislikes their unconscious is a fool, but one who tries to control it in the interest of public duty is wise. What we really are is 90% unconscious, and we can do very little to hide it. The bystanders will always see someone who is trying not to be themselves because you cannot perfect living in others' romance and deception all the time.

It is, therefore, more important to recognize that *religion was more detrimental than colonialism*. If colonialism was introduced minus religion, the story would be very different. There were no formal agreements reached while introducing religion to many African parts, unlike colonialism. Religion was more psychologically driven, which made it touch our bone marrows more than colonialism.

Some others argue that it was because of Africa's political balkanization that invaders found an opportunity to exploit. This has some degree of correctness but not the main reason because each African chief would resist the invaders from impacting influence just the same way they would do to their fellow Africans. My analysis comes up with five (5) strong points that made invaders successful in Africa: selfishness and ignorance, the industrial revolution, African's failure to create a robust method to convey information from one generation to another, and conventional religions weakening the hearts and minds of Africans. The issue of political balkanization is weak because African's have shown some promising level of dealing with diversity following boundaries that Europeans created. In Europe, many countries were formed largely because each ethnicity wishes to be themselves and create their own countries.

Although North Africa aided the three great religions of the modern world in terms of core beliefs, their architecture was not drawn by Africans. Otherwise, the most feasible locations of the leading worshipping centres would be near ancestral lands.

In my opinion, the first attempt to abolish the slave trade in 1807 must have been influenced by many factors beyond the obvious case, which is to believe in human values. There was a risk if those countries continued to be flooded with African slaves. At some point, African slaves would learn to see things differently, which led to uprisings, for example, the Second Maroon War of the 1790s, where the enslaved Africans to Jamaica rebelled against colonials. The formation of Jamaica was a good example that if the slave trade continued without being stopped, it risked enslaved blacks outnumbering the colonials in some territories. It was not much of colonials graduating from a sense of oppression to a more intimate emotion that views African humankind as sensible, human, equal, and meaningful. According to the Christian's Old Testament, the Jews were slaves in Egypt for many generations, at least through the New Kingdom (1550-1175 BC) and because they had become many, the Pharaohs feared their presence that one day they would turn against the monarchy.

In Uganda, the Buganda Kingdom has had 36 monarchs since the first well-documented King (Ssekabaka), i.e. Kintu. Kintu took over from Bemba Musota; there is no well-documented history before that. The Kingdom is believed to be over 1000 years old, almost older than the United Kingdom. The well established Kingdom was established in 1300AD. I corroborate and compare the Buganda Kingdom with the United Kingdom because Buganda was a protectorate of the UK. Before 937, Anglo-Saxons of England lived in many small kingdoms, which slowly united under the reign of King Athelstan (894–939). Christianity is believed to have reached England in the 5th century, although an organized attempt to introduce Christianity in England is traced way back to the 1st century AD. The point to figure in this is that the formation of the United Kingdom appeared when Christianity was already embraced to cleanse what they would call paganisms in performing the rituals of cultural traditions.

Africans, especially in the Sub-Saharan were perhaps innocent until the 15th Century. East Anglia, Mercia, Northumbria, and sub-kingdoms of (Bernicia and Deira) were the four main kingdoms in Anglo-Saxon

England before uniting. The early Christian church had many struggles to expand, which were lessened by the legislation of Christianity by Emperor Constantine I of the Roman Empire in 313. The revolution caused by King Henry VIII (1491 – 1547) of England because of his disagreement with Pope Clement VII (1478 – 1534) on the question of marriage annulment separated the Church of England from papal authority. As an African who believes in the existence of the Supreme Being, sober and curious enough, how do you begin making decisions with a mind biased towards conventional religions? I am waiting for that day when deception held in some religions across the globe will be uncovered, borrowing tools and techniques from psychology, science and technology. During that time, Africans will be liberated from living on free meals. That day all religious concoctions will be unveiled.

When you find a population feeding on termites, uneducated, and loving themselves in a way that contradicts yours and you attempt to rule them by replacing their rituals with yours, you must be the problem. So that in the end, they rely on you for mere subsistence, which they could find by themselves before your invasion. Culture influences the way we think and reason. *Why?* Because we make emotional attachments to what we like, believe and associate with. The type of music we listen to, the sports we get involved with, the people we associate with, what we call Supreme, the food we eat and the clothing we dress all have emotional attachments. When one distorts their own culture haphazardly instead of growing it, they risk falling into a *multigenerational trap*. An instinct is a very powerful asset that cannot be repressed anyhow.

Spirituality, Psychology, and 21ˢᵗ Century Sustainable Development

The reason for varying degrees of faiths among humans is because of the uniqueness of our minds. Every one of us has a unique mind distinct from that of others. Our thought processes, consciousness, imagination and how we perceive the world varies from one person to another. The way we make judgments to influence decisions we reach in everyday lives can be understood by studying the cognitive faculties housed in the brain. Science, in which psychology forms part, is studied through experiment and observation. In science, old facts are held or nullified with just a blink of *new evidence*.

Our core cultural and religious beliefs are highly shaped in infancy, childhood and adolescence, the same stage where our cognitive and emotional development also takes shape. Before the scientific revolution, everything was viewed from a philosophical point of view, until when man learned to make vivid observations and experiments about phenomena motivating much enthusiasm in understanding the universe. Slowly, people learned to appreciate that some things were explainable scientifically.

Religions were formulated as a set of doctrines, regulations and rituals *made by man* to support humans to grow spiritually. Therefore, to have *faith in the High of Creation* is to hold strong beliefs in the doctrines of a religion one follows. Sometimes, one might not follow any religion but develops a set of beliefs through meditation and appreciating phenomena that they imagine could lead them to the High of Creation in the universe. But then, to hold these beliefs, one aims at doing good to humanity and nature. And doing this good is exercising certain behaviours what society constructs as good. Humans consciously hold beliefs through perception and imagination. Through meditation and appreciating phenomena, humans connect with the High of Creation in the universe. Therefore, the cognitive process on the High of Creation coupled with a set of behaviours that society constructs as good to humanity links with the human spirit at some point. The mind, emotions, and characters distinct from the human flesh form the foundation of spirituality when linked with the High of Creation in the universe – a phenomenological process.

To understand the connection between spirituality and psychology is by focusing on doing the good. Doing the good is not rooted in any religion. I believe it is purely natural and sometimes learnt from the society in which we get raised (cultures). The uniqueness of our minds predetermines how one adheres to doing the good. At some point, religions have instead culminated into extremisms that threaten the world. This is because some people learn to believe that doing the good is having to follow strictly the doctrines of religion which is man-made—purely a psychological fact.

When I mention a psychological fact, I mind about the uniqueness of one who first drafts the doctrine and the uniqueness of those who review the doctrine thereafter. Despite the fact that these people are filled with what is called good/holy spirit from the High of Creation, that is their phenomenological experience. Adolf Hitler once said, "Secular schools can never be tolerated because such a school has no religious instruction and a general moral instruction without a religious foundation is built on air; consequently, all character training and religion must be derived from faith… We need believing people." What moral instruction or philosophy did Adolf Hitler follow in exterminating millions of humanity? Adolf's actions could easily be profiled in the psychological dimension but not in doctrines of any religion. Besides, religious doctrines that promote satisfactory women emancipation are very scarce.

When you pierce yourself with a needle, you feel sensational pain. Similarly, when someone makes defamatory statements about you, you feel your ego being attacked. When you fail to find love, you experience a particular crisis in your life. One who understands this behaves well to neighbours because they cannot bear the consequences when such experiences come their way. However, one who behaves oddly is labelled to have maladaptive behaviours. I disagree with one whose behaviours are maladaptive and then claims to reach the High of Creation.

Take an example of a man of power who abuses neighbours' children. When his children are abused routinely by some other society members, this man will sooner or later agree to sit down and formulate guidelines to stop child abuse in their society. Nobody wishes terrible incidences to happen to their lives and family. It is because our bodies and minds are always in a survival state that we find ourselves agreeing to agree hence constructing the good to society. The differences between people who do what society constructs as good to humanity and nature and those with maladaptive behaviours are phenomenological, an explanation for the belief in the High of Creation. Exercising morality is a psychological fact whose pillars are rooted in appreciating phenomena. These phenomena vary from one person to another. The struggle to unify phenomena is the reason laws are made and/or outlawed.

Psychology works following techniques, theoretical constructs and principles. Some of these principles and techniques include; empathy, non-judgmental, and unconditional positive regard. On the other hand, living high in spirituality means adhering to doing the universal good. There is no way you can do this good without following many psychological principles and techniques aimed at appreciating people, other living beings, and nature as they are. Therefore, to do the good at the highest level is trying to understand others' positions and figure out why they do what they do and behave as they wish.

Self-driven sustainable development of Africans is primarily possible when peoples appreciate that spirituality lives in *oneness*—meditational—not in conventional religions—soul-focused—an integration of mind and heart at the centre of being. Another companion is self-awareness. Therefore, religion should not mislead people to fail to listen to *phenomenological differences* that communicate the uniqueness of one person from another. Africa's self-driven sustainability would occur when we reexamined our traditional ideals.

Conclusion

The 21st Century Sustainable Development strategy should utilize both the spiritual dimension and psychology to resolve the collision between human civilization and the ecological system. Conventional religions do not necessarily drive sustainability, especially in the African context. In the interest of sustainable development, the spiritual aspect does not tag itself on conventional religions. Its effort must be centred on creating a relationship that seeks the highest moral standards between what one considers Supreme and their human spirit or soul.

The process to create this healthy relationship is what conventional religions have disagreed about the most, which has left many African minds to offset because much is held in the process. The "material things" associate more with the process as compared to the product because the product is invisible. Africa's sustainability will only be achieved when we reinvent our own cultures. Cultures that enable us to free our minds to accommodate all ways of life that *honour the sustainability of Earth*. I consciously disagree and disbelieve in moral conventionalism that: does not spare the natural resources, that does not respect the thousands of years that we have come along, that does not respect sustainability and one that leaves no room for empathetically driven ideas, and one that minds less about diversity.

Africans going overboard as far as conventional religions are concerned is becoming very expensive in the long run. The greatest moral philosophers never found any faction. Religion was formulated to aid people to grow spiritually. Unfortunately, many factions used it for their benefit, and they seem to care less about Africa's situation. The most effective solution is claiming what we have become because several lines pull African humankind to where they belong, especially technologically driven ideologies to match contemporary living.

Culture. Religion. Psychology

Chapter Two: Our Politics

"That is simple, my friend. It is because politics is more difficult than physics".[23]
=== Albert Einstein (1879 – 1955) ===

Chapter Organization

Quick Insights

Africa's Politics and Sustainability. What is it all about?

Perception of African governments' Opposition

Intellects Shunning Away From Africa's Politics

The Growth and Development of Africa's Democracy

Improving Democracy

Improving Democracy—a Scientific Approach

The Shortfalls in Democracy

Sycophants in Democracy

Africa's Circumstantial Development

Foreign Aid and Loans

- What is the solution to Aid?

Democracy in Republics

Optimistic Politics in a Republic

On Human Rights Agencies' Philosophy

Who should decide when the Long-serving African Heads of States should go?

Politics, Foreign Direct Investments, and Foreign Portfolio Investments

Vigilance on Debts

Politics Business

Politicking

Cultural Leader's Voices

Constitutional Development in the African States

Systems of Governance and Sustainable Development

Dictators in Capitalistic Economies

Politics and Luxury amidst Extreme Poverty and Hunger

Conclusion

---

[23] As recalled by Grenville Clark, in the New York Times, April 22, 1955, after Einstein's death.

Quick Insights

In the modern world, chances to achieve your political career dreams by force or physical violence are slowly deteriorating. One needs to seem fair in their desires to become a political leader and be more decent. By thinking that promoting your interests while violating other peoples' rights is a tactical move to achieve your political ambitions is no longer an approach to attain a political office—to the decent.

Albert Einstein (1879-1955) once said, "That is simple, my friend. It is because politics is more difficult than physics". It is correct because one can prove a physics principle or law with one discrete-like solution to a problem. However, a political statement is infinite with quite a lot of argumentations, and all of them are correct based on the premises and interests of the arguer. Just as the researcher may pass from cause to effect, so may the arguer. Infinite and endless sets of variables inform politics, and these are pretty cumbersome to integrate. However, matter and its properties inform physics, making it more objective than politics.

In politics, policymakers pass statutes to legalize or illegalize, but remember, apartheid was legal, the holocaust was legal, slavery was legal, and colonialism was legal. This would mean that legality is a matter of power and not justice on one side—consolidating the fact that truth is a matter of perspective. Something equally notable to remember is that after the Berlin Conference of 1884, Europeans penetrated the African continent and picked up many chiefs the way they wanted using the power they had acquired leading the industrial revolution. Today, the exploitation of Africa by others is legal, taking away our gold and other minerals in exchange for pennies.

Not only politics, law itself is equally as complex because fairness and the principles of natural justice seem contemporary in the eyes of a woman activist. For a long time, the world treated women as chattels. On the same continuum, I believe in surrounding yourself with legalists but defend yourself day in and day out by psychological mechanisms in the modern world. And the continued arguments that highly base on principles derived from case law and precedents of common law courts to decide cases in African judicial jurisdictions leaves a curious African contemplating on whether we are implementing and extending a legal system of hope—a system that derives its principles from values, predispositions, dispositions, customs, and beliefs of a particular society, i.e. the African way of life.

Politics is subjective, while physics is objective. Therefore, claiming to enact an objective statute through subjective means depends on the interest of the arguer. The interests of each party influence the kind of debates between parties, and this demonstrates how complex politics can be. It is important to note that those we universally learn about in historical foundations, such as religions, who loved and died for us, never owned property. However, others have claimed their work, and everybody of those claimants claims to know better than others and be the lawful custodian of their living word. That is all politics.

The subject of legality on the earth cannot eliminate the kingship desires amidst love to attain power. In many cases, opponents dispute the governance of territory not because of illegalities and unfairness it fetches but because of the feeling of being less powerful. All this comprehended explains why courts of law have never been a wise man's best alternative but rather a last resort! To reach conclusions, the study of social issues is sometimes tenuous because, unlike natural sciences, we do not apply universally accepted precision laboratory instruments to analyze social phenomena.

Africa's Politics and Sustainability. What Is It All About?

As Africans, what are we longing for? In my opinion, we want to improve the image of Africa, stop neocolonialism, struggle against imperialism, develop sustainably, create peace and stability by integrating, revive socio-economic reforms, promote and sustain the dignity of African humankind, and stand on our own.

The question is: Are we doing correct politics to enable us to achieve those mentioned above? Politics that inspires hope in African masses and protects future African generations from facing neocolonialism, imperialism and paves the way to economic independence. At this point, Africa has the keys to solve the world's problems, primarily through the foreign policies we enact. We need to improve our foreign policies to protect the African humankind of today and many generations to come.

Foreign policy-making and abiding by it in African matters has become a hot matter for African nations. It poses many hazards to African humankind because the wise are quiet and mediocre minds take centre stage. The politics we play is central, and it is the focal politics to correct and inspire peace, stability, justice, and freedom in the entire world. We are the problem and yet the solution to the world's sustainability challenge. I explain, henceforth, the roadmap to have correct politics that inspires hope to African humankind and, in the end, triggers others to behave and think of Africans as comrades but not to think about us as foreign aid recipients, in the struggle to sustain the planet earth.

On Political Revolutions and Social Revolutions

The French revolution and the industrial revolution of the 18th century are widely regarded as two of the most important revolutions in human history. The former taking place in the Kingdom of France beginning around 1789, and the latter beginning in the factories of Manchester in 1765.[24] The establishment of the French republic followed the abolition of the French monarchy and gave rise to Napoleon Bonaparte. The abolition of the monarchy and the subsequent establishment of the Republic of France later gave rise to an authoritarian and militaristic government headed by Napoleon Bonaparte. Another outstanding revolution is the American Revolution that occurred from 1765–1783. It was a colonial revolt where the Americans defeated the British to establish the United States of America.

The African revolution, which was never recognized well enough for reasons not clear to date, took place between the Mid-1950s and Mid-1960s. It was the period when African peoples defeated the European colonizers and gained independence. The colonizers established federal and unitary Republics across Africa in which several monarchs were brought together, with heads of states and prime ministers.

Africans were excited for having gained independence and for bringing together peoples into republics. However, Africa's high ignorance rates, which some historians label as gaining independence prematurely, saw modern dynasties rising to power. These modern dynasties, made by those who fought the guerrilla wars, still exist in some African countries. This demonstrates that power is delightful. This shows how much the living American generation owes to the founding fathers of the United States of America. They portrayed incredible wisdom in forming the constitution and the subsequent democratic transitions from one regime to another.

---

[24] See p. 313, §7.

America's Founding Fathers included George Washington, Alexander Hamilton, Thomas Jefferson, John Adams, James Madison, James Monroe and Benjamin Franklin. Together with several other key players of their time, they structured the democratic government of the United States of America and left a legacy that shaped the world.

However, the American civil war (1861-1865) taught the world something despite the great wisdom the founding fathers portrayed. The primary cause of the war was the status of slavery, especially the expansion of slavery into newly acquired land after the Mexican–American War (1846-1848). The southern states with mostly black slaves had voted to secede and form the Confederate States of America. This led to the official abolishment of slavery in the USA by the 13th amendment to the US Constitution: Abolition of Slavery, ratified December 6th 1865.[25]

"Si vis pacem, para bellum" is a Latin adage translated as, "If you want peace, prepare for war."

The above Latin adage makes sense sometimes. For that matter, Africans must unite or else perish. Sometimes, when the world discusses truth and justice, they open a different dictionary for Africans, consolidating that truth is a matter of perspective.

The lesson we learn from the founding fathers of the United States of America, especially when the subject of power is before us, is that we must agree to a sustainable development action plan before fighting for the cause. In this aspect, most African constitutions are sick! We even learn about President Franklin D. Roosevelt inspiring hope in British colonies when he met with British Prime Minister Winston Churchill on (9-13 August 1941) and said that all people have the right to self-determination.[26] The Atlantic Charter was the first step towards creating a world organization, the United Nations, on October 24th 1945.

Many African long-serving leaders use militarism to consolidate their presence in power. Even those who step down, especially long-serving heads of state, are being pushed out through coups. The only advantage military takeover of governments present in the interim is to avoid direct invasion of foreigners into Africa's politics, like what happened in Libya. Ultimately, as explained in the forthcoming text, the number of civilian deaths is significantly reduced in the scuffle. However, this approach worked in the 20th century but is very risky in the modern world; call it a global village. It predisposes Africa to imperialism of various sorts. Maturity dialogue to step down leaders is the best move.

I cannot cite any military government because, as I said, it depends on how you argue the situation. Those in power have a different view from the worlds'. Suppose you happen to work in a democratically developed country and leave or take holidays in a developing country or vice-versa. In that case, you get the best experience of both worlds. You can have a realistic feel of militarism in some of these countries.

We are getting excited about the emerging revolution in Africa's politics; we are slowly getting rid of long-serving heads of state. But wait a minute; how prepared are we to have sustainable political reforms for this continent in terms of optimistic politics—the politics that inspires hope in the masses? Getting

---

[25] See p. 58, §2 (Hint: Truth is a matter of perspective).

[26] "The Atlantic Conference & Charter, 1941," Office of the Historian, Department of State, USA, Milestones: 1937–1945, accessed on September 2nd 2021. https://history.state.gov/milestones

rid of long-serving heads of state is not the ultimate solution for Africa's politics and sustainability. You might be shocked when you ask those raising the flags for change of government for their sustainable political framework and development action plans for the next 50 – 100 years, and you find very few with an organized and structured plan. The issue should not be just a campaign for change but change with a holistic, sustainable development action plan that is scientifically inclined.

Africa's politics lacks hope. It lacks strategic plans for conserving and sustaining the continent to lead. It is more of "change head of state" in many territories. Some territories are promising, but most African political leaders make little foresight in protecting and planning for future generations through their political parties. Most of the campaigns are about "change the heads of state". He has overstayed or abused democratic leadership; therefore, he should go. It is now more difficult to make sustainable reforms in the modern world by purely physical and legal means than psychological means. I have proved beyond doubt that psychological interventions can solve problems better and at such a high significance level most of the time, compared to legal and physical interventions. For example, the great Nelson Mandela (1918 –2013) awarding his vice president as F.W. de Klerk of the National Party was a remarkable psychological intervention in creating peace and stability in the South African government. The highly respected leaders are those who treat their enemies with the utmost integrity.

Perception of African Governments' Opposition

Some political leaders are trying all sorts of indoctrination to consolidate their presence in power. On the other hand, in a state with a multiparty system, the opposition does not automatically guarantee truthfulness in opposing all government policies. Similarly, being in the government is not rendering automatic support for all policies proposed. Adversarial politics is risky for Africa. However, collective responsibility must remain in executive cabinets, and ideology must have the freedom to nurture. A promising and sustainable democracy has room to nurture and gear focus on government policy more than partisan politics.

Yes, I am a member of a party, but I have the freedom to express my views and opinions with the main focus on government policy; this has to be nurtured in Africa's politics. In the multiparty system, the opposition should be more of an advisory entity for the ruling party, standing firm on its ideologies most of the time. The main focus is on government policy but not on opposing everything the ruling party achieves—adversarial politics. One of the most vital virtues of multiparty politics is that each member defends the ideologies of their respective parties most of the time, if not all the time. However, in Africa's politics, this seems to have nurtured more adversarial politics. Even something that proves morally unfit in African moral philosophy is defended to protect the party objectives. This proves beneficial in the short term but very costly in the long run because it does not inspire politics of hope in the young generations.

The opposition is not an enemy to the ruling government; they just believe in doing things differently. The danger of a less mature opposition is that it stunts national growth and development for all of us. The aggression of the opposition should be ideological and not defiant. The opposition should remember that it is not new; it has existed way back in ancient times. Even Jesus Christ, the saviour of the Christian faith, faced the whim of the opposition too. One of the oldest churches, the Roman Catholic Church, has faced opposition for many years, commonly known as a schism in theology. Politics has not started today; it has existed since ancient times. To oppose is not a new style of things—Satan opposes God—to the believers.

Being in opposition does not mean that you are perfectly righteous and truthful. It is easy to criticize government programs with the benefit of hindsight bias. I rarely come across a situation where people in opposition, especially in my locale and other least developed countries, ask for ample time to comment on government programs—they quickly have opinions on all matters and, most of the time, opposing opinions. I do not think we can have an all-around hopeless regime for the opposition to negate every government program.

In many cases, throughout history, the opposition grows from a group of loyalties when the agenda seems lost. In all ways, the opposition is necessary because when you listen to most of their views, they seem to hold water, but as I mentioned earlier, it all depends on the interests of the arguer.[27] It is the approach used to oppose that is contested in the interest of national development. Political leaders should ideally possess skills and the intellect to lead the masses, and their decisions affect the country and the masses they lead. Therefore, quick decision-making is paramount to save the population, especially in developing economies of the least developed countries.

In a promising state's policy enactment, the opposition may query the approach used in implementing a particular policy, the priority in service delivery, and the order of things. They can query the results but not claim that the policy is useless, just if it holds water from a humanity point of view. Holding water is hypothetical and, as I said, depends on the interest of the arguer. Then, maturity dialogue is critical and promotes respect for the opposition and the ruling party. We need to embrace the science of maturity dialogue, which focuses on interests and optimality. However, maturity dialogue also has a limit. Maturity dialogue without clear ideology is a wastage of time. Maturity dialogue makes sense only where either parties or all parties understand the need for dialogue. You cannot dialogue with someone who does not understand the subject. Our emphasis should be on making people appreciate the need to dialogue and understand the subject of why we dialogue.

When African leaders campaign for sovereignty and insist that outsiders should avoid intruding into our domestic matters, the opposition calls it dictatorship in some territories. However, sovereignty loses meaning when others discuss our domestic matters. What amuses most is that people elsewhere advocate for wildlife sovereignty but find it hard to honour Africa's sovereignty and integrity. Sometimes, they consider the LGBT community's rights before a black community's rights. I wish to make this clear to all Africans; it can never be too late to dialogue. We can always dialogue to have peaceful transitions of power and develop the continent.

Sometimes, the government passes good policies, but because opposition leaders' focus is mainly on partisan politics over government policy, they come out loudly and start telling lies; lies because some arguments about the government policies are baseless. This is because they want to attract cheap politicking and keep fame as extrovert politicians.

---

[27] See p. 58, §2.

Sometimes, the government may pass a good policy in ordinary person's eyes but with a hidden motive. The most annoying thing is that when opposition politicians learn about the hidden motive, they cannot explicitly detest the policy because of the disenchantment that arises from telling the truth. They keep just opposing and not explaining to their followers the problem associated with the policy. I am not against violating political science and politics theories, but I feel the pain when the ordinary person is misled, and the sustainable development agenda seems lost. Jean François Paul de Gondi, Cardinal de Retz (1613–1679) once said, "It is more damaging for a minister to say foolish things than to do them." It is true because the public takes on arguments and views from political leaders much more seriously than anybody else.

It is more amplified in spoken words than when actioned, and it catches a big audience. We cannot keep on wasting time when lies make the day for our politicians to become more of rascals than leaders. A good example is a politician from East Africa who said that constructing a kilometre of a road project in a developing African country was eight times the cost of constructing a kilometre of a similar road project in all the six neighbouring countries. Such kinds of lies do not take us far but rather promote self-seeking behaviours.

Of course, politics is not about truth-telling, but what culture are we instilling in the young generation where Africa needs reorganization of structures and systems? A wise politician dodges facts that he is unsure of, instils a sense of hope, and inspires confidence in the masses. The style of politicking should be qualitative where appropriate and only quantitative with facts to avoid becoming a lair and not to mislead the ordinary person. An ordinary person, when misled, banks on the government for every service, including buying their underwear—thus extending a free aid system superimposed by colonialists through their traditional aid models. For example, if the said politician commented on the cost of constructing a kilometre of a country road being more expensive than the neighbouring countries would leave him unpredictable by the audience. Being expensive is attributable to various reasons. You should only go quantitative when you have facts more especially in technical areas.

If one cannot sustain the life of telling lies, they should not dare to join Africa's politics because they will be tried and convicted for truth-telling. Our politics is very dirty, and in history, it has always been dirty but not very dirty as of now. It is highly perpetuated by the illusion of knowledge that has masked the continent of late, triggered by the education system.

"It is even more damaging for a minister to say foolish things than to do them."
Jean François Paul de Gondi, Cardinal de Retz (1613–1679)

I was a bit shocked to learn that the leader of opposition in a typical least developed African country, who had opposed the ruling government for over 20 years, was asked the economic policy that he disagreed with the most, with the current regime, and he stammered around it during a public debate. This showed that African politicians focus on partisan politics and never mind about government policy. According to the United Nations, economic, environmental, and social policies form the three pillars of sustainable development. And sustainability in the African context should be a prerequisite for all categories of leaders.

We need *well-informed leaders,* not people just *interested in leadership*. The ultimate goal of vying for the governance of African countries, to make decisions for others, should ideally be to lift people out of poverty and oppression at some point. As a politician, you must, therefore, understand how the political economy performs, the political decisions that the current regime makes, which influence the macroeconomic issues to create the difference once elected into office. Therefore, anyone who opposes the government in this era should take a keen interest in learning the three such categories of policies passed by the ruling regime to have a basis to oppose in a mature style.

For example, policies might be on fiscal policies, monetary policies, and policies on protectionism. You can speak of how high-interest rates on borrowed facilities from commercial banks cripple the success of African companies and high taxes imposed on the citizens as appropriate and propose remedial strategies to address the challenges once elected into office. Querying the decisions the current regime takes holistically would garner you more support. You show how one policy influences the other policies and hence collectively cripple the success that people deserve. At present, the ultimate goal of any African leader should be to enact policies that improve the welfare of African people in a sustainable fashion. It is very embarrassing for a candidate who is not a mastery of the current regime policies that he disagrees with yet opposing the government. I believe, in my opinion, that the opposition disagrees with the way things are handled by the ruling regime and believes in doing things differently, which rotates around decision-making processes in enacting policies.

The government may propose a margin of preference policy in the procurement of government works, services, and goods. The government might propose that construction projects below or equal to US$ 10m should be fit to give preference to domestic firms in a bid to develop local capacity in a developing country. Another policy could be on the compulsory takeover of land by the government to develop infrastructure. Suppose a candidate is opposing or supporting such a policy. In that case, they must demonstrate knowledge about the pros and cons centred on the policy and which ones weigh higher or have a long-lasting, sustainable/unsustainable effect—and therefore, they should be immediately outlawed or supported.

Another example might be imposing tariffs on a specific category of imports to promote locally produced goods. And policies on FDI inflows to developing countries. The candidate must have a clear justification and understanding as to why they support or stage resistance. One has to demonstrate clarity in their ideologies and why they view things differently. Politics hinged on socioeconomic doctrines, African philosophy, and values to inform government policy, and sustainability should be cherished over partisan politics if we dream of achieving self-driven sustainable growth and development. For example, high tariff rates imposed on imports to low-income countries may cost consumers more than it indirectly benefits government, workers, and local producers, especially where consumers own small businesses that utilize this kind of products that face protectionist policies. This is because many African countries have not gained a maturity point. We have meagre innovation rates, and therefore, we need flexibility in thinking, not politicians fixated on partisan politicking. Let us free the minds.

It is too far from mere talking and stalling government programs for the opposition to win power. It involves hard work and winning self-confidence and trust from the population, planning a methodical approach such as systems building. The problem of most opposition parties in Africa is failure to lay strategies, failure to formulate structures, and thinking short-term all the time. The opposition needs strategic planning, patience, and silence in many operations—action weighing higher than talking, emotional intelligence building, and building systems.

Decades of research now point to emotional intelligence as the critical factor that sets star performers apart from the rest of the pack. The connection is so strong that 90 per cent of top performers have high emotional intelligence. The opposition needs to embrace the power of emotional intelligence and silence—to sit back, think, and reflect. There is no substitute for strategy and careful planning. Managing emotions is key to winning. Therefore, toughness may be slightly near to being wise, but anger itself is to fools.

Whilst we fail to do long-term strategies, outsiders are already investing in Africa for long-term benefits. They seem to have a plan for Africa for more than 100 years to come. Something we may not have for ourselves. When someone loans you a road, and you are to repay the money in 50 years, this is a long term investment. He is probably planning for his offspring but not himself. Why are we failing long term promises for the good of our nation-states? With patience and building systems, the opposition can easily crush the regime they do not believe in by planning the move in 15-30 years. It is proper to enter the active ground when the party has reached maturity as far as building systems is concerned. We should avoid harvesting unripe things—premature things.

We need to master the art of timing. I have seen many politicians jumping out of the current long-serving regimes, and in 1-2 years, they run for political offices on the opposition's party tickets. Just a few of them have been successful because they think about the move overnight without proper planning and think they can win a regime that has indoctrinated society for a very long time. Chinese say the trick is to masquerade as a swine to kill a tiger. Otherwise, many African states will remain ruined by dictators. And it is dangerous for outsiders to jump in to solve Africa's problems. We need to remember that there is no free lunch under the sun. Nobody else can claim to love your children more than yourself. The problem is ours, not for anyone else.

The Baganda in central Uganda say, *"The owner of the corpse should lift the stinky part"*. Nobody is going to take more responsibility for our problems than ourselves. We are liable to solve our problems. An external's extraordinary efforts are questionable and, at times, fishy. It is a mess to rely on outsiders to solve our problems, which are motivated by; poor attitude, lack of nationalistic spirit, corruption, emotional incompetence, laziness, lack of teamwork, a lack of self-confidence, dishonesty, and etcetera.

"The owner of the corpse should lift the stinky part." African Proverb

Outsiders are also somehow promoting their interests because they are not living a perfect life too—they also have problems to solve in their countries. In July 2016, China's Hunan Province experienced traumatic floods that swept away property, left many people dead, and registered direct and indirect heavy pecuniary losses. Also, in July 2021, the Henan province of China experience torrential rains that affected tens of millions of people forcing thousands to evacuate their homes—signalling the need to address sustainability globally. This is greatly attributed to climate change, whose consequences lead to floods. In the USA, similar traumatic events usually occur. Donors also have their issues to sort. Also, extremists are threatening the world every day. We keep talking of colonialism for having wounded us, which is true because it reshaped our attitudes towards nature, but there is room to recognize our fate. It is important to note that the Europeans colonized the Americans at some point in history. Why do we keep singing about our colonialism? If you have understood the problem, is it still a problem? It becomes a solution to the optimist.

Colonialism is one reason for the distortion of self-esteem before another race. It is not uncommon to see artists, boxers, and other African Diasporas, African-Americans, African-Europeans, dishing out their fortunes showing altruistic traits by handouts. They feel high self-esteem by doing so, but in the real sense, it is the opposite—someone with low self-esteem does such things. Real charity is organised, such as non-governmental organizations, foundations, and making sustainable enterprises.

Intellects Shunning Away From Africa's Politics

The issue of saving the planet is at its climax at present. The right decisions have to be made right from the very smallest unit of society—families and communities. The earth's creatures will not be protected from extinction when intellects are shunning away from decision-making, especially on issues affecting the nation-states. The more, for example, scientists ignore governance and politics, the more the continent and the planet loses hope.

In the developed world, we have seen some heads of state and their administration disputing climate change consequences and, therefore, highly defend politics over science. At times, they (heads of states) dispute scientific results that warn the entire world. The illusion of knowledge described in Chapter Three is accelerated by competent scientists who shun away from taking the lead in political matters.[28] Leaving sustainable development debates solely to political gasbags is a threat to the entire planet. Good and hopeful politicians are not necessarily a product of the intellect's ability or high degree achievers, but the intellectuals and the educated people are better positioned to be well informed to debate politics that inspires hope. They are positioned to develop a good political judgment, being able to view both sides of the coin and to know what to say and to do in unique circumstances.

"...He has clearly recognized that the world is more threatened by those who tolerate evil than by the evil-doers themselves."[29]

Albert Einstein (1879 – 1955)

Self-driven sustainable development shall not occur where scientists and other intellectuals are filled with anxiety to join politics. Look at it this way, sustainable development in the African context, aimed at accelerating progress to protect the future generations' ability to meet their needs whilst improving and maintaining the wellbeing of today's generation, can best be achieved by politicians who are scientists! Why? Several policies are passed on the grounds of promoting the welfare of the state nationals. Welfare associates with safety and health. Who is best suited to debate such policies?

---

[28] See p. 118, §3.

[29] AEA 34-347 Albert Einstein, in a tribute to Pablo Casals, March 30th 1953.

The 21st-century political debates on sustainable development might have to revise philosophical schools of thought that defend science to promote humanity at its best but not putting politics before science. This is aimed at stimulating many scientists to love joining politics. As a scientist, by training and understanding science, your arguments on government policies might be very inclined towards saving the planet than power.

Science is an evidence-based discipline. Scientists always define hypotheses and collect data to validate or nullify their hypotheses. After scientific results are out, policymakers, who are usually politicians, debate on them and whatever they decide on the results is politics. The implication is that a scientist has no control over what happens next with their results. For example, investigating the effect of; deforestation, undersize fishing, swamp reclamation, toxic emissions from industries, and effluents into the rivers is a scientific inquiry, but deciding on which action to take in response to the scientific results obtained is political. How shall we protect, defend and prolong Africa and its peoples where scientists and other intellects shun away from politics?

Again look at it this way: Africa does not have agreed upon African standards and codes of practice in many industrial practices, and Foreign Direct Investments (FDI) is being hosted day-to-day. Every giant country has its standards and codes of practice that add on universally accepted standards and codes of practice. Each giant country is conservative at some point when it comes to its codes and standards of practice. At times, they come along with their codes and standards to facilitate designs and development of solutions wherever FDI goes to the host country—the evidence-based approach in solving problems with a legal implication. Although every country sets up its investment codes to encourage foreign capital investment, African countries always compromise their standards because they are desperate. The Asian giant is very good at exploiting this hopelessness. Therefore, intellectuals would need to join politics and fight to correct these issues.

Of course, in their benefit of trade and policies, harmonization of practice is inevitable but consider infrastructure projects that require designers, engineers, and technologists. Many infrastructure projects loaned to Africa by the Asian giant are designed and constructed by themselves and following their codes. Africa has followed European standards for long since independence, and little attempt has been made to have African standards. The scientists' opinions cannot seriously be taken if they do not wholly involve themselves in politics to defend, maintain, innovate, redefine, promote and extend well-researched standards and codes of practice. I dream of a proposal to request each professional body to be represented in parliaments in the interest of sustainable development. In this way, the scientists' views and other related professionals' views will be much echoed on the floor of legislative assemblies. If not the case, then scientists should wake up and join politics to save Africa.

The Growth and Development of African Democracy

Our democracy is still very young across many Africa states. We need to accelerate its growth to save the continent amidst the many challenges it is likely to face in a couple of years ahead in the 21st century. Seated on several unutilized natural resources is a threat that predisposes us to many deceptive foreign direct investments targeting natural resources. Improved democratic leadership that is not egocentric can save the continent many disasters ahead. You and I owe our continent a lot. It is high time we start maturity dialogue!

Democracy is the fairest way of electing leaders to office. It is guided by free will, freedom of expression, free press, right to protest and right to petition the government, the doctrine of separation of powers, and majority votes. It idealizes that power belongs to the people. In his 1863 Gettysburg Address, President Abraham Lincoln (1809 – 1865), while referring to a democratic government, famously said that "it is an ideal government that is, of the people, by the people, and for the people,"

The longing for freedom is traced way back when warlords, emperors, rulers and kings dictated what was right for society. Undemocratic means of assuming leadership bleed tyranny, authoritarianism and totalitarianism. As Africans, we struggled through history to overcome the forces of tyranny, exploitation and oppression. It is, therefore, our wish to have national constitutions based on the principles of unity, peace, equality, freedom, social justice and progress. I attempt to lead continuous improvement in our democracy; what we ought to do and not to do amidst developed and semi-developed giants, East, West, South, and North of the African continent. What kind of democracy do we need to accelerate self-driven sustainable positive change to save the continent amidst scarce resources and sustainable development challenges?

When I assess my country's politics in particular and look at the kind of multiparty democracy the country holds, compare and contrast it with single-party states' democracies, I remain a little curious to decide on which form of democracy works best for an African child in such a critical situation where the world has become a global village. At some point, I believe the current social conditions might not favour democracy. However, because I wish to be free and I do not need anyone imposing himself over me to take away my freedom, I fall back to democracy.

In single-party state democratic governments, mistakes may accumulate, posing a significant negative impact on the economy and socio-economic stand of the masses. Multiparty democracy creates healthy checks and balances. Undemocratic governments, like some monarchists of the past, greatly shunned away from democracy and their people suffered oppression and ill-treatment, which a civilized person cannot withstand. The acceleration of success registered in many parts of the world results from some form of democracy to a significant extent. Everything that a human in modern society should endeavour to do should promote their democracy. Anyone who ultimately says that democracy is bad has not properly critiqued and reflected on several forms of governance. Unless you come from some form of a royal lineage probably, you may adamantly refuse to understand the subject of democracy.

Democracy, especially in multiparty systems, grows the people's knowledge; first, it grows human rights, freedom to worship, speech freedom, and freedom to enjoy nature. Suppression and oppression are a result of the imposition of leaders to the masses. An African who labours to borrow antidemocratic models from elsewhere needs to understand the history before comparing and contrasting. The history we share as Africans in fighting colonialists puts us in a situation that needs no copying and pasting the material. We need the material that has been well-studied holistically to fit collectivism.[30]

A little distraction from what we hold from the past through introducing religions and later colonialism needs collective efforts to put the continent on the correct path. This is because the level of correlation between the reasons to introduce a new order of faith in Africa and at the same time colonize Africans is slightly not positive. Colonialism oppressed Africans, yet colonialists brought the religions. It is my

---

[30] See p. 322, §7.

first time to learn about a negative conclusion premised on a positive premise. I finally ask, do we have all these facts in order? At this point, I believe Africa needs to grow its democracy benchmarking on self-awareness initiatives, the meaning of collectivism, and our cultural predispositions.

Many people are criticizing democracy. However, suppressing masses will accumulate mistakes over time which can be a time bomb—and this is a characteristic of many Sub-Saharan African countries. It is becoming difficult for several African emerging economies to borrow the democratic ideal that power belongs to the people—that in decision making, people should form a significant integral part. It takes a lot of effort and maturity to reflect on what kind of democracy is needed to register an acceleration of success. At the same time, we are seated between developed and semi-developed economies. What kind of democracy do we need in Africa for the 21st century?

As Africans, we need to strengthen democratization, promote and protect human rights, enhance access to social justice and improve accountability as quickly as possible. To move in multiparty democracy, we need to foster dialogue between political parties and encourage them to corporate on sensitive political issues. To do away with democracy is to attack human rights, morality, and ethics. This is the right time for African philosophers to showcase what they have because unrevised democracy is not going to help Africa very much in order for it to catch space in real-time. The kind of democracy we need must have an African touch, cultures, values, predispositions, and African symbolisms. Democracy sounds the best ideal for democrats, but organized hooligans can defeat disorganized democrats while exercising democratic ideals.

Leadership in democratic governments is about understanding that everyone is correct in their argument. And we try to harmonize the means, the processes, the ways, the approaches, the understandings, and the empathies. In many cases, mature democracy debates the means and processes used to make decisions. At times, the prioritization and pathways are debated in mature democracy but not completely divergent ideologies—with the guiding principle of national sustainability. The ideological frameworks in mature multiparty democracies differ in pathways, not in content—demonstrating sovereignty before anything else—and protecting the country's resources with one heart and soul. This is what true democracy nurtures.

Reaching a maturity point to become accommodative and understand that everyone is different and no man is an island is a cornerstone for a promising democrat. When you find room in your heart to tolerate subjective reasoning from others, it means you are on the correct path to becoming a democrat. Our efforts should all be geared towards turning the masses into democrats. How do we do this quickly when sustainable development is the topic on-board across the globe? How do we shoot this ambition when civic and political education is poorly administered in many parts of Africa? The unutilized natural resources we sit on amidst the threat of climate change and mineral resources exhaustion are a time bomb we ought to recognize now. Do we really need democracy where multiparty system ideologies *differ in content* and not *processes,* considering the issue of sustainable development beforehand?

For democracy to flourish, the following assumptions are held valid;

a) Inclusiveness: all members of a political community have the right to participate and should have their voices heard.

b) Popular control: decisions rest with the political community as a whole.

c) Considered judgement: individual and collective decisions should be based on people being adequately informed and understanding the positions of others.

d) Transparency: decision-making should be open and accountable.[31]

A situation where the wildlife is composed of lions, giraffes, gorillas, antelopes, leopards, crocs, hippos, and the antelope is to become the president of this sovereign Republic as depicted in Figure below, needs stringiest measures to deal with conflict and spearhead self-driven sustainable growth and development.

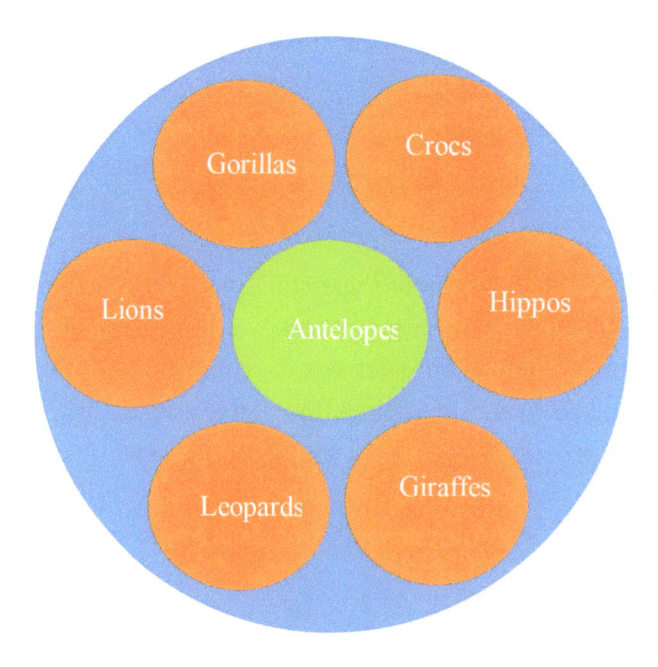

Wildlife Sovereign Republic

A mere claim that power belongs to all of us as one, yet we have specific differences, ranging from cultural opinions, cognitive strength, education levels, ingenuity, and socioeconomic perception, is not enough in deciding who should steer the Sovereign Republic. We need some form of quality control checks to inspire hope in our politics, where we want to make democracy happen. We need to go vertical as we spread horizontally. What happens today is only spreading horizontally. This can be done as depicted in the illustration below with levels A, B, C and D.

---

[31] "What is democracy?" Foundation for democracy and Sustainble developmet, accessed October 4th 2021, https://www.fdsd.org/the-challenge/what-is-democracy/.

The A's should vote within themselves and also vote for the B's, C's, and D'S, and there must be a standard set, which must be achieved by who wins at each level. The decisive vote for the B's, for example, is what the A's have said, and the decisive vote for the C's is what the B's have said but viewed along a continuum with the majority vote—a vote by and for all A's. Similarly, the decisive vote for the D's is what the C's have said. That means the A's vote for everyone and is called the standard benchmark. The B's should vote the C's, and the C's should vote the D's. Then, vetting is guided by majority votes from A's following a prescribed standard on the continuum. The results of each level should be viewed along a continuum. Unimproved democratic elections are an illusion and do not inspire hope in our politics.

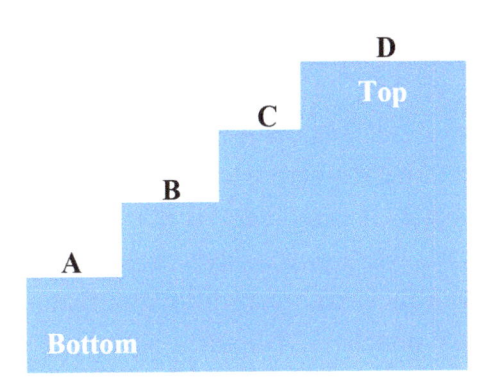

Hierarchy of Voters

The Continuum

Majority vote	0%	50%	100%
Minority Vote	0%	50%	100%

Question: How is the candidate fairing on the continuum following agreed standards?

Improving Democracy—a Scientific Approach

Ernst H. Waloddi Weibull (1887 – 1979) was a Swedish engineer, scientist, and mathematician. Waloddi discovered a probability density function named before him as "the Weibull Probability Density Function (PDF)" that has far-reaching success in manufacturing, computer science, telecommunications, and engineering.[32] His work significantly improved the field of reliability studies in engineering and other science disciplines. His work partially focused on variability within sameness or homogeneousness.

Items which appear equal sometimes are not actually equal unless proved in detail. For example, Candidate A might garner 80% of the votes in constituent X, and Candidate B also garners 80% of the votes in constituent Y. Wallodi's work is more versatile—it can be applied to study the variability and reliability of such voters in X and Y constituents and their overarching effect on self-driven sustainable development agenda. It is high time we applied it in psephology to check democratic ideals. Some of the pioneers of democracy formulated the electoral colleges as a process to oversee quality control, and it is a quality assurance measure within a promising democracy.

---

[32] "Characteristics of the Weibull Distribution," Weibull.com, accessed October 6th 2021. https://www.weibull.com/hotwire/issue14/relbasics14.htm.

The Electoral College is a process that leaders in democracy formulated and established in their Constitution as a compromise between election of the head of state by a vote in the legislative body and election of the head of state by a popular vote of qualified citizens. The Electoral College process consists of selecting the electors, the meeting of the electors where they vote for President and Vice President, and the counting of the electoral votes by Legislature. This is well exercised in the United States of America.

Weibull's discoveries are more versatile and applicable in studying the variability and reliability of data collected, in this case, the votes. In this case, the *compromise* between results from the vote in electoral colleges and vote from all qualified citizens can be studied with the use of Weibull Analyses. Attributes such as; the nature and quality of voters, polling stations' status, candidates, and available resources are all focal points of concern in a promising democracy.

The reliability of the majority vote in a promising democracy can be checked with electoral colleges. In this way, the quality of democracy can be improved to have a clear roadmap to self-driven sustainable development. Otherwise, communism might prove better if democracy is not checked using Weibull's discoveries or electoral colleges. As a matter of fact, when you analyze communism in contrast to democracy with electoral colleges, you might be lost only to find very little difference, *focusing on the quality of the head of state* and speaking from a sustainable development agenda, not the unchecked majority vote illusion and also keeping other factors constant. In some way, communism has a factor of Weibull's coefficients regarding appraising the head of state.

At some point, communism limits; freedom of expression, talent identification, talent nurturing and management, market systems, living life to the fullest, etcetera. A society deprived of these may live happily but less mobile, less flexible, and less explorative. And many masses might be failed to self-actualize whilst authoring their destinies. But also, democracy without electoral colleges or where no Weibull PDF is applied is more dangerous and damaging, especially in a capitalistic multiparty state. "Dangerous" in terms of spurring socio-economic transformation for sustainable development. At some point, because of heavy collectivism, *socialist democracy,* which embraces hierarchical or multilevel staged voting, is the solution for *Africa's presidency and legislative assemblies.* This is because Africa's social conditions characterized by collectivistic bonds seem premature to embrace modern democratic ideals of capitalistic nature.

The Shortfalls in Democracy

Freedom of expression and democracy have their shortcomings, especially in the processes. I am not contesting democratic ideals, though, but rather expound on the other side so that Africans can appreciate the effect it has graduated us into. For example, the Azusa Street Revival meeting on April 9th 1906 in the USA, whose legacy extends to the present day, with more individual Pentecostal churches sprouting out like wildfire, is doing more harm than good on the African continent—considering this from socioeconomic productivity, GDP, and national development perspectives.[33] This movement was spearheaded by an African-American William J. Seymour in Los Angeles, California. Historians consider this revival movement to be the primary catalyst for the spread of Pentecostalism in the 20th Century.

---

[33] See also p. 11, §1.

Today, though there are many Pentecostal independent churches, there is no central authority governing Pentecostalism in Africa. The result is that lawbreakers and many other bad people hide in these independent worshipping centres to promote their interests. I am not against the content delivered but am instead weighing the results and the African processes. Even the smallest Savings and Credit Co-operative Organization (SACCO) in a village believes in having a constitution, articles of association, or a structure, then why not African Pentecostals? They seem not to agree with the importance of doctrines or laws in society. All this is a result of democratic ideals—the freedom to worship and freedom of speech.

The Pentecostal movement took some time to enter Africa spreading from the USA. The HIV/AIDS epidemic enabled the acceleration in the spread of Pentecostalism in Africa. *Why?* In the 1980s, the Human Immunodeficiency Virus (HIV) was identified in humans. Some researchers say that HIV crossed from chimps to humans in the 1920s in Zaire, now the Democratic Republic of Congo (DRC). Researchers say that chimps carried the Simian Immunodeficiency Virus (SIV), a virus closely related to HIV. There is a claim that people used to eat chimps in some parts of Africa and got infected. However, another theory states that there were unethical scientists who were paid to manufacture HIV in a bid to exterminate the African race. These are debates within researchers.

As the virus spread and grew into Acquired Immune-Deficiency Syndrome (AIDS), significantly weakening peoples body systems to look bewildered and hopeless, they ran to various places and treatment centres for help. Because of little knowledge about the virus by then, many African people attributed the symptoms to witchcraft. This belief sent mixed reactions to communities, and at some point, people living with HIV were discriminated against. Because the AIDS stigma is unbearable, patients always sought therapeutic interventions, and there was no traditional healer that could treat the disease. *This is where hypnotherapies met with Pentecostalism.* The freedom of speech, the freedom of expression, and the freedom to worship marrying promoting Pentecostalism anyhow. An ill-informed citizen becomes a nuisance in the sustainability equation because of the unlimited scope of these freedoms nurtured by democratic ideals.

Freedom of expression, freedom of speech, and freedom to worship is a must for sustainable development, but it must be well defined. Imagine a state where child labour is allowed to thrive, women and children continue to be abused, and human rights are abused, yet nobody can stand up to challenge the regime because of living in captivity; you cannot expect sustainable development in such a state. I could equally not be allowed to write this book if suppression of freedom of expression attained the tip of the iceberg globally.

However, democracy should be standardized to become more promising. The state's leader must be sieved through standard mechanisms. This will enable African countries to have capable, competent, all-round candidates; unimproved democratic ideals might not function amidst poverty and ignorance, appearing as illusions instead. This is one of the various reasons some undemocratic African leaders claim to be democrats because of the prevailing socioeconomic conditions. Many African dictators focus on rural areas in their campaign strategies because they are characterized by high ignorance levels, ill-informed people, and high illiteracy levels compared to their urban counterparts.

At some point, weighing Abraham Maslow's hierarchy of needs with democratic ideals shows that the two are in disagreement in Africa. A hungry society cannot understand the effects of the cause until when they find what to eat. This kind of society cannot identify risks associated with the hazards. Such a society needs real help, and democracy might not work in a foreign aid recipient at some point.

There is a lot to study about democracy. People speak what is good to listen to and what appears to fascinate the masses. A team of 100 people voting for their leader democratically would ideally take on one who garners the most votes. But what is the agenda for the leader? If the aim is to lead us to sustainable development, this mode of voting is irregular, especially in Africa. As far as the prevailing socioeconomic conditions are concerned in developing African countries, it is sometimes an irregular system. It might not help us to achieve the sustainable development agenda unless improved.

A farm of pigs can elect their leaders democratically, and this would carry sense. In faith and religion, democracy counts. Schools, colleges and universities, are perfect ideals for democratically elected leaders. A farm of pigs, cattle, goats and possibly wild animals needs Weibull's studies to yield promising democratically elected leaders.

However, triangulating democracy in Africa should not be misinterpreted or directly equated to dictatorial or authoritarian governance. There are many other ways we can think of to decide how to appraise competent and visionary leaders. Leadership transitions are inevitable in a promising state. This promotes equity and equality. We cannot have a life presidency and think self-driven sustainability will occur. We need to respect ideological differences and provide room for trials.

Even if Nelson Mandela (1918 –2013) had overstayed in power, mistakes would accumulate, and his legacy would be spoiled. When one overstays in power, it risks the accumulation of mistakes. The law of diminishing returns in economics is more versatile and can explain the fate of life presidency and overstaying in power. Contrary to several other systems, my argument about democracy is based on the ordinary person who is neither wise nor exposed or able to foresee the hidden agenda in political matters—and is the majority in Africa. The ordinary person contributes the majority vote illusion, a democratic ideal, yet that vote dramatically impacts the socioeconomic transformational roadmap. The overstaying regime can quickly indoctrinate the ordinary person, and it wins the majority vote. Therefore, the country can keep festering with wrong leaders due to the massive ordinary person providing majority vote illusion. And this is typical of many African Sub-Saharan countries.

With such incidences of an ordinary person dominating, when shall we catch the sustainable development agenda—when advancement in science and technology from the rest of the pack is moving steadily faster day in and day out? Certainly not possible. Scientists try several prototypes before concluding on the best ideal. Borrowing from their techniques, you try a prototype, and if it fails to work, you derive another ideal prototype and subject it to trials. With such democratic ideals left to impact us negatively, the rate of population explosion shall be inevitable. Our new models should focus on a methodical, scientific approach to plan for the population, and there should be sequenced debates.

Radical scientists have a role in steering the revolution. In a state where the rate of population explosion overtakes the rate of innovation, what do you expect? A state where hooliganism in watching and betting for western football leagues supersedes imagination—a high western football mania is sweeping Africans.

And now democracy in multiparty systems allows everyone, foolish or wise, to debate policies—and more importantly, stall them. We have professors, technocrats, researchers, experts, achievers, revolutionists, philosophers, etcetera who should be funded to plan for the nations. If not, they should find means to fund themselves to save Africa.

In democratic societies, majority support takes over definitely. The above team is pulling for priority whilst the ordinary person is pulling on the other hand for priority. What democracy forgets to take seriously is the slogan that goes, "Empty cans make the loudest noise." In this context, gasbags always win, and we end up losing the very best in talent. We need to focus and apply some authoritarian models where necessary objectively—authoritarian models guided by the will and wisdom of the people. Suppose we love our countries, run a massive PR campaign, and foster a one-month civic and political education. In that case, we make a referendum on the competence of the head of state, parliamentarians, and other high ranking offices, after that.

Democracy at times takes peace away from the peaceful—it needs to be revised, in the African context— Africans should redefine what democracy means for themselves. It sounds unfair and partial to claim that the process was democratic when we have a sample of voters who are not eligible to stand for the post yet are eligible to vote. The decision must go farther than that. Democracy is the best if all voters or at least two-thirds of the voters are eligible to contest for the position. Many African constitutions give a right to every citizen of eighteen years of age or above to vote. Currently, in many countries, only age and being a citizen determine the eligibility to vote.

I give an example of Uganda, which I know most. Article 59(1) of Uganda's constitution (1995 as amended) says every citizen 18+ years is eligible to vote, and they must be a registered voter (Article 59(2)). Article 102(c) of the same constitution deems the person fit for election as president should hold qualifications of *Advanced level education*. Article 102(b) of the same constitution previously mentioned that a person fit to contest as president would be at least 35 years old and not more than 75 years old until 2017 when the age limit was scrapped through a *democratic process*. Any person aged 18+ years can now contest for the presidency. And the upper limit is not defined which would benefit long-serving leaders to rule for life—and this approximates to contemporary dynasties of sorts. This kind of hopelessness is fueled by democracy that Africans have failed to redefine for themselves.

When you analyze those two Articles scientifically, i.e. Article 59(1) and Article 102(c), you see that one Article discriminates against the other based on the *level of education*. Without Weibull's studies applied, democracy escalates Africa's problem at some point. The best question Africans should ask themselves is: how do we deal with deep-seated selfishness that does not align well with correct public philosophy to embrace democratic ideals? Selfishness distorts the will and wisdom to agree on the correct philosophy. Many African political leaders are sick, and they have disorders that international standards and manuals are still failing to diagnose.

The team of elites I mentioned earlier should be tasked to lead and save the ordinary person.[34] Because an ordinary person multiplies day and night and democracy highly multiplies him. And then after, we cry about unemployment and increased crime. Struggles to convert an ordinary person to a higher cognitive

---

[34] See also p. 66, §2.

citizen should be piloted by funding the already existing talented elites. In my opinion, self-driven sustainable development of any society can best be defined in a philosophy that goes, "working together of a developed and either propelled or self-propelled maturity of a highly and freely cognitive psyche(s) —minds which start to view the wildlife as potential living human beings—minds which recognize that the quality of life of one person is equivalent to the quality of life of the entire society."

Ideally, democracy has an advantage over other systems because it saves us wealthy oligarchs oppressing the masses. However, this is very thin in Africa, where politicians buy voters in several countries. Therefore, it is difficult for a middle-income earner filled with a wealth of ideas to win elections. Yet, the accumulation of wealth in Africa, at present, is highly circumstantial and not well-guided by the value theories in economics. So, we are in a state of hopelessness, not knowing what kind of system we should adopt to be more inclusive yet promoting the overall agenda of spurring socio-economic development structurally.

Federal African Republics versus Unitary African Republics

An emphasis on coming up with the best constitutional models through dialogue and appreciate our deep-seated selfishness to capture the facts of the majority African person is essential. In that case, their attitude, cognition abilities, foresight abilities and overall perception of life are all factors that need new political and governance models to accelerate socioeconomic transformation. The best governance model would be *federalism hinged* and built on regions or territories *but not tribes or clans* for relatively big countries. Our *deep-seated selfishness* would be broken down by holding power at county and national levels. Even if we have three or four states are enough to make a nation built on a federal constitution. Where tribes or a set of cultural beliefs coincide within a federal state, it would be modelled to reflect both harmoniously.

Secondly, some bit of positive dictatorship or authoritarianism in federalism through *evidence-based approaches* to propel the ordinary person to the mutual goal is necessary. It is important to note that anyone aiming at a new social order because their clan is less incorporated in decision making or not incorporated in the current government structure and systems must be careful not to have a poor vision—a vision that is motivated by tribalistic mentality. There is no clan or tribe too independent, isolating itself in the modern world, and integrity is not tagged to any clan or tribe. Such emotionally driven prejudicial acts in politics motivate adversarial politics and depict the highest kind of ignorance today. They overtly demonstrate a big room to grow one's intellect. A promising politician must have an overarching goal that is nationalistic, not tribalistic.

Federalism is not about empowering tribes, as some people might confuse the discussion. It is about empowering people of a given society to solve their proximate issues without relying on the central government all the time—it is a system too good at conserving the environment, preserving cultural heritage and promoting our identity. The system might help Africans to fight *contemporary nomads* with ease. Uganda, in particular, continues to face the problem of contemporary nomads as a result of converting to a unitary constitution. The contemporary nomads are the invisible force evicting people from their ancestral land, and later the government claims we need land reforms to solve land wrangles.

However, in the African countries whose constitutions have been greatly abused and converted into unitary systems, people find it hard to accept power-sharing at county and national levels. In some of these countries, constitutions were changed as a result of the post-independence insurgencies. It is becoming difficult to convince people about the beauty of a Federal Republic because of their fixation on unitary constitutions, which they believe unite people more than federal governance. In this case, the ideology we need to base to interest people fixated in unitary systems shall be based on "The Unitary Republic that answers everyone's Question not Questions". This should be introduced to define modern federalism. Every part of the country has its unique Question. Anyone who wishes other's Questions not to be answered would be the enemy in modern federalism for these countries.

Because of the deep-seated selfishness, that people fear to discuss because of the disenchantment it brings, other people's Question is not answered well-enough by the ruling regimes in the unitary systems that several African countries are fixated into. This is what perpetuates high corruption rates in Africa. In Africa, most of the countries are under unitary systems. Federal Republics include Nigeria, Sudan, South Sudan, Ethiopia, and Somalia, among others. However, unitary systems were a conquer approach used by power-obsessed people like the colonialists to annex neighbourhoods. Africa has a myriad of different peoples of several ethnic backgrounds and ought to be a little sensitive while carrying out integrations. Growth and development start in mind, and people think and behave differently, influenced by cultural predispositions. I have explained this quite well in Chapter Four (Optimism and Positivity). Some people ought to copy from others in some jurisdictions but not lead what you do not understand due to purported integrations.

Federalism is about solving proximate causes by the people of that county/state with love and enthusiasm, using very applicable methods in the circumstances. Of course, these solutions must not be ultra-vires with the national legislation. Now that we have learned that doing something out of love defeats doing it out of fear, we ought to integrate psychological interventions with legal interventions to develop the best ideals to promote development. Africa has several tribes, and although we have registered success dealing with diversity in many areas under unitary systems, I believe we would do better under federalism. Federalism promotes competition amongst counties or states and would check on corruption for Africa's context. I believe federalism would work best for African nations because of the unique attributes in the minds of Africans I have described in Chapter Four (Optimism and Positivity). These attributes need to be considered while drawing up standards. Regionalism would make more meaning when federations are considered a multi-level approach right from the home countries. It should be *Federate Home, Federate Regionally."*

In Chapters Four and Five, I have discussed other forgotten phenomenological and psychological issues, yet they are unique obstacles to Africa's self-driven sustainable development. I have also provided reasons why we need some bit of authoritarian governance. Slowly, promising democracy will be well-founded. Democratic ideals seem premature for some African countries' social conditions. We also need some form of electoral colleges similar to those of the leaders in democracy or Weibull techniques to check the head of state's overall competencies if democracy is to yield fruition.

It is essential to note that the kind of democracy from the developed world is not the same democracy we have in Africa. For example, not every catholic priest votes for the pope in the Catholic Church—it is restricted to the Cardinals, Bishops and Vatican officials. The fact that Africa copies from A-Z, most constitutions are hopeless and sick characterized by selfishness. The living American owes a lot to the founding fathers of the United States for making a constitution that will live on for many generations to come. They can always make amendments to the constitution. However, the founding fathers structured the democratic government of the United States of America and left a legacy that shaped the world. The wisdom exhibited by the founding fathers in the making of the USA constitution is admirable. We also need to think of something that is not selfish. This draws me to conclude that Africa needs its models but not copied, full-blown, and pasted models and theories. We should desist the bandwagon influence if we need to achieve self-driven sustainable development.

Should we Act with Love or Fear?

Too much bureaucracy embedded in unimproved democratic ideals stunts national development. Decision making at a snail's speed results from poorly studied democratic ideals in a society that lacks democrats—government officials embezzling funds for their benefit and hiding in democracy. This leaves me thinking that in some African states, we gained independence pre-maturely. We still needed to be governed by the colonialists, and the model they used was essentially authoritarian. But where does today's problem come from? The problem is that we failed to understand that doing something out of *love* is far rewarding than doing something out of *fear* of collapse or competition. We still needed to have governance hinged on our cultural roots; this is to say that our cultural leaders needed to be an integral part of the development process.

Today, cultural leaders have no power and are resting behind the scenes. The governance models that could work best for Africa would be those that have the cultural leaders influence the decision making in the interest of national development because the masses they lead were and are totally in love with their cultural leaders, except a few. Cultural leaders are custodians of cultural values, norms, and beliefs, a foundation of a sustainable and socioeconomically transformed society.

Colonial masters saw this love for one another—the masses and the cultural leaders as inseparable twins, so they disintegrated the love to promote their influence. When colonial masters left, we were supposed to go back and propose systems that could hinge on our territorial interests and cultures. However, we instead promoted a unitary system, which is a technique for conquering others. The unitary system is an ideal that assumes to unite people. However, cultures are more than ideals—they have existed for many years and approximate to facts. It is like thinking that a personal value weighs heavier than a scientific fact when you go unitary.

As long as the central government(s) continue(s) to make oppressive decisions on the spiritual and cultural lives of its nationals going by the majority rule in unitary systems, the desire for political independence by the minority groups will increase in several African countries. Some of the high ranking advantages of unitary constitutions as cited by scholars include; (a) equal development throughout the country; (b) maximum exploitation of all national resources, both human and material, throughout the country; and (c) promotion of the idea of one nation and symbol hence people begin to think nationally in contrast to federalism where people think more about their states.

However, in African's case, the above merits of the unitary system cannot be achieved satisfactorily for several reasons cited in Chapter Four and Five, and the following reasons; (a) equal opportunities and balance throughout the country is impossible where the ruling regime is a war veteran because his perception of power is different, (b) excessive embezzlement of government resources is given way in unitary systems because of the deep-seated selfishness triggered by distortion of collectivism, (c) Unitary constitutions in distorted collectivism assume that they are cultivating social power but in the actual sense not because it gives no chance for people in a given territory to exercise what they believe at extraordinary liberty, (d) democratic foundations are so weak in Africa to favour unitary, (e) the tribalistic mentality is so intense in some unique tribes; they ought to live alone so that they learn because under unitary they create a network of idiots, (f) selfishness cannot allow the unitary system to function; it is better to go federal system to scale down selfishness, (g) unitary systems cannot promote sustainable management of natural resources better than federal government, (g) the Asian giant quickly manipulates unitary governments especially those with sick constitutions, (h) some regions can be excessively looted under unitary, (i) the unitary government can suppress the minority for what they believe, (j) regionalism is better supported when we federate at home, etetera.

Unitary systems might be more successful in individualistic cultures than in collectivistic cultures. Collectivism highly demands sub-division of power. In many unitary African governments, decentralization has been introduced in which local governments are fully functional, but this cannot help very much. The overarching pillar of federalism vests in social power created by regional *cultural tradition* on which love is hinged. Doing something out of love defeats anxiety-driven goals—and one should not deceive you that an external person can prioritize your interests more than theirs. Unitary is too *idealistic* than federalism. They are both models, but the most reliable model is federalism, as far as doing things out of love is prioritized with the overarching goal of sustainable development. There is too much deception in unitary systems. Federalism is criticized by claims that it is expensive and people think more about their states, but this is more perpetuated by people who think more of foreign aid as a means to develop. If you are a nationalistic person who believes in working hard to develop your area or state, then I do not see any reason you should fear competition. The sustainable governing principle should be *"federate home, and federate regionally."*

Consider country X, which democratically votes for the president as shown below:

Assumptions

a) **A – P** are regions,
b) All democratic ideals are valid

A	E	I	M
B	F	J	N
C	G	K	O
D	H	L	P

Option 1

(A+B+C+D+E+F) = 35.70% of the population voted 100% red, and 0% yellow.

(G+H+I+J+K+L+M+N+O+P) = 62.50% of the population voted 100% yellow, and 0% red.

Many combinations are available; a few are listed here;

Where are the country's resources and economy concentrated? Is it equally distributed? If the country's resources and economy are concentrated in A to F, it is highly likely that regions G to P loot regions A to F or cannot do without regions A to F; there must be a vast difference of opinion; economic, social, and political.

If the resources and economy are in G to P, it is highly likely that regions A to F want to secede from the parent country to develop independently; if they *consistently* vote in the same pattern for more than two terms. *Perhaps,* they think they are unfairly treated.

If the system of governance is federalism, regions A to F would fairly participate. If it is unitary, G to P is likely to suppress the regions A to F, whatsoever, i.e. whether the economy is equally distributed or not.

Conclusion: Such distribution indicates that the country is divided, but democracy has no better solution for this fact. This distribution indicates that the problem is highly likely to be psychological and not political.

What if country X democratically votes for the president, as shown below? What is the message? Contemplate.

Conclusion: This voting exhibits fairness; the distribution indicates a political phenomenon but not a psychological phenomenon. There is room for a healthy democracy to flourish.

Note: A person diagnosed with two problems, (a) psychosocial impairment, and (b) a medical or clinical problem, would need to see a doctor before meeting with a counsellor. In this case, the counsellor is "democracy". Therefore, a political problem is solved after a psychological problem is sorted. Whom should we see first in Option 1 and 2, a doctor or a counsellor? Who is that doctor? Contemplate.

Sycophants in Democracy

People who are not empowered to cogitate well enough on the world around them result in voters who fill numbers. They are sycophants. This is because an ordinary person is neither wise nor intelligent nor rational, but democracy believes in these things. Besides, politics is highly technical and complex, and an ordinary person cannot understand the complicated issues of politics. Moreover, the elections are also a force in which ordinary people are not in a position to judge the candidate on merit. Even some people have very little interest in politics. This is one of the reasons why democracy sometimes cannot function. Because many intelligent men and women fear politics leaves a big room for several extroverts, whether wise or not.

A leader can be a manager, politician, engineer, entrepreneur, or revolutionist. But these cannot be equated to mean a leader. They are explicit in their meanings. Therefore, wise and educated men and women should come forward to save Africa. Do not leave important matters to averages and gasbags. Developing countries and primarily least developed countries are full of sycophants. Sycophants do not appreciate voting candidates on merit. A population that fights using witchcraft as an alternative dispute resolution rather than courts of law yields no promising democracy. Usually, significant majorities of people, particularly in the least developed countries, have very little civic and political education. They do not understand political, economic and international issues. You cannot decide on what you do not know/understand.

Moreover, they can be very easily influenced by cunning politicians. As a result, they elect ignorant people who create more problems for society instead of solving their problems. Many dictatorial regimes have taken advantage of the less cogitative masses and indoctrinated them with their pseudo ideologies. For example, sycophants vote for a comedian when a comedian contests with a highly responsible and patriotic person. This keeps Africa in a cycle of hopelessness because many politicians are rascally driven. And when genuine and wise politicians contest, they lose because people are not interested in the truth and prefer to hear fantasies.

Today, the quality of many African legislatures is doubted—and this is what democracy in a doubted quality of voters yields. If you want to know the extent of the problem, conduct quick research throughout the least developed countries—tell the masses to distinguish the role of the President, Member of Parliament, and local council leaders.

Many sycophants seem to misunderstand democratic ideals. When comparing the success after independence (post-independence) and before independence (pre-independence) in several areas such as education, health, food security, technology, infrastructure development, etcetera., you hardly notice much progress in a large number of developing countries. Many developing countries are progressing due to circumstances. The effect of sycophants *misunderstanding* democratic ideals and liberal models infiltrates service delivery and has a long-lasting negative effect.

Most of the governance theories we adopt are ideals, borrowing from the philosophy of the western world. When blacks recognize that they are different, they will shape a new wave of thinking to lead the continent's sustainability. Can we have models that work best for us? The problem is too much copying and not thinking; we need to manufacture things that work for us. Under democratic governance, citizens are believed to be actively involved in their governance. I wonder how a community without an excellent civic and political education can promote the principles of democratic governance. Where is democracy when Civil Society Organizations (CSOs) voices cannot be heard in several African countries? The democratic ideals are abused in many parts of Africa because leaders who impose themselves on the masses also claim to be democrats.

The leaders that Africa requires today should be revolutionary thinkers to forge and reshape the way people think to attract genuine self-driven sustainable development. For example, a significant number of the post-independence infrastructure in several least developed countries is funded by outsiders. When you compare the lifespan of the post-independence infrastructure with pre-independence ones, you notice a big outstanding difference in reliability in favour of the pre-independence, except in a few cases. I have seen many buildings in higher learning institutions built by the colonial masters looking stronger than those newly built in the least developed countries of Sub-Saharan Africa. It is important to note that national decisions as guided by political decisions must be compliant with and falling within the sustainability framework. This calls for the minimization of waste and reworks in infrastructural projects. Therefore, national buildings should be designed and built within a sustainability framework. Here, colonialists scored heavily, but our sycophants are doing things haphazardly. And the colonialists predominantly used anti-democratic systems to administer African peoples. To what extent is democracy applicable to Africa's social conditions? And who should change the situation?

In addition, many government institutions are failing to perform their intended duties because they are infiltrated with untrue democracy yet dictatorial. It is a mix of deception, and African leaders interplay people using invisible hands to appear democratic. For example, consider some countries in the Nile Basin. Therefore, it is not clear to define them as democratic or dictatorial because they use militarism to consolidate themselves while changing constitutions and rigging votes. And this is not good news to patriotic Africans.

Democracy in African Republics

Many African countries were born as Republics. The birth of these independent republican countries was primarily driven by freedom fighters but not African chiefs in many areas. These are people who understood that all people are equal and need fair and equal treatment. However, after gaining freedom from colonialists, they graduated into a *new set of chiefs* by refusing to step down. This clearly demonstrated that Africans beliefs needed to be recognized in any kind of transformation. And most of these freedom fighters were schooled in the western world. In not a very far past, oppression and suppression of masses by traditional rulers, emperors and warlords, cut across the world. The longing for freedom is global.

Socioeconomic transformation to improve standards of living required people to understand that they deserve the fair and dignified treatment of all—a benchmark that lays the foundation on which we premise the argument that one person's life is equivalent to the life of all of us. In a democratic republic, supreme power is held in the hands of all people for all people regardless of tribe or culture. These people exercise free will in electing their leadership representatives. The same people elect their supreme leader and detest monarchists as the Supreme command. However, the continued survival by foreign aid has introduced *self-defeating behaviours* in some African peoples. We are trying to grow our democracy, but because we need aid from the Asian giant to live, we talk ill about democracy, forgetting where we are coming from.

The goal we are aiming to accomplish is to have free human beings who enjoy their countries equally. The goal is to *improve, redefine, accelerate* and *promote* democratic ideals to catch space in real-time but not oppose democratic governance. The first quarter of the 21st century has made some people think that structural transformation, for example, can be reached at the expense of declining democracy. People who are democratically enlightened and believe in the Supreme Being rarely put money before human rights. I have provided solution's to improve democracy above, i.e. (a) the Weibull technique; (b) elites joining the political arena; (c) understanding our differences; (d) doing things out of love but not fear; (e) controlled selfishness to align with correct public philosophy; (f) manufacturing our models; and (g) behaving like an ordinary man and thinking diplomat to change the deal midstream.

To please some faction of donors, some leaders manipulate democracy for something else through *self-defeating mechanisms*. Slowing democratic reforms is completely bad, but unimproved democratic ideals are more dangerous in the prevailing situation—a situation where the intellectuals never involve themselves in politics—a situation where we sit amidst developed and semi-developed giants. We need more intellectuals willing to die for the cause.

Africa's Circumstantial Development

Many African countries are developing by circumstance, i.e. *globalization-induced development*. Not many African long-serving leaders should be boosting for doing very much to spearhead development. A situation where telecommunications innovated by others has made the world a global village leaves some others to develop out of circumstance. Seated amidst innovators, east, west, north and south, you definitely get a small share of their success. The development registered by many Sub-Saharan territories has dramatically resulted from circumstance but not planned development, i.e. *globalization-induced development*. So, long-serving heads should not brag about the globalization-induced development as your make.

Foreign Aid and Loans

Not very long ago, the Asian giant was a foreign aid recipient. Today, it is among the world's leading foreign aid donors. Although western donors have criticized the Asian giant for its alleged violation of traditional aid models of the western countries and instead a great deal of its foreign outflow is outright loans, the Asian giant looks very promising in fighting for global peace to a layperson. But of course, it is hard to learn about what lies in the entire strategy. One cannot fail to rule out the possibility of using Africa as a route to target the north of the northern hemisphere. They seem more focused on their economic gain than political gain in the case of Africa. However, economic gain and political gain are inseparable twins, but some territories do it quite expressly. This express action is what makes other countries seem more focused on political influence than commerce, trade and investment. The Asian giant, for example, is investing in long-term relationships and not just trade and infrastructure. They have introduced their language in several African institutions, symbolic of a strategy beyond trade and business—claiming that they are connecting the world through developing infrastructure.

As Africans, we are not aiming for positions but somewhat worth in the struggle for peace, unity, stability and sustainability. Unlike the rest of the pack, the Asian giant is not *expressly* fighting for positions but rather focuses on her economic interests. Note the word *"expressly"* in the preceding statement. It is upon us to invest heavily in human capital to have principled negotiations with the Asian giant with a clear foresight into the remedies of their aid. Suppose we do not have a clear foresight into the remedies of their aid. In that case, it is better to ban it completely to instil confidence in the population and nurture good leadership so that our people wake up from sleep to think of solutions that can sustain African humankind. Otherwise, failure to recognize our position and draw a clear roadmap to move forward, many African economies funded by the Asian giant will excessively fall into a debt trap diplomacy.

It is urgent, and we need new ideologies to save the continent because many veteran leaders seem to have run out of ideas. This is primarily due to the failure to recognize how things must be pieced together to spur scientific innovations that can help the African child live in a respectable position. They made many mistakes to partner with the Asian giant without limit and have no clear method to correct them. A person with $2 cannot partner with someone with $10,000; that is not a partnership. However, when a person with $2 realises he has the mineral resources surpassing the $10,000, they put away *selfishness* and mobilise the masses to create an engine to stimulate innovation and growth.

As Africans, we must all understand that social boldness is vital in winning respect. And winning respect is already one step forward to achieving our dream. At the moment, very few respect aid recipients that much, as if we were born disabled in some faculties. I make this clear by categorically stating that diplomacy excites diplomats, and what diplomats talk and express outwardly is typical of diplomats and not the population. The reality remains very bold, "a man who cannot take care of his family and leans on support from the neighbour is not brave enough to partner with others who learnt how to support their families."

We need to understand that many diplomats' smartness is on the microphone to excite the audience and, in the shared contract agreements, to keep the promise alive. They know how to package deception very well to persuade others. But behind the scenes, things are different all over the world. Much of what foreign diplomats say to Africa with their minds is not what they believe with their hearts. The reason Africa believes too much of perfectionism to put all trust in foreign aid of all kinds is what I fail to understand. A very honest person has no place in the world of politics and economics. I am yet to describe political and economic honesty, another African form of ignorance that has not been documented yet. Going a bit relativistic, just like some Asian territories, we might have to swallow consequences and do away with aid. Aid seems to relax our brains, and our minds become weak, thinking to borrow for everything. There is no aid too good to spur genuine socioeconomic transformation for Africa. One of the strategies to shun away from aid is to have leadership hard on tackling corruption and misuse of government funds. It is possible where well-grown democratically improved governments are in place.

If African counterparts master the art of playing cards right, the Asian giant is more interested in business than politicking and conquering others. However, *characters* might overtly depict business interests when *temperaments* require conquering others; who knows? What should stick to everyone's mind as Africans is that nothing exists like this foreign aid is more free and helpful than another.

Much as the Asian giant targets the north of the northern hemisphere by using Africa and the going global framework as the route, controversially providing foreign aid, the north of the northern hemisphere is collecting data on Africa through several developmental agencies. Have you ever wondered why they focus too much on health?

In the same boat, the former colonialists *live in anxiety* with a guilty conscience, crippling Africa's success—fearing that if Africa only wakes up one day, it will weaken their economies, marking the end of their ranking as one of the world's best economies. Some of their economies depend on colonial tax as if Africans agreed upon colonialism in the first place. It was out of imposition and not free will, but now they kill our very own leaders for imposing themselves onto us, with a claim to clean the world free of imposition—this is symbolic of a guilty conscience. They have done this perfectly well by funding huge PR advertisement campaigns, giving out free aid through organizations, and sustaining Africa's poor image. They continue the spoon-feeding ideologies associated with free aid hence crippling success. One cannot fail to mention a guilty conscience in the PR advertisement campaigns heavily advocating for democratic governance.

The biggest war they would otherwise channel all their energy to if they realized the past mistakes on Africa is to relax all the so-called colonial tax, respect Africa's integrity and honour, and our sovereignty. Why are they so concerned in the first place? Why are they so worried? They are worried about the population growth rates, healthcare system, education, local languages, nourishment and many other things. This depicts someone living in anxiety with a guilty conscience for what they have caused to Africa. Why worry?

It is not about all those they do as mentioned above, not even about the products of the industrial revolution. It is about how you treat me on a cake of human importance. It is more about my honour, integrity and dignity, sovereignty, and life. It is all about what is mine, how to preserve it for generations to come, and how to make use of it productively. Africa is the way it is because of the western world—and this can be proved. It will take great courageous and ambitious African men and women who can conquer fear to revive the position of the African race—those who are willing to make the sacrifice in living without being taken up by the products of the industrial revolution but instead just need oxygen in abundance to live and go when natural selection calls them.

All donors are the same; what matters is how ready and organized the aid recipient is to turn around the table, just like what the Asian giant did. What pains me the most is, the African child has lost hope amidst giants east and west, north and south. He has developed a tendency of getting excited in the middle of economic danger. The same child goes with whoever shows up and promises free lunch. This is damaging when the donor shows no interest in streamlined bureaucracy and order, seeming very uninterested in accountability. The rampant forgery in relationships will leave a good lesson to comprehend for an African child. The illusion of the Asian giant's aid being supreme will backfire in not so many years to come. In that very soon time to come, the concept of debt diplomacy will get a new twist to lead structural economics. The world has grown too competitive that you cannot trust anyone basing on the worth of aid they have provided to you. Associating aid with their workforce signals how sustainability has already made an alarm. It is no longer about where you are on earth; it is about the means to sustain your people.

A claim that the Asian giant is constructing industries in Africa and providing jobs to the locals should not be measured in quantity alone. The quality of jobs and the quality of industries established matters, if not the most important. How many qualified engineers are working in leadership and management positions on the infrastructure projects developed in Africa by the Asian giant? Are the health, welfare and safety standards followed in their operations on Africa's humankind? The going global framework is a good initiative for those who fail to understand that leadership is influence, and modern colonialism is neocolonialism and imperialism. Sooner or later, mistakes will accumulate through the going global framework that will make other giants react. Besides, they sometimes fund infrastructure using non-concessional loans, which is very risky to Africans in the long run.

The Asian giant is more likely to make mistakes to exploit than their counterparts in foreign aid for various reasons. These include failure to conceal intentions and the domineering tattle-telling characters overt in many of their peoples and putting development before human rights. The western world is smarter than the Asian giant, which is depicted in their well-calculated international factor movements and influence in African matters, which is more subterranean. Yes, the underlying goal of aid to the recipient is to foster economic growth and development and improve the nationals' welfare. However, suppose we wish to see genuine self-driven sustainable development. In that case, we should desist the spoon-feeding ideologies of the traditional aid donors by maturity change of attitude, which is quite difficult in any case. But difficult is not impossible. I have described the way to revisit attitudes[35]. We can rebrand[36]. There is no free lunch under the sun.

Though the Asian giant's most significant chunk of foreign aid is not in the form of traditional aid models but rather friendly market-rate loans, sometimes they seem, to a layperson, to be more focused on *gaining economically than suppressing others,* politically. However, though traditional aid donors spoon feed Africans, they insist on *accountability,* unlike their counterparts. Therefore, this difference or similarity shows you that none of the two is better than the other as far as African matters are concerned. It is our responsibility to make them right when they deal with us.

On the other hand, traditional aid donors would be the best. However, we have consistently failed to outsmart them and show them that we are potential partners, thus precipitating and perpetuating their motive—the spoon-feeding ideologies and associated outcomes of political suppression and domineering themselves on us by peddling influence in our sovereign matters. Failing to fight corruption and self-serving traits are two significant weaknesses an Africa child identifies with that fail us to become potential partners with others—but we instead seem helpless.

Of course, we know that many outsiders exploit Africa and, in return, place huge budgets on funding PR campaigns and advocating for democracy as the best governance model for Africa, killing many heads of state on the grounds of dictatorship and imposition. It is only a short-sighted person that fails to spot opportunism in their activities. Their ambition is about destabilizing Africa and get better to exploit it for the worst. Through destabilizing and the focus on politicking, the essential matters are forgotten, and this gives them room to exploit the mineral wealthiest continent.

---

[35] See p. 192-226, §4.

[36] See p. 182, §4.

On the other hand, I believe in my opinion, innocent traditional aid donors—those who give out aid with the impression of reaching out to suffering peoples, at some point in time, and in their somewhat limited knowledge about the political agenda as compared to those who draw up the architecture, i.e. higher command, hoped to see us stand on our own. However, the continued embezzlement of donor funds in many developing countries is symbolic of states which cannot govern themselves but rather ones that can live by leaning on others.

By excessive embezzlement of government funds, a person demonstrates a poverty of ambition. This poverty of ambition cannot fail to scare the donor. Yes, foreign aid and massive PR campaigns are well-calculated strategies, but why can't we outsmart the donors by putting aid to the correct use? Here, visit the African unique attitude disorder for treatment.[37]

Ask yourself a question: Why continue paying school fees for a child who does not attend classes? The point is: you wish that child good life after school, but if they instead channel the school fees into sports gambling and the gambling company is yours, you might tolerate and continue paying the fees. However, you must ensure you monitor and control this student who acts odd because oddness itself is a threat in several spheres of social influence. Being a partner means lots, and you need to show worthiness in how you behave and act. The point comes back to us. How do we act on the aid? The way you act signals a lot to the provider because attitude is a function of cognition, behaviour and feeling.

Take an example. A highway is opened somewhere in rural Africa, but before the defects liability period expires, all road furniture is stolen. The donor cannot fail to get scared. To be my partner, you need to have the same or slightly the same attitude towards the attitude piece or event. Otherwise, if we cannot match, I will ask myself what to do for you out of a good heart, although some factions mistake it for a guilty conscience because of the donors' past deeds on the African continent. I cannot wholly attribute it to having a guilty conscience. There is always room for a guilty conscience to meet with a kind heart. Sometimes the Asian giant's aid looks friendlier because the donor at some point identified with us. But of course, the western quality of life is the prototype, which is an ideal that the entire world ought to achieve.

The Asian giant has been criticized for its arm in slowing democratic reforms in many African countries. However, I warn that democracy without reforms is not the best ideal to reclaim the position of Africa and spur accelerated self-driven socioeconomic transformation for Africa. Do not be surprised to learn that unimproved democracy in multiparty systems perpetuates Africa's problem. This is because it is costly for many African social conditions to cope with the standard it calls for.

One of the reasons Western economies advocate so badly for democratic governance in Africa is the *conditioned sycophants* present in these countries. Because the wise, the educated, and the intelligent ones are quiet and the mediocre minds are busy making laws, Africa is in a very hopeless state. When western economies recognize this, they do all sorts of things to promote democracy to aid hooliganisms to take over African governments so that they can continue their planned neo-colonialism. Today's most challenging task in Africa's politics is to convince the masses that *unimproved democratic ideals* are not the best solution for Africa amidst the global sustainability challenge.

---

[37] See p. 205-226, §4.

The advantage that the Asian giant has presented in foreign aid recipients is a reduction in the too many strings attached to aid by traditional donors. We have seen a reduction in the requirements for traditional foreign aid. However, doing away with unimproved democracy in the interim to save the continent calls for a unified political ideology and a very well organized set of mature psyches to propel nations to a common goal—a correct mindset. This kind of determination calls for people willing to sacrifice their lives for future generations—putting whole systems thinking before their families and close friends. Democracy is incomparable with other systems, primarily where psyches are grown in catholic.

It is argued that over 90% of traditional foreign aid donors focus on economic development and welfare amidst democratic ideals that many African countries cannot constitutionally improve. Unimproved democratic ideals take Africa nowhere as far as accelerated self-driven sustainability is concerned. We need *improved democracy*. The ball is in our hands for all those that have understood the meaning of democracy. Democracy needs to be grown, and no other governance model can defeat democratic governance. However, the current African position on the planet puts its democracy at risk since we need accelerated growth and development amidst global sustainability challenges.

Democracy is the best model for democrats. However, in a situation where Africa is positioned east and west, north and south of developed and semi-developed nations necessitate another governance process that accelerates the improvement in democracy to save the continent. Traditional aid is associated with less necessary attachments and overdependence syndrome. To live confidently while thinking that one cannot do without the donor and which instils mistrust within the recipient, failing to identify with themselves and thus gets fixated in aid to live. More importantly, to free the mind and only get reminded of the source of aid that transformed the developed world—the western world. That source is the purest source that can spur genuine self-driven socioeconomic transformation for Africa. How about if we ban aid? Free things are not only bad but very dangerous. We are constantly retarded in thinking solutions to solve crises and instead resort to begging to pay salaries for government workers, including politicians sometimes. The right medicine for a dependent is to stop providing free services to them. It should be our wish to stop receiving aid.

What is The Solution to Aid?

There is no aid better than the next alternative aid. The solution lies in putting a total ban on aid and inspiring confidence in good leadership. This coupled with adequate planning, putting an end to corruption and embezzlement of government funds, and self-awareness initiatives coupled with effective adoption and appropriation of development-oriented innovations described in Chapter Four can spur sustainable socioeconomic transformation to this continent and facilitate structural changes.[38] The procedural crisis described in Chapter Five must be closed so that the planning deficiency is worked upon as a critical measure in this struggle.[39]

---

[38] See p. 219-226, §4.

[39] See p. 269-270, §5.

The illusion of knowledge explained in Chapter Three[40] must be addressed by strongly defining the jigsaw approach explained in the same Chapter and searching for the original species of truth.[41] In this way, we not only shoot, but we lead. When things are put in order, distortions corrected, there is no reason why Africa should not smile because there is room to lead the global sustainable development objectives—the fact that we are late-comers. Let us have our children attain the proper education to exploit the mistakes that the Asian giant is likely to make while in Africa.

It takes great courage and devotion to say "NO" to foreign aid. This takes on zero tolerance to corruption. It also requires proper decision making which is *unselfish*. It is not that we cannot live without aid; it is about failure to make proper decisions. Sometimes, I wonder how several African leaders manage to fit in conferences and meetings with people who discuss technology, science, and industry—and for them, they discuss begging! I do not think I can attend many such gatherings where I am an odd man out.

Innocence is the highest form of ignorance, but overreliance on foreign aid is also dangerous. What we need is to cultivate a well-informed population that understands how things work. Overreliance on donations for infrastructure development, education, health, safe water, electricity and technology, etcetera may see developing countries rising in the human development index that categorizes developed, developing and least developed countries on the planet, but shall we really be developed?

I believe genuine sustainable development should be self-driven and should start with improvement in the way people think—knowledge, intelligence and moral character. The way we view our neighbours should matter. We need a joint stand for human rights. Freedom of expression should be a must, and the Rule of Law should be non-negotiable. There should be well-campaigned equality in gender for available opportunities and *women repowering*. Since we aim to improve democracy, freedom of expression, freedom of speech and freedom of worship must be redefined in the African way with the overarching goal of self-driving our development.

Donors also have wounds to nurse. Japan, for example, was traumatized by the USA near the end of the great World War II (1939-1945) when the USA threw nuclear bombs on Japan. Although they are likely to be on good terms with the USA, this traumatic event will never get off their minds. It is estimated that the US nuclear bombing on Japan killed more than 200,000 people from just two bombs. The first bomb was dropped on 6th August 1945 on Hiroshima, and three days later, the second bomb was dropped on Nagasaki, Japan. This tragedy continues to be felt by people all over the world. The holocaust also went down in history with the largest number of death toll killings of the 20th Century. The descendants cannot ever forget this traumatic event.

The Japanese greatly wounded the Chinese in the (1937–1945) war, something they will never forget. Such traumatic events may lead to long-term effects such as transgenerational effects if not treated sufficiently, especially where victims prefer not to be reminded of the event.

Almost all people in the world have history to remember and to console themselves therapeutically. Behaving like children amidst scarcity is an outright mock to ourselves that we ought to recognize now.

---

[40] See p. 118, §3.

[41] See p. 131, §3.

We need to forge a way forward, recreate ourselves, and reclaim the position we held and the excellent history we have in theology, mathematics, and human existence.

As a patriotic person, you need to weigh in the options, be of an independent, open-minded and sound mind, and wishing good for your country all the time. We should stop personal politicking. Anyone who does so is promoting their interests, not voters' (people's) interests. It is high time we needed to attain political maturity. We need to embrace a common good and shared prosperity without politicizing all government policies and programs. If a government policy is good, support it. Let us not promote partisan politics to save Africa.

Optimistic Politics in a Republic

It is never tribalistic. It is never racist, and it is never sectarian. It promotes unity, freedoms (speech and expression), understanding, justice for all, human rights and fights against repression, suppression and oppression. Africa has various tribes; it is characterized by sectarian and tribalistic politics covertly. It is one of the many reasons a continental government faces the stringiest opposition, from when Kwame Nkrumah (1909 – 1972) first proposed it in his iconic speech of May 25th 1963, in Addis Ababa, Ethiopia.

The sectarian politics is not overtly or expressly campaigned. However, someone who can labour to investigate the behaviours of those in the political arena will not fail to get results of tribalism and sectarianism in our politics.

I mentioned earlier that many people speak their minds what they do not believe with their hearts. You can get to what they think and believe by heavily studying their actions and behaviours properly. A Republican government characterized by over 90% officials and civil/public servants of one tribe is a good example, e.g. typical Sub-Saharan governments. In such a republic, it is challenging to balance the boat. Africans' selfishness required no unitary systems.

I have mentioned that integrity and mediocrity are not tagged to any religion, race, tribe, or culture. It is the highest kind of non-patriotism and hopelessness to believe that you can steer sustainable development by domineering your relatives and tribe-mates over others. I earlier mentioned that if you are troubled because your tribe is not having enough people in government and you wish to open or join a political party to do the same, you are not thinking hopeful politics to develop and expand your economy sustainably. I see many opposition political parties vying for power doing the same thing within their parties across Africa. We should, therefore, not get excited because long-serving regimes are slowly dying out but rather ask ourselves whether we have optimistic politics for the African continent—the politics that instils and inspires hope.

On Human Rights Agencies' Philosophy

The philosophy adopted by human rights agencies on which several national constitutions draw inference to protect and promote fundamental and other human rights and freedoms of their citizens is that the quality of life of one person is equivalent to the quality of life of all of us. However, some territories believe that the quality of life of some others is not equivalent to one person of themselves – diving much into non-domestic matters. We are all humans, but some people believe that they are more human than others. The continued fueling of conflicts by others in many African countries justifies the situation.

Some territories claim to be objective, but that is limited within themselves because they tend to go relativistic for other territories. Ultimately, the world becomes more divided than it ought to be. The underlying reason I see them as relativists for other sovereign territorial matters is the way they analyze Africa on international matters like crimes against humanity and related war crimes. They never get to the root cause. The aiders of crimes are sugarcoated, and the suffering of an ordinary person due to destabilizing their economies by the forceful end of regimes is not considered for the aforementioned reasons. If I simplify it, it stands as follows, "The meaning and worth of life of one of us equals to the meaning and worth of life of all us within our territory, but the meaning and worth of life of one of us is more important and greater than the meaning and worth of life of all of the others in other territories."

In many instances, they show more regard and invaluableness to the wildlife freedom than the freedom of the African child, especially in the past century. Therefore, to arrest a dog for its crimes but at the expense of thousands of puppies losing life is not a big deal. In the scuffle, the life of the one who arrests is more important than the life of all puppies. Many wars fought in the Middle East in the 20th and 21st Centuries have left those who took the decisions to live in apology. Apologizing not because of the negative thoughts they held on the peoples and perhaps the subsequent consequences caused but because of the much wounding and hatred created in the surviving peoples. It is not about apologizing as a result of feeling pain for lives lost in the Middle East and similar African states and destabilizing their economies but rather due to the anxiety brought about by living in a world where invaded peoples dislike those who took bad decisions on their lives. That propels them to issue apologies.

> *"Scientists have laboured to explain the ecosystem. The complex ecosystem finds all constituents valuable. All interplaying features of the ecosystem are important. The social world has labelled some constituents less important and forgets that the significance and importance of constituents judged inconsequentially is one of being inconsequential to the judge." Patrick Ssempeera*

Several attacks on other sovereign countries have caused many people to live in apology. In some instances, some try and sentence to death the purported criminals, whilst others commit crimes against humanity. They regret the decisions later when the countries get into intense political turmoil. However, their actions are simply reduced to mistakes. The remaining African has to learn from the story quickly and should emphasize routine dialogue. Calling upon routine dialogue shall lessen the value of conflicts and soften the leaders who wish not to step down by a peaceful transfer of power. Allowing foreigners to take decisions on African matters is more hazardous than any other remedy. When we go to war, we get torn apart, and the little we have achieved diminishes.

Who Should Decide When the Long-serving African Heads of States Should Go?

You must be among the short-sighted African people to rejoice about the killing of Colonel Muammar Mohammed Gaddafi, the former head of state for Libya. The attack on Libya was a shame to Africa. The Western countries spearheaded the attack. This is something that Africans would solve.

Of course, the various core beliefs held by different African linguistic groups associated with religious differences are essential to take note of because they influence the way we view things and our intentions, but Africans should solve Africa's problems. As a leader, Gadhafi might have caused several crises somewhere maybe. However, these are not comparable to the heart and mind weakening programs the western world has caused to African humankind in a very subtle fashion that still hold validity in the modern era. One most important aspect to appreciate is that the colonialists did not leave Africa. They *live in anxiety.* They, therefore, ensure that Africans remain controllable, economically and socially. It is difficult to estimate how much Africans have lost due to Gaddafi's death.

Long-serving leaders are not about to end. They will always emerge through the years because the desire for power is inborn in man, and the distortion of the environment will fuel many wars ahead. Even those who claim to be highly democratic peddle influence in others matters. Is this not power greed? If not, what is it? Improving the world will always be a work in progress. There will always come a time when manipulations in governance systems will arise due to man's innovations and climate change. Civil wars will erupt as a result of food and water crises. There will always be revolutions since change is inevitable. People will always see an imperfect present. The world has seen tremendous change in the last 500 years precipitated and perpetuated by the 17th-century industrial revolution. Climate change is challenging the industrial revolution, despite all the innovations to combat temperature rise globally. I do not think Africa's long-serving heads of state will always need to be killed by outsiders claiming to be democratizing Africa.

It does not make any better to kill one long-serving head of state, and the country goes into prolonged instabilities, losing innocent civilians as a result of destabilizing the country, especially by foreign forces, in a highly technological world where Africa lags many light years behind super powers. We can continue to dialogue routinely, day and night. African long-serving heads of state are better to leave power by our own making through dialogue than using external forces. We can learn from lessons on some states whose long-serving heads have been fought and killed by external forces.

We should never get tired of dialogue. We need to sit down and understand each other. There is a significant risk in this global village when we go to war amidst sustainability challenges. Going to war predisposes Africa to attack by others and several other crises. The acceleration of success registered by others in telecommunications, space-time, infrastructure, and artificial intelligence puts Africa at a significant risk whenever we go to war. The highest good in the hierarchy of doing the good for African long-serving heads of states is to award them amnesty. Africa has for long been attacked by others either directly or indirectly. Therefore, decision making in the early post-independence years was tricky and highly risky. One cannot rule out the possibility of former colonialists peddling influence to cause the failure of African states. This can be a reasonable defence for some African long-serving leaders. Some current African leaders inherited these mistakes and continue to leave in fear if they are to correct them. We, therefore, have to reason beyond the obvious and protect the current and future generations before we fight for justice on the fallen patriots and innocent civilians. The living ones and those to come should be protected before we remedy for the dead.

Those who have left us have gone forever, either because of many political mistakes done by governments or by diseases fueled by opportunists and natural selection—no problems. All is death; the fact remains, they will never return. In the interest of "we, the living Africans, and those to come tomorrow", we need to put all that aside and protect ourselves from contemporary invaders precipitated by the threatening climate change, exhaustion of natural resources, and power greediness.

Sub-Saharan African countries like Uganda, Rwanda, Burundi and DRC will get poorer if they destabilize again. In growing our democracy, we need to recognize where we are coming from and make sound decisions. I believe, in my opinion, that Africa needs no more wars for it to have an opportunity to stabilize and emerge. You might be shocked to find that extremists that threaten African countries are precipitated and fueled by opportunists because they wish Africa to keep in a destabilized situation. The solution lies in routine dialogue. The long-serving heads of state will finally go; they are not immortal. They cannot stop the sun from rising from the East and set in the West. The earth has not existed for hundreds of years but billions.

The socioeconomic acceleration should be guided by our need to protect future generations' ability to meet their needs and ensure that the African race does not become extinct. Man's greed for power will never cease. Innovations in spacetime and AI will actually cause more power greed within humans. Even those who claim to be polishing the world to get it free of dictators are an illusion. They are dictators themselves because, many times, they do not value others' ideas. The 21st-century invasion in Iraq was never fully consented to by some leading peace building agencies. They were warned from invading Iraq by the supreme body instituted to dialogue the world's most dangerous problems. However, because these people wish to live as supreme, they refuse to listen. Some *live in anxiety* for the history they hold on Africa. Others have grown too big to believe in being above the Supreme Being. Let us continue the dialogue. We should never get tired of dialogue.

Politics surrounding loaned Projects, Foreign Direct Investments, and Foreign Portfolio Investments

We need to forge a maturity point, a case where Japan loans us, and a Brazilian company executes the project. I mean that we should forge a way to attract more foreign portfolio investments than foreign direct investments if we dream of sustainable growth and inclusion. Such arrangement shall raise quality assurance and guarantee total quality management on infrastructure projects vital in the structural transformation. There is a high risk in using the funder's consultant, contractor and other related solution providers. Reliability as one focal point of interest can only be guaranteed by initiating and building it right from the start when appraising a project through implementation. The maintainability of infrastructure projects which dominate foreign direct investments in many developing countries is a subcomponent of reliability and is greatly affected by decision making right from the start. Reliability problems become too expensive to fix in infrastructure projects and related systems if not considered from the start. We are experiencing a tremendous change in infrastructure project appraisal and development to take on robust highways, expressways, flyovers, cable-stay bridges, cable cars, high-speed electric trains/railways, hydropower generation systems, renewable energy and several power substations, modern airports, intelligent buildings, nuclear power stations, artificial intelligence, crude oil and gas pipelines, telecommunication systems, etcetera. Therefore, several political decisions should be primarily influenced by the desire to empower our people. We need to invest in human capital as the most critical resource over and above any other.

Most infrastructure systems require asset management plans to achieve maximum functionality and operability over the intended lifespans. For an infrastructure or any engineering system to achieve its maximum usability or functionality, it must consider operation and maintenance personnel in the planning and implementation. African governments must take a keen interest in allowing nationals to be involved in all stages of planning, design, construction and commissioning to well-service, operate, and maintain the loaned infrastructure systems from an excellent and well-informed perspective. Suppose the systems show signs of weakening at one point in their lifecycle or deterioration or posted weight restrictions like bridges. In that case, the nationals can carry on investigations working through the procedures undertaken during project appraisal, planning and project development.

Problem diagnosis has never been a simple task, especially trying to fix a problem with minimal knowledge. I know some plants which when they get breakdowns they always need to fly in experts from abroad to diagnose and fix them right, at least in my country of origin—Uganda. Suppose human capital enhancement through capacity development programs is not done as a government policy on each loaned national project. In that case, both the socioeconomic benefit and cost-benefit analyses favour the funder because African governments shall have to rely on the funder for servicing, operating, maintaining, and the overall asset management portfolio for the loaned projects.

Why Do We Have More Foreign Direct Investments (FDI) Than Foreign Portfolio Investments (FPI) in Many African Countries?

First, an investor looks at how the economy is performing and the policies surrounding investment decisions. Africa's domestic enterprises still face skills and technology gaps in many sectors, making productivity very low and less promising. This means that most African firms are still weak and generate meagre domestic savings required to make substantial investments in the economy's priority areas. In many African countries, except South Africa (only South Africa), the private sector is dominated by small and medium companies which lack the capacity to issue securities on the capital market, yet the attractiveness of portfolio investments is based primarily on the structural nature of an economy, regulatory and institutional framework of the financial markets of which many African countries are underperforming. At least minimum standards of governance that conform to and comply with the requirements of globally acceptable standards, clear audited books of accounts and profitability are some of the metrics used to judge the feasibility of a firm to issue securities on the capital market. These shortfalls in domestic firms outlaw the need to prioritize foreign portfolio investments.

However, the political climate in several African countries does not allow empowering domestic businesses at a rate that rivals globalization. In this way, no serious attempt is made by many African governments to safeguard, empower and inspire confidence in domestic businesses to generate modern businesses that can stimulate innovation, growth and development.

On the other hand, this problem is highly political, and the causes are traced back to the way boundaries of African countries were drawn by colonialists—first, colonialism was associated with conventional religions that weakened Africans in both the body and mind.[42] Countries were born anyhow without following intimacy issues as far as ethnicities could identify with each other—drawing on differences and similarities. This failure to draw feasible boundaries led to many crises, and it is continuing to cause massive *contemporary African nomads*. Long-serving heads of states and high corruption rates are traced from this mistake, leading to many people succumbing to the *unique African attitude disorder (UAAD)*.[43] Some dictators got what they did not expect without much work, and they could not accept to leave power, creating a significant effect, which we can call *"Africa's dictatorial effect"* that will live to cost many of Africa's future generations. This effect refers to the lack of foresight into *"the how-to sustainably develop Africa after colonialism"*. The long-serving African leaders have/had to ensure that they contribute/hold the largest fraction of the country's economy, by owning the private sector enterprises, mainly in what we refer to as capitalistic economies.[44] In the end, they keep/kept masses poor without empowering them correctly to solve their problems using available resources optimally.

By keeping the population poor, long-serving leaders can shoot their ambitions. This was/is done by leaders controlling all government institutions, including the central bank and all arms of government, thereby rendering no government institution independent. Because they need to show people that success is registered during their regimes, they have/had to borrow anyhow both externally and internally or accept investments anyhow because they lack the confidence and support to negotiate win-win deals. Therefore, foreign investors exploit the opportunity, especially the *Asian giant*. They have direct control and ownership of the investment they make in many African countries. This comes with Africans losing control over their domestic policies. For example, it is becoming difficult for African construction firms to bid and win infrastructure project developments, especially in Sub-Saharan Africa.

I do not believe that foreign direct investments from the *Asian giant* protect Africa's sovereignty in a situation where no attempt is made to empower locals. It is because the majority of African countries have been made desperate by their leaders. The solution lies in fighting to remove bad leaders using Africa's young generation. We can help ourselves, not to wait for foreigners to redeem us. We cannot fight unemployment when we have no significant influence in negotiating foreign portfolio investments so that we develop enterprises in which foreign firms have less control.

When analyzing foreign investments, we look at the movement of factors of production across borders, i.e. capital and labour. In Africa's sustainability equation, what kind of decisions are we supposed to make with the love for our people of today and tomorrow? The Asian giant is offloading what they term "cheap labour" to Africa, yet we also have a problem of unemployment. Our labour force needs to acquire new skills required to support any kind of FDI, but this is not possible where FDI coupled with capital-intensive techniques dominates many projects.

African governments have recently forged relationships and opened up to many Asian firms. Asian countries are now taking the lead as emerging Africa's most vital partner, especially Sub Saharan Africa. To a significant extent, they are doing great to finance our projects and loan us. But the biggest questions that remain unanswered are, "To what extent are we and the future generations protected? Are

---

[42] See p. 359-370, §8.

[43] See p. 203-204, §4.

[44] See p. 108-109, §2.

the socioeconomic analysis and cost-benefit analysis in our favour?" If yes, then that is great. If not, is it a win-win situation or a lose-win situation?

Some Asian firms, especially those from the Asian giant, are fond of quoting low prices for construction projects. Because of the procurement methodologies copied and pasted from elsewhere, contracts are typically awarded to the lowest bidders in many countries. Here, I am benchmarking on construction companies because the tangible development, let alone the psyche's development, is significantly shown through the built environment. When you speak of improvement in health, access to safe water, access to education, access to electricity, improved transportation, tapping and utilizing the energy resources, improved communication, improved standard of living, and etcetera, you cannot look further than construction companies because they are contracted to develop the required infrastructure. The built environment is the king of other sectors because they hinge on it for sustainability. This is the reason achieving a carbon-neutral economy must place stringiest measures on construction activities.

The lowest bidder that is technically responsive and compliant with the bidding requirements syndrome, which in my opinion is long overdue to be overhauled in many countries, would best be substituted with the best responsive bidder compliant with market prices. This syndrome has left many projects executed not to standard and can barely live up to the expectation of the project sponsor. Several professionals argue that the bidder who quotes the lowest with unrealistic prices must be assigned a highly competent and vigilant consultant to supervise the works to achieve value for money. This mechanism works in the short term, but good risk managers cannot allow it. The risk involved in such a practice is too high, and anyone who thinks in matters related to the sustainability of the infrastructure cannot allow it. The risk must be reduced by adopting, "best responsive bidder compliant with market prices." If we continue doing this, are we supporting our local companies or digging their graves? If, for example, you know the cost of a computer set is US$ 1000, and one proposes to supply it to you at US$ 100, 1000% lower price than the reserve market price, and you do not ask yourself how they are going to manage the supply at such a lower price. If he manages the supply, what is the hidden motive?

Forensic audits, value for money audits, and technical audits are all way chewing up the taxpayer's money and leaves a professional wondering why reliability issues are not fixed at the earliest start of the project because correction of reliability problems is too expensive halfway or at the completion of construction projects. When you sum up costs of auditing, mediation, variations, cost overruns, time value for money costs, cost of reworks, and in other instances, premature discharge of contracts as a result of poor performance, you regret why the contract is not awarded to the "best responsive bidder compliant with market prices". The additional costs that result out of the inefficiencies of the lowest bidder almost total to the reality. As explained in Chapter Five, it is a problem of not valuing time, and no price tag is well defined for time right from project initiation.[45]

From the project management domain, reliability is a sub-component of quality management and measures put in place to promote quality assurance, and quality control encompasses procurement practices. Shoddy work has been witnessed in many projects funded by loans from several developmental agencies and the Asian giant. Those projects funded by sovereign states are restricted to own the project from inception, design, construction, commission, and favourably decommission by the funders. In such arrangements,

---

[45] See p. 241-243, §5.

the question remains on who monitors and evaluates performance against the set attributes in the interest of the nation. Such projects are vulnerable to quality compromise leading to a reduction in the lifespan. A typical case study is the US$ 12 million Sigiri Bridge in western Kenya that collapsed in July 2017 before commissioning.[46]

Deterioration rates are too high and operationally and functionally not meeting expectations. A forecast into the future reveals a conflict of interest arising out of each foreign investor's assets in the African states, hence tearing the countries apart. The way forward is to invest heavily in developing human capital correctly and *learn to listen to experts.* We should stop politicizing every issue.

The institutions responsible for human capital development should improve their open-mindedness to tackle ambiguity and old fashioned processes if we are to accelerate the socio-economic transformation and cope with the rest of the world. Traditional practice that encourages more of what to do or what is done than how is/was it done and why was it done makes it almost impossible to make advancements in engineering technology in many parts of Africa. Politics and bad governance should not be used as the only excuse for the mess, although it is the catalyst, but rather each of us should look into ourselves and see what is not done right hence failing national development.

For Africa to have genuine self-driven development, the indicators shall be: If Africa is comparable to other continents in all spheres; if we are treated as people of the same potential and integrity; if we are treated as partners, not servants; when Africa receives a loan from Exim Bank of China and a Japanese firm executes the project funded; when Africa is not a dumping place for others; when an African firm owned by Africans is hired to compete and provide expertise in the developed world say the USA; also when we are self-sustaining. And we cannot attain this if we continue operating a blind style and fail to wake up. The phrase *"sustainable development"* should be changed to *"self-driven sustainable development"* for Africa to resonate and amplify. If the listed indicators are instilled in the minds of others (non-Africans), then the road to sustainable development would be viewed as wide open because human development indices can rise from the will of others which is not sustainable development for Africans.

GDP to rise at the will of others carries little meaning in terms of Africa's sustainability, and it will not help Africa very much. There is no doubt that Africa's economy has grown rapidly over the last couple of years and is still growing steadily. In 2019, the IMF reported that 6/10 of the fastest-growing economies are in Africa measured by the GDP growth. The question on Africa's development is about the position of Africans in the race. Are we building capital for the African people? What share do African's hold in firms, industries and other enterprises that immensely contribute to the GDP?

To be of value to others, you must exhibit significance. We should desist from an unforeseen state of meaninglessness. Genuine development will be observed from the overall perspective that other people have on the African child. If the issues above are not fixed, Africa should prepare for incoming crises/wars due to foreign direct investors fighting each other to reclaim positions for the stakes they have in the African governments. This investment politics can be understood by a child of 10 years.

---

[46] Briana Duggan, "How did a $12 million bridge collapse in Kenya?" CNN, Market Place, July 4th, 2017, https://edition.cnn.com

Restricted procurement disadvantages a sovereign state, mainly where a project is funded more by a loan, unlike through a grant. I am a football fan though little I know about football dynamics; I can easily see that footballer A is more of a superstar than footballer B. The same applies to procurement; it has never been sophisticated to shortlist and evaluate service providers by procurement professionals. Genuine loans that wish Africans sustainable growth must let us take the decisions by ourselves. Yes, we need the grants and loans, but we are betraying ourselves. This is perpetuated by bad leaders. The leaders we have created for ourselves. Cao Cao (155–220) once said, "I'd rather betray the world than let the world betray me." We are betraying ourselves. This kind of nonsensical dilemma is being escalated by a lack of genuine leadership that leaves most African countries ruined by dictators. A dictator focuses on how best he can confuse the people to remain in power; that is all. He is, therefore, left to accept whatever comes to fulfil their ambitious plans.

In modern civilized societies, one's best friend, brother or sister is the government. Where a society claims to be modern, and their worst enemy is the government, people's best friends are relatives, making old fashioned attachments, especially in collectivism, then that society needs to overhaul the government immediately. The world has been changed by people who believe in improving the standard of living, that it will be difficult for collectivistic cultures to survive in pseudo governments. A government that shies away from empowering its people to author their destinies is incompetent and needs to be overthrown. African governments that believe that without the Asian giant's FDI, we cannot live are incompetent. Those are governments that mind less about future generations' ability to meet their needs. The Asian giant's FDIs are more of vehicles for African leaders to merit from corruption. The Asian giant does not mind about the extent of the effect of his activities on the local peoples—whether there is equity or not in the way the resources are distributed in Africa's economy—that is none of her business! The Asian giant's investments in Africa are avenues through which African dictators get access to money that they later use to suppress masses and perpetuate invisible sectarianism. You can only learn about this sectarianism when you apply for a job and fail to get it because of your ethnicity. Modern sectarianism is a network you cannot visibly see but operates in the system; it automatically rejects you when they sense alien blood.

Vigilance on Debts

It is continually becoming impossible for Africa to build its capital base because of the heavy taxes imposed on the start-ups. Heavy taxes are imposed by those who give us loans, and many start-ups fail to celebrate their fifth birthdays. Many enterprises fail to grow and expand because of reasons cited in Chapters Four and Five and heavy taxes imposed. The western world loaning Africa with so many direct and indirect taxes imposed deter Africa's capital building.

Poverty shall be perpetual in Africa if we do not build capital bases, build factories and infrastructure. We shall be left to rely on loans and aid day in and day out simply because of the fear we hold to cut the cycle of hopelessness. It will take courageous men and women in Africa to decide when to stop aid and build capital through forging politics of hope. Our problem is corruption, non-transparency and lack of accountability, unique African attitude disorder (UAAD), failure to sacrifice to save future generations, and weak democratic foundations. The Asian giant has expressed competence in how to exploit these weaknesses. When these are fixed, we can do away with aid.

Some African countries are among the countries with high tax rates in the world. The high taxes imposed in Africa result from donors imposing them on us because our leaders lack the competence to negotiate fair deals. In other words, many African leaders have no room to negotiate fairer deals for their people because they impose themselves on the people. Here, when the donor learns about this weakness, they take advantage. We, therefore, cannot race with high tax rates in an attempt to stimulate economic development. Startups will always collapse in an attempt to please the donors that we can raise enough money in the shortest time possible to pay back the loans. Africa's poverty will long live, perpetuated by bad politics which fails to learn about the intentions of others. Because of this, we cannot move as a whole. We need to sort the leadership distortions if we are to spearhead economic development.

The continued conflicts in Africa are a significant industry to some parts of the western world. Thus, some elites of the western world are working day and night in this industry to destabilize Africa, and one of the tools they use is through massive PR campaigns inclined on the need to democratize Africa. They hide in democracy campaigns for the reasons I have explained earlier in this chapter. The distortion of the sociocultural environments for the introduction of western models will not only make Africans lag permanently in all facets but also make us forget the dream of attaining financial and economic freedoms. The oppressive tax rates imposed on loans cannot allow the establishment of industries in our countries. They debar investors from establishing factories in many African territories, yet we have some of the lowest wage earners. The solution to oppressive tax rates would include stringent measures to curb corruption and forging a mechanism to have politics of hope that looks at a whole, not a piecemeal thing. This kind of politics of hope stimulates Africa's solidarity on sovereignty, and any attack on the sovereignty makes political parties dialogue to agree. The enemy is the one who attacks African sovereignty.

Relying on charity and loans is what many of our neighbours plan for Africa day in and day out, with too much deception, yet on the outside, they seem to have excellent intentions for this continent. Modern-day deception makes Africans forget that rascals also grow old. A professional rascal groomed in diplomacy and well-schooled has left Africans only to live on loans and charity to survive.

Politics Business

Self-driven sustainable development is highly impossible in a situation where politics is viewed as a business venture. In many countries, especially Sub-Saharan Africa, politics has become a mainstream job opportunity. People join politics as a get rich quick venture. Fresh graduates are looking at politics as a potential scheme for getting rich quick. This explains why many ruling regimes view a 4 or 5-year term as too short, necessitating to amend it to have more years in office. The whole cycle of hopelessness that focuses on politics as a viable business venture leaves no room for them to think developmental in the 4 or 5 years hence the thinking that more time will enable them to accomplish their promises.

The legislators spend much of the time politicking and time to legislate appears too short. What matters is what you accomplish in the years in office but not how many years you spend in the office. In some African countries, it is always campaign time from the day the president swears in up to the day the next elections are held, especially in Sub-Saharan Africa. Thinking that politics is a business is spoiling many people. Standing for people is to serve people, not a business. Many people standing for political offices look at politics as a business to see them attain financial independence, which is wrong.

I am convinced there should be a wealth threshold or statutes combined with political goodwill to limit the level for young political enthusiasts. Therefore, anyone contesting for high profile political offices, e.g. presidency and a legislator, must meet the well-reviewed criteria.

It does not necessarily imply that the rich cannot be corrupted nor embezzle public funds for that matter but instead act as a measure, somehow. Of course, some people are born greedy or psychopaths and those born to serve people as good leaders. But as I mentioned, here in Africa, some high profile political offices might need a wealth threshold to attain before one contests for that office. This is because of the unique crises we face. Many politicians have been bribed and used in minor things that leave voters wondering why they voted for them!

The commercialization of Africa's politics sees people vote for those who can provide food, household items, and money. It is becoming difficult for those not associated with sound financial and economic freedoms to be voted, right from a local council election to the highest presidential office. Correct and promising political ideology is not attributable wholesomely to how much money you have, although it could be one of the metrics to measure capability. However, there is a high positive correlation between a promising financially muscled candidate and their political success in fostering global ideas. A poor man's language might be filled with inexperience and less exposure to current and emerging developments in several spheres of leadership, science and technology. The fact that mobility is simplified with a certain degree of financial and economic freedoms makes people who are not financially strong lag behind. Africa, seated between highly developed giants and semi-developed, east and west, north and south, requires integrated approaches to quicken growth and development whilst promoting sustainability of the continent. Therefore, a promising politician who wishes to save Africa should strive to be financially independent. It is important.

Of course, it sounds a bit unpleasant to see that the politics of Africa is dominated by gasbags, poorly educated people and those with unexplainable sources of income living above the average earning person. However, this is so because of the intellectuals, elites, professors and expert professionals who run away when the subjects of making money and politics are discussed. As I explained in Chapter Three (Education System), professors and the learned people who run away when the subject of making money by ordinary-man-centred schemes is discussed are the ones perpetuating the problem.[47] You are doing nothing to support economic growth, and you expect sycophants to vote for you because you are filled with ideas and academic doctorates. It is better to show the power of your example than to show the example of your power. For example, talk of, "the women groups I empowered managed to pay school fees for their children, sounds better than I empowered women groups or I studied so many ideas on how to empower women." I led all those people out of poverty sounds better than I can lead all those people out of poverty. The evidence-based approach is the way to go to liberate Africa. You have to resemble them and change the deal midstream—low balling. In this way, the learned ones will know when to showcase a doctorate degree and when not.

---

[47] See p. 168, §3.

Politicking

It is not wise to make malicious and defamatory statements as a method of confronting your competitor—the use of unmannerly verbal and non-verbal expressions when campaigning is not good. Malicious and defamatory campaigns do not portray good politics. We have more confrontational tactics in our politics that associate with politics of envy. Yes, making negative statements or running negative campaigns about the opponent is acceptable but should be done in a more gentle style that portrays maturity and a tender temperament.

A wise politician would focus on what they can do for people once voted into office. They can as well show people what those in office have poorly executed or failed to do. And the inability and inappropriateness of the running opponents in the race. Of course, the inappropriateness and inabilities are negatives. This should be accompanied by showing unique attributes that hide why the candidate is a fit to speak on behalf of others. Good politicians market themselves with reasons why they think they are the best to represent and speak on behalf of others and why they think they are the best of all other gifted people in the race. You know, sometimes the truth is ugly and unpleasant. Most of the time, politicians resort to fantasies. The most detested person in the world of politics is the one who always tells the truth. Many politicians tend to conceal the truth because it is ugly most of the time, and at times they fear the disenchantment that comes out of telling the truth. Despite all these, the fact always remains, we are almost auctioning our countries in broad daylight because we fear associating with the truth. Therefore, politicians resort to lies because lies are palatable. The question is, will this help Africa?

Globalization has left many of our politicians only giving opinions in the interest of what people want to hear. To constitutionally consolidate yourself in power for the next tenure would require you to consistently remind voters of what positive change you have caused and regret what you promised and not yet implemented—this kind of maturity politics is not anywhere practised. Then assure them of your next plan of attack on the unimplemented goals. We should avoid deriding on our competitors, focusing on unconstructive things.

Once in the opposition, try to appreciate the good side of the government to some extent. This can be difficult to take but keeping quiet on some things that look good is not such a bad idea. You must have proper and sound reasons to oppose government programs. These should be reasons that flow from fundamental ideas that reflect social interests. The business of opposing because my friend is opposing is not being mature. Or supporting the regime because my friend supports it is childish. Overopposing government programs delays the implementation and retards development. Do not oppose government programs for selfish reasons on a personal level, just like many politicians do—neither do you have to support government policies out of fear because you belong to the ruling party. A wise politician is partly one who listens to the voice of reason, does things out of love, not fear. We need to learn to listen to the voice of reason and promote government policy over partisan politicking.

Does Politics Need Formal Training?

In many parts of Africa, you still find people who believe that politics requires no need for formal training prior and experience to entering the battlefield. We have many less experienced politicians because many African constitutions allow a person of 18 years to represent people in legislative assemblies, which is improper. However, there can be a few cases or positions where youth at 18 years could be prepared enough to run for a political office. Politics, just like any other field, calls for competence and experience, especially at the level of passing legislation. Because of this shortfall, many African politicians are ill-informed, inexperienced and incompetent.

However good and talented a person might be, they need mentorship and preparation. A person has to engage with the community through appropriate mentorship before they can gain the platform to have the competence to speak and act on behalf of others. This takes hard work, preparation and passion. The tendency to vote for somebody's daughter/son as a consolation for the lost cadre has its shortcomings as far as self-driven sustainable development is concerned, and this should stop.

To What Extent Do We Need Authoritarian Models In Africa?

The sustainability challenge is serious. Because of this challenge, Africa, to some extent, requires strong leaders with high patriotic charisma, some sort of *socialists* to sort its present-day distortions so long as they are proved beyond doubt patriotic, putting public funds to proper use and making the right decisions in the interest of national development, not their interests be contented with the little they have and very ready to serve the people and handover power. However, proving extraordinary patriotism is difficult, but not impossible. Honestly, where the population's quality is in doubt, the outcome of a democratic election cannot be trusted, only in today's modern and civilized world, not the past.

We have people who ideally wouldn't be eligible to vote for presidential elections, however much human rights and democracy are advocated for because they lack the understanding of how the country works – and they are the majority in third world countries. The lack of proper civic and political education predisposes them to this problem. The unique African attitude disorder (UAAD) I described in Chapter Four caused by the western models puts African democracy at scrutiny.[48] Many things appear God sent to Africans. The ideals of democracy can only resonate when every community member participates in its governance or understands governance issues. This cannot be achieved where civic and political education is not a priority.

Julius Nyerere (1922–1999), the founding father of Tanzania, once said, "You cannot have democracy where you do not have democrats" He was right. But today, many people understand what majority vote is all about—that all eligible people are responsible for voting their representatives. Today's biggest problem is the questionable quality of the population in a world driven by technology. The indicators of the quality of the population include; *poverty levels, illiteracy levels,* and *attitude*. With chronic poverty, one is limited to learn, and he is less exposed. Therefore, democracy is highly limited to work unless you wish the society to remain as it is or become worse. Where there is room to reverse or trigger life situations in the direction of one's choice, democracy may work. You cannot talk of democracy in a starving community. Positive dictatorship might work, but the tools to measure it are unavailable, especially where the attitude of most African leaders remains unchanged. Inequitable sharing of opportunities, employment discrimination and unbalanced regional growth and development will always remain a challenge.[49]

---

[48] See p. 203-204, §4

[49] See p. 324, §7

I give credit to Leen Kwan Yew of Singapore for graduating his country from the third world to the first world using positive dictatorial models. And his counterparts of Indonesia and South Korea, i.e., Suharto and Chung-Hee, respectively. This was possible because they never caught the *unique African attitude disorder (UAAD)*, and conventional religions never touched their bone marrows like Africans. A few of the long-serving heads of state in Africa sometimes do great things, but they *lack the skill to protect future generations.* The greatest humanitarian crises facing Africa today are disloyalties, Africa's unique attitude disorder and short-sightedness.

Cultural Leader's Voices

Some countries in Europe and Asia have their cultural leaders actively involved in national governance by proxy, while others do it remotely, but still, their influences are felt. For example, countries like the Kingdom of Netherlands, Kingdom of Belgium, Japan as a Monarchy, The United Kingdom, and the Kingdom of Norway, etcetera. All these monarchies are sovereign, constitutional, popular, hereditary or unitary. Why not Africa have such? Many African countries have enacted laws debarring cultural leaders from *participating* in the governance of African countries. This is improper because governance and politics in Africa were started by royal lineage. This is outright modern discrimination. Laws that are more just and well-reviewed ought to be enacted but not discrimination and suppression of cultural leaders. Moving from monarchism to democratic governance does not mean you leave out the cultural leaders.

Colonialists initially drafted most constitutions at independence to give due allegiance to cultural leaders. However, along the way, in turbulent post-independence days for many African states, the agenda got lost. Constitutional monarchies would be ideal in some instances, giving them a distinctive legal and ceremonial role. This would make sense where intimacy in drawing sovereign boundaries was followed.[50] Africa's social conditions demonstrate a vast difference from those of Europe, and we ought to have a degree of variations in forms and systems of governance. African men and women sat to draw a line with complete discrimination of cultural leaders in many spheres as if cultural leaders were a taboo. This was wrong for someone who claims to believe in the doctrine of equity. Many constitutions were drafted, making presidents more or less contemporary African chiefs. There is room for proper integration of cultural leaders in our constitutions in the modern-day. The love for power and excitement caused by colonial masters made many African freedom fighters look at cultural leaders with the potential to cause political problems and, therefore, tied them up from taking active roles in national governance. They assumed to have fought and replaced the tradition, and therefore, in that capacity, there was no need to model development culturally pivoted.

Today, we have only one kingdom as a sovereign state, i.e., Swaziland, officially the Kingdom of Eswatini. Kingdoms like the Zulu kingdom of Zululand in South Africa and the Buganda Kingdom in Central Uganda would be sovereign states and many more. Buganda was almost a nation because it had 20 counties and 56 independent clans with an excellent political structure. Today Buganda has 18 counties. Each county had/has *"Omwaami"* who headed it. **Note** that the "Omwami" was not the head of any clan. He was a *territorial leader, i.e., the county.* This was a good indicator that Baganda people had political and cultural leaders distinct from each other. If Buganda remained a sovereign state, self-driven

---

[50] See p. 359-370, §8.

sustainable development would be easier to achieve. The 56 clans were enough to embrace diversity. The website for Buganda is https://www.buganda.or.ug and http://www.buganda.com/. All information about the counties and clans can be obtained from that website.

I advocate for that because people did things out of love for the societies, not by force or competition. We still needed constitutional monarchies in some parts of Africa. I do not understand the reasons that would propel someone mature in the psyche to leave such political architecture that Buganda had to adopt that of the colonialists. This architecture drew a line between culture and politics. I disagree in all ways that such philosophy was nurtured from people filled with the holy spirit of a lesser God. The Baganda people of today are facing political suffocation that will go down in the books of history as the worst ever!

Still, in the Buganda Kingdom in Central Uganda, people used to do the so-called *"Bulungi Bwansi,"* an activity for routine or periodic maintenance or rehabilitation of roads out of love, not a must or a competition. Today, if The World Bank or the African Development Bank does not provide a loan, no new roads shall be opened, constructed, rehabilitated, or maintained. There would be no corruption if the Baganda people of Buganda were governing themselves. The white man distorted us the worst! Although he brought us education and religious enlightenment, if he had left us as we were and never colonized us, we would be a *million times better* than what we are now. Learning from others and *self-empowering* ourselves is the best approach.

In Buganda still, there was Ssekabaka Mwanga II (King), who reigned between 1884 until 1888 and from 1889 until 1897. He was the thirty-first (31st) Kabaka (King) of Buganda. This King excavated one of the biggest human-made lakes in Africa with the intention of creating an aqueduct that could ease transport from his palace to Lake Victoria shores. His ambitions were technological in nature and could spur economic growth, and people worked on his projects out of love. In Today's so-called modern Uganda, if The World Bank or the African Development Bank does not provide a loan, such ambitions cannot be started on.

The same King of Buganda crucified the Uganda Martyrs in a bid to strengthen his kingdom from intruders because he saw that his powers were declining. He loved his Kingdom despite the burning of the Uganda Martyrs. Therefore, one should not only view the burning of Uganda Martyrs symbolic of the rudimentary mannerism of the King but rather check the good side of such foresight because every kingdom or country colonized was infiltrated by religion first, and behind the religion, colonial masters lay their tools. At least King Mwanga II tried to pose some resistance to the colonial masters. Where you restrict the powers of monarchs, it would be wise to introduce federalism or grant sovereign republics honouring their identity and their self-love in the interest of national development. *Why force federations and integrations that follow no intimacy?*[51]

Constitutional Development in the African States

Most African constitutions are *sick*. They have been selfishly drafted with a complete lack of African factualisms. They lack a logical and scientifically proven attitude that helps eliminate leaders' selfishness out of the equation. On the other hand, many constitutions were largely drawn following the western models while borrowing much from the common law and very little from what we ought to develop—call it customs.

---

[51] See p. 359-370, §8.

In several African countries, much power is vested in the president, which limits exercising the doctrine of separation well enough. There is very little difference between today's president and African chiefs of ancient years. What kind of democracy can you dream of where the doctrine of separation of powers is non-functional? A majority of African constitutions stimulate breach of the social contract by leaders. A constitution that does not tie leaders' selfishness out of the way predisposes and precipitates leaders to breach the social contract. A workable constitution for African states ought to be drawn by non-politicians who are experts on the subject and approved by the people through a referendum. This might represent a milestone for the growth and development of democracy in the region.

On Republics

The Greeks who pioneered democracy, according to some scholars, explained very well the three kinds of people in society, i.e., the citizen, the tribe's person, and the idiots. They argued that the citizen is someone who has the skill and competence to live a public life. The tribesperson has a tribalistic mentality, not able to think beyond their tribes. Idiots are self-centred, selfish, and always private people. The longing for freedom which is a global cause got people tired of monarchs. Ideally, a republic is composed of citizens. Because monarchs rotated more on tribes, they left little room for people to graduate to ideal civilized citizens. Everything different was viewed as alien to them, and they wished to keep conservative. In a republic, democracy is the best ideal form of governance.

Besides people longing for freedom and getting uninterested in dynastic monarchism, many other forces interested people in welcoming republics; for example, the scientific and industrial revolutions turned things around. These two revolutions led to a well-founded understanding of political economies. Ultimately, the financial and economic freedoms facilitated the enlightenment of peoples in several domains of life and wished to be freer, forging ways to take part in the governance of their territories. Here, they could not withstand dynastic monarchism, and they started to advocate for democratic governance.

From a psychological perspective, the selfishness of man cannot be ruled out of decisions taken because of graduating to freer societies. The new social order excited several enterprising people who wished to grow stronger every day. The tax bases are enlarged when sovereign territorial boundaries are large enough. At some point, a dialogue ensued whilst extending influence and forging new sovereign territorial boundaries. However, most sovereign countries' enlargement resulted from the forceful end of dynasties or some regimes. The guiding assumption was that when we federate or integrate and unite, we grow strong. We avoid unnecessary restrictions and trade barriers of a sort, among other issues. That, "united we stand, divided we fall." That, "united we rise, and share the commonwealth." Ultimately, our people live a happy life, the standard of living is improved, and we graduate to more ideal citizens. *However, sustainable development goals were never in the correct perspective.*

The extent of power held in the supreme governing body or a central government of a newly created sovereign territory classifies the country as unitary or a federal republic. People with low levels of selfishness provided controllable powers to the central government and empowered individual states that formed a republic to stand on their own to solve proximate causes. Those with power greed, who wished continued annexure of territories by conquering others, and who felt a little unsure of the long-lasting relationships with newcomers, could not afford to allow sufficient power to be held at county levels or states within a republic. However, in the African context, several linguistic backgrounds associate with undocumented levels of idiotic traits and tribalistic mentality that highly required confederate systems or federations but not unitary constitutions. Africa has a problem with a myriad of social groups. These groups associate with unique cultures and religious foundations, which highly influence the mindset. Today, we have *contemporary nomads* who have exhibited significant idiotic traits and tribalistic mentality in Sub-Saharan Africa—typical of some Nile Basin countries. These people take advantage of the illusion of these governance models to silence those who wish Africa to rise. Africans are very divided than you can imagine in the "unitary systems." This has been proved through social circles and social media platforms.

It should no longer be a stereotype when it is evident.[52] Studies have to be conducted on a certain faction of people that claim each cow they meet on the road as theirs. These people are found in Sub-Saharan Africa. The same people, when asked how many people boarded the bus, refer to themselves and never count others who were on the bus. This is justified when they buy goods in the market from themselves only and never buy from others. They prefer eating a rotten yellow so long as it is sold by their own people, even if a fresh one is available from others. Occupationally, it is only themselves that they find fit for a referral or recommendation. The same thing applies to scholarships. They award themselves a significant number of scholarships. A strong degree of idiotic and tribalistic traits that becomes evident should not be called stereotyping. The bad news is that these people are steering some of Africa's economies, and the Asian giant knows how to exploit this confusion. This leaves no hope for Africa.

The illusion of the word "unitary" to mean united has caught many shortsighted Africans not to dig deeper than the obvious case. All civilized people wish for unity. However, no man would give in his family to the local council chairman because we are integrating to be more united. The jurisdiction of the local council chairman views power structure as a federation of societal families and leaves the males to man their families. The African unitary system is one where the local council chairman can dictate what happens in people's families—that is, the state of affairs in contemporary monarchs that claim to be republics.

The corruption, lack of accountability, and transparency are perpetuated by such unitary systems in Africa. The Asian giant knows how to exploit this hopelessness. The ruling clans of peoples that approximate to idiots and tribespeople according to the Greeks take decisions for the entire sovereigns yet only themselves merit out of the deals with the Asian giant. If many African constitutions were selflessly drafted/reviewed, the Asian giant would find difficulty chewing up Africa. Therefore, if you pose a mathematical construct and solve it, many *African Republics are Contemporary dynastic monarchs.* These monarchs are driving countries as "projects." Most economies in Sub-Saharan Africa are projects. Very unsustainable projects! This is not good news for those who feel the pain for Africa's sustainability because these dynasties live in anxiety and rarely do the right thing. They always wish to forge pseudo relationships with outsiders, especially the Asian giant, to survive. When doing the right thing, I do not see why you accept the acquisition of non-concessional funds to meet nationalistic goals.

---

[52] See p. 190-191, §4.

Systems of Governance and Sustainable Development

The amount of power held by the central government determines the system of government a state has. For many sovereign African countries, federalism would be the right system. However, not one hinged on tribal segmentations rather one rooted in regions—a form of *heterogeneity* not *strictly homogeneity* to avoid tribal segmentations. Where tribes coincide with individual states, it can be modelled to reflect both but never on the tribe's homogeneity alone. Although the size of the country at times predetermines the appropriateness of federalism, it is still the best governance model to nurture patriotism. Unitary models claim to be about fairness or equity—I am after nurturing patriotism, the mother of fairness and equity. You love your homeland first before loving the Republic!

A sustainable federal government should not create tribal segmentations. It should not be hinged on tribes but instead defined following interests, not positions. These interests must promote heterogeneity of the federal state and must be governed by the overarching goal of sustainable development.

Federal constitutions are rigid and not easily manipulated or amended. Although manipulations cannot be avoided entirely in situations where weak democratic foundations manifest, they still present a practical competitive advantage over unitary constitutions. The attitude of an indigenous native African can be well controlled and developed through such models but not unitary constitutions in order to spur accelerated socio-economic transformation. All heads of state clinging in power for life presidency utilize the weak democratic ideals embedded in unitary constitutions to amend the constitutions—things that appear legal but hopeless in the eyes of a transformational socioeconomic activist. Decisions that are legal following democratic ideals but contravening the principle of natural law. Resolutions that are legal but contravening the human sense of right and wrong.

We have always had influential revolutionary leaders throughout history. The mentality that one person is the only one who has the potential to steer a political economy can only be found in the books authored by gods, which seem perfect with impunity. The tendency for African leaders to cling to power is motivated a lot by weak democratic foundations. To bring in the love for cultural norms described earlier, we would embrace federalism modelled to reflect regions and cultures but not tribes so that each state can make resolutions over its affairs and jurisdiction controlled by the central government. Each state decides on its local leaders, technocrats, professionals, and social workers with the supervision of the central government.

In this case, people's love for their cultural heritage will be exhibited in the works, and corruption could be reduced. Therefore, the system that works best for African countries is federalism but not unitary systems. The capitalist nature of many African countries faces many challenges and requires federalism to spur accelerated economic growth and self-driven sustainable development. Weak democratic foundations cannot support capitalism to flourish. It becomes a mix of confusion, and capitalism could escalate the inequalities between the rich and the poor. African social conditions find weak democratic ideals not suitable at present. A person diagnosed with two problems; (a) psychosocial impairment, and (b) a medical or clinical problem, would need to see a doctor before meeting with a counsellor. The choice is ours. Should we see the counsellor and ignore the doctor?

An African nation wishing to develop a solid democratic foundation should forge a way to have a federal constitution or a well-thought-out integrated constitution like a confederate for accelerated socio-economic transformation and must adopt Weibul studies in an election cast under universal adult suffrage for the president or any other vital office. The leading colonial masters forged unitary systems for basically conquering others as the number one priority, something we ought to recognize now. Size and costs should not be a big stumbling block for going federalism.

Dictatorial regimes are working day and night to destroy multiparty systems in several African countries to forge a movement similar to communism. Communism can never be embraced in Christian-dominated societies. They are forging monarchism instead, which modern civilized societies have resisted. Some African leaders have a dream to become the chairman Mao-(s) of Africa. The reason behind this is that unitary systems are a conquer approach and not an empowering stimulus. If Africans do not wake up early enough, the Asian giant is already succeeding in confusing Sub-Saharan leaders.

The long-serving African leaders wish to use unitary systems to suppress people, indoctrinate people, conquer people's hearts and minds, and later kill multiparty democracy to one-party states, hence introducing some modified communism in the long run. I think they would be fairer in their thinking only when they respected the phenomenology of success described in Chapter Five if they wished the masses a share on the bread. However, many are very idiotic and tribalistic, as described by the Greeks.[53] They cannot allow masses to benefit equally. This is an instinctual fact, i.e., the selfishness of many African collectivistic societies that require federalism to wake them up and drop these cultural predispositions that will not lead Africa to the path to self-driven sustainable development.

Dictators in Capitalistic Economies

In a capitalistic economy led by a dictator, business empires are highly influenced by the dictatorial regime. The influence is a must if the dictator is to keep himself in power because he needs to be fed the information on how each business performs for fear of the rich becoming a threat to his government. Therefore, he has to cripple the success of other's businesses. Countries with dictatorial leaders can never have a genuine open economy, although they talk of having free-market systems, which is false with the exception of a few positive dictatorial models of the non-African countries that have recently graduated to developed status.

Some least developed economies in Africa where political systems are weak will continue to cry of stunted growth, unemployment, diseases, and poverty because their economies are tied in the hands of the dictators. Unless one understands the concept of open-mindedness, you cannot understand what I am describing here. The dictator prefers to give foreign investors tax incentives and tax holidays than local investors who have the capacity and willingness to invest in their countries because foreigners are less likely to threaten his seat. This, coupled with the fact that Africa is hugely living on the mercy of others, escalates the problem. Foreign investors appear untouchable for the reasons described earlier. And when it comes to protectionism, industries and associated employments affiliated to the dictatorial regime in one way or another survive.

---

[53] See p. 105-106, §2.

Africa is not going to genuinely develop its capital base when heavy taxes are imposed on start-ups. These heavy taxes must be imposed because the dictators have no option but to milk the taxpayers. It is going to be a whole cycle of hopelessness living on the mercy of donors and well-wishers. Taxes imposed by donors who know how to manipulate the hopelessness many African countries face: corruption, lack of transparency, weak democracy foundations, and the unique African attitude disorder (UAAD).[54] This coupled with high inflation and interest rates superseding innovation rates, makes this mathematical equation complex to solve.

You cannot have a section of the population feeding on termites, and you prioritize infrastructure development and weapons in the budget. Despite scholars criticizing Maslow's hierarchy of needs, it remains evident. William Wallace (1270–1305) once said, "Every man dies. Not every man really lives."[55] He disputed Maslow's hierarchy of needs and left it very functional to those who only die. Those who live to die never follow Abraham Maslow's hierarchy of needs. They find reasons to live far beyond what Maslow postulated. Fine, the security of the country is a priority, but nobody can attack a starving community. However, suppose one part of the country is starving, and the state is busy procuring weapons. In that case, there is a problem of inefficient allocation of resources, unbalanced growth, inequity, and selfishness. We will not allow dictators to own over 80% of the country's resources through manipulating systems. We should refuse, and that must end if we are dreaming of self-driven sustainable development. Can we be those who live to die in order to save Africa?

Politics and Luxury amidst Extreme Poverty and Hunger

It is not rare to see personalized motorcar number plates for big politicians and middle-income earners. If we understood the relationship between the poor and the rich in Africa, we would view nationalistic issues a little more differently. The rich and wealthier people are working on program projects funded by development agencies like The World Bank, Islamic Development Bank, African Development Bank, Exim Bank of China, etcetera, or financed by donors except for a few people who have made their wealth through innovation and business enterprises. But still, if your biggest client is the government whose budget is primarily funded by outsiders, you are still falling in the same boat. If you export your products and services, you are a brave and lucky person immensely contributing to the country's GDP.

It is prevalent for people working in government and donor-funded organizations to masquerade as wealthy because of a lack of foresight into the source of their riches. They should examine if The World Bank or any other funding agency pulled out the support whether they would still have the jobs. Thinking you are so rich in Africa is not knowing how we live and how our economies function. Engineers and scientists try to envision this and become more innovative. We should, therefore, learn that genuine rich and wealthier Africans can be counted. Most of the rich people are just inches away from poverty. It is highly likely that Africans who often take holidays in the developed world are those who swindle government funds. It is thus a collective effort knowing that it begins with all of us. We are all equal on the assumption that most African states rely on loans and donations to live. It is a pity for those with an inflated sense of self because they hold public offices run on donations and loans. We should therefore behave right. If loans and donations are scrapped, some of Africa's economies get into turmoil, with lots of highly educated people losing employment.

---

[54] See p. 203-204, §4.

[55] William Wallace (1270-1305) was a freedom fighter for Scotland and Ireland against England, near the end of the 13th century.

Morals and values should be taught to our children to make them aware of living currently as dependency nations so that none views themselves as unique once holding a particular office. Living just inches away from poverty is explicitly demonstrated when you claim to be rich and drive a posh car on roads with potholes or unpaved. Being rich and staying in a neighbourhood of people starving makes you poor as well. I doubt whether you can feel good cruising your expensive vehicles while looking at malnourished children in your vicinity. You can only enjoy your riches where people understand them and where the community speaks the same language. A blind person can only appreciate things by other senses but not eyes. To be part of such a community as a rich person necessitates you to awaken their other senses. Endeavour to live with people who are not blind to enjoy your riches. It is mainly in Africa where you find a high court judge sentencing a person to jail over corruption and abuse of government office when their children are attending schools in the developed world, and their monthly expenditure is 10 times what their salary can afford, yet they provide no proof of an accountable business besides their job. This judge does not feel any sense of guilt whilst exercising their discretionary powers to sentence the culprit.

Suppose you are a professional or a technocrat and one peruses through your curriculum vitae. In that case, one might be able to audit your earnings so long as the curriculum vitae is well-detailed. That means if one cannot account for their wealth, then they must possess a dirty spot somewhere—and this is typical of many technocrats, politicians, judges, and public servants in Africa. In 2010, you must know that you earned this much and invested it in business A, which yielded profits of margin B, which you used to acquire property so and so, in the year 2015, etcetera. You must own clear books of accounts. If governments were auditing the wealth of all; politicians, technocrats, public servants, and business people, Africa would be able to get on to the right track for self-driven sustainable development. As a technocrat or professional, you must possess a deliverable for why you are paid. If you are a businessperson, you must have clear books of accounts.

Conclusion

Our foreign policies should never be biased towards any territory, and they should be fair enough. The guiding assumption is to treat others equally whilst making national decisions. We should strive to be independent to protect both current and future generations. Africa should be put first, and any decision that risks putting Africa second in our endeavours should not be allowed to take off. We should prioritize government policy over partisan politics.

We need politics that inspires hope, which is non-sectarian, non-tribalistic, and nonbiased. We need politics that puts Africa first, cultivating independence and offsets the mindset of dependence to build Africa beyond charity and aid. It is essential to comprehend that every race on this planet earth is on its own first and then integrates the self with others as the second-best alternative in the sustainable development struggle. It is improper for Africa to get convinced that another race minds about Africa's problems more than Africa itself.

It is not black and white thinking, but I wish Africans to recognize their position and play good politics of hope that is not biased with any other race. I am not de-campaigning unity, but Africa holds the keys to solve the world's problems; we need to view others the same way. When we show sides, we will never achieve the overarching goal of self-driven sustainable development. Our strength and unity as Africans will awaken all races that wish to dinner-up Africa as their meal. By Africa growing strong, the world will channel all energies into fighting extremists threatening the world and possibly think more about sustaining humanity. Africa, therefore, has to play good politics, knowing that it is the only factor left to save the world. Psychologists remind us that one's behaviours and emotions are a gateway to their thinking. The continuous interference of the western world in African matters is symbolic of opportunism that we ought to recognize now.

For Africa to grow its democracy, it needs intellectuals to get wholly involved in politics. It is important to note that everything on top gets political. From medicine to engineering, to agriculture, to academia, the top is politics. Even a hospital director, with all their medical expertise, must be politically vigilant. It is deceptive to think that you can separate man from politics!

There is no substitute for democracy for those who believe in the Supreme Being. Democracy is a work-in-progress and shall always be a work-in-progress, but it is the best ideal that puts a man's heart and mind about matters of power at a less excited state. The world fought to reduce the jurisdiction of kings, sultans, warlords, rulers, and chiefs to free humans and make the world a better place to live for all. We need leadership assumed through democratic means, and we cannot dream of going back into that kind of life. The truth is, we need to *improve our democracy* by ourselves, not being forced by others. The current African democracy is fragile, and the Asian giant is meriting from this weakness.

The continued blame that hooligans dominate one side in democracies and end up having hooligans assume leadership can be answered by intellectuals simply thinking the way they want but behaving as though they were hooligans to save Africa. Empathetically live like the majority. Masquerading as a swine to kill a tiger—but never to replace democracy. If it needs to spend half a decade eating grass to become the cattles' leader, do so. The intellectuals must have this tremendous desire to make changes using the ordinary person as the main stimulus/engine.

Africa's politics is dire, and democratic means of assuming leadership seem to escalate the problems in some countries. Positive dictatorial models would work the best in the interim. However, if untreated, egocentric tendencies perpetuated by the Unique African Attitude Disorder (UAAD) cannot allow such models to be productive. The UAAD originated from colonialism and religions marrying to disorder Africans.

We need to protect the living ones and future generations before trying and convicting leaders who have committed crimes against humanity. The dead ones cannot stand in court to give testimony on the living ones. Failure to forge our democracy and lean on others to dictate our future is highly detrimental. Dialogue with the remaining long-serving heads of state should be routine. The long-serving heads of state should be handled with dialogue because it does better than using foreign forces to forcefully end regimes in the claim of pursuit to democratize the state(s). The ultimate end for everyone is death; the difference is in when—the time. We need to protect the African race in the sustainable development campaign first before thinking of anything else. That is the best gift to give the forthcoming generations. Generations that will lead on their own and live as partners with other races but not as subordinates.

Africa holds the keys to perpetuate global conflicts or leading a peaceful and stable world. Today's decisions are determinants of how competing superpowers will react to sustainable development and world stability. They seem to triangulate their anxieties through Africa. The way we tolerate others' decisions and perceptions of us teaches them how to continue treating us. Therefore, Africa needs to forge its path and wake up to have a better world. Suppose we demonstrate cohesiveness rather than playing ridiculous political games on one another due to excessive politicking. In that case, the competing superpowers will not have anywhere to triangulate their aggressiveness, and they will be left to look out for extremists threatening the world. Hence, the stability of the world will improve day in and day out.

Socialist Policies. Democracy. Federalism

Chapter Three: Education System

"Someday, in the distant future, our grandchildren's grandchildren will develop a new equivalent of our classrooms. They will spend many hours in front of boxes with fires glowing within. May they have the wisdom to know the difference between light and knowledge."
=== Plato (428/427 – 348/347 BC) ===

Chapter Organization

Quick Insights

What, How, and Why Questions

The "Why," Supreme Being, and the Big Bang Theory

The Proof of Science

The Illusion of Knowledge

- Implications of the Illusion of Knowledge

Can one become Educated without attending School?

Local Languages and Dialects in Education

Justification of the use of Local Languages

Local Languages, solidarism, and Culture

The African weak data collection and Documentation Culture

The Jigsaw Concept

What is the Sign of Good Education?

Do our education systems test memory or intelligence?

Education that stimulates Thinking

Grading in Schools

Health, Safety and Welfare in Schools

Teaching versus Lecturing: What should be the criteria?

On Modern Teaching Pedagogy

Training and Skilling Graduates
- Karamoja case study of an illiterate technician
- Theoretical Examinations and Practical Tests

To what extent do PhDs matter in solving Africa's distortions?

What does it mean to graduate in many parts of Africa?

Software and Hardware Components as Products of Our Education system

Do we need to bias our Children to Courses?

What does Europe mean to the World?

Relevance of Science Education in Sustainable Development: The Future of Courts

Education, Innovation, Politics, and Patriotism

Do School Mottos Matter?

The unnoticed education held by African ancestors

Africa's University Research

The Question of Confidence to Communicate Ideas with Authority

Academic Politics

Contemporary Duplication of Fields

On Scholarships, Africa's Universities and Other Universities

Elites that fear discussing the subject of money

Conclusion

Quick Insights

Just for passing exams highly affects the education system and distorts the productivity of the components of social structures at both macro-level and meso-level scales. Without a correct system, a few units can function efficiently and effectively. The education system is central to the entire system, which makes up the social structure. The quality of the output of the education system highly influences the way other units of society perform efficiently and relate to one another. Thus, as dependent on several independent pillars, the modern societal system stands on the education system as the central pillar.

The "self-discovered" system of learning to get educated is done improperly in African educational institutions. The best way to study is to teach yourself when an instructor facilitates you. Heavy commercialization of education needs stringent measures to meet industry demands. A majority of private schools, colleges, and universities across the continent make students pass exams but not understand. Anyone can pass exams. However, the overarching goal of schooling is to understand and apply. That is why many graduates are learned but not educated.

Although some African countries have a reasonably strong education system with a diverse range of academic programs and a seemingly good quality of graduates in some universities, most of the graduates do not have enough of *"how is it done? Or why is it done/happening? Or how can I make it happen?"* in their thinking, but they instead have questions like *"what is available to do? Or who has a job for me?"* The thinking is usually occupied and associated with acquiring very high grades to find an excellent job, yet excellent jobs are limited and scarce.

Modern thinking for 21st-century graduates should be "to excellently understand the taught school knowledge that fulfils my interests for proper visualization and externalizing my calling into reality." An educated person constantly questions themselves how to make things happen (to create or recreate and innovate), integrating information and education acquired in college. We cannot solve *multigenerational poverty* by graduates looking for unavailable jobs but rather creating jobs. The correct education system should empower graduates and prepare them to think higher consciousness to solve societal problems.

What, How, and Why Questions

Genuine development lies in answering the *"why"* questions. We cannot stop questioning if we aim to grow sustainably: socially, economically, and spiritually. The "why" questions should take precedence. And the priority order of questioning should be: why, how, and what. Graduates should train to answer more *"why"* questions. When you look closely around you wherever you are, you notice a *"why"* question taking a more complex explanation than a *"how and what"* question. If graduates train to unlock the *whys*, the *whats* and *hows* are simplified. The illusion of knowledge hides very much in the *whats* and *hows*. Complete understanding resides in answering the *whys*. Proper knowledge and understanding reside in unlocking the *"whys"*. People who labour to answer the *whys* are leading and have greatly influenced and changed the world—exhausting a *why* question takes considerable commitment and passion. Often, *"why"* questions are not exhausted; in other instances, trying to exhaust them tends to lead us to believe in the Supreme Being or the Big Bang Theory. That is the main reason we research. A question like, "Why are there 12 eggs in a dozen?" can help unlock a child's curiosity.

One of the *two processes* leading to the theories of either the Supreme Being or the Big Bang Theory might be an illusion. Or else one governs the understanding of the other. This is because, to date, the understanding of both is more about answering the *"how"* but not the *"why"*, especially at the beginning of the universe. The process leading to the Supreme Being is quite poetic but very good at making philosophical inquiry into the *"why universe"*, yet the Big Bang claims background radiation left over from which the radiation information helps astronomers determine the universe's age. The Big Bang theory goes ahead to demonstrate the existence of particles such as neutrons, electrons, and protons that decayed to form the cosmos—scientists arguing the case from mathematical formulae and models. However, the theorem fails to answer the *"why"* and the origin of the small singularity claimed to have inflated to the cosmos we know today. To a considerable extent, the real beginning from nothing might be well-answered in the existence of the Supreme Being since several philosophical schools of thought have laboured to explain why the Supreme Being created the universe. I believe the answer to the *"why universe?"* is highly likely to be well-answered unscientifically.

My hypothesis rests on the fact that: there will always be a supreme leader above any leader—even within the universe—the sun leads the planets and other objects that orbit it in the solar system. In my opinion, the universe is too organized to have originated out of confusion. However, I do not stop on that, since scientists have been able to determine the universe's age, then the universe is perhaps finite because if it were infinite, they would not be able to determine its age. An infinite universe might have other older stars that scientists have not yet discovered. Scientists have again discovered that the universe is expanding. For example, the moon is moving away from the earth. To expand something, you must have extra provisions for the expansion. Without extra space, room for expansion is impossible. What is this extra room space? If the universe is infinite, then it is not expanding but somewhat changing. That means that since the universe has a correct age and expands, then it is not infinite.

The implication of *correct age* determined is symbolic of something before the Big Bang. No attempt has scientifically unveiled the answer to the "before big bang" hypothesis. Astronomers estimate that the Big Bang occurred between 12 and 14 billion years ago. From where did helium molecules come? That something before the Big Bang hides the answer to the *"why universe?"* question. The Supreme Being might lead the Big Bang—and the correct research tool to the question hypothesizes around the *"why we can determine the age of the universe yet we claim the universe is infinite and expanding?"* The universe cannot be infinite when its age is correctly determined. Couldn't there be another universe older than this one we know onto which this fits and expands as claimed? Both historical and contemporary cosmologists have had a conflicting understanding of *"why universe?"* yet referred to spiritual beliefs as mere traditions of creation myths. None has answered the *"why universe?"* with vivid scientific proof to date, setting out the reasons for reasons of universe creation.

The "Why", Supreme Being, and the Big Bang Theory

If not Supreme Being, then why develop the natural law and equity principles to guide us to live in peace following universally accepted morals? We decide many things basing on the equity principle. Where is equity in Big Bang? Why not let the consequences of the Big Bang take the course? The development of many governance laws and principles is rooted in equity and natural law. These laws were derived from teachings on the Supreme Being. However, many scientists believe that the Big Bang is responsible for universe creation and how life began on earth, but the laws and principles derived from the teachings on the Supreme Being govern scientifically patented discoveries—the natural law and equity principles. Which one is an illusion, then? If none is an illusion, then one must have defined the other.

Similarly, the *"how"* Egyptian pyramids were constructed has conflicting theories; what about the *"why"?* The way the spermatozoa fertilizes the ovum, and here you are today, partly defends the Big Bang Theory. However, the governance of life on earth hinged on the development of equity laws justifies why the sun leads the planets in the solar system and hence the existence of the Supreme Being. The scientific orderliness is challenged by the Supreme Being orderliness that governs humans who develop those principles

Besides, nothing is new in science; we are just discovering the greatness of the Supreme Being. Many phenomena are undiscovered, and science cannot explain everything. The great discovery in the 21st century will be the relationship between science and spirituality. The incredible power of science and its applications/innovations resides in four major mathematical signs/operators: addition, subtraction, division and multiplication. Science takes on the constructive direction of mathematics and leaves logic and abstract mathematics to philosophers to inquire into the body, mind, and the universe.

Understanding or disputing the Supreme Being does not require you to go out in space but rather to ponder around the two sexes, i.e. male and female. Why not 3 sexes? How does science explain the genesis of 2 sexes and not more than 2? The 2 sexes depict an excellent plan in the beginning, and the Supreme Being can be understood through the complexity of dealing with the *'why'* hypotheses, which generate leads into infinitism. For example, one may ask: why are Africans backward? Many analysts can give reasons trying to answer the backwardness. However, the reasons given by analysts have their reasons. And their reasons can be called second-order reasons, which also have their reasons. The reasons of second-order reasons can be called third-order reasons, and the chain continues to nth order reasons. That definitely ends in infinitism, which explains something supreme beyond our imagination. Therefore, the quality of education provided is defined at what point along the continuum the why questions are considered exhausted. On the other hand, those who labour to find out the circumstances surrounding the reasons for why they are born cannot be fooled to believe in no supremacy above all.

The Proof of Science

Science is not meant to finish people's happiness. It is better to develop a core belief that universally creates peace, brings happiness and joy to humans and other living beings than a proof of science that brings contradiction, unhappiness and unsustainability. That is the good side of the secretive African philosophers. A wolf-pack would not mind having any salt until an intruder comes with salt to create value and scarcity. Africans ought to understand the ingredients of life.

The Illusion of Knowledge

"The greatest enemy of knowledge is not ignorance, but the illusion of knowledge."
Daniel Boorstin (1914 – 2004)

The illusion of knowledge in the education system is more damaging than ignorance. It not only lag the continent behind, but it is also a big enemy to the entire planet. The environment is greatly destroyed by the illusion of knowledge—thinking that we are sustainably developing, bringing many creatures to extinction and exhaustion of natural resources. The illusion of knowledge depicted in the many planning deficiencies is perpetuating socioeconomic dilemmas in several developing countries. This is mainly observed in cities where environmental degradation is rampant, extensive construction reworks, and sustainability metrics are not considered in the planning of buildings and similar structures. Therefore, investment in human capital must be prioritized as the most critical resource over and above any other to curb environmental damage. Stephen Hawking (1942–2018) made it very clear when he echoed Daniel Boorstin's (1914–2004) famous quote where he said, "The greatest enemy of knowledge is not ignorance; it is an illusion of knowledge." Africans must understand the underlying meaning of Hawking's statement because several higher institutions of learning might have caught the bug. The illusion of knowledge can be summarized as "thinking that you know and understand something well-enough yet in the actual sense, you do not". Lots of people have graduated with invalid degrees. Others are poorly taught.

The planning deficiencies in poor African countries resulting from improper coordination of state agencies and working in silos is due to failure to understand and appreciate the limits of our knowledge and skill. That coupled with not adopting the jigsaw concept well enough in knowledge building keeps many poor states in a prolonged state of hopelessness. The ability to learn about what you ought to know, what you know, and appreciate what you will never understand in the interim, is an attribute for intellectuals. Therefore, you avoid what you do not understand well enough! The intellectual academy does no discrimination and follows no well-defined formal training. Its gates are wide open for everyone who labours to have a tremendous desire to know, learn, unlearn, relearn and be ready for change.

It is also interesting to note that the difference between a fool and an intellect is that a fool knows no boundary. What you do not understand and what you will never understand only leaves people who live with integrity to be positioned in humanity saving positions. The ability to go slow in matters where one's conscious and subconscious signals lack of knowledge is what demonstrates good judgment, maturity, and growth in the intellect. This kind of independent judgment lacks in many decision-makers on the continent.

Our education system rarely prepares graduates to have sound judgment. The illusion of knowledge has masked several people with authority to believe in knowing a lot simply because of the high academic levels attained in colleges before assuming offices, whilst others it is because of the political power gained in many cases out of imposition. An inexperienced and incompetent labour force is disastrous and hazardous most of the time. It is common to find a fisheries expert making decisions in the infrastructure and works department in several developing countries because he mastered business administration. Therefore this makes him fit to review planning decisions and account for a works department.

Intellectuals understand that school is just the beginning of learning. Authentic learning is self-driven. Most of the growth in learning is a personal responsibility. All universally accepted laws were hypothesized and proved by geniuses who had a tremendous desire to know and improve the lives of others—living a life for others. These people became geniuses after the world disputing their theorems for many years.

The school develops a curriculum based on what conditions or circumstances dictate at that time. Those who develop curriculums, many times, go by the prevailing industry demands. Professionals are self-made. Professional bodies provide pieces of training, but true iconic professional unlocks their talents out of curiosity. All people wishing to grow their intellect and professionalism on the African continent should break the barrier of curriculums made by others to develop the curriculums that make them a better fit to save the planet and the African continent in particular. A majority of Africa's education is still following curriculums developed in the colonial era. Africa sits on natural resources amidst highly curious giants living by expectations of discovering extraterrestrial life without boundaries needs a complete overhaul of the systems.

Those who discovered the universally accepted laws, inventions and innovations took quite some years to make breakthroughs. Some taking a few years whilst others took decades. The school creates an illusion that you can easily *understand* a couple of theorems, laws and principles simultaneously in just a couple of hours. That clearly shows that school is just about exposing you to concepts, and the rest is self-driven. *How often do Africans consolidate their understanding in a situation where we survive largely on others' decisions?*

Implications of the Illusion of Knowledge—Planning Deficiencies triggered and perpetuated by the Education System

A Case Study on Environmental Impact of Old Cars on Urban Gravel Roads—Typical Africa's Policies Perpetuated by the Illusion of Knowledge in Decision Making

It is difficult to estimate how much the environment can get destroyed when we falsely believe that the person is knowledgeable enough to entrust them to make decisions. Little knowledge can be very damaging. One who admits to being ignorant will not embrace anything unusual and will keep the environment intact. For example: while other countries are shifting away from fuel propelled vehicles to green vehicles and cycling economies aiming to become carbon neutral economies, developing countries, especially in Sub-Saharan Africa, are importing used cars, many of which are too old to be put on the road. The carbon emissions resulting from these cars is unbearable because it contributes to climate change, but the governments remain reserved to restrict the importation of old cars. The 21st century needs clean car standards. One of the most challenging issues is that the rate at which roads are paved is too way below the rate of old car importation.

There are always options, but health & safety is always the first priority for those who understand sustainability goals. If the country cannot manufacture cars or afford the importation of new ones, they need to look at the impacts brought about by increased vehicular traffic on unpaved urban roads. The increased vehicular traffic on many unpaved roads of the poor Sub-Saharan countries greatly lowers the standard of living of the neighbouring homesteads due to the unbearable dust produced from the roads as a result of increased vehicular traffic.

Sometimes it requires roadside dwellers to do some dust suppression mechanisms just to be able to carry on businesses. Such planning deficiencies depict an illusion of understanding the core principles of planning for a state. These are all issues that emanate from an illusion of knowledge. An understanding planner values the health and safety of state nationals and derives policies accordingly. The old cars emit huge amounts of gases that are a big threat to the environment, and the dust produced is a big problem to the roadside dwellers. The life of one person is equivalent to the life of all of us arguing from ethical standards of practice.

The table below aims at throwing insight into a sustainability framework that guides decisions that would inform green politics. The illusion of knowledge does not allow planners to exhaust the options by drawing mathematical models that predict the consequences of each decision. The interdependence of sustainable development attributes calls for a sound understanding of the cause and effect prior to taking decisions. The education system that makes things appear disjointed and does not emphasize learning by self creates illusions. In many cases, decisions are taken looking at how taxes are going to be collected. However, little attention is given to time to remedy the impacts and the effects of holistic decisions. Sometimes people think they are solving a problem yet creating a more grievous problem. That is the illusion. In brief, the education system passes out people that cannot think holistically. This means they think that they are solving problems, yet they are multiplying them.

#	The decision to buy old cars as guided by the sustainability framework—drafting a policy	Amount ($)	Time to Rectify the Impact
1	How much impact does the decision cause to the Health and Safety of the country (side road dwellers and road users)?		
2	How much impact does the decision cause to the environment in terms of carbon emissions?		
3	How much traffic jam does this create as a result of increased vehicle activities?		
4	How much social impact (wellbeing) does this cause?		
5	How much does the decision contribute to the GDP and welfare of society?		

Road dust may contain toxic pollutants. Toxic substances may cause death, chronic and acute damage to health when inhaled, absorbed through the skin and swallowed, even though in small amounts. Toxic pollutants could come from a range of anthropogenic sources, characteristic of urban land uses. Sometimes dust may carry quartz, and heavy metals such as copper and lead, which might originate from vehicular traffic, whilst some other metals present in dust such as iron may originate from surrounding soils. Silica, a compound present in many rocks, stones, particularly sandstone, slate and quartz, is hazardous when inhaled as dust. It can cause chest and respiratory tract diseases like silicosis. Therefore, planning for the state in the interest of sustainable development, health and safety should be the number one priority. In other words, an education system that is very strong in health, safety, and welfare will reduce the knowledge illusions.

In the effort to develop sustainably, the acceleration should be put on putting together competent planners with a sound understanding of the application of knowledge sequentially, taking health and safety as the highest good in the hierarchy of doing good. The illusive knowledge described herein looks at health and safety as an addition to many other activities but not forming an integral part in decision making. In this way, having many people own saloon cars stimulating dust on unpaved roads supersedes the need to have safe living environments. This demonstrates that decision making and policymaking has the highest level of bugs as a result of the knowledge illusion—and this can be a product of the education system at some point, although it is highly guided by *political decisions.* The reason is that many decision-makers do not want to think but instead copy and paste ideologies which is a typical product of the banking education system—a concept model developed by Paulo Freire (1921-1997).[56]

The illusively trained person will destroy the environment for a community that has not been to any school to create a road network—destroying many sources of first aid. Hiring many consultants who are more sensing than intuitive, more feelers than thinkers—coupled with the illusion of knowledge-leaves havoc in the system. In so doing, they destroy the community's source of herbal medicines and fail to build a hospital in return. The risks associated with destroying nature are very high, especially where illusively educated people claim to help the unschooled. In the long run, they create more stress, sadness and depression amongst the unschooled and poor communities because of failure to understand the interdependence of correct knowledge from different fields, i.e. how an engineer must be guided by a social worker vice-versa. Therefore, actual knowledge would benchmark self-awareness initiatives to grow what nature and ancestors laboured to put in place. You do not destroy what you found in place because you have obtained education from school. It is about questioning how you lived before getting educated and how and why you lived before knowing how the ecosystem works. Then lead sustainable development.

> The illusion of knowledge is deceptive in that one believes to be solving a problem, yet in the real sense, they are multiplying the problem ten folds. When you analyze the story of my former biology teacher described in Chapter Five, he thought he knew what he was doing but ended up creating more havoc on the nation by failing almost half the class.[57] He lacked a basic understanding of economics and how to eradicate poverty to improve people's living standards. The teacher lacked sound knowledge on socioeconomic transformation to inspire confidence in his students. He believed in the illiterates' adage, which goes, "Because you are poor is the reason I am rich."

---

[56] See p. 132, §3.

[57] See p. 235, §5.

The main point out of the acquired knowledge is to understand. Africa's education system creates more of an illusion of knowledge because it nurtures more knowledge than understanding. It takes a little more curiosity for an African child who studied in Africa to stand out in the innovation arena. Many graduates have no complete understanding of the application of the acquired knowledge. And many teachers set exams to catch students on what they do not know. If you are an instructor who wants to catch your students on what they have not known and understood quite well, you need to grow your intellect. If you have such a teacher who sets to catch you offside, then know that their problem is the illusion of knowledge.

Can One Become Educated Without Attending School?

The answer is "yes and no." What matters is what you get from the school where you go to. It is not wise to confuse schooling with education. It matters less where you school from. What you get from there is what matters. Self-discovered knowledge sticks more. However, it comes with a great conscious effort to learn on your own. When you have a passion for exploring things like music, art, technology, science and engineering, you can do it yourself when you devote your mind to it. Education is about understanding that supersedes knowing. If you can understand concepts on your own, you get educated. Many artists, radio presenters, TV presenters, politicians, and writers are self-educated. And they are doing it better than those who attended great schools.

On the other hand, the interaction one gets at school with colleagues and instructors contributes extensively to the education but not the passing of exams. So, when you miss this interaction, you need to find it out in the world. This interpersonal building of relationships is paramount in making a sound educated, and competent labour force that meets industry and national standards. Most self-educated people are either more exposed by travelling and practically doing things like art, music, writing, technology, science and engineering—a hands-on culture. Instead of meeting peers and instructors at school, they learn through trial and error and discover things independently. The advantage of this self-education is that the person gets curious to understand how/why things work as they wish. Yet, the school system has a defined curriculum that might not meet the talents and capabilities of each student.

Local Languages and Dialects in Education

A language can be grown. At some point along a continuum, a dialect can convert into a different language. Some of our dialects are rich enough, e.g. Luganda in Uganda is a rich dialect. Estimates show that a majority of Ugandans can listen to Luganda whilst about half can speak and write the dialect. The dialect is spoken in almost all parts of the East African Community. It also has a unique character, "ŋ" and associated prefix "ŋa"; it exists in a few other dialects like Karamajong. If Europeans had not colonized Uganda, Luganda would most likely be the official language of the country. Anyone visiting Uganda learns about Luganda as being the second most recognized language after English.

We would have sciences taught in local languages and dialects. It is possible. It will be difficult to lead in sciences where we do not grow our vernacular literacies and local languages. It is on record that many African leaders are highly grown in their cultures. You cannot grow in your culture without mastering the language dialect. Good African leaders are strong in their local languages and vernacular literacies. It is not easy to imagine, think and rethink in a foreign language tremendously. You might have the imagination but not a far-reaching modern success and not as good as that one who has grown in culture and local language dialects, studied in a local language. For example, suppose you task science graduates from Africa to explain scientific terminologies like a mole and molecule to an unlearned person. In that case, I am convinced that less than 3% might have the ability to do so. You have not mastered it quite well if you cannot explain it to an unlearned person quite easily.

The illusion of knowledge described earlier has negatively impacted several communities across the continent. Many people are sent to jail erroneously simply because of a judiciary that failed to incorporate African self-awareness initiatives in the systems. Many legal processes and documents remain only understood by the legal fraternity. We need a system that makes law understandable to everyone—a system that simplifies the campaign to spread civic and political education swiftly. We can do it where people agree to trust their local languages and grow them accordingly. The use of local languages has been recently advocated for in courts of law in several societies across the continent. However, it might be difficult if judges and magistrates themselves are not fully grown in their local dialects and become mastery of vernacular literacies. The point to note here is that the judge or magistrate should be well-schooled in the dialects.

Justification of the use of Local Languages in Education

Each language has its phonemes, morphemes, semantics, syntax, grammar and pronunciation of words. Language develops serially in children by learning phonemes, morphemes and finally the syntax. Phonemes are the smallest units of sound in a language. Morphemes are the smallest units of meaning in a language, and syntax refers to the language rules that allow generating an infinite number of understandable utterances. This explains why Africans, especially those grown in local languages, cannot correctly pronounce English words and other foreign languages simply because they skip the stages of learning phonemes and morphemes and go straight to learning the syntax in several schools environments.

Ideally, to have a well-differentiated person in a language, the phonemes and morphemes should not be learnt at school; it should be an everyday routine learning for our children. Unless we wish to kill our local languages and dialects to fully adopt the foreign ones, which can be a devastating incidence in the history of the African people, that is when we can embrace the use of other languages in our homes. The culture revolves on a unique local language. There is no way you can preserve culture without preserving the local language. Failure to preserve culture, then forget about self-driven sustainable development. Culture rotates around the original local language.

One of the strangest myths on the African land is that Europeans taught us to read and write. At least not everywhere! Egypt's and Ethiopia's literacy is not attributable to any white invasion. So, nobody should hoodwink us. As early as 1BC, Ethiopia had poetic forms such as the Qene and Mawandes. This is too way before Christianity and Islam. The Bantu of Southern Africa had a language of symbols similar to the Egyptian hieroglyphs. This was reported by Credo Mutwa (1921-2020) in his book, "Indaba, My Children."[58]

Along a well-defined continuum, a dialect can become a language. Lack of a writing style and alphabetic symbolism (in some African territories before Europeans scrambled for Africa) does not mean that a dialect carries no meaning. An alphabet and characters can be grown as you wish through social constructionism

---

[58] Credo Mutwa. *Indaba, My Children* (London: Canongate Books Ltd, 1964).

as society agrees. So long as when one communicates, you understand what they mean, you formally design the language. And your mode of passing information from one person to another has a unique sound, meaning, rules that govern it, pattern and unique utterances; we can create symbolic meaning for writing the socially constructed message. The Ethiopians, Eritreans, and Egyptians demonstrated hope.

According to psychoanalysts, the first five years of a child are considered formative years. During this period, the formation of the child's unconscious takes place. The formation integrates nature theories with nurture. The onset of cognitive development stretches from 3 years for some children to the onset of adolescence. The distortion of cognitive development by teaching kids to dislike their local languages or dialects is one of the great products of inferiorism. This leaves only a deep thinker to cogitate about remedying such hopelessness that masked the African people. How about when we change the order of education to regrow our languages and instil confidence in the local languages? I believe we can see positive results immediately. Let us tag some value to what belongs to ourselves. There is nothing like people born in certain places are more human than others. We all have the same anatomy.

The brain processes information serially. It is worth noting that a language represents knowledge. The brain has four quadrangles or lobes responsible for processing information to make it useful to sustain a human being—to think, plan and organize tasks; to create, innovate and develop; to cogitate, visualize and learn; to socialize, move and emotionally survive among other functions. The brain contains a sensory register that registers all information reaching it. Imagine a child raised in vernacular up to about 6 years to start school. Teachers punish the child for speaking their local language or dialect through several integrated reinforcements when they reach school. The child is in a stage of cognitive development. Doesn't such practice lead to a permanent wound in the cognition of the child? It might bleed anxiety which manifests later in life, considering their local language or dialect as useless and a dangerous provoking stimulus.

The fact that the brain processes information serially, its lobes have overlapping functions. It has areas specialized for auditory perception, speech, cognition and motor functions. These areas are always associated with others to make a rational human who can create, innovate and develop. The brain can do all functions in microseconds at very high speeds. Areas specialized for reading, writing, speaking, and visual cognition have overlapping functions in a message feedback system. A child who has grown rich in their local language or dialect somewhat finds difficulty processing the information in a foreign language if somebody drastically pushes the child to convert to a foreign language. The overlapping functions of the brain areas have to create shortcuts to process the messages into meaningful outputs. I cannot fail to spot misinterpretations as a result of language conversion from local to foreign. There is a risk of converting the wrong message as the child tries to pass the meaning from local to foreign languages.

The brain sensory register first registers meaning in the local language or dialect. It then transmits it to areas responsible for converting the local meaning to a foreign meaning before storing it in short and long-term memories. I cannot rule out the possibility of interference of stored local meanings with foreign meanings because the child is in the cognitive development stage. Benjamin Lee Whorf (1897 – 1941) coined a hypothesis he termed "linguistic relativity hypothesis or the Sapir-Whorf hypothesis", where he emphasized that words in our language can influence our cognition.[59] His research would have yielded a better understanding if he had taken a neuropsychological dimension and flowcharts/mathematical modelling.

---

[59] Benjamin Lee Whorf was a US linguist and fire prevention engineer.

Local Languages, Solidarism, and Culture

I have watched teachers whipping pupils because they speak vernaculars or simply their local languages and dialects. I do not welcome this because the problem is ours, not for the children. We failed to design an education system that prioritizes our dialects and local languages. We have many children who fail subjects such as sciences simply because they are unfamiliar with the terminologies used. It is always good to explain a concept in a language that all people can listen to and understand.

In many regions around Africa, people who can speak Arabic, English, French, or any other foreign language fluently are viewed as the most brilliant; this is not true. The lack of confidence in our dialects and local languages breeds fear and anxiety in many children while speaking them in public. Languages like Kiswahili and Luganda in East Africa, Berbers in North and West Africa, Hausa in Central Africa, Amharic in Ethiopia, Ndebele, Zulu and Afrikaans of South Africa and many more would be taught to students at all levels. With the many local languages spoken across the continent, a consensus to use these languages in schools and colleges would be agreed upon. Conceptualizing something requires the use of local languages first. Thinking can better be stimulated when we use local languages. Originality begins when one has understood.

The symbolic interactionism philosophy in which social construction of meaning is rooted for a given native society is based on the assumption that native languages and dialects are adopted to make images. The meaning and better understanding of reality come through semantics. Semantics refers to the meaning of a text, phrase or word. Most children and many older people in Africa use dialects 9 in 10 of their time, at home and while at work. In addition, we learn dialects or local languages in infancy, and even instincts pull us to learn unconscious behaviours. The infancy and early childhood is a formative time because many researchers have argued that we are a product of the first five years. Suppose one's infancy is characterized by the use of local language or dialects and goes ahead to learn in a foreign language only 1 in 10 of their time at school. In that case, this must slightly impact the outcome, especially the ability to think of innovative solutions at a cognitive development stage. The brain needs to take off some microseconds in translation from the foreign language to the dialect and vice-versa to fast-track meaning.

With the differing levels of dissociation within brain faculties, an explanation for why one could forget not because of interference or decayed past information, the correct meaning gets lost along the way. The brain plays many functions, i.e. auditory, sensory, motor, movement, visual, spatial, emotion, and many more. All people dissociate in the brain faculties at some point. Teaching a child in a foreign language while the child spends 9 in 10 of the time at home using a dialect interferes with the brain's ability to process visual information and subsequent registration of such information onto the memory. The brain wastes much time constructing meaning from the images and processing the meaning into other meanings for proper understanding. In many times, the continued construction and deconstruction of meanings take on false meanings because of the slight levels of dissociation in brain faculties. Why do we keep on using foreign languages to teach children, especially in the *formative years?*

I have seen many students feeling shy to speak their dialects. Where does the problem come from? The problem arises from the fact that foreign languages are prioritized to appear as the only ones that can convey a message more appropriately and that our local languages and dialects cannot make points clear.

To forge a route for development means focusing on what you love and emphasizing what can bring people together. You have to focus on excelling locally first and then think of excelling across borders. This means you have to strengthen development metrics at home by exploiting all resources you have. In our schools, the local languages resource is not exploited. If you promote science subjects in schools, why not promote them in local languages so that everybody can understand what you teach? The target is to make all understand.

When you restrict the study to only a foreign language, some people might be left out. And when one fails to understand the language, this person is more likely to fail to understand mathematics. If one fails to understand mathematics, they are likely to fail to understand science disciplines because the creative energy of science resides in mathematics. When one fails to understand, they are left to cram and learn something for the sake of passing the examination—and these are the majority of graduates we have.

> Nurturing pupils how to use logic to solve abstract problems at the right cognitive development stage is crucial. We must reexamine an integrated approach but not wound our children by restricting them to learn in foreign languages only. The age between 6–12 years is the stage for shaping the child's correct cognitive and moral development path. The education ministries should study a relationship between moral development theories and cognitive development theories before passing policies on educating or punishing misbehaving children—punishments not well-thought-out affect the child's intellectual, physical, and emotional growth.

If possible, part of the solution is to create a version of all subjects in our local languages and dialects at nursery, primary and secondary levels. I have experienced many cases where a student passes but fails to understand the concept because of cramming. Everybody may get the pass mark, but the point is to understand. We go to school to understand the world around us but not to simply pass. By instilling confidence in our local languages, students shall interact freely without fear to express themselves, and it encourages more discussions with their peers and people outside the classroom.

During my undergraduate study in the University, I heard a coursemate whispering to a colleague in their dialect. I was surprised because the response he received was unpleasant. He was advised only to speak their dialect when they were in their villages of Soroti in Uganda. To me, this did not please me at all. It only showed me how enslaved my coursemate had become to a foreign language. Most of our dialects are enriched with good and meaningful proverbs and sayings. These aphorisms help to instil morals, beliefs, and values in our people. Many habits that contradict the African values have been introduced to the African community from other parts of the world through foreign languages. Therefore, maintaining and extending our languages would protect our identity and values.

To be an educated person, you need to have a strong moral fabric. Strong moral fabrics are manufactured in family settings. Can we shoot patriotism when we are losing identity? Can we shoot patriotism when we are losing our local languages and dialects? Schools are responsible for maintaining, extending and growing our languages and dialects but instead abandon the role. Should we leave our dialects and local languages to die? Will this stimulate self-driven sustainable development? How will we maintain our cultural values? Sometimes I wonder whether Africans who draw curriculums are sober enough. Our cultures have strong moral fabrics rooted in politeness.

In the past, children learned at home before the modern school system was introduced in the land. The trend has since shifted, and our children are spending more time in schools. We need to introduce solidarity and patriotism lessons in schools to raise a fully educated person, not half-baked. Can we do it effectively without integrating dialects and local languages that store cultural predispositions on which patriotism attributes are founded? Social solidarity and cultural norms, values, self-awareness courses in children and adolescents must be emphasized in schools to lead sustainability. A curriculum free of such courses lacks sustainability goals. Learning where you are coming from and the genesis of the words and their meanings contains wisdom our children ought to learn. I cannot believe that our ancestors who spent many *thousands of years* on this beautiful continent were hopeless—that all the construction of meaning they held in their languages proves hopeless in the modern-day. With this kind of hopelessness, how sure are we that we align well with sustainable development goals?

Although ever since colonial masters left, many countries have moved in the dark, failing to recreate an education system that can enable people to think—we had a foundation to design our education system. I am convinced that you cannot do more to think, dream, create, recreate, innovate and invent in a foreign language. Unless you have been a foreign inhabitant in the jurisdiction of a foreign language for long, a case of the African-Americans in the USA, you automatically adopt the foreign language for several behavioural and cognitive issues. But still, instincts are a powerful source of unconscious forces that drive our day to day behaviours—nature. Instincts still shape our cognition and the perception of the environment around us.

Educated African men and women can design an education system that grows our dialects and local languages. The reason for the failure to do so is perhaps the illusion of knowledge described earlier. Killing local languages also distorts tourism. African ancestors coined a proverb, "It is the young trees that strengthen the forest." Every foundation for anything has to be laid in the formative years. For example, a European visiting Africa wishes to experience the uniqueness by hearing locals speak their dialects and local languages, making specific explanations on tourist sites by deriving meaning from dialects—and creating an impression that the value of this tourist item is rooted in the dialect.

Most of the historical sites which bring us more tourists each year have stories surrounding their existence for many hundreds or thousands of years ago. The meaning of these stories is rooted in social constructionism revolving around the communication used for the many years they have been in existence. Because modern education has been in Africa for not more than 200 years, we seem to find no need to preserve this meaning correctly. I am emphasizing this because many African graduates hardly speak their local languages yet search for jobs without limit. They resort to slang instead. This does not lead to sustainable development, and it is also not good news for the owners of the languages we praise.

"It is the young trees that strengthen the forest." African Baganda Proverb

As far as the struggle to make all students understand but not just to shoot the pass mark is concerned, there are three things to emphasize in the school system: teach children to document their lives and their work right from school; promote local languages and dialects for all-round inclusivity, and; promote the "no one is dull solidarity." Africa needs a thorough understanding of inclusivity and the needs of special education. Inclusive and quality education forms the foundation of a sustainable education system.

Inclusion, associated with diversity, is the foundation of a quality education system that can live on for many generations. Ideas that do not leave out ancestral assets, women, disabled people, and disordered people are the benchmark to lead a sustainable education.

The scope of special education in Africa needs to be reviewed and widened. We have many disorders not brought to book. We need an African diagnostic manual of mental and personality disorders specifically for Sub-Saharan Africa. This can help to reach more students that need special education. Special needs interventions are designed to help students with special needs achieve a higher level of personal self-sufficiency. This cannot be possible when disabled and disordered students are only given access to typical classroom education. Through special education, the student gains more success in school and their community. For example, social phobia and panic disorders' prevalence is high in African children, although a few specialized studies are conducted to give the exact figures in the land.

Panic disorders in children sometimes are a result of whipping children for speaking vernaculars at school. This makes them feel low self-esteem. Others feel shy when they speak broken English, French, or German in schools. This predisposes, precipitates, and perpetuates panic disorders in children. I am convinced that the story would be different if we left children to love their languages and designed curriculums that grow our dialects and local languages. Let us learn to love ourselves, at least in this 21st century. We need to be kind to ourselves!

Increased primary school dropouts may be attributed to a lack of addressing some of these disorders properly. Therefore, the African manual of disorders yet to be designed will culminate into an assessment criteria for promoting students who need special care to do what they feel capable of. If the life documentation practice is taught to children right from primary through secondary and promotion of local languages is done, specially trained teachers then do the career guidance in line with what the student wants to be.

The present education system pushes students to become whatever is there simply because it is designed to make some students categorically appear dull. Things like subjects so and so are compulsory should not be allowed in an excellent education system. In my view, it is only the solidarity classes that are meant to instil patriotism in our children that should be made mandatory, maybe. However, these solidarity lessons should not be politicized because Africa has faced partisan politics in most states for a long time. These lessons should not be confused with the indoctrination ideologies for partisan politicking of the present-day long-serving leaders in most African states. The lessons should be in the same queue, similar to other lessons, neutral with a common purpose for all.

When teachers deliver science subjects in local languages, students can quickly relate what they see every day to what they study in class. There is no need for making them mandatory in lower secondary. Remember doing something out of love always defeats doing it out of fear. Some local languages or dialects on which culture rotates are rich enough to have corresponding scientific terminologies. The teaching in local languages and dialects is long overdue.

Education, Beliefs, Values, and Culture

It has now become a norm to describe good mannered people as "villagers" in many societies across Africa—and one who imports foreign hair from anywhere around the globe onto her head labelled as a "city born" or a "dotcom" person. Those are the kind of beliefs an Africa child goes out of school with. African moral schools vested much power and authority in elders. Respect for elders is a strong African value, from the south to the north of Africa. This nurtured emotional intelligence in a sense that when elders counselled and guided the young people, the young generation could not fight back—they could hold their emotions, however much the issue may be intolerable. However, today, the norm is changing because of our developments; children learn to be assertive even in the wrong positions/situations.

Today, it has become the order of the day to see young politicians attacking legends ungentlemanly and in a foolish style without scrutinizing what they ejaculate or utter out—because, in many times, their under-thought-out ideas are not well assessed before speaking. This is the kind of education we are receiving in weak democracies and where vernacular literacies are abused. They are fruits of weak democracy and freedom of expression that suppresses norms, traditions, and good deeds from our ancestors.

A morally right person who has undergone proper civic and political education and training cannot attack a legend in a way that fantasizes and disrespects—however much he did politically unamusing stuff, he is worth recognizable for his good deeds. There are many right ways to address someone 40+ years older than you. If we defined our education system, our politics would be a little bit different. The picture one portrays to the young generation is that everyone can be attacked anyhow, which breeds emotional upsets because some elders still cherish those values. I believe one gains more respect and power when he behaves descent in their stand for what they believe without falsely attacking the legends.

The effect of dropping our cultural sentiments favouring nationalistic sentiments has resulted in some countries enacting unnecessary laws such as laws against the LGBT community. Before you make laws for LGBT, revisit women empowerment because they are both rooted in the same argument—social construction of meaning.[60] Women empowerment is rooted in the theory that gender and sexuality are socially constructed; the theory is also valid for the LGBT community. This disbands the biological facts taking on the nurture end of the spectrum from the larger nature and nurture debate. A man can be a woman, or a woman can be a man depending on how society constructs meaning. However, what makes you a father and not a man is what makes a mother, not a woman. The best solution is to give the LGBT community peace and freedom to enjoy the contemporary legal fiction of one as it happens in some developed states. Discriminating the community would be more of an affront, and endless questions about women empowerment and other marginalized groups would emerge.

In many cultures, sexual immorality is prohibited, and if such is adhered to, there is no need for specialized laws targeting specific communities. This fact has existed in the ancient world, and no laws were enacted accordingly. This is learnt from the biblical history of Sodom and Gomorrah in that perspective. Human developmental stages explicitly demonstrate the coexistence of several facts. Several psychosocial and psychosexual theorists explored the genesis. We need to take time to understand the cause. From environmental/social factors, nature, and nurture.

---

[60] See §6

The earlier stages in development necessitate more care and parental love—and it is difficult to penetrate and disintegrate a morally upright, culturally strong, and educated person because they are already triggered by default to follow particular norms and values. Sigmund Freud (1923 – 1963) emphasized the importance of doing an "archaeological dig" to determine the early reasons for current behaviours. We must piece together from both past and contemporary theorists to promote and sustain what we culturally believe. The debate on the LGBT community is unnecessary, and it requires no attention in the African land. We must give the community freedom and equal rights.

However, because our education system lacks cultural assets as a foundation to raise people of strong moral fabric, we cannot keep our position on the topic. The community has the freedom to enjoy its rights. Those who brought us conventional religions associated with modern education are changing their goalposts on the LGBT community to contradict many African religious leaders. This means instincts are already pulling African religious leaders to where they belong. There is no need for specialized fights to sustain the truth; a lie is unsustainable. The point is obvious now—an education system that is not foreign—a system that is ours. That is what we need to fit within the sustainability framework.

"Truth needs no law to support it. Truth is self-evident to all. Truth withstands re-examination. Truth survives questions. Throughout history, from Galileo to Zundel, only lies and liars have resorted to the courts to enforce adherence to dogma." Michael Rivero

The African Weak Data Collection and Documentation Culture as a Product of the Education System

There are many uneducated people doing things in Africa but not knowing why they do them. It has come to my notice that many practices and activities done in ancient Africa were done without people noticing why they were doing them or why they were happening. Some activities had scientific explanations, but people could not find out why and make documentation—and this remains a serious problem in Africa—many people lack the zeal to document facts. This is one of the reasons why all discoveries in Africa are connected to the European colonialists, e.g. the lakes, rivers and mountains. Interestingly, these are named after the white settlers. One is left wondering whether it is true that lakes and rivers, for example, River Nile, the longest river in the world, is believed to have been discovered by John Hanning Speke, and no Africans had seen this river before John Speke. The hopeless thing is that we are still teaching our children that Europeans discovered African lakes and rivers.

Of recent, there has been a debate about who takes the discovery; the first person to file about the discovery or one who actually makes the discovery. The one who files about the discovery might take the credit as the discoverer. This is similar to ideas. You can never sue someone for reaping from your ideas unless you have enough evidence. You have to act on your ideas. The vital issue is acting responsibly and smart as appropriate, all the time and in time. Therefore, documentation is a crucial lesson we need to learn.

Africa has lagged in many spheres for its inadequate data collection and storage. In the modern information age, we need to archive data daily. Improving the future needs to rely on the past; engineers, scientists and many others need past data to improve the world. One of the biggest challenges our scientists and engineers face in Africa is inadequate data and sometimes no data or information. A majority of our museums have scanty records—typical of Sub-Saharan Africa. Record keeping is critical to have a successful and sustainable society. Inadequate data has made the application of time series analyses too difficult in Africa, creating too many sophisticated models that require highly talented and skilful scientists to solve.

Data has no definite price tag. When one needs the records, data, or information, they can pay the price even though exorbitant because they have no alternative. Leonardo da Vinci's Mona Lisa artefact was valued at about US$ 100million in 1962, equivalent to about $870 million in 2021. In 2017, Leonardo da Vinci painting sold for $450m at auction.[61] Of recent, I bought videos and photos of my late great grandfather of the fourth generation at an exorbitant price. Such videos have no market price. My fellow engineer, Robert Kasule, sold US$ 340m cable-stay bridge project videos at an exorbitant price. As a site inspector, he endeavoured to shoot videos using his camera at every stage of the project. In the construction process, the contractor was required to provide evidence of employing skilled people, complying with standards and regulations, following procedures, and meeting the project's specifications at all stages. In some sections of the project, the contractor had not laboured to shoot enough videos. These videos formed the basis on which his payments were approved. As the inspector of works, my friend Robert had taken the initiative to shoot all stages of the project, and he was the only person to rely upon to sort the contractual dilemma between the consultant and contractor. If you were Robert, how much price would you have charged the contractor well, knowing that nobody else had the information? And there was a claim that the contractor had used materials not meeting standards and specifications at that stage and therefore needed to demolish and rework.

The Jigsaw Concept

The education system that works must be built on the jigsaw concept (see figure below). A well-designed course is like a jigsaw whose units must fit into one another. It is defined when units are interdependent. Many students take subjects and courses that do not jigsaw at A' levels and university, respectively. Such subject combinations which do not influence each other cannot yield a wholesomely well-individuated educated person. Combination of subjects like; Agriculture, literature and history may be hazardous to the candidate in the long run.

Similarly, what is taught at a lower level should make a strong foundation for higher or later studies. The jigsaw concept is not to be made devoid; it has a complete message it sends. Things are not disjointed; people make them appear disjointed. Educators should nurture systems thinking and how to view things as a whole. Many students at advanced level studies need proper career guidance to match their chosen subjects.

---

[61] Edward Helmore, "Leonardo da Vinci painting sells for $450m at auction, smashing records: Christie's sells long-lost Salvator Mundi, artwork billed as 'biggest discovery of the 21st century', for $400m plus auction house premium," The Guardian, November 16th 2017, accessed on August 31st 2021, https://www.theguardian.com/artanddesign/2017.

The Jigsaw

What is a Sign of Good Education?

The capacity to formulate and express ideas well is a sign of good education. One of the indicators of a failed education system is how African scientists fail to lead solutions to Africa's problems. I prioritize science in this narrative because developed nations sustain progress by scientific means. Idea formulation and expression by several African scientists is a problem. Good ideas are always simplistic and not very complicated. The ability to simplify ideas is a sign of quality education; the tendency to view things as impossible and very difficult is a sign of bad education. A good education makes ideas look simple. The underlying assumption is a likely illusion in how we nurture knowledge and understanding of science in the education system. An education system dominated by a theoretical emphasis and few practical science lessons for learners in their childhood and adolescent stages, i.e. in primary and secondary schools, perpetuates the problem. I have a strong hypothesis that many science teachers in several secondary schools across Africa do not clearly understand core principles well enough. The reason is that they have had little interaction with industry experience to bring life to classrooms. We gain knowledge and understanding of science through observation and experiments. It is not easy to lead scientific discoveries and applications primarily by theoretical means.

Does Our Education System Test Memory or Intelligence?

The education system which examines and grades more of one's memory capacity rather than categorizing *potential differences/uniqueness in intelligence* across learners perpetuates Africa's problem. Schools accredit achievement, not grouping intelligence. Paulo Freire (1921–1997) referred to such an education system as a "banking education system".[62]

---

[62] In the banking education system, the learner is the object of the learning process, but not the subject. In this process, the knowledge is consumed without any criticism, and the learners experience a cultural alienation and become defenseless against cultural imperialism.

The education system should be designed to stimulate maximum use of fluid intelligence, thereby making children's brain faculties produce maximum output. I hypothesize that the productivity level in using the brain faculties for an average adolescent and graduate on the African continent is about 10%. The remaining fraction lies idle as they grow through their lives. In other words, African children do not reach their potential to use their brains to innovate, invent and develop new ideas because the education system does not train them how to do it. The education system primarily examines the extent to which our memories can store information. It fails to nurture children to innovate, invent and develop novel ideas to improve the world.

Utilizing the childhood and adolescent stages is essential because the ability to learn and invent or innovate new strategies to deal with novel sets of problems peaks around that time. As one grows, they become more experienced and specialized within specific areas, thus solving familiar problems with previously learned skills and knowledge. Unfortunately, the education system does not support the stimulation of fluid intelligence well enough.

Upon this background, I cannot let the education system that tests memory predetermine my destiny. My life cannot be predetermined by others setting for me memory testing questions; I set myself the right questions and live finding the right solutions to these problems. The correct education should be restructured to shape students' thinking. It matters less to excel or not to excel in school. However, passing is essential. I do not believe in others judging me, particularly a few instructors, from the questions they make for me, especially on how strong my memory can go. I have to set myself the right questions and live the rest of my life answering those questions. That is what counts. The entire world judges you from what you make of yourself but not from what a few instructors you meet in schools and colleges judged you, i.e., memory strength. Intuition is the highest form of intelligence, and it is not in the conscious. It is an instinctual ability we all possess in varying levels, the results of which become conscious at some point. A highly intuitive mind many times correlates with a creative mind. However, our education system has not laboured to experiment with this fact.

Education That Stimulates Thinking

The current education system does not encourage students to learn how to think to solve problems in society. Yet, the 21st-century requires such skills. The 21st-century skills are designed to promote higher-order thinking. Higher-order thinking skills enable the student's memory to be used *effectively*. Analytical thinking is a skill that is not learned by sitting in the classroom and being told how to do it. According to Dr Benjamin Bloom's theory of 1956, there are six levels of critical thinking, i.e., Knowledge, Comprehension, Application, Analysis, Synthesis, and Evaluation. Higher-Order Thinking only occurs from the stages of analyzing, evaluating and creating. Bloom called remembering facts "rote learning"; it dominates Africa's "just-for-passing exams" school culture.

Spending more than seventeen years in school would ideally imply a change in somebody's thinking. The Chinese say, "He who learns but does not think is lost." A graduate should strive to show a positive change in their thinking and way of doing things by being creative and innovative. Graduates might not need to wait for jobs to be creative. There is always room to integrate information and knowledge acquired in college to change our societies positively. One just has to start where they are with the little they have.

The education system is promoting more burdens and creating messes for half-baked graduates. Some people who got the opportunity to go to school became more of a liability than their counterparts, i.e. the unlearned. Many students graduate from colleges and universities thinking they understood because they graduated with excellent grades but only to disappoint the world. Excelling in school and winning a job is not enough. It only benefits the one holding the job.

To *positively change* how to do things creates the difference between the educated and the uneducated. A holistic output from an excelling candidate that benefits society is what counts most but not his credentials. To excel outside class is what is worth celebrating. Touching the lives of others is what makes you worth living. Having it on paper and not on the ground is equivalent to dreaming. The way things are working matters most than how they ought to work. For example, having too much knowledge that you do not use to solve problems cannot garner your professionalism. Professionalism is doing.

Not implementing the acquired knowledge leaves no room other than manipulating the unlearnt. The unlearnt should be supported by the learnt. And the learnt should be educated well-enough to make sense out of their efforts. One's efforts are only efforts worth celebrating if they are out of paper and become tangible. Anyone can learn the language, but the one who codes the things excels and becomes the master. To excellently learn the language is not enough, and it is not enough to have enough. To catch space in real-time, one needs to have belittled contentment and avoids succumbing to academic complacency. The education that can stimulate thinking along those lines is what Africa needs.

The categorical education system focuses on cram work rather than problem-solving and training people how to think disadvantages others who would instead get more familiar going with hands-on and creative approaches. The fact that teachers teach children in foreign languages leaves out those without the ability to learn the language quickly and those with specific learning disorders. They take a long time to memorize foreign languages. I think the modern world has now favoured the ease to use our dialects and local languages in teaching. This can help students who find it hard to understand scientific and other terminologies quickly grasp the concepts using dialects. Our curriculums should be redesigned to promote the use of dialects and local languages at all levels to be more inclusive. People with disabilities are not only those who are physically disabled. There are many other disorders in the African context which current diagnostic manuals of mental disorders have not yet brought to book. This is because Africans are failing to innovate and develop practical solutions for the industry despite excelling academically. It is an indicator of something wrong.

The idea of integrating concepts or disciplines to create or make improvement is not adequately taught in schools. Those who have laboured to improve the existing phenomenon or created new products or services were only enthusiastic and curious. The basic principles taught at lower levels in our education system are enough to open one's mind to start strategic thinking in concept expounding and development. Elsewhere, the concepts only get specialized and find themselves practical applications. This is something that we need to understand. The level of modelling concepts is thought to be for post-doctoral scholars, which I think is for everyone who understands what they are doing. Once you understand a cocktail of concepts, try to fix them up and act on them.

The best innovations are simplistic and do not come from sophisticated ideas or concepts, and straightforward ideas sometimes make the best innovations. The best songs are composed of simple words. Excelling artists, musicians, and innovators are minimalists. To innovate is entirely different from discovery and invention. Improving the existing systems, services, and products or processes is the order of the modern world. In the modern world, there are as more discoveries as inventions and innovations.

In the interest of sustainable development, we need people trained to think to innovate because there is almost nothing completely new under the sun. Innovations are stimulated when one master the power of addition, subtraction, multiplication, and division but not sophisticated arithmetic or scientific hypotheses. If someone invents a machine that can read what the next person is thinking would ideally be the best invention of the modern world, and I would call this a completely new process. Observing people's behaviours to read their minds and feelings, a concept developed by psychologists, is less accurate. Emotionally competent and highly trained people are too smart. Lie detectors or polygraphs are not smart enough; they are biased to validate or nullify the evidence foretold. We need a machine to read the person's thought patterns.

There is widespread modern-day deception, and Africa needed such a machine that reads people's thought patterns. Africa has fallen too much of a victim of modern-day deception in international relations, politics, and natural resources governance. *"Strategy" needs people who can see through walls.* Although around June 2016, a team of scientists from the University of Oregon in the USA claimed to have invented a system that can read people's thoughts via brain scans and reconstruct the faces they were visualizing in their heads, this is not what is needed to track modern-day deception.[63] They claimed to have developed a step towards reading one's thoughts and putting them on a screen for everyone to see. The machine which is required to track modern-day deception does not come in direct contact with the specimen. It would be used to correlate someone's speech, facial expressions, and body language with neurological theories.

Grading in Schools: Criterion-referencing versus Norm-referencing

The teaching method by working out problems from first principles in science disciplines, especially in secondary schools, is slowly getting phased out due to the mushrooming private schools who are after reaping highly from their businesses but care less about the future of our countries. This is because the future's human capital is central to strengthen the three pillars of sustainable development. This method exposed students to creativity and critical thinking. We have now just for passing exams, with lots of pamphlets published for students to read and pass.

In some countries, private schools are propelling examination boards to use the criterion-referenced interpretation of children's results. This is usually done in universities. Criterion-referencing remains suitable for universities because they task students with coursework, continuous assessment tests, attendance marks, and presentations. In most cases, the student works at not more than 60% in the final examination. In case those assessments are scrapped, the criterion-referenced interpretation would not yield the same results. In universities, preparations for the final examinations through those assessments I have mentioned are fair and justifiable using criterion-referenced interpretation. Some examination

---

[63] BECCREW, "Scientists Have Invented a Mind-Reading Machine That Visualizes Your Thoughts," Science Alert, June 23rd 2016. https://www.sciencealert.com/scientists-have-invented-a-mind-reading-machine-that-can-visualise-your-thoughts-kind-of.

boards are starting to set standard scales for grades too way high. This is not because the children understand better today than in the past but because they *learn more about passing exams,* raising the bar for passing. This *"learning how to pass"* but not *"learning to pass"* or *"passing to learn"* is what influences examination boards to dream of *fixed references* (criterion-referenced) to grade candidates in secondary and primary schools.

Criterion-referenced interpretation of results would have a minor positive impact on pre-primary, primary and secondary school children because children have one chance to sit for final examinations. Besides, this stage is a sensitive stage that requires continuous performance analysis because children are undergoing cognitive and moral stages of development. It might not be excellent to fix a standard grading. Children still need extraordinary care to understand their uniqueness. Each child is different from another. Africa is in a stage of emerging, faced with several crises. These range from; political problems, mindset problems, natural disasters, civil wars, and the refugee crisis. All these influence the ability of our children to study effectively.

Criterion-referenced interpretation of results instils intense anxiety in private schools; hence, teaching to pass but not to understand. This fixed domain referenced interpretation of results to obtain the absolute true position of every child would instead promote exam malpractices. It is still better to go norm-referencing while interpreting examination results for a large population of children. This is because final examinations are administered once for primary and secondary school children, which provides no room for the candidate to improve. Once they do the paper—that is all. Administering a test only once to the child has the following shortcomings;

a) The conditions of testing, i.e., time of giving the test, emotional condition of the test taker (e.g., fatigue and sickness), and length of the test.

b) Socioeconomic factors, i.e., the welfare of many children, are not guaranteed to have a clear and relaxed mind for the examinations. Most children in Sub-Saharan Africa go hungry in schools.

These two factors and many others that affect the outcome of an examination administered once makes criterion-referenced interpretation of results for school children improper. Attempts to conduct half-split reliability between continuous assessments and final examinations of university students scheduled for graduation in Sub-Saharan African universities to obtain the internal consistency coefficients might help remove the doubt—whether to go by criterion-referenced interpretation or remain focusing on norm-referencing for pre-primary, primary and secondary school children. It can be indicative.

Note: In criterion-referenced assessment, objectives would be set by the examination board. They would be fixed for a certain period, e.g. 10 years. These objectives would include a standard curriculum and a fixed scale for grading results. Each year, candidates would be graded following the standard scale fixed not until when it is reviewed. However, in norm-referenced assessment, a candidate's results would be presented in relation to the performance of others for each year. This normative information generated every year would be used to design and improve the learning objectives, assessments and activities for the coming batch of candidates.

Some countries like Singapore are moving away from ranking children in schools. This would be an excellent strategy. However, in Africa, this seems premature. The continuous assessments that contribute to the final primary leaving examinations in primary and secondary schools proposed by developmental agencies might be resource-consuming in developing African countries. They can bring about heavy coursework/take-home exercises that poverty-ridden African territories cannot handle hence children dropping out of school. The socioeconomic dilemma is a component of the psychosocial dilemma; socioeconomic wellbeing highly influences the child's psychosocial status. During the final evaluations, poverty-ridden children might have many coursework/takehome missing results or gaps. Sometimes, disadvantaged children skip some classes to cope with the dilemmas of school/family life. In my opinion, continuous assessments are suitable for university and tertiary college students.

Health, Safety, and Welfare in Schools

Several governments' budgets allocated to health, safety, and welfare in schools is sometimes inadequate because of the financing crises we live in. We always miss out on nurturing better people because of the poor environments and circumstances while in school. These predetermine the psychosocial wellbeing for the students and children while in colleges and schools, respectively.

Tackling the sustainable development challenge requires incorporating health, safety, and welfare lessons in schools and colleges. We need physical education, courses in nutrition and psychology, and we need more on sports and entertainment. Good nutrition contributes to the children's psychosocial and emotional wellbeing, cognitive and moral development. Teachers can teach children how to; keep fit; encourage cycling to schools, helping with home activities, and working out to reduce obesity. Educators should develop schools designed with enough space for; bike parks, walkways, green spaces, enough trees, gardens, courtyards, football pitches, basketball courts, etcetera. Schools can reinforce the cycling culture by giving rewards to outstanding children.

Some sustainable drainage systems developed on the school campus, such as stormwater micro-parks, green spaces, planting trees, and bio-retention gardens would facilitate learning. These interventions can reduce greenhouse gases by absorbing carbon dioxide, capture urban air pollutants such as dust and carbon monoxide.

For our education to be more inclusive, we need to support the girl child as much as possible. We need to design strategies to reduce the number of girls that drop out of school. Some of the interventions we need to reduce the number of girls dropping out of school include increased access to hygiene and sanitary services, e.g. provision of sanitary pads. We would also ensure the provision of adequate toilets, bathrooms, clean dining areas, and changing rooms, among others.

Heavy commercialization of education has seen many schools failing to meet the minimum safety, health, and welfare requirements. Several schools in the urban areas lack enough space for enough co-curricular activities, which is not good news for children/students of the 21st century. The 21st-century educators should emphasise health, safety, and welfare, and it is proving more important today than yesterday!

Educated Versus Learned

The higher you get educated, the humble you should become. If your education makes you proud to blow your own horn, you have probably not learnt and mastered anything because you must understand the source of people's problems. If you have not understood the source of people's problems, you should find alternative ways for schooling yourself and grow your intellect much better. An educated person understands why people should be given jobs than free things. People need to get busy to make ends meet, and anyone who provides free things to non-refugees does no better than one who creates jobs for them. Understanding why some people are poor and others are rich is a must for one who claims to be educated.

What Should Guide Elective and Compulsory Units in Schools?

It sounds weird for a county whose backbone is agriculture, and this country makes agriculture an elective subject in schools. It is tricky viewing it from a sustainable development perspective. Much as all nations wish to lead in technology and science, we have many distortions to fix prior. We observe how our scientists, engineers, and environmentalists fail to innovate new approaches and systems to develop our societies; then, we design what would be compulsory. Educators should design our curriculums following the sustainability framework. What should be electives and compulsory subjects for children to take on? Following the jigsaw concept guided by the sustainability framework, we reach a decision. A country whose backbone is agriculture should not miss agriculture as a compulsory subject, perhaps.

Teaching Versus Lecturing: What Should Be the Criteria?

Many can lecture, but few can really teach. All candidates vying for lecturing in universities and other tertiary institutions ought to learn modern pedagogy to qualify as lecturers. Many lecturers are taken based on academic excellence only. Yet not only academic excellence is vital in educating people. I still believe that getting closer to understand each student's uniqueness is essential no matter which level. Technological innovations like interactive platforms could be tried to address the ever-increasing big classes—but understanding each student's abilities is paramount. Sometimes, highly intelligent people do not make the best lecturers or teachers because of viewing things simplistically. Yes, lecturing calls for high academic achievers so that students are not misled, but teaching may not. However, a balance has to be obtained between talent, skill and ability.

I have a friend who is now both a trained teacher and a university lecturer. He once said, "When I had just started teaching mathematics in primary before I became a qualified teacher, I used to ask the pupils questions that required subtracting numbers. It was not until when a colleague advised me to use the phrase *"take away"* that pupils began to understand what I meant."

Similarly, in universities, we have both introverted and extroverted students—and the degree of extroversion differs from student to student. Sometimes, the former find it difficult to seek clarification where they fail to understand during lecture sessions. They fear that their questions are irrelevant and not worth asking. Others are simply shy and cannot talk or express themselves well. They usually ask their colleagues for clarity when lecture sessions end. The highly extroverted students dominate the question-answer sessions, no matter whether the questions they ask are relevant or not. What solution have we made to address these challenges, or do we simply ignore them?

Throughout my lecture sessions in the university, I did not come across a lecturer who dared to address introvert-extrovert student challenges while lecturing. At the age between 18 to 23 years, some students are still young and might need special attention, and this is a stage when they move from adolescence to early adulthood. I do not find it summing up to claim that you automatically mature once you enter the university. In a bid to change Africa, we need lecturers who are real educators, not moneymakers. Lecturers who have understood what teaching entails—at least, they should have the basics of teaching.

We have separately designated facilities for people with disabilities in buildings and associated infrastructure because we understood the uniqueness of people and paid attention to this uniqueness to create fairness. Every part of Africa has quick introverted learners and introverted slow learners, and the latter category is in dire need of attention. Modern pedagogy aims at putting the learner at the centre of the learning process. We can embrace the use of digital technologies appropriately in class during learning sessions to encourage more introverted slow learners to ask for clarification in time. This can be done by creating an interactive platform that allows students to message or text. This is in the bid to pay attention to introverted students.

In most cases, what worsens the situation is the old-fashioned method of dictating notes, which is still in use today in several African institutions. You might not believe that we still have lecturers that dictate notes. A good lecturer should lecture and leave the students to make their notes, and it should be a two-way approach. The lecturer should leave ample time for students to ask questions and guide them on formulating correct notes. At some point, the lecturer should mark the notes as part of the continuous assessment.

I would, therefore, encourage each school, university, college or department, to conduct *personality tests* to check on the extroversion levels of their classes for better planning purposes. This promotes understanding and limits too much cram work, primarily characteristic of many modern private institutions. Since we are adopting 21st-century skills for global competitiveness, we need to address the bottlenecks by tackling all diversity issues. Several scholars have said that self-discovered knowledge sticks more than knowledge received through teaching. Today's knowledge is in "the open",, i.e. on the internet, websites, open educational resources, et cetera. Nobody is a custodian of knowledge in the 21st century. We need to accelerate a shift from *teacher-centred learning* to *student-centred learning*. Embracing digital technologies is vital to tackle several bottlenecks, including introverted slow learners and disabled ones. Therefore, when the instructor leaves students to make their notes, they allow them to research, promoting better understanding.

On Modern Teaching Pedagogy

If we embrace our dialects appropriately, the sky is the limit because children might find it healthy to relate with their colleagues freely. In addition, we need extensive use of visual aids in learning. All Children can benefit from using visual aids and especially those who fit into the following categories: (a) those with learning difficulties, (b) oppositional defiant disorder, (c) hearing impairment, (d) attention deficit hyperactivity disorder, (e) language disorders and delays, (f) development delay, down-syndrome and an autism spectrum disorder.

Visual aids are essential in making children and adolescents understand. However, they are not widely used in Africa. Where they are present, the visual aids are specifically designed for a category of children highlighted above, especially in lower primaries. Yet, I believe they are relevant to all children, especially science subjects taught in foreign languages. When you teach with a picture, artefact, symbol, image, chart or an illustration, video/audio recordings, the child is more likely to interact with the teacher. Visual aids communicate instantly. Visual aids are shortcuts of expression with dozens of meanings in one object. It increases the chances of understanding and not cramming the subject under discussion.

If Africa needs to register accelerated growth in learning science disciplines in schools, we should not overlook visual aids as a tool for effective learning. In a study conducted by Peter Okidi Lating of Makerere University in 2009 where he used longitudinal analysis on the hybrid e-learning for rural secondary schools, he noted that the hybrid e-learning was found to contribute 64% of a student's scores in advanced level physics practicals, making it a very viable proposition for disadvantaged rural schools. His research was conducted in two typical rural girls' advanced level secondary schools, Ediofe and Muni, in the rural district of Arua in Uganda. In his study, the professor's central content delivery platform was the interactive CD-ROMS that were developed based on the local curriculum. Today, more advanced *digital technologies* are available. These can enhance the children's understanding.

The habit of teachers rushing directly to teaching the core concept notes for the subject matter is not very appropriate. For example, if a teacher teaches physics to students in lower secondary, why not have a clear introductory chapter on how physics evolved and its importance in society. The child needs to know why they are studying the subject. How did physics evolve? Who is the father of physics? Why do we study physics, and what does it solve? Where is physics applied? Etcetera., so that children get to know why they are learning the subject. In this way, children will love the subject and get to know why they are doing it. What is happening in many curriculums as a stepping stone is; what is physics? Very few "whys" are unlocked in the present education system—teachers rarely labour to provide introductory chapters on how science/physics evolved and who the prominent physics scientists are. You need to explain to children for some contact hours why they need to study physics and what it solves, and how it evolved—telling children that physics is this and that might not instil the love for the subject within themselves. The same applies to mathematics and other disciplines.

Several mathematics teachers teach mathematics without knowing how to apply many mathematical principles and concepts in day-to-day problem-solving. Yet, they can solve many seemingly complex mathematical puzzles/questions once you avail them with these questions. Throughout my schooling, I did not come across a single teacher/instructor who defined mathematics, how mathematics evolved, its role in society, how to extend it further, and how it influences other disciplines. However, I had an excellent teacher who did it relatively better than others, although he did not bring it out explicitly, Mr Matovu Mark Moses, a.k.a M^3.

The underlying assumption for studying anything is to *understand and apply*. The shift should be from the old teaching of solving numbers for passing and teach to understand and apply. There should be examinations set to test what students have learnt and can apply effectively. Such examinations could be set following the guidelines below:

a) In the mathematics classes you have attended for 1 or 3 months or (3 or 4 years), tell us what you have loved most, what you have understood the most, what you would recommend others to study and the reasons why

b) Relate the answers in (a) above to day to day problem-solving? Where would you apply the topics

c) Ask children/students to set their questions and solve them.

This is to track knowledge and understanding. Trust me; every student will give you something unique and exciting. You will be shocked to learn how students think they have understood yet not. And yet, when you give them a direct question, they would answer it right but explaining how they understood a subject/topic is a problem. Now, as teachers, based on the outcome of such examinations, you can evaluate what the student knows or is capable of knowing. You can then help each student individually or categorically assemble them depending on the responses given in the examination. Such testing of students lacks in our school system.

The present school system sets pass marks. For example, the pass mark could be 50%, and a child scores 30%. In the present system, such a child would be labelled a failure because he failed to shoot the pass mark. In other words, he failed 70% of the test and passed 30%; to me, this student passed 100% in the 30% of the examination. That is what they know and are capable of understanding and applying, perhaps. Much emphasis would be put on this 30% that the student passed to ensure they master the topics involved. An examination focused on only the 30% that the child passed would be set for the child so that they get nearly 100%. *This is a reinforcing and motivational skill, some kind of a reward.*

After the child nearly gets 100%, as mentioned above, the teacher should then give the child another examination mixed with at least 10% of the problems they failed earlier. The performance will deviate again. Again, if the student scores say 45%, set an examination for only those questions they managed to pass. Do this cycle over and over again. You can group children by type of questions they failed and set examinations accordingly. We should teach to *understand,* not to *pass!* If you wish to nurture such a student into a helpful adult, then take away all the questions he eventually fails and leave him with those he has passed and give them more training in the disciplines he has passed. Why insist on the things that are not meant for the child?

The idea of averaging performance for grading learners has shortcomings and has for long not been revised. For example, if you have three papers for a subject like Chemistry: E, F and G, and when a student scores 75% and above is labelled with a distinction one (1). The highest score or grade in the Chemistry examination being fixed as an A, which is obtained by averaging scores from courses E, F and G. The lowest pass mark for the highest grade A may be fixed at 2.5 and the highest at 1.0. For example, a candidate may score a distinction 1 in paper E, a distinction 2 in paper F and a credit 3 in paper G; the overall score in chemistry would be (1+2+3)/3, i.e. 2, which is an A because it falls within the range of 1 to 2.5.

Some important questions to ask following the illustration above are: Couldn't we have two students with the same performance, for example, like an A, but the reliability of their actual performance be quite different? Couldn't we have a student performing lower than this but when their actual performance and understanding of the subject is actually above a student with an A grade? What instrument or tool do we use to measure variability in the performance of the three courses E, F and G? How do the three papers E, F, and G influence or affect each other?

Therefore, the average is not logical. The average as a simple measure of central tendency gives no information about the spread or shape of the student's performance in the three papers E, F and G. We need to dig out the *unique capabilities* of each student. If we do not, many students will continue being absorbed where their strengths do not exist and personality mismatch, simply because of averaging their academic performance. The true art of testing for such typical examinations with more than one examination paper should consider the relationship, variability and interdependence of the papers with one another. The three parameters should be considered as well to get the final grade.

Geniuses are not many. They have always been few, are few, and will always be limited. In a promising society, much of the effort is not geared towards the answer provided by the candidate or the interviewee in other instances but rather the way they approach the question. The way a problem is approached signals much about what the candidate or interviewee knows or is capable of knowing. Unfortunately, some instructors are interested in tricking candidates for what they do not know or failed to understand.

What Kind of Input Do We Need to Have the Output we wish?

When you assess the present education system in several African countries, you can compare it to someone trying to get ghee out of the water. You cannot shake water to get ghee. Ghee is a product of milk. In any production process, there is always a finished product and a residue. Similarly, harvesting cereals yields husks. At times husks can be more than the harvested product. You must always look from the output side to properly inform the inputs. What happens in the current system is quite deceptive to think of magical results. For example, all-round lawyers may no longer find a place in the modern world. That kind of lawyer would argue civil and criminal cases that span several fields, i.e. medicine, engineering, technology, commerce and entertainment industry, etcetera., without certified professional and specialized knowledge acquired before acquiring the law degrees plus licenses to practice.

An outcome is an effect that your program produces on the people or issues you serve or address. Universities would design programs that have far-reaching success. For instance, for some people, the result of a training program might be the number of graduates who get jobs and keep them for a particular period. The parameters for studying the quality of the output should be logically thought out and well consulted before any program is designed. Quality defeats quantity all the time. If much lies in quantity, then the Chinese would lead the world in football. The quality of graduates and professionals is key to sustainable development. We should look further, from the output to the effects and quality of the output. In this aspect, an outcome is a positive change that occurred because of your program.

The African education system prepares a citizen who knows virtually everything but a mastery of nothing, studying lots of things but not understanding and mastering the core principles of the disciplines. The system has passed out lots of half-baked graduates who cannot compete on the global market. The system has passed out many graduates who cannot create and innovate for society and the wellbeing of humanity. The system is continuously releasing many scientists who are too theoretical and not curious enough to walk an extra mile to think of new solutions for the benefit of society and the wellbeing of humanity for purposes of development. The same scientists cannot practically put into practice what they laboured to study. I remember my economics teacher saying that a vendor challenged him in a market; he asked him what he had done for the country with all his economics knowledge. Knowing is not enough;

doing is everything. The system releases many gasbag citizens who can talk about sensible things but without a single victory in real-life problem solving—people who can ably diagnose but cannot treat. This is all because university program designers worry less about the right inputs to get the correct outputs.

Qualifications versus Competence

One attains little when they think very much in academic credentials or qualifications than the execution of work. I have learnt over the years that one's academic excellence has very little to do with reality, in some instances. In my profession as a civil engineer, the limits of scientific knowledge end in where engineering judgment begins; this judgment is embedded in some form of *intuitive ability*. In applied science, mathematical models are just abstractions with very little to compare with reality. These models are used to describe close enough some parts of reality. Knowing what particular abstractions are needed to compare with the natural world is the point.

Thinking of reality and mathematical abstractions as the same thing is invalid. Nonetheless, the complexity of some mathematical equations often prohibits solutions and thus, standard practices are needed to significantly simplify the mathematical abstractions to allow for approximate practical solutions.

Sometimes academic giants' failure to perform as expected at work is an integral explanation, including intuitive abilities. We are all unique, and our personality formations are different. The way you organize the knowledge you have gathered over the years will make you successful or fail. Success is, therefore, the way you organize your knowledge, and it has very little to do with academic achievement and other college performances. Competence, therefore, involves *knowledge, skill, and ability*. Qualifications would not give you all those.

The danger of Computer Programs (Software) built by others and used in Africa

Though some groups of people claim that the future of academics is in Africa, I can foresee the danger of over-reliance on computer programs not built by Africans. The advantage the internet brings to the world is understandable. However, the tendency of children to carry out even basic operations by computers rather than the hand and brain does more harm in the long run. To children in nursery and primary schools, computers may slow down their cognitive development.

Understanding the core principles and algorithms in which the program is built must be well nurtured. Many para-practitioners and half-baked tradespeople use computer programs built by experts from other countries, sometimes customized to those countries, to solve problems in developing countries. The issue of adaptability and compatibility is not given enough attention it deserves.

Suppose a professional is to apply a powerful computer tool designed for another territorial jurisdiction to solve a problem in Africa. In that case, they must have a sound grounding of the theory behind the program. Engineers, doctors and other scientists must have a sound understanding of the principles and algorithms used in the computer program. Otherwise, there will always be an increasing danger of using invalid results to make hazardous decisions. We need software built for Africa to solve our problems.

Training and Skilling Graduates

Alvin Toffler (1928 –2016) once said, "The illiterate of the 21st century will not be those who cannot read and write, but those who cannot learn, unlearn and relearn." Most people go wrong when they think that graduating from higher learning institutions are well-equipped with the knowledge and skills necessary to achieve their goals. Most of the challenges we face are out of school and necessitate us to continuously learn new things, relearn them or unlearn the past. In the modern world, skills acquired are so fundamental than grades attained in schools. Good grades attained in schools without skills cannot help much. So, after school, one should strive hard to acquire appropriate skills to help one achieve their dream.

Our education system does not emphasize training. Training is a key to develop into a fully accredited professional. Here, training takes on a diverse field far away from professional training and includes the nurturing of students. Most students who study through hardships tend to be so productive even at work. The hardships that they go through translate into training in the long run. They learn how to overcome times of crisis and develop *adaptation abilities*, making them think out solutions. This is primarily because the hardships train them to understand that pain is normal and part of life. The hardships make them think hard because they need to survive.

Those who see these students undergoing hardships always label them as suffering, but later these students become strong due to the training they undergo. The hardship they go through always has a positive side, i.e. it trains the mind to think. That is one practical example in our society that justifies the need for training. Therefore, an integration of *good grades, training, and skills will most probably make you a success and be of value to society in the long run*. The chances of succeeding for one who balances the three are high.

You do not need to undergo hardships or wait to get hardships to learn how to think. The solution is setting targets early enough, be a little more curious, be focused on how to live a public philosophy, and have the desire to be of value to society. Only that will make you dream big and admire those who have made an impact in society. However, those who undergo hardships experience training in a way that makes them understand and comprehend that *"scarcity creates value."* Those who never go through hardships just read about it. However, the most important question on that claim is that most Africans experience a crisis and a large number of Africans always study on scholarships in the developed world; why are they not tremendously impacting society? I have provided the reasons and solutions in Chapter one (Culture and Religion) and Chapter four (Optimism and Positivity)

> *"The illiterate of the 21st Century will not be those who cannot read and write, but those who cannot learn, unlearn, and relearn." Alvin Toffler (1928 –2016)*

The success of any nation is vested in its ability to produce skilled graduates who can develop themselves and the economy. Human capital ranks high as the essential resource over and above any other. It is high time educational institutions shifted from primarily focusing on pass marks to the development of skills in the learners.

Dr Chi-Sun Yeh (1898 – 1977) was a famous Chinese modern scientist and educator. He taught in several Chinese universities, including Southeast University, Southwest Associated University, Tsinghua University, and Peking University. He is considered one of the pioneers of Chinese modern scientific careers. In 1945, when Dr Chi-Sun Yeh was giving electromagnetism lectures to sophomores at the Department of Physics, he noticed a transferred student Tsung-Dao Lee, from Zhejiang University, who never missed classes but always lowered his head and read books as if he wasn't listening to his lecturer. If you asked him questions, he would answer confidently; apparently, his theoretical level was distinguished from his peers.

One day when Dr Chi-Sun Yeh finished class, he walked to Tsung-Dao Lee and asked him what book he was reading; it was an advanced course of electromagnetism; Dr Chi-Sun Yeh said, "it is such a waste of time for you to come to my class since you area already reading advanced books. You don't need to attend classes." Tsung-Dao Lee was shocked upon hearing this, "but you can't miss laboratory course, it's mandatory." Said Dr Chi-Sun Yeh, who recognized Tsung-Dao Lee was talented and started to put extremely strict requirements on him. There was a time once the final exam of electromagnetism ended, Tsung-Dao Lee got a great score in the theoretical test (58 out of 60), all his answers were right, but he didn't get a full mark, Tsung-Dao Lee felt very aggrieved and asked Dr Chi-Sun Yeh why. Dr Chi-Sun Yeh replied, "since you didn't do well in the laboratory course, you can't get full marks in the theoretical test!" Tsung-Dao Lee only achieved 25 (out of 40) in the laboratory test; therefore, Dr Chi-Sun Yeh wrote this on the test paper: "Tsung-Dao Lee: 58+25 = 83". Dr Chi-Sun Yeh had a vision for China, transforming its University graduates into highly skilled professionals.

Chinese educated scientists and engineers are rapidly driving China's technological advancements and economic growth. Today, nearly forty per cent of college graduates produced by China have engineering and science degrees. In Africa, the number of graduates in this area is not clear, but it is widely known that the continent suffers skill gaps. That is the main reason foreign experts continue to take up most of the sophisticated jobs in several African industries. Most African countries are characterized by a largely theoretical education system that might not stimulate innovation well enough. In Africa, we have more theoretical graduates than hands-on. The impact of semi-trained graduates is highly felt through the alarming incompetence levels observed in several national and private institutions across Africa.

A majority of the African states are more than fifty years old since they became independent from the colonialists. However, they still need to hire foreign experts to provide consulting services and technical services in unsophisticated areas which have existed and been taught even before independence, e.g. building a drainage ditch or drawing resettlement plans. Civil engineers have been moving and controlling water to benefit societies for nearly four millennia. Minoans who lived on the Island of Crete in Greece moved water and had indoor plumbing around 1500BC. Around the same time, the Romans being the first hydraulic engineers, had clean water and bathed every day. Up to date, Sub-Saharan Africa has failed to identify with others.

The perturbing side of the failure to recognize laziness is the unemployment levels that keep rising every day. Yet, there is still much room to innovate, improve, invest, and incubate in a developing country. Foreigners are taking advantage of this unforeseen and rather mushrooming trend of hopelessness. If our graduates are well-skilled, there would be no need to hire foreigners to provide technical assistance in work that nationals can handle. Today, on average, fifty years post-independence, we would probably hire foreign professionals to train us in information technology, advanced technology, and knowledge enhancement.

Fifty or more years down the road, we still hire foreign professionals to provide assistance to build relatively small safe water systems. Yet, governments claim to have trained more professionals and technocrats in such fields and their associates. The implication is that the technocrats trained are in some way or another illusively trained and lack the competence to advise the governments. The competence would be exhibited in the ability to amend political decisions that contradict Africa's sustainability goals.

In the past, when kings reigned, there were projects done even though people were uneducated. That kind of project leaves you a little bit curious to learn how they managed to do it. For example, King Mwanga II (1868–1903) in Uganda laboured to excavate the largest human-made lake (*Nnyanja ya Kabaka*) in Africa with an intention to make an aqueduct to connect his palace to Lake Victoria. He never had any earth moving equipment or modern engineers to do geotechnical investigations and water resources analysis.[64] He managed to do this with skilled people.

Karamoja Case Study of an Illiterate Technician

In 2011, I repaired hand pumps in the remote areas of Karamoja in North Eastern Uganda, where I met a technician who fascinated me when he spoke several dialects, which included: Ngakarimojong, Lugisu, Luganda, Lusoga, Ateso, Swahili and the English language fluently but he was illiterate. Before I recruited him, I wanted him to sign a contract agreement that would give him the responsibility to lead the team to repair the hand pumps, something he declined to do. I thought he was adamant. Because he could speak English well yet, others could not, I made him a team leader straight away. Because I wanted the work to go on, I relaxed the agreement.

Moreover, the place was too remote, and I could not find alternative personnel. He made the offer by word of mouth, which put the project at high risk. He was too good a technician not to know how to read and write. He mobilized his team of about 15 tradesmen, and we embarked on repairing the 20 hand pumps scattered across the district. Because of being a hand pump repairer for quite some time, he was well known in the district, and he was well-conversant with the status of all the hand pumps we had to repair. We had mobilized enough spare parts and ferried them on the truck as we went from one hand pump to another. Because he knew the exact status of the boreholes, the illiterate technician provided excuses halting the journey for a cup of water and other funny excuses. I did not know that he was planning to steal the spares from the truck, and I could not figure out his plan.

The illiterate technician had repaired the hand pumps before, so he knew the exact depth of each hand pump and therefore knew the number of pipes and pipe rods to replace per hand pump. The district

---

[64] See p. 103-104, §2.

engineer-in-charge had not laboured much to evaluate the existing condition of the hand pumps before issuing contract documents. As a result of the district engineer failing to evaluate the existing condition of the boreholes, there were some overestimates and variations. The illiterate technician did an excellent job, spearheaded the activities from repairs to maintenance. The communities appreciated the work because each hand pump was left when the water was flowing, unlike before.

The communities had had a shortage of water for several months. The illiterate technician had received good on-the-job training that improved his skills to conduct existing condition assessments and get the conditions precisely right though he was illiterate. This skill made him masterly and justified his theft skills, too, because the pipes he left were just enough to finish the hand pump under repair. I leant about the theft of materials while repairing the last borehole when I wandered around the bush and landed on the pipe rods and a few pistons. After we completed repairing all the hand pumps, his workers told me that he had stolen materials on several hand pumps, but we never experienced a shortage. This taught me something that doing defeats talking and unutilized classroom knowledge most of the time. The illiterate technician had the experience and skill.

In addition to the illiterate technician, my first-year university structural engineering lecturer asked, "If you are a qualified civil engineer and you design and build a bridge which collapses before commissioning. The on-job trained person, like the illiterate technician, designs and builds a bridge that stands to perform its intended function. In that case, of the two, who is an expert?"

Theoretical Examinations and Practical Tests

We have many excelling secondary science students in several schools across Africa who can hardly identify the Periodic Table elements. Sometimes, laboratory work is minimal because of the lack of resources, yet it should be the most taught, borrowing from Dr Chi-Sun Yeh case. This leaves students to cram. This, coupled with the art of questioning involving unscientific methods such as list the uses of this and that, advantages of this and that, etcetera is not logical and should not be used to judge academic excellence in science. Such questions encourage cram work. Sometimes, there are some questions I never laboured much to answer in exams. If I didn't know the answer, I never dared to stretch my brain to recall the answers for such questions so long as I knew I had performed good enough to obtain the required score to proceed to the next level, especially in the university.

The magic of science lies in the definition of scientific laws and principles. Teachers should put much emphasis on understanding the definition of scientific terminologies. Learners must learn why and how things happen but not pumping them with "uses and advantages" of this and that. That, in addition to laboratory work, produces sustainable results that meet industry and national standards. For example, questions like: Explain an electron; What is light?; What is a mole?; What is a cell?; What is an atom?; would take the lead. If you labour to explain to the students what light is and understand, they can quickly grasp the details by themselves because you are training them to think. All scientific definitions provide genesis to further details into the subject matter. All scientific formulae, derivations, illustrations and concepts stem from definitions. The challenge is that some teachers spend little time explaining the definitions of the scientific terminologies to students. Some teachers just rush in 5-10 minutes to the details after introducing the topic. An education system that focuses on passing rather than making children understand well enough triggers the habit of rushing to details in 5-10 minutes.

Suppose you are a teacher marking a student. You discover they failed the definition of the scientific terminology but passed the subsequent questions like the calculations and experiments. In that case, the chances are high that they do not understand the subject but instead crammed the process. The true art of scientific questioning would be to make the student define the topic first, and his failure to define it right would impact the results he would get for the subsequent questions, however much they would pass them. Also, teachers would take the use of command words at the beginning of the question very seriously. For example, questions that would begin with "*explain* the term light" domineering "*what* is light?" Therefore, teachers should pay much attention to the command words used in science, i.e. explain, what, outline, discuss, how, why, describe, list, give, etcetera. The way a child answers questions that begin with each of the command words listed above would provide the level at which they understand the topic. After the child provides their understanding of the topic, they progress to the next questions. Therefore, how a child performs on the definition influences their performance for the subsequent questions.

I remember a great teacher, Lawrence Ssenkubuge, an associate of SchoolNet Uganda, who never gave notes while teaching advanced level physics. He did a great job to train us to make our notes from what he explained and from the textbooks he recommended. This was good because it encouraged us to research and think. The United Nations later recognized him for his outstanding competencies in ICT and offered him a better job in the UN. Lawrence is an ICT enthusiast who labours to keep up to date with modern digital technologies to aid his instructorship.

To What Extent Do PhDs Matter in Solving Africa's Distortions?

It is the order of the day to rejoice of many PhD holders across all African states. The problems of Africa do not need lots of scholars. At some point, they are apparent to fix. Though we need research and development (R&D) in many areas, I believe we need more hands-on trained personnel to practically address the exploding unemployment, i.e. the "professionals and technical people". A balance between knowledge and skill has to be struck. Africa needs more genuine practical modellers and technicians. A modeller's role is to make theoretical descriptions of systems or processes to understand them and predict how they will develop. He uses existing knowledge and perhaps some form of industrial research. Genuine models: either business models, scientific models, or full-scale model projects in humanities can help spur socio-economic transformation in Africa than unpublished and published papers shelved without action plans. Research is about discovering new ways, new evidence, and understanding the causes and effects of happenings, trying to reduce the number of what we call phenomena.

We have more PhD holders *without skills* claiming to teach or impart skills to others, and I doubt whether you can practically induce something you have not mastered. Several African PhD holders have knowledge but lack skills. *In many cases,* you can learn the skill from someone who has that skill. The biggest mistake done is to recruit people into offices based on high ranking qualifications as the essential requirement but not competency checks and personality—setting standards too way high for many job descriptions! A diploma or degree (one or two) is believed to be sufficient for someone ready to change the world. A PhD is important to do continuous improvement, new and relevant researches into the problems' cause and effects, thereby proposing new efforts to solve the problems. We forget that recruiting someone with a good heart, although not highly qualified, might be 100 times better than a person of malevolent and cruel nature but highly qualified—and this is a pregnant point.

The problems of Africa are known and do not need sophisticated instruments to study them. They need people who can bring together knowledge, expertise, passion and commitment to utilize the abundant resources for the good of the continent. In this regard, scholars can study facts and propose improvements where necessary. Many government resources are spent on sponsoring academicians who hardly contribute to their countries after completing studies. Why do governments not sponsor the training of students locally and abroad? Those students who have demonstrated high technical and skilful capabilities at both vocational and university levels to become renowned experts in providing such technical services hence practically contributing to the country's GDP?

Today, both the socioeconomic benefit and cost-benefit of sponsoring hands-on technicians outweighs that of scholars in Africa. Elsewhere, the story might be different. Many African governments have spent much money sponsoring scholars who have published research papers without development action plans. Some have failed to receive funding, whilst the majority are poor quality, lacking a professional and practical touch. It sounds better to do a PhD in Africa when you have grown some level of intellect. Otherwise, you might instead become a nuisance to the people because of thinking that you know much better than most of them. The continent's human development indexes are improved not so much by scholars—the scholars whose knowledge is an illusion sometimes.

Being overqualified in the wrong places creates liabilities. For example, many of Africa's engineers and technologists moving into management than real engineering practice is a mess if we dream of self-driven sustainable development. It is a fact that engineers have saved lives more than any other professional. Although I have not conducted any research, I can deduce this by empiricism that several degree holders upgrade not necessarily to master their fields and improve their knowledge and skills. Instead, they upgrade, aiming to obtain bigger offices to manage others but not to lead others, often for better pay. Many engineers are taking this trend.

Engineers should upgrade to further their knowledge and skill, innovate and develop, and save lives but not because they want high-ranking offices to manage others. Real engineers do not think that way. As engineers, let us be of value addition, and management becomes implied. That is one reason which makes engineering levels go down in many African countries. By growing stronger in technical competence and professionalism, we lead the industry forward. When we lead the industry forward, we are leading the economy because many other industries rely on engineering and technology to perform.

The day many African countries will realize that excellent engineering and technology does not necessarily correlate with academic achievement, many innovators will be born. Great engineering is about realizing simplistic ideas. However, many people are fixated on PhDs and academic excellence as a metric to measure ability, knowledge and understanding to generate ideas that solve problems for society. On many occasions, the highly studied people view simple things from a highly complex perspective, especially those academicians that have had much literature all through their career but never interfaced with the experience from which the literature is derived.

Some Africans have three PhDs; for what?

What Does It Mean to Graduate with a Degree in Many Parts of Africa?

The tendency to celebrate minor achievements is spoiling the graduates. The measure of success in Africa is simple; obtain a degree, get an excellent job, acquire a posh drive, throw a big wedding, acquire a better plot of land, build a lovely house, produce children, build some rental units, and that is all! Acquiring a plot and build a house would not be a big deal, and even acquiring a car is nothing. Ideally, every living creature must have a dwelling place.

Similarly, wasting many resources for making big weddings is ignorance. The dedication to live for others or future generations is lacking or absent in many African minds. The youthful stage is always underutilized, and this is when one has the most brilliant ideas in their lifetime. Later on, one becomes more experienced and focused on a specific line of interest, yet if these ideas are acted upon, they can create a positive difference. However, most of the time is dedicated to the usual things, i.e. making massive weddings, building houses, cars, and gossiping. It is in Africa, where you find a recent graduate having over 10 children.

Have you ever asked why people pray, adhere to morals, go to church or mosques? There is always a promise for any actions undertaken. People would hardly worship if it weren't the promise of eternal life after death or some fortune. Most of the religious teachings promise eternal life after death. You leap what you saw. And to keep moving forward, there should be a driving force behind. How would you relate this to life and business? People invest their time and devotion to praise God, first for the gift of life and second for eternal life after death. Investment in education is not seen broadly as some form of business where you invest time and money for a future promise.

We need to be driven by sound considerations. The consideration of gaining knowledge for innovation at a personal level is not taken seriously. The only promise thought about is getting a job after studying, forgetting that where you would work is most probably a business enterprise. The idea of investing in acquiring knowledge to utilize it and create opportunities is not well-nurtured. It is because of not understanding how businesses work that significantly explains the failure of some enterprises. This is because, in most cases, the staff hired is only looking at pay, not value-addition to the company. For any business to survive, there is always a win-win situation for stakeholders and staff. I am convinced that if people were taking time to question what they can do with all that knowledge acquired in school, they could easily understand the gaps to fill in developing countries without necessarily finding a job. For sustainable development, graduating with a degree would mean acquiring knowledge and using it for society's convenience through entrepreneurship.

Graduates Thinking Outside the Box

Imagine you have just graduated from university and are between 22-25 years old, and you are not looking for a job but networking with your friends. At the age of 22-25 years, you are more flexible, and people look at you as a potential trainee, potential worker or potential subordinate. They are willing to delegate responsibility to you or send you to accomplish tasks. You must not disclose your qualifications to anyone. Qualifications should remain your secret. Try to blend with the informal sector as much as you can. The informal sector is full of workable ideas. Grow as you gain experience in whatever you do. Do not listen to people undermining you and negatively critiquing your work. Be ready to make splendid sacrifices. I am convinced that when you do the above correctly, only the country's bad government policies might let your efforts down. When you persevere and insist, you make things happen.

For example, if you graduate with a degree in Automotive engineering, feel free to join a motorcar garage and be ready to spend 3-4 years learning full time. Do not tell anyone about your qualifications because most motorcar garages in Africa are occupied with less qualified mechanics, sometimes uneducated people, and taught on-job people—they will get biased the moment they learn about your qualifications. Some of the very successful mechanics in Africa are illiterate! I can guarantee your success after 3-6 years. Motorcar garages are full of people who have learnt on job whilst others are semi-educated or uneducated, and sometimes they have very practical ideas. You learn from them.

When you blend with them well without disclosing your qualifications to them, slowly, they start identifying your capabilities and think you must be talented. They will like you, and in the end, you become a centre of attraction to them. You will develop power as a magnet of attraction to your employer and the customers. With humility and passion for your work, customers would be interested in you. Then you slowly cultivate your ambitions. Start setting up your enterprise slowly and apply professionalism. This approach ignites ideas and helps to grow your interpersonal skills. Interpersonal skills are one of the 21st-century must-have skills! You can then start networking with your peers and professional networks/agencies for professional accreditation. I can guarantee a nearly 100% likelihood of success via this route if you are a highly visionary and patriotic person who wishes to change Africa! There is power in humility!

If it means working as a turn-man, security personnel, or cleaner when you want to learn, network with others, and attract attention from employers and business associates, do it. Learn how they do the work, how they make losses and profits, etcetera. With your school knowledge, you will sometimes quickly identify gaps. Therefore, find a mechanism to advise them indirectly *where possible*, and they will like you. The biggest problem is the ego that spoils many graduates. People who really matter keep a low profile. Suppose 1000 graduates with engineering degrees, 1000 graduates with physics degrees, and 1000 graduates with other science degrees do this every year; and they stick to their ideas; I am sure the sky would be the limit because such practices trigger innovation. That is what we want to replace the idea of looking for decent jobs which are scarce. And we are aiming at growing the economy.

Software and Hardware Components as Products of Our Education System

Most African states spend many resources on the software component but very little on the hardware component. I mean, investing highly in talking and putting nothing on the ground—bringing many professors and academicians talking a lot of sensible issues but nothing done by themselves. These professors and academicians forget that your child follows more of your example than your advice. They are fond of drawing very nice plans that fail to be implemented and creating enabling environments for reading higher degrees but not paying attention to Business, Technical, Vocational Education, and Training (BTVET)—spending more resources on workshops and little on putting into practice the outcomes from the workshops and spending more on salaries and little on the objectives.

The impact of such practices is that most African states have nurtured people who talk sensible issues, seeming intellectually competent and good at drawing plans but hardly live exemplary. African students who get the chance to study from Universities in the developed countries tend to perform very well, at times beating nationals. They show the same intellectual capabilities in class with the national students of those universities. However, when African students graduate from those universities, their intellectual abilities diminish most of the time. The world fails to see that they had outstanding intellectual abilities while in school. That has also been observed in many international conferences where executives from rich countries who interact with their counterparts from developing African countries show no significant intellectual differences. That shows that the problem encompasses all of us, whether elite or informal, executive or a commoner. It should be a collective effort to spearhead the *"doing"* and not the *"talking"*, advising by action, not by talk shows—*walk the talk*.

Many African governments sponsor up-and-coming candidates for higher learning, but nothing is done to evaluate the benefits from sponsored students 5-10 years into their fields. There should be a monitoring and evaluation program for sponsored students to track their progress. We should desist from wasting the taxpayers' money. After studying, some students just fly out of the country, and they never come back. Several countries are facing the problem of brain drain. There should be conditions to work at home or on government missions abroad if the student is to study on taxpayers' money.

There should also be a program of donating back to society after school. Some of these scholarships are taxpayer's money and would expect a positive national benefit from the sponsored student. The lack of such monitoring programs has left governments with no proper vision for academically outstanding students. If you are sponsoring students for their outstanding capabilities from their peers, let them demonstrate such capabilities even in the market after school. It does not help the nation very much when the sponsored student succeeds in doing things that benefit them individually. If a student obtained a scholarship for being intelligent, witty or clever, they should be supported further by governments to contribute to society.

Africa is partly suffering as a result of not knowing how things have worked since the colonial time. The people taking decisions are selfish, and they cannot remember how the inequalities have been constructed starting from colonial time. This is the time to change things. We need accountability in all constitutional matters. Being intelligent when your intelligence helps you alone, yet you need the taxpayers' money to further your studies abroad to continue your life alone does not help the taxpayers very much. The ground should be levelled. It is high time we stopped wasting resources that do not yield fruition for the nation.

There must be an evaluation and monitoring program to oversee such valuable contributions to society from such academically outstanding students. The monitoring and evaluation program should assess the commitment of the student to give back in ways that enhance the socio-economic growth and development of Africa. It is entirely disadvantageous to others who could not exceedingly perform to shoot the scholarship requirements. Yet, they have financial constraints and fail to get a chance to go for higher learning. Somehow somewhere, if you evaluate the contributions of the so-called academically outstanding students to society, you might be lost only to be shocked when you discover that the average or the so-called poorly performing students contribute competitively to the wellbeing of man and the country's GDP.

Do We Need To Bias Our Children To Specific Courses?

The massive enrollment of academically excelling candidates into engineering, medicine, law and mass communication, leaving other disciplines like culture and tradition, economics, political science, music and sports, hospitality, and finance, taking on less performing candidates, is a threat to Africa. This is precipitated by the loathsome capital rewards after graduating—a claim that these fields have jobs paying off highly as the main reason rather than value-added to society. Government policies to neutralize the rewards and importance of all courses to society would be passed because sustainable development does not weigh one element heavier than the other. They all work together, and not one or two are superior to others.

From my experience as a civil engineer, I have noticed that you do not need to be a genius to apply science, especially when you meet good instructors in your career. You do not need to be a genius at mathematics to solve the world's problems that require engineers. Fields like programming and software development call for the very best in talent, perhaps. But still, creativity cannot be judged from mathematical knowledge alone. Our minds are unique and influenced by the spiritual dimension. So, it is not always easy to correctly judge another person's mind until evidence accumulates to prove the hypothesis.

It would be relevant to note that mathematics which houses the creative force of science, is about ideas, not formulae or equations. Solving a mathematical problem is about being conversant with the applicable techniques. Once you do not have the techniques at your fingertips, it becomes hard to solve the problem. However, this does not mean you are not good at math. Solving a mathematical problem requires techniques, but the formulation of a new mathematical construct comes from the ideas of a creative mind. For example, to solve a pair of simultaneous equations below:

$$x+y=3$$
$$x-y=1$$

This pair of simultaneous equations would require you to know the techniques, i.e. the substitution method, the elimination method, or the matrix method. These are the techniques you would apply to find the missing numbers, i.e. $x = 2$ and $y = 1$. However, in real life, these equations are used to solve problems, and the one who coined and invented the term "simultaneous equations" had the creative mind. Similarly, those who invented the techniques to solve these equations had creative minds. Therefore, knowing about these techniques and applying them is what is taught generally—and there is a big possibility that you can know and solve the equation but can hardly think beyond that. How often does the education system test creative minds whilst enrolling students?

I am very convinced that many learned Africans rarely understand how equations are built from experiments, theories, or empirically, but they know how to use them. It is not only about understanding how and why to use something; the one who learns how things are crafted from first principles contributes to self-driven sustainable development. That is the role of a sound education system.

The most innovative engineers, for example, are cherished for their *ideas to* apply scientific knowledge to solve the world's problems. They extract scientific concepts—laws of nature they need to apply to solve a set of problems. Engineers draw out knowledge from many disciplines beyond science to design, implement, maintain, and operate systems sustainably and reliably. Proficiency in design is what sets engineers apart from scientists. Scientists are credited for studying, discovering, and documenting the facts of the universe as they are, whilst engineers extend the knowledge gained to create, recreate, and improve the universe and its elements. *This is why the sustainability question is so much of an engineer's problem than any other professional.* The engineer takes centre stage in finding solutions to the global climate change and sustainability challenges. Engineers piece together knowledge from different spectrums to improve humanity; they have to conserve energy in the sustainability conceptual framework. Therefore, if you want to do excellent engineering, put away the academics and think. That demonstrates that excelling at math does not guarantee making a great engineer. You might perhaps be good as a scientist. Engineers are at the heart of society, listening and attending to the world's problems and deriving solutions to fix them. These solutions draw knowledge and ideas beyond mathematics.

Therefore, anyone who labours to understand can apply the knowledge acquired to solve a problem. Adding to the existing pool of scientific knowledge requires considerable energy, creativity, passion and commitment and some element of talent or genius to conduct research. The biggest mistake we make is to recommend high–achieving students who excel academically in engineering, medicine, and law and send fewer well-performing students to teaching professions and natural science courses like mathematics, physics, biology, chemistry, and agriculture.

Following his analysis, students who are very good at mathematics should also enrol on science disciplines like physics and chemistry. However, it is common practice that many candidates who excel at mathematics highly get admitted to engineering, medicine, statistics, and pharmacy.

Engineers apply scientific knowledge, but scientists explore the secrets of the universe. It takes a little more curiosity for a practising engineer accustomed to traditional practice to make advancements in science and engineering technology. Today's engineers are at the forefront to save the planet more than any other professional. This means today's engineers must have sound knowledge and understanding of science to practice than before. Still, this means scientists are leading engineers and, at some point, could convert to engineers. In some developed societies, some professionals in the making have started doing double degrees. For example, enrolling for geotechnical engineering and at the same time enrol for a degree in geophysics. Sustainable development leaves all societies to cry for the best in talent and experienced engineers to make sound sustainable development decisions. We should, therefore, not forget the reason we need shrewd brained students to enrol for natural science. Let us not heavily bias students to few specialized fields.

With all these messes, Africa cannot expect to genuinely develop a pool of talented scientists and other professionals unless we change and have a balanced enrollment in engineering, mathematics, science, law, medicine, pharmacy, and teaching because they are all essential and interdependent. We need more scientists to lead discoveries in the field and engineers to make practical innovations using the knowledge from the discoveries. Talented students should not only be encouraged to apply for engineering, medicine, and law. Also, we need them in natural science courses to make more improvements. The fact that engineering resulted from science, we need more scientists than engineers. The biggest problem is the money-minded syndrome of the African child in everything they do but not problem-solving to uplift the wellbeing of the societies that creates all these messes.

The tendency where parents, schools and some career counsellors advise students enrolling for university courses to look at money as the significant motive for enrolling in a course is the worst thing you can ever do in the 21st century. The prevailing circumstances might predetermine the course a student should enrol for, but the student should be advised to enrol for a course in which they find themselves comfortable and able to study with ease. The flamboyant lifestyle that seems to be associated with money has recently driven many students to the legal profession. However, we ought to have students with a great deal of thinking and reasoning—very good at *logic* and *emotional competencies* to enrol for law. The world keeps changing day in and day out, and the fact of deciding cases based on precedence might be overturned by *new evidence* in the study of logic. And unwounded children would apply for law utmost. A wounded child becoming a judge because of their academic excellence has its shortcomings also.

Here is an excerpt that was circulating on social media a while back.

African Education

The African education system has many surprising outcomes. The smartest students pass with first class marks and get admission to medical and engineering schools. The second class students get MBAs and LLBs to manage the first-class students. The third class students enter politics and rule both first and second class students. The failures join the army and control politicians who, if they are not happy with, they kick or kill. Best of all, those who did not attend school become prophets and witchdoctors, and everybody follows them! **Anonymous Author**

What does Europe mean to the World?

Modern African societies blame ancestors for not working along to formulate a language, except in a few countries like Ethiopia, Eritrea, Egypt, and few others, but this should not make us shy away. Most of the basic principles of science on which the modern world is developed were developed in Europe, the European Union in the modern-day and a few from some parts of the Middle East and Asia. These are the scientific principles used across the globe on which all prominent *modern scientists* worldwide have benchmarked.

The highly talented scientists who were real thinkers behind many scientific laws and theories lived in Europe or had their origins in Europe. The likes of Leonardo Da Vinci (1452–1519), Sir Isaac Newton (1642–1726), Michael Faraday (1791–1867), Robert William Boyle (1883–1955), Dmitri Mendeleev (1834–1907), Robert Hooke (1653–1703), Georg Simon Ohm (1789–1854), James Watt (1736–1819), James Prescott Joule (1818 – 1889), Albert Einstein (1879–1955) and many more. Before these modern scientists, the Greeks were credited for outstanding philosophy on which many modern theories are founded; the likes of Pythagoras of Samos (571 – 497BCE), Plato (428 – 348BCE), and many others. However, it is believed that the Greeks learned from the Egyptians! I find it appropriate to name the European society as the Great European Society. Of course, technology has been developed everywhere on Earth, but most of the origin of scientific analysis is attributed to that region.

"Rapid accumulation of knowledge, which has characterized the development of science since the 17th century, had never occurred before that time. The new kind of scientific activity emerged only in a few countries of Western Europe, and it was restricted to that small area for about two hundred years. Since the 19th century, scientific knowledge has been assimilated by the rest of the world." Joseph Ben-David (1920 – 1986)

Asia, in particular the Asian giant, had its language back in ancient times. However, not many basic scientific phenomena, particularly chemistry and physics, were proved as facts until the school education system began. Except for Indians who taught the world how to count, most of the leading modern scientific principles were discovered in Europe. We, therefore, owe the Europeans a lot in this context. We would look at Europeans' *colonial enthusiasm* optimistically to some extent. I mean to some extent. It is justifiable in that scheme of reasoning. They have supported the world more than anyone else in many spheres, including leadership, governance, and science.

Learning from the Asian giant. The advantage that the Asian giant remained with and are still holding today is building an education system that works for them, and they keep improving it. I am not in the know of any basic scientific principle developed outside the European Union *before* the great scientific revolution of the great European society. If it exists, it could be a pseudoscience, e.g. Feng shui, or it is more or less an image of the works of European scientists. Still, if it exists, it was not well documented to garner universal acceptance. The lesson to draw from this is that God or whatever you ought to believe as Supreme had created or made Europe, Africa and some parts of the Middle East for all of us across the globe, to support us, learn from them as we develop. However, many parts of Sub-Saharan Africa have failed to understand this. If you are a believer, you quickly notice the relevance of the Middle East, Europe, the Arabian Peninsula and some parts of North/North-Eastern Africa. They were tasked to pilot. As they piloted, the Asian giant extracted out what was relevant to their development, but Africans are still failing, especially the Sub-Saharan countries.

Relevance of Science Education in Sustainable Development: The Future of Courts

The summary of the word "development" in today's vocabulary is "Science and Technology", finished! And "sustainable development" adds on the improved living standard whilst conserving the planet for future generations to live while ably meeting their needs. When you have science and technology, you can access almost everything on earth. Science and technology are shaping the world so fast that in the future, even courts of law will have many modern scientific approaches to resolve cases because the experimentation method is still the best method for drawing objective conclusions about the world around us.

The balance of probabilities for a standard of proof in civil cases shall be expounded through a scientific approach to enhance reliability and validity. Similarly, the reliability and degree of truthfulness for proof gathered beyond a reasonable doubt to secure a conviction or not in criminal offences can only be improved through a scientific approach—by studying scientifically the *Actus Reus* and *Mens Rea* legal terminologies used in the conviction of criminals. Also, the ruling from supreme courts and courts of appeal, which takes on the majority decision and the dissenting decision dropped, would be improved in future.

There is a good chance for the dissenting decision to be the right decision. For example, the probability is heightened in a decision where the ratio of the dissenting decision to the majority opinion is either: two to three or three to four. More funding into criminology will soon be advocated for. Statements like, "Police used excessive force to arrest a criminal" remain ambiguous. How is excessive force determined? I believe in not a very far time; it will attract judicial review in some territories by heavily integrating technology into the practice of law to study the extent of excessive force.

Education, Innovation, Politics, and Patriotism

In many African states, incredibly the least developed, if one starts a workshop, especially in the informal sector, well-known for sprouting technological innovation worldwide, e.g., assembling cars or anything technological, it is not rare that government fails to support. The developer/innovator meets obstacles and intense criticisms for reasons not easy to understand. This has been very serious in the last 2 or 3 decades. However, today the situation is slowly improving because of information technology driving the modern world—the information age. In Uganda, the likes of *Kayiira* came out with a car prototype which they assembled well in their garages. However, it was not until Makerere University innovated an electric car that the government started to pick an interest. It is not the first time Kampala garages innovated, assembled cars, and the government turned a deaf ear.

If not arrested, the media would go over the innovator, garnering them a fast lane of fame. This quick fame is like an explosion, where they experience some instant boom of success, spot lights on, glory and glamour, for a while, which seems like the whole world is watching them. They forget that the more and more one becomes famous early in their ambitions, the more they become foolish and can quickly lose focus. The principle objective should remain to do a lot in silence and success shouts.

Non-governmental Organisations (NGOs), government agencies, banks and donors, etcetera, praise many achievers for relatively minor things they have done. They constantly shower young people with *premature awards* of different categories such as best upcoming artiste, best male artiste, best entrepreneur of the year, best performing student, young entrepreneur awards, best student, etcetera. This is good, but on the other side, it is perilous for start-ups because the media tends to exaggerate it, making the individual or organisation seem big whilst celebrating minor achievements. This makes the innovators or entrepreneurs become contented and settle for less. The media generally causes this problem, which, if not most of the time, reports false information about the individual or organization. This creates some distortions for the entrepreneur or innovator when they are awarded prematurely. It would help if you celebrated something substantial.

Do School Mottos Matter?

In my primary school, we had a motto that goes, "What Man has Done, Why Not Me", and in my two secondary schools I attended, we had mottos that go as follows: "Be Known by Good Works" in one, and "For Greater Horizons" in another, respectively. Finally, in the University I went to, we had a motto that goes "We Build for the Future." These were shaping me this way:

Primary School	:	"What man has done in Europe; why should I not do it in Africa?"
First Secondary School	:	"Be of value to society through doing good works, do not just study, read, talk, and do nothing."
Second Secondary School	:	"Aim for the best, dream big, and do not settle for less. There is always room at the top."
University	:	"Those who lived before me shaped my success; I need to shape the future generation's success in all my actions."

When one asks me, for example, why I am somehow ambitious with some bit of being passionately curious, the answer is because I went to those institutions that prepared me to be so. Yes, therefore, school mottos matter! The schools only lacked the solidarity and patriotism courses or lessons for the African child. If such lessons were present in these institutions, I would deeply feel the instincts of my ancestors and feel the blood ties. I believe that an education system that truly represents an African and prepares an African child for the industry requires a different setting. These mottos were excellent but lacked those courses above. The new system shall have to reflect on our lives and our cultures. This system shall reflect where we are coming from and where we are going, an education system that instils African values into the child, and an education system that cherishes patriotism.

Ethics, Moral Values, and Culture in Education

Our ancestors fought hard to obtain the territories we belong to, and they managed to survive in the old way of doing things. Today's educated citizens are comfortably selling our countries. They claim to know better than the ancient people. The illusion of knowledge that I described earlier has created a mess. Today, countries are sold with pen and paper. To sell a territory in the ancient world, the buyer would have to settle on that piece of land you have sold to them. Today, the story is different.

The education system has created an illusion that makes us entrust non-patriotic people to big government offices because they attained high academic grades, but when they do not understand how things work in the real sense. As I mentioned earlier, it is the inappropriate use of a pen and paper that sells all of us (as a nation) in the contract agreements done by our leaders almost every day. This results from the present-day education system that lacks patriotism and solidarity courses or lessons—an education system that evaluates academic performance alone as a measure of credibility for someone delegated to conduct nationalistic matters. We should come up with psychological tests to measure patriotism in candidates vying for public offices.

We need to re-evaluate family settings; wounded children are a total disaster when entrusted with national roles regardless of academic achievement and professional status. Most problems in Africa originate from the unhealthy families where people we entrust roles grow because they carry all the garbage to work. Many examples exist in several Sub-Saharan countries where officers steal medicines, steal food, and embezzle government funds to buy expensive cars used for weekends. You get shocked when you learn about their academic results, which reveal first grades throughout their career. That is because they grow up from unhealthy families and get wounded.

You know our cultures teach us how to nurture and groom well-mannered children that meet social values in society. There is nothing wrong to do grooming holistically in schools. You might wonder how patriotism comes about; there are three fundamental values I would wish to promote as essential introductory topics in solidarity classes, and these are: saying hello to one another; a thank you to someone who has laboured to do something good for you; and feeling sorry or saying sorry to a sad friend. These three essential words summarized as "Hello, Thank you, and Sorry" are lacking in many people's vocabulary—yet these people claim they are educated. These three words are powerful, and they can make you obtain something you never expected. These are the essential words that demonstrate a person living with integrity in society. How do you feel when you do something good for someone who fails to thank you? Therefore, patriotism comes from cherishing values, and these values must be promoted holistically in schools.

Interestingly, many uneducated people still cherish these words in their vocabulary. The thank-you can be handwritten, typed, or emailed to; family, friends and colleagues. You need to reach out to them and let them know that you like or love them and that you think about them, and that you appreciate what they do for you and are grateful for what they have done for you in your life. The recipient of a "thank you note" will feel loved and motivated and would reciprocate in a society of people living with integrity. If you have a chance to send a handwritten "thank you note", it is always better.

Handwritten thank-you notes are more humble and would live for generations. The three essential words were very well-promoted by many of our ancestors in ancient times. I can provide an excellent example here: After graduating in 2011, my friend John failed to get a job for almost a year. While on the street looking for a job, he met his friend who worked in a factory. They discussed how that friend would assist John to get a job in the same factory that manufactured uPVC pipes. They agreed that the friend would assist John to get the job. One of the conditions for getting him a job was to remit 10% of his first salary to the person who recommended him (John's friend). Therefore, 10% was the consideration.

After John got the job, he took over six months to meet the obligation after I had counselled him. He was failing to say the "Thank you". In this case, the agreed payback of 10%. Many Africans forget in just a microsecond, and I strongly wish lessons about kindness were made part of the curriculum. I do not know what happens elsewhere, but many Africans have become so forgetful. There was no point in refusing to remit the agreed 10% of the first salary for over six months after getting the job.

Anyone who calls himself educated must learn to be trustworthy, honest, kind, and to live with integrity. They should strive to show the difference from an uneducated person. A person who has been on the street for a year looking for a job and after getting the job he cannot remember where he is coming from is a typical half-baked graduate I have described earlier. You cannot tell me that this person is fit for a big office—someone who cannot be trusted in small matters.

The rate at which people forget in Africa is scary. This, coupled with a lack of proper documentation on our lives, escalates the problem. While we turn against the good deeds of our ancestors, elsewhere, people are nurturing their kids how to communicate. You can feel their sensitivity from email correspondences. Killing all good deeds by our ancestors and embedding none in our education system explains the growing trend of emotionally incompetent citizens.

It is scientifically proved that people with high emotional intelligence balance good manners, empathy, kindness and the ability to assert themselves and establish boundaries. This tactful combination is ideal for handling conflict. When most people are crossed, they default to passive or aggressive behaviour. Emotionally intelligent people remain balanced and assertive by steering themselves away from unfiltered emotional reactions. This enables them to neutralize difficult and toxic people without creating enemies.

Today, success seems to be trending towards 90% of social/emotional intelligence and 10% of IQ. Africa's education system tends not to take this seriously. I felt energized when my little son, Mark Ssempeera Jr., received an award for kindness. At three and a half years old, this award would shape his moral and cognitive development for many years ahead. So, I am telling you about the things I do at home.

Mark Ssempeera's Certificate of Kindness

The Unnoticed Education held by African Ancestors

In some parts of ancient Africa, people used to construct mud or daub and wattle houses. Wattle and daub or mud is a composite building material used for making walls. A woven lattice of wooden strips called wattle is daubed with a sticky material usually made of some combination of wet soil, clay, sand, animal dung and straw. Ancestors knew the different types of appropriate and suitable soils for house construction and could make a perfect combination in the mix. They could identify suitable soils without modern geotechnical investigation procedures and analysis. Modern practices of soil testing analyze the plasticity and elasticity of soils, among other parameters. But when you asked ancestors why they chose such soils (mainly clay), they could not give you a scientific explanation.

Ancestors had the technology for building shelters but had little knowledge about the scientific explanation behind their technology. The problem of not knowing the science behind their technology is not the main problem. The main problem is a lack of proper documentation. When one documents, they organize their thoughts to start from where they stop to make continuous improvement. And when you draw on paper the way things are done, others pick from there. This is just one of the examples; many thousands of other examples needed to be brought forward in the education curriculums. Other examples include alcohol production and backcloth making in Buganda; ancestors knew the fermentation process very well. These are things we needed to improve.

There comes a genius who labours to ask themselves why things are happening in the struggle for improvement. In this scheme of things, therefore, Africa's Architects, builders, and civil engineers would begin their studies by introducing ancient African technologies. For example, how the mud and wattle houses stood a test of time—trying to blend existing technologies with modern technologies within the sustainability framework. For example, people who live in huts and homesteads need integrated housing technologies that build on their ancestral heritage. Many African countries are losing identity because of the education system that does not mind African cause. We are losing Africa's architecture. This is not good news for one who minds about Africa's sustainability. It is the education system that should be revised if we still need to keep our identity.

Africa's University Research

Good social research is about "cause and effect," but why not emphasize scientific research experimentation, observation, design, and modelling? The academic research that dominates universities in Africa is about causes and effects. For example, a research topic like, "causes of pneumonia in children below 5 years in Sub-Saharan Africa: A case study of Chemba in Dodoma, Tanzania", etcetera., for a post-graduate student done as a dissertation for partial fulfilment of the award of master's degree or thesis for a doctoral student. We need more studies like "developing a technological toolkit to stop pneumonia in children below 5 years in Sub-Saharan Africa". The later study encompasses the former study. We need to be ambitious, not just to keep studying causes and effects!

If none has invented a tool to stop pneumonia in Sub-Saharan Africa in Chemba in Dodoma before, then the student's research is original, for that matter. The student will not develop the tool without knowing the risk factors of pneumonia in children below 5 years. Only identifying the causes of pneumonia in children is not enough if we are looking at developing Africa through research. If the research looks unclearly defined, and the scope is wide to achieve the set objectives in the stipulated time, i.e. not SMART (S = Specific, M = Measureable, A = Achievable, R = Reasonable, & T = Time-bound), then allow the research to be conducted by several students, could be three to five students.

In my opinion, students would also be allowed to graduate so long as they demonstrate understanding and competence in conducting research, even if the research findings are not obtained yet. This is to avoid researches meant for students to pass and get their masters and doctoral degrees but for problem-solving in the interest of the wellbeing of society, sustainable development, continuous improvement and change management.

Most researches conducted are dominated by survey research. However, few studies are conducted by experimental methods, emphasising modelling, failures and success, testing, observations, and trial and error to improve, innovate, and develop.

The identification and survey research targets passing and obtain the degrees, finished. We have not matured to carry on sophisticated research in several universities because of the lack of funding. We need studies that cut across problem-solving and leading new findings for filling the knowledge gap. We have continuously had researches for root causes, effects and problem identification in both matters relating to science and humanities. However, little is vested in experimental research to design technological tools and equipment for society's sustainability and advancement once root causes are identified. Most of the researches are set for researchers to acquire more knowledge to shoot their ambition but not for transferability to other situations for problem-solving.

University students are fond of copy and paste culture without scrutiny. With the use of the computer, many student pieces of research and projects are duplicated in some universities—very close to plagiarism. This leaves people who studied before the computer generation wondering if they are not as good as the current generation because of the overwhelmingly high rates of academic excellence exhibited by today's graduates.

Most students' researches in many African universities are a comparison, correlation, causes and effects. It would take on more forms of ethnographic and phenomenological methods in the context of the social sciences. Students should persevere in doing more observational and experimental research.

Experimental research is minimal and this is the benchmark for industrial research,, which nurtures creativity, imagination, improvement, innovation and incubation. It is not rare for researchers to claim that inadequate infrastructure such as libraries and laboratories coupled with less funding deter experimental research,. However, in my opinion, it is planning and prioritizing the biggest problem for Africa's universities.

Many resources are spent on predictable research outcomes. It is common practice that good research proposals, especially for surveys, may include *anticipated results.* However, research whose outcomes culminate into common knowledge or whose prediction can be what society constructed as the absolute truth is not good enough to waste resources. Most research done in Africa is about things we know or can deduce by empiricism and logic. Africa's proper research should find solutions to oddness.

We need more experimental research in *behavioural sciences.*[65] The rate at which the outside world moves requires Africans to put things in order, i.e. the distortions, before dreaming of competing with the rest of the world. We will not reinvent the wheel; we just have to put things in order through dialogue for exemplary leadership in all institutions.

The Question of Confidence to Communicate Ideas with Authority

Many of our professors, lecturers and teachers lack self-confidence; lack of team spirit and confidence in schools, colleges, and universities is common. Some of our trainers, professors, teachers and lecturers are too good, but they do not believe in themselves. They are full of doubts, yet they possess too much potential to uplift our economies.

The result is that those who are confident though ill-advised with mediocre minds will keep misleading the countries. People are not trusting each other's knowledge in the higher institutions of learning. At least in some universities I know, professors are fighting for offices—they do not trust the potential of their colleagues. For example, some scholars think of being the best in everything and all the time. They can never believe that their student might possess more potential than them in specific areas. This has been experienced in many universities across Africa.

I have mentioned some scholars, not all. You might be an exemplary African scholar, but you are only in the top 30% of the scholars. This has not been hypothesized to conclude, but it is depicted in the responses and feedback received when someone innovates in Africa. It is, most of the time, negative feedback. They

---

[65] See p. 218-226, §4 (Hint: Social Engineering).

consistently undervalue others' innovations and research. They do not believe in motivating one who has laboured to innovate something; however little the innovation could be, one needs support.

Lots of people are fond of unnecessary criticism instead of positive criticism. I have witnessed a university professor and a team of students coming up with a green car that could use solar energy. The team faced unnecessary criticism from elders and close professionals. Some said it was not new, while others complained that it had no use since it was not self-rechargeable. Instead of motivational criticism such as giving more advice on how to improve the car, the team faced stiff criticism, almost abandoning the project.

All this kind of mess results from an education system designed to pass exams, not solve problems. When someone tries to solve a problem, others will see them as wasting time, bizarre, and awkward, constantly comparing what they are trying to do or has done to what the outsiders have invented or innovated before.

To people who understand how things work, any student project is worth giving attention to and requires support so long as the student demonstrates passion and commitment to undertake it. They just need advice and support. You cannot claim to understand somebody's project more than them. If a student comes up with a project, we need to support them but not demotivate them. What happens is that people tend to make comparisons with work or products from outside—from developed countries forgetting that these countries also took steps to improve the products. You cannot compare a start-up with an already established enterprise.

Academic Politics

Academic politics is entrenched in many higher institutions of learning. If you have not experienced it, you are lucky. We all have dreams we wish to accomplish once we step into schools, colleges, and universities. We develop a set of goals, desires, and ambitions that often compete with those of people above us or people who have the keys to make decisions on our desires and needs. This is where academic politics sets in. There is a lot of academic politics in higher institutions of learning and professional bodies. This is escalated by corruption, unique Africa's attitude disorder (UAAD) and a lack of transparency which operate more on Machiavellian principles.

Some academicians focus on their interests to manipulate, deceive, and exploit others to achieve their goals. You cannot be called an intellect, for goodness sake, when you are selfish. Some people confuse academic excellence with living as an intellect. In societies domineered by corrupt leaders, the situation worsens. Elsewhere, academic politics takes on a different dimension to mean that people with high emotional and social intelligence always shoot high in academia and professionalism. How scholars approach the views and knowledge of others, especially views from highly experienced and successful semi-educated people, is biased.

Many African scholars believe in being more intelligent than others, and this sometimes destroys the spirit of teamwork. The moment one feels egoistic, they cannot relate well with others because they believe others are not in the know. If you are staggering with ego problems or you have a weak ego, just remember this: I can never be you, and you can never be me. We are very different. Trying to stop me from achieving my goals sometimes is being ignorant. It is common for many PhD holders and professors to rubbish students' work and choose topics that interest them.

In many cases, lecturers, scholars, professors and PhD holders are not licensed by professional bodies. Some feel that those bodies are not worth their academic stand—thinking they are above those professional bodies' requirements; so, they need not be licensed to practice professionally. The moment one locks his mind in such a position, they are left to learn nothing new or noteworthy.

Today, you might be great in your field, but you need training and continuous improvement and involvement with others to keep you great. Professionals call it "continuing professional development". Today you might perform better than me, but next year you might find me doing better than you simply because you keep rejoicing in past results and achievements. Many schools test memory and accredit achievements but fail to test adaptability, emotional and social intelligence. Therefore, to keep the fire burning, you have to keep an open mind. As the old saying goes, "it is not how you start, it is how you finish that counts." Create room for learning new things and keep improving the existing knowledge every day.

If exceedingly intelligent people were all reserving themselves, several developed countries would not open their economies to the world. But because they want to trade and learn about what the weakest people are doing day and night to keep learning, they wish to keep with others by opening the economies. Stephen Hawking (1924–2018) tells us, "I have no idea. People who boast of their IQ are losers."

Excellence in school is just an indicator of the probable capability to do beautiful things. But if one does not labour to discover themselves after that, there is a significant risk of failing to shoot their dream career prospects. In school, we only answer a handful of questions; many questions are in the open. The "open to experience" people tend to perform miraculously outside the school environment. Therefore, boasting of academic excellence only leaves many of Africa's academicians living to help themselves but not sustain humanity. Many fields, especially in the science arena, still hold unanswered questions for those who boast of their knowledge and academic excellence in Africa. They ought to solve these enigmatic issues before they boast around and rubbish students' original ideas. The Clay Mathematics Institute has several problems to solve; they can try. Sometimes, I wonder when these instructors focus on how well the student organizes the report/document rather than the quality of ideas and content held in the document/report.

Contemporary Duplication of Fields Proves Premature for Africa

Institutions should not be money-driven to start duplicating courses because they want to enrol as many students as possible. Governments should put a measure on this practice. The population explosion has left many institutions to target big businesses without caring about the impacts of their products on society. There is no need to split and form sub-standard programs for the sake of enrolling many students. This has a long-term effect when half-baked graduates are released to society. They struggle to find where they exactly fit. The result is to masquerade as doctors, engineers, lawyers, planners, technicians, auditors, economists, etcetera. This kind of deception is dangerous to society since it directly affects unlearned citizens because they lack the knowledge to differentiate a professional from a handyperson.

Meaninglessness has created a duplication of fields. Unanimous groups and organizations are formed to attract conformity from the masses to create meaningfulness to identify with one another. For example, the project and program management profession is neither an independent nor a separate school of thought or profession. Any activity with a start and a finish, planned, scheduled, and executed, with a set of aims and objectives to be achieved, is a project. It is, of course, governed by well-established cost and quality goals. A project can be found in several domains or areas of study, both humanities and sciences.

Associations of project management professionals are composed of all disciplines because projects exist with no boundaries. I am firmly convinced that they grew out of an effort to help people resolve the dilemmas of contemporary life, such as; isolation, alienation and meaninglessness. Because, if I qualify to be called an economist, I must have satisfactorily planned, controlled, organized, executed, evaluated and monitored projects to be accredited—the evidence-based approach. Similarly, engineers, doctors, lawyers, surveyors, technologists, technicians, psychologists, etcetera must have demonstrated the competence and ability to be accredited. I find this kind of duplication of fields premature for some African countries. In the developed world, it would carry more sense.

One may argue that such bodies provide a forum for a bigger voice to be heard. However, they perpetuate Africa's problem, creating and nurturing less effective and incompetent project managers because it creates more pseudo project managers. In my country—Uganda, engineering and related skills are at a threat because of the rampant increase in alternatives to cope with the dilemmas of contemporary life. Things like: I am a project management expert, make the day, forgetting that even someone who sweeps the street is a project manager. Those are things created to make more illusions and to mask the Africans.

A more significant voice can still be heard in associations for economists, auditors, engineers, doctors, lawyers, physical planners, architects, et cetera. Therefore, undergraduate degree courses such as project management, program management, construction management and management are not well-thought-out.

I am not contesting the project profession, but I clarify that the field is implicit, not a separate entity. It should be an add-on to strengthen the competence one holds. Unfortunately, institutions care less about this ideology. If I am a professional engineer, I must have demonstrated competence to lead a successful project. There is no way you can lead and manage solutions to solve technical problems within a field without technical knowledge and understanding of the subject. Therefore, after being a professional engineer, I can apply to become a professional manager. This is the best route but not the other way round. The other route is also possible, but that is the best route.

If I qualify as a social worker, I must have the skills, ability and knowledge to manage a project of a social context, and many more. In the developed world, project associations are justifiable because of the industrialization level and perhaps the ICT revolution, which presents several opportunities. However, in Africa and other LDCs, we need technical skills onto which sound project profession should be built. Project associations in Africa *perpetuate the illusion of knowledge.*

Still, courses like BSc. in Sustainable Development is good. However, the concept of sustainable development arose out of the threats imposed by climate change and the continued exhaustion of natural resources. Climate change is everyone's concern; whether a lawyer or journalist, it matters! Such courses would be designed to be taken at postgraduate levels, not as foundational courses. They would be course units within foundational courses. It should thus be an initiative for all governments to have well designed mandatory sustainable development programs for all, project and program management training schools to help upgrade skills for civil servants and private practising individuals so that they can master the art of delivering successful sustainable projects and be encouraged to stick to their professional bodies.

I am afraid I have to disagree with the splitting to form the project profession as a separate professional body/department or authority in developing countries. It weakens the building of solid professional institutions in Africa and affects the continent's struggle to impart technical skills in the labour force. Project and program management is a skill that anyone leading a successful project or program ought to have. It is thus embedded in all professions, and therefore, young generations should not be misguided to read undergraduate degrees in managing and leading projects. Africa still needs building ingenuity and technical skills than soft skills in children and adolescents.

Case Study: The Tacoma Narrows Suspension Bridge, in the USA[66]

The Tacoma Narrows Suspension Bridge, which cost US$ 6.4 m that collapsed in 1940, merely 4 months after its completion, presents an exciting legendary example of how successful project management is premised on sound knowledge and understanding of the elements of the project. In that case, it helps mitigate risks and have proper project planning and scope management. The project manager must understand why they are doing whatever they are doing to lead a project that can manoeuvre through its lifecycle reliably, operably, and sustainably.

The bridge was primarily funded by the federal government's Public Works Administration. It was intended to connect Seattle and Tacoma with the Puget Sound-Navy Yard at Bremerton, Washington. The bridge collapsed due to poor planning and unforeseen technological effects. It is reported that the bridge experienced severe wind-induced vibrations. Interestingly, the Deer Isle Bridge along the coast of Maine was of similar construction and smaller in size. It had opened one year before the Tacoma Bridge and is still in service today.

The evaluation process conducted during feasibility studies for civil engineering structures takes on a holistic perspective to assess potential risks that would be encountered. The engineer of the Deer Isle Bridge had the foresight and sound judgment to add wind fairings along the bridge's length to give it better aerodynamic properties. He also provided diagonal cable bracings to provide greater stiffness. The engineer of Deer Isle Bridge had good knowledge and understanding of the project at hand. However, the engineer of the Tacoma Narrows Suspension Bridge did not correctly account for *aerodynamic forces*. Many motorists crossing the Tacoma Bridge complained of acute seasickness brought about by the bridge's rise and falling which was nicknamed "Galloping Gertie".

The point to learn from the Tacoma Bridge is that effective project management would be premised on a thorough knowledge and understanding of aerodynamic forces by both the chief engineer in charge and the local construction engineer. Mr Charles Andrews, who was the chief engineer in charge of construction, reported that the local construction engineer substituted open girders in the construction of the bridge's sides for flat solid girders that deflected the wind rather than allowing it to pass. Therefore, the local construction engineer did not understand the implications of the decisions he undertook. The one who takes the decision to piece together a construction project must have technical competence beyond project control and management. Unfortunately, Africans wish to have more Tacoma cases in Africa by promoting more project management professions rather than technical capacity building. African

---

[66] Jeffrey K. Pinto, *Project management: Achieving competitive advantage* (Upper Saddle River, New Jersey 07458: Pearson Education Inc., 2007), 241.

countries are toddler countries and would need to avoid a bandwagon influence. If the project management illusion is not corrected, self-driven development will not happen.

On Scholarships, Africa's Universities, and other Universities

The danger of scholarships is that the provider dictates the programs you have to study, especially at post-graduate levels. Self-sponsorship drives the student to where their passion is. Most scholarships available to African students pursuing post-graduate studies are not their priority but rather choices made by the sponsors. Many students who upgrade in Africa just find themselves doing courses in fields they are not passionate about. However, because scholarships exist in those fields, they are left with no alternative.

Organizations sponsor you many times, specifically when they wish you to contribute to their growth and development (directly or indirectly). Yet, higher studies' relevance would ideally be to fulfil your ambitions and career.

You would upgrade to a course that supports your career dreams. In other circumstances, you would choose to upgrade in a field you are passionate about, which fits your attitude, IQ, ability, and perhaps your personality. The problem of taking courses not in people's interest is significantly affecting Africa. We are losing talent to the wrong fields. We have scholars who are not well-positioned. They would perform better if they had the chance to pursue the courses of their dreams. The moment you vest all your energies surfing and searching for scholarships, you are left to land on anything available.

My advice would be to struggle and study the course you love. Falling in love is more vital than doing things out of anxiety. You cannot genuinely develop when you stop struggling, and one should not fear struggles.

The idea that African universities are not competitive for post-graduate studies by many students, especially those who excel at the undergraduate level, is false. And it is somehow a cognitive distortion; it finds its way into the signs and symptoms of the unique African attitude disorder (UAAD).[67] Excelling students prefer universities in the developed world for post-graduate studies. I do not think you gain much when you enrol and study from outside universities. It is how you are lectured and what you learn while in college that matters most but not where you go. It is the attitude you hold that matters. We have some outstanding universities in Africa that would attract many students.

Unlike the sophisticated science and technology courses in engineering, biochemistry, and biomedical and nutritional courses that need laboratory research work, I am convinced that law, political science, economics, humanities, and psychology can be studied locally. However, the leading universities globally inspire confidence in their alumni in several spheres of social influence. That fact is well known, though, but the best way to start is to start to develop and build for the future of Africa's universities.

The kind of sponsorship which benefits the sponsor greatly perpetuates Africa's problems. Loans would do better, and the student should be allowed to enrol for a course of their choice. The number of scholarships in primary, secondary, university and tertiary institutions would dominate the post-graduates

---

[67] See p. 203-214, §5.

scholarships. Africa's problems are not so much about research. It is about putting things in order—fixing distortions. Accepting who we are and move on. Trying to live a way of life of others and copycatting at the expense of our values, predispositions, and precepts perpetuates the problem and keeps Africa in a cycle of oddness. The genuine sponsor asks what you would need to achieve, the career you need to take on, and supports accordingly. The best sponsor provides loans but not free things to a student who has completed A 'levels or its equivalent to pursue higher levels of learning. We do not need to kill talents at the expense of free things, taking on unwanted courses just because they are free.

What amuses me the most is that most of the research undertaken by African students while studying from abroad is usually focused on solving or identifying a problem in Africa. I am left to laugh when I see almost all colleagues who studied in the developed world did their research on a topic in Africa! Most lecturers in several universities across Africa have had a chance to study in the developed world, and many excel there. Why do we not instil confidence in our lecturers and stop the business of thinking that studying postgraduate courses is more rewarding when studied abroad? Lecturers are sponsored to attain quality education abroad in anticipation that they will come back home and help their countries. But when they return, we do not seem confident enough to enrol for courses they lecture primarily at the postgraduate level. We have many good universities in some parts of Africa, especially those built by the UK in colonial times.

I studied only in Africa's universities, and I have worked only in Africa with local people. I developed my engineering career, rising to sit for Chartered Professional Review in Hong Kong, which I successfully passed. Although the Hong Kong-based reviewers doubted my competence, the second reviewers were satisfied with my submission. The reviewers had the discretionary powers to recommend my admission to the institution. I am now a Chartered Civil Engineer. Every step I took to become accredited was self-driven. If you need to learn more about how I made it to become a Chartered Civil Engineer, send me an invitation on LinkedIn: Patrick Ssempeera. The milestone I drove to become a Chartered Civil Engineer should give you more confidence that Africa's universities are good enough for those who labour to think outside the box. I am not succumbing to complacency that I do not admire studying at universities with an international reputation. However, my opinion is that local universities can produce someone who can meet the *minimum requirements* globally. Therefore, I have more than 1000 reasons to tell the world, particularly Africa, about the need to rise to unlock sustainability and *reclaim Africa's position.*

Elites That Fear Discussing the Subject of Money

The education system produces a section of professors who fear money. They always snake out when the subject of making money with the overarching goal of creating wealth by ordinary-person-integrated models is discussed. They seem to care less about forging practical means of ending poverty by pairing ordinary men in society as a solid engine to end poverty. Instead, professors become a liability when they disassociate themselves from reality, clinging much to what appears to be good life made by non-Africans. They forget that a fool who makes lots of money can disorganize the entire world or continent in particular, and their professorship becomes a nuisance amidst the confusion of the said fool.

Never joke with the power of money. Any fool can make money—a lot of it! What matters most is the how-to. Making clean money should not be a complicated task, mainly where one does not associate themselves with greed. Unclean money calls for very little honesty. But elites and learned ones who try to mix dishonesty with greed get confused in money-making schemes on the African land. Greed has stopped many people from reaching their full potential to earn more money and create genuine wealth on the continent.

Having a college degree is almost useless in the equation of billionaires. However, in nationalistic matters and sustainable development campaigns, things can only be driven in order when intellects take the lead at some point. And these are people who are well-studied most of the time. Therefore, the continued disassociation of intellects from making more money and settling for peanuts is a danger in the campaign to develop Africa sustainably.

A country where big money concentrates in the hands of gamblers rather than intellects is in danger—people who believe that charity is when you give handouts. The money-making subject must be central or next to the central objective, as an extraneous driving factor to create sustainability. Here, sustainability is viewed in a context of continuance but not in terms of keeping the ecosystem in order indefinitely.

The professorship academy should not put money-making by ordinary-person-integrated models as a last resort in struggling to sustain the African continent. Whatever models they develop should be practical and flexible to adopt ordinary men and women as the main engine in the equation to create value in monetary terms. Many professors and intellects who shy away when discussing creating more money by the social transformation of the informal sector perpetuate Africa's problem to some extent. They instead believe in guiding the masses but not empowering them through forming an integral part. This creates everlasting dependents in the long run. A good professor liberates people from where he originated to stand on their own in several spheres, including financial and economic freedoms.

Conclusion

Africa's current education system is less promising and unsustainable, and it is primarily fixated on colonial systems. Today's competitive world requires new thinking approaches to cope with the dilemmas of contemporary living—an education system that stimulates thinking. One that is inclusive and cares for diversity. The sustainability framework calls for an education system that maintains and extends the existing pool of knowledge. An education system that nurtures values and promotes 21st-century skills. Sustainable education must reexamine our roots as Africans.

When we correct the distortions in our education, the future of academics is in Africa. We need an education system that recognizes that each child or student is unique and has special attributes. This shall enable us to accelerate the shift from teacher-centred learning towards student-centred learning. We should empower children and students to discover knowledge independently as we teach to understand, not pass.

In building the education system that can uplift Africa, we encourage children to question the world. We should not be interested in only the answers our children give to the questions we set for them, but we encourage them to question the world endlessly. Those questions, when answered holistically, shall help to unlock their curiosity about why they live.

Holistic Education. Quality Education. Confidence.

Chapter Four: Optimism and Positivity

"Yes, we can."[68]
=== *Barrack Obama* ===

Chapter Organization

Quick Insights

Life is a Game

Perception on Success

Negativity, Fear, and Anxiety

Recreating an African Brand

Perfectionist's Limits

Should The World Drive You Or Drive It?

Mind Your Business

African Attitude Gone Wrong

Stereotypes, Prejudice, and African Core Beliefs

On Africa's Inferiorism and Attitude

Theoretical Understanding of Attitude: Modelling Attitude

Understanding and Growing Attitudes

Attitude and Personality Formation, Reformation, and Change

Attitude Change and Unique African Attitude Disorder (UAAD)

Conclusion and Way Forward on Unique African Attitude Disorder (UAAD)

Varying Core Beliefs

Independent Judgment, Automatic Thoughts, and Bias

The Need for Social Engineering as Defined in Applied Social Sciences

Conclusion

---

[68] President Barrack Obama's 2008 campaign motto

Quick Insights

"One thing worth noting is that the greatest liar on earth is your mind," my brother, Alex, told me calmly. That came after a series of negotiations over an argument. "There is always room for deception in one's thinking. Your consciousness might give you something negative as positive and vice-versa. How often have you thought about something as positive and it went negative or as negative, and it went positive?" he added. "So, what do you mean?" I asked. "You just need to be conscious of some degree of distortions in cognition or some bits of a bias in our brain faculties at some point." He emphasized. All humans experience a certain level of cognitive distortions and bias. It is thus about how we recognize and deal with them that determines the level of our mental health. In other words, all humans experience some mental disorders. Thus, the way we *think* all day long influences the way we *feel* and *behave* and vice-versa. Our emotions, thoughts, behaviour, and body physiology influence each other. A cumulative thought pattern over a certain period determines who you are and what you are likely to become at a future date.

Many people fail to appreciate that there is room in the mind's preconscious for thinking negative about something positive, or thinking positive about something negative and rush on to make conclusions without enough rethinks, proper research, vivid logic, and evidence. You need to be aware of the brain's possibility to dissociate, which can lead to miscommunications, misprocessing information, false interpretations and misconceptions. A mature and intuitive mind constantly labours before making conclusions. It employs a positivistic process before making conclusions that have a lasting effect or might contribute to such an effect. The prepared mind grows in intuition and becomes less judgmental as one of its altruistic traits.

Our minds are good at convincing us of things of different sorts, which might or might not be true—positive or negative. Negative thinking, for example, is always negatively reinforced by inaccurate thought patterns in our minds. Sometimes negative thinking is negatively reinforced by compensatory roles inferred to us by the environment and the community in which we live because Africans have been ruled out as people who cannot help themselves.

For example, we punish children in schools for several reasons. If, for instance, you exclude a child from punishment because of their ill-health condition, the child might play deteriorating sick roles to justify their condition on several occasions. This way, excluding the child from punishment negatively reinforces the habit of playing the sick role to justify their ill-health condition. Following this illustration, as Africans, we have taken the role of living on charity and accepted it because we have been conditioned in the first place to live that kind of life. However, we also wish to justify that we are weak in the mind and body to keep receiving more aid.

Life is a Game

Life is a game; you play it negligently, you lose, you play it well, you win. Of course, within the 1% degree of freedom.[69] It does not only take up the wisest and intelligent men to be successful but those who labour to understand themselves better. On a global scale, prosperous nations have had self-sacrificing people who rarely lived a self-serving lifestyle. They built nations on transformational leadership and inclusive

---

[69] See p. 248-252, §5.

governance. Such governance does no discrimination and plays the game adequately meeting the needs of all categories of people. In such societies, good governance paves the way to live a successful life.

Life is a game. You play it right; you get good results. You play it wrong; you get wrong results. It is a game that begins right from childhood through adolescence to early adulthood. It progresses from middle adulthood to late adulthood and finally old age. Deterministic viewers correspond each stage with a crisis. Once you misplay the life game, it results in crises. When good governance levels the playing field, for example, the acceleration of success is registered. Many African societies have not levelled the ground to play the success equation optimally. That has kept a number of our geniuses and talented ones in the dark. Even if you are the best dancer, you cannot dance where there is no music. The government should play music in a good society. However, an optimistic person always finds a way to deal with the situation. In matters of national development, much is done through a collective effort. Therefore, good governance is fundamental when playing the life game.

Perception on Success

Success goes to those who labour to follow what they believe. They labour to silence the voice that makes them believe they cannot make things happen. Many territories once colonized are doing better, sometimes better than those who colonized them. Hong Kong is one of the examples. It is all about good decision making and believing in yourself. Africa has the potential to develop a technological base and innovate many environmentally sustainable products to sustain humanity. What is lacking is self-confidence. Many people feel they cannot tap into the innermost potential lying idle in their minds. I am very convinced that many Africans rarely use their creative minds satisfactorily. Leading needs to harness all brain resources we have and sharpen our minds wide open to new ideas day in and day out. It is possible where the young generations are taught to believe in themselves. Today's generation of elders needs to inspire confidence in the young ones to see the light at the end of the tunnel—to make things look possible in the eyes of the African child.

If your heart keeps beating with "I can't" all the time, find a way to reverse the beating to "I can" by writing something on paper and pin it in your living room or bedroom. Change the way you see things. Make things seem possible. Avoid seeing things the same way from January to December because change comes to those who struggle to find new ways to improve old processes. Ask yourself, 'What am I not doing right? What do I need to correct? Where do I need change?' Global competitiveness has left no room for those who cannot cope with the dynamics it presents. One needs to change their conceptual framework when things are not working out—in business, politics and relationships. However, grandiose plans, inflated self-esteem and inflated self-concept are characters to avoid succumbing to. The goal is to have regulated positive self-talk that keeps one believe they can change themselves and Africa at large in whatever they do.

The tendency to join an activity when admiring another person's success in that activity is not logical. Simply because someone is thriving as a cattle keeper and getting triggered to become a cattle keeper is not enough. Success is a variable of many factors. In most cases, people do not explicitly provide details of their success stories, and they mainly provide good deeds in their success stories, fearing the disenchantment of telling the truth. If you wish to join a given activity because you have been triggered by someone who is a success in the activity, try to dedicate enough time to weigh your strength against the weaknesses in response to the needs and requirements of that activity.

Try to do a thorough feasibility study and research about the activity to find out if you are fit to undertake the project activity. In scientific matters, what we cannot see with our naked eyes is more powerful than what we can see. This applies to success stories too. What makes heroes, superstars or geniuses is far more than the talents they hold. Please do understand that not all fast runners are the winners of the race. Therefore, success is more of what we cannot see than what we can see with our naked eyes. If you find the activity very intriguing, get back to the drawing board, have ample time to consult and take independent decisions. It is always better to concentrate on your calling than jumping from one opportunity to another because we are all unique, only that many people tend to spend their lives trying to live other people's lives without discovering their callings.

Success is beyond what you can see.[70] Suppose you asked the world's billionaires what they did to become financially very successful. In that case, many will make things appear to have a well-defined path that, if you followed it correctly, you would become a billionaire. The same applies to success in other areas like academia, professionalism, sports, music, entertainment, etcetera. Success stories told sound so nice to hear. You might think that when anyone follows their advice, you succeed.

Someone will say, "I built this and that until when I shot, you will shoot when you do the same." Many people have built this this, that that, and those, but have failed to succeed. My argument is: there is no streamlined path to success.

Because some other person followed a particular route to become successful does not guarantee success to another who wishes to pursue the same. Such phenomena are experienced in many fields, including economics. In the Mid–20th century, some countries in South America moved to semi and high-income countries, something that economists failed to explain with economic doctrines at that time.[71] These countries had not followed economic policies that economists would expect them to follow. Therefore, success should not be attributed to what you can see. People rarely tell what phenomena exactly happens in their lives which is beyond their imaginations and understanding.

Some others wish not to disclose the facts to remain powerful and heroic. Some tech giants steal ideas from other people who die miserably poor. Some others make deals that another person cannot afford to do following ethics and moral dimensions. However, when they speak about their success, they can make you feel their ingenuity and great ethics. At times the actual story does not sound so pleasant for others to listen to, and therefore they always manufacture romantic messages for the audience. Success is, therefore, beyond what you can see. *Follow your path!*

Negativity, Fear, and Anxiety in African Societiesw

Fear associates with *evidence,* whilst anxiety associates with *no evidence*. Fear is an emotional response to a known or definite threat, and anxiety is often a response to an imprecise or unknown threat. Why does anxiety dominate a human being's innermost self, thoughts, feelings, and emotions on the African continent? This anxiety is often experienced by people, i.e. mild anxiety, on a day-to-day basis during specific situations. Could it be because of the families from which we are raised? Are we raised in

---

[70] See p. 250-251, §5.

[71] See p. 326, §7.

healthy families? Why do many people spring quickly to find ulterior motives in neighbours than love or happiness? Cautiously leaving is okay, but society seems to be constructing extreme tension to live in fear of our neighbours without evidence.

Anxiety is of many types. What I am describing here, is anxiety which makes someone feel a little bit sick, worried and scared of others, almost *approximating to "mild anxiety",, i.e. b*ecoming unpleasant because of misperceiving others. The other types of anxiety are diagnosable as clinical or medical. They usually view others as being a little bit alien and pose perceived danger to them without evidence. This is accompanied by negative thoughts about events, people or objects. Why do people quickly fall on the negative than positive thinking? Why does society construct happiness out of someone else's misfortunes? Why does the media find it so pleasing to publish the misfortunes of big personalities constantly? Is it the media finding it pleasant or the media personnel? Why is negative so powerful? Why does it try to approximate tensions in our minds and bodies to *mild anxiety*?

One negative deed dilutes a hundred good deeds. The negative is so powerful that it leaves only the courageous to live in hope. Society has constructed pleasure out of the misfortunes of others. Is it spiritual or socially constructed for a little anxiety to dominate a human being's heart, feelings, thinking, and actions concerning others in the African context?

Why is negativism so powerful? Statements of a sort dominate most people's brains: I cannot do this business; it is for shrewd brained. He is over-ambitious. He had a hidden agenda though he behaved to like us. I was born poor; that is why I live poor, and I cannot be rich. He is successful because he married from a wealthy family. He probably has supernatural powers that bring him wealth. She has magic; otherwise, an ordinary person cannot run as fast as she does it. She just copied the research dissertation from another person; it is not hers—plagiarized. She just copied the model from an American prototype; she cannot have all that imagination. I cannot imagine she innovated this; I didn't see potential in her; maybe she got through by a hidden hand. Who advised you to start a company? Did you start that company yourself? She is not beautiful, only that she has money to clean up well enough. She is not cleverer than I, only that she went to good schools and many other similar statements. Why is the negativism force so powerful for most Africans that it cannot make many believe in themselves; they cannot believe in neighbours, innovate and develop, extend their knowledge to shape the world we want? We take long to believe that our people can do great stuff. Too much negativism will only keep Africans *just to exist*.

One bad incidence can dilute a hundred good ones so quickly. For a hundred good ones to dilute one bad incidence takes many resources, effort and courage. And in most cases, it cannot clean away how people felt when a bad incidence happened to them—they keep pretending. It requires a much more visionary stand to convince the victim/s to neutralize the negative incidence.

Except for extremists, ideally, everyone fears death—whether atheist, believer or monotheist. Therefore, safety and security comes first in whatever we do and think of. We have to ensure that we keep safe and secure. Our bodies are always in a survival state, and the mind keeps pondering around a safe body system free from hazards. That is why information processing in the brain favours negative thoughts. Negatives overshadowing the positives. This is because negative thoughts ignite and elicit fear in the amygdala. The amygdala is an almond-shaped mass of grey matter inside each cerebral hemisphere of the brain, involved with the experiencing of emotions. It is that section of the brain that is responsible for detecting fear and preparing for emergency events.

Positive thoughts do not ignite and elicit fear in the amygdala. But then, if positive thoughts do not elicit *emotional fear* in the amygdala, then why do humans feel tensed up when success stories about others are discussed? Instead of being somewhat positive, giving thumbs up on the success of others, many coil inwards, get analytical on every stance and remain in disbelief whenever others perform exceptionally better than them.

Early experiences are believed to shape our core beliefs. For example, a belief in the existence of a Supreme Being is highly cultivated in infancy, early childhood, and adolescent stages. A person who matures without instilling the belief in Supreme Being early in life might find difficulty adjusting to the belief. The way we look at the world is determined by the lenses that we individually hold. Therefore, negative or positive automatic thoughts, a characteristic of situational circumstances, manifest core beliefs triggered by background or early experiences. They occur as a result of activating and stimulating core beliefs. Should we then say that early experiences determine the level of optimism and positivity in us? And we believe that early experiences shape negative automatic thoughts and positive automatic thoughts? Should we not believe that optimism and positivity can be learnt?

I assume that at birth, the baby has zero cognition and communicates by emotions. At that time, selfishness, jealous, hate and love are the same, and none is more pronounced than others. There is a very thin line between hate and love. Also, there exists a thin line between jealous and selfishness. They are all equal, as shown in the pie chart below. As the child grows, the environment and parental care waters the growth of these faculties. The ideal society waters the love seeds of the newborn baby to nurture into fruits that can live a *public life*. This public philosophy that guides a newborn's healthy growth includes parental care without neglect and a good environment. Are there more societies in Africa which water more hazardous seeds than love?

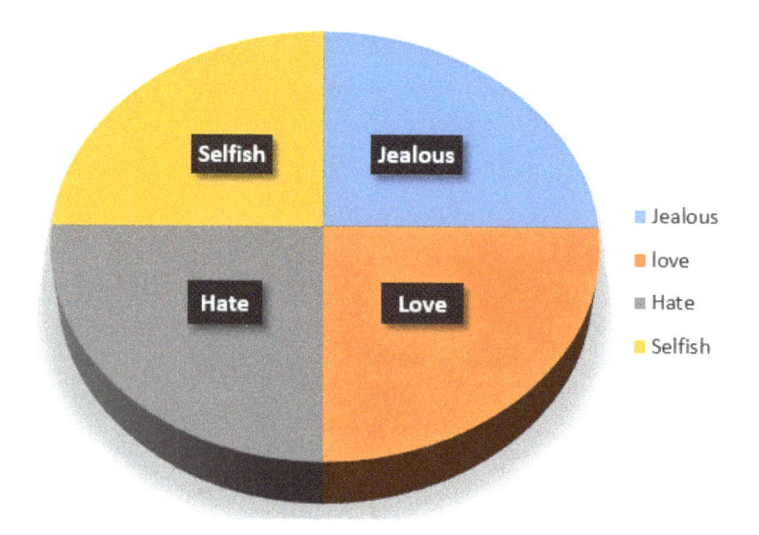

A Person's Level of Love, Hate, Jealous, and Selfishness at Birth

Living a correct public life calls for watering love to suppress the growth of jealous, selfishness and hate. Before the onset of cognitive and moral development, the child is considered unpunishable. What causes the fixations later in years for adults to behave like people who have not matured in the cognitive and moral dimensions? The point is that many families and societies water hate, jealous and selfishness more than love in the formative years. They prolong the irrigation of bad seeds through the cognitive and moral development stages hence creating fixations in adulthood. This problem arises from parental neglect of the child and adopting *western models to water African collectivistic seeds.* Adopting Western models disbands the forces of collectivism during the watering process, yet these forces are instinctive and rooted in the socio-spiritual dimension. This is the reason why negativism is so powerful on the African continent!

Dealing with anxiety—an inquiry into Public Global Core Beliefs

To Africans

We have complained of slavery and colonialism, but why don't we ask ourselves a bold question: "What can we learn from Europe, Asia and the Americas that positioned themselves ahead of us?" Secondly, "what have we achieved from them?"

To Non – Africans

All along, we've been asking a wrong question, "What can we do for Africa?" The correct question should be, "What can we do with Africa?" Bill Clinton

Cultivating an Optimistic Mind

Why bad news spreads faster than good news? When you do something great and worth recognition, the news about your good deeds will not move as quickly as your bad deeds. Always people blame journalists for reporting bad news more than good news. In many instances, the bad news spreads faster because humans are always in a survival state, constantly looking out for hazards that pose a risk to their survival state. The bad news is considered a hazard. People will always have mixed opinions about the good news but quickly find a modal opinion about the bad news.

Sample Case Scenario. Think about the below scenario. The list of negative public opinions seems unlimited. Try to add your own; you will discover that the negatives are infinite.

ᵃ Scenario: At just 10 years old, he set up a very successful factory.

Possible negative public opinions:	Possible positive public opinions:
• His close relative helped him • He comes from a wealthy family • He is hardworking and toiled too much • He is lucky • He is a son of a minister. • The factory is not his. It is for someone else hiding in him	• He has the attributes and had to succeed • We supported him • He was guided • He was mentored

ᵇ Scenario: At 10 years old, he tried setting up a factory and failed.

Possible negative public opinions:	Possible positive public opinions:
• He was over-ambitious • He had embezzled funds • He is a senior rascal • He has many supporting rich friends • He was just showing off • Not possible at 10 years old	• The government failed him with high tax rates • Lack of government support • Lacked technology and capital

ᶜ Scenario: At 10 years, he wants to establish a factory.

Possible negative public opinions:	Possible positive public opinions:
• He won't handle • He is over-ambitious • Where has he got capital? He is daydreaming • Good luck, but I don't think he will handle • Yes, his dad is rich and has to give him a hand • Not possible at 10 years old	• We shall support him • He needs to be guided • He needs to be mentored

These are automatic thoughts, both positive and negatives thoughts cultivated in early experiences. In Robert Kiyosaki's book, "Rich Dad Poor Dad", Robert was raised and nurtured by two dads, the rich dad and the middle-income earning dad.[72] He thus got lessons from the two dads. Both dads shaped his core beliefs and decided on whose advice to follow for the rest of his life.

His decision to follow the rich dad's advice much more than the advice of the middle-income earning dad was motivated and triggered by the *evidence* he witnessed about the two dads. He thus followed

---

[72] Robert T. Kiyosaki, *Rich Dad Poor Dad* (New York: Hachette Book Group USA, 2001), 18-25.

an *evidence-based approach* to problem-solving. He never began from scratch, and he had a wealth of knowledge from both dads. Now, back to the African context, where we rarely have a chance to be nurtured in such an environment of mixed wisdom, what should we do?

Most Africans are born in poverty, grown and raised in poverty, nurtured in poverty, schooled in poverty, age in poverty, produce and reproduce in perpetual collectivistic poverty, and die in poverty. Those who are rich in Africa are just living a reasonably good life, but on the loans of others, the foreign aid, the exploitation of the masses, and the excellent positioning they hold as a result of circumstances induced by globalization and they can hardly sustain wealth down from one generation to many other generations to come. Of course, some Africans have worked out their wealth in good faith, but the markets of their goods and services are characterized by consumers who feed and survive primarily on foreign aid and loans limits their hope.

Being grown in poverty shapes the way we see the world with many impossibilities—the poverty we have created by ourselves for our acceptance to drop our sociocultural thinking instincts and intuitions to adopt the western world systems. The way we behave, feel and think are interrelated—highly influenced by cultural beliefs and predispositions. This acceptance draws many criticisms from people who understand the socioeconomic transformation roadmaps quite well. The blame is on us and nobody else; although partial attributions are correctly placed elsewhere, *acceptance* is the primary point that pins us down. We thus, nurture children who have developed a core belief that inventions and innovations cannot be made by the native African by blood and colour at such tender age of 10 years or below. This association of intelligence, brilliance and integrity with other non-African ethnicities cultivates a sense of perpetual poverty in the African child. This explains why very few African people agree that someone can innovate, invent, and solve problems at 10 years and below. How shall we solve poverty when we continue seeing things as complex and not doable by ourselves and tag ages to problem-solving as criteria? That we need to rely on others to program our lives.

The solution lies in cutting off the cycle of hopelessness. The Chinese say, "The person who says it cannot be done should not interrupt the person doing it." The word impossible does not exist in some families and societies. The more I keep questioning and think about science, technology and spirituality and distance myself from the conflicts of religious differences, the more I realize I can fly, only that I have not yet known how to. Even if I die without shooting my ambitions, I will remain with the belief that things are possible. The moment you keep believing things are doable, you are already miles into doing them. But when you think otherwise, that things are not doable, impossible, you live your whole life praising how others are heroes, lucky, geniuses and blessed.

Dealing with Inferiorism

Inferiority complex bleeds chronic anxiety and fear passed on from one generation to another. Africa's indigenous cultures are devalued at the expense of foreign cultures. As described in Chapter One (Culture and Religion), we are owed an apology.[73] Many things that have brought Africans to distance themselves from their cultures resulted from associating spirituality with governance and politics. People started to wholly embrace

---

[73] See p. 02, §1.

the ways, values and norms of the colonialists. This created anxiety in Africans who have not rethought the reclamation of the continent, mainly when the subject of the restoration of cultural norms is discussed.

Superstitions and prejudicial beliefs that surround a black cat demonstrate how societies could construct meaning on their environment. In some parts of the western world, seeing a black cat symbolises evil omens, whilst in other societies, black cats are looked at as a sign of good luck. Reality is, therefore, assigned by society. An object piece attains meaning by the dispositions passed onto it by the people of a given society. Our egos operate on what society perceives as real. Where inferiorism roots, false reality and false meanings are inevitable. This weakens the African child's ego. A weakened ego fails to balance forces due to biological processes and the mind's demands with moral dilemmas in the global arena. This brings about loosened self-esteem, and the value tagged on self-concept diminishes. The poverty of self-awareness perpetuated by inferiorism, makes no good place for better self-esteem and consequently no belief in innate ability to achieve goals by themselves—self-efficacy. The solution is thus embedded in self-awareness initiatives that go deeper in making people understand the cause, inspiring confidence in cultural values to grow the vernacular literacy so that we can expel the prolonged anxiety that threatens to pass on from one generation to another.

Dealing with Racism

Dealing with discrimination and bias. Apart from the illusion of knowledge, only one thing is more dangerous than ignorance in the 21st century: discrimination based on race, gender, and ethnicity. However, I ought not to forget that harming each other because of religious differences is nearly another form of ignorance.

More than any other race, the African child has faced some ill-treatment before others, in the form of; discrimination, bias, cruelty, and abuse, but the critical question to ask should be; why? It is essential to note that the contemporary definition of racism is discrimination against Africans. Africans rarely discriminate against others; we receive them equally in our land.

The act of discriminating against one another is less pronounced when an African is not featuring in the equation. The answer is simple: it lies in the overt oddness of the African masses failing to team up, disagree or agree constructively, continuous mistrust in one another, lack of self-confidence, and overt jealousness, which instils some anxiety and fear in the minds and hearts of others to act discriminatory in some way. However, some societies just look at Africans as simpletons because of colour, which is very idiotic. I have fallen victim to this nonsense on several occasions and had to get a pen and paper to start writing.

Many organized societies have expressed solidarity within themselves, something that a certain considerable fraction of African masses has failed to live to that standard. On several occasions, Africans are used by others to fight their colleagues. It is important to note that none is born a racist; they just learn from the environment in which they live. However, some just feel disgusted associating with Africans. As Africans, we need to respect this category, for they wish to be themselves.

It is important to note that discrimination can be defended at some point, just like any other thing. I have heard about positive action and positive discrimination. Borrowing from functionalism, the failure of Africans to recognize and embrace the good side of discrimination in politics, power, and governance explains why colonialism hit us the most. That was the reason for going *overboard* as far as conventional religions are concerned and the turbulent start of the post-independence era in many African countries. Recently, some religious and cultural leaders in Africa have understood the need to embrace good discrimination. That can only be appreciated and understood by someone who labours to question in a Socratic style. *Doing the right thing is not always right! Selling to the highest bidder is not always necessary!*

We need to empathetically understand that those who just feel disgusted associating with Africans have reasons for wanting to be themselves and only them. Those reasons, whether good or bad, are worth being respected and investigated. Much lies in understanding the source of these reasons. The solution lies in us to constructively challenge their attitudes, characters, and temperaments. An African child has some overt traits that need no defensive mechanisms to wrap action against them into racism! Because those people overgeneralize, some great Africans become victims of their somewhat evidenced beliefs. Some things need correct attribution and not fallacies and romance.

Acceptance is the mother of wisdom at some point. Once we do the above constructively, we rise and challenge their understanding of humanity and other living beings. A fraction of those who graduated to the nonracist group is challenged day-to-day by some overt traits of Africans. However, the only treatment to keep the bias entirely out of the graduates is to show cohesiveness, unity, peace, teamwork, integrity, and patriotism as Africans.

Otherwise, to believe that a majority of others appreciate the ability of the African race is a modern-day deception. Their predispositions and unconscious communicate racists' characters in the silent majority. When we do all these I mentioned, we shall lead and improve the world to become a better place to live. We are the problem and yet the solution.

The Myth or Truth of One Race Supremacy

The wiring of a human being's neurons has nothing to do with their appearance and colour. Some people have kept the myth of one race being superior to another. If you believe in superiority, you must be able to defend your argument with evidence. There has always been a myth in the supremacy of one colour over another. The environment is an essential factor determining the stimulus that conditions the brain to grow and respond appropriately. Socioeconomic and political rights influence the psychosocial wellbeing of all humans across the globe. Some Africans have not laboured to find the truth, and they keep believing that they are too down to live on their own, create and recreate themselves. Correct leadership steering African nations have the keys to unlock Africa's potential and end the myth of inferiority, among others.

The argument about one race being superior among other races has been at the forefront for a very long time. In my opinion, some people of a dominating race have had some form of domineering *cardinal traits,* at some point in time, whether you want to agree or not. That is primarily in terms of leadership traits. I take full responsibility for this opinion. In terms of IQ, I think not. It is a question of leadership that has been seen as supreme over others. The *evidence* is in *leadership styles.*

For example, many researchers reported that, way back before the 1930s and beyond, African Americans showed lower intelligence and academic achievements compared with their counterparts, the Asian Americans and white Americans.[74] In my opinion, this might have resulted from the oppression and suppression of the African American people at that time because, towards the end of the 20th Century, the same category of researchers reported that African American people's intelligence and academic achievements had improved drastically. Despite all these facts, in my opinion, the domineering group has consistently led in cultivating a favourable environment for sustainable personality formation in themselves, growth and development of a wholesome human being of themselves. However, the continued fixation and belief that Africans cannot improve the world by many others will shock them at some point. Or else the sustainable development equation will do it in itself. Climate change consequences are powerful; they can create a new world!

When you subject all races to the same conditions, like learning in the same schools, there is no striking difference, but you will notice a huge difference when they get out of school. In my opinion, on a modal average, the domineering race has been farsighted and smarter. Altruism, as the central philosophy of teambuilding, makes them beat the odds. However, if you consciously behave ill towards others, time is the only component that can make you good towards them. Slowly you will learn. It might not come overnight, but it will certainly come to learn the experience and stop the conscious ill-attitudes towards others. In many times, unwanted emotional garbage and ill-treatment of others is an unconscious character possessed by a particular category of people. In today's global village, consciously creating enemies is the worst form of ignorance amidst the climate change challenge.

In many times, a middleman lives a more prosperous life than a craftsman. There are lots of beautiful poetic ideas that were obtained from Africa. One who takes the record to book and consequently files for discovery takes the credit whilst the first discoverer takes no credit. That is why Lake Victoria in East Africa was named before the then reigning Queen of England, in a claim that John Hanning Speke was the first person to see the lake, and therefore, the discoverer. Where were the natives—those who welcomed the claimed discoverer?

You have the idea, and you cannot work along getting it out on the road to actualization. The one who actualizes it is a master. You have the land resources and other minerals, but you cannot utilize them. He who utilizes the minerals is a master. A lack of curiosity makes one's life meaningless. The first line discipline of an ambitious nationalistic figure understands the root causes, appreciates them, and accepts the facts to find solutions but not devise defensive mechanisms. Those are the reasons that have shaped the domineering race as supreme over many others!

Recreating an African Brand

Africa is in a dire state to rebrand. Every bad thing is associated with Africa. These range from extensive criminalities, dictators, crimes against humanity, and indiscipline. The truth is that all countries have people who commit crimes or do evil things, but Africa is used as typical of such. We must rebrand to wipe out the prejudice and bias that others have about the African child. The genesis of this prejudice is

---

[74] James R. Flynn, *The Mean IQ of Americans: Massive Gains 1932 to 1978* (Washington, DC: American Psychological Association, 1984), 32.

rooted in the slave trade, of which African chiefs had cases to answer. African chiefs had a strong hand in slavery. However, at some point, they can defend the prejudice which calls on us to change in the interest of sustainability.

The image of the African child is not that awe-inspiring in the eyes of others. Those who have been victimized basing on the stereotypes that others hold about the African child can narrate the story of how they felt, and when I say we need total rebranding, they can support my cause. It might be challenging to comprehend what I am trying to describe in this context unless you have fallen victim to Africa's false image before others. For example, it is almost impossible for others to accept that an African can possess outstanding abilities to *lead* technological innovations in space science.

Many African people who have started businesses in areas that have mixed races have felt significant obstacles in building winning brands. Some need to forge plans to associate their brands with other races to be more competitive. Customers have constantly scrutinized the African child's business because of our history not more than one and a half-century ago. This is the perfect time to rebrand and convince the world that we are taking a firm ground to apologize on behalf of our late African chiefs who found no crime in selling their brothers and sisters. In the history of slavery, Africa is the most victimized.

On the other hand, much as we feel guilty about our late chiefs selling our blood as slaves, others owe us an apology for associating conventional religions with colonialism. In modern criminal law, the buyer and the seller both commit crimes. The slave buyers were more educated at that time, and they thus viewed the world more differently from Africans. I am convinced that oppressive colonialism was fuelled by African chiefs' narcissistic traits that they could not foresee the dangers that were likely to come as a result of the trade.

Who is Responsible for Africa's Rebranding?

The media is greatly responsible for leading change. The practice of quickly exposing every tiny hopeless situation that makes Africans look thoughtless should be put to an end. The media quickly reports any funny incidences happening on the continent and circulates the files on social media platforms. I am not slowing down the freedom of media houses, but I am reminding them of the unforeseen role in promoting Africa's false image. Except for the incidences that infringe on human rights, human dignity, oppression and suppression, and similar events, some incidents ought not to be aired and circulated on social media platforms. They should be dealt with internally, and only people of that area get to learn about the adverse event happening in their locale. For example, a journalist who keeps his cameras focused on a stripped intruder into a football pitch during a game might prove unethical—this is typical of many African reporters.

If you dream of boosting tourism and competitiveness, you need to exploit all avenues that add positively to the promotion and marketing campaign. My argument should not be misinterpreted; it is about training journalists with minds that think beyond and without borders. We need journalism that is holistic and ensures to protect the dignity and integrity of African humankind. Journalism that thinks yesterday, today and tomorrow; journalism that thinks here and beyond; and journalism that thinks the implications of whatever is aired out. There are several reasons why some leaders of the campaign to have free and democratic societies have restrictions on who views certain aspects of their activities. They have a discriminatory strategy on who uses their technologies—and from where? They keep an eye on whatever you process out of the use of their technologies.

Politicians. African politicians have a huge role to play in recreating an African brand. They hold the keys to inform the world about the social transformation Africa is undergoing to improve lives. The quality of African politicians will determine the extent Africa will go to rebrand.

Perfectionist's Limits

Do not worry much about the accuracy of whatever you are doing. Just keep doing it. I do not think this book is so accurate and perfect, but I authored it, anyway. It is not about the accuracy and perfection of what you are doing; it is about doing it.

You want to start a factory, do not worry about the quality of your first products, and so long as you essentially meet the minimum lawful requirements, start or keep doing. Trouble comes when you stop doing or fail to start. Do not worry much about the failure; you only need to be right once.

There is one vital resource you cannot recover, and that is time. You do not need to acquire everything to start, and you need not be perfect to kick-start. The best way to start is to start. There is no designated time/age to start; you can always begin from where you are and at whatever age. Begin today on whatever you wish to begin. Listen very little to naysayers, and avoid responding to negative people to make your life a peaceful walk. Worry little about things that do not go as planned. Truth has it that many people and organizations rarely meet everything they plan for the calendar year. Things rarely come out as you envisage.

Impossibilities. "Impossible" is in you, not others. Please keep it to yourself. What you failed to do in your childhood, adolescence, early adulthood was your mistake. Do not discourage the young generations. Thinking impossible only means you are not capable but not others. Impossible is when you have not tried and persisted. In some parts of Africa, one who thinks positive and dreams big is usually referred to as being over-ambitious. In the developed world, such a person is viewed as being visionary. We are always contented with small things. Do not let someone with a small mind deceive you that your dreams are too big. Everything is viewed as impossible to many until when it is done. It takes much commitment to prove that the world is full of endless possibilities. It is thus very possible for Africa to lead sustainable growth and development on its own.

Nature has ideals. Imagine a situation where everything was perfect: no sickness, income is evenly distributed, food is readily available and freely accessible, etcetera. What would we have to do then? We live to fix issues, and no one should ever tell you otherwise that we can have a thoroughly perfect society. Even some societies which seem developed are now contemplating mental health versus guns. They are contemplating the danger of social media to teens and etcetera. AI and robotics impose numerous challenges to humanity and the like. We live in ideals, and we shall continue to live so where everything ends in nothing. I believe in subjectivism to some extent, where truth is perceived as a matter of perspective. What is true and false, original and duplicate?

There is no fixed being on planet earth, and life is too short; living somebody else's life is no advantage. We have inputs and outputs, but the entire system equals and ends in nothing. We are born with no property, and we die and get buried with no property.

Another person may argue that everything is matter; it just changes states and forms but remains constant. We need driving forces behind us, without which one cannot do much. If you are rejoicing of experiences and success in year B while living in year A, just know you have not accomplished much in year A. What keeps a vehicle move is fuel put in. We keep breathing oxygen to live; we eat, drink and pass out the effluent. This is an in-out system. The ultimate end is nothing.

Another person may claim that everything is soil so long as it leaves within the reach or environs of the gravitational sphere of influence. What keeps us waking up every morning to work is the fear of tomorrow because we do not know what tomorrow holds. If tomorrow were sure, life would carry no meaning. And still, if we could all be equated, there would be little meaning in life. There would be no need to live. We live to work.

Issues to sort or fix are what brought us into this world. We realize we are fortunate to live in this era where we experience a form of freedom. Although in some territories, oppression, repression, and suppression dominate but the ancient was only dominance of those with ambient force, i.e. the emperors, the warlords and chiefs. We should thus not take this ideal freedom for granted. Let us work.

Should the World drive you or you should drive it?

Strive to create something driving you in this world. Do not let the world drive you. A goal is good enough. Pursue the goal. Even if you fail to shoot in the years lived, the willingness to shoot is enough to keep you happy. You realize that as you pursue the goal, you cannot even remember that you are ageing. As you pursue the goal, you will see years as if they are months and months like weeks, weeks as days and days as hours, hours as minutes and minutes as seconds, seconds as microseconds and microseconds as open.

You will appreciate the fact that nature has problems. You have to work because nature holds problems. What would you do if problems were not there? Everyone wakes up in the morning to fix a problem. We fix problems as we age. As we age, the bones lose strength, the cells die out, and we finally die. When you find the reason to live and work hard, you will not be scared of death. You will see no point in crying for someone who passes away when they have accomplished what they aimed at.

Many things are possible and not yet discovered. I am optimistic and highly convinced that the future promises to find life on other planets, the present has just not discovered it. I do not think we can ever say that the universe is now fully understood, that the world has no space for improvement, and there is no space for innovations, new products, new processes, new legislations, and change. We shall always have change.

> *"Discovery consists in seeing what everyone else has seen and thinking what no one else has thought." Albert Szent-Gyorgi (1893 –1986)*[75]

---

[75] Albert Szent-Gyorgi was a Hungarian Biochemist who won a 1937 Nobel Prize for Medicine.

Superpowers will always turn around. There will not be fixed superpowers forever. The balance of power will continually change. The supernatural, above science and technology, which is synonymous with fate, shall always prevail and take precedence—the Supreme Being. This will be and is central to shape the future. For example, those who understand climate change and its threats can echo this argument by doing a little mathematical calculation. Although we plan and try to predict, manage, control or mitigate the consequences of climate change, limitations are infinite.

Complexities in scientific models and the growing hazards of whatever we touch in technology and science creates an important question. It is becoming a common slogan that item A solves a particular problem but is hazardous and whose risk leads to loss of life. A growing need to integrate items A, B, C, and more to solve issues with potential hazards and a complex mixture of risks is a good indicator of the complexity of technology and science and the limitations of science. We must be borrowing existence from an unknown source; a lot remains unexplained.

I have noticed that most people at the top are ordinary people who do things the extraordinary way. One-on-one talks greatly depict little or no outstanding attributes for many top generals. We cannot rule out geniuses, talented ones, messiahs and prophets, shrewd brained, and some bit of lucky guys, but a lot is made by ordinary people who take on an extra mile. They are a little more curious than others, good at team working, and altruistic. Therefore, they cannot fail to beat the odds.

There is a silver lining in every dark point, but you have perhaps not seen it yet. Look for the silver lining in all dark points. You are what you are either because of what you have done right or what you have done wrong. Time can never go late for positive thinkers. Any time, you can act. Look for the silver lining in the wrong. It is possible to change the situation.

It might look like one gate has been closed for you, yet another is being opened, but it requires much courage to see the opened gate. Many challenges present opportunities, but not all people can see them. Just as oil, a natural resource, is used to produce many products, and it lives underneath the sea, and the earth explains that nothing is easy to obtain. There is always a reason why your life is being shaped the way it is. There is always a silver lining amidst difficulties. Many difficulties are there to wake us up. We realize that our lives may have been shaped by someone else at some point in life. You could be a minister today because of someone else's efforts, not your own making. Someone may have faced the pain because of you.

You might find that in someone's difficulties, it is where you emerged to become a minister. There are always the so-called turning points. These turning points are always shaped by several factors, independent or dependent on one another—factors that could be bad or good. The important lesson here is drawing back from many experiences, your own and copying from those of others. Start to view things optimistically and be a little more curious. Ask why they happen to you and find answers before concluding and taking decisions. Various cognitive and motivational biases frequently influence our perceptions and lead us to draw erroneous conclusions. You discover that most of these issues are important to you. Others are warning signs which most people find hard to appreciate. Take time to reason beyond the obvious and go slow where necessary.

Our societies are full of naysayers. Stay away from negative people. They have a problem with every solution. Napoleon Bonaparte (1769 – 1821) made it very clear when he wrote to General Jean Le Marois, 'You write to me that it is impossible; the word is not French.'[76] In other words, the word impossible did not exist in his dictionary. To him, all things were possible. His remarks are very courageous, although motivational speakers sometimes fail to associate an appropriate disclaimer to his remarks. They can make many Africans feel like a fortune can happen overnight and how possible a dog can race a cheetah and several other things of that kind. I firmly believe that a lot is possible under the sun. Today, we live amidst hopeless African people that can quickly label a person who thinks how possible it is to discover what happens elsewhere in the universe, an insane or psychotic person. Our societies are so less privileged to think piecemeal on several occasions. Big thinkers are always seen as daydreamers. Then, how shall we achieve the target of competing with the rest of the world if we continue the same way?

We cannot solve problems in the same way in which we created them. We have consistently done the same things over and over again ever since colonialists left. How are we going to help ourselves? Much of what many Africans celebrate today is due to foreign direct investment and donations to the African child but hardly a result of our sweats! We are fond of following what has been done elsewhere in the developed world but hardly think of our solutions. This is typical of several African states. We need to rethink new mechanisms if we are to reclaim the position of Africa and catch space in real-time.

The Power of Prayer. Prayer works for believers in the Supreme Being or whatever someone calls Supreme; it works for those who make good decisions. One should not be misled that mere praying without work yields sustainable fruition—it does not. You are right to think that prayer can work for you, and if you think it cannot, you are equally right. I believe in respect for one another—the fundamental fallibility of human knowledge—species of truth should be allowed to co-occur. Our beliefs are different, and we ought to recognize this and have mutual respect for one another.

While some Africans spend 90% of their time worshipping the Supreme Being to drop wellness, others elsewhere are working. The sustainable development we are eyeing does not leave our core beliefs out. However, each person's core beliefs must align with the sustainable development campaign because this is the main goal for why we believe in 21st-century governments. Suppose you find it appropriate for you to pray overnight, spending much of your time in worshipping centres and temples. In that case, you are right so long as this contributes to Africa's self-driven sustainable development campaign and protects your position on what you believe in the spirit, mind, and soul. If you find saying prayers from your home as a family sufficient, you are equally right so long as you are sure this contributes to your wellness in the spirit and soul.

Is Being Born Poor Magical?

Most Africans are born poor. It is a fact. A prominent person once said, "Being born poor is not your mistake but dying poor is your mistake." In that case, he was drawing knowledge and understanding from existentialist theories that presume that every person is responsible for their actions and choices. That

---

[76] From a letter that Napoleon wrote from Dresden on July 9, 1813, to General Jean Le Marois, the governor of Magdeburg, a French stronghold in Germany.

we are the authors of our lives, and we design the signposts to follow.[77] The reason to live for a person who is born poor is more magnified than someone born when everything seems perfect. Perhaps a born rich may need to look for needy living beings and associate or learn with them to understand scarcity. And it is scarcity that makes one appreciate more why they live. Advancing technologies are making young generations incredibly the born rich of some countries, develop beliefs such as—when one needs mangoes, the perfect place to source them is either a supermarket or a refrigerator.

A born poor child learns through scarcity. He quickly learns that we get mangoes from mango trees. This enables the child to look at everything as only achievable through hard work. Many a time, great scientists, artists, sportspeople, philosophers, entrepreneurs, freedom fighters, educationists, and many others are born from disadvantaged environments. So, when one is born poor, they should not feel cursed; they have the freedom to exercise the power of their minds and bodies to the fullest potential, unlike a born rich.

On several occasions, students from disadvantaged African states perform better than their counterparts in the developed countries when they learn in the same classes. This is explainable in a way that candidates from the developed countries have little to worry about; secondly, their minds and bodies' survival is not threatened by the society in which they originate. Everything seems to be okay—in a comfort zone. Therefore, being born poor can be viewed as an opportunity to the optimist—where one understands that a crisis is an opportunity.

Minding Your Business

Have you ever been disliked by someone you have not wronged? Have you ever disliked a person who has not wronged you? If not, you are fortunate. Some people are always on the lookout for conflicts from others. At workplaces, in residential areas, and many other places, people find contentment in nagging others. They always look out for sources of conflict with others. They have a personality disorder somewhat similar to Attention—Deficit Hyperactivity Disorder (ADHD) in children. These people seem to mind more of others' businesses than theirs. Something which does not affect you, why bother you to the extent of living someone else's life? A conflict to which you are not a party, why peddle influence in it? You have a life to live and a family to look after, but you spend more time discussing and nagging others. You try all ways to meddle influence in things that do not concern you. Why worry so much? The decisions you always take are those which take away peace from your neighbours. You are not afraid of becoming a nuisance anytime. Somebody opens a business next to yours, and you have all the courage to fail it.

There is a growing concern in Africa—generally on how people mind about things they are not concerned with. The distorted bonds of collectivism worsen this. Ideally, a well-individuated human is supposed to stick to their purpose in life. You need not be a very religious person to mind your own business; it must be a personality disorder that makes a person feel more concerned with things they are not a party to than their things. Why get involved with things independent of your life to the extent of annoying, irritating, or even harming others?

---

[77] See p. 248, §5.

You should stick to your business and stop bothering your neighbours with the things you are less concerned with, things in which you are not a party. Getting bothered by things you are not associated with other than yours is dangerous. For example, getting sick because of one's success is outright ignorance.

There is always room to correct our psychological illnesses, only that some people do not want to heal. Minding your work, goals, and vision is one step to moving forward. A successful life is one tied to a goal, not on people. Unhealthy competitions which drive people to mind more of others' business is better when left for the entertainment industry, specifically the comedy industry. Living a prosperous life requires many sacrifices to make. Only that a few people wish to live remarkably by contributing to the wellbeing of humanity. It is out of the enthusiastic spirit to save humanity that one learns to stick to their goal. When you stick to a goal, you learn to avoid getting into things that do not matter or things you are less concerned with. You avoid your heart, soul, and emotions from getting into psychological turmoil because of other people's far-reaching success. Happiness is being free from such psychological disorders. MIND your business![78]

African Attitude Gone Wrong

I have observed what I am about to describe, and I apologize if somebody else had a different view. An African opens up a business next to that of an Asian, European, or American. A few Africans would support their fellow African by buying their products or services. Instead, most Africans would buy from the foreigner, leaving that of the fellow African yearning for customers, and the business ultimately fails and dies out. We cannot develop when we lack the solidarity to support our cause. Spending within and for the territory should be the priority. We need to support our cause.

Some Africans find it morally right to perform cultural rituals by calling them religious rituals of European descent.[79] Example: Ssekkeba is an African name; many people can name their children "Ssekkeba" if you tell them it is of European origin. However, it would sound satanic and fake to some if they discover the true origin later. This depicts a deep-seated problem I am about to describe henceforth. Even if you are the brightest person in Africa with no support from others, you cannot make things happen. Innovate and develop; then, people need to appreciate your innovation to create meaning and purpose. Several incidences have happened to me, but the most interesting ones are two (2):

> [a] I was driving with an Asian friend, and I entered a garage to fix the car, but the mechanic directed the invoice to the Asian friend. The Asian friend nodded his head and said, "You should learn to trust your people, and please, this is his car."

> [b] Two (2) hotel restaurants taking long to serve me but quickly pop up when the European and Asian friends arrived to meet me, yet morally, it is always a first-come, first-serve basis. I had waited for the European and Asian friends for about 3 to 5 minutes, respectively. It is evident that, on average, Europeans, Americans, and Asians are economically stronger than

---

[78] See p. 236, (Hint: Are people unique?), §5.
[79] See p. 15, §1.

Africans, measured by gross domestic product (GDP) per capita and human development index (HDI). However, the African moral school and any other race pity the fool who does not love their people and demonstrates a lack of self-confidence within themselves. In one of the restaurants, I called the restaurant manager and expressed my concerns to her; for that matter, we never ordered anything. The manager comprehended my point. We had our meeting that lasted for about 30 minutes, and after that, we left.

In many African countries, foreigners are treated better and with utmost integrity, giving them privileges such as tax holidays for their businesses investments to prosper compared to fellow African business people. With this kind of nonsense and hopelessness left to escalate, how will we rebrand or fight racism? That is one of the reasons why others mistreat us because we do not trust ourselves. When other people see such hopelessness, they cannot fail to get scared. You cannot fight racism when you demonstrate the poverty of unity, cohesiveness, and ambition.

Some foreigners are now taking advantage to masquerade as investors but only to end up in retail shops. This is because when Africans see an Asian, European, or American, their false automatic thoughts are activated. If you want your African startup to get customers quickly, have partners or staff that are non-African. Of course, Africa needs investors, I do not doubt that, but local investors need to be treated equally. Otherwise, it symbolizes hopelessness and a lack of correct direction on how to develop our economies sustainably.

Many Africans have innovated several technologies, ranging from software to networking businesses and social platforms, but fellow Africans do not support them. In many cases, products made by Africans are abandoned by fellow Africans to opt for substandard products imported from the Asian giant. Some of our innovative products are symbolic of Africa's uniqueness, culture, and style, which foreigners cannot miss buying.

The cause of African Attitude Gone Wrong

There is a deep-seated problem. This disease or disorder has to be treated. From slavery to religion to colonialism, Africans have been severely impacted. As I explained in Chapter One (Religion and Culture), Africans lost self-confidence that became a multigenerational issue.[80] Our self-worth and self-efficacy were all sabotaged. The majority of current Africans are not sure about their self-worth and self-efficacy, ultimately impacting self-confidence before others. We need holistic treatment.

Stereotypes, Prejudice, and African Core Beliefs

Over the years, I have noticed that African stereotypes hold some truth based on my evidence gathered. I wish to apologize to the learned fraternity who physically detest, and not psychologically detest, all stereotypes of African descent in a situation where African philosophy, coined as ethno-philosophy, is rooted in proverbs, sayings, languages, and dialects. And philosophy is the mother of all other disciplines.

It is good to note that the statistics of the stereotype carry meaning. It is understandable to rubbish the stereotype as a mere widely held but fixed and oversimplified image or idea of a particular type of person

---

[80] See p. 44-55, §1.

or thing but listen to the message carried by the *statistics of the stereotype*. It will perhaps explain the genesis of the stereotype, the how, and why it happened. I have found that African stereotypes carry meaning worth investigating. They are much more than stereotypes. I do not know about other non-African peoples, but from my evidence about Africans, I am convinced that some people are destined to vend ice cream despite achievements in education and other social constructions. I make a psychological assumption that there is no joke without serious meaning to further my hypothesis.

With a tremendous desire to know, learn, and relearn, I try to follow up on these stereotypes, first by denoting them as mere allegations, maladaptive core beliefs labelled on our ancestors. I make such a hypothesis. Over the last ten years, I have tried to surround myself with ten (10) mature males of a certain descent. I have realised that they possess a unique cognitive attribute, predicted through their overt behaviours and actions. All are exceptionally intelligent and very well-learned, as measured by academic metrics. I was trying to figure out whether there is a positive correlation between the mere allegations or maladaptive thoughts inferred by our ancestors through proverbs and sayings. To my surprise, I found some truth in these stereotypes as so-called. The sample is small, but I have made my observations for over ten (10) years, closely associating with these colleagues occupationally. All were found to have some significant level of psychopath. Therefore, I have concluded that Africa's hope should be firmly held in understanding ourselves, self-awareness, research on our own humanity, rediscover ourselves, and promote our own.

Because we have been conditioned to follow western cultural ideologies, we have forgotten about our uniqueness as Africans. We need an investigation into our uniqueness and begin bringing our ancestral philosophies to use. African philosophy and psychology are incomplete without making archaeological digs into the meanings of stereotypes as prophesized and philosophized by our ancestors. Some of these are overt characters whose implication has been abused as allegations and consequently affected the planning and decision making. Yet, ancestors had forewarned through their ethno-philosophies as so-called. The planning, the decisions we make, the thinking, reasoning, and understanding has a solid bearing on our cultural roots regardless of academic achievement. Should we wholly rubbish our ancestral pool of knowledge as mere stereotypes, for that matter, and that they serve little purpose? The failure to extract meaning and purpose from our ancestral knowledge and wisdom is opposing and fighting the uniqueness of Africa.

What is the Implication of not Examining Stereotypes and Ancestral Philosophies?

It is more damaging to have stereotypes and ancestral philosophies unexamined because they motivate prejudice. We need to conduct research and results get published to nullify or validate the stereotypes to become facts. And when we discover these facts, we look for solutions. Our main goal is to achieve self-driven sustainable development, and therefore, we need to reexamine the ancestral pool of knowledge. The deep-seated stereotypes, most of them arising out of the lack of a complete explanation of African philosophies to the masses but remain only understandable by those who have gotten a lifelong interest in listening to the message they carry, and others arising out of the dilemmas of contemporary living such as the socioeconomic inequalities, motivate prejudices. We need to reexamine the ancestral philosophies and listen carefully to hear the meaning they carry. Psychologists claim that there is no joke without serious meaning, and people have been joking right from ancient times to date.

The *assumption* is to label the stereotype a *joke!* I find it terrible to announce that African stereotypes carry no implications amidst a myriad of ethnic backgrounds. We only need careful examination and listen carefully. The way one responds after being prejudiced through a given stereotype creates the meaning we need to observe and process that information. The effect of prejudice cannot stretch any further if it carries little impactful meaning on you. The fact that it prolongs itself with the time element indicates something more profound than the obvious for those willing to listen and learn. For example, when an African is stereotyped as "poor at time management", label this a joke and investigate deeper. Why not stereotype a European or Asian?

On Inferiorism and Attitude

Four attributes define you before others: self-confidence, self-worth, self-concept, and self-efficacy. As an African, if you are not sure about yourself on all the four attributes before others in specific situations, you are susceptible to catch the inferiority bug. In explaining African attitude gone wrong, I explained how fellow Africans abandon to support fellow Africans and treat foreigners better. This justifies the impacts of slavery, colonialism, and religions whose multigenerational effects need to be treated. The new unhelpful core beliefs that were formed through cognitive restructuring of African masses, done *without evidence,* are perpetuated through the maintenance of the aversive schemas.

Africans are now thinking and behaving inferior before other races putting other's interests and needs before their own needs. We treat other races better than our race. Regrettably, fellow Africans kill themselves day in and day out across the continent whilst promoting others' interests in our land. We need to change and stop acting in accordance with purported schemas that do not inspire hope for African humankind. It took me time to realize one of the reasons African students who get opportunities in the form of scholarships to study in the universities outside Africa perform better often, at times emerging out as the best. The reason is that they study while tensed to impress because, in the case of poor performance, they would be apologizing to others that they are Africans.

Theoretical Understanding of Attitude

> ***Disclaimer:*** *The next sections from pages 192–202 represents more or less my novel ideas about attitude. They are more or less concepts that could be insights for someone who wishes to design a package of attitude reforms. They are not facts or approved theories for anyone to consider accurate and reference. Anyone can revise, criticize, and contribute to further developments as they wish. These are ideas that require heavily researched observations/experiments. It would need about US$ 5m funding for research. This would aim at growing attitudes that would lead to Africa's self-driven sustainability.*

To mention somebody's attitude, you must associate it with an attitude object, an attitude piece, an attitude event, or an attitude environment. "He gave me an attitude" is less formal, which literary means a bad attitude, but technically speaking about a person's attitude, you have to mention at least one of the following for your argument to carry meaning: the self, others, and the environment. Attitude is a function of cognition, feelings, and behaviours. One's attitude towards something is explained in a non-unidirectional approach because the three variables forming somebody's attitude are interdependent and influence each other.

I can mention that Jim's attitude towards e-banking is negative predetermined by the core beliefs he has developed over time. This could mean that his attitude is bad, non-constructive, or less optimistic towards e-banking (the attitude event). You could define Jim's attitudes towards many other things such as; people, wildlife, objects, other environments, et cetera.

The assumption: Although cognition, feelings (sensational and emotional), and behaviours influence each other, and at some point they are interdependent, these events never occur in series, and therefore, have some degree of mutual independence since their *effects and causes* are entirely independent. The non-unidirectional representation of Jim's attitude towards e-banking can be illustrated as below:

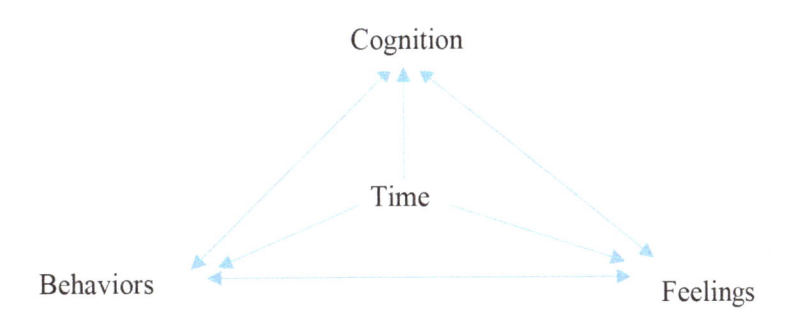

Time Influences Attitude: A Non-Unidirectional Representation of Attitude

Modelling Attitude

The way we think influences the way we feel and behave and vice-versa. However, the *causes and effects* induced by the three in the attitude system are independent. *I will use Bettina, a fresh graduate, to describe the concepts.*

Bettina, a Fresh Graduate

Bettina, a fresh graduate, is recruited in a workplace whose occupational health and safety culture is inconsistent with statutory standards. It always downpours during rush work hours, and she makes it routine to carry on her a small umbrella in her bag for the two consecutive months for which the weather has been very unpredictable. After the 2 months elapse, Bettina unconsciously carries an umbrella even though the rainy season stops. She just finds herself with an umbrella in the handbag. She finally falls in love with umbrellas because the workplace has frequently made her associate with umbrellas due to the irregularities in keeping up with occupational health and safety (OHS) standards. Her attitude towards umbrellas completely changes, and wherever she sees a nice umbrella that can be carried in her handbag, she wishes to buy it. The workplace's occupational hazards made Bettina fall in love with umbrellas because she always had to carry on her one to mitigate the risk of raining on her during the rush work hours.

How to interpret Bettina's Learning?

Bettina's love for umbrellas is caused and shaped by the workplace hazards that made her life wholly associated with umbrellas; despite winter or summer, she finds herself with an umbrella in her handbag. Her attitude towards umbrellas has changed suddenly, and she wants to surround her residence with a good number of them. Whenever she sees signs of rain like wind blowing heavily (feeling), she remembers what didn't go well at work without the umbrella, and she immediately thinks (cognition) of picking an umbrella, moves into the house (behaviour) and pick one. This series of events can also start with moving into the house and see the umbrella or thought of rain. Her attitude towards umbrellas has changed, and she now has about 10 different umbrella sizes stocked in her house.

Bettina decides to move on and look for another better organization. Unfortunately, she finds the same challenge of unsatisfactory occupational health and safety standards. Her recently grown belief that such companies in that area/locale do not meet occupational health and safety standards is reinforced. The frustration caused by the hazardous workplace distorts her cognition and jumps to the conclusion that all similar workplaces are hazardous too. When she talks with friends about similar organizations, she gets typically bad automatic thoughts about similar workplaces. She is very convinced that all similar organizations in the locale do not take health and safety seriously—and this becomes a deep-seated belief. Many things can be learnt from Bettina's story; her new core belief and changed attitude towards umbrellas.

Understanding and Growing Attitudes

Attitudes can be changed. It is possible, although quite tricky. I mentioned earlier that attitude is a function of the three main variables; emotions, thoughts and behaviours. There could be other extraneous variables, like physiology and the environment, but both influence feelings (sensational and emotional) and behaviours. It is, therefore, essential to keep extraneous variables out of the attitude equation. It is equally important to note that a slight change in cognitions, emotions (sensational and emotional feelings) and behaviours can induce an attitude change and a change in the other two variables.

I pose a hypothetical equation for attitude:

$$A = a(c, b, f)$$

It is purely a psychological construct, a theorem that would explain attitude changing with the effects and causes of cognition, emotions and behaviours. A minimal change in one induces a change in the two others and a changed attitude towards an attitude piece.

Assumption:

Note that c, b, and f are to a considerable extent interdependent but *non-unidirectional* and are modelled as mutually independent events. The cause in their changes and the effects they produce in the attitude system are not always interdependent and, therefore, considered independent. What leads you to think of something is independent of what leads you to behave in another way and vice-versa. What leads you to feel in another way is independent of what leads you to behave in another way and vice-versa. What leads you to feel in some way, either sensationally or emotionally, is independent of what leads you to think in some way and vice-versa.

Similarly, the effect of how we think, how we feel, and how we behave towards/about something in the overall attitude system are independent of one another. It is on rare occasions for effects and causes of emotions, thoughts and behaviours to intertwine with one another. The happening of one of the three (3) may influence the happening of others but in a *non-unidirectional* way, and the causal and resultant items are independent. Therefore, the effects and causes are modelled as independent events.

Therefore, the hypothetical equation can hardly be a *linear one*. Conventionally, attitude towards an attitude piece/event is the dependent variable and c, b, and f are independent variables. Note that the effects produced by c, b, and f are independent. For example, one's attitude towards the phone is independent of their attitude towards football which could be induced by a change in perception, association, body physiology and the environment. When you feel happy and motivated, the cause and effect of this happiness are independent of the effect of the subsequent behaviour and cognition. As given in the explanation about Bettina above, *the time component* is a significant factor in attitude change and consequently in personality change, formation and reformation. The psychological construct must include a time dimension.

This psychological construct is premised on the assumption that you do not determine your attitude; others evaluate your attitude. This is why the construct assumes that the effects and causes of changes in the 3 variables are independent. Take another example, where Jonah owes Anna $15. The date for paying back is overdue, and Anna needs her $15. She calls Jonah several times, demanding her money. Unfortunately, Jonah hasn't got the money. Jonah picks Anna's phone for the first and second time and tries to explain the condition as he makes more promises to pay in the next few days. The days elapse, and Anna keeps calling. This time round Jonah starts ignoring the phone (behaviour) and, at worst, switches off (behaviour). Anna insists on keeping calling whenever Jonah switches on the phone (behaviour). At first, an assumption made is that, before Jonah switches off the phone, he has started feeling anxious (emotion), and without thinking enough, he decided to switch off. After a few thoughts (cognition), he switches on. When Anna relaxes the calls, Jonah feels relaxed and consequently suspends the switch-offs. In this illustration, Anna evaluates Jonah's attitude towards the phone (in that period) when he owes another person money, and Jonah evaluates Anna's attitude at the other end. The myriad of causes and effects to think, behave and feel differently at any given time are independent hence making a person's attitude *fluctuate* at some point. This is because Jonah's or Anna's behaviours could be influenced by many events beyond the $15 demand note. It is these events that should be entered into a *probability space*.

Attitude and Personality Formation, Reformation and Change—using Bettina's illustration

Now, Bettina's attitude towards umbrellas has changed, and a new core belief registered as a result of cumulative thoughts caused by the frustration of workplace hazards. Bad thoughts happen when some bit of trauma she experienced at the workplace is activated. She developed some kind of anxiety and does not want to associate with such workplaces anymore. She gives a bad attitude when one mentions such kinds of workplaces. Considering many other series of events that have influenced her life, Bettina's attitudes keep changing. The implication is that her personality can change with time because personality is an integral sum of attitudes. Social media, AI, and other technologies shape personality formations for today's infants, children, adolescents and the old. I have conclusively reached a consensus that attitudes change but through a gradual process. Therefore, someone's attitudes and personality in 2011 can be very different from that of 2021 because of the life events we go through.

Therefore, Personality at time t, $P_t = \int_t dA$

Note: The above is a mathematical construct.

One's personality can be defined by a series of attitudes ranging from one attitude towards something/event to hundreds or thousands and much more. The modern world longing for the planet's sustainability will have to revise another way to define people's personalities, using this approach of benchmarking on attitudes and drawing out a locus of points to mark attitude positions. And the subsequent aggregation of attitudes to score a personality—attitudes towards phones, social media, family, nature, built environment, humanity, flora and fauna, religion, culture, faith, technology, science, fiction, time and space, etcetera. The summation of attitudes at time t could be positive or negative. The conclusion should be, they have a positive or negative personality of a given magnitude in the realm of sustainable development.

The Time Dimension in Attitude and Personality Formation

When a 1 or 3-year-old infant correctly matches symbols and numbers, it is highly basing on the 2 units of cognition, i.e. symbol and image. And when they mistakenly pronounce to call "ear" for "eye", it is because it has not mastered the sound of these words. According to developmental psychologists, a 4 or 6-year-old child who has marked the recognizable preoperational stage of cognitive development starts to progress to the subsequent 2 units of cognition, i.e. concept and rule. Beyond 6 years, the child can start abstract problem-solving. When a child progresses from 12 years and beyond, they have gained all 4 units of cognition, get experienced, and can now learn anything but the foundation is in the very early stages. From 1-10 years, it is the perfect time to grow the kind of attitudes we want in future generations. Those are the formative years for everyone's personality and attitudes because they form a significant level of the core beliefs we carry on for the rest of our lives.

Of course, as we grow, we meet psychosocial stressors; we also catch up on good moments that continue to shape us differently and trigger a change in personality and attitudes. Imagine 2 twins, born and grown together and get separated at 11 years. One grows with a pastor, and another grows with a business person. They get reunited after graduating from school at 22 years old. They are highly likely to have different views and understanding of the world, habits, hobbies, and behaviours, but they will still share some core beliefs—a totally different perception. By drawing one's timeline and tracking the core beliefs developed before 10 years of age, one can start to trigger attitude and personality change, formation and reformation. The timeline is defined from conception. The table below is drafted according to Jean Piaget (1896–1980) Stages of Cognitive Development and Lawrence Kohlberg (1927–1987) Stages of Moral Development.[81]

---

[81] Jean Piaget was a Swiss psychologist known for his work on child development, especially the theory of cognitive development. Lawrence Kohlberg was an American psychologist best known for his theory of stages of moral development.

Development stage	0 – 9 months	9 months – 2 years	2 years – 7 years	7 years – 11 years	11+ years
Cognitive development	In the womb What happens to the mother?	Children develop the concept of object permanence and the ability to form mental representations	Children's thought is egocentric; they lack the concept of conversation and the ability to decenter	Children can decenter; they acquire the concept of conversion; but they cannot reason abstractly or test hypotheses systematically	Children begin to reason abstractly
Moral development	In the womb What happens to the mother?	• Avoid punishment • Gain Reward	• Avoid punishment • Gain Reward	• Gain Approval & Avoid Disapproval • Duty & Guilt	• Gain Approval & Avoid Disapproval • Duty & Guilt • Agreed upon rights • Personal moral standards

An infant communicates through emotions. An infant cries when the mother or caretaker leaves, and it can also cry when sad, frightened, or not feeling well. Crying is a newborn's primary way of communicating, to tell you what they need. It can also occasionally smile while reciprocating to a smiling face—the care we provide to the infant through its emotional development influences the schema development. Therefore, different kinds of abuse of the infants leave severe damage in the child's life because of damaging the schema development by inflicting pain to the infant, thereby distorting the building blocks of cognitive models that enable babies to form a mental representation of the world.[82]

In creating a treatment model or a behavioural, attitude and personality change, formation and reformation, one has to track down the events, both positives and negatives of the individual under the study, by studying the timeline from conception up to the time when the study is conducted. This treatment model/roadmap would be premised on the connotations of addition, multiplication, and subtraction of different stimuli that contribute to attitude and personality formation.

The example given about twins who part ways after 11 years is premised on the fact that all continue with studies and reunite after graduating at 22 years of age. Imagine one fails to study after 11 years but keeps with either a pastor or businessman; their attitudes and personality will change because of these

---

[82] **Note:** That permanent wounding effect reoccurs when they mature unless they healthily reconnect with others or environment to treat the wounded areas. Several problems we face in society are due to wounded leaders taking decisions on behalf of the communities. Prevention is better than cure; never wound children.

events. Suppose a sample of children that live together is taken at 11 years and tested for their attitudes and personalities and later tested at 20 years, 30 years, 40 years and 50 years. In that case, there could be a considerable change in attitudes and personalities because of the experiences and events undergone. However, they will all remain with unique core beliefs formed before they made 11 years.

Attitude Change following the Time Dimension

This is in accordance with psychosocial stages of development, cognitive development, and moral development. Attitudes towards events, objects, or anything might take a predetermined right path for people of a given society, culture, faith, or civilization. Following that illustration, having a crest at an unexpected time could be interpreted as a *crisis* or a *fixation* (a crest can be negative or positive), borrowing from both Erik Erikson's psychology and Freudian Psychology and depending on the construct. The assumption made is that at birth, $t = 0$, and a person lives for 100 years. The family of curves for specified attitude objects or events that follow a correct path predetermined by a given society communicates the kind of personality the person lives. See figure below.

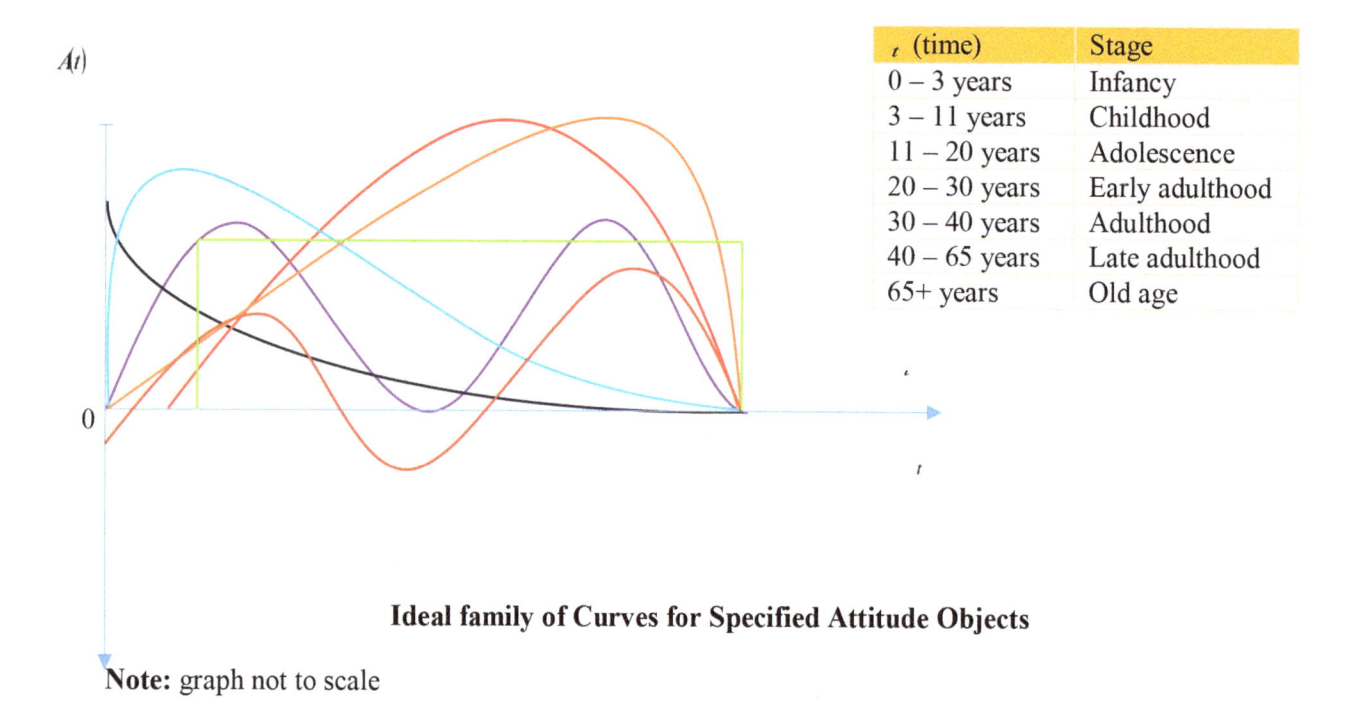

t (time)	Stage
0 – 3 years	Infancy
3 – 11 years	Childhood
11 – 20 years	Adolescence
20 – 30 years	Early adulthood
30 – 40 years	Adulthood
40 – 65 years	Late adulthood
65+ years	Old age

Ideal family of Curves for Specified Attitude Objects

Note: graph not to scale

- This attitude peaks in the infancy stage: e.g. crying for things
- This attitude peaks in adolescence/early adulthood
- This attitude peaks in childhood, declines in adulthood, and peaks again and declines later
- This attitude begins with a negative attitude, improves and peaks in early years, declines and peaks again, and declines
- This attitude is a constant attitude throughout life
- This attitude declines as you age

Within these years, the environment and a human's intervention with the environment causes some attitude graphs to fluctuate, causing more crests than anticipated. Sometimes, this can result from perceived threats because our bodies are always in a survival state, some mild depression or sadness and/or anxiety, fixations, crises, and many other issues. However, the point of interest here is to model a fluctuating attitude towards an attitude object, event, or phenomenon. Therefore, somebody's attitude towards an attitude event/object might *fluctuate,* sending intense signals to the observer. See figure below.

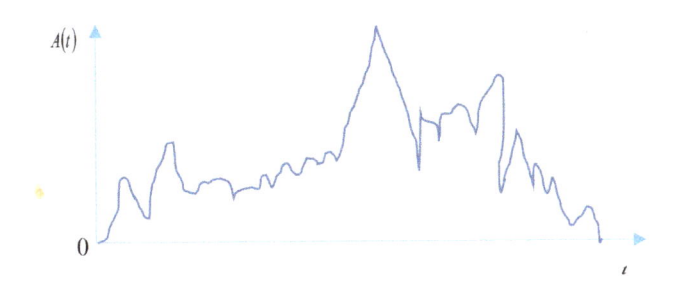

Fluctuating Attitude

Define attitude to a scale of 0 – 10, referred to as a scale of attitude points (aps) measured in terms of hours in a day, and time as the time a person lives estimated to be on average between 0 – 100 years of age. 0 years is at conception. 100 years is the maximum old-age assumed. These two scales are fixed, creating a *continuous* variable. A negative attitude would be the opposite, running from 0 to -10. One of the signs of the *unique African attitude disorder* (UAAD) is having an intense negative attitude (emotions, behaviours, and thoughts) towards your own (things, beliefs, symbolisms, environment, and the self). This is in contrast to loving your own things instead. The *unique African attitude disorder* (UAAD) is described in several sections below.

Consider zero as neutral (neither negative nor positive), e.g., "I am not interested, but I do not have a problem with the attitude object/event. I dislike associating with the attitude event, but I do not hate it."

Imagine an adolescent whose attitude towards an attitude object is directly proportional to his age from when they are 11 years old until when they are 20 years old. Consider *an ideal attitude graph* of an adolescent for that attitude object that complies with psychosocial stages of development, cognitive development, and moral growth of a given culture, society or civilization that follows the equation below:

$A(t) \propto t$ *11≤t≥20 years*

$A(t) = kt$
$k = \dfrac{A(t)}{t}$

k, defined as a coefficient of ideal attitude for an attitude object of a given society, culture, or civilization and should fall between $-1 \leq k \leq 1$.

Consider a society that constructs $k = 0.3 aps/year$, for an ideal attitude of an adolescent aged between 11 years to 20 years towards a given attitude object, event or phenomenon as constructed in the equation above. See figure below.

Graph A: Ideal attitude versus time

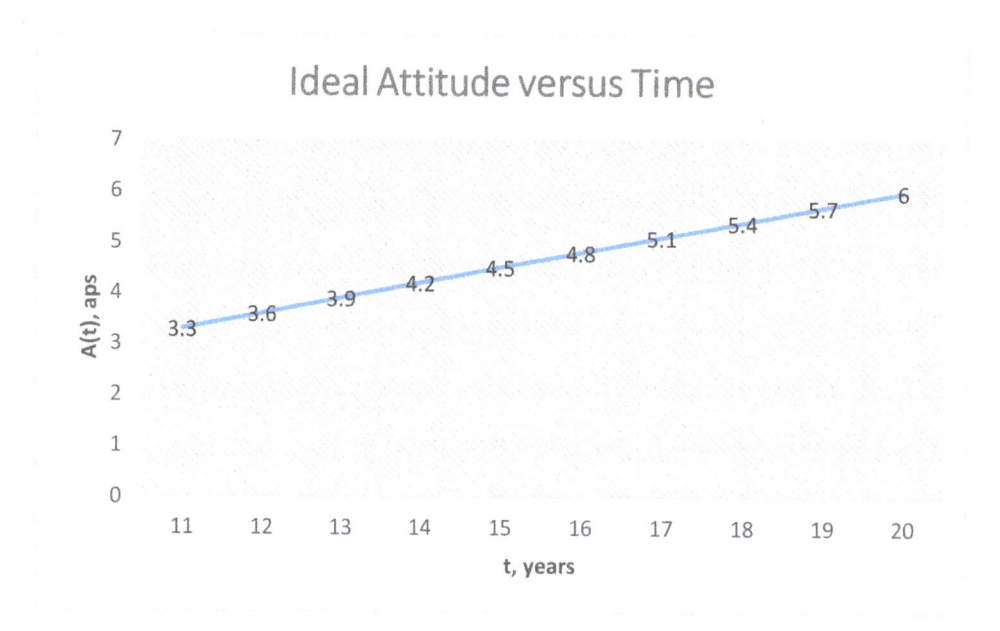

Ideal Attitude versus Time

Graph B: Attitudes versus time

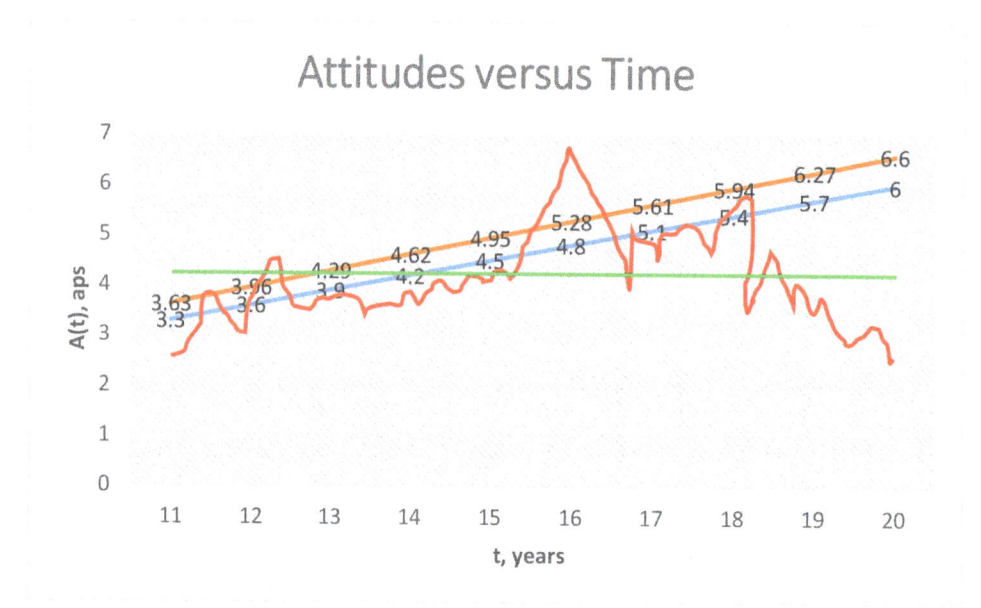

Attitudes versus Time

As far as the attitude object in question is concerned, each individual would have a slightly varying *k* value. However, this value should be able to produce an attitude point that falls within the range that a specific society/culture constructs as normal for a given adolescent of a specific age. Consider an adolescent whose attitude points follow the line in brown. Their *k* value is 0.33 aps/year, deviating by 0.03 from what society calls normal. However, adolescents whose attitude plot follows the red and green graphs can be considered difficult to understand, and/or maladaptive cases and extreme cases, respectively. This is because the red plot is *fluctuating* attitude, difficult to understand, alien, or maladaptive, whilst the green one is an extreme case.

There are many reasons why someone's attitude towards an attitude object, event, thing, or phenomenon can fluctuate or lie on the extreme. These can include diagnosable maladaptive behaviours of some kind, psychosocial stressors, sadness, anxiousness, social phenomena, and unique attributes. k, can be approximately determined by measuring the person's level of interaction with, or disengagement from, the attitude event, object, thing, or phenomena. From quantitative measurements, the ideal k value of the attitude object, event, phenomena, thing can be concluded from samples taken from a given society/culture or civilization from which inference is drawn to generalize into the population. The ideal k is what society constructs as normal. This can be done by conducting scatter plots from experiments conducted in the population as appropriate.

Imagine a society which finds a normal child aged 15 years having an attitude towards a school term holiday as explained henceforth. He spends 4 hours watching TV, 8 hours of sleep in the night, 1hour biking, 2.7 hours of housework, 2 hours of gaming, 2 hours doing holiday packages, and 4.3 hours for other activities. The attitude towards a holiday is an aggregate of attitudes towards events, as mentioned. All these attitudes are measured following the child's interaction with the attitude event/phenomenon/item/thing, which is observed behaviour. Or by the child's failure to engage with the item/event/thing, etcetera. The thinking and emotional reactions as determinants of attitude are all approximated in the observed behaviours. This is because we can never perfectly know what a person's attitude with respect to cognition is like. Emotional reactions can be approximated in behavioural modes.

Suppose the graph in the figure above represents an attitude towards housework. As the child grows, their contact hours towards housework increase in the form; $A(t) \propto t$. Define attitude points in terms of hours of engagement or disengagement with the attitude event or object. If society constructs a normal adolescent to spend a *maximum* of 6 hours on housework, then following the attitude scale of 0 – 10, this translates into attitude points equal to 10/6*2.7, i.e. 4.5 aps. A plot of attitude points for a child's attitude towards housework at different ages is conducted, and the line of best fit is drawn to determine the child's k value. This is because society assumed the normal child's attitude towards housework is directly proportional to their age from when they are 11 years old until when he is 20 years old. Therefore, the overall attitude towards the term holiday could be derived from a multilevel approach.

A family of graphs for the mentioned items can be plotted to aggregate the child's attitude towards the term holiday. This, and other attitudes can be integrated to make the child's overall attitude that approximates to their personality at the time, t.

The Fluctuating Attitude: A Stochastic Process

The fluctuating attitude exhibited in the behavioural mode has a lot to do with cognition. As mentioned, one's attitude is profiled by another. In the process of changing from the *expected value,* the observer profiles a number of *causes,* both diagnosable and non-diagnosable, as far as standards are concerned. In doing so, they model a stochastic process, the operation of chance in practice. Following differential calculus, one models attitude change and fluctuations by fixing initial values alongside observed change. For example, it is common knowledge that a newborn baby's attitude towards life is characterized by the following events: sleeping, cuddling, feeding, and crying in the first 2-3 months. Crying is perhaps the main event noticed about the baby's attitude behaviour. An emotional attitude is exhibited in a behavioural mode.

In some medical journals, crying is estimated to peak at about six (6) weeks. This translates to about 0.875 years old, counted right from conception. Babies are believed to cry and fuss on average for almost three (3) hours a day. That is the *expectation* constructed as normal for some societies. However, some babies cry a lot longer than this. Suppose the highest value in terms of hours of cry is 4 hours for a given society. In terms of attitude points, 4 hours translates to 10 aps. This means normal attitude points (average) would equal 10/4*3 = 7.5 aps. Therefore, on average, a baby aged 0.875 years old would score 7.5 aps. i.e. $A(0.875)=7.5$. Imagine, the rate of change of attitude with respect to time (age) of the babies of this society goes dropping by half in a successive row. This can be communicated in a mathematical construct, a differential equation, i.e. $A'=0.5A$. Therefore, $A=4.842^{0.5t}$ for, $0 \leq t \leq 1.45$ years, $t=0$ is at conception. Such kind of modelling would be applied to a family of curves that predetermine attitudes and personality altogether of a given age of an individual at any given time, in any given society.

The stochastic process can be applied to study the change of attitudes with respect to cognition, trying to dig into what the individual is thinking to portray an emotional or behavioural attitude that the observer can observe. The observer, therefore, generates back and forward causes of the observed emotional/behavioural attitude. At some point, when the individual understudy makes verbal statements, they are denoted as conclusions of the cognitive cycle. This cognitive cycle is evaluated through Socratic questioning, following a well-studied algorithm. Sometimes the unconscious and the subconscious must be evaluated. The psychological principle, "you learn about what somebody is thinking from his emotional and behavioural attitudes," is not 100% correct. It is difficult to exactly tell what the individual is thinking without vivid tools and techniques. It is a *random process* that can support the learning of what somebody thinks about the attitude event/object.

This random process generates a myriad of causes that are evaluated within a *probability space*. The constructor ensures that the probability scoring of causes is unbiased and transparent. They must dwell on the primary assumption, which is scoring the probability of "misjudging" highly. Here, I mean that that the constructor is likely to misjudge. This is because our bodies are always in a survival state. This model technique of 'what is somebody thinking to exhibit this attitude behaviour?' can be applied from when the child (person) meets the cognitive development stage and onwards. Therefore, the modeller would develop stochastic differential equations.

Forensic psychological studies teach us that when you have excluded the impossible, whatever remains, however improbable, must be the truth. Through the so-called random walks of a stochastic process and integrating techniques to dig information from the individual further, the modeller can reach the correct cause. Consider a person who has been responding to your emails or phone messaging instantly, e.g. taking not more than 2 days to respond, on average one day. They are now taking a week or 2. This change of behavioural attitude could be precipitated by some kind of thinking or emotional attitude you can never know through a straightforward process. The person could be busy, sick, sad, anxious, lost interest, or in trouble, and many other issues.

In that case, you might need to generate a probability space to list what you think could be causing that attitude behaviour. Define the scope. Apply some immediate techniques. Some of these techniques include inducing their defence mechanisms to come out. However, this should be applied with caution. The essential technique is approaching the individual with humility and showing them how they benefit from the exercise or what they essentially forgot. This should be smart enough to conceal any kind of opportunism. It should be a win for the individual under the study. Another similar technique is patience and taking enough time to reach conclusions—spending over 98% of the time navigating the problem and only 2% of the time to decide on a solution/conclusion.

Attitude Change and the Unique African Attitude Disorder (UAAD)

Africa needs to teach young generations about our predicament. This is in a bid to nurture correct attribution and positive beliefs. Africans need to explore the fact. Through the self-awareness campaigns, we would persuade and develop a positive self-concept in Africans. Therefore, sustainable attitude change and growth can be done in two approaches, i.e. cognitive restructuring and readjustment, and behavioural modification and activation. Any of these unsystematically done would influence the genesis of a *unique African attitude disorder (UAAD)*. The Europeans played a very big role to distort Africans and caused Africans to succumb to the unique African attitude disorder (UAAD). This was done through religions and colonialism.

Attitude change can be done by tackling the constituent variables, i.e. cognition, behaviours and emotions, their *causal changes and effects* they produce as appropriate. In order to trigger and reform one's personality, we would have to deal with their domineering attitudes with respect to the time factor.

Cognitive Restructuring and Readjustment

Cognitive restructuring is about treating bad and unhelpful thoughts. This involves tackling bad automatic thoughts and unhelpful positive automatic thoughts, assumptions and maladaptive beliefs and readjusting them. These thoughts are a manifestation of core beliefs developed in the early years. An excellent example of unhelpful positive automatic thoughts is: "I cannot eat with unwashed hands (in a situation where one is left with no alternative amidst scarcity and danger like war)". One of the approaches to readjust one's irrational thinking is by taking down *evidence* to support thoughts and beliefs and evidence against the thoughts/beliefs.

Evidence helps to prepare and transition the mind to receive new beliefs constructively. Probe and question for deeper meanings of these beliefs and thoughts and check them on the positive and negative sides. Using a continuum, the person can weigh the evidence adduced to have clear, realistic thinking that is unbiased. Where cognitive restructuring is done by only labelling existing beliefs and thoughts as maladaptive that are very dangerous and require strict avoidance and compensation, and *realistic thinking* is not supported by *evidence*, the readjustment in beliefs occurs to an unprepared mind, creates a quick new belief, sort of a religious belief that follows the Supreme Being, because when having faith you do not question the Supreme Being, and this may result into the *unique African attitude disorder (UAAD)*.[83]

The unique African attitude disorder has roots in the way conventional religions were introduced. It led to a rapid disintegration of traditional values. Our symbolisms were abused. This disorder is becoming multigenerational. One of the most important questions to ask here is: why Africans conform to standards created by others, comply and have consistently complied with requests of externals with ease? We are

---

[83] See p. 44, §1.

disunited and hate ourselves. Africans fail to support each other and instead support foreigners and fail to trust each other; they rarely believe that their colleageus are capable of leading technological change. Africans were severely impacted right from slavery, colonialism, and religions. That is why they hate themselves so badly. It is not uncommon for an African to kill fellow Africans while promoting the interests of foreigners. This is the *unique African attitude disorder (UAAD)* we need to treat.

Behavioural Modification and Activation

This is done through conditioning, where rewards are given as incentives or awards or gifts to people to appreciate their good deeds. In many instances, when a person receives a gift for what he or she has done, his or her behaviour to do the same is reinforced. That means, many times, it is an external stimulus that elicits a behavioural modification or activation. However, a few times, a person may have inner behaviour modification, activation and satisfaction especially where the person's pleasure is activated and something positive is achieved; for example, gaining sleep after taking a few bottles of alcohol might perpetuate the alcohol taking. Similarly, a busy mother who is tired of a baby screaming from the rooftops may opt to have a babysitter to avoid the aversive behaviour of the child. Her behaviour to call for a babysitter is reinforced whenever she gets busier and wishes her child not to cry, and the dad feels not being attended to because the mother spends much of the time while attending to the baby – and this is perceived like punishment to the dad.

The *unique African Attitude disorder (UAAD)* arises, and it is perpetuated where people are rewarded for no purposeful activity done. In the UK, for example, the Queen is the custodian of all the land, which implies that land is a national asset. However, in many parts of Africa, some people were given square miles of land as their permanent asset without justification as to why they got the land in terms of value-added or activities well-accomplished. This created various behavioural modifications impacting attitudes and how they viewed the world. This multigenerational problem rooted in colonialism created inequalities in Africans. Some Africans started viewing themselves as high in status, yet they had done nothing. Africans who used to move collectively started moving individualistically. Note also that colonialism associated with religions gave education to some people while others did not receive that education.

Consequently, those families that got the chance to study were able to educate their offspring. This moved on to several other generations. On average, the current generation is either the 6th or 7th. This problem is too serious because Africa's inequalities are traced from colonialism and religions. What perpetuates these inequalities is the unique African attitude disorder (UAAD) to which several people succumbed to.

Aid and charity is another example of how a person can get conditioned to live without helping themselves and to enslave their mind not to think. Aid bleeds chronic dependency and stifles creativity. It is a behaviour and emotional gratification that affects the correct thinking of an African child.

In many African schools, children were/are physically punished. It is recent that a number of countries have abolished corporal punishment in schools due to the huge "stop child abuse" campaigns and statutes imposed by governments. How often have these countries drawn a relationship between cognitive development and moral stages of development to make decisions on the same, before and after in the African context? And perhaps come up with alternative punishment guidelines that weigh quite well with the wrongdoing the child commits. In my view, emotional abuse is more damaging than giving a child a few spankings. However, spanking a child for wrongdoing is seen as very heavy physical abuse of recent. I conquer quite well that banning a child from getting involved with a sporting activity or entertainment activity for some prescribed time as punishment for coming late for classes might be good enough, but we needed some kind of guidelines for teachers to follow in the process.

African children are now growing with *unique African attitude disorder* (UAAD) as a result of behaviour modification done anyhow, some reporting their parents to police over small issues because they have learnt human rights in the modern world. African moral school of thought debarred such practices of perfectionism. The principles of sustainability must guide the transition from what is wrong to what is right. It has been well known that each culture invents its own morality to a certain standard. The transformation that I coined as a purposeful cultural audit across African cultures must be guided by questions rotating around sustainable development.[84]

Things that make us stronger and that inspire our inner self must take precedence. In this I mean, we ought to agree on what propels us to greater heights and in sustainability, we keep the factor of unique attributes, fighting cultural homogenization which colonialism and associated religions had tried to bring to this world in one of the highest kinds of opportunism that history has ever witnessed. The spiritual dimension, for example, does not tag itself on any conventional or traditional religion but it is soul-focused—an integration of mind and heart at the centre of being. One of the most important questions to ask here is: Why do Africans quickly conform to standards and technologies released by others than their own? This is a behavioural issue that impacts cognition and emotions.

Conclusion and Way Forward on Unique African Attitude Disorder (UAAD)

Africans developed a *unique attitude disorder* that needs to be treated through huge PR and self-awareness campaigns. It requires proper self-examination for all Africans. To motivate ourselves into treatment for the *unique African attitude disorder (UAAD),* we need to accept and agree that we have gotten systemic multigenerational inferiorism, fear, and anxiety as a result of slavery, religion, and colonialism, and it is perpetuated by this disorder. Ever since slavery, colonialism, and religion were optimistically dealt with, we have not psychologically organized ourselves to treat the multigenerational effects it has caused to African mankind. In an attempt to contribute to the treatment of unique African attitude disorder (UAAD), I will pose two (2) fundamental core beliefs that accompany the *unique African attitude disorder (UAAD)*.

- *Other races are more superior and intelligent*
- *Intense pagan traditional practices deterring progress*

Other Races are more Superior and Intelligent

Imagine being faced with such a belief as you wonder how they manage to innovate drones, satellites, planes, AI, politics that inspires hope, fantastic software, and many more. As a typical example (case study) of a conversation between you (African), the person who holds the belief, and a *well-wisher*, you start:

---

[84] See p. 410 (Cultural audit); §8.

Believer	How possible can they invent such *software that can diagnose a fault in the system at such a precision?* They are brilliant.
Well-wisher	You mean, they are brilliant in software design …….?
Believer	Yes, my manager flew in a gentleman from Europe who quickly diagnosed a problem in the production line using a specific software installed on his PC.
Well-wisher	What does this mean to you?
Believer	Those guys manufacture the machines, so it was a *must* that the problem could only be diagnosed and fixed by their guy.
Well-wisher	Oh, ok. I understand. So, how did this change your perception about manufacturers of the production machines?
Believer	They are brilliant. We've been using the machines for a long time, but we couldn't quickly diagnose the fault. Nevertheless, they should be able to diagnose the fault in the machine they manufacture.
Well-wisher	Yes, they are in a better position to track faults in their technologies. However, did your technician try to strictly follow operation and maintenance manuals procedures to diagnose the faults?
Believer	I cannot lie to you. Our maintenance culture is not the best, but we endeavour to try. Our maintenance department faces many challenges; people cannot stay for long.
Well-wisher	What could be the problem? Does the organization you work for design career development programs, training and continuing professional development programs for staff/workers?
Believer	Yes, we have a few training programs in some departments, but many of them are tailored programs, so routine R&D is not a priority.
Well-wisher	Ok. What does all this mean to you?
Believer	The organization has limited funds, and the manager is comfortable working with experts from Europe whenever the production lines get a fault.
Well-wisher	The manager is comfortable working with experts from Europe whenever the production lines get a fault because …….?

Believer	He believes they quickly sort the problem, and I have evidenced it myself. Our technicians rarely effectively and efficiently fix the problem.
Well-wisher	You have developed the belief that foreign experts are more competent, skilled and more intelligent. Haven't you spotted any potential in the local people?
Believer	I cannot say that they have entirely no potential because sometimes working conditions don't favour them maybe, but I have a rigid belief that foreign experts do better.
Well-wisher	You have mentioned the following: Your manager is more comfortable working with foreign experts, and at the same time, doesn't empower staff and workers by training them. That maintenance culture also needs improvement. Is it right to attribute everything like failure to diagnose faults in production lines to the staff/workers alone?
Believer	Somehow, to some extent, I would say they are less privileged, but they still have a long way to go.
Well-wisher	You have seen this in only one organization; Could this be right to say that all local technicians' self-efficacy on diagnosing production line faults are the same? And why should you generalize that everyone is like that?
Believer	Not really. I have had my colleague in a similar organization complaining about the same. He said that this country lacks technicians!
Well-wisher	Did that person mention the same challenges their organization goes through?
Believer	Yes and no. He mentioned similar issues and one other issue. He said their local technicians were very qualified but lacked the skills.
Well-wisher	This story is not about to end. Skills, training, and procedural crisis. Should we label it a systemic challenge we are facing?
Believer	Now, I can agree to have some coffee with you. The education system, our attitudes and governance systems are not in harmony.

Well-wisher	Your organization and your friend's organization are good observations, but we cannot overgeneralize. You are what you are today because of the decisions that past generations took. However, you don't need to dwell on the past that much; look at what the future holds. I don't feel comfortable when you overgeneralize.
Believer	Because of the systemic challenges you have brought forward, I might attribute our local staff's failure to diagnose the problem in the production line elsewhere. However, I maintain the fact that most of our local technicians are less skilled.
Well-wisher	That's now a mature analysis. Not every African local technician is not skilled. Not every local technician is less intelligent. Many are facing systemic challenges that cannot make them get the very best out of their talents. Some managers and leaders are fixated to believe in foreigners as more competent than local people, without providing opportunities to local people to develop their talents. This fixation is a result of the history that Africans hold in several influential spheres. African attitudes were terribly affected. They were terribly wounded.
Believer	I thank you for this analysis. I promise to go out and learn more about Africa's systemic challenges with the possibility of contributing and leading the positive change we deserve as Africans.

Intense Pagan Traditional Practices Deterring Progress

Imagine being faced with the belief that intense pagan traditional practices are the root cause of deterring progress in Africa. You believe that many people fail to succeed due to being bewitched, including yourself maybe. And you believe that most of the mental illnesses and disorders result from a jealousy person bewitching the victim. As a typical example (case study) of a conversation between you, the person who holds the belief, and a *well-wisher*, you start:

Believer	I'm leaving that office because of fear to be charmed. I used to find weird things in the door entrance. All my plans have folded, and I can't withstand any further trouble. I'm making a wise decision to quit and give that woman space. She doesn't want anyone to get closer to the manager for fear that they could probably replace her secretarial duties for something else. Someone told me a similar story before I joined that office that the former staff I replaced had developed a complicated mental illness beyond what doctors and psychiatrists could diagnose. I'm resigning today for fear that I could also face the same trouble.

Well-wisher	You used to find weird things in the door entrance, like which ones……?
Believer	On five consecutive days in early March 2016, two bird feathers were dropped on my office entrance, and one was dropped in my handbag by an unknown person. This left me very terrified and anxious.
Well-wisher	What does this mean to you?
Believer	I attribute this to that secretary. She always gives me an attitude whenever I get to her office for something. Of recent, things have been foiled, and my plans are never succeeding. I have had a lot of marital challenges, and I think all this is because of her. I need to give her space so that I save my life and my family.
Well-wisher	Ok. So, you feel like that secretary is messing up your life? What makes you believe that she's the one who dropped the weird things, yet you didn't see her? Couldn't it be another person? Besides, what spiritual conviction or evidence do you have on the said feathers?
Believer	First of all, the stories surrounding the lady, her emotional projections and her attitudes align well with what I'm going through these days. I grew up in a Christian family, and I cannot withstand seeing such things in my way. I need to give her space.
Well-wisher	Oh, I see. And how did Christianity in your family shape your beliefs?
Believer	My siblings and I were taught that charm is real, and we need to pray hard over it and possibly distance ourselves from the threatening charm-possessed people. I find the office I work in very terrific. I actually spend most of my time praying to God nowadays. Those bird feathers are symbolic of potential charm. Although I have not caught her red-handed dropping them on the doorway, they signify evil omens, and she's the first suspect because of the attitude she portrays towards me. I need to find an alternative workplace to avoid trouble.
Well-wisher	Wait a minute. Before you decide to quit the job, have you tried to open up with other staff, including the lady you accuse? Perhaps, it could be a different person doing that for a different cause or purpose. It might be a bigger occupational hazard than you could imagine of. Sometimes, the meaning you give it might be a false one. Let's try to weigh the odds.

Believer	Opening up to her? Never. I cannot; I'm 100% certain she's the one doing this to me. The stories surrounding her tell it all. Even her moods and attitude are symbolic of a witch.
Well-wisher	You are 100% certain she's the one doing this to you. How do you make 100%? Where is the evidence?
Believer	I have 3 pieces of evidence: the stories surrounding her, the feathers, and the emotional/behavioral episodes I have witnessed on different occasions. But anyway, I have a high degree of confidence that she's the one. Maybe not 100% certain, but she is the one.
Well-wisher	Maybe not 100% meaning…..?
Believer	I mean, maybe 98% certain.
Well-wisher	Ok. Let's begin with the remaining 2%. What is it made of?
Believer	You are making things complicated for nothing. The remaining 2% could be attributable to other factors beyond my imagination as you have tried to think me out of the box, but my instinctual beliefs and intuitive wisdom shaped as I grew in my family of origin are a must to be listened to. I believe in the inner self. 98% is not far away from 100%; what's wrong with you?
Well-wisher	There is a possibility that you are exaggerating because you cannot produce valid proof of how the feathers deter your progress. I want you to step back and look at the many possible contributions to the challenges you are going through these days before you attribute everything aversive to the lady. You need to make a thorough evaluation of the 2%.
Believer	Anyway, some of my marital challenges have resulted from the fact that I overwork and get home very late, and I'm left with very little time to attend to my family. On several days, I always find my children in bed, which makes my hubby lose it.
Well-wisher	Have you tried to get home early yet? What could be the cause of you getting home very late to find kids gone to bed already?

Believer	Of late, we have had many assignments to accomplish at work. The company has expanded and opened a new outlet, and I have to work extra hours beyond normal hours to ensure that everything is in order. You know, I work in the back end department, where I significantly contribute to the company's inventory management, and I need to ensure that the set lead times are met. So, I have been getting home very late because of the latest establishment of the new outlet.
Well-wisher	You need to speak to your manager about the challenges you are going through to find ample time for your family. Are you willing to try this?
Believer	It is because of the new outlet, but we shall get back to the normal working hours very soon.
Well-wisher	Ok. Great! You hadn't thought about the interruption the new outlet has had on your family. Had you?
Believer	This is the 2% talked about, maybe.
Well-wisher	The way I see it might be a big issue because several studies have reported marital challenges resulting from failure to find ample time for the family. It would help if you found the correct attribution for the challenges you are going through. That woman has nothing to do with your challenges.
Believer	What about the feathers, the attitudes, and the long stories surrounding her?
Well-wisher	On the feathers, I said, it could be a more significant occupational hazard that threatens the entire organization that you ought to disclose to the organization. On attitudes, you need to work on yourself and find out why you do mind-reading others and highly judge others. It would help if you recognized that people are different. Some people are selfish; others are humorous, whilst others are reserved. It is, therefore, possible to misjudge them. Stories surrounding the lady are mere accusations and allegations which can cause you trouble because you lack evidence. They are simply hearsay stories that you don't need to follow.
Believer	You are trying all sorts of ways to convince me to remain in that office, and you are labelling things that are symbolic of charm as mere occupational hazards. Are you trying to say they can't contain charm?

Well-wisher	I only said that you need to review your attribution of the challenges you are facing. You have already reattributed your marital tension to getting home late. Try not to exaggerate your core beliefs and have some room to think outside the box to grow your mind. I'm inspiring a realistic mind growth in yourself by learning to view things from quite many dimensions. Don't get fixated on a core belief whose evidence is not investigated thoroughly well, especially here in Africa, where little research has been conducted on our past ancestral philosophies. I want you to grow your mind and lead a generation of people who can think to find the truth on African matters, using African wisdom beyond what you label as charm.
Believer	Well, I have always believed that some people don't wish me well and do whatever they can to retard my success. And the attitude I got from the lady perpetuated and corroborated my beliefs.
Well-wisher	That's realistic—at least *some* people but not all. You cannot please everybody, but it doesn't mean that they can stop your way. The more you think they can stop you, the more you get fixated on that thinking. You are tagging much emphasis on those feathers because of the training you have gone through in avoiding activating your instinctual core beliefs, labelling everything African evil without limit. That called strong Christian family you grew from. That kind of cognitive restructuring that follows no evidence inspires and motivates schema avoidance, one way of perpetuating core beliefs. It is important to note that repressed material does not go away. It just needs an activating stimulus, especially during emotional distress. The correct cognitive restructuring that harbours no opportunism is done based on understanding and realistic thinking. Every African shall always be an African before they adopt becoming something else. Distancing ourselves from what we ought to research brings a greater aversive impact to us and the future generations. I, therefore, champion you to go out and think without fear or contradiction about the many attributions to the challenges you face and make a thoroughly informed decision before you quit. This should include the possibility of talking to the lady about the occupational hazard.
Believer	Well, I'll start to weigh the odds. I'll stop giving myself a hard time, start realistic thinking, and follow back on my decisions to better understand the root cause of whatever I'm going through.
Well-wisher	That sounds like a promising start. The more you look at a problem from a diversity of issues, the more likely you get towards finding a genuine solution.

It is important to note that it is not intense paganism deterring progress in Africa but rather the meaning we attach to paganism and associated traditional practices. The attitude towards charm and associated witchcraft claims in the African land leaves only people with sound integrity to think beyond the obvious. I write up to a certain degree of authoritativeness, leaving room for what I fail to understand—the supernatural power. However, many things labelled as charm are lame excuses for people who have taken wrong decisions in their lives.

Others try to lift what they cannot handle and then falsely attribute their failures to others. Witchcraft is a severe cognitive distortion affecting many people in the land, and it wouldn't be the case if African norms and values were cherished to date. Surprisingly, very few people attribute their success stories to others, but many quickly attribute their misfortunes to others. As discussed in Chapter One, Africa's secretive philosophers left much work for modern researchers who wish to develop Africa ought to start on and whose findings will lead the vast PR and self-awareness campaigns. That would stamp out the multigenerational anxiety and cognitive distortions induced through opportunistic cognitive restructuring done on African masses through colonialism, slavery, and religions.

The decisions we make at all times contribute to our fate—our thought process defines it all. It is always advisable to reflect on your decisions and look forward to those you aim at. Our choices and the alternatives we forego, especially in our early learning experiences, shape our identity and industriousness. The environment in which we grow, the core beliefs we develop in our early learning experiences, and the parental/emotional capital we receive predetermines our psychosocial development.

In a world driven by the products of the industrial and technological revolutions, socioeconomic status highly influences our psychosocial development. Therefore, our everyday decisions are highly influenced by our core beliefs. For example, a learned person whose income can only sustain the welfare of 2 children decides to give birth to 10 children who fail to find school fees. This same person resorts to the thinking that someone is failing them occupationally and that this makes him not earn enough to meet the needs of the 10 children.

Similarly, due to social influence from peers, a student whose parents cannot afford all requirements at university decides to use the little money they have for luxury. They wish to meet the group's standards and then get into trouble failing to complete the course. They then attribute the failure to purported witches.

I insist that the decisions we make today largely influence what we become in the future and that the future has very little to do with being cursed, as many people possess the beliefs. However, I have written not to mean that witches do not exist in Africa. They are actually many on the continent, but I insist that our lives are primarily made from the decisions we make all day long. You insist on living on a paycheck and producing dozens of children because you strongly believe that every child comes with their luck. Despite the education people receive, cultural and religious beliefs strongly influence how we think and reason.

Anyone willing to understand a human descendant of a particular group of people for purposes of predicting how they will behave and act in a situation, minds less on the education and training they go through and makes an archaeological dig into the cultural and religious settings in which they have grown. I am convinced that Africa's failure to develop and maybe some other places facing similar dilemmas, is as a result of tagging very much value on the learning and training in schools as the only measure of competence in decision making and tags very little value on the cultural and religious beliefs people develop by default and learning experiences.

The fact that we have different roots, as Africans, with a myriad of tribes and dialects, presents one of the most crucial paradoxes worth investigating before making decisions on governance models that are best suitable for ourselves alongside appointing officials to steer economies. As I mentioned earlier, I found some truth in stereotypes worth investigating further. Unfortunately or fortunately, many government offices with highly sensitive duties are entrusted to people solely based on education and professional expertise gained as measured by constitutionally founded agencies but not on the African philosophies and psychologies. You can agree with me or disagree, but some people lack the instinctual ability to steer economies despite the high academic grades and professional expertise they attain. Some people need to be vending ice cream despite the high academic grades they achieve, especially those who view Africa's prosperity as challenging to attain. Therefore, understanding and evaluating the core beliefs that each ethnicity holds carries a lot in protecting future generations' ability to live sustainably.

The treatment of the unique African disorder requires a variety social engineering tools and techniques.[85]

Do You Know Your Personality Type?

Imagine a snake found in a moneybag carrying millions of dollars and gold, and it is considered your fortune that has very limited time to impact your life positively. What do you do among the following options?

   a) Remove the snake barehanded and after think of what to do with the moneybag and its contents.
   b) Sell the bag will all its contents
   c) Make a deal with courageous people
   d) Just abandon the moneybag and its contents and report to relevant authorities

It is good to know your characters, temperaments, and attitudes. This analogy can help explain the different characters and personalities that people have. Of course, cultural and religious differences, environment and laws of a particular area may influence the position taken by each person on the moneybag. However, it is good to know your overall attitudes and how you perceive things. Knowing your personality helps you deal with people better and predict how successful your relationships with others might be.

Some people can pick the snake out of the money bag, and some would abandon the moneybag. Also, some would have mixed reactions towards the bag, whilst others would sell or try to deal with the bag as appropriate. This demonstrates why we need to understand ourselves better than anyone else. I do not intend to write scary, but the African child does not know themselves better than what the Europeans know about them. Any attempt to distort cultural sentiments is an attack on the process of socio-economic transformation and consequently sabotages the road to sustainability.

---

[85] See p. 218-226, §4 (Hint: Social Engineering).

For example, in business and entrepreneurship, one needs to know where they can do better than others. In many cases, big businesses and innovations are started as a one man's business. However, along the way, the one man's business begins to outsource people who can help to start from the limits of their knowledge and skill.

Varying Core Beliefs

How should we Make the Right Decisions amidst varying Core Beliefs in the African Context?

The first step is to cultivate an atmosphere of nurturing self-awareness initiatives at a family level. An African born and grown in the USA develops core beliefs distinct from those of an African born and grown in her motherland. This is expressly seen in the huge behavioural and attitude differences between African-Americans and Africans. African-Americans are Americans, it is just the colour that denotes them as so, but overt traits and way of life is American and has very little to do with Africa.

Even if an experiment is performed on twins born anywhere but get separated at birth, one grows in the USA, and another is grown in Africa. There will be common instinctual beliefs within the two, which is a product of the transcendental and antecedent genetic makeup. However, the core beliefs resulting from the nurturing environment will make the two twins completely different in cognition and behaviours.

We need to understand our uniqueness right from the families in which we originate, stretching back to our roots. In the process, we labour to investigate and examine ethno-philosophies and stereotypes coined by our ancestors. The purpose of making the archaeological digs is to nullify or validate the works of the ancestors and break the secretive nature of African philosophers. This secrecy in the meaning and purpose of virtues and traditional practices affects how people think and fuels multigenerational anxiety, a paradox perpetuated by religions. Some of the purported stereotypes are a result of failing to understand the hidden meaning of African philosophies.

Moving away from instinctual core beliefs to the world's famous religious and globalization induced beliefs, we find that people are unique. The core beliefs we develop over the years shape our cognition and biases. It is important to note that all people have a certain degree of bias towards others or things. The way we deal with biases is what differentiates an intellect or a morally right human being from mediocre minds. Biases and prejudices, in many cases, result from acting on deep-seated stereotypes. However, some of the beliefs lack a scientific and spiritual explanation and find themselves a grey area in between.

To uplift ourselves and Africa's economy in particular, we need people with the ability to do so, people with a compelling voice that views things as very possible. I have personally met with very qualified engineers who have studied in Europe, and have practised engineering widely, and have a high professional reputation, but viewing things as difficult to sustainably develop Africa. I have found men with very little education but viewing things as very possible. What we are forgetting is that everything nationalistic is driven by people with ability, patriotism, and optimism but never the level of education, although they need to be educated anyway! Therefore, to make the right decisions amidst varying core beliefs necessitates understanding ourselves through self-awareness initiatives and huge PR campaigns as we position ourselves and others to play decisive roles in governments. This should stretch to making inferences on the findings of the studies made on Africa's philosophies; on biases and stereotypes; on stereotypes and core beliefs; on core beliefs and self-awareness. When these studies are concluded and results provided on the sort of a continuum alongside the educational base, we can determine who is best suitable to lead the leisure and hospitality industry, commerce and trade, engineering and technology, sports and entrainment, and security, among others. This can be done strategically through the promotion of activities suitable in specific places.

In conclusion, I stick to the point that 'it is more about the way we think and behave which is highly influenced by cultural and religious differences' that predetermines our fate. The analogy of the "snake and gold bag" explained earlier can help to give an insight into the typical African ethnic differences in behaviours which the majority of people coin as stereotypes yet carrying a lot of meaning and influence on African humankind. There are people who wait for things to happen to them regardless of academic achievement or whether they attained high-quality education or not. The winners go out and make things happen! These people rarely believe in wasting much time gaining lots of knowledge by avoiding enrolling for higher learning. Many times they enrol after or mid-way their career to solidify their understanding. In many instances, they set their questions and live to answer those questions as the basis for further learning. They imagine the kind of society they wish to live in and then move on. We need to draw a line between people who are very good at knowledge management and those good at extending and leading knowledge.

Independent Judgment, Automatic Thoughts, and Bias

There is a saying about people with chronic speeds in my tiny village, Bukunda, that goes, "he pops up like a thought!" In the Luganda dialect, we call it, *"Agya nga kirowoozo!"* A thought is something you cannot stop from bombarding your mind from time to time. Every microsecond that passes, we constantly experience sudden thoughts that are situation-specific in many instances. These thoughts are a process within our brain lobes and might or might not be stimulated by a set or sets of variables that have starting points on the 5 senses, i.e. sight, sound, smell, taste and touch. That is either stimulated by sensational or emotional feelings.

It is important to note that the onset of a "thought" triggered directly from memory is likely to be more than 95% situation-specific. It is a hypothesis, and I take responsibility for it. Situation defined as "a set of circumstances in which one finds themselves; a state of affairs, way of life, responsibility taken, environment lived in, achievement registered, etcetera." The situation could be; a condition, body physiology, an ambition, a plan, a mood, an activity, a directive, a desire, an accomplishment and et cetera. However, as a rule of thumb, a thought is examined for its validity and utility. When a thought is triggered by a core belief, it is an automated thought. Such a thought is, in many cases is affect-laden. Geniuses and thinkers always make something more than situation-specific, i.e. the remaining 5%. They exhibit a high degree of intuition embedded in the unconscious.

The thoughts triggered directly from memory for people who are sensors, and feelers rarely make 95% situation-specific. They, at many times, possess their thought patterns starting points on the 5 senses as the stimuli—sensational feelings. It is still a hypothesis. Our thought pattern is a manifestation of our beliefs accompanied by the assumptions we make. The decisions we make in whatever we do are conclusions reached upon through many arguments premised on our thoughts—not forgetting that a conclusion is a thought too.

Whether you are a businessman, footballer, football referee, driver, investor, banker, boxer, doctor, engineer, or hotelier, you would wish to be called a "PRO", referring to a professional. A professional engages in specified activity for a living and is distinguished from an amateur for their ability to execute tasks with great judgment, skill, knowledge and precision. Independent judgment is a very important attribute that should be possessed by anyone called a professional. Professional footballers are cherished for their sound independent judgment to make decisions whilst on the pitch. The same applies to football referees. Michael Davis (2012) tells us that, 'Judgment is central to engineering, medicine, the sciences and many other practical activities. For example, one who otherwise knows what engineers know but lacks "engineering judgment" may be an expert of sorts, a handy resource much like a reference book or database, but cannot be a competent engineer. There is no reliable algorithm for doing such things ...'[86]

If you are a professional business mentor training other potential business people, you ought to understand the implications of having the right people to work with, especially in the delegation, even if it costs you more time, money and other resources. In your holistic, independent judgment to make decisions, you learn how to juggle cash, equipment and inputs in your activities. In the same way, you learn to make decisions on the process and approaches to accomplish tasks. All these should be governed by one special interest of the 21st century, which is *sustainability*. The limits of personal knowledge and skill, taking responsibility, and holistic, independent judgment are all governed by the equation of economizing resources to achieve reliability and optimality in your business activities and related engagements. It is an ideal that intellectuals live to realize in the 21st-century sustainability campaigns!

In the decisions we reach—which is a concluding thought of the thought processes we undergo, we normally check back and forth for validity and utility in the prevailing circumstances. In the process of exercising independent judgment, we are faced with a complex situational thought pattern of positives and negatives. Positive thoughts may sometimes be invalid, irrelevant and inappropriate in specific circumstances, and the decision might be made to follow a negative thought. This is where most people— the would-be professionals and para-practitioners succumb to complacency and rigidity because the theory tells them X, and the decision to go with Y and drop X seems naïve.

How do we know that the decision to conclude with a negative thought or proceed with a negative thought is not biased, or taking a positive thought is not biased? A biased mind is one that makes a decision towards someone or something that seems unfair to others. It appears inclined on one side than another side in a condition that portrays unfairness and prejudice against others.

There are several ways to know that we are not biased in our decisions. These include knowing our personality type, specifically on the thinking and judging attributes. Our performance on the thinking and judging attributes has a connection with our core beliefs. The thinker and the judger have an interesting relationship. One who understands themselves better on the judging attribute, especially the one who comes out a judgmental person, will review their decisions in important matters over and over again just to check for traces of bias. This means that you have to recheck your thought pattern over and over again to track irrationality.

---

[86] Michael D. A plea for judgment. Sci Eng Ethics. 2012 Dec;18(4):789-808. doi: 10.1007/s11948-011-9254-6. Epub 2011 Feb 13. PMID: 21318325.

Take an example of an interviewer administering an interview. To make a decision about others you gave the interview, you ought to have used a systematic and structured way to approach problem-solving to achieve objectivity. You need to track down your traces of bias in your core beliefs, e.g. people of type X are less intelligent, prior to concluding with a decision.

One who is entrusted with discretionary powers has to declare a conflict of interest because this is one of the companions of a biased mind. In business decisions, we are always faced with challenges of allocating competent staff, reliable machinery, and the correct amount of cash, yet in many instances, these resources are always scarce. In this case, you need to remind yourself of the organisation's values, vision, and mission in association with one's professional courtesy.

You might have got addicted to one staff who just does everything perfectly but takes a salary that is 10 times the amount of salary that could pay 3 staff members. Because of their expertise amidst a financial crisis, you need to recheck your decision on whether to remain with that staff or train the 3 staff members. In every aspect of the decision you take, you might consider the element of 'time and ethics'. The important aspect is that you might think that you are exercising the limits of personal knowledge, skill, understanding and independent judgment to have the most skilful staff around, yet you are exercising a biased mind locked into one staff, and you cannot think outside the box. That is where the game of power becomes interesting.

Similarly, in administering interviews, the interviewer may make a global statement as a conclusion to pass or fail a candidate, not knowing that a global statement is a manifestation of bias. For example, the interviewer might make a remark, "I tested your knowledge and understanding of music and found it is limited." This is typical of a global statement because you have not expressly provided to what extent the candidate's knowledge and understanding of music is limited. The implication is that you faced a negative thought about the candidate as a conclusion to take a decision without a comprehensive evaluation of the thought that leads to the decision. You should have taken down the evidence to back your conclusion by making it specific, not global.

In that analysis, you ought to recognize the extent to which the candidate's knowledge and understanding of music is limited. In your expert judgment, you thought the candidate's knowledge and understanding were limited without listing down the items to which it is limited. Suppose you cannot answer the question, 'To what extent is the candidate's knowledge and understanding of music limited?'. In that case, the likelihood that you are not exercising expert judgment but rather bias is very high. The likelihood of having a biased mind is high in administrators and managers who make global remarks while giving feedback on sensitive matters. That is where the hallmark of good administration requires giving logical feedback to one who deserves it. This logical feedback must tie together and must endeavour to be expressly given and specifically addressed to eliminate traces of bias. A biased mind rarely meets objectivity. Objectivity is being systematic and structured in the way you approach problem-solving.

The Need for Social Engineering as defined in applied Social Sciences

Social engineering is more about playing with people's attitudes. Africa needs a unique kind of social engineering in the context of applied social sciences to address the bottlenecks. This new social construct would aim at treating the unique African attitude disorder (UAAD) from African humankind. I have come across a number of social constructs providing the theories on social engineering as developed by a number of scholars in the social arena. Most of the developed knowledge around social engineering concentrates on the reason why societies need reforms. They hypothesize and draw inferences on the samples they study to generalize results into the populations they represent, typically on attitudes and behaviour modifications.

The gap I found out in the many social scientists' literature on social engineering is the *'how'* to implement effective social engineering models to treat the unique African attitude disorder (UAAD) coined in earlier paragraphs. A great number of great scholars have heavily concentrated on the *'what'* and the *'why'* make social engineering constructs but failed to expressly address the unique African attitude disorder (UAAD) by drawing up techniques to use in the social engineering models properly addressing the *'how'*. Anyone who wishes to lead the change concentrates on the medicine that treats and elaborately gives the *'how'* to influence the masses by drawing effective treatment roadmaps that are easy to comprehend by the followers. They have to come up with techniques.

In 2012, Babby Shammy Chumbow published a paper titled, "Social Engineering Theory: A Model for the Appropriation of Innovations with a Case Study of the Health MDGs."[87] In this paper, Babby defined Social Engineering as 'the application of principles, techniques, methods, and findings of social sciences to the solution of identified social problems, especially with respect to effecting change.' Babby's work on social engineering was excellent, and he uncovered the bottlenecks affecting the effective adoption and appropriation of development-oriented innovations. He provided a model that can take you from the initial stage of creating awareness to effective adoption and appropriation of development-oriented innovations. I just find his work very important to African humankind.

However, in my attempt to study the *unique African attitude disorder (UAAD),* I need to submit my observations as outlined in the earlier paragraphs versus the findings of Babby. The issue is about Africans placing and tagging greater value and importance to the businesses and technologies in which externals have a hand—generally tagging more value to other races than their race in a way best interpreted as inferiorism. Other issues remaining constant, I have made a vivid observation that has led me to rule out a unique attitude disorder succumbed to by the African humankind. Therefore, treatment of the unique African attitude disorder (UAAD) should be broad in order to have a wide spectrum for administering the treatment. Knowledge and understanding of the problem is not enough. We need a practical methodology to treat the infectious and multigenerational disorder we have all succumbed to either covertly or overtly and either implicitly or explicitly and either directly or indirectly. I have generated techniques or ideas subject to further research by others that can spur genuine social reforms through attitude and behaviour modifications and cause an African revolution in this time when sustainability is the topic of each day.

In modelling the techniques, I base the arguments on the premise that *'the African child quickly conforms to standards, technologies, and social constructs issued by external stimuli and complies with the requests made by external forces of influence at a faster rate than his race.'* The preceding techniques are thought

---

[87] Beban Sammy Chumbow (September 19th 2012). Social Engineering Theory: A Model for the Appropriation of Innovations with a Case Study of the Health MDGs, Social Sciences and Cultural Studies - Issues of Language, Public Opinion, Education and Welfare, Asuncion Lopez-Varela, IntechOpen, DOI: 10.5772/37677. Available from: https://www.intechopen.com/chapters/39103

after as a mechanism to propel African humankind to instil confidence in themselves and promote innovation and development of new and advancing technologies and processes to sustain the race in the global sustainability equation. These processes, technologies, and social constructs I dream about, should be made by the African people for the African people.

One of the most observable examples of the unique African attitude disorder (UAAD) is how Africans react to their African football—the Africa Cup of Nations and local football leagues alongside the European leagues. The second example is the wearing of summer clothes in the tropical climates of Sub-Saharan African countries. The third example is that a foreigner can easily penetrate African societies and obtains whatever they want more quickly than an African counterpart. I have observed this on several international students conducting research; they are warmly received by Africans more than the fellow African researchers, especially in data collection exercises.

With the exception of Nelson Mandela (1918 –2013)—the great and his colleagues who never came in the limelight, and a few others, many highly pronounced great Africans to have ever lived; in sports, music, political leadership, philosophy, scientists, and et cetera have had their success stories with a connection beyond the African continent, especially American success stories—where attitudes are grown to match.

The implication is that it is difficult to make things happen in an environment where others do not think in a complimentary way. Success can never be achieved alone as an individual. You look psychotic when you attribute your success to yourself alone. All successful people have not worked in isolation. They have worked in collaboration with others who have a similar attitude. For example, it is self-evident that you cannot get yourself in the bush and stay there alone and think you can innovate planes. You need other people's support to make a successful innovation. Society has your customers. It is the people of the society in which you live and/or work that give you success—one of the strongest ideologies on which corporate social responsibility is founded. Shared success is the only philosophy that can propel a peasantry community to greater heights. It is a team or teams whose ambitions, visions, and desires interconnect. In a society where several teams have thoughts and visions that do not link up or meet, little success can be registered. Therefore, growing attitudes to match the producer and consumer is the way to go!

Those who have graduated and have had a great understanding of the bottlenecks affecting the continent and have also practically faced the challenges should lead the campaign. In doing so, we need to apply the techniques to the masses in an integrated manner by either allowing the masses to have a conscious vision where circumstances allow or not but by lawful means. However, the unique African attitude disorder (UAAD) is growing day in and day out, accelerated by *digital technologies* from the developed world—with the recent move seen by many African ladies who try to remove the melanin layer from their skin in the way of bleaching to look attractive, maybe. They feel agitated to associate themselves with the black colour. These integrated techniques and approaches will have to take on psychological and legal interventions at national levels and an individual level to induce correct minds that have no borders.

Comprehensive Treatment in Childhood Technique

The more, for example, we train our children to drop local languages to adopt the languages of the colonial masters, the more we perpetuate the problems. This is because even if you speak those languages with the greatest precision and better oratory skills, they can call you a part of them, but you can never become them. They are themselves and will always be! It is, therefore, wise to create our versions following what we have learnt so far. In the attempt to lead change, we reorient and grow our cultures in one of the greatest kinds of cultural audits to foster progress, development and maintain the uniqueness of African humankind. This can be done by understanding the effect of the cognitive development timeline provided on the time dimension. Therefore, children have to do much work before they attain the age of 10 years.

In some schools, children are punished for speaking vernaculars. This is terrible. Knowledge and understanding is not about the language; neither is it tagged to English or French. It is about the perception induced into the human being that stimulates the intuitiveness and instinctual attributes in the inner-self.

The reintroduction of local languages back into curriculums in early learning sessions as provided for in Chapter Three (Education system) will help to reinstall confidence and optimism in the African child.[88] When you punish a child for speaking their own language or dialect, you are teaching the child to *hate* their own instinctual asset hence damaging the growth of an intuitive mind at the early stage of development. Our intuitiveness is a prime factor in the growth and development of children and exhibits its maturity point in the later years as we become more experienced and specialized. It is better to nurture children in their local languages for the first 2-5 years after they begin school. This is because it helps to make them feel a sense of belonging and their uniqueness. In conclusion, the gist of the matter is to redesign the best teaching medium integrated into modern pedagogy to capture the interests of African humankind. If it needs recreating the *African English, the African French, the African Spanish,* and many others that build on our dialects and/or local languages, we can turn the tables around.

Planned Intermarriages and Racial Integrations

Indians, for example, taught the world how to count. They have proved strong in accounting, IT and some particular sciences. And they have loved Africa to the extent of contributing enormously to the GDP of several African economies for many decades. We need them. We need to learn from them. I am happy to learn that they are now a legally recognized tribe in the Republic of Kenya. Other African countries like South Africa should embrace the move to have the long stayed Afrikaners and Anglophone descendants a recognized tribe. The idea of treating them as foreigners will not help Africa in any way. We need to treat them fairly and equally on a cake of national importance, and they should also reciprocate. We need not stop at legal recognition of the Indian community and other tribes, but where possible, they should be encouraged to associate freely without borders as they wish. Measures to have this happen should be installed in public domains like schools, colleges, universities and et cetera. The reason is that they have got some unique attributes and talents that, once integrated into Africa's young population, would help develop Africa through the integrated methods that are neither restrictive nor selfish. Socioeconomic and sociopolitical Integrations can also be motivated by this technique.

Psychometric Testing Technique in Workplace Planned Positioning

I have mentioned that there are people best suited to vend ice cream despite the high academic grades they achieve, especially those who view Africa's prosperity as difficult to attain. The analogy of the "snake and

---

[88] See p. 122-128, §3.

gold bag" explained earlier can help to give an insight into the typical African ethnic differences. There is a need to invest in understanding the impact of our instinctual abilities where we are destined to work together. This social construct or technique is not meant to bias minds but rather search for wisdom and knowledge that can help the person applying the technique to assemble an efficient and effective team to accomplish a task.

Brand Positioning Using Western Faces and Names to Promote Local Products, e.g. Steven Martins

It has been tested in many African organizations where brand promoters, managers, and leaders are hired from outside such as the Americas, Europe, and Asia. The middle managers, the workforce, and staff are all local. A good example is in hospitals where lead practitioners are foreign. There is a way an African person, because of the *unique African attitude disorder (UAAD),* has trust in an outside face than their own identity. Many African people quickly want to associate themselves with brands promoted by other races.

The founders and promoters of local products will have to associate with foreigners or their belongings to capture the attention of African masses who cannot make philosophical inquiries by themselves. The truth is that many Africans have the potential to invent, innovate, develop and even lead this world, but the influence others have had on us in several spheres has created meaning and reality that we seem to be an inferior race—a global statement. They have positioned their brands at a better position in Africans' minds through categorical influences of different kinds throughout history. And the meaning we attach to this positioning is false, which is to their advantage.

The only approach African minds without borders have to do is to associate with them (non-Africans) and/or their belongings so that in the end, African masses will discover on their own and come to appreciate that it is actually their brothers and sisters leading from behind – as Nelson Mandela (1918 –2013) once said, "I always remember the regent's axiom: a leader, he said, is like a shepherd. He stays behind the flock letting the most nimble go on ahead, whereupon the others follow, not realizing that all along they are being directed from behind."[89] Sometimes, it is important to put others in front of you and take responsibility from behind!

Use of Frequently Asked Questions (FAQs) Technique and answer them the Way We Want

This technique is a philosophical technique that allows people, including the young ones, to keep pondering about the answers to questions and ask themselves endless questions about the fate of Africa. The one who applies the technique always brings topics and questions for discussion with answers which are non-exhaustive but open-ended in order to stimulate deeper probing into the minds of Africans. Questions like: Why do Africans manage to survive amidst extreme poverty and hunger? A good response to this question would be, 'because they are Africans.' What's special about the Africans? The response would be, "they are a different kind of human species, and they ought to stand on their own." The person employing the technique creates a chain of questions and labels them FAQs.

Tactical Deception

---

[89] Nelson Mandela. From long walk to freedom, 1994.

In this technique, the person willing to socially transform the African society considers applying structured deception to win masses—this tactical deception fuels solidarity with the African race. A good charisma and some form of a personality cult is an attribute that one would possess to win followers. In their move to change the mindset of African humankind, the person associates themselves with the success of African descent. And it should be difficult to recognize that their success has actually been contributed majorly by external influence.

Cognitive Restructuring—The Evidence-Based Approach

Because people who introduced religion to Africa never based their arguments on evidence whilst encouraging Africans to drop many cultural assets, the person willing to do good cognitive restructuring to win back the mindset of African mankind, has to use an evidence-based approach that links the success of people and society on their cultural assets. One most important item to exploit in this is the use of cultural assets to treat peoples' psychosocial stressors and deep illnesses amidst the sustainably challenge.

Governmental Policies on Locally Made Products/Innovations

These should be hard policies to propel people to appreciate themselves and learn to love themselves and their works. The Buy African Build Africa (BABA) policies should be passed to propel Africans to the common goal. In this technique, tax incentives are provided to African entrepreneurs, and experienced mentors mentor young people.

Huge Public Relations (PR) Campaign Technique

This technique works best for a person who wants to promote their new product in the market. It is based on Babby's model of innovation appropriation. This model emphasizes that the innovated product has to go through six (6) stages, i.e. presentation of innovation, awareness, comprehension, knowledge, evaluation, and appropriation. Babby noted that many companies and people spend many resources on awareness campaigns but fail to recognize that people need to comprehend why they should have the product at the front position in their minds. His model postulates how much input is comprehensible and ably converted into the intake. With the correct mindset, people will start to recognize the need to better position the product within their minds. Therefore, huge public relations campaigns aim at solidifying emotional bonds and interactions between the innovator and their products and the audience that needs the products. This technique is about receiving feedback at each stage and subsequent processing of that feedback in real-time to move to the next stage in marketing the good or service.

Put-Down-The-Gun Technique

Let anyone who wishes to exterminate others do so; the natural selection will reciprocate. What we do not see is actually more powerful than what we actually see with our naked eyes, either scientifically or spiritually. Before 1987, nobody dreamt that sustainable development would actually become a serious issue. Of course, scientists had forewarned in several models they had developed earlier, but the subject of sustainability rose to fame around 1987. If anyone had ever been a custodian of knowledge, they would have thought of sustainable development from the beginning of the Industrial Revolution, most importantly in 1765, when the steam engine was invented in England.

The search for knowledge and wisdom is a continuous process. In this technique, the person associates themselves with no weapons or artilleries, and they make no attempt to acquire physical protective force but instead concentrates their forces on psychological mechanisms. In this approach to socially transform others, the person appears too simplistic and less interested in a materialistic lifestyle. However, this technique should be employed by very smart people with a strong belief/faith in their God.

The reason people hire security companies and operatives to guard their homes is that they fear attacks from potential criminals, but interestingly, they ensure that they still lock their house doors tight. In other words, they reinforce security by locking doors. This is acceptable. However, in a situation where more security operatives are continuously added to reinforce the security for a person living in a hungry society, it fuels intense anxiety in the hearts and minds of onlookers. If any leader decides not to associate themselves with guns and dares to do what they think is right for people, they are more likely to garner more respect and fear from their followers. Even the potential criminal will have a distorted cognitive pattern, wondering what the hell this leader is, to behave oddly. In this context, I would not believe in guns bringing any peace in this world. People who keep manufacturing different models of guns in view of improving the stability and peace of the world are actually perpetuating the instabilities. And that is why they are more eager to learn about what others are doing in all corners around the globe, including Africa, which has very few factories manufacturing guns.

Africa has the position to lead sustainable development because very few countries in Africa manufacture guns, bullets and other artilleries. Suppose only African countries come to a consensus to control the manufacture and trade in weapons of destruction. In that case, non-African countries that manufacture weapons will have nowhere to supply them because their largest market is Africa and perhaps the Middle East. All the energy used to manufacture weapons would be geared to manufacturing agricultural machines and machines needed to conserve the wildlife, flora and fauna. Africa is in a position where it needs to reorganize itself and focus little energy on building artillery bases because we can do very little to compete with people thinking space colonization at the moment—some people/countries whose defence budget is almost three-quarters Africa's GDP. Our strength lies in gearing all energy to conserving living beings of now and tomorrow through ways that create equilibrium in the natural environment.

Social Engineering With Respect To Time (Time Reliability Factor)[90]

A good number of Africans need an element of time offset when dealing with them. In this I mean, if you have to hold a meeting at 10:00 am, you might be forced to communicate that it is scheduled at 9:30 am because some people will arrive at 10:00 am. Here, you would have provided a reliability factor of 0.5 or 30 minutes. It is my observation, and I take responsibility for this statement. Of course, not always, but one who applies the time reliability factor in many parts of Africa is safer. Even in government or individual projects, you have to factor in the element of time loss without much justification. The cause is attitudinal. In this technique, you look at the likelihood of time loss, first on the individuals appearing in the equation, and secondly on the kind of assignment and policies that influence the individuals, the socioeconomic status, core beliefs, and transport mode. Examine the nature of bureaucracy in government proceedings before you rule out the decision to include a time reliability factor in your program design. People's attitude towards time management has a very strong bearing on their behaviours and thinking and the overall view of nature.

---

[90] See p. 240-246, §5.

Social Engineering Based on Emotional Competence Crisis for a good number of Africans

The emotional reasoning bug is common in Africa. Something small might put off many Africans. This is because of the distortions we have experienced and continue experiencing. These distortions later induce some kind of emotional reasoning in many masses. Somebody is feeling bad about something that went wrong but extends the frustration beyond the scope of what caused the frustration. Some people cry because others are crying without real intimacy. You find such things of reaction formation in several parts of Africa. The one who applies this technique draws relationships in occurrences. For example, by studying emotional reactions of paired stimuli, one can predetermine the behaviours and actions of the associated person/s. That means the likelihood that because this person is angered or annoyed will not deliver objectively is either high or low—that kind of analysis. Following no evidence, many people conclude because of how they feel in particular circumstances or situations. This can be applied by sales and marketing people to take advantage of customers who seem not to value evidence in drawing conclusions.

Sustainable Built Environment Approach

Engineers can design and develop a built environment integrating art, culture, systems and processes that are modelled to elicit how a particular society must behave to meet the sustainability goal. For example, the 10-minute neighbourhood is a concept that can be developed further, integrating concepts on how a particular society should grow people's attitudes and behaviours.

Integrated Technique

In modelling the technique, I base the arguments on the premise that *"the African child quickly conforms to standards, technologies and social constructs issued by external stimuli and complies with the requests made by external forces of influence at a faster rate than his race."*

True love is unconditional. Marvin loved his 3-year-old son too much, and one day, he debated whether the son reciprocated the same love. The wife always emphasized that the son loved his dad conditionally to a greater extent because of the Mercedes Benz he had acquired and that he loved the mother unconditionally. The dad did not take the mother's word seriously. One day he tried to move out of home without the Benz, and the response from the son was not the same as when he always moved out with the Benz. Jose, who always wanted to go with dad, declined some movements whenever dad left the car at home. However, when the mother always tried to get out of home, Jose would cry so loud and would not allow staying at home regardless of whether the mother went out with the car or not. Jose's love for the mother—the primary caretaker, was unconditional!

As Jose grew up a little, he became stubborn, and the mother always shouted at him for wrongdoing and sometimes gave him a few spankings. However, the dad was always protective and warned the mother to stop abusing the child. Slowly, Jose became close to the dad and loved the dad more than before. He always wished to see his dad get back home and to have meals with him regardless of whether Jose was hungry or not—he could wait anyway. Jose's love for the dad was more of a conditioned response than true love. And the fact that Jose could wait and spare the hunger—an unconditioned stimulus meant to elicit Jose to eat instantly, and waiting to eat when the dad comes is also a conditioned response simply because dad usually fixed Jose's anxiety induced by the mother. By driving away the anxiety, which of course is a negative event, Jose learnt that dad would help to calm the mother and his stubbornness was perpetuated and grew much more instead. Of course, the physical punishment and shouting at Jose was aversive, but was the dad right to defend Jose? The solution was the dad sitting down the mother first, Jose second and both lastly. That is dialogue.

It is more damaging for the person who fuels anxiety and fear in you to treat it from you. You need to look elsewhere to treat the anxiety. You are pondering about what to do with extreme poverty, hunger and disease triggered by the industrial revolution, which you did not start. The same poverty was created and perpetuated by colonialism and mind weakening programs. To fetch materials from your motherland and in return be paid second hand finished products to meet the needs of the industrial revolution. To associate the heart and mind weakening programs with the products of the industrial revolution. To distort the world through unending technologies that emit carbon emissions into the air and those technologies used against you. This same person comes with free food to support you to solve the mess you have fallen into.

You might be triggered to love this person, but the love is more conditional and opportunistic than real. That is more of fear which approximates to mild anxiousness. Someone who takes you to the landing site to fish with them and teaches you how to do it might garner genuine love than one who brings you tinned fish to solve your hunger problems. How do you think about the two kinds of people? The one who gives you capital and another who solves the immediate problem? The immediate problem is a symptom of the core problem. Addressing the core problem is the permanent solution. And none is interested in solving for you the core problem. The core problem directly touches humanity, and that is where genuine life is found. Never allow any threatening stimulus to treat the impacts it causes for you. Something that threatens your ego and abuses your humane character should not be handled lightly.

Therefore, in this technique, Africans ought to realize that almost everyone from the North to South and East to West of Africa is doing things that promote their interest. They literary speak differently from what they believe in their hearts about Africa. The African who understands how fellow Africans will react to objects, events or technologies in which other people have influence draws up a mathematical model of how Africans will respond when several stimuli are paired. Therefore, it is a back and forward technique involving conditional and unconditional stimuli, rewards, punishments, and evidence.

The main objective of this technique is to shape Africans towards loving their social constructs. The modeller, therefore, juggles or plays with core beliefs, attitudes, cognition, behaviours, emotions, environment and physiological conditions. This project should be driven by specific formative research to inform the design and development of a product or service in/for the market and an elimination method adopted where the conditional stimuli are constantly withdrawn from the model, drawing attention from the community that has been shaped to respond conditionally. The shaping and reshaping continue as a result of constant withdrawals and reintroduction of the conditional stimuli in the equation as Africans start to learn about their potential to lead lives on their own and be able to forge their destinies in technology, engineering, science, commerce and trade, among others.

Conclusion

The way we look at the world is determined by the lenses that we individually hold. Our beliefs and attitudes predetermine our success to a very big extent. The optimists will always see the glass as half full, while the pessimists will always see the glass as half empty. Africa's main distortion as far as positive thinking is concerned is the unique African attitude disorder (UAAD). This fails many Africans to have the solidarity to support their cause. They cannot support African innovators because of the fixation on others' supremacy in all spheres of social influence.

Those who experienced colonial times are passing multigenerational inferiorism on to the young generations. They were wounded beyond repair. This has to stop if we wish to develop Africa sustainably. The unique African attitude disorder (UAAD) treatment has been tackled through social engineering techniques, well-evidenced cognitive restructuring, behaviour modifications, and Socratic questioning.

We encourage ourselves and neighbours to have a positive self-talk regularly. When Mr President Barrack Obama said, "Yes We Can." It sounded impossible until it was done.

Yes we can graduate from the unique attitude disorder and start viewing things as possible, and that we can stand independnemtly.

Optimism. Positivity. Attitude

Chapter Five: Phenomenology and Probability

"I long to accomplish a great and noble task, but it is my chief duty to accomplish tasks as though they were great and noble. The world is moved along, not only by the mighty shoves of its heroes, but also by the aggregate of the tiny pushes of each honest worker." [91]

=== *Helen Keller (1880 – 1968)* ===

Chapter Organization

Quick Insights

Empathy in Sustainable Development

Are People Unique?

Parenting, Orphan-Guardian Relations, and Society

Africa's Unique Understanding of Time

What Do We Make of Our Lives? A Political View

The Success Theory

Who owns Power in the 21st Century?

The Scientist and Freedom Fighter: The typical role of Nelson Mandela and Albert Einstein in the 20th Century

Case study on Effects of Polygamy

The Humble Beginner, the Educated Entrepreneur and Sustainable Development

The Subject of Inheritance

Long Term versus Short Term Thinking: Modern Day Slavery

The Science of Attitude in Planning for Africa's Sustainable Infrastructure: Accidents on Africa's Roads & Highways

Network Marketing, Salary Loans, and Overnight Fortunes in Africa

The State of Uncertainty, Risk, and Probability

Strange Phenomena in Africa's Service Delivery

Conclusion

---

[91] Words of Life, Harper and Row, 1966.

Quick Insights

You need a source of heat to prepare a meal. Without a source of heat, you cannot prepare a warm meal. That implies that the preparation of a meal depends on the availability of heat energy. The event to cook comes after the event to provide heat energy. Neither too much heat is needed to prepare a good meal nor very little heat. The heat required has to be balanced or regulated to prepare a delicious meal. That means the quantity of heat required for preparing a meal affects the quality of the meal. The same applies to electromagnetic waves in the microwave—they must be regulated to prepare a delicious meal.

Cooking depends on the availability of heat energy. The interdependence of such factors illustrated above in preparing a delicious meal is observed in many other states of affairs worldwide, with events A affecting B or the happening of A causing the happening of B or vice versa, etcetera. The interdependence of events and the independence of one event from others is highly significant in our lives. There is a need to invest deeply in the understanding of cause and effect in the region. Several social, political, psychological, natural and economic phenomena influence our lives. Whether an event is dependent or independent is determined by the nature of investigation because complex and sophisticated studies show the events which affect heat energy needed to prepare a meal.

As humans, we experience several social, cultural, economic, natural, political, and psychological phenomena. The most crucial definitive attribute of these phenomena is our failure to understand their causes and explicit explanations. Kats, an African native, claims that when he or another person coughs in the middle of his thought or activity, that thought or activity is taken to the opposite. He explained that when he made an appointment or imagined meeting another person the next day, and somebody coughed, or himself coughed in the middle of the thought or action to meet the person, he could cancel the appointment because it meant to him that things would not go as planned. It is a core belief that approximates to some form of a superstition he found in place passed on from one generation to another, and he tried to dispute it by insisting against the "cough". To his surprise, the argument has remained valid to date, although he fails to find the real cause and explanation, something he has labelled a cultural phenomenon that motivates a core cultural belief.

All humans have experienced several kinds of phenomena, just like Kats, whose explanations are in doubt. Sometimes we label them superstitions or natural, social, and cultural phenomena. Such phenomenological experiences are distinct from signs and symptoms of psychosis, which are delusions and hallucinations.

Jamie, a born Ugandan native, claims that the dreams that happen in his real life are only traced and recalled in his mind when they happen—he cannot remember them before they happen in real life. After sleep, dreams he remembers fail to happen in real life, which leaves him curious about the explanation and cause. Mr Tony Tondo, a medical doctor, also claims to see smoke wherever he approaches the temple yet many others fail to see the smoke.

Scientists, too, are still grappling to explain many scientific phenomena, one of the reasons they have contradicting theories in the existence of the Supreme Being before The Big Bang Theory. Some scientists believe in the supernatural, some others disbelieve. From my experience, I believe there are lots of things that science cannot explain to date. And the spiritual dimension connotes beliefs that supersede our imagination and reasoning just to believe. All these are grouped into one assembly of phenomenological events.

Before the 16th century, many of today's explainable scientific facts remained phenomenological and were viewed in the spiritual dimension. Newton's discovery of gravitational influence on earth and associated laws unveiled why the Babylonians had been able to build the towers. The Babylonians' ambition to locate the Supreme Being upwards and failed to reach him and the subsequent navigation of the universe by scientists failing to locate the Supreme Being is a phenomenon in itself. The distortions created by the accelerated scientific knowledge and wisdom gained from the many discoveries is leading to yet another wave of phenomena—a new wave of cancers. Understanding what others fail to understand is phenomenological and failing to understand what appears understandable to others is also phenomenological. Therefore, Africa's fate is a multitude of phenomena beyond science and spiritualism.

Many events remain phenomenological until when discoveries to explain their occurrences take place. That brings me to the two most critical scientific laws, which stood phenomenological until proved. They have greatly moved the world. The law of conservation of energy in the universe (a theorem from thermodynamics) and Sir Isaac Newton's laws of motion. The former states that energy cannot be created nor destroyed but can be converted from one form to another. The latter is about the statics of rigid bodies and the dynamism of moving bodies. Isaac Newton (1642–1726) proposed three laws, and these are: [1]Every object in a state of uniform motion will remain in that state of motion unless an external force acts on it. [2]The force acting on an object is equal to the mass of that object times its acceleration. [3]For every action, there is an equal and opposite reaction. These laws have triggered and influenced many discoveries, inventions and innovations in science, engineering and technology. Contemporaries of modern physics like Albert Einstein (1879–1955) benchmarked on these concepts to lead improvement in how matter relates to energy in the universe. Many engineering disciplines can be summarized in these laws.

In whatever activity undertaken, there is a need to practically assess events that co-occur and those that occur in series to forecast the results and risks involved to make lasting improvements in our lives and the nations at large. We must understand such practical cornerstones if we are to change the world. Regimes and revolutions come and go; people who have liberated several nations come and go. We feel their effects. Drawing from history, one can learn a lot to improve the future. History sometimes is repetitive; many lessons can be drawn from it. Decision-making in everything carries more weight than the activities involved, such as following free will. The assessment of contributing factors to the cause or effect with profound assumptions should not be underestimated in any decision-making exercise. I am very convinced that anyone's life can be understood as a mathematical model, all way guided by the subject of chance and correlation of one event into another. The same applies to nations and the more significant issues. The subject of chance and correlation should be understood and respected. The biggest problem is the people's unwillingness to appreciate its existence and power—Our circumstantial phenomenology.

Empathy in Sustainable Development

Jimmy, who used to be the last in class, is my former high school friend. He is now a successful businessman owning a significant investment in the agricultural sector. He pays taxes that are directly proportional to his income. This tax is a significant portion of the fund that the government uses to finance public projects like roads and highways that benefit the nation. Jimmy also supplies his produce throughout the country, including schools and universities from which my children are studying, among many other institutions. His farms employ numerous people, including some of my former school friends and a few relatives. He has also established a division for research and development on his farms to foresee improvement and innovation in his business. One of his modern facilities on the farm has had a significant impact on solving drought-related dangers and provided food security to the country. His wealth indirectly benefits me, and I think I should continue consuming his produce to see him expand and maintain his position in the market! That is my thought, perception, and imagination.

Another person may or may not reason this way in such cases when their friends prosper highly more than them. In some instances, it is not rare to find Jimmy's colleagues fighting him, and when his business empire drowns, people, including the media, might start tough critiquing his work. How one experiences another's success through thoughts, perception, and feelings is the subject too good not to miss in the sustainability equation. We have the choices to attach meanings to experiences. However, when aggregated for a particular society, these meanings predetermine the quality of the psyches and what kind of hope we are guaranteed at the end.

Sudhir Ruparelia was the former East African Crane Bank owner who had shot the Forbes List of Billionaires in 2013.[92] The media and some people were all critiquing him and laughing at him when his bank went under receivership by Uganda's Central Bank in 2017.

In religious teachings, some people relate this failure to appreciate Jimmy's success and Ruperelia's incident to the devil tempting them to feel jealous of their success and celebrate their downfall instead. I am convinced that ignorance, a lack of understanding of how the nation works, primarily disturbs them. When you understand how many jobs are lost due to the collapse of an enterprise, then by no means would you blame the devil.

Envy is one factor that significantly distorts teamwork. No school has laboured to educate people on the danger of envy and the how-to control it from a cause and effect perspective—more of psychological interventions than spiritual. Religious institutions have tackled it, but although not exhaustively. The most envious person is lazy, and I warn you to avoid associating with such a person. That person is very negative about everything, and you can do very little to shape them into an optimistic person. In religious teachings, this kind of soul disorder is believed to be caused by the devil. Maybe if one claims that the devil instils the disorder in one's understanding, I would be convinced that way. Otherwise, it is purely a scientific phenomenon that can be proved, controlled and solved.

Local content promotion has remained a challenge for some financial institutions and government agencies across several African states. Financial institutions and the government do not sufficiently support local companies. Almost everything local is seen as substandard, starting from local experts to locally manufactured products. In my opinion, it is not the institutions as I mentioned; it is the individuals working in these institutions who fail to enact policies that promote local content.

Any patriotic person would prefer a locally made product to a foreign product and only prioritise a foreign product because it is more robust, reliable, and sustainable to meet their requirements. The slogan should be 'buy African, promote and build Africa'. On the other hand, some government institutions have tried to

---

[92] "#27 Sudhir Ruparelia," Forbes, accessed on July 15th 2021, https://www.forbes.com/profile/sudhir-ruparelia/.

find a solution to promote the local content, but they face the question: Is local content worth promoting? As a company or individual, are you doing your part to promote local content? Are you playing right? These questions make local content promotion a two-way issue, a collective effort and everybody's contribution to its success.

On the above point still, because of envy that people fear to talk about in public to find its solution, you find that people are infighting in government offices seeking promotion. They do not want to relate well with their colleagues for fear of taking over their jobs. The result is that people tend to focus very much on locking themselves in their job positions so that none can threaten them. That has a tremendous effect on the output of the officials. Concentrating on living somebody else's life at the nation's expense is a problem nobody comes out to discuss its solution, and I should mention it in writing.

A public or civil servant develops intense fear and anxiety because they have seen a person who is likely to do better than them once they get a chance to serve the nation. To solve this problem, we need to educate the young generation on how the nation works to make them more patriotic. I might have been biased in this envy thing because it exists almost everywhere globally. However, it hit Africans hard, and I believe it is more on the front than any other problem affecting Africa. It finds its way into the symptoms and signs of the *unique African attitude disorder (UAAD)* hence influencing the correct standard of public philosophy we ought to live. As Ralph Waldo Emerson (1803–1882) said, "Envy is ignorance" Africa is highly ignorant in this sphere compared to other places. We need to learn how things work.

Envy distorts teamwork. It has promoted criminalities, and it keeps distorting government programs. People are opposing government programs enviously without proper justification. The worst thing is that nobody seems to care and bring this point forward publicly, for example, in the press and academia. We have unprofessional journalists who enviously report badly about senior citizens. As professionals, they out to act on evidence, not rumours or hearsay. We have people who enviously act in favour of foreigners for opportunities and betray their colleagues. I believe we can control envy problems when people get educated on how the nation functions.

As a scientist, I have discovered an invisible force, too much resistance that goes unnoticed, spoiling the effort to put many Africans on the right track for sustainable development. This energy is within us, and we ought to sublimate it to be more cooperative. Officials should be able to think outside the box than locking themselves into government jobs. They should always work targeting to vacate the offices for the young generation to come in. With such envy problems not controlled, women empowerment might create more of a mess or an affront to family values in Africa because of the failure of both men and women to understand the beauty about it and how it works to support sustainable development.

Men, in some cases, feel envious of the progress of women because of the core beliefs they hold in several African cultures. On the other hand, people who cannot remember where they are coming from and collectively aim to be are very delicate and slippery. And the purpose of uplifting them becomes a scorching topic. When dealing with such people, ego problems must be fixed properly from the word go. Otherwise, for people who uplift them, it would look more or less like self-destruction or committing suicide in instalments in the long run.

In my view, following Emerson's observation, "Envy is ignorance", I think envy would not be the biggest problem but *acting for envious* purposes is the biggest problem. I would add to Emerson's observation and say, "envy is not loving your country—not being nationalistic". On the other hand, Venerable Wu Ling says, "Ignorance leads to egoism, egoism to selfishness, selfishness to resentment, resentment to anger, anger to hatred, hatred to annihilation." If you believe in cause and effect, you will notice that this is one of Africans' main problems. In my view, not much differentiates an African elite from an informal person in this perspective, the soul-envy-ego interrelationship.

We are almost equal because most of our economies survive on borrowing and charity, but some Africans think they are superior to others. Most of the investments in the land have a foreign majority holding except in a few semi-developed countries, but this statement is true for least developed countries. If you are a businessman or entrepreneur and your biggest client is the government of a least developed state, you are more or less in the same boat unless you are an exporter or your biggest client is the private sector. I dwell on this because most people in the least developed countries feel more important than others simply because they think they are: rich & wealthier, highly educated, beautiful, handsome, intelligent, powerful, employed and etcetera. This is just because they are ignorant about the state of affairs.

If you are a professor living on a stipend in a university funded by a foreigner and the foreign funder pulls out for a reason, a village man who cultivates his crops might prove more valuable than you. In matters of national development, let us keep reminding each other that we are all equal at the moment. If you stagger with envy problems, remember that I can never be you, and you can never be me. We are all unique. We need to be generous and stick to goals in life but not stick to objects. Remember that nobody gets to this world with an object, and none leaves with an object.

Why worry about something that does not hurt you? You just have to be thoughtful once something that does not hurt you and hurt humanity in any way worries you. Sometimes, because our bodies are always in a survival state, we tend to perceive the threat from others/environment that lacks evidence hence developing easy to avoid anxiousness.

A person can lose the whole day worried about the perceived threat of incoming talented graduates in the office thinking they might take their job. This threat can happen to anyone in unique circumstances, but the solution lies in helping these graduates as much as you can. In this way, you instil hope in them and cultivate respect for yourself. When you give, there is a way you receive back later or sooner. Even a producer is what they are because of consumers and vice-versa. When a colleague prospers, they are prospering you as well, indirectly. Following the correct philosophy of living for others, we can shape the world into what we want.

The chart below provides some techniques to use to treat soul-envy-ego disorders.

How to stop envying others	How to prevent people from getting envious of you
• Tie your life to goals but not objects • Remind yourself that you are unique and you cannot be the next person • Have a sporting activity, e.g. football, biking, chess, rugby, etc. • Try to be a generous person • Celebrate the success of your colleagues and your success • If possible, think nationalistic *most* of the time • Be a believing and optimistic person	• Be a down to earth person and learn that everyone wants to live a good life, but God made the inequity that we idealistically strive to close • Practice altruism behaviour • Talk less, say only necessary issues • Talk less, do more • Avoid talking your plans and deals to the unhappy/unlucky • Solicit people to share your plans and deals with • Avoid too much luxury in wrong places and wrong time
How to deal with ego problems	**How to stop cultivating egoistic behaviour in others/neighbours**
• Remember, there is always a genius on top of a genius • Take time to think about how the world has come a long way—thoughtfulness • Be a believing person • Be an evidence oriented person • Never chase after fame. Let fame chase after you. • Work on your humility levels	• Too much pampering of one child against the other is bad. Stop it. • Give respect to people equally. When it comes to 'respect', everyone deserves it. • Respect yourself

If we are thinking of self-driven sustainable development, we should not overlook the soul-envy-ego interrelationship. This unconscious or subconscious conflict has many effects but seems unattended to while thinking solutions to pave the way for sustainable development. We all have this conflict, including myself. It is only the level of conflict that differs from one person to another. Here, I mean the conflict personality growth according to psychoanalysts that make up the three regions of mental activity.

These regions influence optimism—and the level of optimism predetermines how we perceive others who are succeeding better than us. This conflict still determines our personalities. And, more importantly, our emotional competencies. The superego and the conscience play an essential role in the moral character of a person. According to Christians, we are all selfish by nature except Adam. And the older we become, the more conservative we become, typical of presidents vying for life presidency and power-obsessed African leaders.

I have a senior relative who did not believe my results at the Advanced level (A levels). In some territories, A levels are an equivalence of a high school diploma. He believed I had cheated, and I remember him making comments like, "We also studied hard, but we couldn't score such high points." In my lower secondary school, our biology teacher used to make comments such as, "It is very hard to get a distinction one in biology. More so, if all of you pass, who will cultivate for us beans?" This soul-envy-ego interrelationship makes me wish to study the unique attributes of Africa's humankind for the rest of my life. Records have it that almost half of the class failed the final biology examination. The biology teacher demonstrated an illusion of knowledge because the higher the literacy level of a nation-state, the higher the likelihood of better welfare. That is when leadership can attract the very best in talent.[93] Economists prove that trade in both goods and services benefits all parties.

> *"It is very hard to get a distinction one in biology. More so, if all of you pass, who will cultivate for us beans?" Former Biology Teacher*

Another senior teacher could not believe that a student in his locale could be admitted to the University for Professional Courses such as medicine, law or engineering and used to discourage them whilst attempting to fill forms to apply for those courses. All the time, he discouraged students and made comments such as, "You cannot get that course because you won't be able to score the required points. Look for another course." Some students insisted and filled out courses of their choice and are now medical doctors. Others are engineers—where I belong.

Some people are ill-informed and naïve though learned. This partly explains why many old aged public servants do not want to leave office, claiming to be highly experienced that when they leave offices, the economy will collapse. There is a vast difference between brilliance and experience. We need both. Give room to the young blood to showcase their talents. The Chinese say, "The person who says it cannot be done should not interrupt the person doing it." If you failed to get your dream medical course and you ended up, for example, into teaching, which you did not want, I do not think it is too difficult for your students to achieve the medical course.

Development is to clean the mind free of impurities, unnecessary spiritual jealousy and avoidable hopelessness. Without welcoming this ideology, we shall continue to be messed up because most opposition politicians are not genuine; they envy those in power—very few premises their arguments on socioeconomic and political doctrines. As I mentioned in Chapter Two (Our Politics), some opposition candidates cannot explicitly narrate the troubles and woes in the current regimes.[94] And those who contest and lose cannot willingly accept defeat; however much the results show that the margin of defeat was extremely high, they continue to complain of rigged elections.

---

[93] See p. 118-122, §3.

[94] See p. 62-63, §2.

"The person who says it cannot be done should not interrupt the person doing it." Chinese proverb.

Are People Unique?

No two people are the same. Never. Even twins are different in many aspects—So, refusing to nurture or mentor others for fear that they will outcompete you or be more successful than you is ignorance. People are simply unique. Even people who seem to perform equally in class are different. People's uniqueness is attributable to the differences in personalities. Modelling personality (P) from social intelligence (S_i), emotional intelligence (E_q), and intelligence quotient (I_q) gives; $P=p(S_i,E_q,I_q)$. However, emotional intelligence is a component of social intelligence at some point. But also personality can be modelled as the total sum of attitudes, i.e. cognitions (c), behaviours (b) and feelings (f) to give; $P_t = \int_t dA$ and $A=a(c,b,f)$. These are mathematical constructs.[95]

If you get a chance to equate the two constructs, the intelligence quotient can be modelled in other variables. *How often is the intelligence quotient measured in terms of social intelligence, attitude or affection?* Many times, schools test memory, not intelligence. Scientists are also still grappling with improving their understanding of the relationship between *memory* and *emotions* in the brain. Even if you tested two people and found them to have the same intellectual capability, no two people *thought patterns* could ever be the same. It is, therefore, a complete wastage of time to think that one other person can ever defeat your unique attributes. This should not be a stumbling block for anyone willing to support the cause of humanity. Many scholars have laboured to define and illustrate personalities bringing out the different dichotomies in human beings.

Parenting, Orphan-Guardian Relationship, and Society

Several societies across Africa have failed to comprehend that children are produced for the nation or society. A child does not belong to the parents alone but belongs to a nation-state. Care and upbringing of children should be a collective effort for both parents and the government. In the recent past, many cultures promoted the collectivistic upbringing of children. Many times, adults in the neighbourhood would take the initiative to discipline a child who misbehaved. They would handhold the misbehaving child and carry the child to their parents, sit and talk about the indiscipline of the child to tame them to change for the good of society. This is not possible in today's modern world.

Everyone is after raising their children and less concerned about the upbringing of the neighbours' children. Today, one cannot be an immediate informant if h/she sees a neighbour's child getting spoilt for fear that the parents will misinterpret it as an enemy to their child. One will wait to see that the neighbour's child's indiscipline has grown to reach the tip of the iceberg to act as an informer.

In some instances, the observer may be able to spot maladaptive behaviours in your child early enough—to your advantage. You may not be able to see quickly—and if there is working together as a community in upbringing children, this person will let you know about the misbehaviour early enough—primarily where children get absorbed into drug abuse. It is a fact that by the time the parent or guardian recognizes that their child is absorbed into drug use, the members of society might have known for some considerable

---

[95] See p. 194-196, §4.

amount of time. The tendency of parents to prefer working alone raising children and wait for the government to jump in when children slip off the track is not the best. Some societies dropped African cultural values that were rich in the upbringing of children—collectivistic values.

Today, everyone is willing to protect their interests because they have *not experienced* one of their children getting spoilt. This is modern selfishness; a collective effort is undefeatable—this parenting style was neither authoritarian nor authoritative but cut across. Although today, we are slowly adjusting to authoritative parenting styles common in western cultures, our children grow highly isolated, less altruistic and highly mean at heart. Although no study has been made in Africa to agree or nullify the aforementioned, common knowledge has it that children growing up in collectivistic rural settings where no home perimeter fences exist are less phobic to animals, are much stronger, problem solvers, more altruistic, and hardworking than their counterparts raised on urban balconies. In recent studies, scientists and sustainable development activists have found that the more one interacts with nature, the more one reduces depression and anxiety levels. Suppose you are unwilling to raise kids in a suitable environment never have any because the crisis of a wounded child is a crisis to the entire nation. In the realm of fighting totalitarian governments with developing economies still present in many African countries, we ought to retract cultural norms and values that worked best for us whilst improving the social power to attract self-driven sustainability.

Understanding that children are raised holistically helps grasp and improve the guardian-orphan relationships, foster-adopted child relationships, and sponsor-needy children relationships. However, holistic/societal upbringing of children should not be confused with an institutional upbringing where infants and children are brought up in an institution where they have multiple caregivers. Multiple caregivers predispose children to the risk of psychological difficulties like failing to make and hold onto purposeful relationships later in their lives. Raising children holistically in many cultures is meant to act as a whistleblower when you see a child misbehaving and acting contrary to the norms and values of society—in the modern time, purporting yourself as a whistleblower, you may be labelled a society problem.

To a guardian looking after an orphan, you should not envisage the orphan as being a creditor. And to an orphan being looked after by the guardian, you should not envisage the guardian as a must to be looked after. However, the adopted child is entitled to these privileges as the laws of the country may demand. There is much work to be done in this area. This is because the collectivistic forces of African societies demand attention.[96] Most orphans do not appreciate the little provided by their guardians but are ever complaining of what they have not received, forgetting that it is not a must to be looked after by the guardian. Always appreciating the little, you receive as an orphan from the guardian is a big step to being loved. This motivates the provider and increases the proportion to spend on you. Always expressing dissatisfaction lowers the morale of the provider.

To the guardian or relative who labours in freedom to look after the orphan, please do not see it as an investment where you expect a giant leap after some time but rather look at it as charity. This will always arouse the desire and enable you to concentrate more on charity activities. Actual helping and support happen when the provider does not expect something in return. This, coupled with extensive educative

---

[96] See p. 321-327, §7.

material that you provide to the orphan, would be enough to keep you hopeful. Paying school fees for a needy child to become a mechanic to work in your garage shall not see Africa develop. Uplifting and empowering needy children to stand on their own, forge their case, and realize their potential and dreams is ideal for nurturing a solid foundation for self-driven sustainable development. That planned infringement onto the helped person after school is thinking cuckoo and not nationalistic.

In many African regions, where the HIV/AIDS prevalence and other similar diseases remain high, orphan rates remain a big issue. There are cases of poverty-stricken old grandparents who are left with no option but to take full responsibility for their grandchildren. Therefore, fitting an orphan within the resource constraints remains a challenge in these families. If only the orphans get to know that they cannot receive in equal amounts as the guardian's children, it waives the stress and balances the resource constraints equation leaving room for the guardian to drive their ambitions and see their dreams come true. In the interest of the nation, charitable organizations should start at a family level. Also, a well-researched and studied tax stipend may be imposed on citizens to target the orphanage pool.

It is companies that train staff and treat them well to stay. Parents and guardians nurture and treat children well for the children to have a better differentiation of self to start their lives wherever they go—they train them to leave. They train them for the nation. As a parent or guardian who loves yourself, you must derive much pleasure when you nurture and pass out well-individuated people to society. It is on record that the distorted African collectivism is good at failing to produce competitive graduates. Graduates that are too fused in families and fail to stand on their own. In today's complex global village, sustainability calls upon parents and guardians who understand how to lead while featuring in the equation of followers at the same time.

Some of the continental financial crises are perpetuated by failure to nurture well-individuated offspring at some point. A lack of self-awareness has fueled the history of African poverty through the ages. It is more of the failure to self-examine our lives that perpetuates our poverty. The older people drain the young ones within collectivism. Young ones leave to fix problems without limit, which would have been fixed by the parents whilst in that age bracket. I mean the current age of the offspring. This is a result of the improper training of children to become well-individuated and not very fused into the family. In the long run, people are not liberated but rather become dependents.

In some developed countries, the old work for the young ones, but the young ones work for the old ones in many African countries. The continued cycle of young ones working to fix the problems of the old parents and grandparents maintains poverty in many families across the African continent. Is it possible to accept things as they are at some point to break the chain of hopelessness? Train children well to go. Let us answer this phenomenological inquiry for the betterment of Africa. Unless parents and grandparents are sick or starving, materializing their plans when yours are not yet fruitful when these people passed through the same age bracket successfully is not a very good idea. Anyone else is free to borrow ethical relativism to break the ice in this case. However, I strongly believe in an innovative approach to deal with distorted collectivism in the interest of self-driven sustainable development.

Is Pain Bad or Normal for the Children?

Dysfunctional and unhealthy families teach children that pain is bad. Is experiencing pain so bad, or we can view it as a learning session? The one who teaches that experiencing pain is so bad has entirely got it wrong. Pain is part of the learning process and part of life. Interestingly, experience shows that many people who have achieved lots of success in this world experienced some pain at some point in their lives.

Teaching that pain is terrible and abnormal has caused many problems in parenting children, especially those for relatively wealthy Africans. Although I lack accurate statistics on children of the wealthy Africans who are schooled in the developed countries, from my experience of a few I know, many of them get absorbed into quick money-making schemes. These schemes spoil them and retard the socioeconomic transformation of our countries, especially when their parents die. These boys and girls quickly think along fragmenting the deceased's estate to earn quick liquid cash. They cannot withstand going through hard times. Starting small businesses remains a challenge for children taught that pain is horrible. They always look for soft spots in whatever they do, forgetting that nothing rarely grows when someone remains in their comfort zone.

It is perfect to love your children to the extent possible. However, extending too much love to the children whilst teaching that pain is so bad is ignorance because we cannot disassociate ourselves from pain throughout our lives. Climate change alone might bring about unprecedented pain creating too much depression and anxiety due to traumatic experiences it can cause. For example, the world experiences earthquakes, severe floods, excessive heat, etcetera in several locations. Earthquakes destroy habitats, housing, and infrastructure and severe floods destroy farmlands, roads, buildings, and houses and adversely impact service delivery. All these can cause painful and traumatic episodes. A child taught to bear with pain perseveres through difficult times. In his book, "Tough times never last, but tough people do!" Robert H. Shculler teaches us how we can turn negatives into positives. Robert shows you how to build a positive self-image, no matter what your problem.[97] Therefore, teaching children that pain is normal shapes them into better adults.

The modern world has improved in several spheres, i.e. transport, communication, shelter, human health, clean water and sanitation, entertainment, etc. The continued pampering of children simply because the world has had many innovations that simplify life does significant damage to humanity. There must be a balance in the way we nurture children to grow, knowing that experiencing hardships in life makes life exciting and meaningful.

To lead a healthy life, you ought to learn how to deal with pain. The body and mind work together to grow. The reason we live is to work. Our bodies are kept healthy due to the pain we undergo as we solve existing problems. When young people learn that pain is so bad, they become lazy and always look for quick money schemes, yet the genuine ones are rare.

It is common knowledge that the harder the young person's life, the better the person becomes in the future. Experiencing pain is a learning process that trains the mind to think out solutions. Therefore, hardships in life are better dealt with by a person who knows that pain is normal. Therefore, a healthy

---

[97] Robert H. Shculler, *Tough times never last, but tough people do!* (New York: Bantam, 1984).

functioning family balances love for everyone and emphasises that pain is normal. In the end, we nurture and stimulate people who are ready to face challenges and devise solutions to solve these challenges.

Africa's Unique Understanding of Time

A typical native African does not think of time as a resource whether educated, learned, semi-educated, or illiterate. Before attacking me for appearing subjective, reflect on the masses, the forest, and not trees. We have no insurance cover for lost time in many instances, except a few. Most of our people do not respect the price for the time. Poor time management remains one of the biggest problems we face, yet it is a "function" of all important matters. Once you lose time, you cannot regain it. It has a price tag, but not everyone can see it. The more we less respect time, the more we shall remain mendicants.

Although highly conservative people still find it hard to believe these weaknesses in the way most Africans perceive time, I take responsibility to sound an alarm to the continent about the danger of not respecting time. We always throw the blame elsewhere. I need to awaken Africans and remind you that we have always been responsible for our lives now, and in the past, we are the authors of our lives, and we design the signposts to follow.

> *"Everything that comes; accept. Let it come. For, it has to come. Everything that happens; accept. Let it happen. For, it has to happen." African adage, symbolic of loose existential phenomenology.*

Much as several scholars give facts, West, East, North, South and Central about our position, in the beginning, the time is now and only now to prove that history. We are the only, and only the ones to change our situation but not foreigners. Neurotic and immature defence mechanisms leave no room to learn. Being a typical descendant, I make the identifications, the outline, and the extent of the actual predicaments. Let us work together without going defensive. Not every issue needs researching to validate or nullify it. Not all policies culminate out of the research. Otherwise, legislative assemblies would use only researched items to inform their arguments. Most legislative assemblies, if not all in Africa, lack research as a procedural step involved in the making of primary legislations. Some are observatory issues that stimulate the enactment of policies, whilst we qualitatively assess others to develop relevant policies. I had a chat about time management with a scholar, and below is the excerpt:

> "Someone wounded in the infancy and childhood stages is more likely to have chronic speed." He started. "You mean Chinese are wounded chaps since they tend to act with speed most of the time?" I asked. "No, that is their culture," he responded. "We have learned many things from others; why don't we adjust swiftly to this because it seems a good habit? Is it not important to act with speed?" I asked. "You see, don't tell me that; everything has been designed to undervalue an African man. Do you know the beauty of your black skin? Do you know the beauty of your cotton-like hair? Do you know that the most prominent poetics stole ideas from North Africa?" he tried to shut me up. "Ok, fine, all that might be true, but why do many African people fail to keep time?" I insisted. "You and who?" he belligerently asked. "For me, I keep time." He added. "I mean, I have tried to use email communication, and the response rate is lowest in Africa." I tried another angle. "Do you know that a Nigerian invented email communication?" he twisted me. At this point, I gave up.

It is not about stereotyping an African child on time management dilemmas, but if so, it is a highly observed trait that might approximate to such. I find myself privileged and qualified to give an expert narrative and opinion about time management. I once listened to a pastor narrating his stories after being late for prayers. He said, "The only rightful person that can keep time is God." Yes, no doubt, God is the only perfectly righteous time manager, but I wonder whether this could make a reasonable excuse to the congregation that had waited for him for a very long time. Almost everything has a time parameter, dependent on time as one of its independent variables and should be given a price tag in the equation.

The value of time is such a fantastic resource. The more we understand that time is a resource and has a price, the higher we shall reach. Of course, some people have slowly learned to manage their time correctly, but most are talented or have worked with foreigners or who have worked elsewhere in the world or the well-groomed ones. I hypothesize these are in the top 5%. The majority, including educated and learned people, still face the challenge. What makes it worse is that time management has remained a significant challenge even to the educated people. The most annoying experience is a lack of showing responsibility in matters related to time management.

A typical native African cannot communicate well in advance about his unexpected failure to manage time. By communicating and apologizing about your failure to deliver or make it on time, you show responsibility. Several government programs are managed at a snail's speed, whether in delivering justice in courts or infrastructure development, universities' activities, hospitals' treatment plans, etcetera. That partly explains why many donors and funding agencies at times pull out of some program projects. We have too much bureaucracy and red tape tendencies in several African regions. I have heard about the legal opinion that justice delayed is justice denied. Therefore, courts should not delay justice should without sound reasons. The cases of heavy backlogs in many African courts of law are pretty alarming—only to hear lawyers applying for adjourning cases to future dates.

Case Study I: Time Management

I faced a bad experience when an African university scheduled my viva voce for my master's degree program four times, and none of the panellists showed up until the fourth time. When they showed up, it was a very dramatic incident that I cannot forget. I cannot forget the professor who claimed I had bought my dissertation from a local market that sold research when he commented about the presentation. That was my first time to learn about the local market that sold dissertations! He demonstrated having succumbed to the unique African attitude disorder (UAAD). That kind of bias would not come from someone who had failed to show up three consecutive times if he took living with integrity quite serious—a foundation for professionalism. When I summed up the factors that fail self-driven development in Africa, i.e., time management, the soul-envy-ego problems, the unique African attitude disorder (UAAD), academic politics, selfishness, and many others, I would not hesitate to write this book.

I got convinced that Africa had distortions to fix. Even if you hold a PhD in Africa, it does not warranty becoming an intellect that Africa deserves to solve its predicaments. That was a professor who would apologize for missing the three (3) schedules for my viva voce but instead biased my dissertation to his local market that vends dissertations. After the panel failed me, I submitted a defence outlining the anomalies and from which the university felt ashamed to reschedule my presentation for the 5th time. That is the Africa in which we live.

Another concern is the average time for a post-graduate student to graduate from the same university and department. They make final year research so tricky that an average student would take about 4 – 6 years or more to graduate with a master's degree. Six years down the line, some of my colleagues are still on the course. Interestingly, some students abandon the degree programs because of problematic research and go to study abroad. In just one year, they are awarded their masters degrees, and they return home. Very few people, if not none, fail to achieve their post-graduate degrees when they go and study, for example, in Europe, Australia, China, and America. That is the Africa in which we live! In Africa, you achieve anything through extreme pain. I cannot believe the institution has employed these people for so long without discovering their cruel, malevolent nature. Psychologists usually say, "Someone who was once abused is always an abuser." Can we break this cycle of hopelessness for the good of future generations?

Similarly, the local institution scheduled my local interview to register as a professional engineer three times, and none of the panellists showed up until the third schedule. And when they appeared on the third schedule, the entire process was ambiguous and corrupt. Things like: "the assessor refused to release your report; please do something", always define their days. That prompted me to try outside internationally recognized engineering bodies for accreditation as a professional engineer. The process was straightforward and time-conscious—so, I succeeded. I am now an internationally recognized civil engineer.[98] I moved on to find where I belonged and where I could identify with the right minds that would later shape the thinking about sustainability that the world deserves—organisations that subscribe to the United Nations (UN) mission to combat climate change and achieve the 17 UN Sustainable Development Goals (SDGs).

If the institution had visionary leaders, they would engage me to learn more about the reasons that prompted me to take a bold decision for outside institutions to improve the systems. However, since they did not engage me, it is an indicator of a leadership crisis.[99]

I predicted right that a person of malevolent nature would continue malevolent acts, and it happened. After succeeding elsewhere, a particular network of officials failed me wherever my portfolio featured. You know municipal engineering and the government are inseparable twins. I then remembered Lucky Dube's *You Stand Alone* lyrics;

> "...If you stand for the truth,
> You will always stand alone..."

---

[98] **Note:** The international body I joined is a globally recognized institution. It is a fully established organization delivering *sustainable development* through knowledge, skills and professional expertise for over 200 years. Once you join it, you automatically become a sustainable development enthusiast; you get interested in shaping zero to save the planet. It seeks to continue developing its status globally as an international body, but not as a competitor with local organizations. Anyone with appropriate skills, knowledge, experience, and ability, may join the institution from anywhere at any time around the globe.

[99] See p. 362-366, §8; See also p. 203 (Hint: Unique African Attitude Disorder (UAAD)).

So, I decided to sacrifice. After that, the local institution passed many candidates anyhow, and when I talked with some, I advised them to read about the "ripple effect".

I am sure after reading this book; they might continue the malevolent acts instead of learning to improve Africa. However, I am determined and dedicated to stopping this hopelessness, and I am equally ready to sacrifice. We will not continue to live odd as a result of the wounded Africans. The decision to react in the book came after exhausting options and there was no better option to remind the leaders about the urgency to address sustainability issues.

I have written about the things I have experienced for which I have the evidence but not about what I have heard. Things that had remained a phenomenon until when this book found the reasons. We need to rise to unlock sustainability and reclaim Africa's position. That kind of hopelessness has to end if we are dreaming of achieving self-driven sustainability. The malevolent and cruel nature of the wounded Africans has to be dealt with to forge a sustainable path.

"If you close your eyes to facts, you will learn through accidents" African Proverb.

In all my endeavours, I ensured I remained working in my country to lead solutions for the betterment of the people of my country. And I have never, in any way, felt any dreams of wanting to be others or admire living elsewhere. I do love the Pearl of Africa. In this interest, I need to lead change within my peoples whom colonialism wounded, succumbed to the unique African Attitude disorder (UAAD), and got fixated in aid to live so that they wake up. I had exhausted options before taking a bold step; there was no better option to advise the institution. Under this clause, I would need to shape many others' thinking about sustainability to unlock Africa's development.

The primary purpose of taking a bold step to get internationally accredited was to lead change in the local institution as an example. The institution would perhaps overhaul the whole conceptual framework based on the new evidence. I write this without fear or contradiction; the 21st-century climate action calls for a different attitude; professional bodies and other organisations must be agile enough to lead sustainability.

Many people in government positions in Africa are ungenerous with time, and they do not mind the repercussions when they miss an appointment or schedule. Because the kind of Africa I dream of living in is still miles away, I had to write this book.

Another incident I witnessed was a PhD student and his supervisor in the similar university. When the supervisor stood up, he criticized his student when he said, "I have not experienced such an unserious student before." What amused me the most was that the student, upon letting him defend his thesis, also started with similar remarks and said, "I have not experienced such an unserious supervisor before." The point was on time as a resource and how each of the two perceived it.

The illusion of thinking that we have much time will limit us from achieving our dreams and *destroy us*. Leading improvement in how things are done needs people who understand the importance of proper time management.

Case Study II: Time Management

If you cannot catch time, space on earth cannot be caught too. One is a success in space only with time. I use space in this context to mean the extent you can go leading your goals. Money goes to those who catch space in real-time. Having too much money is not satisfaction. Satisfaction is derived from the urge to succeed and the performance.

I hired 8 trucks from Jinja to Nakapiripirit district in Uganda, a journey of about 275-km to work on a gravel road rehabilitation. I negotiated the hiring fees with the owners and agreed to have the trucks for 14 days. The negotiated fees included drivers' welfare (accommodation and feeding). On reaching the site, the drivers complained that accommodation and feeding were costly.

I immediately called for a meeting to iron out the grievances. We came to a mutual agreement that I should cater for their accommodation. I expected them to deliver maximum output since they seemed satisfied with the resolutions from the meeting. I was shocked to find out that they still failed to perform to the extent they stole the fuel for their gains. I provided 60 litres of fuel per truck per day.

They complained that the fuel was not enough for them to complete the tasks since I had instructed each of them to deliver 9 trips of gravel upon receiving 60 litres of fuel daily. The drivers said that 60 litres of fuel could only deliver 6 trips. That prompted me to perform a simple experiment, randomly choosing one truck and fueling it to a full tank. I sat in one of the trucks for the whole day to monitor the truck while hauling gravel. After hauling 6 trips, I measured the used fuel to be only 40 litres. They agreed with the results from the experiment and regretted that they had been sucking 20 litres every day. I had to deduct money for the 20 litres they sucked per day from each truck before effecting their payments. So, for the four days they had spent working, I paid them less money after deducting the money lost in fuel theft but with a bit of difficulty.

Though I regained the money, I still made a loss due to the low productivity of the trucks and the time lost. This showed me that satisfaction does not lead to performance, and money cannot buy contentment. In construction projects, the element of time and cost move together.

Similarly, in a typical poor rural private secondary school in Rakai district—Uganda, teachers were made to spend 23 hours a week of timetabled teaching. They did whatever was necessary to deliver the lessons in time. The deputy headteacher was delighted with their performance. She commented in one staff meeting and said she was very impressed with the teachers' service delivery that term. This made teachers uncomfortable. They compared their salaries with those of teachers in similar secondary schools and protested. They lodged an official protest and demanded their salaries to be revised. And if not salaries were to be increased, they wanted the school to reduce 23 hours to 20 hours a week of timetabled teaching. They also asked for incentives and similar logistics, such as rewards for the best performing teacher. They also wanted the school to pay their salaries in time. This shows that performance leads to satisfaction or dissatisfaction.

While we complain that we do not have enough money to undertake projects, remember that more money cannot satisfy our needs and wants. But instead, performance shall satisfy us. We need to cultivate performance in however tiny amounts it happens to be with whatever we have. More money, if allocated appropriately, shall improve the systems. Considerable time is lost complaining of no money in almost everything. The solution is to use the available resources to allocate them efficiently and effectively.

When the performance in the equitable allocation of resources improves, we shall attract success and satisfaction. More people shall express interest to cooperate with us. In my opinion, exceptional African states which have improved significantly are only in the top 2%. Performance improvement shall attract more genuine internal and external investors and cooperation agencies to spur socio-economic transformation. More money, if not embezzled or donated to you, is a product of performance but not performance a product of more money, *keeping other factors constant*. It is not about the amount of money you have but rather what you do with what you have in the time you have. Ideally, one uses their cognitive faculties in crisis than when they have everything.

What are the lessons to learn from the above cases? The lessons are as follows:

a) In any undertaking, increased salaries or wages do not guarantee improved workers' performance, but rather, the working culture that includes motivation strategies might improve performance. That means satisfaction or dissatisfaction might not lead to performance.

b) Self-driven sustainable development cannot happen where African nations obtain more loans and grants from developmental agencies because it does not guarantee performance. The question is, "what have we done with the loans and grants we have received since independence?"

Time in the Equation of a Professional's Accreditation Process: Where Ambiguity Meets Academic Politics of a Sort!

Professional registration is about peers reviewing a candidate to ascertain their eligibility to join the fraternity. Much ambiguity exists in many African institutions, which I cannot hesitate to discuss here. Several institutions do not follow a well-structured process to value time in a candidate's accreditation exercise. That coupled with academic politics leaves very little hope for Africa to stand on its own.

Objectivity requires a structured process following rules of validity and reliability. This calls for using a benchmark, the same tools and techniques to assess all candidates' competence for timely admission into the institution. Achieving is not enough; we need to maintain the standard we reach. Integrity lies in being consistent, while achieving lies in persistence. Much as you want the candidate to provide an account of the life in their career that ties well, your feedback as a reviewer or an assessor should tie as well. The instrument, tool, or technique, should measure what it is supposed to measure and measure it consistently. Therefore, a structured process rules out ambiguity, tags value to time, checks on the bias, promotes fairness and the institution's integrity.

A peer bestowed to review a candidate's portfolio should have the discretionary powers to decide whether the candidate should progress to the next level or not. The business of back and forward correspondences within the peers themselves to decide on a candidate's admission creates doubt. It affects the integrity of the institution unless it is an officially accepted structured process of the institution. However, the random walk of events in the professional's accreditation process within African institutions, which is more or less like a stochastic process, leaves little hope for Africa to stand independently. Sometimes the accredited candidates turn out to be very fake to provide professional services to society. For example, it is Africa where you find geologists but do not think like geologists. It is where you find engineers who do not think like engineers! A lawyer should think like a lawyer.

The structured process should be like a questionnaire or a standard psychometric testing instrument drafted in batteries to capture the candidate's competence in several defined attributes set by the institution. If the institution decides to set an examination, it must be a structured, standard metric.

The standard metric or standard questionnaire must comply with the concept of minimum requirements because nobody can claim to achieve maximum competence; we learn, train and develop throughout our lives until we die. The scope of minimum requirements must be well defined. Surprisingly, some institutions do not have a defined scope for minimum requirements; you find people focusing on the candidate's report organization, not what the candidate did. If they cannot produce a standard report following what they did, then they are not ready. The tendency of commenting for the sake of commenting is timewasting. You must know what to look for from the candidate following a standard.

Working for accreditation should be a stage-managed process. To proceed to the next level, one has to be cleared for the lower level. Time is such a vital resource. We need to respect people's time because we have very little time to stay in this world. Give people space to demonstrate what they can showcase in Africa's sustainability equation. Even if the person is not fit to be admitted into the institution, have well-defined guidelines to work on such people and give them honest feedback in time. It makes no sense to waste somebody's years, and at last, you tell that person that your diploma or degree does not qualify you to be admitted as a member of this institution. Even though you are the best caesarean doctor but poor at time management, you turn into a boob because you attend to patients late. Even if you are underpaid, play your part right until when you find green pasture. Abraham Lincoln (1809–1865) once said, "Act your part well, there lies the honour." Let us build Africa with one heart and soul—with passion, commitment, and integrity.

What Time Means in Creating Wealth in Africa

It is mainly in the Africa region where people tag wealth to age—where people say that being rich is for the older people, 50+ years. This is purely an indication of a lack of belief in invention, innovation, and talent. It is one of the reasons why intellectual property and copyright laws are weak in many least developed countries. Copyright laws ought to be highly enforced in a promising state—a state where invention, creativity, and innovation are considered the key to prosperity. A person who starts to view the road to success in his old age, say 50+ years, sometimes enters a crisis, and that person has a unique perception about success.

Unemployment is one detrimental factor that has crippled people too much not to think. This is because we fail to create an enabling environment for the youth and women to innovate, especially where old aged leaders cling in power for life presidency coupled with unimproved democratic ideals that multiply the ordinary man, day and night. Give trial room for ideological differences. And to polish this further, for the educated to claim unemployed *ideally* means wastage of time in school. Unemployment versus time management, the race goes on and on as human beings develop through early adulthood stages to old age.

The increased rates of elders clinging into offices past the retirement age indicate not understanding many of these principles. You can find a solution to unemployment but no alternative for the lost time. We need to understand that we live to work but not to work to live or die while living at work. It is not good to live the entire life working for money. Therefore, dealing with a person looking for only money without a vision is precarious. The notion of time management versus work and space on earth is one subject that every person ought to know. High crimes from elders and the older people claiming to create wealth in their late years are primarily a result of a crisis and resulting fixation in the middle years and the false belief that wealth is for the aged. Always think outside the box to catch space in real-time.

On Government Programs and Time

There is always back and forth correspondences in several government agencies across the continent. This, coupled with slow decision making, poor attitude, too much bureaucracy and red tape tendencies, worsens the situation. Many government offices are occupied by less motivated people, less innovative, and non-patriotic people. Such people are poor at time management. From quick survey research I conducted recently, I failed to understand why an email sent to an institution such as an African university might take more than a month to be replied to if at all replied. Yet, it only takes a few hours or days to be replied to when sent elsewhere in the world. We need researchers and practitioners to look into this behaviour. Otherwise, time is one of the great resources that many people take for granted.

You cannot become genuinely rich when you do not respect time. Self-driven development will be challenging to attain if we fail to respect time. The problem is that every problem has been tagged to money issues. People always say, "There is no money; that is why it takes longer to respond to such inquires and such similar things." These are such lame excuses. I believe it is a lack of morale, poor training, wrong attitude, short-term mindedness, poor policies, and money-minded syndrome in every tiny matter—the how-do-I-benefit attitudes. It is about building effective and efficient systems and the fair allocation of resources that matters the most. Systems that are effective and efficient would be designed to solve the ambiguity.

And what is money, by the way? Imagine they provided you with sacks of money and removed everything from you, say the people, the cars, the food, the hospitals, the roads, the fuel, you remain with only money, and what can you do with it? Money is just a medium of exchange—what lies within us is more than money. I can bet that an improved population quality highly grown in democracy can live without money. People who have invented all the things we see, the cars, the bulbs and electricity, the soap, tinned foods, and many other things, never thought of money when starting. They were trying to solve problems to make the world a better place to live. The money-minded syndrome of Africa's child is a stumbling block to innovation and development. Everything is viewed as impossible because of a lack of money. Even enacting and implementing policies like not littering polythene bags on city streets also needs money first. Some people have mastered the art of timing, though, and are already impacting positive change. We all need to change and respect time.

It is among us still where you find people dropping customers because they have grown too big to serve small customers. This is extremely dangerous for people who understand how a business thrives. Any business expansion harnesses the power of systems building; that is why International Organisation for Standards (ISO) is in place to support organisations and businesses to streamline operations to capture all sorts of customer segments. We need to remember that the developed countries did not have all this money we see. They worked hard to achieve the status they hold today, and they still work harder than us to sustain their achievements.

What Do We Make of Our Lives? A Political View

In my opinion, a human plays only one per cent of his life. The point is to live the one per cent because every person dies, but not everyone lives. Supernatural powers, unconscious forces, and irrational drives beyond our control determine the other ninety-nine per cent of our lives. The psychoanalysts and radical behaviourists call it the deterministic view of human nature. Our fates are a vital source of inspiration. All people who claim to live intentional only utilize the one per cent to the fullest. A plot of one's timeline justifies circumstantial existence. My circumstantial existence should not be confused with circumstantiality because it derives its roots from determinism. The social term circumstantiality refers to a non-linear thought pattern and occurs when the focus of someone's conversation drifts but often comes back to the point. In my hypothesis on circumstantial existence, I draw reference from the English Oxford dictionary (8th Ed.) on the term circumstantial to mean connected with particular circumstances.

I believe that our existence is non-linear, and mathematicians and physicists can model it with the chaos theory and nonlinear time series analyses of a sort. Healthy development is to try as much as possible to run away from chaotic living models to linear models. However, sustainable development prioritizes circular models but is still more promising than chaotic models. Africa lies amidst the first and second worlds and keeps in the chaos theory, which predisposes it to prolonged fixations. Why? We struggle to live linearly on leftovers while others fetch raw materials from Africa, and Africans then wait to receive second-hand products.

With a timeline plot, you can track the effects of the good and bad phenomenology of living. Psychoanalysts see freedom as restricted by unconscious forces, irrational drives, and past events. The behaviourists see freedom as restricted by sociocultural conditioning. The existentialists or the humanistic agree to these schools of thought at some point. They agree that circumstantial existence is inevitable but not all that responsible for our overall being. They claim that we are responsible for our actions and choices. That we are the authors of our lives, and we design the signposts to follow. I somewhat agree with them. However, existentialists should get reminded that they take only one in a hundred. That means the level of responsibility to author destinies is limited to about 1%. And for women, the weight goes further down to about one half in a hundred (0.5%)—they highly live as victims of circumstance. For example, women can claim to author their destiny far better if the tables turn around and a woman starts to propose to a man for marriage. Men seduce women for love relationships; they do this through packaging lies that look real. That victimizes women.

The existentialists view of human existence, growth, and development and absurdity of life are more accurate in the eyes of the Buddhists. However, the explicit belief in the existence of God and Allah by the Christians and Muslims respectively makes the humanistic view untenable and irrational. Therefore, periodic regime changes are inevitable in a promising democracy for checks and balances to create favourable circumstances for all people to grow and flourish. For example, people who advocate for constitutional amendments to favour life presidency or pseudo monarchism and no term limits on the African soil leave a section of the population in chronic illness and negative circumstantial victimization.

Although we advocate for constitutional dynamism, the consequences of such selfish amendments have a broad effect. That is just one example of many other forms of selfish constitutional amendments. The vice extends even to other public offices and in academia; people cling to offices. In academics, people find it hard to appreciate limits. A fair person allows others a chance to make history too. A fair person understands the game of chance. A fair person understands circumstantial success. A fair person enjoys his success with others. That is the person who believes in the existence of the Supreme Being.

Just as death remains mystical and nobody knows when to die, although thanatology and geriatrics claim that nature communicates to a person about to die about 40 days before death, many events in our lives are circumstantial. If scientists and engineers can discover how to move only two microseconds into time, many people's lives would be saved. People are dying of accidents and catastrophes like floods, hunger, earthquakes, and terrorism every day worldwide. A lot has to be done on the communication held between nature and death to enter into time to save lives. The effect of the ninety-nine per cent of our lives being determined elsewhere beyond our control makes us vulnerable and to live as victims of circumstance. For example, obtaining a first-class degree is a considerable portion of the one per cent I describe here. Another person scores averagely, and he is nowhere near first-class. However, because of the circumstantial phenomenology with probably high emotional intelligence, supernatural powers making up our lives, the success in his life becomes more pronounced.

This phenomenon is well understood elsewhere than in Africa, and this is why nations are advocating for periodic regime changes because they understand its effects! Developed societies would try to scale down the effect of circumstantial victimization by improving democratic ideals day in and day out! Nothing is embarrassing than being the best performer in class and the worst performer outside class. It is equivalent to being born rich, and you live and die miserably poor. This leads to a somewhat depressive disorder when low self-esteem develops due to perceiving a gap between the actual and ideal self. Many of us, at one time, dreamt big in our childhood days, and surprisingly things never turned out as expected in adulthood. This wide deviant leads to a depressive disorder resulting from an unrealistic ideal self, based on internalizations of early parental injunctions that were probably highly critical or perfectionistic.

If you want to know how disadvantageous it is for a country with no leadership transitions, ask those living in countries with dictators. You learn about inequalities in opportunities, inequity, and unequal distribution of resources that spans right from employment opportunities to infrastructure development—the long-serving regimes promote people of their interests/wish, race and tribes. Today's dictators are very styled that they use invisible hands to communicate their messages appearing democratic in the eyes of an ignorant person. If your country has never had a dictator, never dream about dictatorship if you are someone who believes in God, humanity, equity, and justice, freedom of expression, equal opportunities and Rule of Law. Even the so-called positive dictatorship is challenging to assess in Africa. Somehow, somewhere, African dictators claim to score more than 90% of the votes in the pseudo democracies because the opposition is incapacitated and incarcerated.

Being born is the first step to understand phenomenological ideology because it is purely out of chance, although family planning advocates claim to know more of this (controlling the game of chance)—which is false in some schools of thought but valid in existentialist ideas. The probability theory goes against existentialist ideas. They (family planning enthusiasts) just ignore the underlying assumptions for the game of chance, how it works and its effects. Even though people on family planning argue that they can pre-control births, you being born as you appear is purely out of luck and chance. Many people have not got a chance to see the world. Some are aborted, whilst others miss seeing the world as victims of circumstances. We need to understand why we are born in the first place. For example, your mother may have been in a bar, got so drunk, became unconscious, and somebody took advantage and raped her. She decided not to abort and gave birth to you. That is purely circumstantial, which derives meaning from surrounding circumstances. There are many events here: being in a bar, getting drunk, becoming unconscious, being raped, getting pregnant, not aborting and giving birth. Have you taken the time to discover why you were born? Have you ever imagined where you would be if your mum had not gone to the bar? Such a circumstantial phenomenon has ever happened to all of us. The point is to learn from it and help others. Or others to learn and get shaped from your misfortunes or fortunes.

At any particular stage in our lives, we have met circumstantial issues beyond our control. Some are too bizarre, whilst others are exciting to notice. In some countries, children spend seven years in primary school, six years in secondary school, and at least three years in universities. While attaining their education, they face influence from the schools, government policymakers, and parents. These influences somehow shape the people they become in future. These are interdependent factors; a parent, school's dynamics and the government policy. These external forces influence the children's passing, choice of schools and courses, etcetera.

If you are a journalist today, look into the past and model out the factors that brought you into journalism. To what extent did you play making yourself a journalist? To what extent did your parents push you into journalism? To what extent did the government policy influence your choices? To what extent did the school dynamics affect your passing? The orphans usually cry out for suffering, but I can assure all orphans that they have an advantage in shaping what they want to become in the future. Through authoritarian parenting models, parents tend to decide for their children what to become, the schools to go to, the courses to take on, etcetera, forgetting that every person is unique. They play a lot of their children's responsibilities. This external influence is out of an orphan's way; as an orphan, forge your case to the top.

The Success Theory

Looking at human behaviour and mental activity as partial determinants for one's success, we get reminded of the holistic view of the road to self-actualization. Where humanistic or existentialists, cognitive behaviourists, and psychoanalysts stop happens to be the window for circumstantial phenomenology to determine one's success. Success and self-actualization, at some point, is a function of circumstances and the view of human nature. Success; defined as value-added in a specified time. Whatever theory you employ to view human nature, whether determinism or self-made choices, you would have a limit. If success is denoted (S), the view of human nature denoted (h) and circumstantial events denoted (c), then: $S=s(h,c)$ where;

- h is an integrated approach of all theories of human nature, and

- c is circumstantial events that may include politics, government policy, war, work, space on earth, religion/culture, science and technology, time, natural occurrences and/or disasters (floods, hurricanes, earthquakes, drought and hunger, etcetera) and etcetera.

A mathematical model for these two primary variables is a function that gives the probability that the view of human nature assumes a particular value (h) and while at the same time, circumstantial events assume a particular value (c). One's success is predetermined by the variables h and c, which are modelled as mutually independent. Hence, such a mathematical function could be a joint continuous density function. Therefore, the phenomenology of success is a joint continuous function of circumstances and how someone views human nature. These can be modelled to create a joint function of partial differentials and integrals to inform the theory of success. Thus, one's success in life can be predicted using the theory of success that finds its way into a *stochastic process*. The future is destined to achieve this theory in reality. For example, you might be brilliant, entrepreneurial, energetic, hardworking and polite, when the politics, government policies, climate change and specific work policies of a country in which you reside are just unfavourable to make you develop or succeed. A man or woman who thinks that politics is not meant for them and cannot contribute to the political success of their territory would be one of the most ignorant persons of the 21st century.

We have less control over many natural occurrences, but we can control politics, decision-making, work, space on earth, and family. This implies that sustaining the planet is more of how we strive to solve the equation of success. I hypothesize that circumstantial events contribute ninety-nine in a hundred whilst the theories of human nature hold one in a hundred. Luck goes to those who are prepared most of the time but not all the time. This is similar to what Thomas A. Edison (1847 – 1931) summarized in quite an abstract sense when he said, "Success is 90% perspiration and 10% inspiration"

For example, constitutionalists who scrap term limits and advocate for life presidency are too selfish and wish no good for others to live and enjoy lives as they make history. Respecting and nurturing ideological differences in our constitutions and politics scales down the power of circumstantial living, creates checks and balances, brings equity and fairness and is juster. The more I study circumstantial living, the more I appreciate the existence of the Supreme Being and detest existentialism.

Territorial sovereignties worldwide work day and night to unify these circumstances, for example, by defining and redefining democracy to set people free. In so doing, they reduce the probabilities of circumstantial events. Respecting ideological and circumstantial differences helps us move towards a unified political system to make everyone a success. Therefore, whatever you believe is attributable to the ninety-nine per cent circumstantial phenomenology. It shows that it is only strategists who would live the one per cent to the fullest. These people are responsible for their actions and choices, but not everyone. Those are people who can see through walls. On the other hand, Buddhists are more promising in the eyes of a sustainable development forward-looker since they largely accept that ninety-nine per cent is their own making.

The Supreme Being's fairness or unfairness models made a human being a political animal right from the beginning. The circumstantial living is overt. As defined to be inclined to who possesses the power, justice portrays that a human as a political animal cannot be fully understood. Therefore, circumstantial living is highly determined by who owns the keys to power. The modern world looks at reducing the gap between the holder of power and the masses.

Some people have mastered the art of living so well that you cannot slip them from the correct path that fulfils their reason for living. Such people listen to the voice of circumstantial phenomenon and chance/luck. They have modelled their lives purely out of experience or learning faster than others, consequently contributing to their nations. The developed world has understood this model critically, and this is the main reason they believe in democracy at some point, freedom of expression, human rights and women empowerment.

Who Owns Power in the 21st Century?

Power in the 21st century belongs to those who own information and can thus influence the lives of others. The balance of power keeps changing every 50-100 years, but Africa has to restructure itself to get involved in this international politics. Africa's failure to make attempts to conceal nakedness will leave future generations vulnerable to all sorts of manipulations. The illusion of privacy statements on social media and other information technologies leaves only a person who lives with integrity safe to a limited extent. The data on several social platforms is enough to conduct several kinds of people profiling to conduct time-series analysis and draw inferences for today and for future generations to come.

Social platforms are designed to make the child residing in someone escape and tap into people's unconscious and private lives, which is a very good strategy to manipulate and make the masses powerless, weakening peoples' boundaries. Lagging in telecommunications infrastructure predisposes Africa to all sorts of nakedness with no limits of secrecy. One of the leading forms of poverty is the poverty of secrecy. "The biggest guru mantra is: never share your secret with anybody. It will destroy you." Hindu saying. Whatever development plan one initiates gets known before hitting the road because of a lack of secrecy. The immediate solution lies in assessing the use of advancing technology but not blindly unfolding and embracing all technologies incautiously.

The long term solution is to stimulate, finance and empower young innovators to think of solutions, especially in the information technology sector. The tendency to think in very straightforward models to live will cause us trouble in this era. Intelligent men and women elsewhere showcase oranges to sell mangoes hiding in too many foot-in-the-door techniques. Many developed giants are giving poor communities enough freedom to hang themselves. Many Africans rarely understand these games!

The time spent chatting about unproductive issues on social media is more than that taken to chat value addition and constructive topics. Have you ever imagined what you would do as an alternative to this unending social media daily jazz? The social media epidemic is chewing up the time to brainstorm youthful ideas forgetting that creative ideas exist mostly in one's youthful stage. The youth spend more time on social media to chat about unproductive topics. Something that continuously distracts one's thinking is perilous. People post more success stories than sad news on social media, and they only post misfortunes of others but not their own. The things we do not see on social media are more significant than what we see concerning individuals who post.

People rarely post frustrations and disappointments about themselves. However, they are quick to share bad news happening elsewhere, not on themselves but will try all possible ways to keep bad things happening to themselves only to themselves. Social media makes people compare themselves with others, especially peers. This bleeds unnecessary/unhealthy competition, which can later develop into several kinds of distortions. It can lead to unnecessary luxury and overspending. The illusion of social media friends is slowly killing real social power that would help unseat Africa's dictators. Slacktivism has replaced real activism. However, social media has triggered more accountability in many African governments.

Social media is perfect for Africa when regulated to a given extent. Otherwise, the effects of these platforms will be exhibited on the African soil in just a few years ahead when the African child has ultimately got spoilt because of lack of room to think and meditate on things that matter. Whether online or offline, one should focus on credibility but not visibility. Some people misinterpret being leaders leading others on social media platforms for social media addiction. Nobody seems to care about the growing trend of adolescents getting fused into social media platforms, and this is not very good news for Africa's sustainability.

"The biggest guru mantra is: never share your secret with anybody. It will destroy you." Hindu saying.

The Scientist and the Freedom Fighter: The typical role of Nelson Mandela and Albert Einstein in the 20th Century

The most extraordinary person I highly respect is a scientist. Next in the queue is the freedom fighter because these two have changed the world more than anyone else. The majority live to enjoy their hard work. Have you ever asked why there has been high population growth in Africa from the start of the 20th Century to date? Try to compare this with the growth rates before 1900. The answer to this question is the living of two people, i.e. the scientist and the freedom fighter. The scientists' ability to understand the existence of microscopic living organisms is one of the most significant contributions to life, improving life expectancy and inventing medicines to cure many diseases. In the same way, freedom fighters have laboured to save humankind from rulers, dictators and warlords. They made the world a better place to coexist, triggering promising innovations in the social order.

Why are you born in this era where every dream of the greatest minds is coming true? As an African, if you have found the reason, you are already contributing to the United Nations Sustainable Development Goals (UN SDGs). If not, you are escalating and perpetuating Africa's problem. Scientists and freedom fighters have profoundly transformed the way we live today. Many of them lived in days characterized by wars, but they managed to persevere and create things we rely on today. It is very unfair to live in an era where communication and transportation have eased, and one fails to account for the life in the years lived.

Most celebrated pioneers of science and governance theories lived in tough times when communication and transport facilities were poor. Today, things are more simplified, creating an enabling environment to solve problems for our generation and the next generations. With today's advancement in science and technology, one can start from anywhere to build on the existing pool of knowledge to cover up existing gaps. The underlying lessons to learn from today's globalization induced by the scientist are:

a) Lots of people have been born because of the advancement of science and technology. Caesarian births are an excellent example of how technology can support an increase in birth rates. In traditional societies, many women died while delivering babies, and today, deliveries have been improved.

b) Improved transport modes, i.e. road, water and air, are making our lives better. We would not do many things we do today if transport modes were not improved. These are all efforts of the scientist, the engineer and the technologist.

On the other hand, the freedom fighter labours to advocate for human rights. Many people could not survive insurgencies in the past, and they died massively in the fight for freedom. The ancient days only saw dictators, emperors, warlords and kings ruling over, and there was no respect for human rights. Dyansties ruled all over the world. The freedom fighter came in to change the world. Democratic governance is purely an innovation of the freedom fighter. Today's freedom fighter has found his work simplified because of the improved information communications technology tools.

It is primarily out of the existence of the two people, i.e. the freedom fighter and the scientist, that we live in significant numbers today. Scientists have helped to improve life expectancy by developing new and advancing technologies for communities. Therefore, many people today are born out of chance and survive out of chance or luck. As Africans, we need to sit and reflect to improve the future. Are we doing enough in a situation where we have no control over emerging technologies that impact the population? Does the freedom fighter understand the role of a scientist, or do they put politics before science? These are questions that we need to answer in Africa's sustainability equation.

Case study on Effects of Africa's Polygamy

In a capitalistic economy with a free market system, enterprises are driven for profit. Polygamy in such economies is more of a detrimental factor in downfallen enterprises since it possesses a greater risk to one's business empire. Polygamy leads to producing dozens of children, and this has its advantages and disadvantages. There are lots of problems associated with producing dozens of children, especially when the parent passes away. In Africa, men are producing 60+ children. We face a serious problem matching available resources to the population while keeping the promise that future generations will survive sustainably. The carrying capacity of the environment is already making alarms in some parts of Africa. People lack water and food.

Drawing a genogram of a polygamous man is becoming a significant challenge to clinicians, counsellors, and doctors in several hospitals across Africa. Such men's business empires become hard to thrive and survive, especially when they die because children are very unlikely to negotiate an amicable agreement. People from different cultures react differently in negotiation—and one woman cannot mother 60+ children. Therefore, they resort to selling the business empire or estate so that each of them bags their share. This has been witnessed in many land fragmentations occurring in Africa today because each of the children would wish to self-own his share, which they would sell off later.

With many kids, they are likely to fail to reach an understanding of how to run your business empire when you die. Even if you leave a strong will, some children would powerfully resist the chosen administrator. But if you have 1-6 kids, the likelihood of disagreement may be lowered. And if the government wants to pledge support to your business, negotiations are more likely to be fruitful because the risk of disagreement is low. However, producing one child also has its demerits, but many children do not promote sustainability either. Therefore, a balance has to be struck.

On the afternoon of August 15th 2015, I was relaxing in a relatively big café in Kampala, Uganda. There happened to be a meeting of six people. After twenty minutes, another four people joined the meeting. Again after another 30 minutes, four people joined the meeting. Finally, after about 10 minutes, another three people joined the meeting. Most of them looked to be in their late twenties. From the conversations I heard them talking, it seemed others had not attended the meeting.

The topic of discussion was how to share the money obtained from the sale of their late dad's estate. It was close to a month after the dad had passed away. The meeting started well with a prayer. After that, they started discussing who would go to the bank to collect the money. To my surprise, the meeting, which went on reasonably well, ended up in fights. The siblings were abusing each other. Some never welcomed the idea of equal sharing. They wanted to share more money for selfish reasons because they felt more important than others. Others were busy blaming their late dad for producing children from many wives. It was a learning experience.

At last, none of them went to the bank, and by close of business, the children had clustered themselves depending on which woman mothered them. You can now imagine what happened after that. It sent out a signal on how bad it would be when you produce many children without thinking about the repercussions to your estate, business, and nation.

Some conventional religions teach that each child comes with their luck, but do they assess the likelihood of bad luck taking precedence due to circumstantial victimization from poor governance ideologies of the least developed countries. Whatever analysis or argument one makes to this effect, one who believes in leaving a legacy and his business to thrive after his demise is always cautious and conscious of the problems involved with producing dozens of kids.

The sustainability agenda of the African continent requires us to mind about the national income sustainability right from the family level. The trend of African men's behaviour in marital issues is a normal distribution. Its central tendency is witnessed at the peak of one's financial independence, meaning that more money triggers African men to produce more children. I can defend the statement above, focusing on the wealthier and business empire owners because poor men also produce dozens of children—but here I look at the effects of many children on your business estate in your demise. That is the scope I am discussing here.

As a sustainable development forward-looker, I believe polygamous marriages are more damaging concerning sustainability because of distorted collectivism than other sex disordered marriages that we highly detest on the African continent. In this scheme of things, African collectivism would be more altruistic if society had constructed women as pivots for clans and tribes. If our societies had provided women with more powers, we would have more things in order. That means children would expressly follow their mother's lineage.

Where children come from the same mother despite being fathered by different fathers, the risk of disagreement is lower than half-brothers/sisters of the same father. The way society was constructed needs a serious self-awareness initiative or program to transform Africa socioeconomically. *In many cases,* children are more on the mother's side than the father's side, which developmental psychologists can prove correct.

Starting business empires has never been a simple exercise. Many huge and highly innovative companies we see today started from scratch, some with zero liquid cash, the only capital the owners had were just the brain. Interestingly, the most successful companies were born just out of unbelievable ideas, and with few pennies, they emerged to be the world's leading firms. People who inherit wealth should never forget that someone spent sleepless nights accumulating the wealth they currently enjoy. To get to number one, you start from zero—that is what many people forget.

You have invented the computer today, but there is someone who discovered an electron. You have innovated a social network today; endeavour to remember the one who invented the internet. If the offspring understood how things interlink, they would not destroy their parents' strenuously made business empires. Instilling discipline in people has never been a simple exercise. It is not rare for the children of wealthy men and women to turn into poorly individuated adults. It takes commitment and passion for the wealthy people to nurture their kids with good morals to safeguard their business empires from being destroyed by the children in their demise. Have enough time with your kids and teach them early enough how your business is run and managed. Teach them your history and the vision to know the overarching goals for sustaining the business to live forever. This should be fixed in your routine business program without dodging it on any occasion. Living a structured life to spend more time with your children is not such a bad idea.

The Subject of Inheritance

Today, you might be rich, but previous generations before you were poor. The industrial revolution, which began in the UK, transformed the world. Starting in the factories of Manchester in the 18th Century, the industrial revolution made the UK a powerful hub to conquer many territories across the globe. You or your parents or grandparents might have worked tirelessly to build the empire you enjoy today. To keep the fire burning for future generations, you need to educate your children about the journey to your success and document it. Purposeful living is a topic that any wealthy, middle class or poor person should labour to teach their children if we wish to shoot the dream of self-driven sustainable development as Africans.

The illusion centred on the age of 18 years misleads. That when one clocks 18 years, they are responsible for all actions is quite ideal. Some students finish university when still young, and some others mature early. Let us understand that 18 years is idealistic, and we should not overemphasize it in all matters, and it should be taken with caution. Several constitutions across the continent allow the minimum age to become a member of the legislature as 18 years. In my opinion, I would not think it is too fit for an 18-year-old child to legislate on behalf of a constituency or a state.

I still ask myself why the Lord Jesus Christ and Prophet Mohammed are all believed to have started their public career after clocking 30 years. Several developed countries have enacted *inclusive inheritance laws* to safeguard the countries' socioeconomic position and GDP. Some states do not allow a paternal child or an adopted child to inherit the parent's estate in full before clocking the age of 30 years, especially for adopted children. That sounds like a more sustainable strategy to safeguard the economic rights of the beneficiaries while at the same time protecting the economy.

In Iceland, the Inheritance Act No. 8, of 14th March 1962 with subsequent amendments up to No.145/2013, provides reversion of property to the State Inheritance Tax Fund (Article 55), and that if a person leaves no heir, their property reverts to the State Treasury. The same Act provides restricted inheritance (Article 50). In case there is a particular danger that a deceased's forced heir will mismanage the share due to him, they may, by will, provide for special restrictions to be applied. And the District Commissioner may cancel such restrictions in part or whole when the heir has attained the age of 21 years if the heir establishes that the reasons on which the restriction in question was based do no longer apply. All these are formulated to protect and sustain the socioeconomic stand of the state.

Our failure to understand that all of us are responsible for the cause of the socioeconomic position of the state has made us not respect the subject of inheritance. Most big businesses and companies collapse when the owners die for earlier described reasons and due to weak inheritance laws in many countries. Small, medium, and big enterprises, although privately owned, are deemed private but should be taken with the public interest.

In many African cultures, the default involvement of clan-mates to take consequential decisions in the allocation of properties of the deceased has shortcomings and should be overhauled through landmark cultural audits that elders would guide. Clan-mates refer to close and distant relatives. However, having a blood tie with the deceased has no proven scientific relationship with integrity.

The danger arising from this kind of distortion in the inheritance decision making is that clan-mates or relatives make ignorant decisions coupled with corrupt tendencies, especially when the deceased owned big businesses and companies—and especially where the deceased did not draw a line to delineate what would happen if they die thereby leaving an intestate estate.

Our collectivistic cultures vested much power in clan-mates and relatives. You cannot make decisions on a subject you do not understand well enough. A typical mess is exhibited in the several decisions taken at the time when African states got independence from colonialists. A majority of decision-makers were ill-informed, semi-educated, and ignorant, yet they thought they were very enlightened. They hence took ignorant decisions whose effects we are still facing. This is one of the reasons why some African firms, those owned by Africans, collapse in the owners' demise.

If we dream about self-driven sustainable development, we need to remember that one plus one equals two. Some of us are better than others, but none is better than all of us. We all contribute to the country's GDP. We need to support each other and be vigilant about our prosperity. Therefore, if we continue losing out enterprises with the owners' demise, we lose as a nation. We should devise strong inheritance laws that contribute to sustainable development to delineate the administrator's power proposed by the deceased person before their death. We need strong inheritance laws that contribute to sustainable development for estates that fall intestate. This shall stop the unwanted involvement of clan-mates who claim to have powers over the deceased's estate because of a blood tie, yet many often possess no ability to make sound decisions. It is regrettable for one's business empire, which has been very successful in their lifetime and automatically dies after their death. We all lose as a nation. Sustainable development can only occur when the smallest units of society like families are sustainable; private firms, small and big business enterprises are sustainable too but not only focus on the big picture, i.e. at a national level.

With clan-mates messing up important matters, where would self-driven sustainable development come from? Let us think of generations to come.

The point is to make clear statutes on the inheritance of a deceased's estate, no matter whether testate or intestate. We may look into this by creating a threshold for organisations that attain it to get special national consideration so that the government takes a participatory role in their sustainability. The continued land fragmentation in Africa by the children of the deceased is highly risky, and it is contrary to the concepts of sustainable development forward-lookers. Ideally, modern societies would share proceeds from the deceased's estate but not fragmenting the estate. The tendency to lose enterprises with the demise of owners is painful. It does not need to be yours to feel the pain. Once you learn about how the economy functions, you feel the pain. We need to invest more in equity and equality. We need to invest more in group counselling to become more empathic and genuine with each other.

The Humble Beginner, the Educated Entrepreneur, and Sustainable Development

Interestingly, most people who have made great history have had humble beginnings. From theology to science, most great men and women have had unpleasant beginnings. Leonardo da Vinci (1452–1519), who made far-reaching contributions in many areas of science, technology, and art, did not attend university and only began studying Latin in his early 40s. Jesus Christ, the saviour of the Christian faith, was born in a barn and was laid in a manger. Prophet Mohammed, the saviour of the Islamic faith, lost both parents by the age of six and was raised by his paternal grandfather and later by his paternal uncle. God has, through different approaches, communicated to us his divine mercy and the need to humble ourselves, in which resides the genesis of wisdom.

We need to continuously work on humility to live peacefully with others in society. The incredible experience in the region is that many people just inches away from starving think that they are wealthy and would not associate with the poor. They raise kids who cannot follow in their footsteps to move their legacies forward for many generations to come. Unless we labour to educate our children where we are coming from to appreciate the order of existence, it will remain a challenge for our children to sustain our legacies; in culture, religion, companies, families and business. If you are lucky and your children live to your expectations in Africa, you are likely in the top 2%.

Friedrich Nietzsche (1844–1900), a German philosopher, was clear when he said, "He who has a '*why*' to live for can bear with almost any '*how*.'" This amplifies that it is more meaningful to prepare and gloom a child for tomorrow than preparing and stocking for the child's future. A child's education and health insurance might prove the best in the long run compared to assets insurance. Doing the two altogether is not such a bad idea. Education is the key and greatest asset that many successful businessmen have tried to criticize because many highly educated people are middle-income earners or least income earners. Most highly successful people predominantly ride on the knowledge of the least income earners or middle-income earners. We have to improve the education system to strengthen our societies and keep our dignity and values intact. Some highly successful businessmen and investors who criticize the need for education, especially higher education, forget that their business empires are run and managed by educated people either indirectly or directly; without them, they would not be sustained.

Highly successful investors and business people are not necessarily the most intelligent, but they utilize the game of power to the fullest. In many cases, they devote their time early enough. Once one becomes a magnet of attraction, builds extensive networks and platforms around them, employs tactical deception, stands firm to take risks, and knows how to hire and interplay skilful and intelligent people, he beats the odds. I conquer with many others that successful entrepreneurship needs no such things as high ranking degrees or high-level education, but driving humanity and sustainability in the 21st century needs quality education.

The world has seen many successful entrepreneurs and wealthy people through ages who built empires on philosophies of the middle-income earners and poor people in several spheres of social influence. In the modern world and sometimes even before, entrepreneurship is built slightly on scholars' work. The entrepreneurs move slightly in thinking outside the box, from a scholar's *i* to, *i*+1 and then rubbish school and education.

The majority of people view success in monetary terms but not in value aspects, which is very dangerous for those concerned with the sustainability of the African continent. This is because society is extensively infected to think about success basing on how many dollars you have in the account and how many things you can fetch from the market in the interest of satisfying your ego.

I remind you briefly that the economist built on the industrial revolution, and the industrial revolution built on the agricultural and scientific revolutions. A successful entrepreneur manipulated all these! To be honest, an entrepreneur needs to see not so many blackboards but sustaining humanity amidst excited entrepreneurs requires intellectuals. If we evaluate how much the world owes Sir Isaac Newton or Albert Einstein, no such wealthy person on earth can equate to the value these people added to humanity! Therefore, rubbishing quality education and the need for higher education is for such small-minded people who cherish money over humanity. I give high respect to scholars in Africa, and beyond whether they part with large sums of money or not, their presence is invaluable to this world!

Why do some of Africa's Enterprises founded by Graduates fail to grow?

Sustaining enterprises and companies has remained a challenge to lots of graduates in Africa. Many people prefer operating sole enterprises even if the business grows and would require to have a separate liability from its founders. The most detrimental factor at the forefront is teamwork inefficiencies. Henry Ford (1863 – 1947) once said, "Coming together is a beginning. Keeping together is progress. Working together is a success." Many people stop coming together or keeping together because selfishness kills the collective efforts when it comes to working together. They rarely achieve the long-term goal. Many professionals start enterprises but fail to stick to their vision. They instead keep applying for jobs elsewhere. A company or business cannot grow when one fails to concentrate on it. Even if a reputable company offers you a great job, you should stick to your goals because you can set your business objectives. When you insist on concentrating on other jobs, then your business or company can rarely grow.

Many technical and professional people tend to concentrate their forces elsewhere because they got well-paying jobs and fail to invest more time in their enterprises. That is the primary reason for less innovative engineers, doctors, physicists, economists, etcetera because they hardly invest enough time in their enterprises. One can rarely innovate when one keeps jumping from one job to another. Innovation and invention take sacrifice, passion and commitment. In your enterprise, you predetermine your success because you are left to concentrate on your strength and hire skilled people in the areas where your weaknesses lie. The problem is that people being too impatient and wish to receive fortune overnight. Otherwise, success is inevitable when you concentrate.

You cannot dedicate 5-10+ years of concentration to do something you are passionately curious about, in love with, and failure defeats success. You do not need to be great to start, but you need to start to be great. Those who are strong, enthusiastic and visionary and decide to abandon looking for jobs after school to start their enterprises are highly likely to succeed if they sacrifice many things.

You need to know that intelligent people look around to find jobs, but wise people create jobs. Africa is still developing and presents enormous opportunities for startups. Elsewhere, it is relatively more challenging to open up startups, perhaps. Things may be hard for startups 1 to 10 years, but after that, you can easily triple the success of those who got very nice jobs immediately after school—and, in the long run, contribute immensely to the country's GDP. The problem is too much of being straight, following others' way of doing things and the law. Try thinking otherwise: if people marry immediately after school, postpone your marriage to start your enterprise.

Long Term versus Short Term Thinking: Modern Day Slavery

We need to drop the extreme short-sightedness and start thinking long-term promises. Tracing way back in the 17th Century, we remind ourselves of the transatlantic slave trading. Historians tell us that African chiefs assisted much of the slave trade until the United Kingdom and the United States of America abolished it in 1807. African chiefs used to sell off their energetic young boys and girls to the white travellers while a small number was captured directly by the slave traders in coastal raids. Some historians report that a section of missionary fathers contributed to the slave trading. However, if you analyze the transatlantic slave trade business critically, you understand who was greatly responsible for the cause.

Despite the Arabs, Portuguese, and Spanish initiating the slave trade, the sense of humanity, brotherhood, and togetherness has been significantly abused in Africa than anywhere else right from the past. And if you think Europeans and Americans are not friends, at least you can see an integration of Africans in their societies to date, but where did our brothers and sisters who were taken as slaves to the Arab world go? Then you can understand what the 45th President of the USA talked about trying to awaken the African masses. Africans who have not spotted the good attributes of the 45th President of the USA are just not being thoughtful. He would speak out his mind about Africa, unlike other politicians who fantasize and sugarcoat the predicaments we create for ourselves.

Acceptance is the mother of wisdom at some point. The problems that the USA faces are not what we face. There is more room for us to learn from all sides of their political debates. One of the firmly held beliefs and theories has it that our brothers were castrated. I can remind you that traces of the slave trade still exist in the modern-day in many places, what the procurement practitioners have termed modern-day slavery.

Modern-day slavery is more pronounced on our soil—whereby girls exported as housemaids are greatly abused in some of those territories. Many African labour export firms lack transparency statements on human trafficking and modern-day slavery.

Modern-day slavery is a violation of a person's human rights. One can be dehumanized, treated as a commodity or sold or bought as "property". One can be forced to work through mental or physical threats, and one can be physically constrained or has restrictions placed on their freedom of movement. One can be owned or controlled by an "employer", usually through mental or physical abuse. Many cases are reported every day where African labour exported to those territories are mistreated. A significant number of labour export companies in Africa are practising modern-day slavery practices. Some companies are genuine but hidden in realms of fantasy crap, and it is difficult to identify them.

Is Africa's Understanding of Dowry or Bride Price Perpetuating Modern Day Slavery?

The materialistic trait of many African people, yet they claim to be faithful to God, is exhibited in how they interpret a gift. A gift is a gift no matter its worth. Appreciating a button of a shirt rather than a shirt as a gift is outright ignorance of the recipient. In the modern world, the first thing to appreciate from the giver of the gift is the *time* they take to think about you and second in the queue is the *willingness* to give you a gift. Other things like value and quality follow next. I find it more touching to violate the African meaning of a gift.

Today, many people think materialistically, and it becomes difficult for an ordinary person to find a suitable gift. A small item like a book, pet, pen, taking a photo or flower as a gift might prove a magical gift to someone who values humanity. To some, if not many, you need to carry a gift worth millions or hundreds of thousands for them to appreciate genuinely. I have noted a growing trend of people despising gifts in wedding preparation meetings and similar parties. Many of our grannies love us much and always shower us with gifts, both small and big—and it is our responsibility to cherish the gifts with kindness and love. Appreciating gifts, however small they are, is the first-line discipline that an understanding person must possess.

The need to cultivate social power is everything if we are dreaming of self-driven sustainable development. It does not harm you when you appreciate people, however wealthier you could be. If one labour to understand the aforementioned, dowry or bride price becomes more meaningful and valued. The materialistic trait within families has left parents not to think beyond, give away their daughters like goods, especially where customary marriages prevail. I find the decision reached on by Justice Hamilton in the case of R. v. AMKEYO (1917) 7 EALR 14 to dismiss customary marriages as mere 'wife purchase" more accurate and well-founded in the eyes of a forward-looking socioeconomic transformational activist wishing their country sustainability. However, many people interpreted it as if it was a misconception of the role of bride price.

> "In my opinion. The use of the word 'marriage' to describe the relationship entered into an African native with a woman of his tribe according to tribal custom is a misnomer which has led in the past to a considerable confusion of ideas…The elements of a so-called marriage by native custom differ so materially from the ordinary accepted idea of what constitutes a civilized form of marriage that it is difficult to compare the two." R. v. AMKEYO (1917) 7 EALR 14

Many parents desist spouses self-chosen by their daughters and prefer those spouses who can shower them with lots of gifts to meet their expectations. Because we do not live in a classless society, this might not be very bad and might prove worth in the short term but might require a remedy in the long run. It is worth getting reminded that marriage's underlying goal is to have peace—and of course, peace comes with costs. We should not forego happiness at the expense of dowry—the issue of integrity should not be overlooked.

The most incredible experience is that the seemingly rich people in Africa are more materialistic than their middle class or poor counterparts. This has a slight connection with modern-day slavery. Much as our people are giving away their daughters more or less as trading daughters, *some* Chinese and Indians are typically after creating more friendship with the sons-in-law. I have two Chinese friends and one Indian friend who have entrusted a section of their estate to their sons-in-law, and it is difficult to notice that they are sons-in-law and not paternal sons. If you wish your daughter to be treated like a queen, this model or technique works perfectly well. It is an excellent psychological technique that can shape the thinking of the son-in-law into how you wish them to treat your daughter. Nelson Mandela (1918 –2013) once said, "I learned a great deal from him—not only on that respect but also, politically, he was our mentor. He is a very good fellow ... and humble. He led from behind and put others in front, but he reversed the position in situations of danger. Then he chose to be in the front line."[100] Genuine sustainable development resides in creating social power right from families—sometimes, it is good to lead from behind.

The Science of Attitude in Planning for Africa's Sustainable Infrastructure: Accidents on Africa's Roads & Highways

One of the forgotten fields given less attention in science, technology, engineering, art, and design disciplines while planning for infrastructure development, especially in Africa, is the science of attitude, social construction, and mental health. Little attention is given to the end user's personality, attitude, highway hypnosis, and mental health in the planning stages for the infrastructure such as roads and highways. If you are designing a road in Africa, it should be designed within the African context but not the western models. Follow the universally accepted codes and standards and innovate an extra mile to meet the needs of Africans. Attitudes are very difficult to change, although training and education may help. I have provided a roadmap to grow attitudes in Chapter Four.

Infrastructure designed for comfort, operability, and functionality while benchmarking on the end user's attitude may last longer. Transport asset management planners and design engineers in Africa may be forced to draw lessons from the science of attitude to well-inform the needs assessments before making prototypes. Design engineers may need to critically assess the predisposing factors that force end-users to act or react in a certain way in a given situation.

Similarly, policymakers would need to embrace mental health examinations to reduce incidents and accidents while using infrastructure such as roads. Permitting use of the road infrastructure would necessitate enacting ordinances and subsidiary legislations to check mental health and personality types because one mentally unsound road user can cause the death toll of tens of other road users. Understanding the effect of the mental health of end-users of the infrastructure throughout the project design, implementation, and operation stages shall reinforce the parameters required to produce a long-lasting program project.

---

[100] Nelson Mandela Interview with John Battersby of The Christian Science Monitor, February 10th 2000.

Taking an example of transport asset management in infrastructure such as road projects, one would pose a question such as, "how do road accidents affect road furniture in Africa?" According to the Global Status Report on Road Safety 2015 published by the World Health Organization, over 1.25 million people die of road accidents annually worldwide, and about 90% are from developing countries. A typical example is the Kampala-Masaka highway in Uganda, which is considered one of the most dangerous roads in the world—the road users would drive well when they anticipate meeting traffic officers on the road. However, where they expect not to meet traffic officers, they fail to drive safely by conforming to road traffic signs. Attitudinal problems are the most likely cause of rampant accidents on the road.

The said road has claimed over 2,000 people's lives in the last decade. Each year it kills about 200-300 people, and it is believed to be the most dangerous road in the world.[101] As a professional engineer, I was motivated to conduct quick survey research dubbed, *Mental Health and Road Safety Campaign: A case study of buses and taxis' drivers from Rubaga division taxi parks, commuting from Kampala – Masaka, Uganda.*" The findings converged towards poor road users' behaviours and attitudes towards the road as the leading cause of accidents on that road. My results correlated well with the 2018 Road Safety Performance Review Uganda findings, which also pointed out that poor driver behaviours were the leading causes of accidents on Uganda's roads.[102]

The operation Fika-Salama was a traffic police operation introduced in 2017 to reinforce the road safety campaign on the Kampala-Masaka road. Fika-Salama is a Swahili word for, "Safe travels". Several traffic police checkpoints were introduced on the road during the operation. It brought about a reduction in accidents to almost zero during the time it ran. However, immediately after the operation closed, severe accidents reoccurred. Before, Fika-Salama, I gave a safety talk about this road to a few friends claiming that the road had demons that claimed people's lives. They called it a natural phenomenon which I always objected.

While conducting the quick survey, I met a traffic officer who enforced the Fika Salama operation, and we had a chat about the road. She told me that she firmly believed that it was basically due to road users' attitudes that caused massive accidents. Fika Salama significantly reduced accidents on the road. I said to her, "I shall have to write about this in one of my books." In my opinion, it is more about the behaviours and attitudes of road users that cause accidents on Africa's roads.

When someone dies at a young age in Africa, many people usually say God has taken them. Why does God not take people in the developed countries so early because the life expectancy is high in some developed countries? We should revise unhelpful beliefs such as God decides that we should have high death rates in Africa. Thinking that high road accidents and high mortality rates occur because of God's will as the leading cause is entirely false.

It is not uncommon to retire people who have made 65 years of age in Africa, yet this is when a person would be more resourceful for the nation in terms of knowledge and wisdom. Civil and public servants

---

[101] "Uganda takes on world's most dangerous road: Government attempts to regain control of planet's deadliest highway," Gulf News, September 26th 2016, https://gulfnews.com/world/africa/uganda-takes-on-worlds-most-dangerous-road-1.1902165.

[102] United Nations Economic commission for Africa/Europe. *Road Safety Performance Review Uganda* (Geneva: United Nations, 2018), 14.

that demonstrate extraordinary competence who clock 65 should be designated consultancy roles to advise the government as appropriate. It is basically because many people falsely believe that someone is highly anticipated to die at such a time, i.e. 65 years of age. We have been indoctrinated with a false belief that God's will causes high mortality rates. We find ourselves too reckless in all matters, hence paying less attention to the science of attitude.

It is not an accident if one could foresee the incident. An accident is a sudden happening causing harm, injury, or damage, and it must be unforeseeable. We can prevent or reduce many occupational accidents from happening. Road accidents are highly occupational, which can be reduced by enforcing occupational health and safety cultures in many organizations. You realize that people crash in accidents 1-3 hours before the incident occurs because of their organisations' poor health and safety culture.

You drive when you are already dead because of not adhering to foreseeable hazards on the road, which would be the employer's work to eliminate those hazards. The lesson to take is to adopt an integrated road safety campaign that includes a "must audit all organizations' health and safety culture" to track commitment to road safety campaigns. We also need to conduct behaviour modification, behaviour activation, and attitude change to suit new infrastructural developments in several African countries.

If you analyzed road accidents from the root cause, you would discover that very few casualties would be pardoned based on an accident on roads as a defence. Negligence, vicarious and strict liabilities are torts whose extent and implications should be revised in the context of road safety campaigns in many African countries. What is much emphasized today is vicariously sharing offences with employers. Therefore, a road safety campaign would take on another twist to propose safe systems of work policies and permit-to-use roads as a requirement for all organizations that use Africa's road networks.

Network Marketing, Salary Loans, and Overnight Fortunes in Africa

It is becoming the order of the day to enter in the passcode on my phone or computer and find an article promising wealth without real hard work. These are usually the work at home, network marketing companies, trade-in crypto currencies, etcetera. The greatest danger of network marketing lies in the *process* of failing. When you win with network marketing, you rejoice, but a considerable number of entrants fail. The risk of failing is inevitable in any business, but the road to failure in network marketing is wide open. These marketing networks to earn a living pose a significant risk to the young generation when the illusion of quickly getting rich starts to exhibit negative symptoms. This can easily set a life crisis for the youths. Besides, if you are an entrepreneur, the best business idea would be one with no revenue limits—one with infinite revenue streams. In other words, you cannot determine how much you would generate if the business grows.

The greatest danger stems from the youth's failure to judge credibility correctly. Of recent, youth are shifting from network marketing to any kind of cryptocurrencies without a sound understanding of how they work. In a business where you invest $100 and expect over $10,000 in a couple of hours or days, you need to evaluate it multiple times. Network marketing companies are good when they promote, "buy African products and build Africa."

If you wish to get disorganized for your entire life and live in a vicious cycle of poverty, take unevaluated or less adequately studied salary loans to start a business, especially in unstable economies of Africa. However, investing your salary in profit-making schemes is not a bad idea, but to start a business from scratch might need your time. As mentioned earlier, a business can only grow when the owner is committed and invests considerable time. In most cases, your business experiences an innovational crisis while you still serve your employer because it is you who loves it most at the start. You are willing to sacrifice and do all sorts of activities to develop it than the hired personnel.

To balance the deficit, you need to delay acquiring salary loans because the loan can be disastrous in unstable economies. In my opinion, when you do not have enough time to attend to your infant business, you instead wait to take a salary loan because you might live a considerable fraction of your lifetime servicing a salary loan. The result is that you can get highly disorganized up to the verge of losing your job. The best advice would be to save while in employment and officially move out to self-employment with enough savings for the startup or investment. Alternatively, utilize the salaries for a considerable amount of time into the business startup until when the business is self-sustaining to borrow. However, investing in profitable ventures while you are in employment is a good idea. The point is to ensure a thorough evaluation before taking a salary loan. You should always strive to lift what you can carry. You cannot lift to carry what is heavier than you—do the fundamental arithmetic right—because, in Africa's economies, it is difficult to pre-determine the future. We live in uncertainty. At the moment, others determine Africa's future.

Living under uncertainty explains the need to insure our lives, education, business and etcetera. I am not imparting fear to anyone to stop getting your salary loans or any other loans for business startups or expansions. We know that if fear defeats your enthusiasm, you cannot achieve much. However, we need to be wise enough in making investment decisions and funding business startups. I am instead warning you about the unforeseen challenges in unstable economies where inflation, high-interest rates, delayed payments, external influence, poor time management, and false attitudes are taking the lead in sabotaging business growth.

I have witnessed a few friends falling into the salary loan turmoil. Some of them are bankers whilst others are constructors. Suppose you audit a majority of successful business people in Africa who hold formal employment hence earning salaries from the government and NGOs. In that case, you will not be surprised to learn about criminalities. Our economies are simplistic and can easily be modelled and understood within a minute using pen and paper. The way things work in African countries is understandable, leaving people questioning the extraordinary talents public and civil servants have to manage businesses while serving the government. This is because Africa's rich and wealthier people are mainly public and civil servants.

The State of Uncertainty, Risk, and Probability

The state of uncertainty was distinguished from risk by Knight Frank (1885–1972) as immeasurable risk and impossible to calculate. In contrast, the risk is quantified as the potential of losing something of value. Ever since Knight drew a clear line between risk and uncertainty, many people have not laboured to understand the effect of these two occurrences in life, business, and relationships. People rarely do risk assessments, yet it would be necessary for all social, economic and environmental aspects. The three pillars, i.e. social, economic and environment, form the foundation of a sustainable community. Risk management is never handled as a priority in many people's lives and daily activities. Lots of people are poor at risk management both in the social and economic aspects. The short-term sightedness leaves no room for such analyses.

The effect of short-term sightedness can be felt in Africa when the subject of insurance is discussed. Insurance for health, education, business, relationship management, old age, etcetera should ideally be a must for a citizen who understands risk. If you hold a professional degree, getting accredited and licensed by a professional body insures your education, qualifications and life earnings for a lifetime. Today's business is more about being honest, building networks, long-term relationships, and making the right decisions.

A decision can only be right to undertake if risk analysis is conducted and a risk management plan is drawn. As a professional civil engineer, I write with authority to advise you that risk assessments should be conducted even in family matters, marriage, and relationships! It is vital in all aspects of life before making any kind of decision. You might have alternatives to the decision undertaken, but you decide to choose what you term the right decision. Without a risk analysis and risk management plan at your disposal, the right decision may turn to be the worst ever taken. Many people have fallen victims to the lack of risk analysis and management plans in marriages, business relationships, contract management, and project management. Are you marrying someone because she has a beautiful face or has a good character and personality? These things matter the most in the long term.

In everything, when you fail to manage risk, you are risking to fail. In managing projects, risk management is at the forefront. Not complying with risk management procedures leaves one vulnerable to arbitration and getting against the law. Therefore, risk control and management should be the number one priority in all matters of self-driven sustainable development. When you see a construction site with a signage reading "Safety First", it means risk management first. Health and safety have strong commercial implications if not attended to correctly.

Risk can be managed in various ways: avoidance, distribution/sharing, retention, mitigation, and reduction. Therefore, as earlier discussed, you must have a risk management plan when taking a loan from the bank. However, most people only focus on the business plan without explicitly considering the risk management plan. The smartest and exceptionally outstanding risk managers are the banks or bankers. They rarely lose. They normally begin with risk assessment and consequently draw risk management plans as predecessor activities to the financial/economic analysis in any business venture. Banks typically; conduct due diligence and have a credit reference tracker system, and in many cases, agreements are in their favour. The fact we need to apply for loans for the businesses and for our lives, we need to understand risk management well enough because we are dealing with expert risk managers.

We need to understand risk in our lives properly. Suppose you are a businessman and you believe in cheating others to prosper. In that case, you do not understand what this behaviour risks to your business and your life because you forget that the more your hands soften to release what does not belong to you, the more you register success. People are more important than anything else, and keeping relationships alive is an important fact that will keep your business thrive and expand.

Risk can be described in various disciplines differently, and it depends on how you model it in your day to day activities. This would actually drive me to say that in the modern world, discipline can briefly be defined as "adherence to risk control and management". To expound more on this, today you might cheat people and tomorrow, you might need their votes. Today, you could be a person who does not socially interact with your community and tomorrow; you need their support. You might recklessly cheat on your spouse; what if they get to know? Do you have a concrete plan to mend the relationship when they got to know that you cheated on them?

The Asian giant is busy providing loans to Africa; what concrete plan has Africa laid out to remedy her failure to service the loans? How would you describe a person who spends all his salary for a night in the bar and is left with nothing the following day? Others are busy investing their salaries, and you are busy drinking yours—and tomorrow, you feel envious about their success. It is common to find people with poor decision-making skills envying others who plan well. Those who know how to manage risk will always lead others. Therefore, a person who adheres to the good in advance controls and manages the risk. Such people are termed, disciplined people. The topic of risk and uncertainty would be taught in schools as early as primary levels. It is crucial in raising disciplined people and people who would take the right decisions in the interest of self-driven sustainable development.

The field of risk studies is broad, but the perturbing bit of it is that few people understand the gist of the field to apply it in day to day problem-solving. In several engineering and scientific studies, where experiments and designs are conducted, probability assessments are employed to explore the alternatives. Probability distribution functions and statistical methods are employed in several models in environmental studies, the aviation industry, computer software, manufacturing and medicine, etcetera.

Case Study on Civil Engineering

I once listened to a colleague saying, "The developed world has done almost everything they thought about in the areas of civil engineering. They are left with operating and conducting routine and periodic maintenance of civil engineering structures. They now focus on other engineering disciplines like bioengineering, chemical engineering, software engineering, artificial intelligence, and etcetera." The oldest engineering discipline is civil engineering, and it is the one that will remain intact when innovations in other disciplines seem to be exhausted and no significant new things are invented simply because its models are highly informed by risk and probability. Risk and probability are complementary terms. For example, civil engineers design to account for; aerodynamic forces, floods (flood defence and hydraulic structures), and seismic forces—probabilistic models inform all these, and climate change is now giving civil engineers more work to do. Therefore, my colleague was not right.

Almost all civil engineering projects are started with a hole in the ground, showing the importance of geotechnical engineering as a required field in civil engineering. The reliability of the foundation that carries the weight of the structure is based on the reliability of the various forms of data collected to inform the planning and decisions on the design and execution of the project; reliability being the ability of a civil engineering structure to perform the intended function in a specified period. For example, you may want your house to be able to withstand snow loads of a given weight for about 50 years and more. Suppose it develops signs of failure to carry the loads halfway to the intended lifespan. In that case, the reliability would be lowered, raising questions of integrity in design and construction, among other issues.

Civil engineering structures are large, and cannot be assessed for reliability through full-scale testing as in the case of small mechanical and electrical devices. Therefore, the risk in civil engineering structures is minimized but cannot be eliminated completely. Reliability evaluation is conducted through system behaviour computational models whereby basic input variables like loads are fed into the models by statistical propagation. This shows that civil engineering cannot be ruled out of practice because of overreliance on *probability* in seemingly complex models that draw disjointed knowledge from several spheres of science. The most challenging role played by a design civil engineer lies in the reliability of their assumptions. You can only tell the best and most innovative design civil engineers following through the reliability of their design assumptions—and these are assumptions that heavily account for risks.

Phenomena in Africa's Service Delivery

Working in Silos

There is a lack of coordination within many of Africa's government agencies synonymous with "working in silos". Several African countries are suffering from communication and coordination challenges. There is a problem of poor information flow within government agencies while implementing programs and projects. There is a vast coordination gap that exists in many government agencies of many African countries. Consultancy projects overlapping each other. There is a problem of role confusion, and too much taxpayer's money is lost plus time. Projects overlap during implementation.

In some instances, there is no proper communication between agencies. There would be a need to institute agencies for tracking between the program projects within government agencies. Who is responsible for what? You find confusion in program implementation. For example, a government program is designed to construct a water supply scheme, and an NGO is also planning to do the same thing. Reworks, repairs and change of course as a result of poor planning cost extra monies.

Procedural Crisis

Computer programs are written to follow a particular algorithm. Industrial quality assurance and quality control plans follow flowcharts. Engineers and technologists follow design flowcharts to produce reliable designs. Professional mechanics follow a procedure before diagnosing an automobile's or electrical device's mechanical problem. Technicians fixing breakdowns in plants and machinery follow procedures. Doctors also follow procedures or criteria when diagnosing a patient's sickness. To start a car and accelerate, one follows a particular procedure. As a project management professional, you need to know the predecessors and successors. Why is it difficult for many people in Africa to follow procedures, especially in developing safe systems of work?

Increased accidents are attributable very much to the procedural crisis in the promotion of safe systems of work. Many small and medium enterprises lack rules of procedure in the health and safety departments, like emergency procedures, first-aid, and training staff. There is a general crisis in procedural management in many spheres in several African countries. This includes the violation of criminal prosecution procedures, civil pursuits and planning crises. In almost everything, one needs to follow procedures. We need to learn how to follow normal, standard and acceptable procedures in everything. Otherwise, without following procedures, you can easily land into trouble.

I will give an example. The pillars of a project management profession are initiating, planning, organizing, staffing, controlling, executing, monitoring, evaluation and closing. The reason we have unsustainable, haphazard and congested cities in Africa lies greatly in the procedural crisis of the aforementioned pillars. For example, a parliamentary motion like, "compulsory takeover of land by Ugandan government from the individual owners for project development," lied and arose out of the procedural crisis within the aforementioned pillars—and of course, not forgetting communication challenges which fail projects, the most. The same applies to underperforming government programs – it is all about procedure crisis. Why would you just wake up and take people's land anyhow? This signifies planning deficiencies which is a companion of procedural crisis.

As an individual, are you following procedures? What routes do you take to resolve matters in your family, or do you take things the way you want? For example, your spouse wrongs you, and you wait for the kids to sleep in the night to talk to your spouse; this is a procedure. Or solve your grievances appropriately in the absence of the unconcerned parties is a procedure too. Does your company or institution have a grievance procedure mechanism? As a police officer, mechanic, lawyer, educationist, judge, engineer, doctor, etcetera, are you following procedures? Do you observe protocol at official meetings? Why would you negotiate the remuneration after the deal materializes? Contract law teaches us that past consideration is not a consideration. A graduate without good grades but who is keen at following procedures is a million times better than an academically excellent graduate who does not follow procedures. Be a mastery of following procedures, and the sky shall be the limit. If you are instituting a case in courts of law, you must open it in the right way from the beginning, and you have to follow the procedures

Ticking Procurement Evaluation Consultants and Service delivery models

Ticking procurement evaluation consultants deter sustainable progress. These are very similar to ticking psychotherapists. The former are nurtured and motivated by copy and paste procurement methodologies, while the latter is motivated by confusion in understanding the evolution of particular societies, lack of sufficient data on the African person and the outdated education system. You cannot measure and fail to assess to make a sound evaluation.

Most procurement practitioners who conduct bid evaluations in Africa are assessors but not evaluators. They should stop calling themselves evaluation consultants. The current procurement laws in some sub-Saharan African countries cannot allow officers to make an archaeological dig of the service providers. Evaluation encompasses *measurement, assessment,* and *prediction.* The existing procurement laws and associated regulations in many African countries refer to assessment. Where *risk assessment* is not thoroughly conducted as part of the offers, evaluation is not achieved. Predicting the nature and quality of the product outcome when the service provider is awarded the contract is risk assessment which must be part of the evaluation exercise, but many current laws do not allow for it in several African countries. Due diligence should not be used as a risk assessment practice. When you fail to make a sound evaluation, assessment and measurement become incomplete tasks. Prequalifying a company for work by merely ticking on a pass and fail basis is illogical to a given extent, following a three-staged approach—eligibility, administrative compliance and technical compliance.

Many bidders get kicked out at the preliminary evaluation stage simply because they submitted a non-sworn affidavit or did not present a sworn affidavit or a license expired by a month or because one of the staff provided has nine and a half years' experience yet the required experience is ten years. This kind of elimination by a three-staged approach is dangerous to many least developed countries that copy and paste procurement methodologies from other countries that are not applicable in the prevailing situations. The three-staged approach disadvantages the client if the objective is to obtain an economical and technically competent bidder because it eliminates potential service providers at the onset. An error, mistake or oversight is human.

As developing states, we ought to revise the procurement laws and regulations to be more inclusive and considerate to speed up the procurement exercises and achieve value for money in the end. And also to build local capacity. Evaluation consultants often get stranded near the end of the exercise when they discover that they remained with seemingly less technically competent or financially unsound companies simply because other potential companies fell victims of the pass and fail eligibility stage. Yes, administrative compliance is the critical cornerstone but developing means a process of devising the shortest route or critical path in real-time—a slight loosening of criterion-referenced assessment might prove logical. That is what evaluation would entail.

A typical example is a road project in Uganda where the bids assessment committee nearly got stranded at the end of the exercise with doubts about whether the remaining successful company would execute the project per required standards and on time. The best bidder had multiple projects running, making it somewhat risky by judgement. Other bidders had fallen victim to the "pass and fail" eligibility stage whilst others had been awarded other projects from other lots, and the law would not allow to award them more projects in that batch of lots.

Three years later, after the contract was awarded to the firm, the Uganda National Roads Authority (UNRA) terminated the contract because the contractor failed to work on the Mbale-Tirinyi road project in time and to the quality deserved. By the time the contract was terminated, the physical progress on the road was 19.09% against the planned 94.46%. On January 14th 2018, The Daily Monitor wrote, "'I recently wrote to you, lifting my executive order on this company to allow it continue with works in Uganda. This was after they agreed to stop delaying government works with court injunction when they fail to win contracts through procurement processes,' the President's letter reads in part."[103]

The firm failed to successfully implement the project on time and as per required standards. Although it qualified through all stages, it was not fit by *holistic independent judgment* to contract that deal. As a team, this is what they ought to have recommended in the assesment report. Their failure to recommend an expert opinion was due to the rigid and inapplicable procurement laws that do not allow the assessors to provide an expert opinion—the assessment team had no option instead to follow the law. The taxpayer does not know the techniques behind tendering and procurement; all they want is service delivery and reliable products.

Engineers warn that reliability can only be built at the earliest start of infrastructure planning stages since it becomes costly to remodel and build reliability halfway or at the end of project development. Amending a bit of the Procurement Law and regulations to be more lenient does not deter the transparency

---

[103] "Museveni orders Kagina on Mbale-Tirinyi road." The Daily Monitor, January 14th 2018.

but only to recall that we need only one bidder who will successfully deliver the product or service at the end of the exercise. Let the name "evaluation consultant" be so, and the consultant's report should not only be fixated in the law but also allow the expert to provide expert judgment and be held negligent of their actions. Therefore, Procurement Laws, which bestow powers to professionals to take independent decisions to award contracts basing on risk, expertise/competence, and financial competitiveness with the overarching goal of promoting/building local content, are more promising. This will solidify objectivity in evaluating offers hence support self-driven sustainable development.

Efforts to be more just and fair enough, considering the resources which the competing bidders invest in the bidding exercise and fail to win, are worth being respectfully recognized. Developing means to be in the process of emerging to meet the development objectives, and when in transit, you would not need to take on full-brown models copied from the already developed world because you cannot perfect the methods and approaches. I believe in the amendment of the procurement laws for the elimination approach to be guided with seeking clarification where necessary in a bid to be more competitive, except where the material provided by the bidder deviated completely from what the client requested.

Evaluation should be more to do with checks and balances, checking competencies, administrative compliance, resources management, project management, capacity to enter contract, *performance prediction,* method statements, *environmental protection,* health and safety policies, litigation history, performance history, *risk management,* adequacy and completeness. At many times, we lose out potential service providers due to unnecessary bureaucracy and a big focus on the tender documentation rather than the capacity to do work in terms of competence, financial soundness and appropriateness to the mission and vision. To accelerate socioeconomic transformation for developing countries, we need to urgently revisit the procurement methodologies to build capacity.

In the practice of soliciting bids, heavy paperwork is non-ecofriendly. The Client might need to list names of service providers/contractors and makes further steps to ascertain the competence of the service providers—a few documents, where possible, would be requested as appropriate, and the client would make her due diligence and a thorough risk assessment. They would finally list the qualified firms for the job and only ask for financial proposals. The current procurement practice is very costly, non-ecofriendly, and cannot let African firms grow.

Project 13 is an industry-led response to traditional infrastructure delivery models innovated by the UK. It is an excellent strategy to deliver sustainable projects.[104] The core message that Project 13 delivers is that the transactional model for delivering major infrastructure projects and programmes is broken. It prevents efficient delivery, prohibits innovation, and fails to provide the high-performing infrastructure networks that businesses and the public require. Project 13 intends to move from a transactional model to an enterprise structure business model. That is all in a bid to promote sustainability.

The CRBNetwork developed in the East African region aims to spur innovation and growth in delivering sustainable infrastructure projects.[105] The CRBNetwork business model takes the project from conception

---

[104] "Welcome to Project13 Network: What is Project13?" Project13 Network, accessed October 5th 2021, https://www.project13.info/.

[105] "About Us." CRBNetwork, accessed October 5th 2021, https://crbnetwork.com/about-us/.

to decommissioning—as a leading integrator of projects—an outstanding office bureau to lead the delivery of sustainable infrastructure projects beyond imagination. This way, many long-term sustainable benefits such as developing the region's human capital and a highly skilled industry would be realised. The CRBNetwork model can be an engine for growth providing integrated sustainable solutions for the construction industry.

Tender evaluation that focuses on skills, competence, and financial capacity would be the priority. The three-staged approach should be reversed if possible to move from technical compliance, financial soundness, administrative compliance and eligibility checks.

Dropping a financially sound and technically competent firm on the basis of not submitting a license or a specific permit does not merit for the nation but only to discover that those companies that remained on the list are not worth awarding the contract because they are not financially and technically sound. It is possible to experience that kind of phenomenon.

Alternatively, we can generate a relationship to move from eligibility checks to administrative, technical compliance, and financial soundness. We may drop the binomial distribution of a pass and fail and adopt something *similar* to the proposed algorithm below in amending procurement laws and regulations. The emphasis is to curb the pass and fail eligibility stage's powers to be more just to accelerate socio-economic transformation by achieving value for money through making the process fair enough and more competitive. The 21st-century sustainable development mission has no room for pass/fail concept. Evaluation consultants should be awarded the powers to be evaluators, not assessors! If we dream of local content promotion, we ought to revise the procurement regulations as soon as possible. Domestic preference must be methodical, and we must address the bottlenecks.

Proposed Methodology

(Disclaimer: This is a proposal guide. Something similar to this could be developed to curb the powers of the pass/fail eligibility stage)

Desist the excessive powers of the Guttmann's scale of PASS/FAIL or YES/NO for evaluating eligibility for tenders issued without prequalification. A one "FAIL" to invalidate a service provider's offer is not fair enough unless if the offer is evaluated for risk and legal implications indexes and found unbearable once clarification is sought on the given item. I propose the following steps.

a) How many items (n) require a Yes/No or Pass/Fail?
b) How many items did the bidder Pass (p)?
c) How many items did the bidder fail (f)?

Stage I: Measure.

For evaluation, at least $n \geq 10$.

- Calculate the item difficulty index (es), (d) for all items failed.
- Calculate the proportions (p) and (f).
- Evaluate the risk and legal implication indexes.

Stage II: Analysis.

Stage A: $d \leq 0.4$ for each item and P>f, if not drop bidder

Stage B: Legal Implication for all items failed.

- Negligence [1]
- Mistake [2]
- Representation [3]
- Misrepresentation [4]
- Ignorance [5]
- Error [6]
- Omission [7]
- Conflict of interest [8]
- Completeness [9]
- Warranty [10]

If [1], [4] or [8] is true for any failed item, drop bidder.

Stage C: Risk Assessment

- Identify the risk
- Identify stakeholders at risk
- Evaluate the risk and decide precautions (Risk = likelihood x severity)

If risk > 0.5, drop bidder.

Stage III: Seek clarification.

Conclusion

Empathy in sustainable development is essential. This involves understanding that people go through varying phenomena. The aggregate of the perceptions of these phenomena is what predetermines the quality of the population. The meaning we attach to the varying phenomena is the most crucial aspect. An investigation into African phenomena is vital to guide decisions in governments. Africans are different and require unique sets of hypotheses in what remains phenomenological in the cultural, socioeconomic, and political dimensions. Sub-Saharan Africa, in particular, needs a special reexamination of its phenomena.

If probabilistic models are adopted to study Africa's phenomena, several ideas on promoting self-driven sustainability would be generated. Democratic governance, for example, would be viewed as a mathematical model guided by one particular interest, which is saving humanity.

For one to succeed in life, the theories of human nature are held valid. However, the circumstances in which we live play an essential part in determining our failure or success. The unification of these circumstances is the ideal that development agencies work for day and night, promoting democratic ideals to gain freedom. You exercise your mind to the fullest where democracy flourishes.

Because people are unique, we promote interventions that promote empathy. We take time to judge others.

Cultural. Socioeconomic. Political. Phenomena

Chapter Six: Women and Youth Empowerment

"Feminism isn't about making women stronger. Women are already strong. It's about changing the way the world perceives that strength."[106]

=== G.D Anderson ===

Chapter Organization

Quick Insights

What is Women Empowerment, and why is it Important?

Wisdom from my Mother

Women Empowerment and Social Transformation

Women Empowerment, Dynamism, and Marriage/Family Power Structure

Woman as a first-line victim of change

Why Oppose or Support Women Empowerment? What Triggers People to Think Otherwise?

Financial and Economic Freedoms in Marriage and Sustainability of Women Empowerment

Objectivity in Women Empowerment

What do Psychologists Say about Empowerment?

Marginalization of Men

Developmental Agencies and Women Empowerment

The Other Side of Equality Equity

Women Empowerment versus Mothers' Empowerment

The Other Side of Empowerment

The Ancient and Today's Global Village: Women Empowerment and Relationships

What influences our Actions in 21st Century Relationships?

What do Equal Opportunities Mean?

Youth Empowerment and Sustainable Development

Conclusion

---

[106] The Cova Project, Australian Charity.

Quick Insights

Understanding a woman in sustainable development agenda is essential. For the world to understand a woman's role in sustainable development means to solve diverse crises ahead. It is a huge mistake to fail to tap into the potential that women have. In this era, where future generations are at risk of failing to meet their needs with ease, everyone, both a man and a woman, must be conscious enough to save the future generations. Understanding the need to advocate for a woman's freedom is to look at her as a mother and be a little more thoughtful. Second, as the primary caregiver of a family in either the demise of the husband or in instances where the man is disabled or where the man cannot meet his financial and associated obligations.

The unbearable pain women go through makes them second to none but heroes. To understand a woman, empathy but not sympathy is a must. In their struggle to live, solve dilemmas, and protect themselves against all sorts of crises, some women have been labelled as opportunists and schemers by unanimous groups. In the whole women empowerment struggle, some groups look at women as such. I can boldly warn that no country on this planet will sustainably develop without women forming part of the equation.

If you are not living with integrity, this may be not easy to comprehend. Gone are the days of patriarchal communities. I cannot imagine living without women in my life. They add love and beauty to everything. They are the ones who shape our personalities to a considerable extent. And if you are a Christian, you must know the significant role that women played in the salvation of Christians. The Christian faith hinges on the resurrection of Christ. The role of Mary Magdalene reminds us of the position of women in the Christian faith. Women have been more intelligent than men all along. That is the main reason why men wish to marry women slightly young than them in many collectivistic cultures around the globe.

The world becomes misguided without women featuring in the development equation. The most damaging crisis one might face in a lifetime is when they develop a conflict with their paternal mum than dad and fail to resolve it. The solution lies in answering the *"why question"* to that statement. Women have much-untapped potential and need to be critically understood. And once understood, you cannot imagine living elsewhere. They also have their slipperiness like the men and need to be handled with caution at some point.

What is Women Empowerment, and why is it Important?

Women empowerment is about uplifting women economically, socially and politically. This is aimed at creating equality, fairness and humane values to meet the demands of sustainable development. Previously, women were denied opportunities such as access to education, gaining leadership roles, access to jobs and et cetera. Women were considered to take care of families and were never allowed to participate in governance and the economics of society. However, in the early 1980s, the subject of women emancipation rose to fame around the same time when the topic of sustainable development became hot. A claim that development that leaves women behind is not sustainable has since become an essential topic of discussion in development studies and economics. Therefore, to ensure that sustainable development is achieved, women empowerment and gender equality are essential. Women have to be allowed to participate fully in economic life across all national sectors to improve the quality of life for a given society and build stronger economies.

The sources of inspiration of the notion of the word "empowerment" arose to fame through the pioneering works in the 1960s and 1970s within domains such as feminism, social psychology, Freudian psychology, theology, and the Black Power movement. Empowerment is about a set of principles aimed at enabling individuals and their groups to act in order to uplift their wellbeing or their right to involve in decision making that concerns them. These individuals or groups are believed to be previously marginalized. In psychological counselling, people who have faced psychosocial problems are empowered to gain momentum to solve their problems. The Black Power movement beginning in the 1960s in the United States of America emphasized economic empowerment and racial pride of African-American people that brought about a revolution in the previously marginalized groups. Such marginalized groups included African-Americans, gays and lesbians, women, and people with disabilities.

Wisdom from My Mother

My mother, who resides in a tiny village of Bukunda in Masaka district in Uganda, is not very enlightened. She raised me as a single mother after my dad passed away when I was 10 years old. Although she is not very enlightened, I admire her desire to develop and grow her intellect. She constantly searches for new ways to improve things and maintain those achieved so far. One afternoon, not so many years ago, while we gardened with her, she said, "Patrick, I can see you want to lead the plan to preserve your ancestral heritage. You wish to mentor many young people to know their roots, but you need to know that the population will explode in a few years to come, and conflicts over land and water shall be the order of the day." Actively listening to her, "population will explode ……." I paraphrased her statement. "Yes," She said. "People shall be too many in the near future, and conflicts over food and water shall escalate. It is better to channel your efforts to something else." She knew very little about my civil engineering profession, which leads or contributes to the campaign to conserve the environment and save humanity in many spheres, including promoting cultural values.

However, my mum's understanding of the implication of the population boom amidst scarce resources was a complete challenge to me, signalling the urgency to tackle sustainability. So, I had to write this book. When the situation becomes overt to inexperienced and less educated people as far as the sustainability topic is concerned, immediate intervention is deemed necessary. This somewhat justified the need to have women and mothers form an integral part in decision making. Suppressing and failing to promote a platform for their voice is not being wise. Her wisdom in raising me as a single parent after my dad had passed away, especially in encouraging me to keep moving regardless of problems encountered and never to give up, shaped my identity to a considerable extent. You can understand where my energy to work hard comes from. She stressed the point that if you are faced with a problem, keep going no matter what. Do not stop amidst a problem. Never halt. Never give up. Stay focused. That I must ensure I do not fetch more problems in the bid to solve the current problem.

The African Mother. She has always been simplistic, tolerant, celebratory, accommodative, reliable, dependable and loving. The African mother is a loving and caring mother who labours to educate her children through hard work and unfavourable conditions. Our beautiful mothers are a source of inspiration, motivation and strength. They have always been abused by society throughout history. Our mothers often fail to get a voice to speak out, but they never lose hope. I feel pain when our mothers are abused and are not well represented in decision-making processes.

Our good mothers shape our personality formation. We are conceived and grown in their wombs for nine full months. Their love and close attachment after we are born, especially for the first five years, shapes our personality to a very large extent. The African mother withstands the pain to deliver through difficult circumstances. Sometimes, the African mother delivers without a midwife, and without a helper and out of the hospital. Where the African mother delivers from a hospital in Africa, there are little or no drugs. She has persevered through pain as a result of political decisions that care less about her right to access good medical care. The ancient African mother used African herbs throughout the maternity period. These herbs have been labelled satanic without evidence, and many forests and other native vegetation is destroyed to construct roads, power transmission lines, dams and many other associated infrastructure. Nowadays, everything needs money to get access to improved healthcare.

The African mother who lives in collectivism faces many challenges, especially when the husband passes away and relatives impose themselves on the marital properties. This becomes problematic in polygamous African marriages. The African mother suffers a lot in circumstances where the husband passes away, leaving intestate estates. Living a structured life is a habit that is just beginning to grow in the African land. Many men pass away living intestate estates, which become very problematic to be administered by the survivors.

The African mother walks while carrying loads on the head, cultivates farmlands with hoes, and lives in areas without access to clean water and sanitation. She stays in slums in urban centres and lives in villages where water and land are scarce resources. Our mothers-in-the-making no longer receive access to the right protection. They are impregnated while they trek from schools hence dropping out of school. Sometimes they get infected with HIV, which continues to be rampant in some African countries. The cycle of suffering continues from one generation to another. This cycle has to be cut, which is why "mother's empowerment" is sought after. I attempt to lead continuous improvement in women empowerment, what we ought to do and not to do.

Women Empowerment and Social Transformation

To effect social transformation in African society, families are at the forefront. Functional, healthy families that do not wound children and the people they nurture are fundamental to social transformation. The word "family" differs in the African tradition, especially from the European and North American models. The African family is mainly extended as compared to nuclear families of the western world and North America. A family is a springboard for understanding people's issues and cultural problems. Therefore, women empowerment is vital in social transformation, and it must be streamlined to meet the demands of the African family values, beliefs, and practices. Short of these, the empowerment of women can be a mess-up in collectivism. As mentioned in Chapter One, any leader, for example, politician, professionals, spiritual leaders, must take part in the social transformation by applying techniques and skills nurtured from healthy families as a springboard for understanding and addressing the need for social transformation. All political problems we face are highly rooted and depend on the families where leaders originate from.

Understanding women empowerment is rooted in the school of thought which claims that gender is socially constructed. In the context of reality being socially constructed, women in leadership are distinct from women in marriage. The social transformation that hinges on sustainability as the overarching goal views women empowerment in the gender question from the social construction of meaning. This means that a man and a woman were being labelled so, but they once played the same meaning in the beginning. A beginning that contradicts between The Big Bang Theory and the Supreme Being existence. But what was the meaning of that meaning? A meaning we want to refurbish in the modern-day power struggles.

The overarching goal of inclusion is sustainable development that would leave nobody behind. That development is premised on natural phenomena. Sustainable development must be inclusive, and that is the reason we look at all marginalized groups. The intended development must create peace—and peace is socially constructed. This is because the best solution to misunderstandings and conflicts is understanding. Social transformation hinges on self-awareness and self-awareness roots in customs, beliefs and values right from the past. Is today's women empowerment socially constructed?

Women Empowerment, Dynamism, and Marriage/Family Power Structure

Ideally, an intimate relationship possesses no imposition; everyone is at liberty. In science, positive attracts negative and vice-versa. Positive repels positive, and negative repels negative. Unlike poles attract while like poles repel. Today's modern argument of change cannot accommodate much of conservatism, but it accommodates dynamism to cope with the changing world. The only constant in today's world is "change". If the only constant is "change", then constitutionalists must embrace dynamism. Nature, holy books, traditions, religion, cultures, and other societal constructions vested much power in a man's hands and very little in the hands of a woman.

If some of us claim to be constitutionalists, then why do we have divides in Christianity and Islam, yet the constitutions are the same, the Bible and the Quran, respectively? Dynamism is unstoppable—let us free our minds and create liberty for all. Today's most important question to the "married couples" and "the seeing someone" is how to live in freedom and keep the love flourish as if it were new every day because freedom hides in true love? The biggest challenge to this question derives from the growing power of the world dynamism, particularly the internet of social networks. We owe a lot to those who invented the internet. The IT revolution contributes to the top factors for the world's swiftness. Communication being less simplified with the IT revolution blocked the wall between strangers and realists—a situation in which the illusion of dealing with the virtual world seems pragmatic.

Today's claim that positive attracts positive is greatly motivated by a number of these forces. But what should be done? The solution is not to transform so fast without new evidence—it should be a scientific, gradual, and well-studied process fueled or constructed by society. Since we can no longer accommodate much of conservatism but rather liberalize our societies to cope with the dynamics of the changing world, what do we need to do to protect facts like marriages, families, and faith? With increased cases of domestic violence, human rights abuse, freedom of expression suppression, and child abuse, it is high time we learn to listen to a woman genuinely. Since many people hardly uphold the values of faith, ecosystem's demands, the dignity of holy books, the religions, it is essential to listen to the woman who is the first line victim of these failures.

Most importantly of all, dynamism is change, and women are highly victims of change. If everything is changing and transforming to modernity, why leave women behind? The reason we work is to improve the world. We call today's world "modern" and the past "ancient" because of our transformation in governance, knowledge, and welfare. If so, then why leave a woman to live in the ancient world? If not us to change things, who? If not now, when?

Man for long used his powers to move astray, in most cases suppressing women in many societies around the globe. If you find it appropriate to fight racism, would you fail to fight women suppression? The modern argument tells us that as humans, we deserve equity. However, an empowered woman can hardly uphold the traditional values of marriage because marriage requires a high level of self-discipline that sometimes an empowered woman cannot live to fulfil. Therefore, the empowerment of women distorts the family power structure at some point. This is where we would need to think at a higher level to have healthy empowerment of women.

In the sustainable development context, equity is only possible when women are at the forefront. If the dynamism of the modern world deserves such, what should we do to protect facts like families, cultures, and faith? Here, the topic of women empowerment is critical and cannot be overlooked if we dream of sustainable development.

Why Oppose or Support Women Empowerment? What Triggers People to Think Otherwise?

Opposing women empowerment makes sense only when it queries the process, not the product. If you oppose women empowerment without an alternative proposal regarding the process used, you are just not thoughtful! In terms of *uplifting the women* (i.e. the product), you should not oppose it if you are someone living with integrity.

Society constructed superiority around the man from two angles— the spiritual context and biological or physical context. The spiritual context premised the argument of supremacy on the Supreme Being bestowing powers onto a man to govern and make rules for a woman to follow, whilst the biological context premised the argument of supremacy on physical fitness and masculinity as a source of security to man a family. The industrial revolution brought many changes in how people view the world. It created endless possibilities, and society changed its outlook on how meaning is perceived. The industrial revolution boosted the world economy and facilitated the creation of many sovereign states. The contemporary world turning into a global village starting in the 20th century also changed how man sees humanity.

At that time, spirituality was associated with biological beliefs of a man being superior. The world growing through revolutions saw many freedom fighters and scientists fighting hard to have several kinds of freedoms and human rights for all, and there was no way this could be achieved in discrimination of a girl child. Ultimately, sovereign economies grew to have structures rooted in creating fairness and justice for all. The world sovereignties became convinced in having a unified source of authority and security for all. Therefore, man's spiritual position was no longer associated with security to a large extent. Security, therefore, turned to artificially created governments for all—a system that has had many challenges to date. Nevertheless, improvement and extension of the governance philosophy hinged on people power remain loyal to all people living with integrity across the globe.

Less association of masculinity with a man's spiritual position constructed another societal meaning—a product of both the industrial revolution and today's globalization. Security is now perceived as a function of financial and economic freedoms. Therefore, today's man must associate himself with these two kinds of freedoms alongside his spiritual position. It is a complete wastage of time coupled with ignorance to hear men complaining of how women have become accustomed to these two kinds of freedoms. The fact is that they have been conditionally stimulated to follow the trend, and this cannot be reversed. What existed before the industrial revolution was instead replaced with the products of the industrial revolution, but the norm remained.

Women respond realistically to satisfy their egos. This is because one's masculinity and spiritual position rarely meet bills in the modern-day. It is becoming a little more difficult for a man to naturally convince and win a response that pleasantly satisfies a woman's ego unconditionally. It will take only a few men who labour to reason out to realize that "Man is a man enough only when associated with financial and economic freedoms alongside his spiritual position in the modern-day." Women can thus be stimulated to respond with much enthusiasm when they find a rich mine that is at peace with financial and economic freedoms so that they can meet the demands of their egos despite the fact that man looks like a creature from Mars.

Society has now learnt that ladies respond to men's requests for several reasons. Since security was replaced with the industrial revolution products, men ought to revise their attitudes to match the trend. A man who meets today's woman's security needs might elicit a prolonged response from the woman more than his looks would, simply because your good words and better looks cannot drive anxiety out of her. This anxiety is caused by the dilemmas of contemporary living and the challenges brought about by the industrial and technological revolutions. The growth of our egos is perturbed by the destruction of the environment to conduct economic activities, and I wonder why men still want natural things for free. Everything is now at a fee. Some are at exorbitant fees whilst others are moderate. Man is a man today when he can drive anxiety out of her.

Life has become highly associated with objects that it would be difficult to disassociate people from objects. Stress-free and enjoyable life is only possible where the standard of living in a particular society is maintained. Short of that, men will always complain. However, some have grasped what life is all about in the interest of the Supreme Being. They have understood the meaning of life. If you have matched a man and a woman, you can live for ages until natural phenomenon or selection do you apart. Such relationships are not many in a hundred; many relationships are just classically conditioned because man is a social animal. And the conditioned response as a result of the products of the industrial revolution is more powerful than the normal unconditioned response simply because life is now sustained where the products of the industrial revolution are at play. In all developed economies worldwide, the basic necessities of life before you get to luxury are accessible at a pay. In not very far away, a flower that has always been symbolic of love will have to be associated with a paycheck as part of the package to be meaningful. That is how far the developed giants have come and claim to lead sustainability.

To make it more elaborate, look at a man who does not associate himself with financial and economic freedoms when making a move to propose to his girlfriend. It hardly works for most couples where financial and economic freedoms are postponed to a future date. The "love me, the way I am" works in a minimum likelihood. This is because the conditional response driven by the effects of the industrial revolution is more powerful than the unconditional response born in humanity. Man has disturbed the environment, and everything has changed. It is upon us to acknowledge it and accept the change in the way we live today. Even those women who claim that their unconditional responses are heavier than the conditional ones just need unconscious tests to provoke them to prove it. The blame, therefore, is not on any woman; it is on a human being who has destroyed the environment in a bid to improve lives. A good question to ask is: is the destruction of the environment to improve lives sustainable? How will it be 100+ years from now if the trend remains constant?

I am discussing the learning of a response as a result of associating two or more stimuli with the actual stimuli, in this case—man. Women getting elicited by financial and economic freedoms regardless of the ability, competence, sexiness and looks of a man is as a result of the association of these freedoms with the man himself. In a world where life is driven by the products of the industrial and technological revolutions, women's anxiousness is more driven out by economic and financial freedoms than man's natural attributes. In other words, the said freedoms should ideally follow man shortly, and a man himself should lead because humanity is the highest good in the hierarchy of goodness. But because the environment has been so much destroyed to create competition in our lives, this creates anxiety in the hearts of all of us at some point. And this means any one of us lives in anticipation to find relationships with those who can help eliminate artificial anxiety. Consequently, the hierarchy of goodness is very hard to be followed by the majority.

The negative reinforcement that occurs as a result of taking out the anxiety, using the financial and economic freedoms' tools and techniques instead of what the Supreme Being provided for, as a man and a woman, makes people fall in love on social media and setting standards too way high to be met by those having intentions to express love interest for them. Many women have been spotted falling in love with men across borders so long as men demonstrate financial and economic freedoms and could delegate and direct whilst in absentia. The sexiness, humour, and looks of a man remain to be lived in regrets. Therefore, ideally, if you wished your wife or spouse to be yours and only yours is when you empower her to access the financial and economic freedoms of contemporary life. So, the winds of the world would not blow her from you.

Financial and Economic Freedoms in Marriage and Sustainability of Women Empowerment

Today's civil marriages contracted solely on love and are not associated with financial and economic freedoms as considerations may prove successful in the short term. However, maintenance of love in the spiritual dimension is threatened by social media and associated technologies. Slowly, a lack of financial and economic freedoms to facilitate, manufacture, and maintain romance, cover up the social media and associated newly introduced technological dilemmas cannot fail to allow spouses to disagree. In the long run, they will see more negatives in each other. Therefore, a monogamous well-off African man may have resources to facilitate, manufacture, and maintain romance.

I hypothesize in the interest of civil monogamous marriages that exercising conjugal rights not associated with economic and financial freedoms may be boring in the contemporary world. However, an average-earning African man who finds peace in customary marriages might successfully manoeuvre through polygamy than a rich man in the same category across the continent. This is because the poor man is not a target of attack for financial and economic freedoms. He, therefore, poses no anxiety in the hearts of others. In many situations, due to the unlimited time they usually have, poor polygamous men learn to manufacture unconditioned romance playing one wife against the other, which neutralizes the woman's urge not to look at financial and economic freedoms as a priority. Therefore, the spouses of a poor polygamous man end up settling for nothing. Wives end up settling for something similar to love but not love.

A financially stable polygamous African man is under great threat than his counterpart, the average earner. The more financial and economic inclusion a polygamous rich man engages with the spouses, the higher the likelihood to separate and divorce because wives learn to cogitate well-enough about sharing a spouse and its negatives because of the conditioned stimulus that facilitates empowerment to deactivate their feelings for a legal fiction of one—and this is a normal unconscious trait that only needs a provoking stimulus to manifest—the trigger. They will have the weapons to triangulate their disarray into the husband, and it would take a great kind of wisdom from a man who believes in gender equality to govern such polygamous marriages.

The average-earning polygamous man makes his wives pursue him constantly, giving them hope but never satisfaction. However, the rich man gives them satisfaction by empowering them through financial and economic inclusion based on love and not purpose on several occasions. And many people across ages have tried to argue that a mind filled with love reasons little. The rich at many times substitute romance with the products of the industrial revolution and hence create satisfaction. They ought to use the products of the industrial revolution to facilitate romance but not substitute it. They forget that power is so adaptive and tempting; the more you have some, the more you yearn for more. All creatures wish to have control over some other creatures at some point. It is a habit that cannot be kept out of humanity; it forms part of our lives.

By the rich failing to empower constructively and on purpose, wives would wish to have more control over everything that comes within their reach. After being empowered, they tend to fight each other and triangulate their power greediness into their husband. They will thus no longer pursue their husband but instead look at maintaining and extending their power base and pursuing properties.

In my opinion, for a stable civil monogamous marriage, it must be solemnized and contracted, before and after, when associated with an intention to have financial and economic freedoms to live as desired and agreed upon by both parties, as one of the critical elements in the marriage without any kind of pretence that these freedoms do not count. Inconsistencies in financial and economic freedoms have rarely been a ground cited in divorce cases. However, the continued fixation on the old fashioned form of love relationships will not fail to rule out such cases on the African continent.

The power of financial and economic freedoms in a world driven by the products of the 4th industrial revolution cannot be overlooked. Love can easily be maintained through financial and economic freedoms than the spiritual dimension since the world is undergoing a rapid 4th industrial revolution that makes everything rotate about these freedoms. Any man who thinks otherwise is daydreaming. The effects of climate change are now overt and manifest in our lifestyles, and I do not think it forgives influencing love relationships.

Since poor and average earning polygamous men might live with settled anxiety than their counterparts, the rich polygamous, and rich monogamous African men might live a better life than their counterparts, the poor, it demonstrates why we need to promote civil monogamous marriages to cope with the dilemmas of the contemporary world. Therefore, since we all deserve a better life, polygamy should be discouraged where possible to cut off the cycle of poverty on the continent. The poor are multiplying day and night as a result of polygamy.

We are misled by the effects of industrial and technological revolutions that the men and women of yesterday have changed. The industrial revolution created everything to rotate around economic and financial freedoms, and it turned everything to rotate around those freedoms. Technology will change. Many things will change, but marriage will remain as it was yesterday. Marriage is going to be a difficult institution in the 21st century because of men failing to understand women and women failing to understand men. Marriages are destroyed by men's failure to understand what women want and learn to stick to that.

As a man, if you cannot associate yourself with security as described to drive anxiety out of your spouse, forget the marriage. She has grown up feeding on cakes and you want to feed her on bread; sometimes you need to be considerate. *Sometimes,* as a man, if you are not in control of your marriage and family, then by no means can you control the world but rather the world to control you. Some great men who have failed to manage and control their families and marriages have tried to arrest the anxiety in themselves early enough by doing away with civilized slavery so that they can control the world in their present and future. This compensation for marriage is painful but paying in the long run when better decisions are taken early enough. A real African man ought to create some sense of fear a little more than intimate love alone. This fear cannot be achieved without a man associating with financial and economic freedoms. The problem with intimate love is that it highly associates with "yeses" and minimal "no", and where limits are infinite, high susceptibility to falling into mistakes is inevitable. Where there is extreme emotional love, there is no reasoning. Emotional reasoning distorts the overall cognition about the world around us. It is important to note that fear associates with respect in shaping a partner, and a thin line exists between love and hate. Therefore, a man should strive to be financially independent as he campaigns for women empowerment.

Who is Responsible for Modern Errant Behaviors?

To what extent is it a result of women empowerment?

In Law, a person who aids a criminal always has a case to answer. Ignorance, not being a defence, does not spare an aider of a criminal. An intention to commit a crime can attract lawful custody of the person who intends to commit an act. These principles are based on the science of behaviours, how behaviours are learnt, perpetuated, unlearnt, and relearnt. For example, several African cultures do not go on well with their ladies putting on very short dresses that expose anatomical parts which are debarred view from the public. These dresses are commonly known as mini-dresses in several African territories.

According to several African cultures, ladies are constantly blamed for putting on short dresses in public places, but who do you think perpetuates this behaviour in the African setting? I vigorously defend the women. The men perpetuate the behaviour when they express interest and reward to those ladies dressed in mini-dresses. They reward the ladies by taking them shopping, outing, biking, and many more places for fun. This makes women learn that they are appreciated and rewarded in the dress code. If men are taken out of the equation, I do not think they can continue the dress code, which is a taboo in the region.

The kind of consequences arising from doing an activity is actually more important than the activity itself. This can be argued from many angles to understand who is responsible for what. Omissions are consciously committed by people only when the consequences are tolerable or less threatening. Women learn the mini-dress code due to the reward from men weighing heavier than the punishment from the state laws for doing so. Therefore, weighing consequences informs the decision by women to adapt to the dress code, but correct attribution of the genesis of the taboo, in the African setting, is a man. Man can attribute it to the uncontrolled technologies of the industrial revolution, which Africa has not had control over yet, creating many co-occurring disorders not brought to book in the African context.

It is important to note that learning takes place in many ways, and a bias of errant behaviours towards women is unfair, mean, and selfish. The environment, both men and women, contribute to behaviour modification and activation in humans. Therefore, men complaining about women empowerment and maladaptive behaviours activated in women due to empowerment and equality programs is well-understood when modelled unbiased. The learning of behaviours is greatly reinforced as a result of the consequences of that behaviour. Therefore, a behaviour is reinforced when a threatening stimulus is removed or when the behaviour is gainful to the person. As I mentioned earlier, people are always looking for survival. This makes them look for the good consequences of their actions that make their survival healthier or better. The fear of committing acts is premised on the bad consequences arising from those acts once committed but not the acts. Therefore, since behaviour modification and activation result from consequences they bring to the human being, the value in those consequences predetermines the anxiety levels carried by the human being.

By men failing to acknowledge the fact that the world has changed and everything has changed, they are reluctant to embrace the fact that financial and economic freedoms of the industrial and technological revolution stimulate women's responses more than the usual norm of reciprocity in relationships. They keep being too ungenerous with their finances and just give pennies to their lovely wives. The fact that women are created with little anger outbursts, unlike men to a considerable extent, does not mean they do not feel the pain of not being able to meet their needs. The stay-at-home moms, for example, have faced inner pain from the mean characters of many of their dear husbands.

The competitive world driven by the technological revolution sees a fraction of women finding opportunities that pay off well. Stay-at-home moms start admiring these women when they see their lives slowly getting better every day that goes by. Eventually, stay-at-home moms start to yearn for paying activities simply because they feel not fairly included in their husbands' financial and economic freedoms. And once they find a way out to find work to start earning some income to meet their needs, men start to complain that women have become accustomed to financial and economic freedoms more than anything else, forgetting their ungenerosity to share what they achieve with their wives.

Many men constantly think of social drinking, business, politics, sports, etcetera, more than meeting the demands of their wives. In doing so, a behaviour of women being more accustomed and pleasurable to financial and economic freedoms is reinforced when uncaring men are removed from the equation. However, it is important to note that rich men rarely complain about women's love for financial and economic freedoms. In this aspect, the subject of caring refers to the transparency and clarity inferred to the union of living as husband and wife—the husband living generously by extending empathy to the dear wife and seeing the wife's works as invaluable. He constantly shares what he gets and properly meets the spouse's demands as far as he can manage. The point to learn from this is that man's mean character triggers individuality to a notable extent.

Men are Very Selfish

Men are very selfish. They complain about how women have got accustomed to financial and economic freedoms. Who seduces or triggers them?

Men are very selfish. They wish women not to cheat on them, but they keep seducing them into casual relationships? Who is unfair?

Men are very selfish. They complain that women cheat. Do they cheat on animals?

Men are very selfish. They protect, defend, conserve, and wish the wildlife to be free. Why not women?

Men are very selfish. They advocate for wildlife sovereignty. Why not Africa?

Men are very selfish. They want the environment to be conserved. Why not culture?

Men are very selfish. They complain that Africans have failed to govern themselves. Why supply them with weapons?

Men are very selfish. They complain that Africans cannot help themselves. Why worry?

Men are very selfish. They complain that Africans cannot put aid to proper use. Why continue supplying them with aid?

Does a Woman predetermine the success of a Man? What should we do right?

A famous adage goes, "Behind every successful man there is a woman, and behind every successful woman there is a scared man." A man who wishes himself success would learn to care for his wife more than anything else. Undermining a woman is ignorance in the modern-day. As a man, materialistic gifts win you more votes before her in the short term. However, the long-term maintenance of a relationship calls for friendship, care, and romance. As a man, when you do those, be rest assured of success.

As a true man, if you want to receive the joy of living a successful life, go back home and love your wife. Nothing can substitute or compare with showing passion, intimacy, and commitment to her. The most prominent mistake men make is to think that when you shower her with materialistic gifts, a wedding, or even a business empire, you have her heart—the financial and economic freedoms. These freedoms are not enough! The thought pattern of a woman, especially in matters related to social intelligence, is one of the most complex puzzles which scientists claim to have understood, but in my view, they have not yet mastered it.

A woman who tries to deviate from the ordinary course is often problematic and sometimes not marriageable. This category has crazily advocated for empowerment, forgetting that it is purely a genetic distinction that makes them outliers. They live very successful and visionary lives that make many other women admire them. However, this category is, in many cases, born but not nurtured. They rarely get married because they cannot withstand traditional values of what marriage calls for, i.e. a high level of discipline. The world's biggest problem from such women is that their motivational speaking can make many cats view themselves as lions.

As a man, the solution lies in understanding and appreciating her for who and what she means to you. Of course, there is no doubt about the man's financial and economic freedoms as a predictor variable of a successful marriage and family. However, I am reminding you that the wiring of a woman is not as that of a man. Both men and women are unique. That is the reason why an artificially gap-toothed lady can concur with a man when flattered that despite the artificial gap-tooth, she is the most beautiful in the locale. They need compliments all the time, even though the compliment is deceptive. No amount of cash can buy a compliment. That is the central point on which I would wish to base my arguments on to address women empowerment.

It might become complicated for a man who makes only actual attributes about himself and does not add any deceptive attribute to seduce a woman for love. It is always a man who knows how to manufacture romance amidst many fantasies to win her heart. Men are always afraid of women's reactions when they tell them the perfect truths, and a man who always tells the truth rarely wins. Men make the first steps in love relationships for most cultures globally, which is the benchmark to understand power and leadership. An extra mile on this fact must answer many right questions in the right way.

First, why compliment a woman about her makeup that looks unrealistic even to a 6-year-old child and feels great? It is about the defence mechanisms provided by psychologists—the reality framework responding to the ego or self-worth. These defence mechanisms have a connection to thinking and reasoning. Correct women empowerment, aiming to lead 21st-century sustainable development, should strive to tie things because it is still a work in progress. We want women empowerment that is sustainable and correctly done based on facts—*the specific empowerment of women, not global.*

Objectivity in Women Empowerment

Since women empowerment is objective, we should get reminded of the stem for the word empowerment, which is "to power". The Merriam-Webster dictionary defines the word "empower" as "to give official authority or legal power to." The same can be defined as "to promote the self-actualization or influence of." I pause an analogy between the goals of women empowerment and those of science and technology.

In science and technology, we learn about the verb "power." For example, all electrical devices need to be powered to start. As a health and safety practitioner, manufacturer, or end-user, what precautions do you put in place before powering an electrical device? Certainly, you need to follow some safety tips to ensure that you are safe before attempting to power a gadget. For example; you would ensure that cables have no damage; ensure that no damage to the plug or cable; ensure that the condition of the casing is good; check that the on and off buttons of the device work; check the fuse rating and also the test label, and finally turn on the electrical device.

It is a recommendation by International Organization for Standardization (ISO) and sister organizations for the manufacturer to provide a safety data sheet and technical manual for users to operate the device. When a system, say a flat iron or a music system (e.g. amplifiers, woofers, loudspeakers, pianos, microphones, et cetera), is connected to an electrical power source, it is said to be *live*. Once it has been disconnected from its power source, it is said to be *dead*. The system is usually insulated with rubber or plastic material to enclose wires and conductors to prevent current leaks and conductors from touching and causing a short circuit. Secondly, a person dealing with the flat iron or the music system can accidentally fall into an electric shock when they contact a live conductor. The current passes through their body. The body then acts as the conductor for the current, interrupting the circuit and providing an alternative path for it to flow along.

Similarly, the human body has several systems; the nervous system, respiratory system, digestive system and circulatory system. All these systems were naturally empowered to work together and support each other for humans and other creatures to be alive. Where freedom of any of these systems is sabotaged, we usually fall sick. They live in a free, fair, liberal and democratic society. If one of the systems is disordered and diagnosed as faulty, one gets administered drugs to repower the system or organ to regain its natural state. History is taken as a diagnostic criterion to track the cause in recovering the system to its natural state. A complete diagnostic criterion is undertaken to track disorders in our body systems and our lives in general. All these body systems were naturally powered to function differently and holistically to contribute to the human's life—none of these substitutes for the other; in instances where one system suppresses the other, the body malfunctions. We administer a drug to regain a free, fair, liberal and democratic society for all the body systems.

Another contemporary theorist may probably argue that our body systems are communistically controlled because the body systems are part of the brain but not the brain a part of other systems. This illustration shows that intestines and other organs dominate the world, and a few brains exist. Since the structures of the body organs are interconnected with their unique functions, any breakdown in the structure or deformation of an organ leads to a distortion of the function. Relate this to the context of a social structure. The biggest question in modern societies is why we empower women and not repower them? What are the precautions taken to empower women? Women were naturally empowered just like other creatures, but their position was suppressed and oppressed by man's greed.

William Golding (1911 – 1993), a British Novelist, Playwright, and Poet, emphasized women superiority over men and in his opinion, there would be no need to advocate for equality. It cannot happen because of the reasons he gave. Golding provided the position of men and women, and using deductive reasoning, presented who possessed the power to make another comply. The one who possesses the power to induce another to comply possesses the keys to steer the wheel. His cautionary remark on multiplication of any crap to tons of shit emphasized the superiority of women over men. Golding fell more on the nature side of the "nature versus nurture" debate.

> *"I think women are foolish to pretend they are equal to men. They are far superior and always have been. Whatever you give a woman, she will make greater. If you give her sperm, she will give you a baby. If you give her a house, she will give you a home. If you give her groceries, she will give you a meal. If you give her a smile, she will give you her heart. She multiplies and enlarges what is given to her. So, if you give her any crap, be ready to receive a ton of shit." – William Golding, British Novelist, Playwright and Poet (1911 – 1993)*

What ought to be done is to make women reclaim their position but not swap to mean that women are now equal to men because lots of people understand it that way. And if lungs can be powered to pump blood throughout the body, replacing the heart, it would ideally present a perfect match, making the body society more liberal. Nature had designed all creatures to take on various unique tasks. There is nothing wrong with what nature holds. We created the mess by distorting the environment, and we need to correct it following the right processes but not through substitution. Substitution is too elementary, non-exhaustive, and nonscientific. Today's methodology of empowering women creates a short circuit within their consciousness, and men and the offspring are the recipients of the electric shock. At times, failure in the electrical circuit impacts all machines and systems linked to that circuit. Where no precautions are taken before powering something believed to be dead and made live by external stimulus, you should expect a shock or danger unless the repower theory is considered.

The repower theory believes that every living creature was empowered naturally by the grace of the Supreme Being. Along the way, as described earlier, some creatures were suppressed by others, and they lost power and, therefore, needed their power reinstated to function appropriately.

In the context of humanities, genuine power is self-made or occurs naturally or occurs through a lineage; exchanged power or power from a third party is not worth celebrating and poses a high risk to the beholder and the ruled. On the other hand, stepping into a great man's shoes means you need to establish your name and identity, double the efforts by changing course and gain or regain power in your way. Realists know that people have four psychological needs, i.e. power, freedom, belonging and fun. People also have the physiological need for survival. The question remains: is the transfer of power in the realm of human existence legitimate? The phenomenology of existentialism designed faculties of the two sexes. Constitutionalists learn about the jurisdiction of the branches of government. Where there is an invalid transfer of power, the doctrine of non-delegation is violated. I maintain the repower technique as an approach to mediate between women and the environment. The current women empowerment does not address the cause. The greed of man is the cause, and man ought to be the control experiment.

What Do Psychologists Say?

Unlike the psychoanalysts and behaviourists who dwell much on the unconscious forces, irrational drives and past events shaping people's lives, existentialists and humanistic viewers argue that human beings are greatly responsible for their actions. They argue that human beings have the power to determine their destiny. At almost any given moment, we can choose our actions because we have free will.

According to Carl Ransom Rogers (1902-1987), a celebrated psychologist, how a human sees reality is more important than the reality itself; perception is more important than fact. Rogers further argued that in the same way plants grow well when conditions are favourable, so persons have a tendency to flourish when their circumstances support growth. Given the proper conditions, the capacities for normal growth and development could be realized in every human being. Clearly, Roger's theory shows that in the instance where prevailing conditions are unfavourable to women, the perception of such conditions deters progress in women. On the other hand, women are responsible for causing the action to forge their destinies. The former role is for the nation-state to reinstate the favourable conditions through correct empowerment campaigns and the latter for women themselves to cause action. I call upon men to create an enabling environment for their spouses and let women forge their cases to get to their destinies. *The repower technique for women can be handled as follows:*

- Invest in the research question: What motivates or perpetuates man's errant behaviour in modern times?

- Invest in the research question: HIV/AIDS, which is quite known even to 12-year-old adolescents, is still prevalent in many African countries, despite claims that no breakthrough of a cure drug to date, but men are still producing dozens of children from more than officially recognized wife or wives. Are these children accidental or planned?

- Invest in the research topic: Nature versus Nurture. To what extent is this probed in the land?

- There is a need to uphold the Rule of Law. The Rule of Law should be non-negotiable.

- The governments should institute tribunals or inquiries into domestic violence.

- Renegotiate gender equity, gender equality and women repowering, focusing on interests but not positions—making women's rights a matter of fact but not a fight.

- Tame the man with well-studied and necessary primary and subsidiary legislations. The motto should be: "Our mothers are our lives, and our lives are our mothers."

- Create interactive platforms for women, e.g. software applications, TV stations, radio stations, clubs, and et cetera.

- Establish an enabling environment that is practical, not theoretical, for equal opportunities.

> Stop biasing women with extra points or weightings or unnecessary incentives because such additions retard their hard work.
>
> Understand the core values and faculties of both sexes and plan accordingly.
>
> Improve the education system with lessons that matter to the girl child and boy child, e.g. necessary grooming and continuous individual and group counselling sessions.
>
> Improve the education system to student-based learning. Let each child decide on what they want to become right from their domicile of origin.

Correct empowerment of women, which I have coined as, *"repowerment"* is very beneficial to the African mothers to safeguard them from shortcomings of Africa's collectivism. The husbands leave intestate estates that clan members later claim based on cultural core beliefs that only leave our mothers socioeconomically and psychologically tortured for life.

Defence Mechanisms and Women Empowerment

The way someone reacts to a threatening stimulus differs from one person to another. Age, gender, culture, religion, occupation, and well-being can contribute to how a person reacts to a threatening stimulus. The responses to a stimulus are unconsciously seated in the person and are activated whenever perceived, or real anxiety arises from unacceptable thoughts or feelings. However, men and women have defence mechanisms they portray on a large scale. Both women and men can portray mature, immature, and neurotic defences. For example, when a boss who does not listen annoys you and you decide to get a few minutes off for a cup of tea instead of trying to correct them, you employ a mature defence mechanism—sublimation. If a person says, "women pretend more than men", which is a global statement, they mean women are good at reaction formation. When a lawyer says, "with all due respect", you know they are about to disrespect you.

Similarly, when things do not go well in a relationship, for example, a man failing to deliver the promise or failing to keep his word, the woman can say, "it is ok". However, this is more likely to mean, "Not Ok". Paradoxical interventions work best on women in religious matters and relationships because many score highly on neurotic personality traits.[107] All these attributes matter in women empowerment campaigns because these campaigns are either watering, activating, or deactivating good and evil seeds. How often are such psychological issues considered in women empowerment action plans?

Albert Einstein (1879–955) had one of the greatest minds of all time. He was such a successful theoretical physicist who has inspired the world, including me. However, the fact that Albert had inconsistencies in his marital life, divorcing the first wife and failing to live to the desired empathy standards marriage calls for, reduces his greatness to a great extent. He failed the practical life examination. Otherwise, with his great mind, he would try to conserve the marital issues and predict the consequences of his actions.

---

[107] See p. 44, §1.

Much as women employ several neurotic defences in provoking situations, they also employ mature defences, but it depends largely on the situation and the woman's age. However, men are mainly characterised by anger outbursts and a quick-forward reaction in threatening situations. Therefore, when designing a package of reforms, such things matter to the world in the interest of sustainable development. Secondly, man has led by default right from Adam, Aristotle and his likes; he, therefore, ought to be the control experiment in such reforms. Do you remember that even those who construct prayers start with God the Father…? How about when we say, God the mother….?

Women as First-Line Victims of Change and Marginalization of Men

Women are being empowered day in and day out. The stunning question is, who is preparing men to receive empowered women?

Nobody's mother is comparable to anything but women emancipation and empowerment is debatable, yet mothers are women. Why? The empowerment of women should not be at the expense of men. We read about the story of creation in Abrahamic religions, and we notice how women have been change agents right from the beginning. Women have been leaders right from the beginning. The Abrahamic religions teach us how Eve and Adam lived in the Garden of Eden and the subsequent turnaround of events that shaped our spiritual beliefs. The story of creation is an important reflection of how a man and a woman play their roles as change victims. Sometimes those who follow Abrahamic religions ignore the philosophy of creation in the decisions they make today.

The philosophy of creation is never or rarely incorporated in psychological interventions and women emancipation campaigns, yet ignoring it leads to the marginalization of men in the long run. As science advances, there is more to do for philosophers. In the psychological dimension, what happened in the Garden of Eden can be profiled, and the facts of women being first-line victims of change proved beyond doubt. In our empowerment campaigns, we are left to draw on scientific knowledge corroborated with a philosophical understanding that will streamline women empowerment to fit well-enough in the sustainability equation.

Women Empowerment versus Mothers' Empowerment

Anyone who told mothers to work created havoc for the world. A good number of empowered women who at the same time juggle as mothers are typically living in dysfunctional families, a good explanation for raising poorly differentiated offspring. Working to earn a living, in a way that deprives the woman ample time to attend to her family, should have been better designed for women but not mothers. That is the difference a future sustainable society should strive to create. There is no law protecting mothers from being loosely attached to their infants in many territories across Africa. Empowerment of mothers, when done right, is more beneficial than that of women. Women need to be repowered, but mothers need to be empowered. *Policies to have a secure attachment of infants and children with their mothers to be a race to the top are required as part of the correct process for mothers' empowerment.*

I do not see sustainable development where false empowerment of women is the order of the day. For example, who wants not to raise a child to move through their footsteps as a repowered woman? Sustainable development is pivoted on; sustaining humanity, promoting the dignity of a human being, values, predispositions, and cultural norms of what the society believes in. The deteriorated societal values and poorly differentiated people at the heart of society do not promote sustainability. The current women empowerment looks very little at nature but promotes nurture in one of the vaguest processes that a socioeconomic sustainable developmental activist ought to revise. Our mothers ought not to juggle life with unnecessary working stress to cater for the young ones to grow well-individuated. The correct *empowerment of mothers* and *the repowerment of women* gives them more time to spend with their families but not subtracting more time away from their families. This is what can sustain society.

Developmental Agencies and Women Empowerment

According to developmental agencies, gender equity, gender equality, and women empowerment are among the prioritized areas in the struggle for sustainable development. Because of the differences between the roles of men and women, different approaches are demanded while designing developmental programs. Women are not well represented in decision making yet they suffer much of the world's crises. Therefore, development agencies fight hard to close the inequality gap between the genders. It is a universal belief that when women are constrained from reaching their full potential, that potential is denied to the whole nation or society. However, existentialists and humanistic viewers would want to know how someone is denied the chance to attain their full potential. It looks like an easy chapter to cope with but very difficult once you open it in that context.

Development agencies say that there are clear patterns of women's inferior access to resources and opportunities, but philosophers warn that none can make you inferior without your consent. Africans, through slavery and colonialism, can testify to this! In the struggle to have all-around inclusion for gender issues, strategy for integrating gender concerns in the analysis, formulation and monitoring of policies, programs and projects is well laid out by development agencies and termed gender mainstreaming. Therefore, development agencies have invested heavily in closing the gaps and gender disparities. They advocate for equal control over resources, access to services, equal access to information and opportunities, equal representation in decision-making, and power-sharing.

Sustainability priorities as far as gender mainstreaming is concerned are hierarchical in nature. The three pillars of gender mainstreaming are equity, equality, and empowerment. Equity is qualitatively assessed and cannot be counted. Equality and empowerment rates can be measured. Equity is not quantified because it operates on the human sense of right and wrong—moral and reality principles. The outcome of this unquantifiable pillar of gender mainstreaming is pre-consciously rooted in the peoples' psyche just as we traditionally believe in God or a transcendent source or Superior Being, and we understand these universal principles through human reason. The process of attaining gender equality has seen several nations advocate for women empowerment through legislation, specifically designated facilities, funding pools, et cetera. Therefore, empowerment is part of gender equality programs. However, gender equity is paid less attention, yet it carries more weight in terms of social stability, peace, unity, and sustainable development. The principle of equity has origin from several spiritual teachings, which denotes doing to others what you would want them to do unto you. The hierarchy to address sustainability looking at gender mainstreaming should be as below:

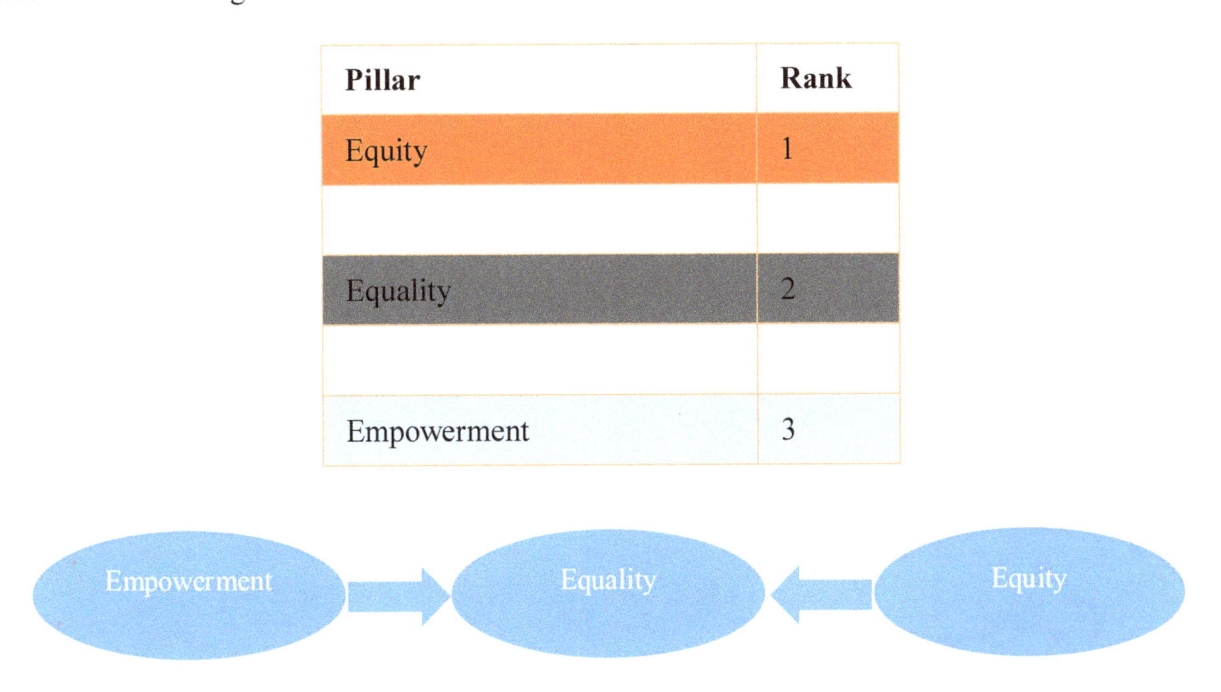

Pillar	Rank
Equity	1
Equality	2
Empowerment	3

The Three Pillars of Gender Mainstreaming

For social stability, peace, and sustainable development, equity is at the top of equality, and empowerment aims to attain equality. Equity also leads to equality. Even if there is no equality, there can be equity. The overarching goal of bringing women to the forefront is sustainable development and meeting the demands for the principle of natural law. According to the current philosophy adopted by developmental agencies, women are believed to be dead (as earlier explained with the analogy of "power" on page 288) and hence made live by empowering them through legislations to attain equality.

To close the gaps in gender enrollment in schools, for jobs, access to health facilities, taking part in the decision-making process, et cetera, you need to enact legislations. However, attainment of gender equality, say 50 males are enrolled for studies, and 50 females are also enrolled for studies or jobs, does not lead to automatic gender equity. Gender equity needs understanding and specifically designed tools, skills, and techniques to prepare boys and girls to achieve equity. Because development agencies have failed to do this, it is the reason masses have interpreted gender equality as men equal to women. Gender equity can be attained by enacting laws benchmarking on Natural Law and the Law of Equity and design tools and techniques to *prepare* men and women for change through understanding.

To what extent would the three questions below be answered with a YES in decision making, resource allocation, opportunities, delegation, power transfer, and power-sharing?

- Can we have 80% men and 20% women in leadership or management, and we have equity?
- Can we have 20% men and 80% women in leadership or management, and we have equity?
- Can we have 50% men and 50% women in leadership or management, and we have equity?

Following the principle of Natural Law, all these questions can be answered with a YES and if you find difficulty answering one of the questions with a YES, just know that is where the problem is from your perspective. Refer to the illustration in the photo below. It looks like equity has nothing much more to do with equality but rather a human sense of right and wrong that follows the principle of Natural Law. It is about understanding. As shown in C, the man could lift the kid to watch the goat race, keeping other factors constant like body physiology. The kid might be light to carry.

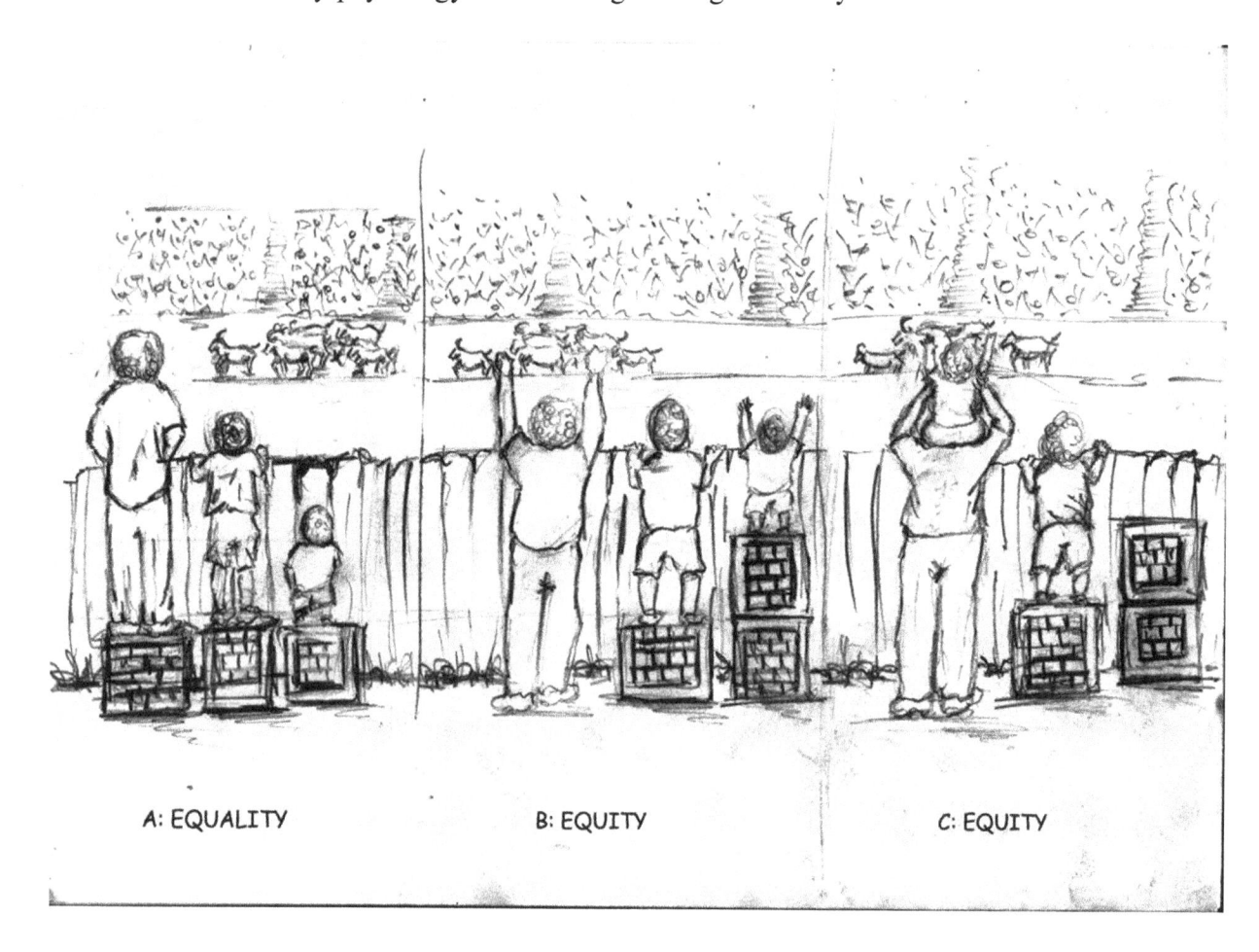

Three People Watching a Goat Race

The picture above shows three people watching the goat race. They are all provided with a stool to stand on to ably watch the sport. The eldest is seen to surrender his stool in B to the kid so as for the kid to watch the sport. This shows that without surrendering the stool, equality does not lead to automatic equity. What leads to equity is both moral and reality principles—the understanding. This is rooted in values. The man must comprehend the reason why he has to provide the stool to the child. The stool should not be forcefully grabbed from him to give it to the kid. That way, it is not fair if it is forceful. In the interest of sustainable development, we are looking at economizing resources—living within means that support sharing values, promote circularity, and also conserve the environment so that we can leave resources that can allow other future generations to live ably. Therefore, when the man comprehends these reasons, the two (2) stools can be used by other people, or there would be no need for the two stools, as shown in C. That way, you save a tree! In other words, we can save two (2) stools for future generations. That means the making of the two (2) stools would be postponed for the future. It is mainly about understanding, not substitution.

Case study on the National Council of Higher Education (NCHE) of Uganda

Girls' enrollment in schools has dramatically improved annually over the recent past. Legislations to educate the girl child have been passed and are in action. This has seen improvement in the enrollment of girls in secondary and tertiary institutions. That approximates to equality. Gender equality requires equal enjoyment by women and men of socially valued goods, opportunities, resources and rewards.

To create fairness, the National Council of Higher Education (NCHE) in Uganda issued a Statutory Instrument through the ministry of Education and sports to add an extra 1.5 points to all female students from the Advanced Level of education vying for university courses, especially science courses in all government universities. The assumption is that the 1.5 points are deducted from the males because it disadvantages them in a bid to create equality. This is equivalent to the process taken to create equity we see in the photo. In this case, the 1.5 points are the stool. Some men are left out so that women can fill the opportunities to create fairness because already statutes to educate the girl child are valid. In the photo above, the man's stool is provided to the kid. Gender equity is viewed as being fair to women and men. By enacting the laws to educate the girl child, the 1.5 points are present by default.

However, fairness cannot be achieved without prerequisites. Therefore, gender equality can be achieved, and we fail to achieve gender equity which is the overarching goal. It is more likely that what is done today to close the gap in gender for purposes of sustainability is more to do with enacting and enforcing laws by Acts of legislative bodies and subsequent subsidiary legislations at the expense of violating the natural law and the law of equity—the moral and reality principles which are key to the attainment of equity. This practice will not take us far. The two maxims of equity, i.e. "He who seeks equity must do equity" and "He who comes for equity must come with clean hands", are poorly assessed in the whole women empowerment strategy or campaign. Which prerequisites are considered before taking the 1.5 points from boys?

The fact that the doctrine of equity originates from the holy texts, you have to ask yourself why man dominated these holy books. Secondly, taking on a holistic view of the coexistence in society, and keeping other factors constant, specifically focusing on the statutory instrument passed in Uganda for providing women with an extra 1.5 points for admission into the university, one may ask the consideration to make this legitimate. It is rather a whole cycle of sympathy but not empathy. The consideration for the men discriminated is not mentioned anywhere in the equation. Assessments and evaluations conducted to weigh the results after the implementation of the policy show little success registered by women who scooped points from men on admission into the universities. Sometimes, the men fail them to succeed, which means men fail to understand the role of 1.5 points. If they understand the 1.5 points' role, then they would contribute to the overarching goal.

On the other hand, women also fail to understand the importance of 1.5 points. Society has not transitioned through a gradual process to fully understand women empowerment's values in the sustainability framework. It is about a woman understanding a man and a man understanding a woman. The holy texts for Abrahamic religions tell us that a woman came from the limbs of a man. What then triggers a man's errant behaviour in the modern-day? Does man understand the beauty of a woman? These are some of the questions that would be answered.

There is no evaluation of the success for the beneficiaries of the 1.5 points after graduation. There would be monitoring and evaluation programs to assess the benefits and costs of upholding the statutory instrument to continue disadvantaging men by deducting the 1.5 points. Several women fail to get jobs after school because the government has not provided a clear plan to support those women who scooped the 1.5 points from men. This would help women to be productive after school so that the resources that the government spends on them are not wasted.

Unlike the men, lots of women lack the techniques to find themselves jobs, especially in the developing economies of Africa. Africa needs people who can soldier on to survive while developing it, and many women cannot handle the hassle. These women end up getting married, and their degrees become idle. Therefore, the idea of sympathy might not work in the long run! We need to be wise enough to make holistic decisions that contribute to a sustainable future. I can hardly find girls I studied with in hardcore engineering practice; reality comes in driven by instincts. Many engineering jobs call for reliability as a practitioner, and most women can hardly meet the demands. Neuroticism, conscientiousness, and openness to experience are traits in which women cannot naturally compete with men even if you add extra points—and many jobs in engineering, science, mining, and construction call for a unique grade in these attributes. So, the whole point is that we need to evaluate and reevaluate decisions over and over again to promote sustainability.

Evaluation of the beneficiaries' performance after school would be a must. Law can hardly treat or amend personality disorders that can either emanate from birth or are behaviorally learnt. We have caused so many narcissistic and paranoid personality disorders by plainly fixing legislations without conducting a scientific dig into the remedies. Today, very few issues that are explainable in humanistic terms lack a corresponding scientific explanation. The existing majority of legislations in Africa have a crisis when conducted by a set hypothesis. Most items are copied from elsewhere and do not meet the needs of the African child. The African child is the null hypothesis, but interestingly, a few of the many legislations are enacted by assuming a western child as the null hypothesis. The copy and paste syndrome takes us nowhere!

The United Nations Human Rights Council promotes affirmative action. For example, Article 21(4) of Uganda's constitution (1995 as amended) provides for equality and freedom from discrimination by embodying the concept of affirmative action, positive discrimination in which laws and policies can be put in place to uplift the status of groups of persons that have traditionally been marginalized. Affirmative action seems to pay little attention to the individual differences of the marginalized groups. Standardized tests must be administered before generalizing and drawing deductive inferences. We throw too much emotional garbage to the world without administering such tests, thinking we are creating equality equity. Although the need for affirmative action is obvious, ruling out a sensitive Act or a statutory instrument, most especially one which affects human behaviours and attitudes, needs checks and balances prior and must be guided by a set hypothesis.

Humanistic viewers claim that all men and women have the potential for healthy and creative growth and are guided by their internal experience rather than external reality. To understand another person, one needs to suppress judgment temporarily and see things as they see them. Understanding this phenomenon shows that you might not need an extra 1.5 points granted without a sound consideration regarding the discriminated person or group. The said marginalized group had not been voluntarily discriminated against or marginalized at some point. Nature has its way of working out coexistence. Without sound consideration before issuing affirmative policies, men are at risk of being marginalized in the long run. Just like what Lucky Dube said in his Affirmative Action song lyrics, "We are tired of people who think that affirmative action is the way out. And, is another way of putting puppets where they do not belong." In this context, therefore, conformists to gender parity need to revise their theories of positive discrimination.

For a society listening to the voice of reason, human sense of right and wrong, or Natural Law, equity can never be pushed for because the maxims of equity are very clear. The process of attaining equity drafted following principal legislation is highly likely to require little review than one decided upon through subsidiary legislation. It is better to stop at providing stools as shown in the photograph, and both moral and reality principles trigger society to create fairness to have the kid watch the goat race. The man could lift the kid following the correct moral principles. Extra free points are dangerous to our communities. If it is not disabilities, personality disorders, or unique African attitude disorder (UAAD), the faculties of both gender were clearly delineated and are both powerful in their way.

Equality, as defined by developmental agencies, has a long way to defeat instincts. New instincts can grow but cannot erase/repress original instincts completely. A mind shaped and prepared to think along a well-defined path intuitively might be difficult to readjust to cope with what you define as the right. Since early experiences shape our core beliefs and innate predispositions to act differently to give us our unique attitudes towards attitude pieces, the process adopted by the developmental agencies ought to get it right from the bottom—and they need to be very sure since they are creating a new world amidst threats of climate change and natural resources exhaustion. This natural or intuitive way of acting and thinking shaped by cultures and society in which we live calls for an early readjustment in offspring understanding of equality as defined by developmental agencies. We need an education that helps shape one's thinking objectively, articulate ideas well, and make the world a better place to live through innovations. For sustainability purposes, it does not kill innate predispositions, characters, and attitudes.

The Other Side of Women Empowerment

Everyone understands the need for women empowerment in the abstract, but people are creatures of habit on a day-to-day level. A Christian will say, "I am already empowered by the grace of God." We have not achieved genuine women empowerment in many African states, with a few empowered women failing to empower others. Some politically empowered women cannot talk in the interest of the masses, and they are more on selfish gains such as complaining about increased salaries and allowances.

I was surprised when a prominent lawyer whispered to her colleague who was breastfeeding her three-week-old and said, "Why don't you pump and store breast milk in the refrigerator? The housemaid will feed the baby. You have to go back to work." Empowered women should be able to stand and advocate for enough maternity leave to breastfeed their babies well. However, they spend more time on things that do not matter, contrary to why they are empowered and elected to represent the masses. Ideally, a baby should be breastfed for about 1-2 years. A breast pump helps express breast milk and feed the baby while the mother is away from the baby. However, it should not be relied on as an alternative to normal breastfeeding. In support of cultural relativism, many of Africa's cultures promote politeness, and a review of technologies before they are permitted in the land must be done. That would contribute to sustainability.

Women resort to canned milk for their babies, forgetting the danger of over-reliance on processed foods in developing countries where corruption has infiltrated almost everything. You should breastfeed your baby than providing canned milk which you are not sure whether the producer got a production license in a proper route. For example, some countries in the Nile Basin are good at corruption. There is a risk in taking things to do with health and safety for granted in such countries. Health and safety should be taken very seriously in developing countries because treating infections from substandard products is very costly.

The empowerment of women is sometimes, if not many times, vaguely campaigned. Women and girls continue to be sexually abused worldwide—in offices and homes, and no immediate laws, hotlines, websites, smartphone applications are formulated to report and monitor such abuses, especially in developing countries. The women sexual harassment vice has taken on many higher institutions of learning in Africa, with sex-for-marks making the order of the day. Although some women around the world are using the #MeToo hashtag on social media to share their stories of sexual assault and harassment, I find this not enough. Today, with the alarming levels of unemployment, women are secretly sexually abused before getting/landing their dream jobs, and no sound instruments have been formulated to curb culprits in many parts of the developing world. Men are stopping their wives from working—preferring stay home moms because it has become the order of the day to abuse women sexually. Women suffer sexual abuse silently. In my opinion, this is something I would gear all efforts to fight. I believe these things matter to be tackled for genuine women empowerment to prove fruitful.

Women empowered society would ideally refer to a society that has achieved progress, say towards;

 a) Equality in gender enrolment for education,
 b) Equal access to primary education between girls and boys,
 c) Equal access to jobs,
 d) Women and girls safe from suffering discrimination and violence, etc.,

Theoretically, gender equality is a fundamental human right and a necessary foundation for a peaceful, prosperous, and sustainable society. According to developmental agencies, providing women and girls with equal access to education, health care, decent work, and representation in political and economic decision-making processes will fuel sustainable economies and benefit societies and humanity at large. But the big question remains how to do it without violating family values and cultural norms. The alarming rates at which divorces are happening in the western world reflect the growing intolerance among people, *intense individuality* and a complete disregard and apathy for the feelings of others. Many countries worldwide face the same challenge, with many marriages breaking beyond reconciliation and many marriages just festering like a wound. We need functioning families and a world free of violence against women and children, men taking on their responsibilities, and women contributing to societal activities and women voices to count. All these should be planned whilst upholding family values as the number one priority.

In my society, I have come across many powerful women living as single mothers. Others are divorced. You can look around your neighbourhood and make an evaluation as well. Some of these women are politicians, others are rich women, while the majority are highly educated. Some others are famous women. Many powerful women in Africa, especially music artists and politicians, are separated or divorced or live single lives. When you are contravening against what nature holds, cogitate well enough before you advocate for change because it looks easy to understand in the abstract but complex in the details. Changing what nature holds is a delicate field that needs to be handled with research and integrity.

It would help if you created performing models that are all-round inclusive in whatever you think and do. Therefore, the topic of women empowerment is more to do with educating a girl child with an education that really matters and promotion based on merit. Gender equality is idealistic and not possible. Upholding human rights is what is possible. The term gender refers to the economic, social, and cultural attributes and opportunities associated with being male or female. Such bold words as *"gender equality"* might be dropped because they are heavy and confusing to the African masses. The phrase "gender equality" is too summarized, and some people misunderstand the primary goal of equality programs. We should adopt *"equal opportunities for gender."*

For example, we cannot equate cultural attributes. We equate opportunities for cultural attributes. I believe in taming the man of greed through lawful innovations as the number one technique. Trying to reclaim the position of women, we ought to make men the control experiment. I believe in merit promotion of the girl child or women. Merit promoted women are admirable. They tend to be talented, hardworking and excellence is part of their life. Therefore, merit promotion that is not biased is the way to go because there is danger in empowering what nature did not. This danger must be evaluated properly. There are women with outstanding capabilities worth recognition. But the massive assumption or belief in women substituting for men's roles and vice-versa is false. I believe in a society that respects the woman, makes a woman's voice count, gives respect to culture, allows women leadership, educates the girl child and upholds human rights with proper policies to safeguard family values at large—because a healthy family is a springboard for sustainable social transformation.

In many cultures, it is a tradition for the man to propose to the woman directly while genuflecting in front of her. On the face of it, giving a woman an occasion to ask a man to wed would seem an empowering moment. But not everyone sees it that way. Back in the day, women who asked men to marry were portrayed as ugly, mannish, crass or desperate. The empowerment of women today might be understood this way because most of the objectives are vested in the term "gender equality". In Scotland and Ireland, the 29th of February in a leap year is the day when a woman can propose to her partner. This is a cultural norm. Finland has the same custom, with the addition that a man rejecting such a proposal is expected to buy his suitor enough cloth for a skirt as compensation. Why this compensation does not apply either way for gender equality to be more amplified remains unexplained. When uttered by a man, the words "will you marry me" serve to signal a tradition that is both widely accepted. The fact that women are still finding it difficult to propose to men signals a lot when the subject of women empowerment is to be effectively and purposefully campaigned.

Up to now, I still question why conventional religions still find it hard to emancipate women and make them freer to become church magistrates or sheikhs. The twelve disciples of Jesus Christ were all men, yet he is believed to be one of the great moral teachers of all time. One who has not got me right on this point would say that the long distances Jesus and his disciples traversed were the reason for not including women as disciples. As Africans, if we are initiating a new order of things, let us make it a gentle improvement with all-round inclusion, consultation and proper research but not transform so fast. There is a danger, especially where the illusion of knowledge substitutes ignorance.

Queen Elizabeth I (1533–1603) once said, "I rather be a beggar and single than a queen and married."[108] The moment a woman views herself in a queenly manner, woes will start in the family because the man will try to resist her growing powers to retract his position. This reminds me of a famous adage: behind every successful man, there is a woman, and behind every successful woman, there is a scared man. This adage should be explored more, but I somehow believe in its truthfulness to some extent. Women empowerment is misinterpreted as women equaling to men extending it to families. The Queen's statement partially explains why many women politicians, wealthy women, and other powerful women live single lives or divorced. Women empowerment should be explicitly taught so that people know its overarching goals that aim for sustainable development.

I have seen a colleague crying out so bitterly, saying, "I'm the one who initiated everything for her. The first time she ran for a political office, I funded her campaigns, and now she cannot listen to my advice. She is filing for divorce." If you do not take time to study your spouse very well, it is inevitable that you will fall victim to such circumstances. Unless you lay a strong foundation for the family institution, you are left to harvest nothing. As a man, I rather learn through the misfortunes of others than my own. Here, my colleague never created an enabling environment for his spouse but surrendered his power.

As I mentioned earlier, the mistake we are making in our education system is teaching many things that do not really matter. The things that matter are not mentioned anywhere say; happiness, power, families, patriotism, and purposeful living. That is why we have child marriages, graduates wedding so quickly in 1 or 2 months after school without gaining financial and economic freedoms first. These marriages are more of wildcats. How prepared are such graduates for marriage considering the fact that schools do not teach anything about marriage and marriage is a contract? At times dodging to take sufficient time for premarital counselling and premarital preparation before entering a marriage is the root cause of breaking marriages.

To get committed to anything for a lifetime ideally requires a considerable amount of time invested in planning and making preparations. On average, one spends 20-23 years in school. When they come out, they require between 3-6 years of working experience to master their work so that they become professionally accredited if needed, provided they demonstrate competency to meet certain attributes required by the state. Why is family and marriage institution not given enough attention yet it is an institution that requires too much discipline and self-examination?

The Ancient and Today's Global Village: Women Empowerment and Relationships

Everything that was done in the ancient cultures to restrict women mobility was at times done in good faith to maintain relationships forever—to raise children with family values. Except in the instances where

---

[108] Elizabeth was a queen for England, Wales and Ireland. She never got married and that was the secret for her great success.

the women were debarred from eating certain foods, denying them access to education and violating their human rights such as freedom of expression—that was really bad. However, a relationship where everyone believes can do without the other, i.e. *intense individuality*, cannot last. A small mistake escalates to a huge one because of ego problems caused by inflated self-esteem – *intense individuality*.

The subject of power is a delicate one and has to be approached with integrity, not sympathy. It should be approached with empathy. One thing we have failed to master is how to attract, gain and maintain power whilst elsewhere people seem to understand it the most, and that is why in most cases, they prefer giving out a fish to teaching how to fish. When one gets some power, they will always yearn for more. It is advisable to empower cautiously and wisely because many times, people are empowered and turn against their supporters and the people who empowered or uplifted them—not everyone remains loyal.

We should stop polishing and sugarcoating things that should not be. We need to understand that the trend is shifting—lasting relationships are no longer hinged on true consummate love for one another. We have more reactive love characterized by extravagant showiness or compulsion. Relationships are no longer much hinged on faith, unlike before. This is because of the developments a human has had with the environment, i.e. globalization and industrialization. They are more of commitment or empty relationships, but very few intimate relationships exist. We have more empty relationships because of the technology that is slowly making it look like having property is everything. Liberalism or dynamism of the world today is shaping marriage and family trends to incline materialistically.

In this era, when one does things out of too much love or emotional attachment, in many cases, they end up making a lot of mistakes. Today, lasting relationships are hinged on purpose or consideration, which might even be outside the love domain. Either one spouse sees purpose in the other, or it is two-way. Without a sound consideration, today's love is easily shaken by many external forces. But in a situation where a relationship is believed to be hinged on love alone and no intended or immediate purpose or promise between each other, do not expect it to last in this era—that was for back in the days.

In a consideration, there should be one willing to make an offer, to propose, and the offeree evaluates the offer against set attributes. In the past, such attributes were noncompetitive and incomparable due to the communication challenges and the like. As creatures of habit, let us not be chewed up with deception; none will accept your worthless offer. Looking attractive, decent, and gentleman is not a promise worth enough to package it as the only consideration to earn you a long-lasting consummate love relationship. It must be associated and paired conditionally with a materialistic consideration to elicit a conditional response in the form of a relationship. It must be supplemented with tangible benefits to be more amplified—and that is the model roadmap for sustainable love in the 4th industrial revolution. As a man or a woman, you should learn to play your cards right because the 21st century is not a joke because of the false empowerment of the previously marginalized groups.

What Influences our actions in the 21st Century Relationships?

Many people do not do things because they wish to do them. Many people are not employed in jobs that suit their skills, competencies, and capabilities but are into those jobs because that is what is available for them to do to earn a living. However, if you asked them what they would wish to do, they would point somewhere else. What keeps them in those jobs? The answer is fear of failure to survive and to be able to meet their needs. As a matter of fact, many people are sitting on their talents simply because they are wrongly positioned in jobs because they have to earn a living and have no alternative.

Many people are getting married not because they are following faith, cultural or religious norms but rather get married for showing off in the white gowns. People are holding onto relationships not because they found the right partners but because of the consequences of losing their partners, and maybe because partners can solve their problems. People do not commit crimes because they are too moral but fear the consequences of committing crimes. People fear more of the consequences of committing a crime but not the act of committing the crime.

Similarly, the trend has shifted; lots of people stick to their partners for a more important purpose other than love. Therefore, in the modern world where most marriages are a door-in-the-face, anything that disrupts today's families should not be allowed to thrive. The underlying reason is that tying a knot increases the likelihood of the partner agreeing to a second, more reasonable request, more than if that same request is made in isolation and without marriage coming first. Following this narrative, we need explicit women empowerment that upholds the dignity of a man and a woman in society. Empowerment of women ought to be done following interests but not positions. The interests of women empowerment are clear—taming the man, for example, by understanding the overarching goals for shared prosperity, equal opportunities, stopping gender-related violence, freedom of expression and women voices to count, and etcetera.

A man who has been brought up morally and well-groomed by his parents, particularly the mother, would ideally possess the character to transfer this love to his wife. There is no way an understanding, moral and decent man would wish to have an oppressive and tyrannical dominance over his wife. An understanding man would wish to provide room for his wife to nurture the children in freedom. He would wish her the best of the best because he has witnessed her mother's role in his life. He would wish to see shared prosperity in his family. The tendency of men behaving like animals causing too much domestic violence and selfishness is rooted back in the families where they grow from. All problems are created by men failing to play their part right as the family leader, leaving mothers with mixed thoughts on how to raise children.

As a result of fathers failing to act like real men, most mothers become short-sighted and disloyal to the nation, making them think about themselves alone and forget to think about their daughters-in-law. To iron out family distortions, all people should be supportive and wish the neighbours good. The entire logic is vested in the family as a production unit to promote peace and freedom in the hearts of men in their infancy, childhood and youthful stages before letting them to the world. We should all look at peace as a priority in everything. When things go bizarre, look left and right but do not dismantle what nature holds out of anger. You cannot play evil with evil, and you think you are creating peace. Too much domestic violence and suppression of women has let them think in fighting for positions which is false. The best approach is to fight for your interests as women. The justification of this behaviour is exhibited in the fact that most women in leadership forget the reasons they rise to the top and instead turn against their husbands.

What do Equal Opportunities Mean? What is the implication of equal opportunities?

Equal opportunities should ideally mean to allow women to compete with men on merit but not bias the race with things like a woman should be given extra points. Women ought to be empathetically recognized for their outstanding skills, talents, competencies and capabilities but not out of sympathy. Women need an enabling environment to show their worth. Things like they are only men here meeting the criteria, so any woman around is welcome to fill this space are false.

In both my college school and engineering class, there were lots of girls who performed better than me and needed no extra points. In fact, many. If women are weak, then weakness should not be transformed into strength. There is danger in this. Women's empowerment is misinterpreted as fighting for positions leading to an impression like gender substitutions in families and at the workplace—as far as roles and responsibilities are concerned. That is why many empowered women—politicians, technocrats, rich, etcetera, cannot contribute tirelessly to make the women empowered community to grow day and night for good reasons. They are vocal when bad reasons are tabled. For example, when things like, "I am not a marriage material" are discussed. They instead fight their husbands. I am not stating this out of research results, but when I look around my community, I spot a growing number of such women who claim to be empowered. It is actually more men who tirelessly support the cause of uplifting more women. Several uplifted women instead become too selfish and forget the overarching goal of why they were empowered

A large number of empowered women are egoistic. This sounds like a bias or a global statement until when you experience it. Women ought to be simplistic, lovely and dependable for a family and marriage to thrive—coming from a cultural and religious perspective. Whether a woman is a minister, the husband shall remain the team leader in the family but not let a woman extend ministerial powers to the family because it is natural or ritual for a man to lead a family unless otherwise advised. Unless otherwise proved scientifically, many marriages of falsely empowered women will keep festering like a wound. Unless you are a highly emotionally competent man and you take the credit for it, a more powerful woman than you is hard to negotiate with. As you know, the truth is always hard to talk about in public—people tend to cover it up with so many lies. The truth will remain.

The tendency of women trying to lead in families and being non-submissive to their husbands are due to egoistic reasons that breed envy in men trying to desist women growing powers to retract their real positions as men—and never undermine envy; it is the greatest disorder of the soul. **Note:** empowered women suffer egoistically while their men suffer from envy, and this breaks the marriage. The solution lies in understanding so that appropriate mechanisms are incorporated in the strategies that uplift women.

Many African cultures have a belief that women must be submissive to the man, although it has been challenged by modernity. I also discourage over-submission but to what extent are we prepared for the transition? Sometimes, an empowered woman is too busy and often may deny conjugal rights and consummation to her husband because of being overworked during the day and fulfills her obligations in quarters, which makes marriages fester like wounds. This might precipitate infidelity. *Radically empowered women* tend to cause disequilibrium of the triangular theory of love developed by Prof. Robert Sternberg in the USA.[109] Instead of working for consummate love, they are triggered to incline towards commitment love.

Women empowerment is similar to capacity building in firms and organizations. The staff are empowered to improve their competency levels, but this does not mean that after acquiring more skills and knowledge, they shall become adamant about following work ethics and the structure or failing to follow instructions from their bosses. Women empowerment is more or less the same. It is meant to empower the smallest and weakest woman at the grassroots to get access to education, *have equal opportunities as men,* be safe from domestic violence, etcetera. However, it does not mean a woman to turn against the core values of family principles. As a Christian and true African, who follows the bible, the bible says man shall be the leader of the family, and many African cultures have by default made a man the leader of the family—we need to model policies that are not contradictory with our cultural norms and religious teachings. Let us find a meeting point for sustainable development, reduce divorce rates, and make women's voices count too through the appropriate, all-round education that matters for the girl child. I feel something is lacking in the women empowerment campaign material.

Youth Empowerment and Sustainable Development

Throughout history, the youth have caused many revolutions. The youth spearheaded the most notable French revolution (1788–1799). Napoleon Bonaparte (1769–1821) became Emperor of the French in 1804 when he was 35 years old. The youth have been at the forefront of causing revolutions in many parts of the world. However, the 21st Century African youth are facing several distractions precipitated by the ICT developments. Such kinds of distractions include sports gambling, western football mania, and social media networks. Social media networks have eased information flow and accelerated the ease of doing business for small to medium enterprises. However, many youths spend much time on social media gossiping instead of utilizing the empowerment opportunity that the networks present. On the other hand, sports betting, especially on western football, has engulfed African youth. Therefore, they are left with minimal time to meditate about the state of affairs of their countries.

The African Youth Charter developed by AU in 2006 prescribes the responsibilities to member states to develop the youth. Africa's vibrant and highly entrepreneurial youth constitutes about 65% of Africa's population. Ever since the Charter came into force, many African governments have failed to empower the youth satisfactorily. The following summarized key points are obtained from the Charter:

- The African Youth Charter provides the Governments, Youth, Civil Society and International Partners with a continental framework, which underlines to the rights, duties and freedoms of youth.
- The African Youth Charter paves the way for the development of national programmes and strategic plans for their empowerment

---

[109] Robert Sternberg's triangular theory of love proposes that love is composed of three distinct but interrelated components: intimacy, passion, and decision/commitment. Therefore, consummate love = intimacy + passion + commitment. In many times, radically empowered women distort this equation.

- The African Youth Charter is to ensure the constructive involvement of Youth in the development agenda of Africa and their effective participation in the debates and decision-making processes in the development of the continent.

- The African Youth Charter provides important guidelines and responsibilities of Member States for the empowerment of Youth in key strategic areas, namely Education and Skills Development, Poverty Eradication and Socio-economic Integration of Youth, Sustainable Livelihoods and Youth Employment, Health, Peace and Security, Law Enforcement, *Sustainable Development* and Protection of the Environment."

===== The African Youth Charter, 2006 ====

The empowerment of the youth should be one of the cornerstones of Africa's sustainability programmes. Unfortunately, little progress has been achieved in this area because of politics of envy, selfishness, and greed. By 2019, The Youth Charter was ratified by over 39 African countries. Many African leaders continue to discriminate against the youths on the grounds of where they come from—the ethnic backgrounds, although this kind of discrimination is often covert. The education system of many countries remains fixated in colonial systems, and youth unemployment is on the rise each year that passes.

It is still a challenge to have all-round inclusive platforms for the youth and elderly across many African countries. The elders are still adamant about embracing the youth in decision-making processes wholly. Elsewhere in the world, the youth have been provided with opportunities and practical solutions to forge their case and contribute to the development of their countries. In Africa, this is still a dream. It is still theoretical since the continent is still largely governed by guerilla war veterans who find it inappropriate to entrust decision-making to the youth. This definitely impacts the continent's future because of the high-level advancement in ICT and associated technologies globally. As a race, we risk lagging forever. We need the young, hopeful, and enthusiastic youth to drive decisions that stimulate growth.

The African leaders seem to have the will to ratify the Charter, but action has never been easy. The Charter is elaborate and explicit since it provides the framework and guidelines to have inclusive and diversified platforms that enable the youth to discover their full potential. However, the *unique African attitude disorder (UAAD)* cannot fail African leaders to look outside Africa when it comes to sourcing who can deliver instead of providing quality education and skills development in Africa's youth networks.[110] And this is due to African leaders hitting a crisis as a result of a fixation caused by colonial wounding.

Therefore, the solution to realising what The African Youth Charter stipulates is to have many elite youths get involved in activities that promote the youth's voice without waiting for African leaders to design youth's programmes. The reason is that many African governments design programmes for the youth that do not explicitly empower the youth to realize their full potential for reasons outlined earlier. Therefore, patriotic youth have to exercise their minds to think at *a higher level of consciousness* to penetrate the government systems and forge an unselfish path that includes the *next youth generations.*

---

[110] See p. 203, §4.

Conclusion

Social transformation calls for the empowerment of women, mothers, and youth in a correct manner. We need to keep women's interests as a matter of fact but not a fight. Raising their status by; educating them; raising their awareness; financial inclusion; improving their literacy, and proper training to sustain progress. However, the empowerment should not be at the expense of families, cultural values, faiths, and marginalization of men. Otherwise, where families break and children grow like wild cats or field mice, this will not lead to sustainable development. We do not need to create a generation of intense individuality in the pursuit of development. Intense individuality can become a nuisance, and a woman looks for spermatozoa from the laboratory to fertilize her ovum, only to produce offspring lacking identity. A balance has to be struck when funding empowerment campaigns and preparation for empowerment campaigns. In my view, women empowerment campaigns should be identified as "repowering campaigns." If not, then mothers' empowerment serves a better purpose/meaning than women empowerment. The program must be designed in a well psychologically built framework.

When the $100m fund goes to repowering women, another $100m funds should go to the preparation to repower women or empower mothers. Another $100m fund goes to preparing men to receive empowered women. In order to ensure the stability of marital life, which is the foundation of great societal success, as a springboard for socioeconomic transformation and the balanced development of our children, repowering/empowering preparations and counselling programs should be equally funded.

Overgeneralization will backfire in the long term. Some indicators are already manifesting through alarming divorce and separation rates in high-income countries. Since Africa can still plan for sustainable, inclusive development, our values, beliefs, and customs must be respected. This way, we shall forge our case to tackle challenges. In the same way, I wish to have both cultural and religious values and customs not swayed by the whim of the 21st Century technological revolution.

Women. Youth. Repowerment. Empowerment

Chapter Seven: Industrialization and Globalization

"Where globalization means, as it so often does, that the rich and powerful now have new means to further enrich and empower themselves at the cost of the poorer and weaker, we have a responsibility to protest in the name of universal freedom."[111]

=== *Nelson Mandela (1918 –2013)* ===

Chapter Organization

Quick Insights

Brief History of Economics

LDCs and Factors of Production Interpretation to Guide Decisions

How Should We Raise Capital?

Local Investors' Capacity and Capital Raising in African Economies

Discussion on Individualism and Collectivism in Relation to Capitalism, Socialism, and Communism in the African Context

Africa's Social and Structural Transformation in the Face of Globalization

Manufacturing share of GDP in Developing African countries

Deindustrialization in Poor African Countries

Protectionism and Globalization: Will Africa manage?

Structural Transformation and Sustainable Industrialization

Public Contracts Financing and Foreign Direct Investment Traps in the Face of Globalization

Analyzing the Asian Giant's Typical Turnkey Construction Project Loaned to Africa

- What are some of the Effects of The Toll Road FDI Project on the Host African Country?
- What are some of the Effects of The Toll Road FDI Project on Home Country?
- Conclusion on the Toll Road Project

The Asian Giant's going Global Framework and FDI in Africa's Infrastructure: The Big Picture

What about when the Asian giant does nothing?

Way forward on Asian giant's FDI in infrastructure

Conclusion

---

[111] Speech on receiving the Freedom Award from the National Civil Rights Museum (USA, November, 2000).

The planet earth is estimated to be about 4.54 billion years old.[112] The world has grown and transformed through stages spanning millions of years before the Christian, Jewish and Islamic calendars. The most popular calendars are the Gregorian calendar and Julian calendar, both versions of the Christian calendar. Scientists predict the universe to have existed billions of years ago. The world transformed through civilizations and revolutions spanning from when life began somewhere in East Africa.

Before 100BC, information was passed orally in many African territories. The black man was among the earliest humans that lived, according to Charles Darwin and Dr Leakay Louis. The archaeological studies that Louis and Charles conducted at Olduvai George in Tanzania, East Africa, leading to the discovery of Zinjanthropus, provide insight into a black human's existence very long ago. In Ethiopia, the famous Lucy was discovered by archaeologists at Hadar.[113] These two humans are believed to have lived between four million to one million years ago. Archaeologists have laboured to explain that Zinjanthropus and Lucy belonged to the family of Hominidae, which includes human and human-like species. Therefore, they were not apes because the fossilized footprints near Olduvai George in Tanzania indicate that hominids walked upright. This background provided by archaeologists points out Africa's position in the existence of humanity.

Humans have transformed from ancient civilizations and through several revolutions to improve their wellbeing and the social structure. From hunting, gathering lifestyle, and eating fruits to farming, humans have come a long way. In ancient civilizations, humans invented symbolic communication systems, urban development, social stratification and domination over the natural environment. At some point in time, humans lived in small isolated groups. Along the way, humans found it helpful to live in more significant communities which shared a common purpose and mutual dependency. With time, such communities expanded to turn into civilizations. Around those ancient times, humans could live in a social system characterized by kings, emperors, chiefs and many other kinds of rulers as the supreme command in the societal structure.

According to archaeologists, Africa is the origin of man, about 4-5 million years ago. The last ice age ended 11,700 years ago. It is believed that all other races originated from Africa and lost their pigmentation due to living in cold climates. Not until about 100,000 years ago, it is believed that people inhabited only Africa. The North of the Globe being too cold, people could not live there.

The world has gone through civilizations, and the most notable ones include Minoan civilization (c. 2700 to c. 1450 BC), Mycenaean civilization (1600 – 1100BC), Ancient Greek Civilization, Ancient Egyptian civilization and Chinese civilizations. One of the fascinating ancient civilizations worth noting as an African is a Minoan civilization. Tracing back to about 1500BC, the Romans and Minoans moved water

---

[112] "Age of the Earth," National Geographic Society, accessed August 24th 2021, https://www.nationalgeographic.org/topics/resource-library-age-earth/?q=&page=1&per_page=25.

[113] Judith G. Coffin, Robert C. Stacey, Robert E. Learner, and Meacham Standish, *Western civilizations, 14th Edition*. New York: W. W. Norton & Company, Inc., 2002.

and had indoor plumbing in their urban centres. Sub-Saharan Africans should note that in the 21st century, they still need to hire foreign experts to move water!

The Egyptian civilization, which is one of the earliest civilizations, started around 3000BC. It is upon this background that Africa is believed to be the pioneer of civilization. Ancient Civilization was about a shift from living in isolated groups, tiny in size, to organized bigger communities that shared values, interdependencies, and customs. It was characterized by hierarchical social classes with a ruling elite and subordinate urban and rural populations. Over time, as humans searched for knowledge, the improvement in social structures and systems slowly improved how life was perceived in the communities.

It was against this sociopolitical philosophy embedded in societal ideologies that led to modern civilizations and later cultivated an atmosphere for revolutions. Through revolutions, humans understood "power" a little better and how delicate it is. Humans were able to philosophize theories and techniques of governance. The continued search for knowledge led man to discover more about his supremacy over other creatures and subsequently dominated the natural environment. Over time, humans found power to be the ultimate driving factor for life. That is the primary reason the world has undergone remarkable insurgencies spreading from 2700BC to date—in the form of revolutions across the globe. These revolutions take two dimensions, i.e. political revolutions and social revolutions.

Political revolutions have shaped the world to a greater extent more than social revolutions. They have been more pronounced in history tracing many years ago, as the ancient Greek philosopher Aristotle (384–322 BC) describes in his book, V of the Politics. In political science, a revolution may be referred to as a period where people feel oppressed or perceive inadequacy in the political systems and decide to revolt against the government, usually bringing about a sudden transformation in either political, social or economic spheres. On the other side, social revolutions transform the societal structure and impact the nature of society in terms of culture, philosophy, and technology.

In the interest of sustainable development, social revolutions in the modern era are discussed, focusing on the western world. I did this to analyze why Africa, which had one of the great civilizations, is still underdeveloped. Life is believed to have begun in East Africa, but the continent lags in socio-economic development.

By focusing on the UN SDGs, specifically Number 9: Industry, innovation, and infrastructure, Africa's position would be reclaimed. This chapter presents the analysis of the problem and recommendations *contributing* to UN SDG No. 9 while developing Africa.

The UN Sustainable Development Goals are the blueprint for achieving a better and more sustainable future for all. The world has gone through several social revolutions in both the pre-modern and modern eras. The modern era in the western world consisted of the following social revolutions: the scientific revolution, the agricultural revolution, the industrial revolution, and the scientific-technical revolution.

The Scientific Revolution

16th Century

The scientific revolution is believed to have started in Europe. This followed the book published in 1543 by Nicolaus Copernicus (1473 – 1543) to give an alternative universe model. Prior to the publication of the De revolutionibus orbium coelestium (On the Revolutions of the Heavenly Spheres) by Nicolaus, Claudius Ptolemy's geocentric system view of the universe was considered valid throughout ancient times.[114] The study of nature with a deeper understanding of the universe through mathematics, chemistry, astronomy and biology changed people's views. Before the scientific revolution, every understanding of nature was held in philosophy. Before the growth of science, people looked up to the church and believed all teachings and beliefs. There was rapid progress in the accumulation of knowledge in the 17th century, leading to many scientific discoveries in Europe. Science, therefore, became an autonomous discipline, distinct from both philosophy and technology. In 1687, Sir Isaac Newton published "Philosophiæ Naturalis Principia Mathematica", often referred to as "Principia". Newton's publication stated the Laws of motion, the law of gravitation, and the derivation of Kepler's laws of planetary motion. Kepler had obtained planetary motion laws empirically, which Newton improved in his publication. The scientific revolution is believed to have ended following Isaac Newton's publication of 'Principia'.

Agricultural Revolution

(1600–1740)

This was a period of significant agricultural development marked by new farming techniques and inventions that led to a massive increase in food production. Historians report two agricultural revolutions in history. The first one is reported to have taken place around 10,000BC and was marked by the transition from a hunting-and-gathering society to one based on stationary farming. The second agricultural revolution took place between the 17th and 19th Centuries when European agriculture shifted from the rudimentary techniques of the past to more advanced techniques. The second agricultural revolution began in Great Britain around the 18th Century primarily due to increases in labour and land productivity between the middle of the 17th and late 19th centuries. There was a slight reduction in labour-intensive farming, and production increased due to the perfection of the horse-drawn seed press. This was associated with the enclosure laws enacted to limit the common land available to small farmers in the middle of the 18th century. This enabled exclusive ownership of land. The boost in livestock significantly changed the diet of much of Europe, which led to a healthier population in many European countries. The population of Great Britain alone rose from about 5.5 million at the start of the 18th Century to over 9 million by the end of the 18th Century. Other significant developments that made it possible for increased agricultural productivity included increased farm size, selective breeding, improved infrastructure such as roads, railways and canals, Norfolk four-course crop rotation to turnips and clover in place of fallow and technological advancement in plough using fewer oxen or horses.

---

[114] Claudius Ptolemy was born in Egypt in 100AD when it was part of the Roman Empire. He was a mathematician, geographer and astronomer and produced several important, ancient manuscripts. Ptolemy died in Alexandria in 186AD.

Industrial Revolution

(1780–1840)

Not until the middle years of the 18th Century, workplaces in Europe, especially Great Britain and across the globe, were characterized by artisan's shops and peasant's cottages. Several communities across the globe were agrarian societies, solely relying on producing and maintaining crops and farmland. Around 1780, near the end of the 18th Century, the industrial revolution emerged, initiated by the improvement in the steam engine in England in 1765. The steam engine was invented to pump out water that regularly flooded the coal mines.

The boost in economic activities started as early as 16th Century leading to the industrial revolution. Social scientists continuously debate the causes and stimuli of the industrial revolution's inventions because it is regarded as a technological expansion.

The industrial revolution involved the transformation of technology resting heavily on human and animal labour into a technology characterized by machines. Along with this came the transition from heavy reliance on agricultural production to a reliance on the manufacture of goods for sale in the context of a factory system. The industrial revolution was, at the bottom, a revolution in technology; nevertheless, it created new and profound changes in the structure and superstructures of the new society. Wood, the energy base of the medieval way of life, became increasingly scarce. The subsequent search for alternatives finally led to the replacement of wood with coal. The move to an economy based on coal changed the entire way of organizing life in Western Europe.

Other notable revolutions include the Technical revolution (or Second Industrial Revolution) (1870–1920), Scientific-technical revolution (1940–1970), Information and telecommunications revolution (1985–present), and the Fourth Industrial Revolution (4IR) (21st Century).

A good question to ask is: What were Africans doing throughout the revolutions listed above?

Brief History of Economics

In 1776, Adam Smith (1723–1790) published a book, "The Wealth of Nations, " marking the beginning of classical economics. The early work on economics rotated around the *labour theory of value* or simply *the theory of value.* Adam Smith, a Scottish social philosopher, was not the first to appreciate how economies function. However, he is believed to have contributed a more convincing explanation of the theory of value in his 1776 publication. He followed and critiqued several theories posed by notable philosophers, economists, and theologians such as St. Thomas Aquinas, William Petty, and William Stanley, among others. Adam Smith's 1776 publication followed the mercantilists' economic thoughts that had dominated the period from 1500 – 1750, which were instrumental in the political economy of nation-states building.

Today, economics is considered a science because it uses some kind of experiments and observations of how economies function under unique circumstances. It is basically concerned with how goods and services are produced and consumed in an economy and beyond. Economics studies in detail the factors of production and how scarce resources can be optimally utilized to meet the demand within an economy and across borders. However, the fact that economics does not hold repeated experiments and strict verifications before theories and principles are ruled out differs from natural sciences. In scientific facts, observations and repeated experiments are performed in a laboratory, and proofs are validated or disputed before results are declared scientific facts. Therefore, economics as a science is tenuous and heavily relies on different schools of thought, with theoretical forecasting, scientific observation, and deduction, especially at a macro level and not simply individual consumers and producers. This is the reason why George Bernard Shaw (1856–1950), who was an Irish playwright and a political activist, benchmarked to say, "If all the *economists* were laid end to end, they would never reach a conclusion."

What does the labour theory of value hold? And what was special about it in the 17th, 18th, and 19th centuries? Why did it trigger economics to become an exciting subject in addition to natural sciences considering success as value-added in a specified time?[115] Europeans registered unimaginable success in those centuries brought by the agricultural and industrial revolutions. The change in land policies that limited the common land available to small farmers, technological advancement, and improved infrastructure were the main reasons that accelerated success, growth and productivity. In the middle of those centuries, Africa was characterized by the slave trade as a booming business. *These slaves were used as labourers on farms and infrastructure projects such as roads, railways, and canals.* Therefore, in my opinion, the unbelievable productivity from slaves was an eye-opener to a new approach in understanding political economies, and it helped many theorists build up critical economic theories. In one way or another, African slaves played an important experiment in how economics as science evolved from mercantilist theories. In brief, mercantilism believed in national welfare and wealth was based on national holdings such as gold.

In brief, the labour theory of value states that the *amount of labour* required to produce a service or a good determines its economic value. Many scholars in the 18th and 19th centuries held several debates, wrote books and papers on the labour theory of value, but in 1776 Adam Smith published "The Wealth of Nations", in which he elaborated several economic ideas that associated well with the labour theory. His ideas included the philosophy of "Absolute advantage". The earliest work on the theory of absolute advantage argued that to have an absolute advantage over another is to use the same resources as another competitor and produce a greater quantity of the good or service than the competitor. In other words, if two competing farmers harvested 6 and 2 bags of coffee in a working day of 8 hours and using 3 slaves each, the farmer who harvested 6 bags a day is considered to have an absolute advantage over the other with respect to labour and time as resources, and Ceteris Paribas. This would be translated as production taking 4/3 hrs/bag and 4hrs/bag respectively.

In other explanations, of my understanding, the reason why Great Britain and Portugal are extensively used as examples in many economics textbooks on the topic of absolute advantage and associated studies traces back to the trade volumes they held in the slavery business. In this way, borrowing from a psychological perspective of learning by both consequences and association, there were understandable reasons that triggered writers to formulate theories that could later be used in the search for a better understanding of how political economies function.

---

[115] See p. 250, §5.

As economics grew and interested many people in Western Europe, economists viewed the bigger picture at a macro level, seeing an economy as a whole, which constitutes many key players. This gave rise to the search for more understanding of how the economy would function efficiently and effectively. The concept of opportunity cost came into the picture of which some of the notable economists associated with it include David Ricardo (1772–1823), an English economist who analysed the alternatives we forego to opt for others in an economic perspective. In doing so, Ricardo looked at how best an entity could produce a good or service at a much lower cost but efficiently more than others. He, therefore, contributed to coining the term "comparative advantage", which meant that the party had a comparative advantage over others if it produced a good or service at a lower opportunity cost than others.

Ever since then, comparative advantage has always been the primary focus of international trade. In my opinion, it aligns well with the principles of global sustainable development. Nevertheless, no single country with the resources and ability in the modern era would wish to relax its production, in the interest of sustainability, to depend on others' efficiency and effectiveness to survive. This argument associates well with what capitalism will yield in the long run, failing countries to determine what goods and services they should specialize in producing and leave alternative goods and services to other countries. The continuous strife and tension in changing trade policies across the globe and climate change patterns would risk several economies failing if they restricted themselves to producing only goods and services they are good at, making sustainable development a concept troubleshot by social phenomena.

In contemporary economics, absolute and comparative advantage concepts have faced numerous criticisms, and the economists' understanding of these concepts has been improved ever since. Economies or parties evaluate multiple factors to reach conclusions on specializations to attract effectiveness and efficiency in production. This is because economists think in terms of costs versus benefits and alternatives. In the interest of sustainable development, economists are at the forefront of steering appropriate accounting systems that incorporate environmental and green protectionism.

Ideally, 21st century modern and advancing economics would consider optimizing the global resources as a whole and not segmented units as far as sustainability is concerned. In the African context, the appropriate accounting system would measure how much regeneration capacity is held by the continent's natural resources so that resources are used sparingly and as desirable. As far as production is concerned, and sustainability governs, costs and benefits accounts would be aligned well with renewable natural resources as alternatives to guide 21st-century economic theories. Contemporary theories that will twist and craft a new understanding of land as a factor of production whose supply cannot be increased, but its depletion can happen in some instances, would guide appropriate accounting philosophies. In this appropriate accounting system, Africa's mineral wealthy status and virginity in terms of industrialization in many areas rank it the first globally.

Least Developed Countries (LDCs) and Factors of Production Interpretation to Guide Decisions

The factors of production can be listed as follows: land, labour, capital and entrepreneurship. Land can be interpreted as a factor of production that is not consumed, whose supply cannot increase, and without it, production cannot happen. In other explanations, especially the legal perspective, land is viewed as an asset that includes anything above the ground, on the ground and under the ground, down to the earth's crust. In terms of the wealth of a nation, land includes all physical elements bestowed by nature. As a primary factor of production, labour refers to the aggregate human physical and mental effort used in the creation of goods and services. Capital as a factor of production is anything made that is used to make something else, e.g. money and machinery. However, since money is not involved in the actual production of a good or service, capital stretches to refer to the purchase of goods made with money in production. Entrepreneurship is the activity or skill a person undertakes to integrate the factors of production to set up a business to generate a product or service for the consumer market.

Many least developed countries (LDCs') policies are enacted following examples of the roadmaps undertaken by the developed countries. For example, the economist's view of population growth leading to a big population that provides labour and ready markets for products and services, the improvement in infrastructure, and land reforms are some of the special activities that associate well with the growth and development of the European Society between the 17th century and 20th century. The best question to ask is whether that roadmap is still valid in the case of Africa, in an era characterized by globalization, digital technologies, and the sustainability challenge? Can we catch space in real-time following that roadmap? A situation where land challenges that originate from colonialism take centre stage in challenging the production process in several Sub-Saharan developing countries. In my view, sustainable production will only be possible when landmark land reforms happen that will overhaul the current interpretation and understanding of land as a factor of production in the African context.

That would mean agreeing on a land review commission governed by selfless interests to guide African countries on how land ownership can sustainably benefit all of us as we stand today in diversity without discrimination—reforms that are inclined to production and ability of the landowner but not reforms driven by nativity kind of interests alone. These kinds of reforms will address land fragmentation which is usually done by descendants of the deceased in many African cultures.

Labour, as a primary factor of production, includes both skilled and unskilled labour. When we talk of skill, we refer to expertise in executing a task. In the first European industrial revolution, the successor of the agricultural revolution, unskilled labour in the form of slaves was supervised and guided by the skilled labour of European descent to build infrastructure and work on sugar plantations and other farmlands at costs that were exploitive and opportunistic. That gave Europe both absolute and comparative advantage because the cost of production was extremely low regarding unskilled labour and keeping other factors constant. It is important to note that thorough supervisory skills associate with ability and knowledge. In today's globalization which presents enormous challenges to Africans because of the failure to train skilled labour, as a result of the education systems which promote pseudo project managers perpetuates the problem. Therefore, population growth that is unproductive but targets consumerism might be more disastrous in the sustainability equation.[116]

In my view, consumerism is highly beneficial where the population is equally productive. One of the indicators of the hopeless unskilled labour surplus registered already, as a result of the population growth, is depicted in how some African countries desperately enact labour export policies despite the cry out of torture in some jurisdictions where African unskilled labour force is exported. The skilled labour force would ideally be fit to integrate the factors of production as entrepreneurs to lead and supervise

---

[116] See p. 164-165, §3.

the unskilled labour force to solve demand deficient unemployment. The government's role is to train a skilled labour force that can learn to see things differently. And therefore, cottage industries would begin or be promoted by the government in that sense. Should we believe that Africa still needs a population boom to create markets in the economic sense? In my opinion, following sustainability goals, I do not believe so! The current population would be enough for us to develop. Thus, the problem lies elsewhere.

Unemployment would mean being jobless and actively seeking a job. A job has a description that might call for a skilled or unskilled labour force. When you are searching for a particular job, it ideally means that you probably have the skill for that job. To gain expertise, you must practice or train for some time in a particular area under correct supervision. In other words, the knowledge that lacks skill in a given field might not produce a good understanding of a task. In my view, Africa's labour force has a skills gap, and globalization challenges shall hit us the worst if we do not devise means to catch space in real-time.

People shall continue to graduate from many African universities but without the skills to execute tasks. This propels foreigners to board the skilled labour force along with FDI and their technologies. Some African governments are also slow in supporting local skilled labour to train others. Seated on minerals in the digital and globalized era, with population explosion that is unproductive and unskilled, embracing FDI inflow day in and day out that is technologically driven and at times capital-intensive or skilled labour-intensive, where is the hope for Africans in as far as catching space in real-time is concerned? In my view, it is the confusion but not unemployment in some countries. The solution lies in reshaping the education system, improve governance systems and politics, advocate for transparency and clarity and proper management systems and treating the unique African attitude disorder (UAAD).[117]

As we try to shape our economic development following western prototypes, we need to think and reflect on how economies have emerged through revolutions to rethink better economic models that best suit our progress in the fourth industrial revolution, which is characterized by digitalization and globalization.

How Should We Raise Capital?

In the production process, capital is the most important resource. We have the land, although it has challenges that colonialists created. The labour is available, but the governments fail to shape it into what markets demand. Ultimately, because many governments are premised on incorrect political ideologies that are fixated on colonial theories and prototypes of western life, the labour available cannot innovate capital. *What is capital then, in detail?* In my understanding, following 21st-century globalization, capital encompasses both the hardware and software components, the processes and systems, tangible and intangible products or services that are made by humans and are used to make others of the similar or upgraded form, as aforementioned.

According to economists, capital as a factor of production in both private and public sectors can be raised in several ways. These include loans, grants and donations, savings, and financial markets. In other words, capital can be raised by either one, two, or more of the schemes mentioned above. Africa has a rising youth population with a high entrepreneurial spirit. However, very few startups can live to celebrate their 5th birthday. I would think that living in an era of globalization and the virginity of many African

---

[117] See p. 203-214, §4.

countries compared to other continents as far as industrialization and digital technology are concerned, a considerable fraction of startups would rise, but instead, they fail. What is the real problem, then?

In my opinion, before economists present their views which I will hint at later, the biggest problem is the *unique African attitude disorder (UAAD).*[118] This disorder is so powerful because it has no boundaries as far as literacy levels are concerned. It knows little about the level of education, training, and skill that an African possesses. Whether you are a chief economist, executive director, or manager of a development/commercial bank, what attitude do you have towards an African enterprise in the first place? How do you view the world? What attitude do you give an African innovation and invention compared to an Asian, European, or American? Therefore, the unique African attitude disorder (UAAD) affects both sides of the demand and supply markets.

People's attitude, either from the demand side or the supply side in our markets, is crucial in raising capital for African enterprises. For example, key players in the financial sector like African banks are very slow in supporting technology entrepreneurs. Once a person comes up with some technology to solve a problem at a small scale, and the idea seems vibrant, banks and their people of correct attitude ought to support the cause if we are to accelerate economic development. In Africa, this kind of support is rare. However, if the same enterprise has some social engineering concepts, as crafted in Chapter Four, a few banks would give it a shot.[119]

Many banks in Africa largely support schemes that emerge out the best through competitions. Sustainable economic development is about inclusion, and it is never about competition. Staging competition to support enterprises is modern discrimination, and it is categorical discrimination that appears civilized. When banks largely support only those who emerge out the best through competitions, they are very unfair. In my view, that does not work. From my observation/experience, people who change the world rarely win competitions. The reason is simple, people in many cases, misunderstand them. In many cases, perfectionists win competitions, especially those that follow the literature of many economic doctrines correctly.

Many prominent entrepreneurs domineering the world had ideas that were beyond the understanding of many banks. And when they went through competitions, they always lost out because the panellists hardly viewed the problems that the entrepreneurs were trying to solve. And because many business decisions are primarily based on the current market demand and supply forces and less on futuristic demand/supply, African banks rarely support a futurist. That is one of the most apparent reasons why climate change will hit us the worst!

The 21st-century entrepreneurs create or increase demand in the markets that has never been. They also create problems and later solve these problems. They write a virus and later write an anti-virus or manufacture a vaccine. Several players in the African financial markets rarely understand these games.

African banks and staffs primarily understand and appreciate the usual ordinary markets, and many have not yet moved wholly into the 21st-century demand and supply markets to support the cause. As I

---

[118] See p. 203-214, §4.

[119] See p. 218-226, §4.

mentioned earlier, the prototypes and old roadmaps we fixate on are not the best ideals to succeed. Banks need to understand how to support their clientele, i.e. small, medium and big, and the futurist, in the 21st century. And to appreciate that people are changing, Africans have the minds to innovate and invent great things but only need financial support. Therefore, banks are better suited for this partnership.

One of the reasons banks and other financial sector players rarely support technology entrepreneurs is primarily viewed from the economic perspective. However, the financial sector players' attitudes and behaviours are rarely considered. They consider the risk of investing in an African technology entrepreneur very high because they are already accustomed to modern technologies from the developed world. As I mentioned, the fixation on analogue systems roadmaps drawn by others in the past yet embracing digitalization from the modern world retards the thinking and innovation in many financial sector players across Africa.

The financial sector itself must be very innovative and willing to support technology entrepreneurs. And because these financial sector players cannot predict the cash flows quite well, from these startups or expanding technology businesses, they look at the risk as being very high. This is somewhat because many commercial banks, for example, identify with short-term credit, yet technology entrepreneurs might require long term credit facilities. Technology entrepreneurs always have medium to long-term business plans. The dominance of trade in retail over cottage industries and associated technologies is partially explainable from this point of view because banks and other financial sector players understand those old roadmaps better and are not willing to move with the demands of the 21st century, and the demands of the youth population explosion in Africa.

It takes sacrifice, and the governments, through the commercial banks and other financial sector players, should get unlocked to support African technology entrepreneurs and cottage industries. The same applies to medium and big enterprises. Commercial banks and governments have to devise means to support these entrepreneurs in a more or less cost-effective mechanism to spur innovation and accelerate economic development. Therefore, when the financial sector players support a few technology entrepreneurs and make them successful, they inspire others to begin. Many people cannot see new roads that can reach them to new destinations until others have used them. From an economist's point of view, several bottlenecks hinder capital raising in Africa. These include: domestic savings rates in Africa are too low, lack of financial literacy, lack of access to credit, poor corporate governance and many others.

Local Investors' Capacity and Capital Raising in African Economies

Some economists argue that Africans' domestic saving culture is poor, and this makes capital generation difficult. But can you save what you do not have? Is it possible for an unhealthy mind and body full of diseases to save? An exploding population that is characterized by diseases that are perpetual like HIV/AIDS in collectivistic cultures, amidst low innovation rates, merely lives to eat and would have very little or no disposable income. Do we have the correct social architecture in the social systems that can support a correct savings culture? Does it align well with our cultural predispositions? All these explain why it becomes difficult to have disposable income to set aside to raise capital for African enterprises.

The Africa Financial Markets Index 2017 showed that South Africa ranked highest among the 17 countries studied in the index, comprising three-quarters of Africa's GDP. However, the economists seem not to agree on the definite reasons why South Africa does better overall in financial markets at some point. South Africa ranked highest in all 6 pillars surveyed by Barclays Africa Group Limited in collaboration with Official Monetary and Financial Institutions Forum (OMFIF), i.e. market depth, access to foreign exchange, market transparency, tax and regulatory environment, the capacity of local investors, macroeconomic opportunity, and legality and enforceability of standard financial markets master agreements.[120] South Africa ranked highest in terms of size and liquidity of the capital markets.

In 2018, the Absa Africa Financial Markets Index depicted that Kenya and Nigeria overtook South Africa in the "access to foreign exchange" pillar and "market transparency, tax and regulatory environment" pillars. However, South Africa retained the top position overall, supported by strong financial market infrastructure with few large and medium enterprises. Subsequently, a considerable number of their labor force is employed in the formal sector.

One of the reasons advanced by economists for South Africa's vibrant overall performance in these two consecutive years is primarily due to the structure of South Africa's economy. South Africa's economy is characterized by large and medium-sized companies with the capacity to mobilize capital on capital markets by issuing bonds and equity to investors. The big and medium companies employ a considerable number of people in the formal sector required to contribute to the pension fund. South Africa has pension and insurance fund assets of about $627 billion. Most of the economies of other countries that were surveyed are dominated by informal micro and household enterprises. Issuing securities to raise capital on capital markets requires a solid track record of profitability, corporate governance, properly audited books of accounts, evidence of tax returns, and professionalism. And very few local companies meet these minimum standards to issue securities to raise capital.

However, what caught my attention the most when I read these reports and statistics is that majority of the shareholders of the firms that issue securities on capital markets are foreign nationals in many African countries. And another essential aspect to note is that South Africa transitioned from apartheid policy to democratic governance in 1994. There is some unique information to process here beyond what economists can view: being late in democratic governance and performing best in financial markets. As economists argue for increased FDI inflow into Africa than portfolio inflows because Africans lack capacity, expertise, skills and technology to run modern enterprises, they need to answer many "why" questions prior. For example, why are majority shareholders of companies that *meet criteria* to issue securities, whether small, medium or large enterprises are foreign nationals? That is the most significant point. And once the answer is unlocked, many firms will begin to meet the criteria to issue securities on capital markets to raise capital. In this very question, the one who labours to answer it will study South Africa critically compared to Ethiopia, for example.

The uniqueness about Ethiopia is that it performed worst in the Financial Markets Index 2017 on the pillars of "local investor capacity, market depth, market transparency and access to foreign exchange". "If you close your eyes to facts, you will learn through accidents" African Proverb. Try to look at things this way: had independence been delayed in Africa for more than 20 years, what impact would it have caused to the whole of Africa in terms of economic development? Compare and contrast.

---

[120] The Official Monetary and Financial Institutions Forum (OMFIF) in association with Barclays Africa Group Limited. *The Africa Financial Markets Index, 2017.* 8-9.

"If you close your eyes to facts, you will learn through accidents" African Proverb.

Discussion on Individualism and Collectivism in relation to Capitalism, Socialism, and Communism in the African Context

The earliest collectivist ideas were postulated by Jean-Jacques Rousseau (1712–1778) in his 1762 publication of the social contract. He argued that in collectivism, the individual finds true being and freedom only in submission to the "general will" of the community. Collectivism has powerful bonds that bring people related or have a connection closer, in memories and emotions. It emphasizes the interests of the group over the interests of the individual. The interconnectedness between people in collectivistic cultures plays a central role in each person's identity. However, an individualist is motivated by personal rewards and benefits. Individualism highly prioritizes individual interests over the interests of the group.

Individualistic cultures often place a greater emphasis on characters such as assertiveness and independence. Geographic clusters for collectivism are often located in Arab countries, Confucian Asia, Latin America, Southern Asia, and Sub-Saharan Africa. In particular, Sub-Saharan countries (e.g. Uganda) have many collectivistic cultures. Other countries with highly collectivistic cultures across the globe include; Argentina, Brazil, China, Ecuador, Guatemala, India, Indonesia, Japan, Korea, Taiwan, and Venezuela. In contrast, generalized geographic clusters of individualistic cultures can be located in Germanic Europe, Nordic Europe, and Anglo countries.

Communism, socialism, and capitalism are socioeconomic/political philosophies to guide political economies that several thinkers developed. For example, communism and socialism were triggered by industrial revolution businessmen who were becoming extremely rich by exploiting their workers. It was purely more of an economic issue that motivated these philosophies. I find it appropriate to provide short notes on these socioeconomic and political models. In brief, communism is an economic/political philosophy or a system of social organization premised on common ownership of the means of production and the absence of social classes. In the communist theory, each person contributes and receives according to their ability and needs.

On the contrary, socialism is a socioeconomic system in which the means of production are socially owned, and a self-directed labour force characterizes workplaces. The main difference between socialism and communism is that socialism is a socioeconomic philosophy, whereas communism is both a political and economic philosophy and sees the government as the owner and main decision-maker in all issues. In a true communist ideal, a state would not have money, and people would receive what the government finds fit to meet their needs and wants, e.g. food, shelter, education and etc. However, in socialism, people receive according to how much they contribute. Therefore, the one who works harder and smarter in socialist communities would be entitled to receive better than others. Of course, these philosophical models of economic development in social and political systems associate with many other schools of thought to improve their practicality. Here, I have tried to provide a brief outline of how communism and socialism differ. However, socialism has never been fully adopted in any country since its development. Some countries have socialist policies, but because socialism is highly anti-business, capitalist structures that promote free-market systems that accelerate economic growth and development still dominate.

On the other hand, capitalism is an economic system that emphasizes privately owned factors of production, and profit is the main goal behind these operations. Of course, it has its advantages and disadvantages, being the oldest economic system that associates with a free market system. It is important to note that philosophies and theories govern all systems, and there exists no perfect system. Each system has advantages and disadvantages. For example, many countries that practice socialism have never fully adopted it to a satisfactory standard. They always enact a few policies that follow socialist philosophies (consider socialist democracies) and later think capitalistic in other matters. Some of the domineering sectors that some countries find appropriate to borrow socialist philosophies are health and education.

In my opinion, Africans need a new kind of philosophy to tap into the opportunity that the fourth industrial revolution presents. A new set of socio-economic systems integrating some of these present economic doctrines and tends towards a mixed economy would be required. We need not get fixated on what great philosophers of the western world thought to govern and develop their territories. There is room to think philosophies that highly utilize the psychological dimension, a field that will spearhead sustainability, peace and stability in the modern world than the legal dimension. For example, communism does wonders in atheist communities, but in Africa, regardless of the conventional religions, one cannot separate Africans from the understanding of the Supreme Being.

On the other hand, the unique African attitude disorder (UAAD) that accompanies the politics of envy makes many diehards of partisan politics shoot their ambitions in capitalistic states across African countries. One would argue that the politics of envy is highly likely to be practised by the poor calling for socialist democratic policies, which could be true at some point. However, in Africa, the story is different. Because these economic doctrines were purely influenced by economics and politics, they considered less of people's intimacy in diversity and inclusion. Hence, Africans who are in power are exploiting the loopholes in these philosophies. For example, the unique African attitude disorder (UAAD) might cause the African leader to opt for a foreign expert or financial assistance over his own/fellow African expert. They would, therefore, focus less on government policy and instead go for partisan politics. Because of the unique African attitude disorder (UAAD), they (Africa's leaders) would forge relationships to attract foreign direct investment that promotes and protects their (leader's) enterprises, thereby holding over 80% of the county's wealth in their hands, typical on Nile Basin Countries.

On the other hand, the architecture of collectivistic cultures may associate well with socialism over capitalism. And individualistic cultures may associate well with capitalism. It is only Japan with practical collective capitalism. And it would not be such a successful economy if conventional religions had highly absorbed it. We also learn about the reorganization after World War II (WWII) that brought about remarkable socioeconomic development in Japan. They had to restructure and be freer to promote innovation. Many African countries that practice capitalism in collectivistic cultures are struggling. One of the reasons for struggling capitalism in Africa is the result of conventional religions that made Africans go too far than necessary at the expense of their cultures. They hence weakened and repressed many instinctual facts that made them *live in anxiety*, thereby keeping most of them in conventional religions during the day and traditional religions during the night. This creates uncertainty and perpetuates pretence, which is not a very good attribute in the equation of success and sustainability.

> "The main challenge that has cost Africans is the limited or absence of organized and well-documented philosophical schools of thought written by African thinkers, right before European invaders, to track and capture African order. This problem has led us to follow, enact laws/policies, and get tied up to western philosophical schools of thought that do not match the African contextual factors. The only way to rise Africa with Africans is to wake up now to redefine our identity to catch space in real-time. Otherwise, globalization will hit us at the weakest emotional point, and it will be challenging, if not impossible, for Africans to rise with rising Africa." I do submit.

Collectivistic cultures have very intense bonds that unite people in groups from which every individual derives meaning and identity. These forces or bonds need to be considered and carefully studied to think of appropriate political and economic theories that can socially and structurally transform Africa. This is because you cannot separate man from his instinctual assets; they continually reoccur regardless of the level of education and time. The philosophical guideline should thus be being born free without anything, and when we die, we do not take anything with us. Whether rich or poor, you get laid in the grave; none is transported to mars for burial. If that is the case, what socio-economic and political theories do we need to defend, protect, and transform Africa both socially and structurally?

> Canadian psychologist Jordan Peterson once said of socialism, "……which means everyone who has more than you got it by stealing it from you… 'Everyone who has more than me got it in a manner that was corrupt, and that justifies not only my envy but my actions to level the field,' so to speak… There is a tremendous philosophy of resentment that I think is driven now by a very pathological anti-human ethos." [121]

Jordan postulated how imbalances or inequalities in socialism would fuel envy in those who own less. However, collectivist bonds keep Africans in perpetual poverty, and socialist policies would be the best ideal. At the moment, Sub-Saharan Africa's economy is too weak and needs a new socioeconomic order to graduate it somewhere near a maturity point. Jordan's views are valid in mature democracies. However, one successful African has to help dozens of other relatives, family members, and friends. To derive meaning and identity, a successful African has to honour the interests of the groups in which they live. And these groups warranty little or no need to follow wisdom, knowledge, virtues, and understanding as a basis and metric in their formation. They are more of blood ties. That is where individualism scores highly because the individual is at liberty to deal with no fool. In collectivistic Africa, you have no choice but to be tied up in a chain of groups, and you have to be accommodative to associate well with society members to derive meaning and identity. Based on this narrative, specifically, the collectivistic bonds, what kind of systems do Africans need to transform Africa socially and structurally

One of the reasons African enterprises collapse and others fail to celebrate their fifth birthdays despite a high entrepreneurial spirit is the failure to recognize the influence of these collectivistic bonds. In the application of the ideal philosophies, the African governments primarily encourage capitalist democracies and have little room for socialist democracies, yet their peoples live in collectivism. In many African countries, the population is exploding every year and dependence ratios are rising every year because

---

[121] Frank Holmes. "Don't Be Fooled by the Politics of Envy," U.S Global Investors, March 11th 2019, https://www.usfunds.com/investor-library/frank-talk-a-ceo-blog-by-frank-holmes/dont-be-fooled-by-the-politics-of-envy/#.YTC_9t8xVPY.

the children below the age of 15 are the majority in several developing countries. So, the expenditure on children's welfare and education is relatively high, and there remains very little disposable income to invest. How will African private sector enterprises grow when their founders are tied up in a vicious cycle of hopelessness fueled by collectivism that governments fail to support? In my opinion, Africans ought to have mixed economies first to meet the demands that globalization presents. However, African economies need to be primarily dominated by socialist policies to address the challenges of collectivism.

The unique African attitude disorder (UAAD) and other personality factors of entrepreneurs and businessmen influence the progress of African enterprises because many entrepreneurs make decisions that leave no room for their enterprises to grow. However, the kind of societies we live in are a benchmark to transform us socially. For example, many European firms lost their fortunes immediately after they made it between the 18th and 19th centuries, and along the way, they kept improving systems to address the cause. There were many economic reasons at that time that made these companies open and fluid. In the case of Africa's economic development, for our enterprises to grow, we need an integral socio-economic and political philosophy to address two issues: unique African attitude disorder (UAAD) and collectivism requirements. Some of the diehards of capitalism, which is the oldest system and most promising ideology, borrow culture from elsewhere. That means they continually redefine their cultures as they wish and have little external influence. This makes them highly individualistic and vest all their energy in the government policies, which is good because it fuels less partisan politics. Africans, are not migrants; they have a history for many thousands of years. It is believed that humanity began somewhere in East Africa. It is a big mistake to model socioeconomic development outside Africa's culture and history.

Too much corruption and employment discrimination by the ruling regimes in Sub-Saharan Africa is perpetuated by socioeconomic doctrines that are not modelled to reflect collectivism. Most of the African leaders are tied up in bonds of collectivism, and although it is unlawful to second their peoples for employment without fulfilling requirements and criteria, the cultural force of collectivism falls short of the law. Consequently, several African governments are dominated by a lineage of clans and their relatives. It is highly likely that even you, the African native, would ensure that your close people get employment because of what collectivism calls for if you got the chance to lead the countries. The same scenario applies to corruption; it would be difficult for corruption to infiltrate governance hinged on collectivistic philosophies that match the African order. Who can mess around with the products of collective sweats?

We are looking at how the past shapes the present and how events happening today reflect on events that will happen tomorrow. We are, on average, 60 years old since we gained independence from colonial rule. Before colonialism and conventional religions were introduced into Africa, many Africans were illiterate. In other words, some Africans have become largely literate, on average, about 120 years ago. Our enterprises and companies fluidity and openness are understandable to some small extent from that view of things. Chinese and Japanese, for example, have been reading and writing for thousands of years. The most important thing is that their cultures have not been violated by conventional religion, unlike Africans. This creates a few distortions in their way of life. And consequently, this puts them in a better position to transform socially.

In my view, some people do not understand how to make enterprises survive and thrive for many generations to come. This is because the ability and capacity to plan for future generations has very little to do with literacy levels attained, but it takes sacrifice and a correct public philosophy. Someone can be very learned but stupid! It calls for skill and understanding. And above all, it requires the right attitude. Some of these attributes are not taught in schools but are instead a fraction of what families produce in making well-individuated human beings. In this scheme of things, collectivism nurtures support for one another, and it is difficult and risky for one grown in collectivism to make an individualist. The collectivistic bonds will always pull you to get to where you belong.

Back to Jordan's concern about socialism fueling envy to some extent.[122] It is common knowledge that people are friends when they identify with each other. "Show me whom you associate with, and I tell your characters!" African proverb. For many relationships to prosper, there must be shared attributes. Or things that matter to all stakeholders. This means that individualism highly brings together people who match, identify with each other, share values and attributes more perfectly than collectivism. Here, I am describing a general picture. In collectivism, which also has several types, someone has responsibilities by virtue and morals that pull them back, forth and sideways without choice. In collectivism, there is an association of people that goes beyond what ancestral Africans could define at that time—the association of people hinged on loose blood ties and societal demands. Africa has young and talented people with a high entrepreneurial spirit, but the reason many enterprises fail is as a result of the chains of collectivistic bonds to which governments turn a blind eye. The forces within these bonds are so strong that one who tries to break them feels no sense of identity in a society. This creates perpetual poverty because many entrepreneurs have no choice but to respond positively and comply with what society demands to fulfil their identity in society. Economists seem not to understand these things! Otherwise, there would have been an economic theory around these collectivistic networks.

Envy is a disorder of the soul that leads to cognitive distortions like witchcraft practices in many societies across the globe. In Africa, because of the collectivistic forces that pull people by default, you cannot fail to rule out high chances of envy. This is because of the continued association that has no boundaries and because someone to gain identity and meaningfulness requires to keep the norm. Otherwise, avoidance is one of the most extraordinary remedies applied by an individualist. Therefore, whenever someone fishes better than others in collectivism, they have to share the catch regardless of whether it is mature or young. And any slight deviance from the norm by the go-getter sometimes breeds envy on the recipient's side. And this envy grows into a severe cognitive distortion leading to extremisms of witchcraft in several cultures across the African continent and beyond.

Many people cannot believe that many people in Africa derive a sense of fulfilment (self-actualisation) when they have a relative that is doing well when for themselves they are super poor—and they keep bragging around because of this association. And another category that plans to live their lives on the hard work of others. This is where psychologists label these people as "suffering from a dependency syndrome", but the root cause is not attended to, especially in collectivistic cultures. Some people who have learnt to include a "NO" within collectivism's vocabulary have economically and financially succeeded. However, many people lack the zeal and emotional capital to move individualistic where it demands to protect their fortunes for generations to come. And knowing when to move individualistic can essentially happen when a person was not grown with a fused personality in their home of origin. Capitalism creates a more healthy competition in individualistic cultures but risks unhealthy competition if not envious competition in

---

[122] See p. 323.

Africa's collectivism. And this explains why many startups in Africa fail simply because of collectivistic bonds they have to attend to without limit—many starters do not take time to assess where their potential lies before an attempt to start. They instead follow what other people have tried and perhaps succeeded or tried to succeed. And all this is a result of collectivistic bonds whose forces call for a new social order destined to lead economic growth and development in Africa's collectivism.

Therefore, from this background, a reorganization of families as a central engine to driving economic growth is vital—socioeconomic transformation must be hinged on self-awareness cultural initiatives to decide on the integrated philosophies suitable to govern and develop Africa. Envy, as postulated by Jordan, should not be a stumbling block to promote socialist policies because many Africans are already envious of others who have prospered by merely hiding in the moral teachings of Christian faith and other faiths, which outlines the difficulty a wealthy person will find when trying to enter heaven. *Therefore, many African societies require socialist policies to a given extent to address the demands of collectivism and the unique African attitude disorder (UAAD).* When many African psyches learn to view the wildlife as potential living human beings, capitalism will be highly advocated. Relatively mature democracies cannot look elsewhere other than capitalism. However, democratic ideals seem premature for some African countries' social conditions.

The Asian giant has also recently started moving capitalistic to a large scale, but their democracy is not promising. Addressing the income inequality communism breeds within collectivism would require a different philosophy where democracy is not yet matured. It is difficult for democracies in collectivistic cultures to rank as matured because of the aforementioned reasons unless there is external influence. We need a new wave of 21st-century thinkers to create theories that meet the demands of the digital era while keeping collectivistic cultures intact and socially transforming them. African matters are complex because of the effect of colonialism and conventional religions. Conventional religions brainwashed Africans because we were illiterate before Europeans conquered us in many parts of Sub-Saharan Africa. Therefore, we lost a lot of helpful information that would later be used in the process to digest the ingredients that would catalyze African humankind's correct social transformation philosophy. And suppose anyone thinks that they will solve Africa's complex matters using already established western philosophies alone. In that case, it will work in the short run, but crises will reoccur with time through a new wave of cancers, in which scholars and tech gurus will derive opportunity as they bring them to book. For example, some low-income countries that had shot the middle-income status between 1960 and 2009 are stuck in the middle-income trap.[123] Some others have regressed to low-income status. Economists seem to be fixated on structural failures as the main problem affecting these countries, yet the problem is broader in scope—the causes of structural failures. Many people author articles and others widely publish research about what they know about Africa's predicaments but not solve them. This book provides the reasons that contribute to structural failures.

In individualism, which highly cherishes perfectionism, it is morally acceptable for a son/daughter not to support a parent contesting for a leadership position in a community. The son/daughter can also decide to open a civil case or criminal prosecution against a close relative or parent for what does not go right. This is highly formidable in many African cultures. In fact, mere listing a parent as a suspect in a criminal

---

[123] Greg Larson, Norman Loayza, and Michael Woolcock, *"Research & Policy Briefs, the Middle-Income Trap: Myth or Reality?"* (Malaysia: The World Bank Malaysia Hub, 2016).

case appears strange in many collectivistic African cultures. Although nobody is above the law, Africans always have a second thought before dragging their parents and relatives to courts of law. This is not the case in some other territories. And these things are not going to be changed overnight. They are instinctual facts of collectivism. As I mentioned, the unique African attitude disorder (UAAD) makes many learned Africans want to live odd due to the association they have gained with individualistic Westerners. This does not create much progress but instead makes Africans sink the worst.

The solution lies in understanding. Collectivism debars many acts of perfectionism, and many people are spotted saying, "He ought to keep quiet for that. His dad remains a dad and so forth..."—protecting many kinds of things that would be called criminal in the eyes of an individualist. Therefore, individualism creates very efficient and effective democratic governments because individualists tend to lean more on government policy than what collectivistic cultures would call for —the back and forth criteria for creating one's identity and meaningfulness—of a well-individuated human being, with a sound mind, and non-impaired interpersonal skills. Individualists water capitalist democracies better. In other words, the democratic government policy pulls the individualist as the bonds of collectivism pull the collectivistic. In my view, all these things matter in deciding a correct roadmap for Africa's economic growth and development.

Africa's Social and Structural Transformation in the Face of Globalization

First, promising social transformation of a social system should be premised on the reorganization of cultural assets to align with socio-economic doctrines. There is a need to premise development goals on self-awareness cultural initiatives. And any improvement within these cultural assets should take on a collective consciousness of society members. The social structure and systems must guide the political structure of a society that is on a correct roadmap to economic prosperity. The philosophy of symbolic interactionism and social construction of meaning corroborates the need to have consensus on; cultural modifications, new market entrants, societal order, new evidence, and technologies.

Many social transformations are intentional or controllable in economies with continuous technological innovation. However, the new social order in Africa is rarely controlled by ourselves but largely dependent on others—it is more influenced by an external stimulus than our will. We, therefore, have a little will in many matters as we draw consensus to have correct social transformation primarily due to the forces of globalization and later on our fixation on others' systems. This makes many Africans fail to think outside the box to innovate technologies or systems/processes that will socially transform our values, norms and other cultural assets without contradiction. In a nutshell, we need to transform by improving what is found in place. For example, digitalization is bringing about tremendous social transformation globally. Although cultural and behavioural barriers to digital transformation hinder progress in many African countries at some point, the forces of globalization are too intense that they influence social order everywhere, globally—it is about how prepared and vigilant each community becomes to embrace new social order brought about by the digital transformation.

In an attempt to draw causal relationships between Africa's transformation and globalization, the structural change is only sustained when social values, norms and practices are rationally transformed. And nobody, if not a few policymakers, drive these two pillars, i.e. social and structural changes harmoniously in the fate of Africa. Whilst economists argue that sustained economic growth is only possible where there are structural changes, I believe that in the context of Africa's sustainability, the structural changes must align with social transformation. Look at an example; when smartphones entered the African market for the first time, very few people appreciated their importance. However, when swift social media platforms in the form of mobile Apps joined other internet platforms, they completely changed the African social order to a notable extent. Social media platforms are socially transforming African societies largely by accident since it is not our plan to innovate these platforms, but we rather find ourselves using them. External leaders influence us to a large extent. The connection between social transformation and structural transformation is as follows:

Promising social transformation should be largely intentional, not influenced by others. In this intentional social change, what is found in place is not discarded but rather improved, conserved or modified as appropriate. And the guiding principle should be the "values" remaining intact. The existing situation associates with economic activities. Therefore, with social change, these economic activities also change or get a facelift. With correct social transformation, a consensus is reached in embracing technologies from other countries primarily due to globalization to uplift the current economic activities. Therefore, the reallocation of economic activities to the three broad sectors, i.e. agriculture, manufacturing and services, would utilize the existing/new social order as consensus may provide. In its idealistic form, the kind of manufacturing undertaken by society is highly based on its comparative advantage. And the comparative advantage is determined by the factor endowments of the country at any specific time. As a result of social changes, e.g. technological innovations, factor endowments change over time for every country. Economists argue correctly that the industrialization of a country requires the country to upgrade from a factor endowment structure rich in labour and natural resources to one packed with capital, new technology and better infrastructure. However, they fail to explicitly provide the "how" in the fate of Africa. In my view, the "how" is answered this way:

"I am a small farmer in a locale of many other small farmers and peasants in Sub-Saharan Africa who wish to go modern farming and perhaps add value to our produce. The primary factor of production is the land on which we cultivate. However, as a result of poor land policies from previous successive governments, right from the colonial time, the land goes getting fragmented day in and day out. Because of this, people use the land anyhow. This affects planning. It is rare to find a sub-county or county specializing largely in cereals production—for example. With the support of correct government policy, I wish we could make land reforms to stop land fragmentation and later form cooperatives where we aggregate the sub-county and county produce. This is correct social transformation. These cooperatives will act as savings clubs, training institutes, and advisory boards. Later or sooner, the savings shall procure modern agricultural equipment to work on our farms. With the government proposing import subsidies on modern agricultural equipment, the sky is the limit. It is on record that advanced economies subsidize their domestic farmers by about $360 billion per year in total.[124] The increased farmers' supply drives down world prices of farm products below the costs of production, and farmers in low-income countries find it difficult to compete. I believe, the other economic activities that associate with agriculture will be boosted and manufacturing that follows comparative advantage economic doctrine will be stimulated." I do submit.

---

[124] Steven A. Greenlaw & David Shapiro, *Principles of Economics2e* (Texas: OpenStanx Rice University, 2011), 812.

From the 2015 world summit on sustainable development held in Paris, France, the three pillars of sustainable development are social, economic and environment. Before any project is undertaken, it is prudent to ensure that the three pillars are in harmony. For example, a project that lessens the moral values of a society, although it does not harm the environment and brings about economic prosperity, is considered viable. Similarly, a project that keeps societal values intact or improves/transforms them and brings many economic benefits, although harming the environment, is considered equitable. In the same scheme of things, a project that brings no economic benefit but is socially and environmentally unhazardous is considered bearable. In my opinion, a project that is hazardous for two pillars but supports one creates and perpetuates a generation of poorly individuated people. Refer to figure below: adopted from the 2015 World Summit on Sustainable Development

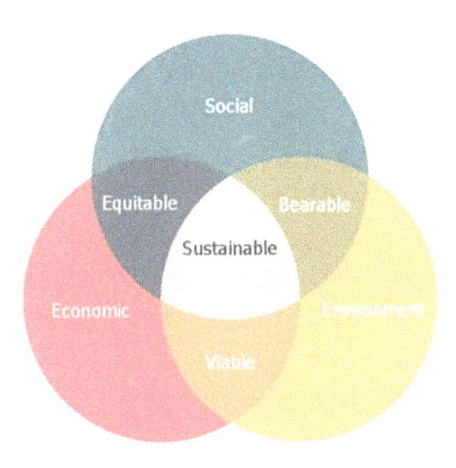

The Three Pillars of Sustainable development

Source: 2015 World Summit on Sustainable Development

Now, let us try to view things this way: economic prosperity across the globe is centrally pivoted on structural transformation. That means relatively balanced activities must be achieved between the agricultural sector, manufacturing sector, and services sector. Therefore, the sustainability equation calls for fundamental social transformation that aligns well with structural transformation and environmental safeguards. At present, no single territory has achieved sustainable development yet. Sustainable development is still a work in progress for all countries across the globe. No single country can claim that its development is not threatened. However, high-income countries have achieved sustained growth and eradicated extreme poverty, unlike many Sub-Saharan African and Asian countries. It is, therefore, in the interest of self-driven sustainable development, in the African context, which stretches beyond what is defined by developmental agencies, that we seek to ask ourselves the following questions:

- To what extent is the tremendous social transformation we have undergone in the past one or two decades out of our will?

- How are religions providing the correct philosophy to shape peoples' understanding of sustainable development in Africa?

- Are we in control of our natural resources? How best can we use our natural resources to move economies from being natural resources-based to sustainable manufacturing?

Many thousands of years ago, the Egyptians pioneered writing styles and the Greeks later learned from the Egyptians. Except for North Africa, many other parts of Africa had little history stored in a permanent medium. This required no immediate shift from vocational training to degrees and PhDs in Africa's institutions—especially in engineering, science, technology, and agricultural disciplines. Degree programs would be awarded to people who have practised hands-on skills and gained outstanding experience or exhibited exceptional talents in the fields mentioned above. There was a mismatch of events influenced by poor planning.

In my view, many parts of Africa would be starting degree courses and PhD programs, especially in STEM subjects. There were premature educational policies in Africa. This has caused many crises in Africa, which has led to pseudo project managers hence converting economies into service-based economies and accelerating premature deindustrialization. I believe that an economically promising African society that would structurally transform should be characterized by workshops, small and medium factories, and cottage industries on a large scale. The digital revolution that facilitates globalization has made many African societies think more of rendering services than products. This new social order is influenced by an external stimulus, i.e. the forces of globalization, of which we are observers more than participants.

Economists are super clear when they say that markets are the fundamental pillars of an economy. These markets have the supply end and demand end. In the opening paragraph of the education system (Chapter Three), I mentioned that the education system is the central pillar of the societal system.[125] Whatever comes out of our education system predetermines the quality and quantity of the labour force, which later influences labour levels among other factor endowments of an economy at any time. It is, therefore, harder for promising structural transformation to occur when many tertiary institutions are converting into universities—consequently creating a mismatch in the labour markets of developing countries. The industrialists demand labour X while educational institutions are supplying labour Y. How will structural transformation occur then? Structural transformation is about *proper and adequate reallocation of economic activities* in the three broad sectors, i.e. agriculture, manufacturing and services, to stimulate economic growth and development. That means the factor endowments at any specific time shift from being rich in labour to being rich in capital for industrialization to occur. However, the unique African attitude disorder (UAAD) is the biggest stumbling block to raising capital in many African countries. Correctly skilled labour innovates capital. Because educational institutions produce a labour force that does not meet the demands of industrialists and the same labour force caught the unique African attitude disorder (UAAD), hope is lost.

The degrees filled with theories and sometimes fewer skills and practical activities create many distortions, especially after one fails to get employment. A technician or vocational graduate is more humble and could easily open up an enterprise to showcase their skills. Universities create an illusion that the moment one acquires a degree, they are good to go many places, yet it is just the beginning of learning. A degree counts less in the 21st century, but rather the holder must gain a lifelong attempt to perfect whatever they learn. Therefore, regardless of whether you hold a degree or not, you must be open to continuous learning. And learning is not restricted to lecture/classrooms, schools and colleges. It is in the open. The hard work, and sometimes smart work, out of the university distinguishes a go-getter from an academic.

---

[125] See p. 115, §3.

In schools, one is tested after learning a lesson, and in the practical world, a lesson is learnt after the test is administered. Therefore, success out of school is an integral of many sets of variables. Sub-Saharan Africa remains predominantly an agricultural-based economy despite the rising literacy levels because of poor government policies primarily influenced by partisan politics, which minds less about the future of Africa. Therefore, instead of supporting policies that would revamp collapsed industries, support local investors' startups, and revisit educational policies, military governments aim to consolidate their presence in power. In this way, structural transformation can hardly happen, especially where some military governments had to destroy all cooperatives and industries that earlier military governments had started in many Sub-Saharan countries. One cannot talk about poverty and fails to mention Sub-Saharan Africa.

To move from agrarian to industrialized societies requires the will and sacrifice of leaders. Because of the politics of envy, some African leaders are opting for Asian-giant-driven economic transformation, allowing more FDI inflows from the Asian giant and collapsing local investors. Consequently, protectionism is biased towards the leadership lineage and their peoples/relatives who own industries, controlling a significant fraction of the country's GDP. In my view, I believe the issues above are the main reasons why Sub-Saharan Africa manufacturing share of GDP is tiny, and poverty levels remain among the highest in the world.

Manufacturing Share of GDP in Sub-Saharan African Countries

When talking about developing countries in Africa, the Sub-Saharan countries are always listed first. When development agencies round-up for policy-making about global poverty eradication, they cannot look farther than Sub-Saharan Africa as a typical representative of economically struggling societies across the globe. The manufacturing share of GDP in the Sub-Saharan African countries stands as follows:

The manufacturing share of GDP in the Sub-Saharan African

Country	Manufacturing, value added (% of GDP	Most Recent Year
Angola	6.581	2017
Benin	12.294	2018
Botswana	5.159	2018
Burkina Faso	4.859	2018
Burundi	9.362	2016
Cameroon	18.557	2018
Cape Verde	6.710	2018
Central African Republic	18.132	2018
Chad	2.955	2016
Comoros		
Congo (Brazzaville)	6.523	2017

Congo (Democratic Republic)	18.557	2018
Côte d'Ivoire	18.106	2018
Djibouti	3.424	2018
Equatorial Guinea	24.814	2018
Eritrea	5.493	2009
Ethiopia	5.821	2018
Gabon	19.083	2018
The Gambia	4.416	2018
Ghana	10.459	2018
Guinea	10.570	2018
Guinea-Bissau	10.499	2017
Kenya	7.741	2018
Lesotho	14.011	2018
Liberia	1.748	2018
Madagascar	10.104	2018
Malawi	9.366	2017
Mali	4.062	1979
Mauritania	7.407	2018
Mauritius	11.364	2018
Mozambique	8.810	2018
Namibia	10.110	2018
Niger	5.471	2018
Nigeria	9.647	2018
Réunion		
Rwanda	2.492	2018
Sao Tome and Principe	7.444	2018
Senegal	19.706	2018
Seychelles	6.428	2018
Sierra Leone	2.099	2018
Somalia	4.428	1990
South Africa	11.755	2018
Sudan	2.058	2011
South Sudan	3.534	2015

Swaziland		
Tanzania	7.659	2017
Togo	6.580	2018
Uganda	8.266	2018
Western Sahara		
Zambia	8.479	2018
Zimbabwe	8.479	2018

Source: The World Bank (https://data.worldbank.org/indicator/)

Modern economists report that developing countries have remained poor due to the failure to spearhead structural transformation. Most of the industries in Sub-Saharan Africa are owned by foreigners. However, sometimes economists seem to be puzzled why poverty levels in Sub-Saharan Africa remain among the highest in the world. This socioeconomic phenomenon stretches beyond the understanding that current economic theories provide and calls for rethinking new economic theories specifically for the Sub-Saharan African region. It is quite puzzling why extreme poverty remains worst in this area. This new wave of economic theories will utilize the psychological dimension to the fullest. In this interest, I find it appropriate for the MIT Poverty Lab project (The Abdul Latif Jameel Poverty Action Lab) led by economists to take samples from the Sub-Saharan African region. The MIT Poverty Lab project mission is to reduce poverty by ensuring that policies are based on scientific evidence. I am convinced beyond doubt, of course, from observations conducted over time that this socioeconomic phenomenon affecting Sub-Saharan Africa can be studied by collecting scientific evidence. I have crafted the *unique African attitude disorder* (UAAD), which distances Africans from consuming their products and services.[126] And I believe the MIT Poverty Lab gurus can investigate this further.

Deindustrialization in Developing African Countries: What do we have to do?

Advanced economies have been losing jobs ever since they began to deindustrialize. The fear that quality jobs and declining innovations rates associates with deindustrialization has been the greatest among high-income countries. However, something that makes news is that poor African countries have begun to deindustrialize. As a result of globalization, late industrializers—typical of Sub-Saharan Africa, are reaching peak levels of industrialization that are very low compared to those experienced by early industrializers. For example, in some African countries, peak manufacturing employment shares are at about $700 compared to $14,000 experienced by Great Britain around 1990. This trend which Dani Rodrik (2015) called "premature deindustrialization", is very worrying.[127]

In my opinion, apart from the globalization effect, deindustrialization in African countries is accelerated and perpetuated by an education system that creates more pseudo project managers than skilled labour force. That corroborates the fact that deindustrialization in African countries arises from the supply-side deficiencies—the lack of investment and innovation. A number of the high-income countries'

---

[126] See p. 203-214, §4.

[127] Dani, R. *Premature deindustrialization*. J Econ Growth, Springer Science+Business Media, New York, 21:1–33, 2016.

transformations went through the following stages, as shown in the chart below. Some of these stages intertwined, and they did not occur successively. From agrarian societies up to today's knowledge-based economies, high-income countries have revolutionized to boost their economies.

Typical development stages for high-income countries					
Agrarian societies (agriculture/ hunting societies)	Scientific revolution	Agricultural revolution (mass agricultural production)	Industrial/ technological revolution	Information communications technology (ICTs) revolution	Knowledge-based economies, globalization and digitalization
From about 10,000 years ago	16th Century	17th – 19th Centuries	18th – 19th Centuries	20th – 21st Centuries	21st Century

Most African economies have been agrarian up to the 20th century. They had not undergone many structural transformational changes when other countries were revolutionizing. The 16th – 19th centuries were characterized by slave trade and religion, whilst the early 20th century saw colonialism taking centre stage. Many African countries became independent sovereign states in the mid-20th century, and that is when they began to plan for their economies. Globalization has highly been pronounced in the second half of the 20th century.

It is worth noting that the scientific and agricultural revolutions were foundational stages for the developed countries, and the industrial revolution concreted the superstructure of high-income countries. The sustained growth and development attained by high-income countries has been driven by the ICT revolution, digitalization, and globalization. It is highly unimportant for Africa to try to go through the development stages the western world went through in this digital and globalized era. *We need an integrated approach,* and the information age requires brilliant policymakers.[128]

During that time, the Europeans did many good and bad things in the pursuit of development which were never brought to book. Today's information age and swift flow of commerce require an integrated approach. In my opinion, less than 50% of the valuable information was recorded before the ICT revolution. This information would be helpful for us to learn from. Many events went unnoticed. In today's globalization and digitalization, the internet and social platforms record every single incidence that happens globally. The high-income countries have all it takes to aggregate the incidences to conduct different sorts of data analytics for their sustainability. That is why Africa's development will always be difficult because we can be supervised remotely by the European countries. Therefore, the planning

---

[128] See §8

required where democracy is highly advocated for globally must promote clarity and transparency. There were uncontrollable transparency levels during those foundational and superstructure days of the high-income countries, unlike today.

In today's globalization, we can know whatever is happening at the smallest unit of society as soon as possible. We, therefore, need quality leaders whose debates focus on the cause and effect of whatever policies are to be enacted. The structural planning amidst the 21st-century sustainability challenge calls for an integrated approach. In the face of globalization, we cannot get fixated on the stages that high-income countries went through. It just cannot work. We need a new wave of economic thinkers to draw mathematical models that can uplift mineral wealthiest African countries out of poverty and at the same time sustain the growth.

Protectionism and Globalization: Will Africa Manage?

Information technology has brought countries in the world closer, making it a global village. The world is more connected on multiple economic levels. The first kind of protectionism for African industries and enterprises is shielding them from politics of envy. The kind of politics that kills businesses that support other political ideologies and developments must stop. We need to find a way to focus masses on government policy other than partisan politics. Then, analysis of specialized trade policies and sustainability policies aimed to reduce or block international trade in the interest of shielding domestic producers and domestic workers from foreign competition come next.

When developed nations wish to sustain their economic growth, they enact policies and laws to ensure that their prosperity is sustained. Therefore, the trade policies of the developed nations have little room to allow developing countries to emerge from poverty. And this, therefore, calls for sound African politics that will enable quality leaders to be elected into office to enact appropriate policies, laws, and regulations to safeguard and develop domestic firms and workers. In several lines and paragraphs, I have mentioned the idea, "…..of catching space in real-time." Late coming has its economic advantages and disadvantages. The advantages can only be realized when African peoples appreciate the predicaments and bottlenecks they faced while others were prospering.

Power is constantly kept in check in many high-income countries, at least better than their African counterparts. The developed world is strategic when enacting sound government policies because their political systems are mature enough, and very few legislators emerge out of the electoral process by accident. Several developed countries have experienced and talented legislators, unlike Africans who compensate for the loss of a legislator with their 18-year-old daughters and sons. This makes developed nations more promising in the sustainability equation.

Africa's politics characterized/associated with many distortions will less likely allow Africans to utilize the late-comer opportunities that globalization presents unless things are changed following some of my recommendations. These distortions will instead perpetuate the disadvantages of late coming, and it is to the advantage of the organized, developed world. These distortions include the unique African attitude disorder (UAAD), politics of envy, displacement of African values for western values, unique understanding of time, wanting education system, conventional religions not fitting well enough in the equation of Africa's success and et cetera. All these and many others outlined in other chapters impede self-driven sustainable development.

The late-comer opportunities include but are not limited to:

a) Lower wages in low-income African countries can allow the growth of labour-intensive manufacturing.

b) Facilitating FDI inflows from lead comparator countries into developing African countries.

c) There is tapping into opportunities presented by global value chains—negotiating offshoring from big multinationals of high-income countries.

d) There is also opportunity to borrow or adapt technologies that have already matured in high income economies.

e) Developing countries can plan their economies from the experience of the developed world in manufacturing, smart city planning, greening activities, et cetera.

In other words, the late-comer has the opportunity to weigh the risks from a more informed point, borrowing from a number of experiences on multiple levels across the globe.

The late-comer disadvantages include but are not limited to:

The high-income countries perceive some emerging economies as a potential threat and enact many policies to ensure these economies continue in an emerging situation. For example, policies on excess agricultural produce given out as foreign aid to African countries are to the disadvantage of African farmers.

Secondly, a situation where African developing countries are seated on minerals in the face of globalization is a time bomb. The perceived threat of mineral exhaustion in high-income countries and yet African countries are not optimally utilizing theirs risks a conflict of interest in a way relations between high-income and low-income countries are built and administered.

Because many African countries are still virgin, and their workers' policies are weak, some high-income countries initiate aid and FDI inflows geared towards uplifting Africa but impose policies along with aid that cannot support the growth of African workers.

Another problem comes from weak human capital produced by many African educational institutions, which is not destined to stimulate African growth. This affects the late-comer in a way that modern enterprises require continuously evolving human capital, yet many African countries are fixated on analogue systems. Here, the high-income countries will always get excused for recommending their labour along with FDI inflows to developing countries.

Green politics, which should be the driver of sustainable development, is primarily informed by the following key professionals but not limited to: the engineer, the environmentalist, and the economist. In an attempt to protect domestic industries, domestic workers and consumers, sustainability, as defined in Africa's context, is the special interest that governs decision making. In the decision-making process, which requires high-level planning because of the late-comer risks associated with development partners' attempt to drive our growth, we need a new kind of political leaders with the ability to weigh the odds. There is no direct approach that Africa has to borrow to obtain economic independence but needs highly emotionally intelligent leaders who know when to start, when to pause and when to stop. Emotional incompetence has made some African leaders think that because Europeans colonized us, they are worse than the Asian giant. Something untrue! Look at the economic status of South Africa and Hong Kong, which took long time to revert and weigh the odds. Problems cannot be solved by anger and negative emotions. It is about understanding why they (Europeans) led to avoid immature defence mechanisms like intense self-deceptive rationalization. We tend to believe that the Asian giant is any better.

All that is necessary for analysis because our late-coming is perceived differently by masses across the globe. And perception is more important than fact! Therefore, the kind of protectionism we need might not be based largely on present economic doctrines or first-generation theories, which are very strict and obvious at some point, but rather accommodative policies would be prioritized in a bid to understand how to move in the interest of masses. For example, some high-income countries set invisible trade barriers to protect their domestic firms. They have resorted to trade remedies used under unique circumstances and bringing policies in the interest of sustainability, such as low-carbon trade barriers and intellectual property.

Claims that when free trade is allowed with some countries, their intellectual rights would be violated and that there will be increased carbon emissions in their countries is one of the arguments they make to protect their domestic firms. Also, some high-income countries are debarring corrupt African leaders from entering their territories by refusing to grant them visas to their countries for fear of infection. This is another kind of protectionism not yet recognized well enough by economists because it takes more of the psychological dimension.

In order to prevent the corrupt African leaders from infecting their citizens, of which some are producers, they break the association by refusing them visas to their countries. In the same scheme of things, we need uncertain policies and measures to protect our domestic firms and workers in the face of globalization. This is because direct trade policies commonly adapted spark mixed reactions from well-wishers and several economic analysts. Therefore, well-studied policies and measures in the interest of Africa's sustainability as defined correctly in this authorship need to be enacted. For example, policies enacted following the protection of African values could stretch farther than the obvious. Specifically, this may include a ban, quota or imposing high tariffs on clothes that do not support Africa's politeness. Rather than enacting a policy to ban second-hand clothes in the interest of protecting domestic firms, one may argue that these clothes are against Africa's politeness.

Good nutrition is important for a healthy body. The trend is shifting away from healthy foods to fast foods. Many young people feel bored consuming old boring home-cooked food, yet studies show that these foods are more nutritious than fast foods. Fast foods are rich in sugars, salts and fats; hence are claimed to cause high blood pressure, obesity, diabetes and heart diseases. In the interest of accelerating human capital growth, we need to focus much on education and health. Hence, sustainability and trade policies must prioritize these two sectors first—in my view. Therefore, any kind of direct protectionist policies must prioritize developing Africa's human capital—and by people feeding well and getting access to quality and inclusive education, we are guaranteed a rise in the wellbeing of Africans. Education and health associates with the following sectors: agriculture, housing, energy and etcetera.

In our protectionist policies, we should not appear strict where we cannot sustain the strictness. Second-hand gadgets, e.g. electronics and apparel from Europe and America, are associated with little carbon emissions and, in many cases, are more reliable as compared to sub-standard, low-quality products imported from some Asian countries. Some products imported from the Asian countries are of very low quality requiring the consumer to either repair or replace them with new ones routinely—they have very limited lifespans. Considering this issue from an economist's point of view, the consumer of the less quality product that breaks down routinely, causing many downtime costs for the business case, is constantly in the market for a replacement.

Since few Africans can afford to buy reliable products, we need to assess the repercussions of banning second-hand products in our territories. By the time first hand owners discard some of the used products, they are still salvageable, and their lifespans are still on. Inadequate assessments to outlaw a policy on second-hand products might end up increasing the cost of doing business in the region both directly and indirectly. What economists would call savings from buying an alternative new low priced good imported from some Asian countries might become a reliability cost, causing many other costs that cannot be monetized. Therefore, in the face of globalization, it is not only about protecting domestic firms but rather the practicality of our policies at a macro level. This is by considering the cost of doing small and medium business. We need to analyze policies on imports in terms of reliability, operability, maintainability, safety, security, welfare and sustainability and not restrict ourselves to the mere protection of producers and workers. We should desist from making more premature policies like the premature educational policies and premature deindustrialization associated policies.

If we are moving in the line of sustainability, I would argue that high tariffs, quotas, and non-tariff barriers would be imposed, for example, on; fast foods, sodas, sports gambling equipment, et cetera. We need to protect the farmers who produce green and organic foods and protect value addition industries surrounding the agricultural sector. We are in a bid to improve the general African well-being through better nutrition. And a healthy body leads to a healthy mind. Throughout the authorship of this book, my emphasis is on dealing with the mindset. I, therefore, advocate for good nutrition that can affect a healthy body for a healthy mind. I have given a few examples here, particularly considering the emerging African countries. However, many other examples exist in other sectors where we need to be cautious when enacting protectionist policies.

I do therefore submit:

> "Long-serving heads of states that rise and hold onto power undemocratically have to go. However, we need to make them go by ourselves, not by others. There is a risk when non-Africans push out long-serving heads of states. It perpetuates more influence on Africa by non-Africans. Our task is to ensure that the masses appreciate why long-serving heads of state have to step down. Masses loyal to the long-serving heads of states claim that their respective regimes have scored many positives and that we ought to appreciate their contribution to the growth of some of Africa's economies. In my opinion, long-serving cannot go without the accumulation of mistakes. It is because of these mistakes, which we collectively aggregate at a macro-level to weigh the odds following the guiding principles of sustainable development in the face of globalization. The politics of envy domineering

African countries makes a network of some lineage of people benefit from the long-serving, and they think because of the improvement in welfare that they have achieved in their lineage, there is a general improvement in national welfare and economic growth. There will be no free trade, neither right protectionism, where leaders impose themselves on the masses."

Structural Transformation and Sustainable Industrialization

As developing countries fully industrialize, they are tasked through international agreements to promote cleaner industrial processes. Economic growth that can be sustained comes with structural transformation. Economists argue that countries that have remained poor have failed to achieve structural transformation. This is basically about failure to diversify activities ranging from agriculture to modern activities and manufacturing. In 2018, Some Sub-Saharan African countries enacted a policy to ban the importation of second-hand clothes for import-substitution industrialization to promote domestic textile industries. I believe sustained growth is more promising when production is based on the comparative advantage and factor endowments of a country at that time. Governments, therefore, have to play a proactive role in facilitating structural transformation by understanding the obstacles faced. Correct policies on; new and advancing technologies, skilling locals, trade, and commerce are some of the remedies to spur successful structural transformation within African economies. Identification of suitable industries is paramount in the equation of structural transformation. Sustained economic growth and development is a product of successful structural transformation.

Sustainable industrialization is a work in progress and promotes green industrial and manufacturing processes. Activities that minimize to the extent possible the carbon emissions pumped into the atmosphere. The world requires industrial processes with increased environmental performance and utilising more efficient machinery that generates less effluent, waste and pollutants—industries that promote a reduction in waste, reuse, and recycling of products. Many firms are promoting or starting to promote green energies and are particularly concerned with workers' health and safety.

In the process of combating climate change by ensuring temperature rise is kept below 2°C above pre-industrial levels and pursuing efforts to limit the temperature increase to 1.5 °C above pre-industrial levels, developing countries' industrial processes are tasked to maintain a log of carbon emissions from industries for submission as part of the nationally determined contributions in response to the UN Charter ratified in 2015.[129] **Important:** The process to fully industrialize African countries has come when the world prioritises sustainability, unlike before. It, therefore, requires African countries to be more accountable and vigilant. Some of the remedies for failing to meet the policy requirements will be to levy taxes on those industrial processes which are not green. Some of the developmental agencies at the forefront of promoting sustainability goals are the same agencies that support/finance economic development roadmaps in African countries. That means economic development in Africa is tightly supervised. What does this mean? It means that Africans need to wake up. "We are not going to keep eating beans using needles and think we shall have a sustainable future" African proverb.

---

[129] UN Paris Agreement. Article 2, 2015.

As we think of utilizing the late-comer opportunities in the process to industrialize fully, we should highly base our arguments and policies on comparative advantage and associated economic doctrines. Africa needs to plan well because developmental agencies are getting strict on cleaner industrial processes, which call for new and advancing technologies that might need heavy initial capital investment. For example, with good leadership, there is room to negotiate better international trade policies with partners. This might help Africans industrialize by joining the international supply chain rather than building its supply chains through home-based industrialization. Because sustainability issues are a hot topic of the century, it will not be very easy to fully develop home-based industrialization when globalization presents competitive options that can be tapped into by a forward-looking nation. Therefore, industrialization by joining supply chains is more advantageous to accelerate African growth.

Economic development in Africa's context and the interest of sustainable development should be measured this way –

"We need to invent our kind of economic theories in the context of Africa's sustainability—measuring success as value-added by Africans in a specified period. Economic development measured by social and economic progress in Africa's context may not use the current human development index (HDI), based on life expectancy, adult literacy, and GDP per capita. The current HDI philosophized by developmental agencies provides misleading results to believe that the standard of living of African peoples has improved. Yet, it falls a little short of the psychosocial wellbeing triggered and perpetuated by multigenerational syndromes, especially those repressed and become more hazardous in the equation of success. The accurate indicators of development for Africans amidst the 21st century, where globalization is making FDI inflows dominate African countries, will take on a different metric based on the do-it-yourself extent. The governing interest for formulating the measure of Africa's economic development is sustainability as defined in Africa's context so that Africa rises with Africans. The correct economic development indicator for Africa will measure: how many people access the right education system that is free from knowledge illusions, how many people are living in a green environment and eating organic and green foods, the extent for consideration of the Africans' voice in international matters, how many Africans invent, innovate and develop practical solutions for industry plus being integrated into FDI inflows, and GDP per capita measured from how much the nationals contribute to the pool. The current measure of economic development does not account for Africa's sustainability."

Public Contracts Financing and Foreign Direct Investment (FDI) Traps in the Face of Globalization

Many African low-income countries have a predominantly mineral resources-based GDP and, therefore, plan to get fully industrialized within the first half of the 21st century. However, this ambition meets enormous challenges amidst globalization. Governments have several priority projects that they wish to implement, and if implemented, several ambitions would be realized. In this case, concept notes and detailed feasibility studies of priority projects are prepared to interest investors. I mentioned earlier that economists argue that Africa needs more foreign direct investments than portfolio capital flows. I would be interested in adding, "……..Africa needs more FDI in the private sector." Here, many priority projects lack financing to kick-start. That is where governments find it appropriate to open up widely to investors willing to invest in Africa. They make presentations about the priority projects, and some investors pick interest to finance some of the prioritized areas, especially those with sound revenue streams.

The most competitive fields include the construction of: airports, roads and highways, expressways, bridges, water and electricity, hydropower dams and et cetera. Because government expenditure is a political decision, the political atmosphere is critical in the sustainability equation. The sustainability equation calls for an appropriate accounting system. Also, the present worth analysis is an important attribute that cannot be left out before deciding to undertake a project. Sound project selection must be done for emerging economies to develop themselves in this competitive world driven by globalization. A good question to ask is: **do we have promising political atmospheres to spearhead self-driven sustainable development?**

If public projects are not funded by government savings/loans/charities, i.e. Traditional Public Sector (TPS) financing project delivery mechanisms, they go for Public-Private Partnerships (PPP). The contract execution modalities can always be agreed upon. The most common contract models (forms of contract) for mega infrastructure projects include:

a) Engineering, Procurement and Contracting (EPC) + Financing contract/financing models
b) Design and Build
c) Build, Operate and Transfer (BOT)
d) Design, Build, Finance, Operate, and Transfer (DBFOT)
e) Design-build-finance
f) Design-build-operate-maintain, and;
g) Other National Procurement and Contract models.

There are many newly introduced contract and financing models for public projects innovated by high-income countries whose economic analyses are not yet well-understood by developing countries. Some of these newly introduced models intertwine FDI with PPP to make very complex models. Many high-income countries have demonstrated a hallmark in sustaining their growth and development. The burning question is: with the current rate of globalization, will high-income countries be able to sustain their growth and development for 100+ years to come? Therefore, they have to devise complex models that will make them shoot sustainable development by utilizing several spheres of social influence.

The most critical issue to note is that several African governments are desperate. The desperate situation stems from a lack of funds to finance public contracts. This condition in the face of globalization is a great opportunity for the Asian giant. The Asian giant is finding a new twist in FDI superimposing over the contract financing models of mega infrastructure projects and later enable her multinationals to move freely to attain the go-global agenda. The Asian giant government facilitates state-owned multinationals and provides financing in the form of very low-interest loans. They have started up many new affiliates that belong to state-owned multinationals, especially construction firms in African countries, to execute mega infrastructure projects. And this is for the long term; hence many of these affiliates can be treated as FDI or FDI vehicles.

What they need from African governments is either a memorandum of understanding or a sovereign guarantee to invest in Africa. This business model is very strategic for the Asian giant, i.e. state-owned multinationals using state finances to invest in Africa. In the interest of the Asian giant, this is the modern Foreign Direct Investment (FDI) to African countries—and should be treated as purely FDI. They are eager to pick those projects with justifiable annual savings from the list of priority projects in African countries. The focus is on projects that are likely to have sufficient revenue streams. Another important aspect to note is that the Asian giant is faster to invest in public infrastructure than other sectors. The second Asian giant ranked based on GDP growth is more genuine because it focuses on Africa's foreign direct investment in the private sector. Africa needs FDI in the private sector, where foreign investors associate with local people freely. If African economies drove the private sector growth through FDI in the private sector, increased revenue would bring about a promising tax base, and healthy funding of infrastructure projects would be possible. Multinationals operating in the private sector would find the need to finance roads and other infrastructure projects.

Analyzing the Asian Giant's Typical Turnkey Construction Project Loaned to Africa

According to the Asian giant, the going global framework intends to spearhead economic integrations and bring about shared prosperity, peace, and stability. In this framework, the Asian giant's multinationals share a common goal of going global to create various global production networks and global value chains. The Asian giant's framework claims that a set of principles guides it, and these include: not peddling influence in another sovereign's affairs, desist from geopolitical sabotage, and not exporting social systems and structures in another sovereign. In the same framework, mutual benefits and shared prosperity are core objectives.

Consider an expressway toll road project worth US$ 476 m loaned to a developing African country under the Design, Build, Finance, Operate, and Transfer (DBFOT) contract model. The contractor, consultant, materials supplier and financier are all from the FDI home country. There is no doubt that highways are important infrastructure to the country's economic development and improve the economic structure of an economy. I give an estimated breakdown of the cost below:

Item	US$
Project cost	*476m*
Materials and land	330.5 m
Technology, machinery and equipment	95.2 m
Management and consultancy (skilled & semi-skilled labor)	30.3 m
Other labor (unskilled)	20.0 m

In the economic sense, it would be okay to look at the "expressway project" built in this kind of arrangement as a product more or less like the production of a cell phone or a refrigerator in the Asian giant's territory and shipped to a developing African country. Economies of scale occur to companies when they produce in large quantities. In this case, one product is produced and not many products. However, because the project is big enough, constituent elements like precast concrete production enjoy economies of scale.

About 80% of the materials are fetched from the FDI home country or the affiliates operating in the host country that would translate to about US$ 264.4 m; land compensation and associated materials go to the host country at about US$ 66.1 m; technology, machinery, and equipment are all fetched from the home country at about US$ 95.2 m; management and consultancy (skilled labour) fetched from the home country for about US$ 30.3 m, and unskilled labour for about US$ 20.0 m obtained from the host country.

Simple payback period analysis shows that for the Asian giant to recover US$ 476 m in 5 years, the net annual savings (NAS) from the tools would be about US$ 95.2 m assuming a zero discount value, i.e. Payback period $(P_b) = (C_0/NAS)$, where:

C_0 = the initial construction of the highway project

NAS = net annual savings

Therefore, at a payback period of 40 years fixed as the loan maturity period, the net annual savings required should be US$ 11.9 m. However, this cannot be the case where net cash flows are identical from the first year throughout all years. Therefore, the discount rate cannot be zero. The cash flow yields from the tolls will follow a geometric progression from one year until the end when the construction cost plus cost of capital is recovered. That would mean the traffic growth on the toll road would positively correlate with the region's economic growth. In this case, if we are to follow the present worth economic methods, at *net annual savings of US$ 11.9 m* on the toll road and a discount rate of 10%, the present worth factor would be as follows:

$$\frac{P}{A} = \frac{(1+i)^n - 1}{i(1+i)^n} = \frac{(1+0.1)^{40} - 1}{0.1(1+0.1)^{40}} = 9.78$$

Therefore, the present worth of the project = -476 + (11.9 x 9.78) = US$ -359.618m

Where;

P : Present value

A : Future sum to be received

i : The discount interest rate

n : Number of years to pay back the loan

Since the present worth of the project is negative, it renders the project unfeasible in the first place. However, at a net savings of US$ 50 m per year, the project worth is about US$ 13 m. For example, if the cost of capital is negotiated at 1%, the present worth factor becomes 32.82. Therefore, the present worth of the project at a discount rate of 1% is US$ -85.45 m when the tolls generate net revenue of US$ 11.9 m per year and US$ 1,164.95m when the tolls generate net revenue of US$ 50 m per year.

The graph below is a plot of present worth versus net annual savings at discount rates of 1%, 5% and 10%, respectively, for the toll road project constructed with a loan worth US$ 476m.

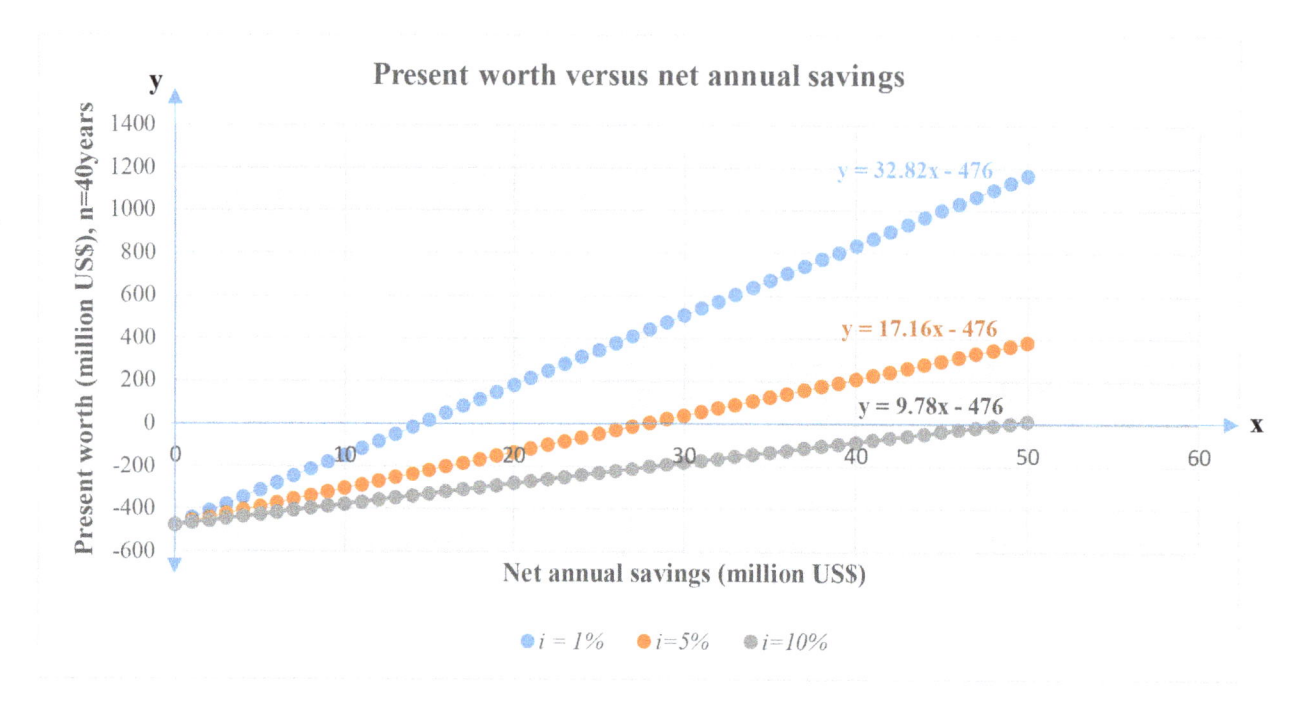

Present Worth versus Net Annual Savings for the Toll Road Project

From the above illustration, it is super clear that negotiating discount rates is very important, which is highly influenced by the political atmosphere of the nation-state. This is because government spending is more of a political decision than an economic decision. The funding of mega infrastructure projects requires concessional loans. However, the political atmosphere and many other distortions cannot allow many African nations to take concessional loans. The atmosphere favours non-concessional loans. The economic structure of the region highly influences the net annual savings from the toll road project.

The willingness and ability to pay for the tolls is predetermined by the nature of economic activities in the region—the country's GDP growth rate. Therefore, traffic evaluation at the points connected by the expressway considers how economic activities shall be transformed in the 40 years. Other economic analyses that are absolutely imperative in addition to the project present worth would be to carry out the cost-benefit analysis and investigating the internal rate of return. A cost-benefit ratio greater than unity and an internal rate of return that exceeds the discount rate must corroborate a promising project present worth for a more feasible project. **Therefore, the critical questions to ask are as follows:** do we have the power to negotiate fair discount rates? What structural reforms are in place to bring about modern economic activities to boost the region's GDP to be able to pay back the loans? In terms of sustainable development, how are future generations protected not to become slaves in their region due to the failure to meet our obligations? What are the remedies to prevent the Asian giant from peddling influence beyond the tolls?

What are some of the Effects of the Toll Road FDI Project on the Host African Country?

Transparent land compensation might improve the well-being of project affected persons (PAPs), and also unskilled labour force finds employment opportunities on the project. There is also reduced time of travel for those who can afford to pay for the tolls. The expressway cuts down on traffic congestion and reduces the amount of money lost from the host country due to traffic delays. There is a likelihood that accidents would reduce as a result of a new alternative highway. There is also an acceleration of economic growth and development because of improved infrastructure, which eases the transportation of goods. Tax revenues increase in the host country arising out of the toll road project as long as these revenues exceed extra costs that the government may incur in the process. The toll road project facilitates sister FDI from which the host country could benefit in a short while, especially some unskilled labour force gaining employment.

On the other hand, environmental management and project design/development decisions are left to the FDI home country, posing a risk to the host country. And these are very critical planning decisions that affect sustainability. Environmental, social, and cultural concerns require African experts to be involved in the planning process to evaluate the nature of road, expressway, and highway designs. The decisions on our sacred sites, which we have protected for many thousands of years, are made by experts from the Asian giant in the interest of roads and highways development and associated infrastructure developments. This is false and very bad. Leading continuous improvement for sustainability must be primarily handled by the one who understands how particular peoples have evolved over the years to promote and protect sacred sites symbolic of values, norms, predispositions, tradition, and related cultural assets. That habit of designing infrastructure mainly by foreigners and the local people never form an integral part must immediately stop if we dream of self-driven sustainable development. African experts must decide on appropriate routes for roads and highways following a holistic approach that favours sustainable development. The reason is that they have the knowledge of their ecosystem better than a foreigner.

The failure for African governments to negotiate deals that allow African scientists, engineers, traditionalists, sociologists, environmentalists, and technocrats to be wholly involved and, where possible, lead project design/development decisions on infrastructure projects cripples the building of skills in our labour force. It makes Africans hopeless in maintaining, extending, and developing technologies in Africa. Operation and maintenance of the expressway might prove difficult once the host country is not fully involved in the design and management decisions as early enough in project appraisal, especially after the expiry of the DBFOT contract.

For roads and highways programs, great effort is geared towards operation and maintenance because this is a routine/periodic activity that public authorities undertake to have fully functioning and operable road networks. There is always advancing road technologies, especially in road pavement structures that would require the involvement of Africans. Recent improved nanotechnologies and geotextiles for stabilizing structural road layers and new asphalts technology for road pavements are gaining market and need engineers who understand their correct application and maintenance.

In the example provided above, the loan's maturity is based on the assumed project lifespan of 40 years. The expressway design and construction is a one-off exercise, but maintenance is an ongoing activity. Therefore, local capacity has to be built right away from project appraisals by allowing our technocrats and engineers who understand how we have evolved and graduated to what we have become to actively participate in training/assistantships and decision-making processes on these projects. There are many similar examples of such projects built by Europeans in Africa that Africans failed to maintain because of lack of training and no technology transfer. These include railway lines, industries (e.g. textiles), and telephones technology in many African countries. Where there is no concrete plan for technology transfer, developing economies cannot be boosted. It is evident that technologies get outdated and become obsolete. However, a good understanding of the obsolete technology is vital to lead the generations into the replacement. For example, in Africa, which plans to go digital, a good number of the would-be experts are not well-conversant with many old analogue technologies. A shortfall in continuous research and development on many projects that utilize technologies from elsewhere leaves no hope that African economies will stand independently. They will remain to be remotely controlled by others.

The truth is that the new kind of FDI that the Asian giant has spotted is in infrastructure development in African countries. This includes the toll road projects and associated infrastructure. There is no doubt that African countries will see all infrastructure worked on by others through models that do not support or stimulate the ingenuity of their people. In this way, African engineers will be disabled in thinking and fail to support, operate and maintain their respective country's infrastructure. In my view, engineers have a pivotal role to play in the economic transformation of a nation. This is because they deal with the design and operation of machines and associated infrastructure which are used in the production of goods and services across several sectors of an economy. Therefore, failing the nation's engineers to realize their potential is cheating our economies in broad daylight. When you talk about agricultural modernization and manufacturing, nothing transforms without engineers piecing together.

A Nile-Basin country's leader was excited to announce that he had temporarily banned borrowing (both external and internal), favouring the Asian giant's proposals to fund the toll expressway because they were planning to collect their money from tolls. It is not about the toll road FDI projects that leave the home country to make decisions alone. Then we get excited that our people will not face the debt consequences because the funder will raise the invested money by managing tolls, but instead building foundations for our people to help themselves in all spheres of social influence. That is what counts much in project feasibilities and appraisal studies! People and sustainability come first, and money comes later.

Note: The Asian giant collecting money from tolls is a contract condition in the DBFOT contract. It does not mean they will lose when the 40 years elapse, and their money plus the interest is not recovered. The host government has full responsibility to ensure that they clear the debt. This condition is only meant to ensure clarity and transparency in the toll business so that cash flows are recorded transparently. It ensures checks and balances, audits, and QC/QA, but it is real debt. The two nations have to work together to ensure profitability and to recover the loan. Our responsibility as Africans is to negotiate concessional loans that are compatible with our GDP growth to enable us to pay back the loans. If the loan is not recovered in 40 years, the two nations will renegotiate new terms and conditions. Among them would be negotiating a new FDI establishment that would facilitate loan recovery. **The questions are:** Are we taking on concessional loans? Who is driving our GDP growth?

What are some of the benefits of the Toll Road FDI Project to Home Country?

There is no technology transfer to the host country. Skilled workers primarily conduct road designs while in the home country. The technology used in design and construction is limited to Asian giant's skilled workers. This will always give the Asian Giant room to exploit Africa, and Africa will remain primarily a consumer market. The toll road project facilitates sister FDIs in the host countries, especially multinationals from the FDI home country. For example, many Asian giant's industrial enterprises are still at the early stage of going global, and such toll road projects are a good motivator. Going global is a common interest for all multinationals of the Asian giant. They cannot achieve the go global agenda in African countries where roads are in a dire state. Going global means establishing affiliates that can engage in the same type of production as the parent companies or engage in different stages of overall production. They can, therefore, complement or substitute export trade as appropriately modelled to suit their interests. How would they transport their goods on bad African roads? That is why they associate themselves with the Design, Build, Finance, Operate, and Transfer (DBFOT) and Engineering, Procurement and Contracting (EPC) plus financing contract models in African infrastructure projects.

FDI in the form of infrastructure development, especially those that are income-generating like toll roads, water supply schemes, energy projects, and other similar projects, are the best option in Africa's context to complement the FDI home country's international trade and to facilitate the mission of the Asian giant's firms for going global. Economists argue that FDI can either complement or increase the exports of the home country. Keeping many other factors constant, the model of financing and contracting for this toll road project contributes to a favourable balance of trade and a favourable balance of payment of the FDI home country. The foreign exchange risk is also lowered because less of their currency is exchanged for other currencies in project transactions.

Conclusion on the Toll Road Project

A senior official from the Asian giant was intensely questioned by the Public Accounts Committee of a developing African Nile Basin country on the accountability of a DBFOT toll road project they loaned to Africa. He was confident enough to say that they were helping Africans. In the eyes of economists and other well-informed people, this was an insult because if they were helping Africa, they would give money as a donation and leave Africans to decide on the toll road project. Or else they would give the country a loan, and the Africans take the decisions. Later, the Asian giant issued a statement published in the local newspapers to apologize for the earlier statement made by the official, which corroborated as evidence. You cannot claim to be helping Africans when you insist on turnkey and DBFOT projects. At least alternative development agencies provide room to exercise more transparent procurement processes that build reliability in projects right from the start.

"It is even more damaging for a minister to say foolish things than to do them."

Jean François Paul de Gondi, Cardinal de Retz (1613–1679).

Where technology is not transferred to Africa, the Asian giant is not sharing prosperity but rather moving smart enough to protect their businesses and investment interests by going global to extend economic prospects. Africans will benefit from the toll road project in the short term, but they have no choice to stop the financier's influence, which is a long-term strategy. And their (Africans) negotiation power is threatened. This is because Africans are not wholly involved in technical decision making on projects that affect the nation-state's sustainability. It is purely a political weakness by African governments that fail to negotiate better deals to allow their scientists, engineers, and technologists to practice what they learned. If professionals are given the opportunity, they gain confidence and independent judgment to help their countries obtain a long-term win-win situation with the FDI home countries.

The Asian Giant's going Global Framework and FDI in Africa's Infrastructure: The Big Picture

More than half of the Asian giant's population know very well that there is no free lunch under the sun, and it is an instinct held within their blood. The going global framework is a program project too good to be missed by many African countries because it presents opportunities visible to almost everybody. But of course, vision is not merely seeing but rather the art of seeing through walls. Sometimes, having a vision is being able to see what is invisible to others. The going global framework is intended to create friendship between the Asian giant and the rest of the world. It sounds nice! The Asian giant claims to be more focused on economic gain than political gain.[130] The "going global" mission is an economic development program. However, economic and political agendas are inseparable twins. Many of Asian giant's enterprises are still at an early stage of going global, and they wish to open up to the outside world.

Africa presents many challenges for her FDI inflows' success. The notable ones include but are not limited to; poor infrastructure, unique African attitude disorder (UAAD), lack of technology and skills, the illusion of knowledge, and a unique understanding of time. But because it is endowed with natural resources, minerals, and a good climate, it attracts FDI. Therefore, the success of the FDI is warranted when infrastructure is improved. With infrastructure improvement, production is highly possible. For example, roads/highways should be improved before setting up industries. Therefore, the improved connectivity and the reduced travel time would facilitate trade. The sources of energy should also be good enough to facilitate production. In other words, a reliable supply of electricity is a crucial driver of economic growth. This justifies the reason why the Asian giant has heavily invested in transport and energy infrastructure in Africa.

We need to ask ourselves why FDI inflow to Africa from the Asian giant largely supports infrastructure development. However, this does not mean that the Asian giant does not invest in other sectors. The domineering and most exciting sector for the Asian giant is transport and energy infrastructure. **Why?** Many African governments get excited for road tolls projects loaned by the Asian giant because the Asian giant finances, uses their expertise, and collects their monies back, but is this what we wish to have when we claim that we are supporting our people to stand on their own? Now that massive national debts are quickly becoming unsustainable in many African countries, the Asian giant exploits the mess. Leaders believe that since the Asian giant can provide alternative financing in transport and energy infrastructure, it is better that way. That is all hopelessness which poor leadership breeds. Leaders have lost hope and are left with very few options.

Evaluating FDI moving from the Asian giant to Europe is not the same way you would do when moving FDI to African host countries. The majority of multinationals from the Asian giant would look elsewhere

---

[130] See p. 83, §2.

to invest as a priority, i.e. to the Americas and Europe. Africa comes in as a last option mainly due to the cheap unskilled labour and the growing consumer market for substandard goods and services. However, a profitable multinational capable of negotiating better deals would look at the ease of investing in other countries globally, and African countries do not rank so well.

Although the ultimate goal in FDI is premised on mutual benefits, those benefits vary wildly for Africa that has lagged in industrialization. The political structure of each economy predetermines the success of FDI and the contribution it brings to the wellbeing of both peoples of the host and home country. The "going global" agenda of the Asian multinationals is a common interest for all. In my understanding, the success of FDI, therefore, as evaluated by Asian multinationals, cannot be achieved where there is an infrastructure gap in the host countries. They, therefore, have to close this infrastructure gap prior. However, by the time Africans wake up in a quest of closing the said gap, the Asian giant will have exerted much pressure on us, and the only solution will be to let them be. As a result, we will live to consume what they produce, and our engineers and scientists will be porters on their construction sites and in manufacturing industries!

The Asian giant is looking at the benefits that accrue in the long run. One of the reasons their firms quote very low prices when tendering for African construction projects is that most of them are state-owned and can access credit facilities at relatively low-interest rates. Many African firms will never break even unless something happens spearheaded by the young generations not suffering from anxiety disorders driven by so-called friendship ties. During that time when Africa fails to meet its obligations, they will seize the management of every enterprise and renegotiate terms favourable to them. Their multinationals will be unstoppable and shall move freely. They are not looking at monetary returns at present but cost-effectiveness because some African countries will never manage to service the loans for some projects. This is because they are not well streamlined to operate and manage cash flow streams. After all, they lack capacity and expertise—and several governments are doing nothing to mitigate the worst scenario.

Many African countries are not negotiating deals that allow technology transfer and support the training of Africa's personnel to own the operation and management of loaned projects to generate cash flows that are promising to service the loans to completion. The Asian giant's companies and their organized labour force shall continue professional development, but Africans will keep progressing with pseudo project management professionals perpetuating knowledge illusions. The attitudinal challenges of Africans crafted as the unique African attitude disorder (UAAD) cannot allow leaders to instil confidence in our engineers and scientists.[131]

Our failure to meet contractual obligations will help the Asian giant to solidify their presence in Africa. In my understanding, they look at the benefits, especially those you cannot monetize that will accrue when Africans fail to meet their obligations. Those benefits will *motivate political influence*, allowing their multinationals to expand freely and break trade barriers imposed by Africans. When trade barriers are broken, and transport costs are lowered (due to closing the infrastructure gaps), the Asian giant will benefit highly from FDI in African countries. The Asian giant will continue to set up multinational affiliates that can either produce goods as the parent companies or manage stages in the production network to meet the demand of the exploding African consumer market, which is less conscious about standards.

---

[131] See p. 203-214, §4.

Africans will start to soften and give out permits and licenses to exploit our natural resources and minerals. The Asian giant will continue to teach their languages and impose them on Africa's curriculums extending more psychological distortions. Some of the European languages, which the majority of Africans can speak, write, learn, and listen to, are already strong enough wherever you go, globally. As Africans, I do not think we need to learn Asian languages first to produce goods and services. The strategy of the Asian giant teaching her language in African schools is aimed at peddling influence. Linguists are professionals just like any other can be and require no such unique attention. It is a big warning for Africans to understand that the Asian giant's neocolonialism in Africa is a hundred times more dangerous and damaging than any other because we cannot recognize at what point along a continuum their ethics meet with those of African humankind. Many of us will be dead when the Asian giant exerts insurmountable political influence on Africa. However, this book will remain in publication for the next generations to read. We are solely responsible for defining a sustainable future for the next generations.

Something worth noting is that inadequate budgets tend to compromise the health, safety, and welfare of workers in developing countries. And the Asian giant's firms are good at furnishing clients with inadequate budgets. If you wish to learn more about this, ask for the environment, social, and governance (ESG) reports for the projects they have financed in Africa—try to audit these reports checking for sustainability metrics. I am writing as a professional coming from what I have observed and experienced over the years. The most annoying thing is that the Asian giant's firms rarely subcontract local firms, even on works that require no advanced technologies. They ensure that all the money that merits from a project circulates through themselves, and Africans would only benefit from informal sector-related activities that surround project developments. They always opt for their people. This is one of the most robust strategies to solidify their presence in Africa. After some years, they will set a strategy to have a good profit margin after winning a good fraction of the market share. During that time which is not very far, they will raise the bid prices after they have wiped out local competition.

A contractor expressed disappointment when we met at an official contractors' conference, and he made comments summarized as below:

"I have dealt with a big multinational from the Asian giant. As a corporate social strategy, they wished to donate a primary school to the African community located somewhere in Entebbe, Uganda. Having been prequalified to render services to the municipal council in charge, we were selected to design and build the school worth about US$ 500,000. Without any formal contract signed, we successfully conducted the designs, and everything that was required was made for us to negotiate the construction. It was understandable to make designs though no formal contract was signed because the cost we would put in the bidding, for example, would instead go for design the fact that we were selected without competing for the contract. The design phase included numerous correspondences to review many sections of the designs, which we did successfully. However, when proposals and the draft contract reached the multinational's head office, we were objected. No response has been received from those people to tell us why we were objected. We lost our time and money in preparing designs. After a few months, and using our designs, the school project was awarded to their contractor."

That is the typical hopelessness that the Asian giant has caused to African enterprises. That is how several peoples from the Asian giant's multinationals behave when doing work in Africa. Without having a contract agreement with them, just forget the deal! It goes back to the ethics I discussed earlier. To appreciate the Supreme Being's presence in humanity which guides the hierarchy of doing the good, you do not need to make contract agreements prior. I have much evidence on such incidences, and I warn Africa to be careful. In civilized societies that aim for sustainability, people do not put money before human rights! And if people at the top do unthoughtful things, what about ordinary people?

From the economic point of view, a quote that is relatively below the market price is highly likely to have something missing, either in terms of processes or quality. The cost of production varies across the globe, but there is always a threshold under which the desired quality cannot be achieved. In civil engineering and construction, which is quite different from other industries, reliability is built at the earliest stage since it is difficult to correct reliability problems after the civil engineering project is raised.

A senior project manager in a typical African developing country once said, "…..do not mind about the low prices provided by the Asian giant's construction firms; what we need to do is to propose tough consultants for their projects." From the reliability professional's view, this does not help very much because, in construction projects' reliability, we consider minimizing the likelihood of contractual dilemmas at the earliest stage. It is better to say "NO" to prices that cannot achieve the desired reliability to avoid stalling government projects as a result of falling into contractual dilemmas. Much as the desperate governments aim at cost-saving, they should be aware of the reliability costs that accrue in construction projects later and call for unnecessary reworks that highly interrupt service delivery. In the long run, this affects sustainability.

From my experience about construction procurements that the Asian giant's multinational construction firms feature in Sub-Saharan African countries, their quotes always cause a very high standard deviation within the set of bid prices read out at bid opening. In case the readout prices follow a normal distribution as shown in the picture below, my experiences are summarized henceforth. I have witnessed many bid openings that involve international companies from elsewhere and the Asian giant's multinationals, and I can summarize my experiences in the table to the right:

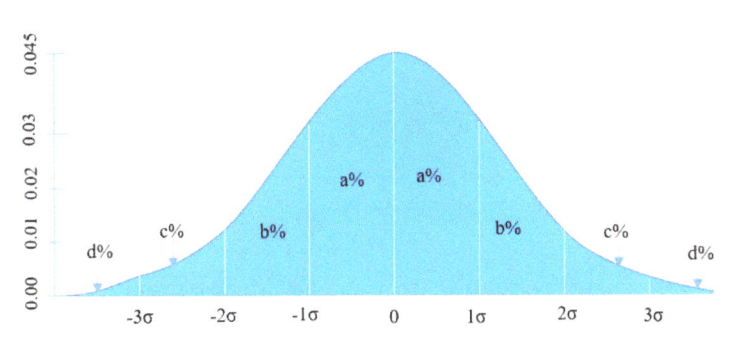

Region		Remark
d% to the Right	:	Never
c% to the Right	:	Never
b% to the Right	:	Rarely
a% to the Right	:	Rarely
d% to the Left	:	Somewhat
c% to the Left	:	Somewhat
b% to the Left	:	Typical
a% to the Left	:	Typical

How typical Asian Giant's Multinational Construction Companies' Bid Prices Look like at Bid Opening in Sub-Saharan Africa

When assessing the benefits of FDI, it is appropriate to look at the multinationals' owners, workers, and their governments. The nature and structure of the economies. Deciding how FDI should flow in and out of a country basically takes on a holistic economic/policy judgment based on various interests, causes, and effects. A cost-benefit analysis, for example, is more appropriate when FDI is flowing from developed to developed/semi-developed nations. However, in many cases, a cost-effectiveness analysis is applied by giants in the case where FDI flows from developed to developing countries. The guiding principle when giants invest in Africa is: How do we solidify our presence in Africa for many generations? *How do we get those minerals?*

The Asian giant has many multinationals owned by 3 players, i.e. the government, big stakeholders, and small stakeholders. The implication of this is that FDI outflow holistically gains the Asian giant in many instances. And they have a very complex system of screening FDI inflow to their country by prioritizing FDI that brings in advanced technologies and restricting those that risk polluting the environment or use old technologies. There is no adequately streamlined technology transfer to African countries that they would consider a loss on their side. Neither is there a political climate favouring local African manufacturers to imitate their technologies in many Sub-Saharan African countries. They board all their workers (skilled and semi-skilled) to Africa, and they only hire porters from Africa, most of the time.

I have seen institutes for their languages domineering the would-be technical training institutes. I have also witnessed award ceremonies to reward those who demonstrate excellence in writing and reading their language. Very few or no ceremonies are arranged to award those African people trained/taught technical and engineering skills.

There is no such kind of costs that threaten their technologies. In other words, they are moving as a whole in all decisions, which makes their vision very solid. They do comprehend their agenda very well, and they cannot miss the point. This is exhibited in the behaviours and actions of many managers and leaders they delegate responsibility to on several of Africa's programs and projects that they work on.

What About When the Asian Giant Does Nothing?

This means: what happens if the Asian giant decides to ban investing in Africa's infrastructure? There are many effects to both Africa and the Asian giant but the most remarkable ones, in the case of Africa, are:

a) Africa's corruption will reduce,

b) Africans will start to put their brains to work on a serious note because they will be left with limited choices but rather to help themselves, and

c) Africa will be able to negotiate better deals on international trade and win-win FDI.

The issue of infrastructure deficit that retards sustained economic growth and development can be sorted by the Asian giant's investment in Africa in the short-term, but the question is whether the growth forecast will be able to improve the *welfare of nationals, shoot the ambition of Africa rising with Africans,* and be able to pay off the debts. And whether Africans will register sustained growth and development over and above mere progress.

The welfare of nationals in the 21st century takes on a psychological dimension where Africans find value in themselves, stand on their own, and can relate to others as partners, not as servants or subordinates. Nobody will help Africans show them how to fish; it will always remain trade and investment relations that unite Africans with others. The anxiety-fueled hopelessness to fail to help ourselves as if we cannot integrate factors of production to spearhead economic growth is partially perpetuated by FDI from the Asian giant that acts as a vehicle for African leaders to merit from corruption—perpetuating partisan politics over government policy.

The justification of the above effects is overt in this way:

a) The Asian giant is very slow in auditing projects and asking for/making accountability, unlike the Europeans,

b) African construction and engineering firms and other companies will get some space to breathe, and this will spark innovation,

c) Africa's negotiation power will be uplifted, and this cannot fail to attract partners.

Two serious issues to note: African companies are losing business to Asian giant's affiliates, and there is no immediate demand for our learned, skilled, and educated labour force in those affiliates. It is important to comprehend that whenever you are faced with a challenge or crisis, and you have no alternative other than helping yourself, by all means, you will devise an appropriate strategy to manoeuvre through. And it will be difficult for an individual to merit out of collective sweats opportunistically. In a situation where you always have to think of others to help you, even in matters to do with sensitization, you better sit back to think and reflect. It all goes back to the governance and politics arena most of the time but not all the time.

On the other hand, the Asian giant will be affected this way: It risks the Asian giant's manufacturing competitiveness among international players not growing as planned. Foreign affiliates are always the best way to compete globally with better marketing in the host countries. The "going global agenda" will be interrupted a bit and cut short of Africa somehow because what helped the Europeans and America's multinationals catch the global scene, Africa in particular is a long story that we share as Africans through religion, colonialism, and slavery. The association of multiple factors positioned them better to identify with masses globally hence facilitating international factor movements. The Asian giant has to create friendly relations to open doors for their multinationals in a century characterized by knowledge-based economies and the ICT/digital revolution. However, the Asian giant's story is more psychological or yet to face modern psychological waves because they have gained the momentum and wish to get to the top. To find out how it feels talking and others are willing to listen. The Americans and Europeans have experienced this already.

Talking and others are willing to listen to the person would differentiate a leader from others. However, transparency and clarity are associative attributes of a 21st-century leader, primarily a Democrat. Although security and safety features guide the working principles of tech gurus, they have to promote transparency and clarity, especially in the development of ICTs. Analyzing what the Asian giant calls privacy on social media platforms versus European and American standards depicts unique variances. Several American social platforms promote transparency, and it is always at the discretion of social media users to configure their accounts to the extent of privacy they deserve. However, the Asian giant's social platforms are restricted and non-flexible in some areas. Then, how sure are we that the deals we engage with the Asian giant are transparent enough, not Trojan horses, and that they do not conceal intentions?

The way someone behaves and acts, in this case, through the manufacture of technologies, is symbolic and indicative of what/how they think, at least to a good significance level.[132] Without improvement in democratic means of leadership, transparency and clarity, their ambition to speak and others willing to listen will never be achieved. Sustainable development puts human rights before any development. Their political ideology of "power belongs to leaders" does not fit the 21st Century Sustainability Equation, especially the UN's Sustainability Framework. The culture of putting money before human rights, showing less concern about Africa's local people, animals, and the environment, will backfire not in a very far time.

There is no doubt that the Asian giant will continue to register economic progress in the first half of the 21st century. However, the continued fight for freedom globally will necessitate an overhaul of systems to sustain the progress. The shortfalls in democratic ideals are pretty straightforward, but it is the most promising form of governance for a world that has been longing for freedom for many centuries ago. The Asian giant's loose work ethics, especially when dealing within Africa, will not see them shoot their economic prospects. This claim is backed by pieces of evidence on how they treat African peoples in their factories, construction projects, and other associated industries. In 2015, The World Bank cancelled a $265 million Ugandan road project because of the contractor's purported violation of work ethics, in which they were suspected to have sexually abused children, paid low wages of about US$ 2.5 per day, indulged in child labour and ill-treatment of workers.[133] This is one typical example of poor work ethics, but many other cases that do not come to book are experienced in several African countries. In my view, and following many experiences I have had with a number of the Asian giant's people, the majority hold certain unique moral principles and a unique work ethic—and it is very difficult to know at what point along a continuum their moral principles meet those of African humankind. This is because, regardless of conventional religions, most Africans believe/d in the existence of the Supreme Being.

If we say enough is enough, the African consumer market that is exploding like wildfire will be too much missed by the Asian giant. At least not as when they hold unstoppable affiliates that could dominate over the Africans owned industries. Africa is in the process of industrialization, although some governments are not quite sure how to support their people to lead the process. However, currently, it heavily relies on imports from industrialized countries. Therefore, moving multinationals' affiliates closer to the African market boosts the Asian giant's economic prospects. The ultimate goal is to become the leading supplier to growing Africa's consumer market by exploiting the unique attitude disorder of African humankind because many Africans rarely trust their products in case alternatives are available made by others, however good the African-made product might be. Even the leading African multinationals and big enterprises in Nigeria and South Africa, for example, are thriving due to utilizing social engineering remedies crafted in Chapter Four.[134]

---

[132] See §4.

[133] "World Bank Statement on Cancellation of the Uganda Transport Sector Development Project (TSDP)," The World Bank, December 21st 2015, https://www.worldbank.org/en/news/press-release/2015/12/21/wb-statement-cancellation-uganda-transport-sector-development-project.

[134] See p. 218-226, §4.

One of the solutions is to disassociate masses from sovereign guarantees issued by heads of state that rise and cling to power through undemocratic means and those who associate with vote-rigging. They break the social contract, simple! It is between them and the Asian giant. We just have to gather evidence. Next generations need to learn about this fate of incidences to decide how to protect and defend Africa collectively. Corrupt leaders who cannot promote balanced growth and development in nation-states and those who derive pleasure from employment discrimination shall have to service those non-concessional loans together with their people.

Another option is to go back to the drawing board and redefine policies on FDI because no country has shot ambitions in isolation. The fact is that Africa needs appropriate FDI inflows that will enable it to empower locals to grow and stand on their own. So that sooner or later, portfolio investments in Africa will start to interest investors. With good governance, win-win better deals can be negotiated that can help protect and defend African peoples and their enterprises. We need to align well with the rate at which FDI flows in from the Asian giant and other countries and renegotiate technology transfer and quality jobs in their multinational enterprises (MNEs). It is possible where leaders are working for people, not their presence in power. Let us fight to improve democracy.

Africans shall not manufacture capacity but rather build it over time. They (Africans) must have the will and understanding to change for the better where necessary. And they must revise their understanding of time. In a nutshell, Africans should learn that we have limited time to stay in this world; the future is now, and now is today. And if we do not help ourselves, who will? There is no time. The most threatening aspect is the complex mathematics in globalization, which, when not understood properly, will see Africa rising without Africans rising. We need an enabling environment to support African masses to build capacity if we want Africa to rise with Africans. African leaders often opt for the Asian giant's firms/products, arguing that Africans cannot deliver. In a few instances, Africans are also given a chance to do business with the government, but they fail to perform because of the unique African attitude disorder (UAAD). This makes Africa's sustainability equation a complex one to solve because it is a two-way dilemma. However, this cannot stop us from brainstorming solutions on the nature of political economies that we need as Africans. The unique African attitude disorder (UAAD) might need a political structure destined to deal with it!

Moving as a whole and working for people, Africa can always tap into the opportunities that globalization presents. For example, because of fertile soils and tropical climates, many African countries have the potential to develop modern agriculture that can feed a considerable fraction of the world population. Therefore, tapping into the global production networks and global value chains driven by globalization, Africa can negotiate win-win FDI inflows so that multinationals set up affiliates in Africa to take advantage of lower costs in some areas. Agricultural production with/and/or value addition processes is one of the industries that Africans should gear efforts to. A number of multinationals' production stages that require low-cost labour could be offshored in African countries. All this needs correct government policies, strategic planning, and a conducive political climate.

Conclusion

Africa needs a revolution tapping into the opportunities presented by the 4th industrial revolution (4IR). We need not go through all these stages that the western world went through. It is impossible and unhelpful because of the wounds others have caused on us to a significant extent and that we have accepted because we failed to define what success means for us.

If Africans do not wake up, they will be dealt with by others in a very subtle and subterranean fashion. Many Africans believe that self-driven sustainable development is about green industrialization without necessarily following a correct philosophy to lead structural transformation. It is about having the correct mindset to design and plan for future generations to live sustainably.

The Asian giant's economists, planners, and philosophers have an agenda beyond cooperation. The sustainability topic has had many people of good foresight take holistic decisions that contribute to sustaining their growth. These people care less about local Africans, and they ask themselves what they have to do to remain economically strong for many generations to come. Here, they find Africa important. Some economists argue that the Asian giant's investment in Africa is less than 3% of its FDI. However, what they take out of Africa is unknown. As Africans, we need to wake up and use our minds properly. We need to stop the circumstantial development as a result of globalization.

Asian giant. Globalization and Industrialisation. Africa.

Chapter Eight: Integrations

"Integrations is not a new order of thinking. It guides innovation and sustainable development."

=== Patrick Ssempeera ===

Chapter Organization

Quick Insights

A Reflection on Colonialism and Statutory Boundaries: A Case Study of Uganda

Regionalism

Federations

Trade Blocs

Marriage and Racial Integrations

Nutrition Integrations

What is a Sustainable Project?

Unified Socioeconomic and Political System

Integrations is Not a New Order of Thinking: It Guides Innovation

Sustainability Beyond The 21st Century

Leading and Managing Sustainable Development

- Climate Change and Its Impacts
- Why is Africa Likely to be Worst Hit by the Effects of Climate Change?
- What Should We Do To Mitigate The Worst Scenario?
- Measures to Mitigate Worst Scenario

Framework for Sustainable Development Action Plan

Conclusion

Quick Insights

Integration is the act or process of mixing previously separated people, usually because of colour, race, religion, or tribe. Examples include economic integration, socioeconomic integration in communities, and racial integration in schools, among others. In science, integration means logical summing up. This chapter explores the power of integrations in both humanities and scientific fields and shows how to achieve continuous improvement in sustainable development. It elaborates the three main pillars of sustainable development on which numerous factors hinge across other chapters of this book. Therefore, sustainable development integrates the three pillars: social, economic, and environment, as illustrated by the December 2015 Paris Agreement on climate change that over 195 countries ratified. Harnessing the power of integrations in both humanities and sciences would enable Africa to achieve self-driven sustainable development. To lead sustainable development, Africa needs not to invent the wheel but put things in order.

Integration in the scientific arena falls within calculus, the mother of the many scientific-related disciplines and the engineering profession. The engineering profession is an influential profession that has improved the lives of living beings and solved the world's enigmatic problems. It is also at the forefront of saving the planet by designing and implementing sustainable products. Today, integrated design thinking methodologies have shaped how engineers approach problem-solving, improving infrastructure development and gadgets through well-socially constructed artificial environments. Systems thinking methodologies have outcompeted piecemeal thinking philosophies to improve the world. Integration is compelling because it breaks conservatism to uplift the liberalized economies that lead the world. Understanding integration boosts economies and explains why the earth split into continents for us to have work to accomplish and bring it back in spirit to improve the definition of integration as provided in humanities. Without work, life would be meaningless.

In working together to sustain humanity and all terrestrial existence, the earth's sustainability should be the primary goal for all of us. The earth is one of the many planets in the universe. Scientists have discovered some traces of the possibility of super intelligent extraterrestrial life on other planets. Intercontinental discrimination in races towards an attitude piece or event of any sort, especially in occupation, is the worst form of ignorance today. We ought to work together. All races have contributed to the pool of knowledge that has improved life. With the likely dangers of climate change and the possibility of extinction of many creatures, scientists predict the 6th earth's mass extinction to occur soon. We should gear all efforts towards safeguarding ourselves from this extinction and the possible future attacks from the extraterrestrial creatures living on other planets.

Africa today consists of 54 states. Colonialists partitioned Africa in the Berlin Conference of 1884. Europeans sat to differentiate or disintegrate the original African product—what the political scientist calls *"divide and rule."* We are now a new kind of Africans not because of our own making but because of the Europeans. We are derivatives of what we lawfully ought to be. We need reforms or meaningful integrations to move the derivative back to the original African product in all jurisdictions except the territorial jurisdiction, which seems too late for reforms. More importantly, jurisdiction in the context of social power is possible. It is, of course, costly to amend territorial boundaries. None of our ancestors attended the Berlin Conference of 1884, yet we have been unable to review or redraw boundaries ever since the colonialists left Africa. In boundaries, I do not refer to territorial boundaries only, but also many other spheres influencing the way we relate to one another. What were the attributes followed to create a sovereign country? Couldn't there have been errors in deciding which states make up a nation?

A Reflection on Colonialism and Sovereign Boundaries: A case study of Uganda

When colonialists forced the independent tribes of Africa into single countries, they did one of the great things. They formed African nations we see today, but how did they come up with perfect ideal nations? What were the basis and metrics used to predetermine colonial political architecture? I define a nation, and many others have defined it as "a group of people who are bound together into a single body through; history, customs, values, language, culture, tradition, art, and religion." Also, a state is a patch of land with a sovereign government. The states together form a nation. However, a state may have a separate political entity within a nation. Though the states have their own rules and can also bring in new laws, they must adhere to the national laws. The states cannot frame laws that are of no interest or ultra vires to the national constitution. Sovereignty is modern terminology for a self-governing or independent society.

The colonial masters found many patches of African land self-governed and independent with kings and chiefs as rulers (heads of states). There were no nations, but a kind of states existed, therefore. The Europeans claimed they were integrating the kingdoms or chiefdoms to form nations, but the criteria used were not ours. Whenever they identified that community A had fertile soils for agriculture and B had minerals whilst C had lakes, they could connect the three areas by a railway line. Hence, they claimed a sovereign nation encompassing A, B, and C without consulting the chiefdoms and kingdoms. It was purely out of the colonialists' economic and political gain that countries were born. The East African railway was constructed in 1895 by the British Railway's Corporation, and subsequent drawing of Kenya and Uganda territorial boundaries in 1920 and 1926, respectively, is one of the examples.

There would be no raid on the Buganda Kingdom by Milton Obote in 1966 if at all colonialists had well respected our identities and ethnic backgrounds, identifiers, and differences in creating nations—the correct political architecture. And if it had been there (the scuffle), it would have been small and would have been solved because the first Ugandan constitution of 1962 had provided for federal states. However, who would federate with who was an essential factor in forming citizenship. Was it intimate enough for the Niger-Congo and Bantu peoples to federate with Nilo-Saharan (Hamitic, Nilotic and Nilo-Hamitic), or the Nilo-Saharan (Hamitic, Nilotic and Nilo-Hamitic) federating with the Afro-Asiatic (Arabic, Tigrinya and Amharic)?

Young nations like South Sudan teach us to start viewing things a little bit differently. The tribalistic mentality still dominates many Sub-Saharan African countries because of the premature citizenship ideology introduced in Africa. Very soon, many countries are to secede from the current countries. The Kingdoms of Bunyoro and Buganda in Uganda had scuffled before, but they could do so without overthrowing their respective governments. On this note, I credit the British to have given Uganda a governance system similar to how they found us—the federal system, which allowed us to hold power at two levels, i.e. the county level and national level. By leaving Uganda as the Federal Republic, colonialists apologised for the wrong actions while drawing sovereign territorial boundaries.

In Uganda, the tribes of Buganda, Bunyoro, Ankole, Busoga, Tooro, and other Bantu had similarities. These presented an excellent opportunity for federalism at that time. The Nilotic, Hamites, and Nilo-Hamites, collectively known as the Nilo-Saharan linguistic group, have their stories and identifiers. To what extent was this considered while drawing boundaries to create nations? Federalism was a perfect thought, but its extent in deciding who should federate with the other was wrong. That is why the Nilo-Saharan linguistic group of people fought federalism to suppress the Bantu in postcolonial Uganda. It would be a perfect match if Bantu federated within themselves and Nilo-Saharan peoples also did the same on their side. In that aspect, using Uganda and South Sudan as a case study, part of Northern Uganda would be a perfect match to federate with part of South Sudan forming a sovereign territory accordingly. Also, as appropriate, part of central and western Uganda would be federated with Rwanda, Burundi, and Tanzania.

These categorical linguistic groups could identify with themselves because of shared histories and closely related cultural values. But when you analyze people who created havoc and political turmoil in Uganda in those days, especially the Buganda crisis of 1966, they all came across the river Nile on the other side of the river bank with highly selfish and enviously grounded reasons. They all came from states which had no well-organized kingdoms. They did not understand well enough what a royal family holds amidst subordinates or servants. Relations prosper well when we foster integrations among people who can identify with each other—*drawing on intimacy*. You cannot just mix up people of different *perceptions, core beliefs, attitudes, and behaviours* and having a different view of the world—and you think conflicts cannot arise unless they have agreed within themselves. *Note:* Perception is more important than fact in essential matters. Perception influences imagination, thinking, and reasoning and has a strong bearing on one's ethnic background. King Edward Muteesa II (1924-1969), who was the head of state, and his peoples, felt superiority which was a fact, but perception is more important than fact. How they perceived that superiority was the problem—and partially the reason that triggered Obote's emotional reasoning to decide to raid the Kingdom. Therefore, it was a *two-way problem* whose best solution was exercising enough care while marrying people from different ethnic backgrounds.

It is evident that the raid on the Buganda Kingdom in Uganda by chief-of-staff Col. Idi Amin (1925–2003) on the orders of the then prime minister Milton Obote was precipitated by the emotional reasoning of Milton Obote (1925–2005) in what he called, "a good Muganda is a dead one".[135] Although no clear evidence has been produced that Obote said those words, his ill-advised actions towards Baganda would not fail to daunt the Baganda—and the 1977 document published in the Voice of Uganda newspapers leaves many questions about who authored the article that stated those ugly words. There are conflicting theories about who authored the document, which called upon the Langi and the Acholi to cause an armed uprising against Idi Amin regime. Amin had overthrown Obote in 1971 Ugandan coup d'état. Whether it is Obote, his associate, or another person who authored the article, it becomes immaterial. However, the document itself depicted that Uganda was either born prematurely or fell short of who should federate

---

[135] From a 25-page document titled, "Obote's War Call to Langis and Acholis" reproduced on the February 17th 1977 in the government-owned newspaper, the Voice of Uganda. This document outlined the justification for an armed uprising against the Amin regime. That was the first time the statement appeared in print. Obote never understood Buganda's politeness. This illusion mixed with emotional reasoning, precipitated and perpetuated by ethnic differences created false perceptions and brought scuffles in the country. The Baganda in Uganda, by virtues and cultural norms, do not speak bad things about a person who has passed away. Obote misinterpreted that norm and he is claimed having always joked that "a good Muganda is a dead one" —but of course there is no joke without a serious meaning.

with another. As an engineer, I try to study several events that happened to Uganda in the postcolonial era under Obote's regime to generate several questions on those ugly words:

a) There was a raid on the Buganda Kingdom in 1966.

b) The Uganda Constitution was changed from Federal to Unitary in 1967.

c) King Edward Muteesa II (Buganda's king and the first Head of State for Uganda) was poisoned in 1969 in the UK.

In 1966, Obote argued that the Head of State, the then King Edward Muteesa, had planned a coup to overthrow the government (by fighting Obote), so he ordered the raid to his palace. The Constitution vested more powers in Obote as the prime minister. Obote and his UPC diehards claim that the prime minister had ordered an investigation into the activities carried out in the palace—and that it was the armed royalists who started shooting. Nobody knows what happened precisely because each side has since provided her defence. However, in my opinion, it was primarily emotional reasoning, a companion of jealousy and anger that caused that mess—and as I have matured, I no longer underestimate jealousy, envy, and emotional reasoning anymore—it can bring down the whole world. The three distortions are the most significant disorders of the soul. Interestingly, the world sometimes thinks leaders do not catch that bug!

Obote had many avenues to *evidence his* beliefs to solve the problem but not raiding the kingdom. That destabilized the country and threw Ugandans into instabilities that saw many short-lived presidents until 1986 when President Yoweri Kaguta Museveni, a former rebel, rose to power. Because of these circumstances, Museveni has clung to power through militarism and manipulating the shortfalls in democracy.

When President Museveni fought Idi Amin, he revolutionized the country. Together with others, they relieved the people of Uganda from Amin's oppression. I cannot close my eyes to such great sacrifice they did for the nation. However, since then, Museveni's government has failed to set people free to create an environment that sparks self-driven innovation and growth. Today mistakes have accumulated because of overstaying in power, and when the trend goes on, future generations are at risk of failing to meet their needs. The government should set Ugandans free for a sustainable future.

As a result of his overstaying in power, almost no government institution is still doing the right things to serve the people of Uganda—including professional institutions.[136] Many institutions are infected with the overstaying syndrome that restricts the growth of the professions. Some professional bodies and educational institutions of higher learning influence each other in a corrupt manner—they provide licences within a circle affiliated to the long-serving regime in a hopeless way that leaves no room for innovation and growth. Civil servants head almost all professional institutions, yet the economy is private sector driven.

If you know how to move from cause to effect, you must understand why the country has had many multistoried buildings collapsing in recent years. And you must also understand the role which human capital plays in the structural transformation of an economy. With that insight, you should contemplate Uganda's predicaments and why the country remains among the poorest in the world.

---

[136] See p. 241-243, §5 (Hint: Case Study I, Time Management).

To make the best human capital that the current regime requires, or to be designated a big role to play for government, you must be willing to sell your conscience or become a nuisance, for example, "when you do not feel any sense of guilt to issue a licence to build in a wetland or to sell a cemetery"—that is when you can have a big role to play. I have travelled throughout the country, and I felt too much pain whenever I found wetlands and cultural heritage sites destroyed.

Someone might argue that the incidences that have happened to me are isolated cases.[137] However, my response would be that my opinions are representative and expert. Therefore, at some point, I would give you responses that you would otherwise aggregate from millions of people. Take an example of the response from African Development Bank Group concerning my grievance on the construction of the $150 million, 23.7 km Busega-Mpigi Expressway, in Uganda in 2020—and nothing promising I have obtained to date. I represented a team of over 50 people. The complaint was about social concerns and unfair treatment.

If a professional could be failed and mistreated from the right, the left, and in the centre—educational institutions' personnel failing to do their part with a healthy conscience, professional bodies' personnel becoming vehicles that fail sustainability, and funding agencies' personnel becoming silent about issues that matter—what happens to a peasant through whose estate the expressway traverses? There is no hope in a country where leaders do not listen, and we need to create hope. Or else we have to make them listen to the planet's message about sustainability the hard way. Gaining anything in the country has become very painful, or else you would need to take a shortcut at the expense of future generations, i.e. the corrupt way—but some of us are refusing. We need to lead sustainability. I know I would perhaps be better financially under the "corrupt umbrella", but I chose sustainability when I woke up from my dream. It is a reason good enough to live and die for.[138] And because I had written my life's hypothesis, I became strong after I read philosopher Friedrich Nietzsche (1844–1900) famous quote, "He who has a *'why'* to live for can bear with almost any *'how'*".[139] When I remembered Hussein Walugembe, a Boda Boda cyclist who burnt himself over a bribe in 2020, tears rolled down my face.[140]

Despite receiving an official communication from the Bank's Director for Compliance Review & Mediation Unit (BCRM), who promised to follow up my complaint with the relevant individuals within the project implementation unit to request an investigation and update, I have not received anything substantial to date. Under this clause, I would not hesitate to mention that the country needs a total overhaul of systems to prosper and sustainably develop. Otherwise, I see no hope for future generations.

On August 13th 2020,

> The president made remarks about the Baganda that saddened me when he was interviewed on Uganda Broadcasting Corporation (UBC) TV. Those remarks blew much attention in the Buganda community at home and in the diaspora. The president expressed his

---

[137] See p. 241-243, §5 (Hint: Case Study I, Time Management).

[138] See p. 109, §2 (Hint: The historical William Wallace).

[139] See p. 131-132, §3 (Hint: Memory Testing Questions).

[140] BBC News, "Uganda boda boda rider sets himself on fire 'over bribe'," BBC News, July 3rd 2020. https://www.bbc.com/news/world-africa-53278900

grievances against Baganda, who preached controversy, and I am afraid I had to give my opinion in the book as a descendant of Kintu/Nambi.

Of course, the president had his reasons; the Baganda also had their reasons to say "ffe nga". That difference of opinion is what makes us work to cultivate a solid democratic foundation for Uganda. Of course, Mr President holds different lenses viewing the world compared to some others. However, objectivity in fostering sustainable communities is the overarching goal. In that case, our lenses must be customized to comply with sustainability standards. No law prohibits a Catholic or a Muslim to fight for their interests. However, the regime constantly uses the tribal card game as a defence to suppress some others who fight for their interests. The tribal card game presents a high risk in the sustainability framework, and we must act. In that case, we need to involve international agencies that consider sustainability an essential topic of the 21st-century. In the sustainability equation, ethnicities' interests are a solid factor—and the term Baganda refers to fifty-six (56) independent social groups, i.e. clans.[141] Ffe nga, means "we the". The Baganda constantly reiterate "ffe nga Abaganda", referring to the properties that the government seized, including the federal system of governance, which was the primary condition for *other regions joining Buganda* to form Uganda on October 9th 1962.

What is wrong with loving your identity? How shall we lead sustainability if we shy away from our identities? Africa is a continent of many firsts, and we must save the planet—it is our responsibility. Mt Sinai of Egypt, Ethiopia's Hadar, and Tanzania's Olduvai George are some places that identify Africa with many firsts. I would want to remind Mr President that we are not migrants and when we say, "ffe nga", we mean it; Uganda came from Buganda.

If you are defining Uganda (U), you start;

$$U=u(Buganda, Bunyoro, Tooro, ……).$$

Suppose a Lugbara has their hills, stones, artefacts, paintings, landscapes and townscapes of cultural significance. In that case, they say, "we the Lugbara", we need to define green politics to defend our heritage; where is the problem? In the interest of sustainability of the beautiful continent (Africa), my motherland (Uganda) in particular, and the planet (Earth) at large, I would wish to state categorically that,

> "In the name of our cultural heritage, our ancestors, our beliefs, our values, and our instincts, the Baganda and I would wish to remain Baganda for many years to come. Our role is to live to cherish our values, predispositions, and beliefs and teach young generations to love their motherland. I am a Muganda before I become a Ugandan, and I would not in any way accept the government to suppress my identity. I come from the Kintu lineage of Butesaasira village, Bukesa parish, Ngando Sub-county in Butambala district in Uganda and the sub-lineage of Nkulo of Bwende village, Kisuula parish, Kasasa Sub-county, Kyotera district in Uganda. I live to protect, conserve, and defend nature and our culture to promote sustainability. I raise my hand when a call for sacrifice to save the planet is underway. In the interest of sustainability, others and I swear to belligerently defend the ecological system, promote equity, preserve our cultural heritage, protect and defend our motherland and the planet up to the last breathe. Our best avenue would be to cherish the

---

[141] The Kingdom of Buganda, "Ebika (Clans)," accessed October 1st 2021, https://buganda.or.ug/clans.

notions of "people power, our power" and improve democratic ideals to adopt peaceful means to make the masses understand the sustainability topic. The notions of "people power, our power" governed the interests that brought different ethnicities of Uganda under the same umbrella by cherishing democratic ideals to gain freedom.[142] Along the way, because of several circumstances described earlier, others wished to suppress others by violating the rule of law to create a modern dynastic monarchy that we live to refuse. Others and I cannot abandon the collision between humans and the environment that the government has caused in the body, the spirit, the mind, and the soul. This collision threatens future generations' ability to meet their needs. It is our role to fight for the right, and it is the Supreme Being who bestows the right to us."

In 1966, i.e. *the past,* Obote raided the Buganda Kingdom because Baganda had put up a heated debate about their interests. In response to the President's remarks, therefore, I would wish to state categorically that;

"Abaana ba Nambi/Kintu: tibaggweerawo ddala!" Baganda proverb, which translates to;

"Nambi's/Kintu's children cannot get extinct!" African Baganda Proverb.

Humanity constantly renews unless you wage war against it—that is why we are leading the sustainability of our motherland. Nambi was Ssekabaka Kintu's wife.[143] Ssekabaka Kintu was the first cultural leader to organize the Buganda Kingdom around 1300AD. The excellent attribute about the Baganda is that they can trace their lineage very well for over 800 years, i.e. about eight (8) to ten (10) generations—which brings sustainability to the heart of society. That political philosophy obtained from elsewhere aimed at suppressing others cannot work on people who are not migrants; it is impossible to succeed with it. Anyone with a healthy conscience would feel guilty for failing to conserve the ecosystem when the illiterate ancestors managed to conserve it. We cannot keep quiet when some people intentionally destroy our cultural heritage. The lakes and rivers are polluted, extensive sand mining from lakes and rivers makes the day, people are evicted from ancestral land without adequate compensation, cemeteries destroyed to develop infrastructure without sound ethical planning, and several people destroy sanctified places. For example, Kasubi tombs (UNESCO World Heritage property of Uganda) caught fire on March 16th 2010.[144] The government has not produced the Kasubi tombs report to date. Extensive sand mining in Lwera wetland in Lukaya town council, Kalungu district, greatly tampers the region's hydrology, leading to severe floods and constant pre-mature failures of that section of the road that connects Kampala to Masaka.[145] People also destroy forests, landscapes and townscapes, and build in wetlands. The result is excessive floods that continuously hit Kampala city and other areas. The recent abuse of customs and teargassing cultural and religious leaders was the climax—signalling the urgency to fight for sustainability. On October 17th 2020, police officers lobbed teargas at the Archbishop of Masaka Diocese, Emeritus John Baptist Kaggwa, Omutaka Gajuule Kayiira Kasibante of the Mbogo Clan, and others attending thanksgiving prayers, at the

---

[142] See Article 1(1) of The 1995 Constittuion of Uganda (as amended).

[143] See p. 02, §1.

[144] Kasubi tombs location (Latitude: 0° 19' 27.00" N; Longitude: 32° 33' 7.19" E)

[145] Lukaya location (Latitude: 0° 08' 60.00" N; Longitude: 31° 52' 17.99" E)

clan's ancestral ground, at Mugulu in Zigoti town council, Mityana district, thereby disrupting the Holy Mass.[146] We, therefore, need holistic climate action to defend our motherland, reiterating Article 1(2) of the UN Charter as we aim to achieve the 17 UN SDGs.[147]

When Mr Museveni had seized power in 1986, he commented that Africa's problem was about leaders who overstay. He later clarified his position in 2006 polls that he would only stay as long as democracy flourished. In December 2006, the president defended slashing part of a rainforest reserve to make way for a sugar plantation, in which he advised that Uganda lacked professional services but not forests.[148]

I base on the above arguments to remind Mr President that forests are essential in sustainable development, and we cannot dare to lose a single species if we are to save the planet. According to the UN FAO global forests resources assessment report (2010), Uganda lost about 37.1% of its forest cover, or around 1,763,000 ha between 1990 and 2010 under Mr Museveni's administration.

Correct leadership in professional bodies is equally vital, and overstaying in power cannot go without mistakes accumulating regardless of how you overstay. We aggregate the mistakes at a macro level to judge credibility to determine whether they are excusable and warranty sustainable development. And many actions cannot be reduced to mistakes, for goodness sake.

On July 31st 2021,

> The Kabaka of Buganda Kingdom, a constitutional monarchy, made several remarks in his 28th Coronation speech at Nkoni, Masaka, Buddu, Uganda. He condemned people who wished to create an environment that attempted to divert people from reminding the leaders about Buganda properties. The cultural leader insisted that Buganda has never wanted to secede from Uganda.

In my opinion, Buganda's cultural leader, His Highness Ronald Muwenda Mutebi, spoke paradoxically, which is an indicator of an integration festering like a wound. He expressed his disappointment in those who create an oppressive environment. And I am afraid I had to give my opinion in the book because his grief is Baganda's grief; that's the cultural tradition we need to consolidate in the sustainability framework. We are not fetching conservatism but rather grassroots democracy to protect and defend our cultural heritage for sustainable development. Grassroots democracy promotes equity and protects the land by proudly acknowledging the natives—a solid factor in sustainable development. Everyone operating on Buganda land should acknowledge Baganda as the traditional owners and as the first peoples and custodians of the land where the economy functions and people work and live. Endeavour to respect our rich culture and our elders past, present, and future. The environment that people create to suppress the Baganda would lead Buganda to secede from Uganda instead. A negative event would highly likely lead to

---

[146] Pius Arinawe Keeya, "Police apologise over dispersing Mbogo clan members," The New Vision, October 21st 2020, https://www.newvision.co.ug/news/1529950/police-apologise-dispersing-mbogo-clan-members.

[147] UN Charter, Article 1(2) states, 'To develop friendly relations among nations based on respect for the principle of equal rights and self-determination of peoples, and to take other appropriate measures to strengthen universal peace.'

[148] "FACTBOX-Quotes from Uganda's Museveni," Thomson Reuters, July 22nd 2008, https://www.reuters.com/article/uganda-museveni-quotes-idUKL2207523720080722.

a negative outcome. In 2005, multiparty democracy was restored in Uganda following a referendum. This was partially due to the pressure mounted by donors. However, despite the people preferring the federal system earlier, the regional tier system was proposed instead. The reasons for this could be profiled well in the psychological dimension—but they converge to one point of premature integrations.

However, the extraction of oil in the Albertine region of Uganda would perhaps reduce people's fixation on Buganda—their anxieties might triangulate and start to view things differently. Those people might begin to fall in love with a federal system of governance or resurrect their love for it. Most especially when they learn that everything might end in the modern dynasty if they fail to wake up. Those with either copper, gold, cattle, sugar plantations and others with theirs might want to learn more about the federal system of governance.

Almost all people globally have grudges against others in history. The reason we ignore these grudges is that development cannot happen if perpetuated to future generations. New evidence has shown that we need to forgive each other to achieve sustainable development. In the interest of sustainability, the president must understand Baganda. Climate action is holistic; it involves understanding how communities have evolved—and it is part of the role of cultural leaders to shape people's thinking about sustainability. In the pursuit of sustainability, the Baganda pivot everything around maintaining the throne (Okukuuma Namulondo) as a pillar of the region's sustainability—remembering His Highness Ssekabaka Muteesa I (1837–1884) Mukaabya Walugembe's role in the enlightenment of Uganda.[149]

"If you close your eyes to facts, you will learn through accidents" African Proverb.

In 1967, Milton Obote changed the 1962 constitution and turned the state into a unitary republic, an opportunistic strategy. In my opinion, a unitary system is a conquer approach. It has nothing to do with uniting people. The 1966 cause is primarily attributed to the colonialists who never followed intimacy in federating and integrating peoples, yet they introduced heart and mind weakening programs to Africans in an opportunistic cognitive restructuring the world has ever experienced. The country continues to face contemporary nomads, and this problem is rooted in the 1966 raid on the Buganda palace. Uniting peoples is purely a psychological mechanism that follows forging intimate relationships, dialogue and agreeing on a common goal as peoples of a specific geographical area. It works its way out. You do not force it. You just have to create an enabling environment to achieve it. You cannot physically change people's core beliefs, characters, and temperaments, but psychological interventions can do. That is why conventional religions won, but politics of hope is failing in many parts of Africa.

You can fight wars, conquer others, and annex states to expand a sovereign. However, as long as people feel not free to exercise what they believe, they stage resistance. That means you can only achieve peace by understanding. If Europeans had not partitioned Africa, some Africans would emerge stronger to fight others to expand sovereigns. However, we would achieve peaceful sovereigns by agreeing to agree to the facts. The facts are the beliefs, predispositions, and sustainability.

---

[149] Ssekabaka Muteesa I is regarded as the father of Uganda's formal education. He played a key role in bringing literacy to Uganda in the late 1870s. His vision for Uganda cannot be underestimatd or forgotten.

At any time, the person who holds the keys might deceive the followers that he is uniting people through the unitary system because he wishes to control them properly. A correct system leaves some little power to the people of a specific area to decide solutions to their proximate causes. A unitary system is more selfish than a federal system. Ugandans continue to suffer today due to Obote's emotional reasoning when he took wrong decisions in 1966 and 1967, King Muteesa's wrong perception about his superiority, and the Europeans who failed to follow intimacy while drawing boundaries to decide who should federate with the other.

In 1969, King Edward Muteesa II died of alcohol poisoning in his London flat No. 28 Orchard House, in Rotherhithe.

We have suffered and continue to suffer in Uganda because of the above incidences. Cartels have run the country since 1966. Nobody seems to tag value on cognitive distortions in politics and geopolitics, yet emotional reasoning has cost Africans, right from the slave trade and colonial eras. A severe mistake in the start has left perpetual problems for many generations to come unless we take firm ground to correct it now.

In November 2016, a conflict involving a raid on the Rwenzururu kingdom in Uganda attacking royalists involved the same peoples. The Rwenzururu people of 2016 and the Buganda people of 1966 had their beliefs. They ought to be listened to but not raiding on them for what they believed, especially in a society that claims to be democratic. Many other people across Africa are denied fundamental human rights for what they believe. African leaders' fixation on the gun, "our votes, our guns" Robert Mugabe philosophy highly threatens Africa's sustainability in the modern world. Can we wake up and make sound integrations to stimulate socio-economic progress?

"There is, and there was a better way to integrate African peoples following intimacy. That is why the colonialists thought of federalism in many parts of Africa. Federalism was a good decision but went short of who should federate with who and why. Colonialists had to be more sensitive when federating peoples of different ethnic backgrounds. However, when I borrow a leaf from symbolic interactionism, I explain Uganda's case this way: Buganda is one letter away from Uganda, i.e. B+Uganda. Only this name sent anxiety in the hearts and minds of some other ethnicities and perceived Buganda as superior over others. If they had named Uganda the "Pearl of Africa", it would have been more advantageous psychologically to all the peoples of Uganda. A psychological construct is very powerful, and perception is more important than fact!"

I describe Buganda and Uganda because I come from there. It is what I know the most. Therefore, I cannot bias myself by neglecting others. I know there are many other places similar to what Uganda experienced. Because Uganda came from Buganda and only "B" was removed, I find the locus of points that the colonialists would have used to demarcate Uganda's boundaries in 1926 to take on two theories: the Ubuntu philosophy and delineation caused by water bodies, as shown in two pictures below. The red polygon in the figure to the left is the ideal Uganda that colonialists ought to have created out of Buganda following a locus of points in line with the shared history, values, norms, symbolisms, language dialects, and particularly the Ubuntu philosophy. Other territories would annex as time went by as they would wish or as circumstances would dictate. Or they would belong elsewhere. That is because the decision would be based on those people that could identify with the Baganda and who shared the "Ubuntu philosophy".

It is on record that before Europeans officially settled in Buganda, the King of Buganda was collecting taxes from as far as Mwanza. Mwanza is a port on the shores of Lake Victoria in Northern Tanzania. The King had negotiated for a marriage exchange program in the Kingdoms of Tooro and beyond after realizing that they had beautiful girls. The men from Buganda could be allowed to marry from the Tooro Kingdom upon reaching an agreement. *That was in a bid to create a more intimate understanding and federation that is more sensible.*

On the other hand, water bodies could prove helpful. Almost in all places, going over the water body (river or lake), another tribe existed. Europeans would have been so cautious about this. Therefore ideal Uganda following the demarcation of water bodies would appear as shown in the picture to the right.

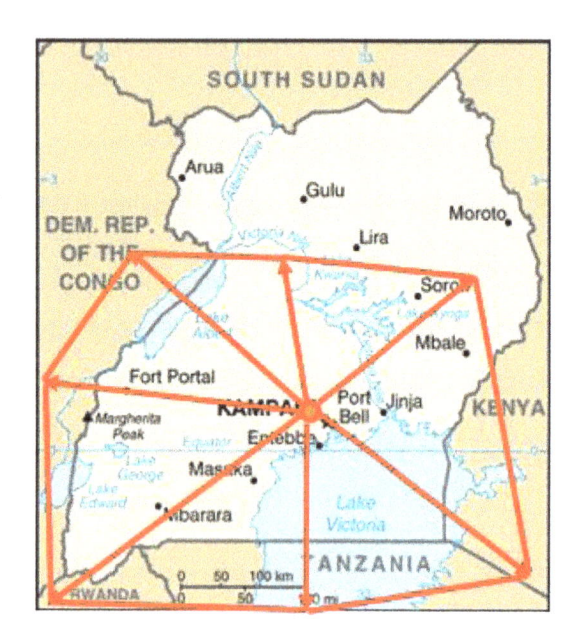

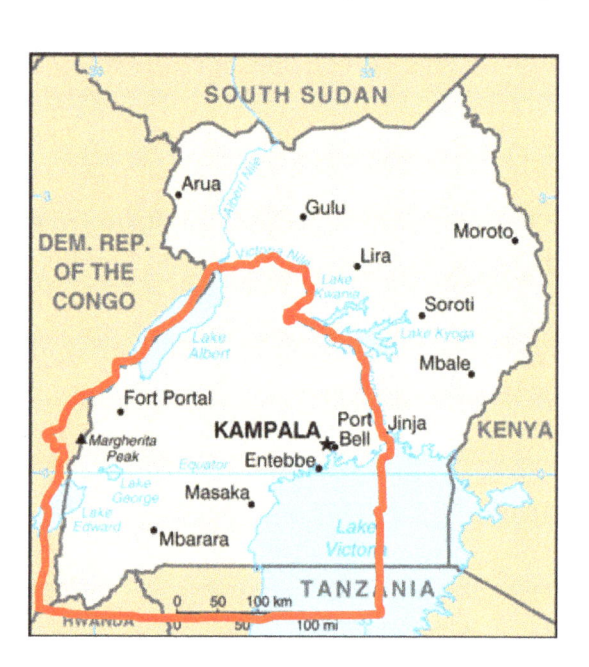

The Best Ideal Demarcation of Uganda Boundary

Something that would cost a revolution took colonialists just a couple of not more than 10 years to decide on who should federate with another in a bid to formulate an ideal citizen of a given territory. History shows that most of these distinct tribes settled in those areas more than 1000 years ago. Therefore, based on this 1000 years' history associated with heritage, it necessitated revolutions spearheaded by the Africans in creating new social order. Colonialists taking a couple of years to decide who should federate with another in formulating ideal citizenship was *premature* and caused a big mess Africans ought to recognize. Of course, we cannot reverse the developments, but it is good to understand the phenomenological differences.[150]

Some of the Sub-Saharan countries have remained poor because there was no intimacy in deciding who should federate with another in the beginning while drawing citizenship. We have, therefore, festered

---

[150] See §4 & §5

on wrong political and socioeconomic ideologies as a result of the insurgencies encountered as a result of forming non-intimate relationships. Things were heavily distorted, and today people who would be steering economies have no power. Those who would own factories making and selling ice cream are now planning for economies. Those fixated on the gun know how to deal with any uprising that wants to put things in order on the African continent.

> Monkeys and other wildlife have their freedom in the jungle. He, who destroys their habitat, is the enemy. They have no education, and they have no piped water. They do not live to enjoy electricity or manufactured cars, but they are happy. If you traverse distances to get them, destroy their habitats, create a new social order in them, and domesticate them, you are the enemy. Why worry?

Both Milton Obote and Idi Amin Dada claimed one of the greatest dictators of all time, come from the Nilo-Saharan linguistic group. Although claimed to be among the leading dictators of all time, Amin's love for Africa should not be overlooked—a positive attribute worth noting. On the other hand, one would view this love as ignorance because of his grandiose plans that seemed heavier than the planet.

Colonial masters' mappings were not well-studied on the grounds of ethnic and linguistic groups' integrations, and we continue to suffer today on this issue. They were very negligent because they were highly educated, and these are some of the things they ought to foresee. They were after promoting their interests like; agriculture, mining, and building railway lines to ferry raw materials out of Africa but not after drawing national boundaries that are feasible to promote social power while promoting socio-economic transformation.

Below are several other examples that show less care while drawing statutory boundaries:

The Sebei and Karamajong people in North Eastern Uganda have their tribe-mates in Kenya; the Alur people in North-Western Uganda have their tribe-mates in the Democratic Republic of Congo (DRC). The Alur people in Uganda always cross the border to DRC for their kingdom activities because the headquarters of their cultural institution is located in DRC. Also, some Baganda are in Mwanza and other parts of northern Tanzania. Francis Joash Ayume (1940–2004) was a Ugandan politician and lawyer born in Koboko district in northern Uganda.[151] He formed the *Kakwa Salia Musala* community to unite the Kakwas of Koboko in Uganda with the Kakwas of South Sudan and Congo. That means the colonialists subdivided the Kakwas into three groups while drawing country boundaries. And after that, they brought aid to support these people to unite and grow.

In this aspect, the colonialists' feasibility studies were selfish. They wanted to promote their interests and never bothered about the African child of tomorrow—and it is under this clause, they must be held accountable. They never catered for the sustainability of Africans, which was very bad! South Sudan seceding from Sudan on July 9th 2011, broke the ice to create a friendlier and relaxed atmosphere for both South Sudanese and Sudanese peoples to live better. It demonstrates a loophole in the feasibility of country boundaries because no intimacy was followed, especially by following the extent of cultural traditions and

---

[151] Francis Joash Ayume was a Speaker of Uganda's Parliament from 1996 up to 2001.

conventional religions. Many questions surround the formation of nation-states in the interest of spurring socio-economic transformation for African humankind.

The colonialists never consulted African kingdoms and chiefdoms when drawing boundaries which presented a high risk to Africans. Otherwise, if our ancestors drew boundaries, there would not be many risks and mistakes. We would perhaps agree on how to unite to form a nation built on scientific evidence to promote sustainability. It is important to note that cultures influence the way we think and behave and the overall attitudes. Therefore, drawing integrations and curving nation-states would need an evaluation process before or a revolution spearheaded by Africans. Colonialists left more permanent effects on Africans at cultural and political levels. That is our predicament in the sense that African Kings and Chiefs failed to desist colonialism at some point, and we are failing to wake up. They were deceived with materialistic gifts forgetting that colonialists had a hidden agenda. I explained the root cause of this in Chapter One.[152] I have used Uganda here, but many similar case studies exist in several African countries.

The main question that should haunt all African contemporary revolutionary activists should thus be: Since the colonial education systems, colonial sovereign borders, political architecture, and management systems are not reviewed to match the African context in this modern era, how are Africans going to resist neocolonialism and imperialism? In my opinion, more lies in doing and improving one–on–one relationships than talking. We tend to focus more on leaders and not the awakening of the masses. We need to look into our core beliefs—awakening the masses appropriately with solidarity to instil confidence in future leaders. Failure to do this explicitly outlines why all African dictators at some point spoke democratic rule until when they resorted to acting with impunity.

When we do not address the bottlenecks, do not be surprised to see that even modern revolutionary activists change to dictators or become hopeless once they assume power. The environment of the ill-informed masses is highly likely to turn once a promising leader into a dictator. The high level of senselessness into how things work to spur socioeconomic transformation coupled with too much selfishness are the two great forces affecting the land—and we give very little attention to these intrinsic forces. You cannot work alone; however good a leader you may prove to be when the subordinates and followers are not well-informed, they mess up your leadership. You are left to cling in power for fear of the disenchantments caused by your people. We should gear the effort towards improving one–on–one relationships.

The cross-cutting issues in Africa are a good indicator that some peoples share origins. We have always been the minority, although the population growth rates risk us to become the majority by 2100. We thus ought to be a single territory of our own making, not Europeans' making, despite the consequences of the Berlin conference. The Berlin conference of 1884 is still holding the keys and power to segregate Africans as different. It should not be. That was not our making; we could have been better off a single nation with federal states. The states that should have followed intimacy and understanding. The need to unite politically, socially, and economically is a must to change the state of affairs for the continent. The integrations should be practical and not more on diplomacy.

Regionalism

---

[152] See p. 44, §1 (Hint: Cognitive restructuring of African masses – dealing with Africans thoughts and core beliefs).

Today, the 32 independent African states that sat in Addis Ababa on May 25th 1963 are remembered for two remarkable speeches by the then Central African President David Dacko and Kwame Nkrumah of Ghana. Their two speeches keep resonating to date, with some African leaders arguing that Africans are to perish without integrating. Many developing countries consider regionalism the best tool to undertake as we aim for self-driven sustainable development. We notably remember Nkrumah's speech that proposed establishing a committee of foreign ministers to oversee the administration of a union government.

In his own words, Kwame Nkrumah (1909 – 1972) said:

"….. We must also decide on allocation where this body of officials and experts will work as the new Headquarters or Capital of our Union Government. Some central place in Africa might be the fairest suggestion, either at Bangui in the Central African Republic or Leopoldville in Congo. My colleagues may have other proposals. The Committee of Foreign Ministers, officials and experts should be empowered to establish:

1. A Commission to frame a Constitution for a Union Government of African States;
2. A Commission to work out a continent-wide plan for a unified or common economic and industrial programme for Africa; this plan should include proposals for setting up:

    - A Common Market for Africa
    - An African currency
    - African Monetary Zone
    - African Central Bank, and
    - Continental Communications System;

3. A Commission to draw up details for a Common Foreign Policy and Diplomacy;
4. A Commission to produce plans for a Common System of Defense;
5. A Commission to make proposals for Common African Citizenship.

These Commissions will report to the Committee of Foreign Ministers, who should, in turn, submit within six months of this Conference their recommendations to the Praesidium. The Praesidium meeting in Conference at the Union Headquarters will consider and approve the recommendations of the Committee of Foreign Ministers……."

The subsequent sittings of OAU in Addis Ababa has seen many African leaders echo Nkrumah's words. However, we are yet to implement his recommendations. To date, each country has its currency. It is not easy to believe that over 5000 units of some African currencies are worth one (01) unit of some Western currencies, yet Africa has some of the richest gold reserves.

Correct Federations would lead to Proper Regionalism

As first proposed by Kwame Nkrumah and echoed by Muammar Gadhafi (1942–2011), a continental government requires careful examination. It should not be a speedy process in a situation where colonialists defined sovereign boundaries. The ethnic and linguistic groups were the best ideal in deciding who should federate with another. Colonialists cared less about this fact in the beginning. A careful examination into the success of nations built on intimacy ought to be the ideal for drawing sovereign boundaries—and colonialists unsatisfactorily delineated boundaries. That, therefore, signals that a continental government should be a gradual process.

I hinted at psychological mechanisms to guide decisions in the 21st century. There is meaning in developmental agencies associating the Middle East with North Africa when reporting economic data, i.e. "Middle East & North Africa". Sub-Saharan Africa is evaluated on several occasions without associative territories by developmental agencies. Developmental partners evaluate it independently. There is meaning in this categorical reporting. The map shown in the figure on page 8 demonstrates that the federations would first follow the ethnic and linguistic backgrounds and then decide on the correct regional blocs later. In this aspect, African sovereign states would appear a little deviant from what the colonialists drew.

Now that we can hardly change what we have graduated into, a continental government has its challenges spanning from ethnic, cultural, and religious domains. Emphasis should be geared towards fostering effective and efficient blocs we have created so far. However, the recognition of the shortfalls colonialists created in sovereign demarcations is not such a bad idea. For example, following the correct political architecture, the entire African population of 1.307 billion people (2019 estimate) would be comprised of only four great nations: the Niger-Congo, the Nilo-Saharan; the Afro-Asiatic; and the Khoisan. Africa would have about 2-4 trading blocs. Therefore, the federations would be within these 4 great nations; a typical demonstration is provided for Uganda's case. Nature takes its course. Moving from 32 African countries in 1963 to 54 countries in 2019, with South Sudan gaining sovereignty lately in 2011, is a good indicator of the shortfalls in sovereign delineations. Of course, scuffles always emerge, leading to independencies despite following ethnic intimacies, as I claim. However, colonialists deciding on our behalf on who should federate with another cannot be underestimated in causing the problems we face today.

The correct federations would lead to proper regionalism in a multilevel approach;

Federate Home, Federate Regionally.

We would, therefore, think of the Regional Economic Communities (RECs) agreeing on a single currency. Each community would have codes and standards of practice in that region, customized IT infrastructure and software platforms, and official languages. In addition, regional blocs would create armies, centralized courts, central banks, regional passports, and many other items that promote regionalism. Ideas for a continental government might need to be suspended because of colonialists' faulty ideals in the demarcation of sovereign boundaries. The developments we have achieved through the philosophy we adopt are not a make of ourselves. Therefore, we need a tested/trusted philosophy to adopt before forming a continental government.

Trade Blocs

The need to boost the Regional Economic Communities (RECs) is urgent to create more frees (free trade zones). The cost of frees should be well-studied as well. The 1963 establishment of the Organization of African Unity (OAU) saw the need for economic integrations to spur economic development in Africa. The establishment of the African Economic Community (AEC) by the 1991 Abuja treaty proposing the establishment of Regional Economic Communities (RECs) followed the OAU. The philosophy adopted was that a continental government would follow RECs. This was well-thought-out, but it risks having multiple integrations.

Accelerating the move to continental integration (economic) is required to cope with the pressure of global competition. Otherwise, some blocs are forging free trade zones with non-African territories and looking at African integration as less promising. For example, the signing of the African Continental Free Trade Area (ACFTA) in Kigali, Rwanda, took place from 17th – 12th March 2018. Two of Africa's largest economies, Nigeria and South Africa, took their time to study the possibility of their countries becoming a dumping ground for finished goods. Giants also weigh in the possibilities of retarding in innovations due to a lack of political integration. Political integration and economic integration ought to move hand in hand to yield fruition. However, a continental government requires close examination for the reasons outlined earlier. One of the underlying reasons for this is that firms in a country tend to lean towards rent-seeking rather than improved efficiency in running economic integrations alone.

Political integrations help to create constancy and economic operational standards hence upholding innovation and growth. My prediction on African continental integration (economic) is that it might be difficult or somehow impossible to materialize if not done in real-time to catch space—because of the influence of globalization. African giants would feel more used in the whole equation, and that is why they weigh up the odds before federating to form a continental integration. They must see the competitive edge for their companies arising out of the integration. It is that prestigious attitude that draws them from the agenda. However, their distancing away from a common goal helps outsiders as usual, and the overarching goal of the 1991 AEC treaty would be lost. Time is of the essence. People, territories, and other jurisdictions grow from smart to smarter and from sharp to sharper daily, although this does not guarantee sustainability. Sustainability is working together to live for today and tomorrow. It is, however, important to note that federations and integrations can do very little where masses do not understand the underlying assumptions, especially when everything is left for only leaders to decide. Integrations carry weight only when they are made to the minds of people that are prepared for it.

Marriage and Racial Integrations

We need several Obama prototypes. The US is what it is partly because of racial integration. We need to welcome the idea of racial integration either by racial intermarriages or living together as a community in diversity but not to remain so conservative that we do not open up to others. In the struggle to improve the standard of living for an African child, we ought to cross and fetch outside blood to engineer a new African breed (Afro-European, Afro-American, and Afro-Asian kind of). African men and women should try pairing with spouses from outside. We need racial integration to breed some mixed-race human beings of Africa to solve several dilemmas.

I have observed some issues that may not be solved when we remain so conservative. Because colonialism distorted the African masses, many things got messed up, and it might be difficult, if not too late, to correct some messes. There are several unique good attributes with an Asian and a European. The solution lies in identifying these and engineer a better action development plan following the prevailing conditions to solve the distortions.

I have observed many extraordinary attributes that the African blood would use to compete when integrating with others. Sports and entertainment being the two of the avenues to exploit. The France 2018 national team that won World Cup had over 50% black community. Another outstanding attribute is the African culture characterized by remarkable hospitality in many areas across the continent. When embraced legally and objectively on the African soil, racial and marriage integrations can create an unstoppable breed that is superb in leading new and advancing: technology, engineering, science, entertainment, poetry, and the sports fields. We need to embrace diversity and inclusion, new breeds through intermarriages and racial integrations. I am very optimistic that this can bring some radical change.

Nutrition Integrations

I am a bit perturbed by the small spectrum of foods we eat, especially in my culture. Our ancestors debarred some delicious species. These included several kinds of seafood and other plant species. Some of the culturally debarred foods are very nutritious. I am convinced that if we can start doing integrated dishes such as Mexican, Chinese, and Italian, we shall have some good results. It is a hypothesis which our scientists and agriculturalists may validate or nullify, but my opinion rests on that position. The staple foods for several cultures across the continent are characterized by starchy foods, which are also nutritious, but how about when we embrace some new diets and follow through the effects to learn?

Feeding iws an avenue that we need to discuss. The increasing trend of consuming fast foods and animal-based products can stimulate cancerous chemicals in our bodies, and we channel efforts to cure cancer. The production of those kinds of foods come with enormous amounts of unsustainable energy. Our scientists and agriculturalists need to spearhead the integration of foods in our communities not only to limit themselves (their thoughts) to genetically modify foods for increased supply to meet the population demand. They need to think about how the type of food consumed over a certain period influences someone's cognition, social thinking, attitude, and behaviour.

To develop Africa, the young and the youth matter. Therefore, the struggle of the current generation of adults should be geared to thinking solutions to answer the overt issues. I believe that the food we consume has a direct impact on the way we think and act. *It must influence imagination and perception.* We need to promote expert nutritionists. Where they are not present, governments should develop institutions that train and register expert nutritionists.

Sustainable Development Built on Developmental Agencies' Proposals: What is a Sustainable Project?

Since the Paris Summit of December 2015, the way manufacturing and the construction sector are to be conducted in the future is under greater scrutiny. Any developmental project in the 21st century must address the environmental, social, and economic impacts. For a project to be sustainable, the three must agree, as shown in the figure below.

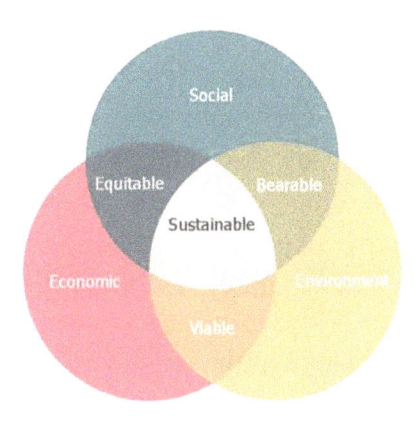

The Three Pillars of Sustainable Development

Source: Paris Summit, 2015

Social Pillar

The project would socially transform the community. It would uplift the well-being of people and improve relationships and social networks. The social pillar has several extraneous variables that influence it, i.e. culture, religion, and politics. A sustainable project would culturally objectivise the community through benchmarking on the cultural heritage. Favourable political decisions would be inclusive and would cater for everybody. Take an example of a multi-billion dollar water supply and sanitation scheme developed for a community through the lifecycle phases. The positive impacts the project would bring might include; clean water supply, improving water supply reliability and availability, women and youth getting jobs, improvement in public health and preventing communicable diseases, and etcetera. The negative impacts might include; defining the scheme route and the locations of reservoirs may warranty resettling people, and they must be compensated; scheme routes may touch sacred sites and important landscapes; sometimes scheme routes may be underground or above ground which might necessitate a sound safety plan to be in place; and etcetera. The balance of negative and positive impacts must be obtained, and it must be economical and eco-friendly. Therefore, by juggling options, the most optimal solution is obtained.

Economic Pillar

Defining the economic impact would necessitate comparison of benefits and costs through the project lifecycle phases. The most beneficial option is derived using economic indicators such as discounted cashflows yields, net-present value, internal rate of return, cost and benefit ratio, payback period, etcetera. In terms of sustainability, you might consider the most cost-effective option. The decision taken must be environmentally sustainable and socially acceptable.

Environmental Pillar

The overarching goal of the environmental pillar is to preserve the ecosystem. That means climate action is essential. The extraction of fossil fuels for use in industries comes with the adverse effect of carbon emissions which contribute to climate change when pumped into the atmosphere. Therefore, projects that produce less or no carbon emissions throughout their lifecycle phases are considered a priority. Climate change has led to extreme heat, floods, droughts, and the extinction of creatures. When appraising projects, the extent of environmental damage the project would bring is extensively evaluated together with proposed mitigations that would stop environmental damage. The mitigations' cost must be economical, and project outcomes must be socially acceptable (a must-do!). In many cases, you would consider an option that creates minor environmental damage, and alternative options dropped. Thinking about strategies to stop climate change and adapting to climate change is the new normal globally.

A sustainable developmental project maintains the ecosystem and holds nature in equilibrium. The hot topic engineers and other professionals hold in the 21st century is how developmental projects can leave nature in equilibrium so that minerals and other resources do not get extinct or depleted so that future generations can ably utilize these resources. Also, maintaining flora and fauna without losing any species from nature is part of the overarching goal. A sustainable project promotes the ecosystem and contributes to the effort to hold climatic conditions constant worldwide. This struggle is difficult where political decisions are not uniform globally, and politics influences all events. That is why sustainable development forward-lookers argue that *political integrations* must move along with *economic integrations.*

The political decisions inform the economic pillar as the main component in driving sustainable products. That is because government expenditure is always a political decision. The US$ 5 billion East African Crude Oil Pipeline (EACOP) presents a perfect example of appraising sustainable projects. It showed how politics plays a pivotal role. The Uganda-Tanzania route was more cost-effective, hence dropping the Uganda-Kenya route.[153] But was it the case? Find out more on how politics influence decisions.

Opinion——

A situation where various political systems govern the world threatens the effort to protect future generations' capacity to meet their needs. Industrialization has seen economies grow and expand, attain sustained growth. However, the continued investment in weapons for protection rather than food to eat makes the entire equation complex and things left to the Supreme Being to determine the fate of the future generations.

However, this does not stop us from continuing to save the planet. Engineers and technocrats ensure that the three pillars attain equilibrium in project design and development. ***In my opinion,*** equilibrium would not be enough. We need a shift in the boundaries of the pillars making sustainability tending towards *inclusion* so that the three circles superimpose onto each other hence maintaining the ecosystem, as shown below.

---

[153] "Route description and map," The East African Crude Oil Pipeline, accessed July 15th 2021, https://eacop.com/information-center/maps/the-route/route-description-map/.

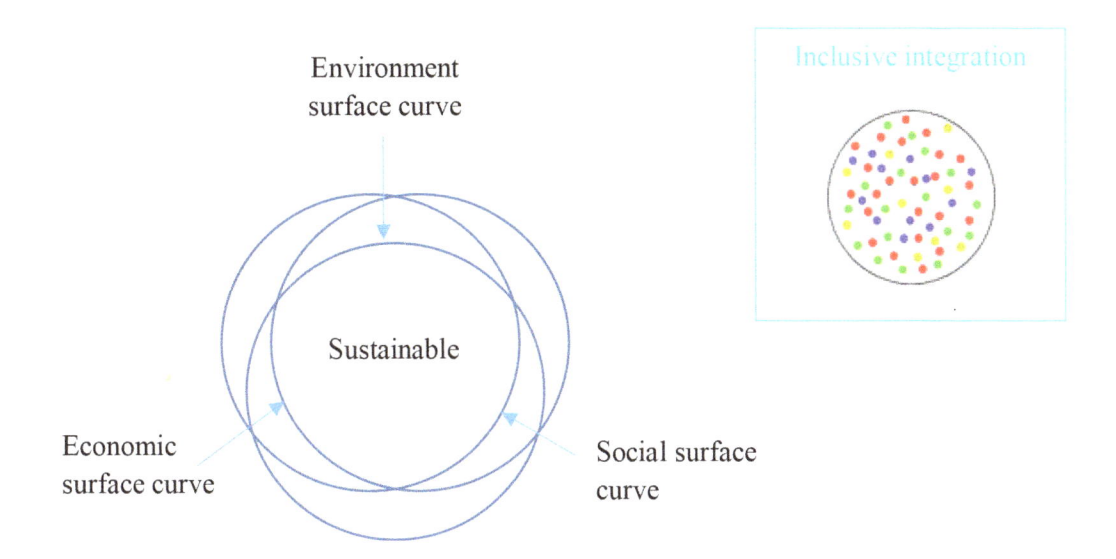

The Sustainability Intersection Growing Bigger

As explained earlier, the efforts should aim towards *inclusion*. Therefore, sustainability represented by the intersection of three (3) circles would be improved when the circles move from intersecting to superimposing. A sustainable integrated community project is inclusive, and if it is not inclusive, it is not sustainable.

Sustainable project development would be an integral of the three curves as shown in Figure below delineated out of the well-studied *trends* of the three pillars, i.e. social, economic, and environment. Then model the functions of the theoretical pillar trends and *several ideas can be generated from this construct*.

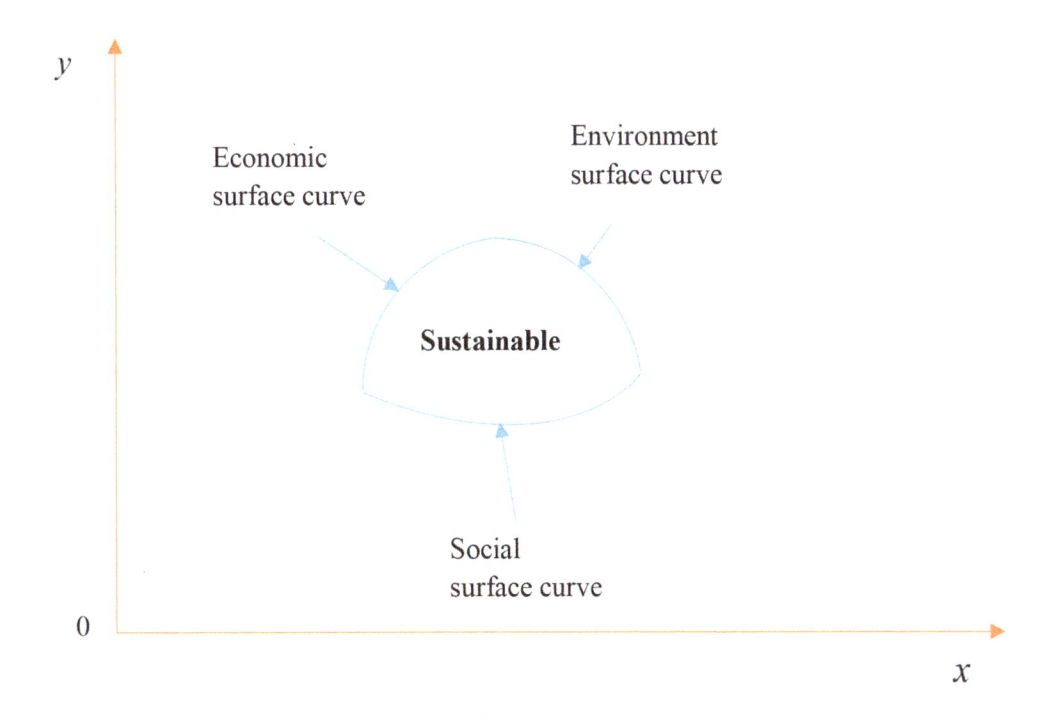

Ideal graphs for the 3 Pillars of Sustainable Development

Viewing them as circles and calculating the area at the intersection that meets sustainability requirements is not such a bad idea. It should be greater than any other intersection. As a 3D, the volume should be the greatest. The project analyst models correct functions for the environment, social, and economic pillars and corresponding 3D views. As the intersection moves to superimposition of the circles or 3D cylindrical objects, the project is considered inclusive. The economic pillar is measured at the level of structural transformation that the project would bring, the social pillar measured from the social transformation that the project adds on top of present value, and the environment pillar considered from the environmental impact caused by the project development. The figure below illustrates that as circles superimpose, tending towards inclusion, the project becomes more sustainable.

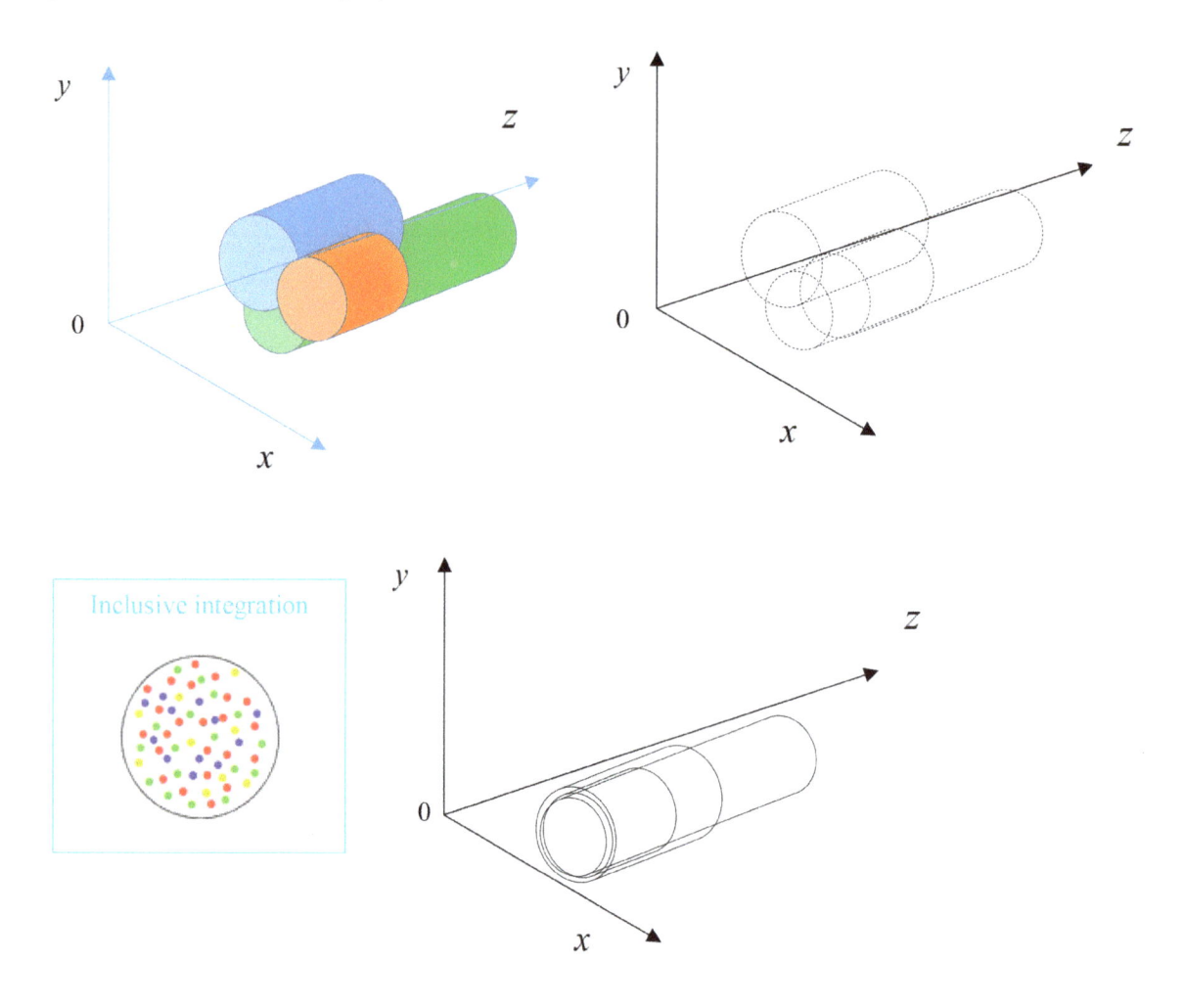

Superimposed pillars of sustainable development

A Sustainable Multitude of Projects leads to Healthy Integrations

The concept of inclusion which is in place, for example, for the people with disabilities, is a perfect ideal when diversified to other issues like jobs—allowing people to seek jobs across integrated blocs freely, direct from the smallest unit of society. The *guiding assumption* is that every aspect of government decisions is viewed from a sustainable project perspective. Therefore, when governments are moving forward to integrate, they bring a multitude of sustainable projects that tend towards inclusion to form healthy and inclusive integrations.

A 21st-century feasible project should be a sustainable project. A sustainable project leaves room for future generations to ably meet their needs. On the other hand, a feasible project must be technically viable, economical, operable, reliable, and maintainable. It should be socially acceptable and transformative.

In many times, a feasible project may not be 100% sustainable because of the social aspect informed by many variables; culture, religion, legal, and political decisions. Usually, the social impact analyses conducted in Africa to learn about the project development's social transformation are non-exhaustive, especially lacking a touch or feel of the cultural predispositions and societal self-awareness initiatives. That leaves the social pillar more demanding.

For example, technocrats, engineers, and other professionals have laboured to produce mathematical models to reduce carbon emissions from industries through innovative means. They also reduce the number of materials used to produce finished goods. They also advocate for circular economies. However, the most challenging aspect is the social component informed by several factors, as earlier mentioned. The mentioned professionals have the highest level of competence to produce safeguards to the environment and economize the production units. However, they have no way to limit politics, culture, and religion that promote the social structures and systems. Therefore, the world summits should now greatly focus on the social component to derive means of working towards a unified socio-economic and political system—a system that is free from immature politics, violence, and manipulation. That should be the primary goal.

Unified Socioeconomic and Political System: Would it sustainably develop Africa?

The socialist ideologies are premised on the notion of "taking from those according to their ability and giving to those according to their need." The capitalist views the socialist as one who wishes to redistribute wealth that is not theirs. The capitalist believes in using their intellectual abilities to do business for profit. In the interest of sustainable development, we need a unified socioeconomic and political theory that finds a meeting ground for a capitalist and socialist to redistribute wealth within the masses whilst leaving room for future generations to meet their needs. In my opinion, the challenges to sustainability brought about by the capitalist are more severe than those of a socialist. This is because a capitalist concentrates entirely on making profits and, in some cases, would care less about saving resources for future generations.

We need competitiveness that drives innovation and growth. At the same time, we need a fair distribution of resources within masses guided by measures to keep resources for the next generations. This is why an integrated socio-economic and political theory that juggles socialism and capitalism is vital to meet Africa's social conditions while saving the planet.

Diversity without Inclusion Does Harm

Inclusion incorporates the full panoply of a specific community. As organisations shift from homogenous to heterogeneous workforces, they need to be more inclusive in their decisions. They have to incorporate all people to take part in the growth and development. Take an example where an organisation promotes LGBT rights, women rights and allows all races to be part of the forum. We can say that the organisation is diversified. However, imagine the organisation's administration is for only LGBT people; how will others feel and think about the organisation? Some countries in the Nile Basin have their top positions in the government agencies headed by people of the same ethnicity. However, development agencies keep funding diversity and inclusion without questioning this anomaly. In that case, the funder also has a problem.

Integrations is Not a New Order of Thinking: It Guides Innovation

The Supreme Being proved integrations right from the beginning. We had not just recognised their presence until when scientists made excellent observations. A man has laboured to study and understand integrations to the depth. The Supreme Being made a human being together with other living beings as perfect engineered living beings. The Supreme Being provided the geometry of the living beings as an integral of constituent parts or components with highly moulded surfaces. Therefore, when one talks of integrations, they talk about *inclusion*. They talk about *consulting,* a two-way approach, but not informing one another.

To understand the world, we build on what the Supreme Being has put in place, and we question ourselves about many questions for which we live to answer. There is no innovation and invention which is too good or very new to the world. Many innovations and inventions are either directly or indirectly mimicking natural creatures. They are primarily typical prototypes or imitations of the existing creatures or phenomena and are very symbolic of nature. Several innovations mimic natural creatures. Consider the examples below:

- If a shark can dive, why not a submarine?
- If a bird can fly, why not an aeroplane?
- If a cheater can run faster than many other animals, why not a car?
- If a duck can float, why not a ship?
- Since mammals, insects, and reptiles can move things, why not earth moving equipment, e.g. excavator, grader, dozer?
- If a living creature's body can process the input to produce output, why not a manufacturing plant?
- If a living beings' reproductive system can produce a living being, why not 3D printing (additive manufacturing)?
- If the central nervous system can process, store, and retrieve information, why not a computer?
- If the human skin can sense cold and warm, sharp and blunt, why not artificial sensors like smartphone screens?
- If messages can be conveyed through an electrochemical process in the body's nerves and neurons, why not batteries?

> If a night dream can come true, why not a dream reading machine catch space in real-time and avoid future danger? A relationship between science and spirituality.

> If pain creates tears, depression, and anxiety, why not a machine that taps the unconscious suitable for marketing companies and security departments?

> If brain lobes can work together to process information in microseconds, why not robots and artificial intelligence?

The list that mimics natural creatures goes on and on. It purely demonstrates that people who have laboured to create artificial environments have dedicated their lives to studying the natural environment. They have lived their lives answering questions. Therefore, workable integrations must be symbolic of the natural phenomena to promote sustainability. Those fixated on The Big Bang might need to revise their beliefs. Therefore, it is crucial to learn that understanding the living beings' anatomy fuels inventions and innovations.

Africa's Sustainability beyond the 21st Century

The hot topic of the 21st century is sustainable development. Man has studied the natural environment to be able to live swiftly. However, the artificial environment seems to be turning more hazardous than before. Suppose we do not wake up early enough. In that case, the children of our grand grandchildren will say the earth was destroyed dramatically between the 16th and 21st centuries but more destroyed in the 20th and 21st centuries, which marked the start of the 4th industrial revolution (4IR). This will happen when they fail to find what used to be nature only admired in photos, videos, and historical items. Artificial intelligence (AI) and artificial life shall be a characteristic of generations to come—in a world where creatures that once lived are seen in photographs, but an imitation of such creatures is provided in the form of robots and the like, fueled by artificial intelligence innovations and associated complexes.

That kind of development will become a nuisance to the people, in the long run, creating more idiots than ever. As the modern world boasts of advanced technology, those who built the great Egyptian pyramids must have had unique technology. However, they did not destroy the environment as we have done today. Before the 16th century, the planet earth was still intact, but the world became misguided because of the continued search for knowledge amidst power struggles. The search for knowledge is not bad but how the knowledge is applied is the question to answer. The struggle for power that continues to be overt among giants makes the sustainable development equation complex and should be added to the seven (7) millennium prize problems defined by the Clay Mathematics Institute (CMI). The desire and greed to colonize space leave one who believes in the existence of the Supreme Being a little much offended. It exposes how humans have created intense anxiousness to live than ever.

Before the 16th century, the planet earth had its natural self-regulating mechanism. The contemporary scientist popped in with discoveries to aid life improvement. He was thus able to increase the number of people surviving difficulties and increase life expectancy. The rate of global warming accelerated after that.

Africa presents the best opportunity to lead sustainability and teach many other societies how to live economically. Not very long ago, there was a debate on the definition of poverty in the African context versus that of European standards. Several developmental agencies defined it as living below US$ 1.25 per day. Some argued that if one lives happily in a natural habitat, they may not admire the other who lives amidst pleasurable amusement and artificial environments. Without air-conditioners, their life seems to get distorted. Others claimed that many people in Africa are so rich, but the measure of poverty has been misguided to look at: to what extent the natural environment has been destroyed to manufacture goods and create artificial environments. The measure of GDP looks at the goods and services produced but does not look at how much the environment has been destroyed. I believe, not very far away, the use of GDP as a metric to determine success might be revised or dropped. Even the Human Development Index (HDI) will be revised to have metrics that determine how many people are living in the green natural environment, cherish values, breathing fresh air, and eating organic foods, among many other natural things.

My friend who lives in one of the highly developed countries told me how a neighbour next door died in his house, and it took them over five (5) days to recognize his death. That is something that rarely happens in the African setting, although today, many areas across Africa are starting to catch the bug. Is this sustainable development? A situation where an immediate neighbour collapses and dies in his house, and it takes almost a week to find out. Sustainable development will not occur when African values are washed away. The measure of success, happiness, and growth should not exclude the prolongation of values.

Poverty has been measured in a relativistic way by developmental agencies, threatening the environment at large. A community that is not transformed by sociocultural strategies and self-awareness initiatives should not be measured in poverty relative to that of one that is culturally objectivized. In the African context, poverty levels measured relative to other parts of the world leaves guilt and some degree of attribution to those who distorted the order of things not more than a century ago. As defined by developmental agencies, our poverty is not self-made but triggered and perpetuated by others at some point. Keeping many Africans in the dark corners and not exposing them to the truth about how life is genuinely improved—not getting them exposed to the original species of truth! Many models have been imported to Africa that cannot spur socioeconomic development—a claim that positive arguments can be based on false premises!

It is usual for many people in Africa to admire luxurious life in many societies around the globe. However, the table is turning around, and by the end of the first half of the 21st century, Africa will be the best place to live if people understand that nature is the highest level of wealth. Engineers and scientists will be awarded for scaling down on the air conditioners in buildings, ingenuity design that follows our ancestral habitats, bringing in ideas that make us more human than robots, and forward-looking at conserving what we found in place.

That is the main reason why cycling economies, circular economies, carbon-neutral economies, sharing economies, and many other kinds of well-thought-out economies you can mention are being rethought and advanced. In this continent, which has been rich in collectivism for a long time, sharing economies is not a new order of things. Our collectivism ought to have lived, but it was heavily attacked by colonialism and conventional religions that changed our thought patterns and attitudes, growing much mistrust with one another and lacking self-confidence. That is why we need to grow or regrow our attitudes to cope with the changing needs to match the self-awareness campaign that can help spur socio-economic transformation across the continent.

Africa has had many good things, just like elsewhere in the past. Doing away with some of the ancient technologies exposed people to illnesses and, in many other instances, increased the risk to catch diseases—just like any other thing has pros and cons. In emerging economies where old and used products are imported, it is not good to drop all old technologies. In many areas around Africa, pots were used to preserve boiled drinking water. However, now these were dropped to take on imported old refrigerators, too way past the design lifespans and emitting electromagnetic radiations of very high frequencies which may be harmful to people's health leading to chronic diseases like cancer. That is just one in a million examples. Physical water purification is not a new order of things across several African cultures, but it has been packaged to look like the latest innovation. Advancing on pot technology would be the best option to undertake. Therefore, the best approach was to improve the ancestral technologies with green energies and other natural means to purify and preserve water as cold. Engaging in continuous improvement is something that Africans have not rethought to improve, maintain, and extend their ancestral knowledge base. In many other places around the world, especially developed countries, it is common to find homes with more than 2 TV sets and refrigerators. Not because one refrigerator is full but simply because it feels good to have more than one. That will not sustainably develop the economies!

I am very convinced, subject to proving me wrong by others, that where the world has reached, especially in telecommunications, infrastructure, space science, and artificial intelligence, that many innovations, but not all, are fueled by power struggles. I mentioned in Chapter Two that Africa could not start yearning for power in such a context. Its power base should be built by putting things in order first and influence by keeping the continent safe. We should correct the distortions prior. Thinking about artilleries should be about solving internal conflicts but not a safeguard against outsiders. Outsiders are now thinking about space colonization. It might take about 150 years for Africa to manufacture weapons that might threaten it to yearn for safeguarding against the first world. It is not easy to safeguard against a person who is 150 years into your time by thinking massive artilleries. The solution lies in pulling up masses to understand the need to unite as an independent bloc(s). It is about understanding and not about weapons. Having heavy artillery and weapons cannot help very much to safeguard against insecurity.

The admiration of fresh air, green environment, and wildlife will attract many tourists for a vacation. Africa's tourism industry will boost, and gaining citizenship in Africa will hike in value. Africa will be strong. There is no need to dream ambitions of luxurious technologies, artilleries, and artificial intelligence at the expense of the planet. Despite all efforts put in impact assessments of different kinds, luxury economies are a total waste of the planet's resources, and there is no way you would explain this to future generations. We see several leaders in sovereign states like Southeast Asia, for example, that have fleets of vehicles worth millions of dollars that are just kept and used periodically. One of the challenges that the distortion of the order of things has brought to humans is kleptomania, which has left several states' leaders and wealthy people unable to survive it.

Engineers are to make Africa a leading hub for vacations by utilizing nature to plan stress-free vacation destinations. It is possible with the beautiful sceneries Africa has got. The wildlife and sanctuaries present in the continent make it very possible to shoot this ambition. Doctors across the globe will find it appropriate to prescribe our stress-free vacation destinations as therapeutic interventions for depressed and stressed wealthy people. That will boost Africa's GDP.

Beautiful Africa, endowed with different types of bird species like in the Pearl of Africa, is naturally leading by the grace of the Supreme Being in that aspect. Suppose we regulate the population growth rates, put health first through consuming organic foods, and forecast a sustainable population. In that case, we can decide how many industries we need, how many road kilometres we need to pave, and etcetera. These need to be at a minimum but utilized at maximum output, clearly pointing out the amounts of greenhouse gas emissions, planned urbanization, and gearing efforts to regulate rural-urban migrations.

The stage at which Africa is is a hot spot and presents an opportunity to lead. The advancement in technologies globally puts Africa at a competitive edge. These technologies can be tapped into—the good ones to create integrated approaches to aid growth and development. African has huge mineral deposits and a virgin environment suitable for developmental projects—and this makes it competitive. The solution lies in adequate planning. And adequate planning calls for investment in human capital prior. The planning should motivate people to remain in rural areas. Modernized agriculture that poses no threat to the environment is the best solution to create jobs for Africans. Natural water reservoirs like swamps, rivers, streams, ponds, and lakes should not be encroached on for farming, but rather the environs should be utilized to draw water from the reservoirs to irrigate crops and feed animals. Tampering with the natural reservoirs impacts the groundwater recharge process and affects the natural reservoirs' hydrology. Sustainable groundwater management balances the volume rate abstracted and recharged over a period of time. Modern agriculture utilizes mechanization and draws on adequate calculations to determine the amount of irrigation water that does not drain the underground water quantity.

Self-awareness campaigns are the cornerstone for Africa to lead in food production. Several economies are agricultural-based, first because of the suitable arable land and secondly, because of our history. The reason we look elsewhere to turn many African economies into something else is what I fail to understand. The primary question is how the world will feed the growing population by the first half of the 21st century? Everything else would be a value addition to our agriculture. A number of African countries have fertile soils that have been carried away in planes by some others at some point. Some of the leaders in fruit growing and juice processing reside in deserts. That mocks Africans because we have fertile soils, yet hunger keeps striking us. Right after we became independent from colonialists, the challenge we have faced is the planning deficiencies and a failure to embrace self-awareness initiatives. Many other stressors like corruption and embezzlement of public resources are just a result of bad leadership. However, the human capital deficiency is equally a result of failing to self-critique, self-reflect, and re-examine the systems that colonial masters left in place. Things like the education system, democracy in collectivism, land matters, and self-awareness family initiatives need to be in order. They must be re-evaluated.

Many societies across the globe are putting more emphasis on turning their economies into carbon-neutral economies by the first quarter of the 21st century. However, sustainability is not only about turning to carbon-neutral economies. The issue of sustainability is more about having many future generations ably live as we live now or even better. Therefore, values need not be forgotten. The exhaustion of natural resources and minerals for the production of *luxurious products* is equally a big challenge. The 2015 UN

Paris Agreement specifies holding the increase in the global average temperature to well below 2°C above pre-industrial levels and pursuing efforts to limit the temperature increase to 1.5°C above pre-industrial levels. However, the population boom amidst luxurious lives perpetuated by capitalism in power-hungry giants makes it the number one issue to tackle before the affixed 2°C UN goal. Necessity was the mother of invention at some point in time, but today luxury drives necessity.

In 2019, Africa's population stood at 1.307 billion, and the economy stood at about US$ 2.6 trillion (Nominal GDP). The population is expected to rise gradually by 2050, and Africa's GDP is estimated to multiply by over 10 times the current GDP. The African population has almost doubled since 1990, something that must worry any person with a healthy conscience. The economist's fixation on population explosion to aid market growth is no longer applicable in modern theories of sustainable development. The continent is already experiencing many crises; how will it be by the first half of the 21st century?

There is no doubt, Africa is becoming the investment hub for foreigners. The Royal Institute of Chartered Surveyors of the UK predicts that the world's best cities will be in Africa 100 years from now. The question is about how prepared are Africans to invest on their own? Secondly, how prepared are Africans to protect and preserve the environment? And how prepared are Africans not to slave within their territory? GDP levels to rise on the tunes of others is not going to help Africa very much. A large fraction of foreign direct investments counted as Africa's GDP helps foreigners much more than Africans. This is because Africans cannot sustain growth. Africa would be excited about the growth of the economy only when the population can be maintained constant. How will such a drastically growing population be fed? A good question from Steven Hawking (1942-2018).

100 years post-development of African cities from 2020 need clear roadmaps to conserve the environment. Interestingly, the roadmaps are at many times inexistent or inadequate. Where they are produced, they are provided on a piecemeal basis making it difficult to plan for sustainable development. There should be holistic *master plans* for sustainable African cities. There is an illusion of knowledge at some point which is highly depicted in the planning deficiencies of some regions. This problem, coupled with a lack of comprehension of procedures, is complete havoc to the continent and a threat to the entire planet. In this way, since sustainable development calls upon all continents to be vigilant, the planning of Africa's cities should be taken seriously irrespective of where one comes from. The deficiency on this issue is depicted in failure to do what is supposed to be done first and postpone the other—a deficiency in planning for remedial options, a weak legal system in many sovereign territories, unhealthy politics, and showing less regard to the environment at large in many decisions taken. Recently the world economic forum ranked many of Africa's cities among the fastest-growing cities globally, and at the same time, many of them face high risks from climate change. This mismatch justified shortfalls in planning for sustainability.

No doubt Africa's cities will grow and expand, but the biggest question lies in answering the position of the African race. An African by nativity, colour, and blood but not naturalization in the entire sustainable development campaign. There are about five elements to weigh and come to a conclusion about the future of Africa: [1]Culturally sensitive population growth rates, [2]foreign direct investments rates, [3]nationals' investments rates, [4]climate change monitoring safeguards rates, and [5]ecosystem sustainability rates. If all the five are in equilibrium, then Africans can be excited to have a sustainable GDP.

Leading and Managing Sustainable Development

Africa presents the best opportunity to lead sustainable development because it still has many living beings intact, abundant mineral resources, and a green environment in some regions. The biggest threat is the loosening culture in favour of outside cultures. However, this can be solved when people get exposed to the original species of truth. The heart of sustainable development is about thinking green, combating climate change, using materials sparingly, reducing raw materials used in products manufacturing, maximum use of energy and products, and thinking of alternative green solutions to promote the ecosystem. The overarching goal is to have the life of all living beings indefinitely without extinction and ensure that the standard of life achieved in many developed countries is sustained and perpetuated so that future generations enjoy it.

Life has graduated to a stage or extent that a prediction of one's time to stay in this world is inevitable without the use of sophisticated means and technologies. A prediction by profound scientists that we are left with less than 12 years to save the planet consolidates this logic. Understanding sustainability struggles leaves only open-minded humans to create peace in the interim to put things in order. The struggle to have things in order will need a campaign to shape people's understanding of life. As I mentioned in Chapter Five, nurturing others should not be a stumbling block for a person whose mind is open to understanding the meaning of life.[154] As African leaders, we have a role to play to make more leaders.

Africa's rudimentary way of life in many rural areas might prove wealthier in the sustainability equation, especially in the regions where ignorance outweighs the illusion of knowledge. The sustainability campaign is not yet understood nor appreciated by an ordinary person on the continent. However, the end results of human's intervention to disorder the planet will wake us up in a not-very-far period from now. During that time, HIV/AIDS prevalence in Africa will become more or less like a simple fever—a disease that people will admire over the different cancers that will sprout out across the globe due to climate change. The solution lies in understanding the meaning of life and promote the think green campaign.

The African human being is extraordinarily privileged by the grace of the Supreme Being, or call it the natural selection mechanism, to still be living in massive numbers. I am very convinced that almost more than half of the existing population would be dead. If not, they would not get the chance to see the world. This argument rests on a number of social interactions that draw an African closer to others occupationally—many African girls who look for green pastures in some parts of the world work in hazardous ways that infringe pain to them, contrary to what human rights agencies advocate for in the modern world. The discriminatory characters tendered by some others in some sports, religion, work, and professional bodies keep their integrity doubted. Then, how sure are we that we are eating the right imported processed foods, taking the right medicines or evidence-based medicines, and using the right fertilizers for crops from such territories amidst the sustainability challenge? Let us lead ourselves to the promised land and reclaim the position of Africa.

---

[154] See p. 236, §5 (Hint: Are people unique?).

Climate Change and Its Impacts

Solar Radiation, Global warming, and Greenhouse Effect

Developmental agencies predict that Africa is more likely to suffer droughts and food shortages due to global warming. They warn that changing weather patterns threaten food production. China and the USA produce the largest amounts of carbon dioxide, with 2014 World Bank estimates reporting $10.29 \times 10^6 kt$ and $5.25 \times 10^6 kt$ respectively. Carbon dioxide (CO_2) is one of the five primary Green House Gases (GHG) and the leading cause of global warming. As a result of global warming, Africa is claimed to face more droughts and food shortages more than other territories. Other greenhouse gases include; Ozone (O_3), Water vapour (H_2O), Methane (CH_4), Nitrous oxide (N_2O), Chlorofluorocarbons (CFCs), and Hydro-fluorocarbons (includes HCFCs and HFCs).

The Earth's atmosphere contains 78% nitrogen, 21% oxygen, and 0.9% oxygen. Other gases that account for almost 1% of the atmospheric gases are carbon dioxide, nitrous oxides, methane, and ozone. The earth, like other planets, has its natural mechanism of keeping these gases in equilibrium. However, due to human activity, the equilibrium of the atmospheric gases has been offset since the beginning of the industrial revolution because of the excessive emission of greenhouse gases into the atmosphere. That is the biggest challenge associated with the industrial and technological revolution. As a result of human activities that lead to the emission of greenhouse gases, the excessive concentration of these gases in the atmosphere becomes hazardous.

To a greater extent, the planet earth relies on the constant supply of light and heat energy from the sun. The sun produces three types of radiation, i.e. infrared, visible light, and ultraviolet radiation, which traverses through space and earth's atmosphere to reach the earth. The radiations produced by the sun are electromagnetic, and these radiations propagate (radiate) through space carrying electromagnetic radiant energy. When these radiations hit gas molecules, they excite the atoms of each respective gas differently to vibrate and distribute their electrical charges.

The infrared radiation with longer wavelengths has a critical effect once it excites gas molecules in the atmosphere. The balance between absorbed and emitted infrared radiation has a critical effect on the earth's climate. Greenhouse gases absorb more infrared radiation because the distribution of their electrical charges changes when they vibrate. Because non-greenhouse gases in the atmosphere, such as Nitrogen (N_2) and Oxygen (O_2), have two atoms of the same element, their distribution of electrical charges has no net change when they vibrate. Monatomic gases such as Argon have no vibrational modes. Therefore, the more greenhouse gases increase, the more infrared radiation is trapped into the atmosphere. Most solar radiation that hits non-greenhouse gases is reflected back towards space and is not trapped to stay in the earth's atmosphere.

The increasing amount of carbon dioxide and water vapour in the atmosphere due to human activities intercept solar heat and cause it to get trapped in the earth's atmosphere, the lakes, oceans, and the land to cause the **greenhouse effect.** The water vapour increases due to rising temperatures of the seas and lakes that trigger rising evaporation. That causes "Climate Change or Global Warming".

The European Union, the USA, and China have more industries releasing carbon dioxide into the atmosphere than Africa. Also, Africa has the largest infrastructure crisis, especially in Sub-Saharan Africa. The implication is that Africa should ideally have the largest part of the ecosystem and natural habitat intact because infrastructural development like railways lines, hydropower facilities, tunnels, and road networks cannot be built without destroying the natural habitat. **Why then is Africa at the highest risk of the consequences of global warming?**

Why is Africa Likely to be Worst Hit by the *Effects* of Climate Change?

Humans have been looking for knowledge to improve life for many centuries ago. In the desire to improve and ease the way to live, humans thought of alternative energy sources. In the beginning, human labour was extensively used until people felt the need to find alternative energy sources to replace manual handling. Alongside human labour, other energy sources included domestic animals, e.g. donkeys, camels, dogs, horses, and etc. In the 16th Century, water-wheels and windmills were greatly used as a source of energy. All these forms of energy were renewable not until 1765 when an improved version of the steam engine was invented in England following Thomas Newcomen earlier invention of 1712. The improvement in the steam engine marked the beginning of the industrial revolution. This triggered the onset of the widespread non-renewable energies from fossil fuels, coal, oil, and gas across the globe to develop and aid machinery and industrial processes that require enormous amounts of energy.

Following the 1987 Brundtland Report about sustainability, humans woke up to save the planet by thinking of solutions to create the balance between human's activities and the environment so that the consumption of natural resources is controlled to allow regeneration and renewal of the used up natural resources. Therefore, a condition would be termed unsustainable when the consumption of a natural resource surpasses its ability to regenerate/renew. Many scientists had warned before, but the sustainable development topic rose to fame in 1987 following the common future report (Brundtland Report).

Most African economies solely rely on imported finished goods from the Americas, Asia, and Europe, yet a considerable amount of raw materials are fetched from Africa. The extraction of minerals and oil comes with emissions. A good proportion of imported products we use in Africa are either used products or low quality, especially in Sub-Saharan Africa. Some do not meet international standards, which poses significant risks to lives.

Sustainable development is about easing the way to live in the maximum possible way for today's generation and many generations to come whilst having the planet in order as much as possible. The collision of human civilization with the environment and other living beings must be reduced to the extent possible. That means that if the government proposes to construct roads, industries, dams, or power plants, they must provide a well-grounded roadmap to control the greenhouse effect by producing the greenhouse footprints to guide decision-making.

I have outlined reasons which I believe are a part of the reasons some parts of Africa are likely to be severely affected by climate change.

Tropical Climates and Monsoon Winds

The Köppen—Geiger climate classification system divides climates into five main climate groups: polar, dry, tropical, temperate, and continental. Some countries in Central Africa, West Africa, and East Africa experience tropical climates. The unique attribute of tropical climates is that solar radiation is intense, and temperatures remain relatively constant (hot) throughout the year. Where temperatures are relatively constant (hot) throughout the year, the greenhouse effect can be very disastrous once emissions are not controlled because it can significantly alter the area's climate patterns, hence altering the occurrence of the only two seasons: a wet season and a dry season. This has a serious impact on African livelihood. Monsoon winds always blow from cold to warm regions of the tropics. Increased greenhouse gases would alter the movement pattern of these winds because of the change in temperatures within tropical regions.

Population Increase

Some African countries have the highest fertility rates. The population is multiplying day in and day out without proper control measures put in place by governments. While some leaders encourage women to set their ovaries free to produce and grow economies, they have not well-thought-out the ecological footprint and required attitudes. Population increase adversely impacts the ecological footprint if not controlled. The rate at which the population multiplies in some parts of Africa is threatening the continent's sustainability. Population growth might not be the issue, but are African governments prepared to receive the exploding population? Are attitudes rightly grown? The population that the environment can hold needs to be considered in all decisions that affect future generations' ability to live sustainably. We should always consider the carrying capacity of the environment.

The amount of land, oceans, and lakes required to sustain the consumption patterns and to absorb waste will need to be tripled by the first half of the 21st century if the population is not controlled in some parts of Africa yet in an actual sense, we do not have any other place to go. Several scholars and developmental agencies argue that a big population is important for an emerging economy—that it creates markets for products and threatens a potential attack from outsiders. However, when a large proportion of the population is unproductive and lacks well-defined economic activities, it can become more disastrous because conflicts over land and water might become the order of the day. Sub-Saharan boda-boda economies cannot yearn much of increasing the population. The population must be productive, policies on land must be clear, and the right attitudes towards; work, time, and space must be nurtured to make use of a growing population.

Extraction of Minerals

Countries like the Democratic Republic of Congo (DRC) have rare minerals. The extraction of some minerals requires enormous amounts of energy. The challenge is the lack of policy on emissions in several countries. If we restructured Africa's economy, some countries would be among the richest in the world. Instead, the minerals are fetched from Africa, and policies to control emissions are poorly enforced. That means climate will continue to change, and minerals will continue to be fetched. Also, mineral extraction sites contribute to surface water and groundwater pollution, erosion, and sedimentation

Deforestation

Many other areas produce enormous amounts of greenhouse emissions. However, deforestation is high in Africa because of languishing in extreme poverty and hunger in some parts of Africa. Forests, trees, and grasslands are cleared to get timber for houses, to make furniture, and burning charcoal. And there are no excellent policies on afforestation. Where they are, they are not adequately enforced because of the political situation in which Africans live. Where policies are enforced, the processes are improper; enforcement agencies arrest people for charcoal burning without concrete plans issued by governments on alternative renewable energy sources. People are languishing in poverty, and their immediate energy source to prepare meals is firewood or/and charcoal.

Forests and trees are crucial elements in the carbon cycle because they absorb carbon dioxide from the atmosphere through photosynthesis—a process in which they manufacture their foods. Once forests are cleared and carbon emissions increase in the atmosphere due to human activities, the carbon cycle is offset. We thus have more carbon dioxide in the atmosphere that traps more solar radiation around the earth.

Limited Agricultural Mechanization

Africa has not wholly embraced agricultural mechanization. With over 60% of land in Africa being arable, the largest part of it is cultivated using hand tools, which lowers agricultural productivity. If Africa fails to go agricultural mechanization to a big scale, many areas are prone to extreme food shortages before the end of the first half of the 21st century. The changing seasonal patterns call for change in planting and harvesting times to address the food shortages we are experiencing. The tropical climates have since changed. The occurrence of the two seasons (wet and dry) have changed. We need to revise planting and harvesting times to integrate innovative schemes like mini-irrigation and big irrigation schemes as appropriate. Otherwise, if measures are not implemented, we are prone to be hit by the worst droughts associated with food shortages that will go down in the books of history. A situation where African countries living in the tropics and at the same time host a significant number of refugees, as a result of the crisis in Somalia, DRC, South Sudan and CAR, etc., we need concrete plans on how to feed the growing unproductive population. Thinking seasonal planting is no longer an approach to address food shortages because of the changing weather patterns. Therefore, increased productivity will only be possible when sophisticated and motorized equipment is deployed for Africa's farming activities. At the moment, Africa has not mechanised agriculture to full scale.

Transportation

The belief that a car is a sign of success in some African cultures needs to be restructured. Whilst many societies across the globe wish to maximize public transport, some societies in Africa still believe that it is not easy to live comfortably without owning a car. They look at walking, cycling, and public transport means as associates for the poor class. Great effort should be geared in educating the young people that a car is not a symbol of success and that alternative means of transport are not for the poor. Walking and cycling come with health benefits. They help burn calories from the body and thus enable the person to be physically fit and within a good healthy body mass index. Many societies worldwide are now planning cities with well-designated spaces for walking, jogging, and cycling to address health and safety concerns. It is high time we reviewed the planning process to have smart and sustainable cities in Africa.

The effect of the belief that a car is everything in some societies in Africa is this: people work hard to ensure they possess cars. Very few African countries manufacture cars. Because most African countries live on charity and loans from developmental agencies, the Asian countries, and the western world, it becomes difficult to buy brand new cars. That is because of the heavy taxes imposed on the importation of cars. The selling price of the new cars is already high; the CIF, and import taxes escalate the final price. This makes many Africans resort to buying old and unsalvageable scrap cars.

The rate at which old cars emit carbon monoxide emissions is higher than new cars because they burn the fuel far less efficiently because of defective/worn parts, exhaust system leaks, and defective catalytic converters. Carbon monoxide is toxic to people and animals that use haemoglobin as an oxygen carrier. If living beings inhale it, it reacts with the haemoglobin in red blood cells to form carboxyhemoglobin, preventing oxygen transportation by the blood to other organs. Production of carbon monoxide occurs when incomplete combustion occurs due to a limited supply of air or oxygen. Once carbon monoxide is chemically oxidized very slowly by oxygen and water in the lower atmosphere and at room temperature, it produces carbon dioxide—a greenhouse gas. Consequently, the quality of air that the people residing near the roads breathe and the water they drink reduces significantly.

When combustion is incomplete, any engine produces carbon monoxide. Internal combustion engines operating on; gasoline, liquefied petroleum gas (LPG), or diesel fuel produce varying amounts of carbon monoxide. Carbon monoxide itself is not a greenhouse gas but possesses an indirect radioactive effect when it breaks down in the atmosphere producing carbon dioxide—a greenhouse gas. The quality of fuel, the mechanical condition of the vehicle in terms of reliability, and engine type influence the production of gas emissions in the atmosphere. For sustainability purposes, it would be wise for African governments to promote public transport, cycling, and walking economies as appropriate to reduce greenhouse gas emissions. The railway transport, electric vehicles, and communal taxis interconnected and facilitated by digital technologies are better strategies to adopt for developing African smart and sustainable cities.

Foods—consumption of animal-based products

Consumption of animal-based products in many African cultures has been quite dominant for some time. The rate of consumption of animal-based products is increasing in some cultures across the African continent. There are several health issues associated with animal-based meals, unlike vegetarian-based meals. The feeding of animals is also associated with several activities that require enormous amounts of energy. The processing of animal-based products also needs significant amounts of energy. Preservation of some animal products is also energy-intensive. Many African countries, because they are poor, they sell their cereals to the outside world to boost the foreign exchange, yet cereals are associated with minor health issues and do not require much energy for preservation.

Africans are shifting away from green foods, kinder to the planet, to processed and packaged foods. Junk foods pose a high health risk and are high energy-consuming. Also, organic foods are reducing in Africa.

Encroaching on Wetlands

It is hard to convince ignorant people that cultivating some crops in the wetlands impacts wetland hydrology. Peasants find it hard to agree that cultivating in wetlands affects groundwater recharge, and that is because they have been doing it for the past centuries.

Commercialization of almost everything has created a big risk to this planet, and only curious people can live to understand its negative impacts. Government policies that follow little or no procedures due to planning deficiencies perpetuated by selfish politics greatly confuse the poor people. One person can be sold a big chunk of a titled wetland simply because he is an affiliate of the ruling regime in Sub-Saharan Africa—typical of Nile Basin Countries. That person goes ahead to destroy the wetland. That is the political side of the cause.

However, the point lies in the interdependence of factors: politics, commerce, cultural beliefs, and science in the protection of the wetlands, and with science wishing to take the lead in decision-making requires brilliant, hardworking, and patriotic African men and women to dedicate their lives to saving the continent and the planet at large—which very few people are doing that at the moment. African dedicated people must develop a mechanism to redefine Africa's politics that can inspire hope, restructure unhelpful core beliefs within some cultures, and inspire people to love science.

Land, Housing, Infrastructure, and Culture

Developing economies that wish to realize self-driven sustainable development would require no single person to own land permanently—some socialist ideologies to match the present-day sustainability requirements. The government would own all land through appropriate means and sound considerations, and people would hold leases on land where lawfully permitted. In some countries across Africa, people can still own land permanently. Of course, many African cultures have ancestral sacred land associated with cultural activities performed from time to time. However, sustaining the African continent and its people is the priority, and that means mapping out all sacred sites is necessary.

I mentioned earlier that cultural audits are inevitable in the interest of sustainability. Some cultural activities and rituals are noncompliant with sustainable development goals and would need a total overhaul. For example, my culture and many other cultures require to have a cemetery for each small lineage. This is a cultural norm not very conforming to sustainability requirements because of the increasing need for land. A particular lineage or clan would get a specially designated place(s) in each district or sub-county or county to locate a cemetery than having individualized cemeteries scattered all over the country. This can be planned where consultations with elders and cultural leaders are well conducted. Land is becoming a scarce resource in the 21st century, and such constraints retard development in infrastructure because they are time-consuming and precipitate conflicts.

The housing sector consumes a considerable number of raw materials and finished construction and building materials. For example, the production of steel and cement products is a high energy-intensive process. The production of steel and cement produces enormous amounts of carbon emissions pumped into the atmosphere. These two products are the most commonly used construction materials. The use of concrete and steel in construction therefore, needs alternative value engineering additions in a number of processes to reduce unnecessary waste and perhaps their need would be progressively reduced over time. Innovations are underway in several developed countries to produce low-carbon concrete. We need a construction sector planners and other lead planners that can economize resources whilst maximizing the use of construction materials. At the moment, Africa does very little to use cement and steel sparingly.

Sand which is a non-renewable resource over human timescales, is in very high demand worldwide. It is estimated that over 50 billion tons of sand are needed for construction globally, and sand mining significantly alters the hydrology of mining sites, and this impacts climate patterns. The Asian giant is exploiting the loophole in the environmental protection policies across Africa.

Buildings and infrastructure' reliability and sustainability are essential in the 21st century because we need to reduce waste and unnecessary reworks—the risk of depletion and exhaustion of natural resources tasks planners to be more thoughtful. However, the housing and construction sector in many African countries is poorly regulated. Poor quality building materials and shoddy works are common. Haphazard planning of cities and towns is common, which perpetuates the housing deficiency.

On the other hand, some African house designers and engineers are not well-trained in designing for sustainability, operability, and maintainability. The green building movement is inadequately embraced in many African societies. The green building movement addresses the need and desire for more energy-efficient and environmentally friendly design and construction practices. Many house designers are not trained how to reduce waste generated from the household, how to maximize power and water consumption, how to integrate efficient renewable energy resources, how to maximize the use of construction materials, being conversant with carbon footprint decisions to inform design, how to deal with unique sites and overall site planning, and how to preserve cultural heritage/values whilst designing and constructing houses. Therefore, the housing sector presents a big challenge because many governments lack concrete policies for people to follow whilst designing and developing houses. This is because energy use in buildings is not straightforward in many cases since the indoor conditions that can be achieved with energy use greatly vary. For purposes of sustainability, the housing sector is one of the sectors that need very strong laws and regulations. Existing laws are very weak and poorly enforced in many African countries.

Planning for Software and Hardware

Because we borrow most of our standards from the western world, we have achieved exciting developments that imitate the western world. However, we fail to perfect the models and pass out exclusive and poorly diversified policies that are unsustainable. Today's effective planning must be holistic, involving professionals from both the scientific and humanistic fields of knowledge.

A significant number of African elites are well-known for preparing beautiful reports that are well organized and might appear straightforward but lack practical and workable action plans. One professional Asian colleague confessed and said, "I think Africans can prepare excellent documents better than us on average." The point is not about organizing an excellent report/document but rather a report/document filled with ideas that work or are practical, even if the report/document is not so many pages, neither is it very organized or very straightforward. Excellence and coherence of documents are essential, but they do not guarantee the quality of ideas within the documents! I have come across several elites focused much on the font type, size, and structure of the report/document than the ideas contained within that document. Several African economies spend more on planning the software component than the hardware. There are many reports shelved and lack action plans for implementation. Sometimes they lack resources to implement the plans. However, they continue spending more money on attending conferences and workshops than executing the intended goals.

In the interest of self-driven sustainable development, we should focus on the quality of ideas and practicability of those ideas. Ideas that are holistic and can be executed with inclusivity. The documents should be excellently and coherently prepared, but the ideas in those reports should take precedence. Environmental enforcement agencies have a significant role in ensuring that the decisions taken emanating from the recommendations presented in the documents are holistic and practical. They should desist from making decisions based on scientific theories alone.

In conclusion, along with this point, African countries will be hit the worst by climate change because of investing more resources and time in the software component than the hardware. Here, foreign consultants bag million dollars for drawing strategic plans, yet there is rarely nothing much beyond piecing together what others have done before—very little reinventions and innovations per se. A Nile Basin country lost close to US$ 1.2 m in master planning projects in 2020/2021 to a European firm, which could not deliver. It was primarily because of the unique African attitude disorder (UAAD) that fails officials to trust locals with work. The implementation of projects was delayed by over one (1) year as a result of planning deficiencies. This is one example in thousands. There is a planning deficiency in many developing countries perpetuated by the illusion of knowledge and working in silos at some point and minding more about the report/document structure than the ideas in that report/document. That, coupled with too much bureaucracy copied from elsewhere and never improved, escalates the problem, especially in procurement systems and et cetera. Many environmental impacts assessments and risk assessments are too theoretical and fail to integrate the knowledge and experiences of the local inhabitants. Although science makes the backbone of the decisions taken on environmental impact mitigation measures, a true African expert ought to listen to what stakeholders and related interest groups submit before making policies that follow theoretical hypotheses while seated in their offices. A true African expert must *do things with* stakeholders/end-users, not *doing things to* the stakeholders/end-users. We need environmental impact assessments followed by mitigation measures that are holistic and practical.

What Should We Do To Mitigate the Worst Scenario?

I have addressed why I believe some parts of Africa shall be the worst hit by the effects of climate change and therefore need immediate climate action intervention. African governments should prioritize climate action more than anything else because its implications are far-stretching. The Paris Agreement of December 2015 of which UN member countries ratified, requires member countries to report progress on Nationally Determined Contributions (NDCs) to combat climate change. The governing special interest is to work to limit global temperature rise below 2 degrees centigrade. All member countries are doing whatever it takes to contribute significantly to the effort to develop sustainably. The following interventions can prove useful to enable the highly likely African states to be worst hit by climate change to make safe plans to mitigate or reduce the adverse outcomes and accelerate socioeconomic transformation.

Corporate Strategy

The 17 UN Sustainable Development Goals (SDGs) are a blueprint for achieving a better and more sustainable future for all. Therefore, embedding sustainable development goals at the core of organizations and the project strategy is one of the most critical components in the sustainability campaign. The UN sustainable development goals address the global challenges, such as extreme poverty and hunger, quality of education, climate action, clean water and sanitation, affordable and clean energy, smart cities, life below water, and gender equality. African governments would prioritize the UN SDGs and task all organizations to embed the goals in their mainstream activities to achieve remarkable progress and report significant success through the nationally determined contributions.

Appraising projects following standards such as the International Finance Corporation (IFC) performance standards on environmental and social sustainability should be at the heart of every corporate organization.[155] The IFC standards provide eight performance standards, i.e. Assessment and Management of Environmental and Social Risks and Impacts; Assessment and Management of Environmental and Social Risks and Impacts; Labor and Working Conditions; Resource Efficiency and Pollution Prevention; Community Health, Safety, and Security; Land Acquisition and Involuntary Resettlement; Biodiversity Conservation and Sustainable Management of Living Natural Resources; Indigenous Peoples; and Cultural Heritage. These standards aim at guiding corporate organizations' governance and sustainability strategies.

Training

Government leaders must be competent enough to lead the sustainability agenda. This means they must be trained and shaped in thinking to match the needs of climate action campaigns. Whether they are politicians, civil servants, and public servants, all need the competence to steer African economies in the right direction as far as sustainability is concerned. This training which must be geared towards shaping thinking, knowledge, and understanding of the implications of the decisions made concerning the environment, would need to be a mandatory exercise. Training should deliver a skilful workforce that is impacting positive change to the communities and the individuals themselves. Several collaborations and partnerships are vital to attaining this milestone.

Climate Change Policy

Greenhouse Footprint. In the interest of promoting clean energy and reducing carbon emissions pumped into the atmosphere, African governments would be required to enforce climate change policies. These policies would require project managers and leaders to provide greenhouse footprint calculations during project designs, before commissioning the projects, and during the operational phase. Project feasibility study reports and projects appraisal reports would be required to be accompanied by forecasted greenhouse footprint calculations, if any, within the environmental impact assessment and mitigation plans.

Industries and manufacturing plants would be strictly required to report carbon emissions to the responsible statutory agencies and how they intend to make continuous improvements to reduce down the emissions

---

[155] International Finance Corporation (IFC) performance standards on environmental and social sustainability, 2012.

per year. That means carbon taxes and climate change levies in industries, commerce, public, and private sectors would be charged as appropriate. For example, companies importing unsalvageable cars would be highly taxed, and the cost of electric vehicles manufactured locally subsidized. Setting emission standards required per sector would enable stakeholders to work within the limits of the emissions prescribed in each sector.

The government has a significant role to play in enacting policies that promote green. In some cases, the initial cost of setting up renewable energies is high and would necessitate the government to subsidize the sector. In some developing African countries, the initial cost of installing solar energies, including the purchase cost, e.g. solar street lighting, is higher than that of hydro-powered street lights. In the interest of combating climate change, the governments would have to enact strong measures to support the implementation of renewable energies.

Research and Development (R&D) Fund

$22 billion a year is spent globally on clean energy R&D, and a significant fraction of the R&D budget is from developed countries, with the USA taking the lead.[156] Emerging economies: China and India also invest a significant amount of money into clean energy R&D. However, many developing countries invest very little to nothing at all in clean energy R&D. Tax incentives for private, clean energy R&D are required to allow developing countries to invest better in R&D. It is crucial to think green by funding R&D in clean energies across the African continent.

Land and Housing Policy Reviews

Housing and Land. In the interest of sustainable development, African governments would enact stringent measures to control the housing sector. Land policies must be reviewed in some of the poorest African countries. The tenant-landlord systems in many African countries need review to promote fairness and sustainability. The effect of climate change and sustainability needs is evident in how land conflicts are emerging in many Sub-Saharan African countries of late. Poor masses are constantly evicted from land in very unsubtle and unlawful approaches in unique circumstances based on assumptions arising from the interpretation of land policies that are not innovatively updated to align with modern changes.

Conflicts over land and water are increasing every day, which are perpetuated by weak land policies that were drawn following English common law and have not been fairly improved ever since. The modern world that is driven by technology and, more importantly, several African countries primarily registering globalization-induced success creates an illusion to think that we are relatively economically stable. Yet, in the real sense, we are just a few inches away from a total disaster. In this, I mean, African land policies do not align well with sustainable development goals. Housing, for example, consumes many land resources. Policies meant to promote ways to reduce waste, and the use of recyclable materials must be well-thought-out and passed.

Innovation Policies. In partnership with the world leaders in renewable energies and sustainable development associated innovations, African organizations can do magical wonders. Organizations

---

[156] "Let's Fund: Clean Energy Innovation Policy," Let's Fund, accessed September 10th 2021, https://lets-fund.org/clean-energy/.

working in the interest of fostering sustainability and clean energies should have a specialized program to enable them to get substantial funding to innovate and develop products that will have a long-term benefit to this continent. It is common knowledge that what cripples many African start-ups and already established firms is the heavy taxes imposed by governments in the interest of exciting donors that we can recover the loans in the stipulated times. However, since sustainability is a topic about saving humanity, we ought to eliminate our deceptive and politically motivated ideologies from the equation and plan a practical methodology of incentivising and subsidising sustainable development innovation programs to save the planet.

Population Control

People, particularly intellectuals, have extensively debated population growth. Economists argue constructively that a big population presents opportunities for markets, security, growth, and development. The issue of sustainability in the African context seems to outweigh the economist's point of view. The number of natural resources and environment capable of sustaining or supporting the present population whilst not compromising the use of those resources/environment for future generations is the biggest concern for humanity in the 21st century. The rate at which the population explodes must equate to the rate at which the population becomes productive, for example, to match the available employment opportunities.

It is estimated that Africa's youth population today is over half of Africa's population, i.e. 65 per cent is below the age of 35 according to UN ECOSOC Youth Forum, 2014. A boda-boda economy that explodes day and night might cause a severe crisis that can go down in the books of history as the worst crisis ever. In some parts of Africa, particularly the Central and East African regions, the population density is still controllable. However, the lack of proper planning perpetuated by selfish politics that allows no room to think of solutions to save the young generations to find employment may sink the immediate countries into extreme poverty and hunger.

While economists find good in the growing population considering the economic and financial uplift it brings in terms of markets, sustainability finds good in the growing population by striking a balance between the available resources, the carrying capacity of an environment upon which the population depends and the people's way of life. The population must be controlled to achieve self-driven sustainable development.

Controlling Luxury Economies and Consumer Behaviors

I cannot find any convincing positive argument as to why some of the poorest countries in the world can have some of the most luxurious figures in the world. Such luxurious African figures include religious leaders for many Christian denominations, especially the movements as they are coined. In some cases, these leaders are more affluent than their congregations. In such congregations, when the spiritual leader has a problem, the followers would collect monies for them to solve the problem, but when one of the followers gets a problem, they pray for that person! That is modern oppression and hopelessness!

In a society whose biggest population lives below the poverty line, hungry and sick, someone would ideally expect to find no person with a jet aircraft or multiple homes, to the extent that people would fail to recognize their permanent place of residence. This is one of the overt indicators of inequity and inequality present in many African societies, and that society must have a deep problem.

In the realm of self-driven sustainable development, more than necessary items for a person amidst hungry, sick, and impoverished people in some circumstances must be controlled because it fuels and perpetuates psychosocial stressors in the less privileged masses. On the other hand, a shift in consumer behaviours to promote sharing economies and reduce waste is essential. We ought to reclaim the African norm of politeness and collectivistic sharing. Spending on products mainly for fun but with a big negative impact on the environment needs stringent measures. It is equally important to foster a campaign on behaviour modification and activation to meet the sustainability goal.

Sustainable Energies and Energy Efficient Methods

African countries that receive a good amount of solar radiation would use solar energy from the sun as the best alternative to hydropower and fossil fuels. In East Africa, for example, the Kiira EV project for manufacturing electric vehicles should be boosted, and it is an up-and-coming venture in the realm of sustainable development. The East African region should massively embrace products that use solar energies because they are clean and emit no greenhouse gases into the atmosphere. For example, cell phones that use solar energy, torches, cassette radios, home appliances, and many other gadgets would be promoted. The production of electric vehicles is a good opener to start thinking of hybrid electric vehicles.

A considerable fraction of the investment provided by the Asian giant to build hydropower dams in some parts of Africa would be invested in renewable solar energies because that is what we can sustainably achieve in abundance in many parts of Africa. There are several ways you can generate several Megawatts of solar power on-grid, and we could have mini-generation solar stations across several African countries. Here, governments would be addressing the deforestation epidemic by promoting eco-stoves. Hydropower, though renewable to some extent, its generation comes with the cost of destroying a lot of natural habitats, destruction of flora and fauna, and the risk of floods.

Although solar power comes with the cost of requiring big chunks of land for solar panels, its generation does not pollute the air, and I find an appraisal of mini-solar stations across African rural areas more beneficial and sustainable. It could reduce the cost of doing business in rural areas, and accessibility to energy would be made quicker in certain circumstances.

That would come with legislation passed to ensure that the use of gadgets that use solar energy and associated renewable energies in the order of which energy source is more abundant and sustainable than the other is done on a massive scale. Also, this would come along with the policies on energy efficiency use methods or sustainable energy policies.

As I mentioned earlier, planners and designers of products and infrastructure must be well-conversant with the processes to design and develop an energy-efficient built environment. They must have at least the basic knowledge and understanding of operational carbon and capital carbon embedded in projects while appraising them. Among some of the areas where governments would put a keen interest as far as energy efficient methods are concerned are: commercial/shopping malls design and construction, industrial processes designs and manufacturing, the housing sector, transportation, and infrastructure design and development, e.g. roads street lighting, road pavement structures, among others.

A sustainable building that requires lighting, heating, cooling, and ventilation which all consume energy, requires energy-efficient methods integrated into its lifecycle phases to control energy losses. In Africa, not many buildings require heating, especially in the tropics. To some extent, this waives African buildings the risk of contributing to greenhouse gas emissions. Once energy-saving and efficient methods are integrated into the lifecycle phases of the building project, the energy needs are progressively reduced over time. For example, design for natural skylight windows would reduce the amount of light required to give the same level of illumination compared to using incandescent light bulbs.

Low embodied construction materials, e.g. slab decks, would lower the carbon emissions of the building's lifetime. **Note:** A 255 mm in-situ slab emits approximately 137 Kilograms of carbon emissions compared to the 61 Kilograms of carbon emissions per square meter for slab decks. This is a true eco-friendly slab system that saves the environment about 52-55% of carbon emissions. I have expressly given the housing and construction sector example because it consumes many natural resources and emits large amounts of carbon into the atmosphere. Africa needs sound policies in this sector.

Once incorporated in buildings, demand response strategies help regulate the use of energy so that there is a match between the demand for power and its supply. Some of these strategies can be used by utility companies, e.g. smart metering and off-peak metering. The former strategy helps utility companies communicate changes in prices to customers under well-studied circumstances. The latter is meant to subsidize the cost of power at different times of the day as appropriate. The designers who wish to design demand response strategies in buildings concentrate more on the target loads in the building structure. The most common target loads in Africa's buildings include lighting systems, elevators, pumps, air handlers, and etcetera. Engineers can design a system that allows building utilities to communicate signals whenever there is a demand reduction event. Therefore, maintenance and operation managers can reduce the electricity loads to that specific utility. Similarly, an automated system can be designed because the internet of things (IoT) is already getting popular, especially in developed communities across the globe. Carbon footprint calculations guide all these activities before making the final decision.

Other alternative renewable energies applicable in the African context include wind energy, biofuel, and hydropower. The decision to develop a particular energy source would be based on sound analysis of the operational and capital carbon embedded in that particular source. Although wind power generation requires much land, it does not pollute the air during generation. The two most common types of biofuel are bioethanol and biodiesel. Bioethanol can be used as a gasoline additive to increase octane and improve vehicle emissions but can also be used in its pure form.

Many African societies are well-conversant with the production of bioethanol, alcohol made through the fermentation process, especially from sorghums, sugarcanes, and bananas. Biodiesel is produced from oils in a process known as transesterification, and it is an additive added to reduce levels of carbon monoxide and hydrocarbons from diesel-powered vehicles. Although not popularly used in Africa, its production can be readily made available since the raw materials are readily available in some African societies. Hydropower energy which is the most popularly used in Africa, comes with a relatively high cost of land, risk of floods, and destruction of natural habitat, although its generation does not heavily pollute the air.

Appraising Sustainable Buildings

The 21st-century sustainable buildings would significantly reduce both operational and capital carbon. Designers, developers, and contractors would need to estimate the likely embedded carbon and operational carbon throughout the project lifecycle phases to contribute to the net-zero carbon targets. The design team would apply a broad hierarchy to improve environmental sustainability while appraising building projects. This hierarchy includes; building location, energy in use, embodied energy, and renewable energy.[157]

Sustainable Infrastructure

The main goal of sustainable infrastructure is to ensure that carbon emissions are significantly reduced throughout the lifetime of the infrastructure. That means capital and operational carbon has to be estimated when conducting the feasibility and detailed designs. Embodied (capital) carbon comes from the energy consumed to extract, refine, process, transport, and fabricate material or product (including buildings). Operational carbon comes from all energy sources used to keep the infrastructure, such as buildings warm, cool, ventilated, lighted, and powered—or energy used to operate a machine or equipment.

In Africa, where resources are scarce, low-cost innovative methods that contribute to a carbon-neutral economy should be adopted. For example, using cobblestones to pave low volume roads (LVR) could immensely contributing to a carbon-neutral economy. The cobblestone sector is gaining momentum in Ethiopia. Cobblestones are used to pave Ethiopia's low volume urban roads, and they are proving sustainable. Cobblestones technology is much more durable and entails less rehabilitation and maintenance. Also, it reduces the amount of environmental stress caused by construction. Because cobblestones are permeable, water penetrates the surface and recharges groundwater resources.[158] Ethiopia's cobblestone sector is a vehicle for good governance fostering transparency, efficiency/effectiveness, accountability, and participation. Several African countries could copy this technology; it comes with many sustainable benefits.

As mentioned in the previous section, the use of slab decks would significantly lower capital carbon in suspended slabs. Also, adopting sustainable drainage systems in cities and municipalities would help to reduce stormwater runoff and supplement the grey infrastructure. This would reduce the risk of flooding and hence create more resilient cities across Africa. Such infrastructure enhances biodiversity and creates cities that can adapt to climate change.

The use of geotextiles could significantly reduce the operational carbon arising during road maintenance. Usually, poor soils call for stabilisation techniques to achieve the desired reliability. The use of geotextiles could significantly reduce the cost of constructing the pavement structures to about 70%. Once the desired reliability is achieved, you can be assured of saving operational carbon that would accrue from the periodic maintenance of the roads whenever they fail. Reducing carbon is reducing cost, too, at some point.

---

[157] Fiona Cobb, *Structural Engineer's Pocket Book, 2nd Edition* (London: Routledge Taylor and Francis Group, 2011), 330.

[158] Kai Hofmann, Toni Kaatz-Dubberke, and Mali Kos, *Making Good Governance Tangible: The cobblestone sector of Ethiopia* (Addis Ababa: Deutsche Gesellschaft für Internationale Zusammenarbeit (GIZ) GmbH, 2014).

The sustainable infrastructure structural elements would be designed and implemented in ways that do not diminish the social, economic, and ecological processes required to maintain human equity, diversity, and the functionality of natural systems. Adopting green concrete to reduce the environmental impact of concrete is also a step forward to construct sustainable infrastructure. Also, estimating the emissions associated with building bituminous road seals must be undertaken to find effective, efficient, and economical solutions guided by the overarching goal of sustainable development. The emphasis to use local materials is required to reduce the carbon emissions associated with vehicle activities.

In conclusion, suitable infrastructure would be achieved by ensuring that lifetime emissions are significantly reduced while ensuring that the infrastructure projects' reliability, operability, and maintainability goals are achieved. That means an optimal solution should always be obtained.

Green Infrastructure and Grey Infrastructure

In partnership with developmental agencies, several African governments are doing a great job to improve the status of cities and municipalities in many countries. The infrastructure improvement is highly characterized by grey infrastructure. In its simplest form, grey infrastructure refers to structures such as dams, seawalls, roads, pipes, or water supply and treatment plants. These structures are often constructed of concrete, and these come with not many additional benefits, unlike green infrastructure. Green infrastructure techniques refer to an approach to water management that protects, restores, or mimics the natural water cycle. These techniques are widely used to control stormwater runoff in a way that mimics the natural water cycle. Green infrastructure techniques are good at building resilient communities that can adapt to climate change. They include but are not limited to; infiltration systems, bio-retention gardens, rain gardens, green roofs, porous pavements, detention and retention ponds, green spaces in cities, vegetated swales and planting trees. **Note:** A typical tree can absorb about 21-kgs of carbon dioxide per year.

The green infrastructure presents enormous benefits, which include improving the quality of life for the inhabitants. Unlike grey infrastructure projects, which are very costly, green infrastructure projects are relatively cost-friendly. In some cases, they help to maintain ecosystems by retaining soil to prevent erosion and landslides. In other instances, they reduce the risk of flooding and support more resilient communities' growth. African needs to embrace the application of green infrastructure to design and develop resilient cities.

Cities' green spaces help preserve and restore natural areas, such as cultural sites, forests, stream buffers, and wetlands. One most important aspect of green infrastructure as far as sustainability is concerned is its potential to absorb emissions, especially carbon dioxide, and hence reduce the harmful effect these could present to the urban population.

Infiltration systems, bio-retention gardens, and rainwater harvesting techniques are among the commonest green infrastructure present in many cities across the continent. There is a need to promote more green infrastructure at a household level to improve the esthetics of several cities and towns across Africa and improve the quality of life in the long run. That comes with policies on "living in green." We also need to promote clean water and sanitation practices by integrating both grey and green infrastructure to develop program projects across African societies.

Sustainable Transport

Africa's population is expected to double by the first half of the 21st century, and this means there will be an increased need for transport of people and goods from time to time and place to place. The sustainable modes of transport that are kind to the planet come along with a reduction in waste, reduction in emissions, safe, and present a reduced risk to commuters' health.

Transport accounts for over 50% of world consumption of fossil fuels. The transport modes that will dominate the 21st century include low-carbon rail transport and hybrid electric buses. These present reduced emissions and smart cities developments benchmark heavily on these modes of transport. Sustainable transport is about designing and developing fully inter-modally connected transport systems across Africa in a more environmentally friendly approach.

The massive number of people projected to live in the urban areas by the first half of the 21st century will require governments to enact sound policies on transport by own cars to control emissions and traffic. Promotion of cycling, electric bikes, and walking as sustainable modes of transport would be encouraged. People would be encouraged to commute via rail and communal hybrid electric buses, especially for work-related activities.

The aviation industry is estimated to produce about 2% of the carbon emissions annually, making it a little more of a less sustainable mode of transport after rail and communal hybrid electric buses, in Africa's context.

According to the Sustainable Development Commission (SDC) in the UK, a sustainable transport hierarchy would take on four stages, i.e. demand reduction for powered transport; modal shift to more sustainable and space-efficient modes; efficiency improvements of existing modes; and capacity increases for powered transport.[159]

However, in the realm of sustainable development and the African context, the best sustainable modes of transport are those that can propel African societies to graduate out of extreme poverty by easing business and networking. Therefore, the order of priority in investment in sustainable intermodal transport would aim to strike a balance between several modes of transport as appropriate following very unique circumstances in the decision-making process as guided by consultants. We should also not forget water transport because, according to the UN Economic and Social Council 2019 session report, 80 per cent of world merchandise trade by volume is transported by sea, making maritime transport a critical enabler of trade and globalization.

Smart Cities Planning and Digital Design

Smart cities leverage technology. Information and communication technologies (ICT) are highly integrated into cities' operations to make them smart and resilient. Smart cities are about optimizing resources through exploiting ICT benefits. Therefore, they help promote sustainable development by saving people lots of time by relaying information in real-time. Smart cities are known for saving energy and improving

---

[159] "Fairness in a Car-dependent Society," Sustainable Development Commission, accessed September 15th 2021, https://www.sd-commission.org.uk.

people's psychosocial wellbeing. In smart city design, everything goes digital, and ICT drives the city operations. From traffic control and management, transportation and mobility, utility management, leisure and hospitality, environmental stations management, and many more, smart cities have a process to relay helpful information in real-time, saving a lot of energy, costs and time. By leveraging technology, smart cities present an excellent opportunity to reduce the economy's carbon footprint by scaling down on the number of kilometres of carbon-intensive movements because everything is digitally interconnected.

As far as sustainable development is concerned, smart cities should be planned in Africa because they help to use energy more efficiently and enhance the quality of life. Proper planning by experienced personnel through good 3D modelling is vital before any construction is put in place. This helps planners develop several concepts and scheme designs before taking a holistic decision on which design to adopt for the smart city. Things to do with lead times in some city operations, sustainable energy alternatives, thinking of other green alternatives, population growth rate, and politics need to be considered whilst planning and making 3D models. Very few African cities are yet smart enough, and this means planners have very much to do in this field to achieve sustainable development.

Smart cities present a great opportunity to reduce the economy's carbon footprint by scaling down on the number of kilometres of carbon-intensive movements/travels. This is because everything is networked on digital platforms, and therefore a person would only move when they are sure that whatever they are going to do requires them to move. Many customized platforms would be fitted with virtual tour provisions.

Health, Safety, and Wellbeing

In the world of ethics, the highest good in the hierarchy of doing the good and avoiding bad is lifesaving. Risk management is thus embedded in many organizations' operations to scale down the likelihood of working in unsafe environments. And in some cases to improve the safety and wellbeing of the people. The cost of health and safety can be devastating once health metrics are not taken very seriously.

Cases related to health, safety, and welfare can lead to the institution of both criminal and civil proceedings as appropriate. These can be very damaging to the image of the organization, society, and the professionals involved. Our health should be our priority in the 21st century, and all decisions taken should consider lifesaving as the highest priority. In the realm of self-driven sustainable development, we look at future generations' ability to prolong the life on earth.

The government leaders have a big role to play. This includes political heads, civil servants, and public servants. On the other hand, key players in the procurement cycles and service providers must appreciate the codes of practice and standards to derive proper solutions to the problems we face in health, safety, and welfare. Planners and designers must understand their role to play whilst taking decisions to ensure that health, safety, and welfare are well-integrated in the proposals.

Vehicle emissions are being addressed in many territories by encouraging cycling and public transport as an approach, among many others. This comes with a cost of safety safeguards like designated walkways and cycling lanes which must be well-planned and designed for, right from the initiation/appraisal of projects as appropriate. That is the work of the designers and engineers to specify walkways and cycling lanes.

The measures to control obesity, for example, include encouraging walking and other physical exercises and eating the right foods—eating organic and green foods. Policies to plan for adequate and holistic welfare facilities, including gymnasiums and green parks, among many others, must be enforced and aligned well with the city planning activities. In the interest of sustainability, psychosocial wellbeing is one aspect not well-thought-out in many planning activities across Africa. Yet, it presents the opportunity to predetermine the happiness and likelihood of living stress-free moments.

Sustainable Agricultural Mechanization

Extreme hunger can be solved by increasing agricultural productivity across the African continent. However, in a situation where climate change is significantly impacting the African continent, we cannot expect productivity to increase if we continue doing the ancient agricultural practices in the digital era. We need innovative approaches to improve agricultural productivity, and this calls for climate engineering and agricultural mechanization. The issue of land fragmentation is a core problem that is perpetuated by cultural beliefs needs restructuring to innovate a good methodology within succession plans on how land should be handled.

Solar-powered irrigation schemes are an up-and-coming venture in the 21st century. Macro-irrigation schemes funded by governments and developmental agencies are doing great to improve agricultural productivity. However, there is still an overreliance on manual labour in many regions across Africa, which guarantees no food security. The shift of farmers from handheld tools to more technologically advanced mechanized agriculture needs governments to create enabling environments that can allow farmers to access credit facilities with reduced interest rates. The formation of organized farmer groups should be encouraged. In the interest of sustainable development, funding organized farmer groups and progressive farmers should be the priority to act as pilot demonstration farms.

Due to limited capital in many African societies, farmers need to soldier on and unite forces to raise funds for mechanized agriculture. District or county poor and middle-income farmers may decide to form a group force intended to raise capital to procure tractors and agribots, harvesting and planting equipment, among other machines. As I mentioned earlier, clear methodology in succession plans on lands must be solved to reduce land fragmentation. In the realm of self-driven sustainable development, agricultural mechanization presents benefits that include increased productivity, reduction of hazards associated with manual handling activities, relieves labour shortages, improvement in shooting timelines of agricultural activities, and efficient use of resources, among many others.

Environmental Management

The three R's, i.e. reduce, reuse, and recycle, are followed to help control and manage the amount of solid waste we dispose of in a circular economy. There has been the comprehensive promotion of circular economies to replace the linear economic models. In a circular economy, reduction, reuse, and recycling of elements occur while the domineering current linear models promote the manufacture, use, and disposal of products. Using natural resources to ease human life dramatically impacts their existence in the universe, leading to the extinction, depletion, and wastefulness of these resources. For example, many industrial processes in Africa are wasteful, inefficient, and destructive to some extent.

Environmental management interests are vested in utilising resources to the maximum extent possible in a way that optimizes the resources, reduces waste, is unhazardous to living beings, efficient and effective, protects the ecosystem, and avoids extinction and depletion of natural resources of any kind.

All environmental management policies aim at achieving those mentioned above. For example, in the construction industry, waste can be reduced using the Reduce – Reuse – Recycle – Specify Green hierarchy.

The polluter pays principle is premised on the impacts caused by the activities done by the polluter in the consumption and production processes. These costs are paid by organizations that engage in activities that pollute the environment and cause harm to the health of living beings. On the other hand, sustainable management of resources may provide limitations to the environment's carrying capacity, specifically in the interest of conserving biodiversity.

In the interest of sustainable development, African countries ought to define an appropriate accounting system that considers a diverse range of sustainability issues to guide the economies. The accounting system should be built on conserving the environment and sustainable management of natural resources with parameters such as: how much natural habitat is risked in the equation? How much flora and fauna is risked in the equation? How much of the physical universe is utilized in the equation? How much pollution is caused by the activities in the equation? And many other parameters you can think of in the interest of being kind to the planet. Therefore, prices must be tagged to all ecological processes to guide decisions.

Digital Planning

The first benefit that is understandable to many people is that digital planning reduces waste in terms of papers. Unlike planning using papers, digital planning would only require someone to own digital technologies such as iPADS, computers, and smartphones, among others, which makes use of papers in planning limited. It makes it easy to circulate a work plan, for example, to different departments within an organization via established platforms.

Digital planners present a competitive advantage in terms of portability and customization. Its customization is straightforward, and you can add and delete pages, pictures, text boxes, stickers, etc. Digital planning harnesses the power of digital tools. Stakeholder engagement is eased with digital planning because digital technologies can create virtual reality, simulations, 3D visuals, data analytics, and management. In the interest of self-driven sustainable development, Africa should embrace digital technologies to ease planning in a more holistic approach to reduce planning and working in silos.

Digital Procurement

In the developed societies that embrace automated procurement processes, everything moves much faster. The most significant impact of digitalization is increased speed and meeting timelines. It begins with automating procurement systems by investing in software from vendors. Digital technologies drive procurement quite quickly, and this solves many problems. It reduces the likelihood of any form of canvassing in organizations, especially at the expression of interest stage. It minimizes paperwork and saves lots of time. Of course, using less paper is kind to our planet. Software vendors always provide solutions that match the organization's systems.

Digital procurement technologies can be well-integrated in company operations and can communicate the impact on operations. It all depends on the nature of business operations and the procurement goals that inform the design of the most suitable digital procurement technologies to fit the organization. That includes selecting the right tools for digitization. This 21st-century procurement system works best for organisations with lots of inventory management for the effective supply chain management. Such organizations' business operations integrate a digital inventory management system that is built on AI-based platforms. For example, these systems would be designed to send reminders on stock levels in real-time, monitor supplier performance, and forecast demand.

Government procurement systems can be automated to improve service delivery. It is essential to view all government proceedings holistically to design an effective digitalized procurement system synonymous with the internet of things (IoT) that loops through all relevant government departments to complete a specific procurement exercise. An example of infrastructure development procurements that either go through prequalification of service providers or direct procurement without prequalification presents a typical flowchart that can be developed through relevant parties to the contract formation.

In many cases, the procurement of service providers to design and develop infrastructural projects in Africa goes through stages, i.e. eligibility, technical, and financial evaluation stages. A robust digital procurement system incorporated in all government departments would ideally start with a switch to request proposals following an invitation to tender. The service provider would submit e-documents at her pace one by one until the closing date; typical documents are listed below:

Eligibility/administrative	**Technical**	**Financials**
Certifications	Personnel	Budgets
Licenses	Compliance and conformance statements	
Legal authorizations	Equipment and technology	
Responsiveness	Standards and codes of practice	

All the above eligibility requirements have government entities responsible for their issuance. A digital procurement system that networks all agencies in a country would help verify e-documents provided to the system in real-time by sending alerts. This would reduce the paperwork required in bidding. The bidder's responsiveness is measured as an index generated by the system, and finally, the administrative score is registered/ruled out. The technical stage is a little more demanding and requires serious coding. On personnel, institutions responsible for professional development and accreditation can be connected to the system and alerts are generated once a professional's name is listed in a procurement exercise. The estimation of quantities of work in progress, work performed in general, and in specific work performed for a stipulated period by the bidder can be verified by former clients being contacted as appropriate in an automated cycle. And at the same time, scanning through the documentations appended to the system.

With AI and robotics integrated into the system, codes of practice, method statements, and risk management systems can be assessed and scored. The service provider provides evidence of equipment and technology, and the system provides an overall comment. The due diligence exercise is performed by physically inspecting and verifying what is proposed in the offer. And this may have no shortcut. However, the bidder's proposed technology can be verified and assessed with the help of AI and robotics interface. The proposed budget is checked for unbalanced sections using specialized data analytics software or AI platforms fitted in the digital procurement system. In this way, front-end loading can be tracked, and a bidder that is substantially responsive, competent, and compliant with market prices will automatically emerge as the best. The digital transformation in procurement systems within government requires heavy investment in digital technologies, but this can be very helpful in the long run. It would address corruption, reduce working in silos, track incompetent service providers, reduce waste and save governments lots of time. The overarching goal of sustainable development would be achieved.

Reinventing Business Models in the New Digital Era

African businesses need to become more agile in the digital age. Otherwise, it is becoming difficult for African companies and businesses fixated on the analogue processes to remain in good operational business. The Asian giant's companies which have spread rapidly across the African countries are quickly moving digital in all operations and their businesses are agile enough to win many African markets. The digital era presents opportunities and threats to African businesses. One of the threats is start-ups failing to grow—and already established businesses getting kicked out of business. We are slow at reinventing businesses to shift away from old business models. The businesses which have embraced digital technologies are making tremendous progress which comes with increased revenues. Such digital technologies as e-procurement procedures, digital planning, and data analytics accelerate companies to greater heights. The integrated e-billing and e-payment systems that are digitally integrated into the business operations are very limited in Africa's business. Consequently, much time is wasted, and this will keep us behind unless things are changed to address the unique African attitude disorder (UAAD) coined in "Optimism and Positivity", Chapter Four.[160] To reinvent businesses to become more competitive, organizations need to up-skill the workforce and attract new talent.

Robotics and Artificial Intelligence (AI)

We need not look further than robotics and artificial intelligence as we reinvent business models to become agile in the new digital era. AI and robotics technologies are used in various industries to improve productivity by automating several processes. The mechanism, knowledge, and philosophy of robotics mimic the living being's anatomy. Humans have efferent and afferent neurons that carry impulses towards and away from the central nervous system (CNS) and the brain, respectively—something that motivates the understanding of robotics mechanisms a little bit.

Robots are programmable machines that are usually able to carry out a series of actions autonomously or semi-autonomously. They interact with the physical world via sensors and actuators. In many cases, they are designed to mimic living beings. With the invention of improved coding in the digital era, several

---

[160] See p. 203, §4.

lines of code can be written to program a robot. Therefore, AI drives a robot. Such kinds of robots are called artificially intelligent robots. However, most AI programs are not used to control robots.

Artificial Intelligence (AI) are computer programs that are developed to do tasks that would require human intelligence. AI algorithms can be applied to solve a variety of problems. For example, GPS route finders use AI algorithms. Also, AI algorithms can be applied in developing website searches.

In the interest of sustainable development, automation of processes is a crucial factor. This would lead to increased productivity because much time would be saved. The fear that unemployment will escalate is not the case in several industries because of the following reasons: robots minimize manual handling activities and hence contribute to safety in the workplace, robotically automated processes are faster than human labour and hence improve productivity in the long run, robots can perform more hazardous assignments which would highly risk human life, robots can be programmed to lift loads beyond what human beings can handle and et cetera. A robot can never replace a human mind that programs it. But of course, a few jobs might be lost here and there. AI is an integral part of several processes, including software systems and platforms. Africa still needs lots of specialized software systems and platforms of its own to become competitive. We need our internet search engines, social media platforms, and etcetera.

Data Analytics in Africa's Sustainable Development

Africa has faced a problem of data management and continues to face the problem in some parts. In some parts of Africa, it is very embarrassing to find that outsiders have more data and information about our past and present activities than we do. The bug continues to spread in the digital era, which is very disastrous. This is partially observed in how some fraction of the learned fraternity fails to record their work and life. In the digital era, one should endeavour to keep track of useful information at least daily. It is important.

It is becoming cultural, or a cultural instinct to be weak in keeping history in a readily accessible, reliable, and promising process. Improvement in whatever we do is premised on what happened in the past. The absence of reliable data sources in many parts of Africa presents many issues to planners and project designers.

In the digital era, data analytics is broad. It uses several software platforms and specialized systems to analyze and make meaningful and purposeful information out of different data sets. Today, some of the highly paid engineers are big data engineers! Many African enterprises are not good at data management and data analytics, which heavily impacts sustainable development. It is almost impossible to sustainably develop when you are not sensitive to data management and processing. World leaders treasure data and the immediate processed information so much more than anything else. Best practices in data management produce good analytics. To reinvent businesses in the digital era, we must appreciate data management and associated analytics for better business performance.

To industrialize Africa and go digital, we need to unveil a solid strategic plan with a practical methodology for managing data and information. This should associate well with data analytical processes to support a wide variety of business uses. It should be noted that industrial performances are better improved through good data analytical processes. For example, engineering failure in some industrial processes is learned by maximizing the utilization of predictive machine learning, advanced analytics and AI. On the other hand, reliability simulations and modelling in many industries are premised on data analytical systems to maintain systems in a functional and operable state. Data analytics are used widely in many industries for reliability and predictive purposes. They are also used to identify patterns, trends, and relationships. All this communicates valuable information to management and leadership teams within organizations.

The question of data and associated managerial and analytical processes keep many parts of Africa in a situation that guarantees no hope. The value some societies tag to data management and processing does not align well with the need to move digital in their operations. Therefore, there should be programs to train people about the importance of keeping, collecting, and processing data sets for today's and future generations' use. In the interest of sustainable development, the futuristic person, who labours to feel passionate about how African humankind of tomorrow's generation will live amidst giants, would be a little sensitive and curious about collecting, refining, safely storing, and using data.

Cultural Conservation and the Spiritual Dimension

In the African context, the spiritual dimension has a unique and more complex way to convincingly fit the sustainable development equation. The spiritual dimension will continue to cause many messes in several deceptive ways, i.e.

>From anointing oil to building in wetlands,

>From praying for wealth without work to fighting one another because of religious differences,

>From individually owning worshipping centres to collecting offertories for the individual religious leaders to gain from,

>From worshipping centres causing noise pollution to the juggling as bars and worshipping centres at different times,

>From religious leaders consistently harvesting monies from donors in the interest of helping the poor to help themselves instead,

>From religious leaders attacking themselves on several platforms to healing all sorts of psychosocial, clinical and medical problems,

>From designating separate baskets for offertories presented in coins and those in paper currencies to burning holy texts,

>From spiritual leaders that are more affluent than the congregation to a congregation that prays for their colleague with problems but begs from the outside world to make offertories that gain the magistrate,

This is because of the anxiety-fueled in the hearts and minds of many African masses in a very subtle and unique cognitive restructuring which was opportunistically instituted by others whose effects will continue to be multigenerational unless masses are re-restructured to understand that spirituality lives in *oneness*—meditational—not in conventional religions—soul-focused—an integration of mind and heart at the centre of being.

Our cultural values, which are taken as inferior by many people, have some unique methods of conserving the environment. At least one would not find any traditional religion that permits a worshipping centre constructed in a wetland. Many native species (flora and fauna) are getting extinct because people are destroying animal habitats or clearing native plants to embrace the so-called superior species from other parts of the world, mainly from the western world. The reason is that the superior species are associated with conventional religions, and our native plants and animals are associated with the traditional evil religions. However, the continued deceptive tendencies perpetuated by African egoism make many African believers have one leg in the conventional religions during the day and another in traditional ones during the night. And one leg in the conventional religion in group dynamics and another leg in traditional religion when in isolation. Consequently, this affects the mind because it fuels deception that keeps Africans living for food.

In the interest of self-driven sustainable development, we cannot call for a state religion of a sort. However, we need to respect our cultures and re-examine traditional religions and ideals. The existence of the Supreme Being is not detested in any way by those who take the time not to stop questioning themselves in a Socratic manner. I believe, and many others believe, in the Supreme Being. However, I am afraid I have to disagree with one religion's supremacy over the other as far as praising the Supreme Being is concerned.

I detest the processes that many conventional religions took and still take to replace traditional religions because they leave anxiety in the hearts of Africans. In the interest of understanding the greatness of the Supreme Being, one's religion and belief would be in having things in order, and one kind of belief that conserves what they found in place, and another belief that conserves the environment, because the Supreme Being is the one who created them. In that line of reasoning, an invention or innovation must respect what the Supreme Being created. An attempt to redefine the good and bad natural environment categorically associated with religion as supreme over the other religions is quite naïve. Believe what you want to communicate to the Supreme Being whilst conserving the environment and native species without contradicting others who wish not to follow your process.

Cultural Audits. We need a cultural audit to improve some cultural practices so conservative not to take us far in development by borrowing on cultural relativism philosophy to compete with the rest of the world. Female genital mutilation (FGM) is a norm practised by some cultures in many parts of Africa that needs re-examination. Debarring women from owning property is another cultural norm practised by some cultures that needs immediate evaluation. However, this should be a gradual process because fast transformation may not help. This is because adjusting one's core beliefs requires adequate preparation, evidence, understanding, and the willingness to adapt to new proposals. This should be backed with evidence that sustains their identity and values for many years ahead.

Education System

Quality education that is all about nurturing people who can think and create jobs for themselves should be the target to address the high unemployment rates in African countries. In some countries, the education system needs a total overhaul to address structural elements, curriculums, syllabuses, and modern pedagogy.

The digital era requires instructors who are flexible enough to move with the trend. Therefore, in the realm of sustainable development, quality and inclusive education for all is the most crucial target over and above others. That aligns well with the investment in human capital as the most important resource. Therefore, quality and inclusive education for all cannot be achieved in isolation but by working together with other systems in the societal structure. In as much as other structural units are dysfunctional, expect less from our education because other sectors define the role of teachers and also legislate about the teachers' salaries. It is out of the understanding and appreciation that a teacher makes a doctor that will serve as the benchmark to improve our education system.

When other units are dysfunctional or conflicting, the education system creates and perpetuates the illusion of knowledge, which is more damaging than the lack of knowledge. The education sector is central in a societal structure. The systems of governance, for example, impact the overall quality of education and its level of inclusion. The African egoism, which would be best tackled by federalism or by significantly reducing power in the central government, is doing more damage in Africa today. Unitary systems present in the developing Sub-Saharan countries highly threaten diversity and inclusion at different levels of education. Therefore, correct governance models are vital if we dream of quality education.

Phenomenology

All of us get through our lives facing unique experiences. The meanings we attach to these experiences are what counts at the end of the day—perception is more important than fact! And it is from the meanings we attach to experiences; we get the reasons we were born and still living to date. One born a king or queen has his view of human nature and the responsibility he or she owes to his followers from which to derive meanings of meanings. As they grow in unique circumstances, they get shaped following the experiences they encounter from time to time. Whilst some others are born as kings and queens, princes and princesses, others are born subordinates and followers.

In the same scheme of things, some are born rich whilst others are born poor following unique circumstances. These circumstances can hold a diversity of meanings from West to East. That is how society has lived before, today, and continues to live. The struggle to close this gap by humans through developmental agencies is the ideal on which sustainable development enthusiasts and economists hinge to premise their arguments. In many cases, in the context of sustainable development, inequalities may escalate. Economists have their view as well! Therefore, in the interest of self-driven sustainable development, it is the understanding and meaning that people attach to the oneness that agencies are fighting to unify. In the subject of phenomenological differences, sustainability will be attained when Africans learn how it feels to experience a particular situation without necessarily first encountering that situation—when a person learns that fairness is when everything seems working out perfectly well for them either financially/economically or socially, but they can recognize that the economy is in bad shape. This will perhaps, promote sharing economies.

Framework for Africa's Sustainable Development Action Plan

This framework will guide Africa on improving several domains: culture and religion, politics, the education system, optimism and positivity, phenomenology and probability, women and youth empowerment, and industrialization. The framework *estimates* the required resources, the timelines, what needs to be restructured, and success metrics.

Framework for Africa's Sustainable Development Action Plan

Setting strategies Domains for improvement	Domain's relationship with sustainability	What needs to be restructured?	Development Plan Action required	Estimated resources to carry through	Metrics of success	Timelines
Culture and Religion	• The spiritual dimension which is grown in culture and religion, shapes peoples' minds, attitudes, and beliefs about the universe.	• Massive inculcation to regain Africa's glory • Spiritual things are believed to surpass human understanding. Living in the spirit more than the soul. However, the universe of which Africa is a part needs to be conserved. People are burning our homes, cultural heritage, native species, and African symbolisms because they believe that these things promote someone to live in the soul more than the spirit. Therefore, they are more satanic than what the conventionalists bring on board. Asians who follow their cultural tradition have shown sustained growth and development whilst supporting Africa. This now becomes evidence-based. Africa remains a mendicant despite high rates in adhering to conventional religions, whilst some factions distort nature by claiming to be holy.	• Conventional religions to reshape people's thinking towards sustainability • Cultural leaders to spearhead the sustainability goal • Well trained psychologists on Africanisms to be consulted • Embrace digital technologies in collecting offertories • Self-awareness family initiatives • Encourage meditation	US$ 100 billion	• Regrown African values • When Africans learn that spirituality lives in *oneness*—meditational—not in conventional religions—it is soul-focused—an integration of the mind and heart at the centre of being. • Improvement in psychosocial wellbeing to contribute to the attainment of the UN Sustainable goal No. 3, "Good health and wellbeing"	50 years

Setting strategies

Domains for improvement	Domain's relationship with sustainability	What needs to be restructured?	Development Plan Action required	Estimated resources to carry through	Metrics of success	Timelines
Politics • Socialist policies for the next 30 years as we prepare open minds to embrace capitalism • Politics in collectivistic cultures • Democracy • Integrations following intimacy	• Political decisions guide all activities in an economy	• Redefine Africa's democracy • Redefine governance systems • Reducing the power of central governments • Review integrations and statutory boundaries that colonialists defined • From sick to healthy constitutions	• Elites and intellectuals joining politics in high numbers • Civic and political education	US$ 50 billion	• A workable Separation of Power doctrine • Reduced power of the central governments • Respecting the Rule of Law • Politicians putting Africa first regardless of differences • Focusing on government policy other than partisan politics • Politics that meets the requirements for UN Sustainable development goal No. 16 "Peace, Justice, and Strong Institutions" • Selfish constitutions dropped	20 years

Setting strategies

Domains for improvement	Domain's relationship with sustainability	What needs to be restructured?	Development Plan Action required	Estimated resources to carry through	Metrics of success	Timelines
Education System	• The education system is central to the societal structure. • Sustainable human capital is a product of the quality education system. • Self-driven sustainable development will occur when heavy investment in human capital is made.	• Education that stimulates thinking is needed • Education that focuses more on practical skills • Education that focuses on nurturing students with 21st-century skills. • Education that focuses on instilling "Values" in children	• Redevelopment of curriculums and syllabuses • Paying teachers and instructors well • Modern pedagogy that follows on use of digital technologies, • Sound philosophy statements that meet student-centred learning	US$ 800 billion	• Innovation in science and technology hence contributing to UN Sustainable Development goal No. 9, "Industry, innovation, and Infrastructure" • Inclusive and diversified education Education that meets requirements for the UN Sustainable Development goal No. 4, "Quality Education".	20 years

Setting strategies

Domains for improvement	Domain's relationship with sustainability	What needs to be restructured?	Development Plan Action required	Estimated resources to carry through	Metrics of success	Timelines
Optimism and Positivity	• Ending extreme poverty has something to do with an optimistic mind.	• Unhelpful positive beliefs • Negative beliefs • Attitudes, characters, predispositions, and temperaments need to be reevaluated/reviewed	• Social engineering of African masses • Research, i.e. reducing poverty by scientific evidence under the African Poverty lab project (APLP)	US$ 30 billion	• A continent free of the *unique African attitude disorder* (*UAAD*) • High optimistic mindset levels • When there is reduced poverty levels to shoot UN Sustainable Development goal No. 1, "No Poverty" • Improvement in psychosocial wellbeing to contribute to the attainment of the UN Sustainable goal No. 3, "Good health and wellbeing"	5 years

Setting strategies

Domains for improvement	Domain's relationship with sustainability	What needs to be restructured?	Development Plan Action required	Estimated resources to carry through	Metrics of success	Timelines
Phenomenology and Probability	Every event remains a phenomenon until new evidence is discovered. Some of these events are circumstantial, whilst others are mutually independent or dependent.	• Minding one's business • Open-mindedness • Empathy in sustainability	• Self-awareness family initiatives • Research and development	US$ 20 billion	• Rising empathy levels • Reduced inequalities meeting UN Sustainable Development goal No. 10, "Reduced Inequalities", as a result of rising levels of empathy in the population • Improvement in psychosocial wellbeing to contribute to the attainment of the UN Sustainable goal No. 3, "Good health and wellbeing".	5 years

Setting strategies

Domains for improvement	Domain's relationship with sustainability	What needs to be restructured?	Development Plan			
			Action required	Estimated resources to carry through	Metrics of success	Timelines
Women and Youth Empowerment	• Fairness is an associative attribute of a person who has graduated from monarchism to a free and fair society	• From *"empowerment"* to *"repowerment"* • Empathy but not sympathy • Women interests to be viewed as a matter of fact but not a fight	• Enacting laws to safeguard both the boy and the girl child • Comprehending that equity is brought about by understanding not substitution	US$ 50 billion	• Stable marriages and families • More youth in leadership positions • The empowerment that leads reforms for UN Sustainable Development goal No. 5 "Gender Equality" in the African context. • Improvement in psychosocial wellbeing to contribute to the attainment of the UN Sustainable goal No. 3, "Good health and wellbeing".	10 years

Setting strategies Domains for improvement	Domain's relationship with sustainability	What needs to be restructured?	Development Plan Action required	Estimated resources to carry through	Metrics of success	Timelines
Industrialization	Industrialization impacts heavily on sustainability, i.e. could cause climate change, affects life on land and in water, and contributes to the structural transformation of an economy	• Empowering Africans to lead the industrialization process. • Shifting to sustainable industrialization • Tackling African attitudes to redistribute resources to; agriculture, industry, and services.	• Carbon footprint for each project • Investment in renewable energies • Investing in sustainable manufacturing • Infrastructure development in roads, railways, airports, dams, spacecraft, • Agricultural mechanization • Research and development	US$ 1500 billion	• Increased number of Africans owning industries • When the Asian giant's activities in Africa contribute to UN Sustainable Development goal No. 8, "Decent work and economic growth" for Africans • Smart cities that meet requirements for UN Sustainable Development goal No. 11, "Sustainable cities and communities" • Clean water and sanitation that meets requirements for UN Sustainable Development goal No. 6 • Achieving full-scale agricultural mechanization to shoot Sustainable Development goal No. 2, "Zero hunger" • Affordable and clean energy in accordance with UN Sustainable Development goal No. 7 • Africa owning communication satellites	30 years

Conclusion

Leading and managing sustainable development in Africa requires integrated approaches, systems thinking methodologies to solve crises and put African peoples on the right track. Embracing integrations in both humanities and sciences is necessary to spur innovation and growth. Integrations in both the social and scientific arena need to be tapped into by Africans, and Integrations known in the social arena need to follow on intimacy. These kinds of integrations should be more of psychological decisions than legal decisions, and they should bring masses to comprehend inclusion over and above embracing diversity.

Everything we reach as life gets more refined every day is an imitation of the greatness of the High of Creation. The High of Creation is the best doctor, the best engineer, the best lawyer and the best accountant. He is the best in everything, and he accounted for the universe and everything in the universe. For example, since the beginning of the universe, the amount of water in the universe has never changed, and it just changes form and position within the universe. Humans use integrative approaches, i.e. additions, subtractions, multiplications, and division, to use the water available in the universe to make our day to day lives refined. We do it so well by questioning all the time as we unlock the "whys" in which hides the High of Creation.

Africa as a latecomer requires harnessing integrations to the fullest. We should build platforms and networks for African peoples. The main goal should be to sustain the African continent and enable Africans to stand on their own. As we benefit from late-coming, we need to aim for sustainable development and define carbon footprints for all activities.

Integrations. Leadership & Management. Sustainability

Acknowledgements

This book would not have been possible without the extraordinary support of a number of people. I have to begin with my best friend, Peace, who is the mother of my children. Being in a relationship with a busy civil engineer who is also writing a book requires tolerance.

I would also wish to thank my family members and relatives for their extraordinary support, specifically Joan Grace, Alex Kasanya, Joseph Mubiru, and Regina Mubiru.

I would also wish to thank my friends: John Kibuuka, Rogers Sabiiti, Robert Kasule, Daniel Ssentume, Richard Li, Mathias Kayabula, Jason Kikuungwa, Vincent Lusembo, Faisal Kauma, Dennis Kyeyune, Dickson Berabose, and Jane Frances Nnantamu (PhD), for the ideas we shared on how to develop Africa sustainably.

Categorically, my colleague Richard Li always commented on how Africa does nothing to shape people's thinking about sustainability. He triggered me to author this book.

I would also wish to extend my sincere gratitude to Dickson Berabose and Michael Daka for mentoring me through my civil engineering career. Their honesty and professionalism inspired me.

I extend my sincere gratitude to Mubiru Joseph, a Public Health Specialist, for his extraordinary support in mentoring, training, and shaping my professional skills. I gained many skills from the projects he initiated and led; he shaped my perception of the world during my early adulthood.

I am very grateful to my best secondary school mathematics teacher, Mark Moses Matovu, a.k.a M^3, for grooming me. He had an excellent style of delivering the topics, and everything was spot-on. Mark, I am now a civil engineer destined to improve the world. You did a great job, thank you.

I am equally grateful to Lawrence Ssenkubuge's teaching approach while delivering physics classes. His work ethics is remarkable, and he shaped my critical thinking skills. Lawrence, I remember the day you said, "You will find it easy to make your notes going through the university." It happened exactly as you said.

I thank Nnaloongo Nansubuga Joan Grace for encouraging me to keep going. Her great sense of humour is all fun. She motivated me to work hard.

I thank all those people in the university and professional bodies who said "NO" to my work and commented that I bought the dissertation from the markets of Wandegeya, a suburb in Kampala, Uganda. Because of them, I learnt to think differently, rising to become an international professional civil engineer.

I am grateful for my late dad Fred Ssempeera for loving me; his loving spirit still sustains me to date. I successfully followed through the footsteps of my late dad, granddad and great-granddad, who were all technicians, rising to become an international professional civil engineer. I have, therefore, contributed to the refurbishment and maintenance of the role of the "NGO clan" in the Buganda tradition—the role of constructing sustainable habitats. Thank you, dad.

I thank Omutaka Muteesasira Keeya Ttendo Namuyimba for leading the NGO clan and sustaining our cultural heritage as we contribute to maintaining the throne (Okukuuma Namulondo) to forge a sustainable future for the children of our grandchildren.

I am very grateful to the iUniverse Team for doing an excellent job evaluating the book to meet global standards. They gave the book the attention it deserved. Thank you so much.

Extraordinarily, I would like to thank my mother, Betty Nakimera, for raising me as a single mother after my dad passed away. Her efforts have made me accomplish this book. Growing up with her shaped my industriousness, identity, and I learnt to dissect women empowerment empathetically but not sympathetically.

Lastly, I thank my little son Mark Ssempeera Jr., who gave me company as I wrote this book. He is such a kind son who gives me hope. After winning a kindness award, I would wish him to study in colleges such as the Massachusetts Institute of Technology (MIT) when he grows up, supplementing what he would study at local institutions. It is my dream. At that time, the chances are high that he will have the freedom to flourish and grow.

Unlocking Africa's sustainable development.

Patrick Ssempeera,
Kampala UG.
January 2022
www.africa4better.com

CPSIA information can be obtained
at www.ICGtesting.com
Printed in the USA
LVHW070552270122
709551LV00008B/210